Microsoft®

Coding Faster: Getting More Productive with Microsoft® Visual Studio®

Covers Microsoft® Visual Studio® 2005, 2008, and 2010

Zain Naboulsi

Sara Ford

Published with the authorization of Microsoft Corporation by:
O'Reilly Media, Inc.
1005 Gravenstein Highway North
Sebastopol, California 95472

ISBN: 978-0-7356-4992-7

1 2 3 4 5 6 7 8 9 M 6 5 4 3 2 1

Printed and bound in the United States of America.

Microsoft Press books are available through booksellers and distributors worldwide. If you need support related to this book, email Microsoft Press Book Support at mspinput@microsoft.com. Please tell us what you think of this book at *http://www.microsoft.com/learning/booksurvey*.

Acquisitions and Developmental Editor: Russell Jones
Production Editor: Adam Zaremba
Technical Reviewer: Kevin Stevens
Copyeditor: Richard Carey
Indexer: Ron Strauss
Proofreader: Nancy Sixsmith
Cover: Karen Montgomery
Compositor: Ron Bilodeau
Illustrator: Robert Romano

First and foremost to God and Jesus Christ for making this all possible.
To my mom, Helen Naboulsi, for always encouraging me to go above and beyond to reach my goals, and to Russell Chandler for being the greatest nephew anyone could ever have.

Zain Naboulsi

Senior Developer Evangelist, Microsoft

To my parents, Jane and Louie Smolensky, for encouraging me to program on the computer when I was 5 years old, and to Beulah Bourgeois and Annabelle Fayard for being the best babysitters a little girl could ever hope for.

Sara Ford

Contents at a Glance

Table of Contents

Part II Extensions for Visual Studio

Foreword

Visual Studio is quite possibly the most powerful and comprehensive software development suite available. No matter your discipline—developer, test, architect, etc.—Visual Studio provides the tools you need to help get your job done.

However, Visual Studio handles such a large number of development tasks for so many platforms that learning it can be an overwhelming process. Many learn just enough to solve the problem at hand but don't delve deep enough to unearth the gems that enable real productivity.

Visual Studio contains numerous features and options that can help you perform your tasks more effectively. Some are prominently advertised, but many of the real time-savers are buried in obscure dialog boxes and triggered with arcane keyboard shortcuts. While most of this information can be learned by wading through hundreds of pages of documentation, many of the more powerful features are yet undocumented. How can we possibly navigate the vast forest that is Visual Studio? A guide is needed.

Fortunately, we have two.

For several years, Sara Ford has championed productivity with her highly successful Visual Studio "Tip of the Day" blog. Between July 2007 and December 2008, Sara blogged nearly 400 Visual Studio tips and tricks that were essential for many of us (myself included) to get closer to attaining Visual Studio mastery. After Sara completed her journey with Visual Studio, Zain Naboulsi picked up the torch. Zain continues to blog Visual Studio tips and tricks, digging into features in the latest releases and covering some of the popular Visual Studio extensions that are available.

I vividly remember my first encounter with Zain. I had just joined Microsoft as a Program Manager on the Visual Basic and C# IDE experiences and received an email from Zain saying that he was taking the mantle from Sara and starting a Visual Studio tips and tricks blog. My first thought was, who is this guy? Sara was an alumnus of the Visual Studio team and had a great deal of "inside knowledge" to share. How could Zain go to the same level of depth that she had? I wasn't prepared for my initial impression to be shattered so thoroughly.

It didn't take long for me to realize that Zain really knows his stuff. After that first email, Zain kept in touch regularly with me and other members of the Visual Studio team. As he systematically pulled away the layers of Visual Studio to find the golden nuggets of productivity beneath, he would ask questions or confirm the tips that he found. Often, Zain would find features that I didn't even know existed. In some cases, he even found bugs where something had been unintentionally left in the product (e.g., the infamous Debug.cleartextonfoo command).

What you hold in your hands is the crème de la crème of the sum of Zain and Sara's Visual Studio knowledge. In these pages, you will find a sure compass to help navigate the treacherous peaks and vast oceans of Visual Studio. By putting these tips, tricks, and techniques into practice, you'll grow closer to attaining Visual Studio mastery and learn to travel in style.

Dustin Campbell
Program Manager, Visual Studio

It's hard to imagine but if Sara Ford had her way, there never would have been a "Visual Studio Tip of the Day" blog. Back in 2005, we were colleagues on the Visual Studio Editor team who shared an office and a passion for making developers more productive. We both became intrigued by an email with customer feedback, which was remarkable because all of its suggested features were already in Visual Studio but the customer hadn't discovered them. We realized that many of the great productivity features that we developed in Visual Studio 2005 such as Code Snippets and Smart Tags would go unnoticed by many developers who weren't looking for them. We brainstormed several different ways that we could help customers discover all of the hidden functionality in Visual Studio until we arrived at the ultimate solution: Putting a Visual Studio Tip of the Day on the Start Page.

At the time, the Start Page was being completely rewritten to include an RSS feed which would be the perfect mechanism for users to learn how to use Visual Studio better one tip at a time. We lobbied hard to have the Start Page point to a feed of Tips & Tricks for Visual Studio. Unfortunately, there was too much skepticism that there were enough tips to generate new content every day and so the idea was rejected.

Defeated but undeterred, Sara was determined to demonstrate that not only were there enough hidden gems but that there was a huge audience for a "Tip of the Day." She had recently started blogging and challenged herself to blog every workday until she ran out of tips. Initially, we wrote a list of about 50 different tips before she set out on her challenge. Over the following months and years, Sara has worked tirelessly to find hundreds of useful tips, created an engaging blog and helped thousands of developers become better users of Visual Studio.

As we were putting the finishing touches on Visual Studio 2010 last year, I was reassured to find that Zain Naboulsi had stepped in to create the next generation of the Visual Studio Tips and Tricks blogs. He's engaged directly with the Visual Studio team to highlight each of the new features that were introduced in the latest release and the greatest from previous versions.

Based on their years of experience evangelizing Visual Studio Tips and Tricks, "Coding Faster" distills this knowledge into one easy-to-read book which will make you a better user of Visual Studio. Using the described techniques, you'll learn to write code with fewer keystrokes, manage projects and documents with ease and powerful debugging techniques. It also introduces Visual Studio Extensibility which allows you to create your own extensions or find those provided by the community.

In retrospect, it's fortunate that the tip of the day didn't make it onto the Start Page as it led Sara and Zain to write great blogs and this brilliant book to help everyone code faster.

Sean Laberee
Lead Program Manager, Visual Studio

Introduction

Visual Studio is sexy. In the world of Integrated Development Environments (IDEs), it stands as a beautiful example of how environments should work. Yet many of the features created to improve productivity, I believe, are largely neglected. Most developers use only a small percentage of the capabilities in this wonderful product—not because they don't want to use them, but because developers don't know they exist.

In most books that address the various .NET languages or technologies, Visual Studio seems to be mentioned almost as an afterthought; to be fair, its focus is primarily on the language or technology that's the subject of the book, not the IDE—which is as it should be. On the other side of the coin, books written about Visual Studio do focus on the product, but tend to be broad in scope, describing features, but without saying much about their actual use.

The goal of this book is to arm you with techniques that you can apply immediately to improve productivity. Use the content in this book anywhere, anytime, to dramatically reduce the time required to perform just about any task in Visual Studio. You won't find an exhaustive treatment of every feature in Visual Studio in this book, but it contains sufficient coverage that we're sure you'll find something useful, regardless of how you use the product.

This is much more than just a tips and tricks book. Within these pages are—for the first time ever—the keyboard mapping shortcuts, commands, and menu paths for features, along with detailed descriptions of how to use them. We worked very hard to present the information in a way that makes the book easy to read cover-to-cover or as a quick reference.

Who Should Read This Book

If you use Visual Studio 2005, 2008, or 2010, you should read this book. There are over 365 tips in this book (including the additional online Appendix), all selected with the single goal of helping you be more productive by showing you how to use Visual Studio features. The contents in this work are great on their own or as a prefect complement to any course, book, or other learning tool as you explore Visual Studio.

Assumptions

This book assumes you have, at a minimum, Visual Studio Professional 2005, 2008, or 2010 installed. Specifically, it covers techniques that can be used in Visual Studio as well as examples in C++, C#, and/or VB where appropriate.

With a heavy focus on helping you get work done faster, we assume that you have a basic understanding of how to use Visual Studio, and have had exposure to one of the many languages supported in the product.

Organization of This Book

This book is divided into two sections. Part I, written by me, Zain Naboulsi, called "Productivity Techniques," provides information that can be used in your daily work with Visual Studio; these techniques range from very easy to quite advanced methods of using the product. The chapters are organized to take you through the most common daily tasks you perform. Within each chapter the information is arranged, essentially in order, from beginning to more advanced optimizations:

- Chapter 1, "Getting Started," shows key skills to have when starting up and using Visual Studio.
- Chapter 2, "Projects and Items," shows ways to create and use projects and items more effectively.
- Chapter 3, "Getting to Know the Environment," gives guidance on how to organize the environment to best advantage.
- Chapter 4, "Working with Documents," illustrates how best to navigate and manipulate document windows.
- Chapter 5, "Finding Things," is a collection of tips on how to find just about anything in your code or code related in Visual Studio.
- Chapter 6, "Writing Code," the largest chapter, shows a host of techniques for using the editor more efficiently.
- Chapter 7, "Debugging," the second largest chapter, shows you great techniques to improve your debugging experience within the IDE.

Part II, "Extensions for Visual Studio," written by Sara Ford and other authors, contains an examination of selected extensions from the Visual Studio Gallery that you can install to further accelerate the Visual Studio experience.

Finally, we have included an entire second book of tips in Appendix B (downloadable at *http://go.microsoft.com/FWLink/?Linkid=223758*) that were cut from the main book so that we could keep the print size manageable. You are literally getting two books for the price of one.

Finding Your Best Starting Point in This Book

Each chapter—and in fact, almost every item—in Part I of this book stands on its own, so feel free to begin reading wherever you like. However, I suggest that you start by choosing the tasks that will have the greatest impact in your daily work. If most of your day is spent debugging, then start with Chapter 7, "Debugging," first. After you have a good handle on using the features built-in to Visual Studio from Part I of this book, look in Part II to see if there's an extension that can help you advance your goals even further. Visual Studio has many extensions that can improve your overall experience.

Conventions and Features in This Book

This book presents information using conventions designed to make the information readable and easy to use.

Keyboard Settings

Throughout this book I refer to the keyboard settings often, so it is important to know the connection between development settings and keyboard mapping schemes. When first installed, Visual Studio asks you to choose a collection of settings, as shown here:

The settings chosen are directly related to Tools | Options | Environment | Keyboard within the "Apply the Following Additional Keyboard Mapping Scheme" dropdown list. For example, when you choose Visual C# Development Settings, you will see Visual C# 2005 as the keyboard mapping, as shown here:

The following table lists the setting collection and its corresponding keyboard mapping scheme:

SETTINGS	ADDITIONAL KEYBOARD SCHEME
GENERAL DEVELOPMENT SETTINGS	(Default)
PROJECT MANAGEMENT SETTINGS	(Default)
VISUAL BASIC DEVELOPMENT SETTINGS	Visual Basic 6
VISUAL C# DEVELOPMENT SETTINGS	Visual C# 2005
VISUAL C++ DEVELOPMENT SETTINGS	Visual C++ 6
VISUAL F# DEVELOPMENT SETTINGS	(Default)
WEB DEVELOPMENT	(Default)
WEB DEVELOPMENT (CODE ONLY)	(Default)

Summary Information

One of the unique features of this book is the summary information at the top of every item. All tips will contain a table with one or more pieces of summary information that looks like this example:

DEFAULT	Ctrl+Alt+F1 (help settings); F1 (view help)
VISUAL BASIC 6	Ctrl+Alt+F1 (help settings); F1 (view help)
VISUAL C# 2005	Ctrl+F1, M (help settings); Ctrl+F1, Ctrl+M (help settings); F1 (view help)
VISUAL C++ 2	Ctrl+Alt+F1 (help settings); F1 (view help)
VISUAL C++ 6	Ctrl+Alt+F1 (help settings); F1 (view help)
VISUAL STUDIO 6	Ctrl+Alt+F1 (help settings); F1 (view help)
WINDOWS	Alt, H, S (help settings); Alt, H, V (view help)
MENU	Help | Manage Help Settings; Help | View Help
COMMAND	Help.ManageHelpSettings; Help.F1Help
VERSIONS	2010
LANGUAGES	All
CODE	vstipTool0120

Here is what each piece of information means:

- **Default to Visual Studio 6**—Keyboard shortcuts assigned that are mapped to the choice made for development settings. These settings can be found at Tools | Options | Environment | Keyboard. If absent, implies there are no keyboard shortcuts that apply.

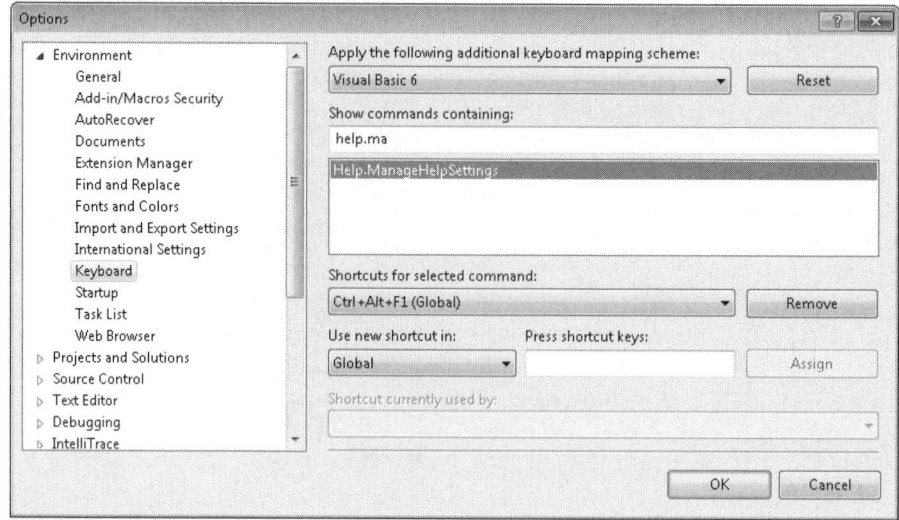

- **Windows**—Keyboard shortcuts that navigate the Menu Bar for commands. If absent, implies there are no Menu Bar shortcuts that apply.

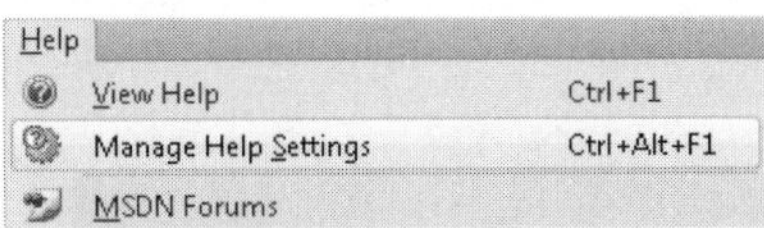

- **Menu**—Menu Bar path for using a command. Help | Manage Help Settings means click on the Help menu and choose Manage Help Settings item underneath it. If absent, implies the item can not be accessed from the Menu Bar.
- **Command**—Visual Studio command used to assign keyboard shortcuts, aliases, run macros, etc. Found at Tools | Options | Environment | Keyboard. If absent, implies there is no command available for this activity.
- **Versions**—Versions of Visual Studio that support the information given in the tip. If absent, implies all versions are supported.
- **Languages**—Languages supported (C++, C#, and/or VB). If absent, implies all languages are supported.
- **Code**—Unique identifier for each tip for looking up references to the tip in the book, online, etc.

Additional Information

- Boxed elements with labels such as "Warning" are used to tell you about items that may impact you negatively. Be aware that these activities are done at your own risk.
- Boxed elements with labels such as "Note" provide additional information or alternative methods for completing a step successfully.
- Text that you type (apart from code blocks) appears in bold.
- A plus sign (+) between two key names means that you must press those keys at the same time. For example, "Ctrl+Alt+L" means that you hold down the Ctrl key while you press the Alt key and the L key.
- A comma (,) between key names means you press each key separately. For example, "Alt+T, O" means you hold down Alt while you press T then let up on the keys and finally press O by itself.
- A vertical bar between two or more menu items (e.g., File | Close), means that you should select the first menu or menu item, then the next, and so on.

System Requirements

You will need the following hardware and software to complete the practice exercises in this book.

Software Requirements

- Windows XP (x86) with Service Pack 3—all editions except Starter Edition
- Windows Vista (x86 & x64) with Service Pack 2—all editions except Starter Edition
- Windows 7 (x86 & x64)
- Windows Server 2003 (x86 & x64) with Service Pack 2
- Windows Server 2003 R2 (x86 & x64)
- Windows Server 2008 (x86 & x64) with Service Pack 2
- Windows Server 2008 R2 (x64)

Supported Architectures:

- 32-Bit (x86)
- 64-Bit (x64)

Hardware Requirements

- Computer that has a 1.6GHz or faster processor
- 1 GB (32-Bit) or 2 GB (64-Bit) RAM (Add 512 MB if running in a virtual machine)
- 3 GB of available hard disk space
- 5400 RPM hard disk drive
- DirectX 9 capable video card running at 1024 x 768 or higher-resolution display
- DVD-ROM Drive

Depending on your Windows configuration, you might require Local Administrator rights to install or configure Visual Studio.

Acknowledgments

From day one this book has been a community-driven effort. The readers of my (Zain) and Sara's blogs have been a constant source of content, comments, and ideas. Our heartfelt thanks for all our readers have done to make this book a reality.

I used to make fun of those people who win awards on TV because they always have a huge list of people to thank and never seem to get through them. It looks like it's my turn now and I *know* that I will forget someone, so let me just say that behind every effort like this you will always have a great deal of people helping you in one way or another. Below is just a partial list of people Sara and I want to thank for contributing, directly or indirectly, to the effort:

Russell Jones and Adam Zaremba—Editors at O'Reilly Media, who herded the cats to make this book happen.
Kevin Stevens—Who came up with the name of the book and was instrumental in the technical review process.
Paul Millsaps, Bill Needels—For doing some of the technical review for the book.
Sean Laberee—Senior Program Manager Lead at Microsoft who helped both Sara and me get started with Tips and Tricks.
Dustin Campbell—Program Manager at Microsoft who continues to be a constant source of information when I get stuck on a feature or concept.
Brittany Behrens—Program Manager at Microsoft who helped me during those first tenuous days after I took over Sara's work.
Matt Manela—for writing the content for the Snippet Designer extension.
Andrew Steele—for writing the content for the Productivity Power Tools extension.
Jim Christopher—for writing the content for both the GhostDoc and the StudioShell extensions.
Terry Leeper—Principal Architect, Windows C++ Team, my main contact with the C++ folks and a good friend that has helped me resolve questions about features since I started doing the tips.
Lisa Feigenbaum and Beth Massi—Program Managers at Microsoft who constantly provided guidance and support as the content of the book evolved.
Brian Moore—Director, DPE Central Region, for providing support and being a great manager.
Clint Edmonson—Senior Architect Evangelist at Microsoft who I have toured with throughout the country delivering Visual Studio talks to thousands of people.
Phil Wheat—My best friend at Microsoft and a constant source of information. Phil is easily the smartest person I know.
Jared Bienz, Mike Azocar—Very good friends who have been great to bounce ideas around as I worked on the book.
Rob Bagby, Mike Benkovich, John Weston, Keith Combs—My old Microsoft Across America buddies.

Finally, Sara Ford wishes to thank Dr. Terrance Delaney and Dr. Michael McMurray for fixing her chronic shin splints during the course of writing this book.

Errata & Book Support

We've made every effort to ensure the accuracy of this book and its companion content. Any errors that have been reported since this book was published are listed on our Microsoft Press site at oreilly.com:

http://go.microsoft.com/FWLink/?Linkid=226221

If you find an error that is not already listed, you can report it to us through the same page.

If you need additional support, email Microsoft Press Book Support at *mspinput@microsoft.com.*

Please note that product support for Microsoft software is not offered through the addresses above.

We Want to Hear from You

At Microsoft Press, your satisfaction is our top priority, and your feedback our most valuable asset. Please tell us what you think of this book at:

http://www.microsoft.com/learning/booksurvey

The survey is short, and we read every one of your comments and ideas. Thanks in advance for your input!

Stay in Touch

Let's keep the conversation going! We're on Twitter: *http://twitter.com/MicrosoftPress*

Part I

Productivity Techniques

In this part:

Chapter 1

Getting Started

"A beginning is the time for taking the most delicate care [...]"

—Frank Herbert, "Dune"

This chapter addresses tasks that would be immediately beneficial as you work in Visual Studio. The main themes here are exporting your development settings, learning the Start Page, adjusting your performance, and other key tasks.

This chapter is arguably the most important one you will read in this book—and yet, I suspect, the one people will think they need the least. If you have been using Visual Studio for any length of time, you might easily feel that the tasks in in this chapter have little application to your situation. But whether you have been using Visual Studio for ten days or ten years, these tips will help ensure that all your other efforts go smoothly, so taking time to absorb the contents is definitely worthwhile.

01.01 Running Multiple Versions of Visual Studio Side-By-Side

VERSIONS	2005, 2008, 2010
CODE	vstipEnv0054

People often ask whether you can run multiple versions of Visual Studio side-by-side on the same machine. The answer is yes you can!

You can find documentation on MSDN, in the topic "Installing Visual Studio Versions Side-by-Side," at *http://msdn.microsoft.com/en-us/library/ms246609.aspx.*

The recommendation is that you install multiple versions from oldest to newest. So you would install Visual Studio 2005, 2008, and then 2010—in that order.

01.02 Getting Table of Contents in Visual Studio 2010 Online Help

DEFAULT	Ctrl+Alt+F1 (help settings); F1 (view help)
VISUAL BASIC 6	Ctrl+Alt+F1 (help settings); F1 (view help)
VISUAL C# 2005	Ctrl+F1, M (help settings); Ctrl+F1, Ctrl+M (help settings); F1 (view help)
VISUAL C++ 2	Ctrl+Alt+F1 (help settings); F1 (view help)
VISUAL C++ 6	Ctrl+Alt+F1 (help settings); F1 (view help)
VISUAL STUDIO 6	Ctrl+Alt+F1 (help settings); F1 (view help)
WINDOWS	Alt, H, S (help settings); Alt, H, V (view help)
WINDOWS KEYBOARD	Alt, H, S (help settings); Alt, H, V (view help)
MENU	Help | Manage Help Settings; Help | View Help
COMMAND	Help.ManageHelpSettings; Help.F1Help
VERSIONS	2010
CODE	vstipTool0120

I have to admit I don't like the new online help in Visual Studio 2010. Not that I think it's bad per se, but I was just used to the old help system's look and feel—particularly the table of contents list.

If you are like me and want to get that classic help look-and-feel back for online help, you need to do two things.

Online Help

First, you need to set your default help to online help (you need Internet connectivity to use this feature) by selecting Help | Manage Help Settings. Then click Choose Online Or Local Help.

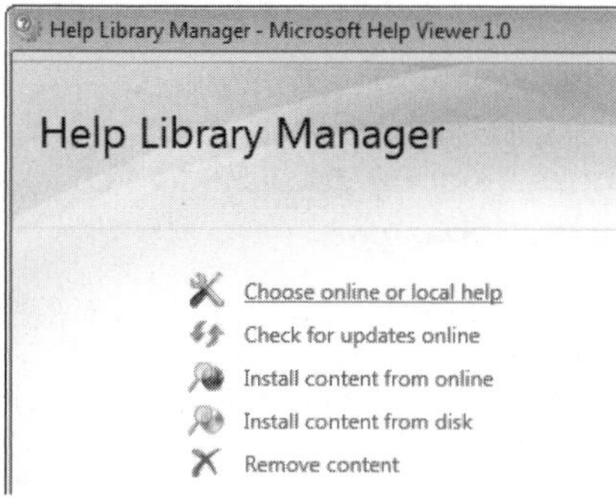

Select I Want To Use Online Help, and click OK.

I want to use online help

I want to use local help

Using Classic View

Now that you are using online help, Go to Help | View Help to see a page similar to the following:

In the upper-right corner of the page, if you see the Preferences link, click it.

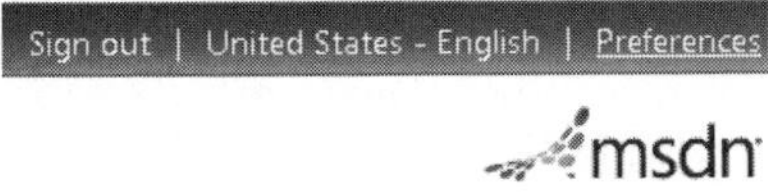

Note You may not see the Preferences link but instead just three links to Lightweight, ScriptFree, and Classic. In this case, just click Classic and skip the next step.

Choose Classic and click OK.

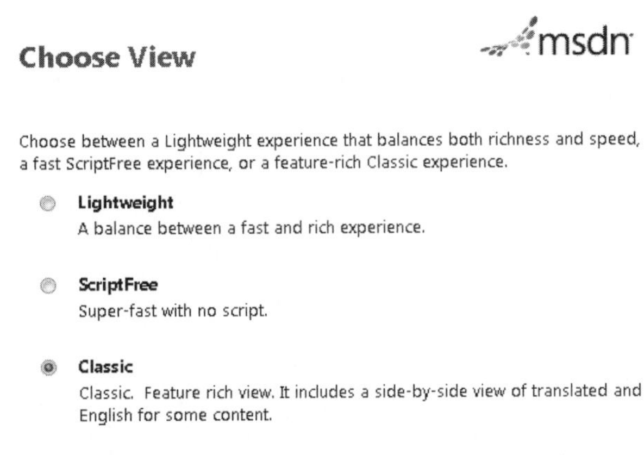

Now your help will use the old-style contents list.

01.03 Exporting Your Environment Settings

WINDOWS	Alt,T, I
MENU	Tools | Import and Export Settings
COMMAND	Tools.ImportandExportSettings
VERSIONS	2005, 2008, 2010
CODE	vstipEnv0021

Exporting your environment settings is a great way to back them up. You can export your settings by selecting Tools | Import And Export Settings Wizard.

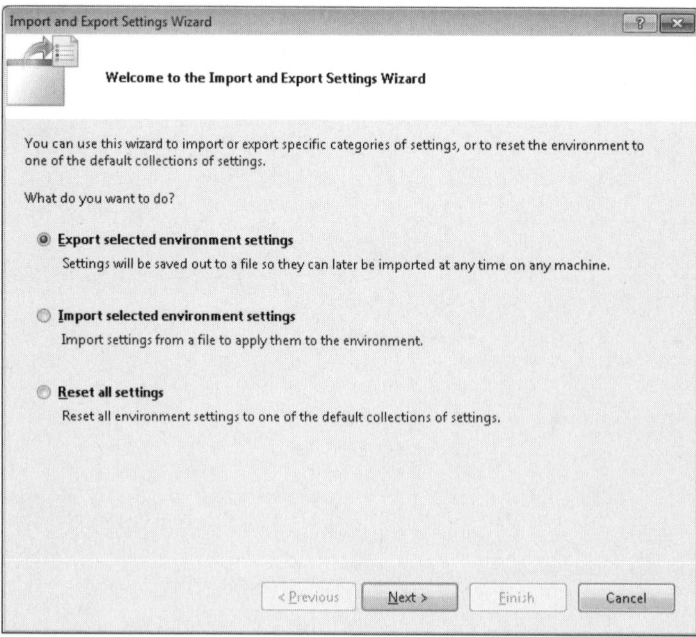

The Export Selected Environment Settings option lets you save your settings to a .vssettings file.

Click Next to see the Choose Settings To Export dialog box.

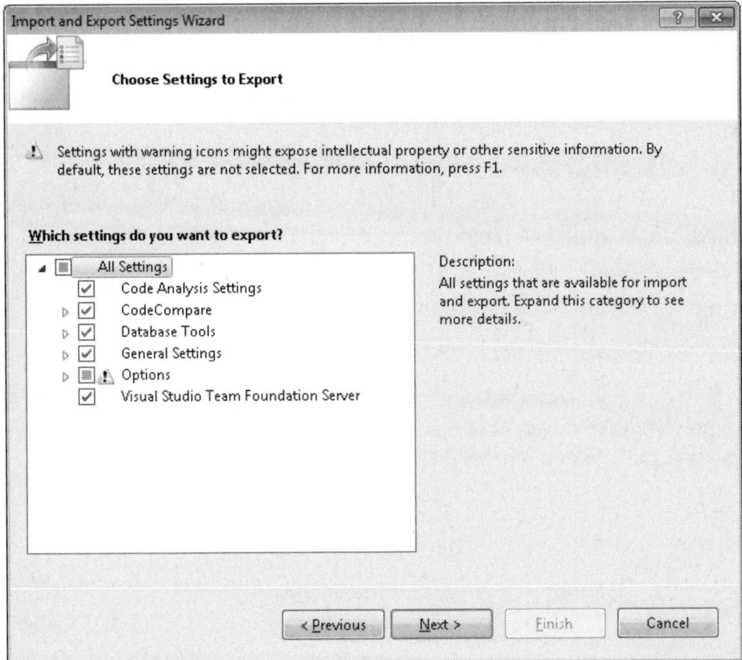

You can expand the areas to choose the items you want to include or exclude.

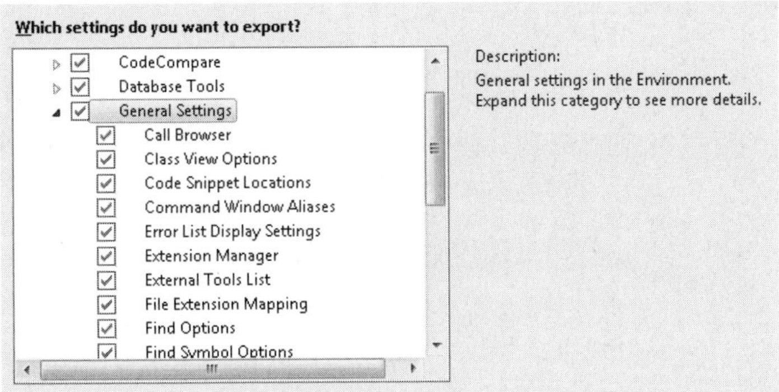

By default, almost everything is selected except for items that could expose sensitive information. You can tell which options these are by the yellow warning symbol icon next to the item.

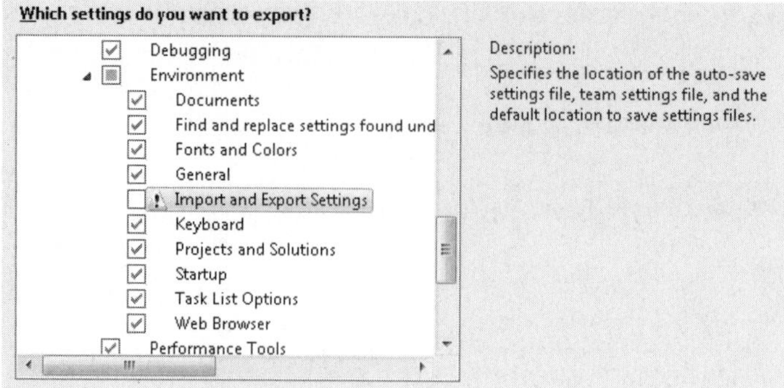

After you make your choices and click Next, you can pick the location (C:\users\<current user>\documents\visual studio <version>\settings, by default) and the filename (the current date, by default) where you want to save the exported information.

Warning If you don't give your exported settings good names it will be hard to figure out what they are for later. For example, if you are just exporting your favorite black theme fonts and colors, a name like "Fonts and Colors (Black Theme) 2010-07-05" would make sense.

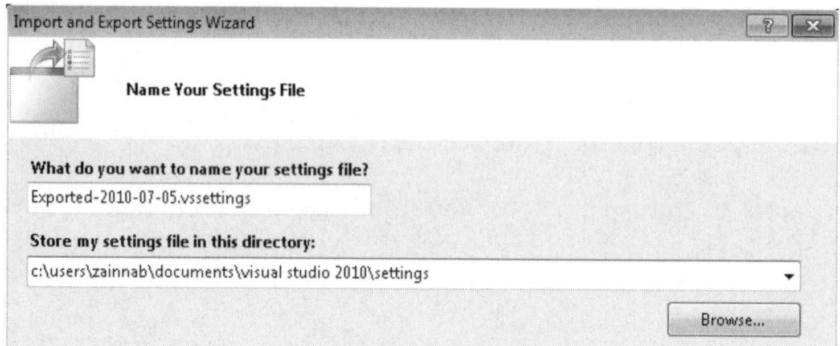

When you click Finish, Visual Studio exports your settings, and the following dialog box appears.

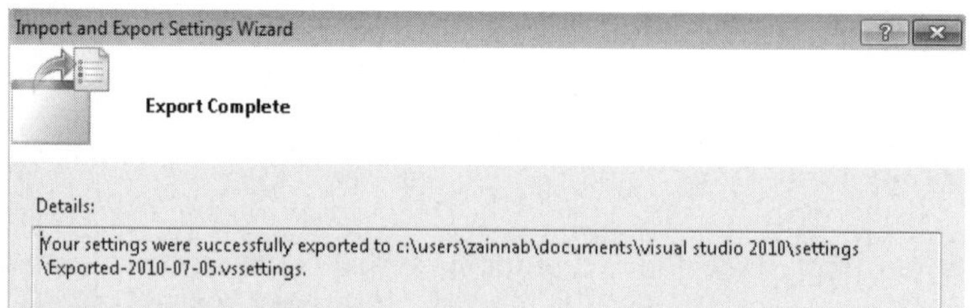

If you are curious, the exported file is just an XML file. You can open it in Notepad and see the contents, as shown in the following illustration.

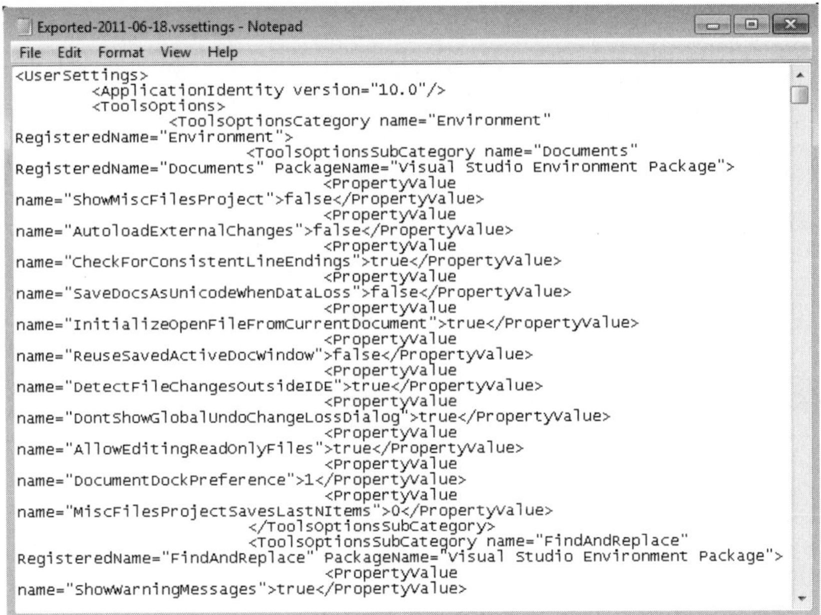


```
<UserSettings>
        <ApplicationIdentity version="10.0"/>
        <ToolsOptions>
                <ToolsOptionsCategory name="Environment"
RegisteredName="Environment">
                        <ToolsOptionsSubCategory name="Documents"
RegisteredName="Documents" PackageName="Visual Studio Environment Package">
                                <PropertyValue
name="ShowMiscFilesProject">false</PropertyValue>
                                <PropertyValue
name="AutoloadExternalChanges">false</PropertyValue>
                                <PropertyValue
name="CheckForConsistentLineEndings">true</PropertyValue>
                                <PropertyValue
name="SaveDocsAsUnicodeWhenDataLoss">false</PropertyValue>
                                <PropertyValue
name="InitializeOpenFileFromCurrentDocument">true</PropertyValue>
                                <PropertyValue
name="ReuseSavedActiveDocWindow">false</PropertyValue>
                                <PropertyValue
name="DetectFileChangesOutsideIDE">true</PropertyValue>
                                <PropertyValue
name="DontShowGlobalUndoChangeLossDialog">true</PropertyValue>
                                <PropertyValue
name="AllowEditingReadOnlyFiles">true</PropertyValue>
                                <PropertyValue
name="DocumentDockPreference">1</PropertyValue>
                                <PropertyValue
name="MiscFilesProjectSavesLastNItems">0</PropertyValue>
                        </ToolsOptionsSubCategory>
                        <ToolsOptionsSubCategory name="FindAndReplace"
RegisteredName="FindAndReplace" PackageName="Visual Studio Environment Package">
                                <PropertyValue
name="ShowWarningMessages">true</PropertyValue>
```

01.04 Remove Projects from the Recent Projects List

WINDOWS	Alt,F, J, [Number]
MENU	File | Recent Projects and Solutions
VERSIONS	2010
CODE	vstipTool0017

In Visual Studio 2010, you can now remove projects from the Recent Projects list on your Start Page.

Just right-click the project, and select Remove From List, as shown in the following illustration. That's it. The project is removed from the list but not deleted. If you want to permanently delete the project, you need to do that yourself from the filesystem.

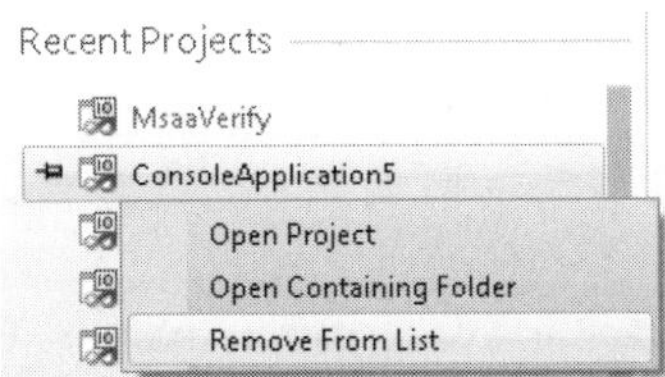

01.05 AutoRecover

WINDOWS	Alt,T, O
MENU	Tools | Options | Environment | AutoRecover
COMMAND	Tools.Options
VERSIONS	2005, 2008, 2010
CODE	vstipEnv0019

AutoRecover can be a real life saver if the development environment crashes or if a power outage occurs. It's simple to use: Just go to Tools | Options | Environment | AutoRecover.

To turn this feature off (not recommended), you can clear the Save AutoRecover Information Every check box. Here's an explanation of what the other options do:

- **n minutes** Determines how often Visual Studio saves AutoRecover information for files. The default is to save every five minutes, but you can adjust that interval up or down depending on your needs. There is an inverse relationship between this value and the frequency of your updates to code. If you make frequent code updates, you should set a smaller save interval. Conversely, if you make relatively infrequent code updates, you can increase this interval. It's better to err by using an interval that's too short rather than too long; in other words, it's better to take a performance hit from file I/O than to lose a ton of work.
- **n days** Determines how long Visual Studio keeps AutoRecover files in the Backup Files directory. The default is seven days, which is adequate for most situations. If you work with a lot of projects over a short period of time, you might want to decrease this number to keep the Backup Files directory from getting too cluttered. If you're not sure about what you need for this value, it's better to guess high and later reduce the number as needed.

I want to be clear about what exactly gets saved and where it gets saved. First, recovered files are stored at My Documents\Visual Studio <version>\Backup Files\<projectname>. But not every file is saved here. The backup folder is empty when you first create a solution in Visual Studio.

When I make a change to a file and save the change, I wait five minutes to see the result.

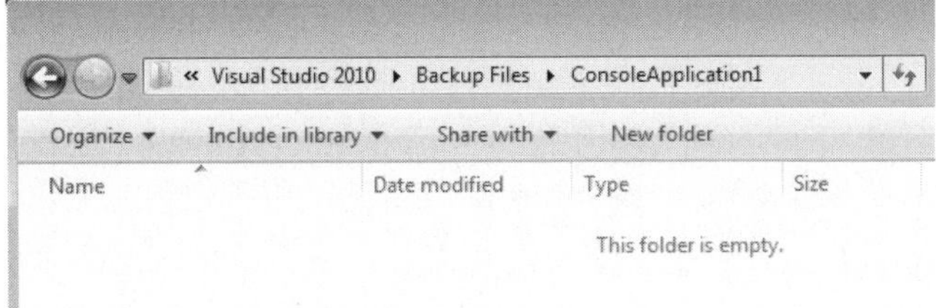

There's still nothing there, because Visual Studio knows there is no need to recover a saved file. But if I make a change to a file without saving it and wait another five minutes, here is what you see:

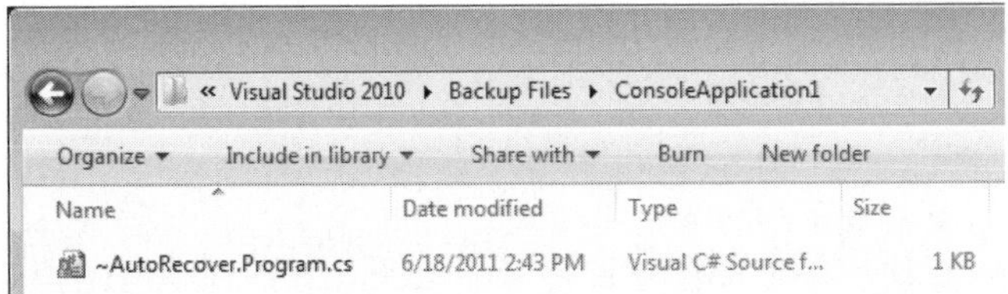

At this point, the AutoRecover information appears because there are unsaved changes. If Visual Studio crashes now, you would need to make a decision about whether to recover the unsaved changes or keep the last saved version. Giving you that choice is the essential function of the AutoRecover feature.

When you do finally have to recover a file, you will see the following dialog box.

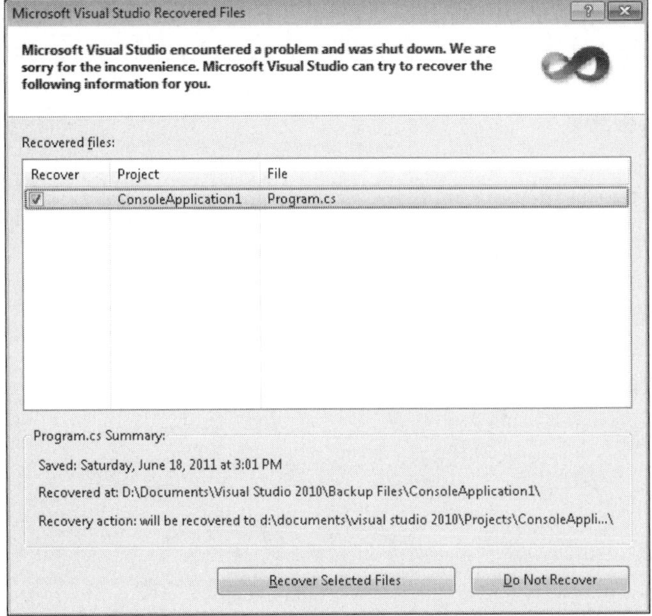

To explain the terminology in the preceding dialog box:

- **Recovered files**
  Lists the file(s) that can be recovered. Use a check box to select or clear the files you want to keep as well as to see some basic information.
- **<File Name> Summary**
  Shows detailed information about the currently selected file, including date/time information, location of the backup file, and the destination location where the recovered file will be saved.
- **Recover Selected Files**
  Performs a recovery action on the selected file(s), copying the recovered source file to the previously indicated destination.
- **Do Not Recover**
  Closes the dialog box without recovering any listed files.

01.06 Improving Performance by Changing the Visual Experience in Visual Studio 2010

WINDOWS	Alt,T, O
MENU	Tools | Options | Environment | General | Visual Experience
COMMAND	Tools.Options
VERSIONS	2010
CODE	vstipEnv0017

Visual Studio 2010 automatically adjusts the visual experience depending on the situation. For example, it might eliminate or reduce the use of gradients and animations when running in Remote Desktop or virtual machine environments. It also makes use of hardware graphics acceleration when that's available.

In some situations, you can improve Visual Studio's performance by changing its Visual Experience manually. To change these settings, select Tools | Options | Environment | General | Visual Experience to see the following dialog box.

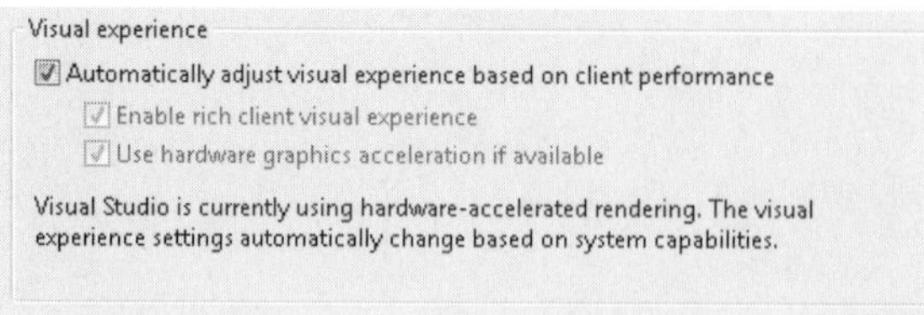

Clear the Automatically Adjust Visual Experience Based On Client Performance check box.

Note As you work with the preceding options, the message at the bottom of the dialog box does not change until you click OK to commit the changes you have made.

Following is a brief explanation of what each option does:

- **Enable Rich Client Visual Experience** This option gives you gradients and animations (also known as "eye candy") for elements such as sliding tool windows and so on. If you leave this option selected, Visual Studio uses these rich animations in all scenarios—including remote sessions. You should usually turn this option off in such situations to get a bump in performance.
- **Use Hardware Graphics Acceleration If Available** This option lets you decide whether Windows Presentation Foundation (WPF) hardware acceleration is something you want. If this can benefit you, you'll notice a clear change in performance when you enable or disable this option. Make sure to test both scenarios.

Note If you have a system whose performance doesn't suffer when animations and gradients are turned on, a little eye candy can be a good thing, so this tip is really for those folks who are having performance issues in their Visual Studio experience, either locally or remotely.

Now that you have played with the preceding options a bit, you might be wondering whether you can actually see how much they can improve (or hurt) performance. The Windows SDK includes a tool called WPFPerf that enables you to measure WPF performance. You can find a great article on how to use it at the Microsoft WindowsClient.NET site, at *http://windowsclient.net/wpf/perf/wpf-perf-tool.aspx*.

Also, when using Visual Studio 2010 over remote sessions, you should definitely read the article titled "Optimizing Visual Studio 2010 and WPF Applications for Remote Desktop," at *http://blogs.msdn.com/b/jgoldb/archive/2010/02/27/optimizing-visual-studio-2010-and-wpf-applications-for-remote-desktop.aspx*. This article provides important information about how to dramatically improve performance over Remote Desktop.

01.07 Change Tool Window Animations

WINDOWS	Alt,T, O
MENU	Tools | Options | Environment | General
COMMAND	Tools.Options
VERSIONS	2005, 2008
CODE	vstipEnv0018

In the tip vstipEnv0017 ("Improving Performance by Changing the Visual Experience", page 14), you saw a discussion of how you can improve the visual performance of Visual Studio 2010. Now let's look at Visual Studio 2008 and 2005. You can change the animation speed of tool windows in Visual Studio 2008 and 2005, but why would you want to do this?

The answer is that you can get a performance boost by speeding up or completely turning off the animation. Select Tools | Options | Environment | General, and locate the Animate Environment Tools option.

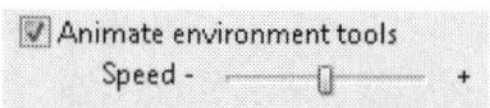

I suggest you turn off this feature to begin with, to see whether you notice any performance improvements. Later, if you want your animations back, turn on the option and set the slider to the far-right side (the fastest speed). As you test the performance, you can adjust it back to the left to determine the best setting for you.

01.08 Importing or Changing Your Environment Settings

WINDOWS	Alt,T, I
MENU	Tools | Import and Export Settings
COMMAND	Tools.ImportandExportSettings
VERSIONS	2005, 2008, 2010
CODE	vstipEnv0022

Assuming you have exported your settings (vstipEnv0021, "Exporting Your Environment Settings", page 6), you can import your settings by going to Tools | Import And Export Settings Wizard and selecting Import Selected Environment Settings:

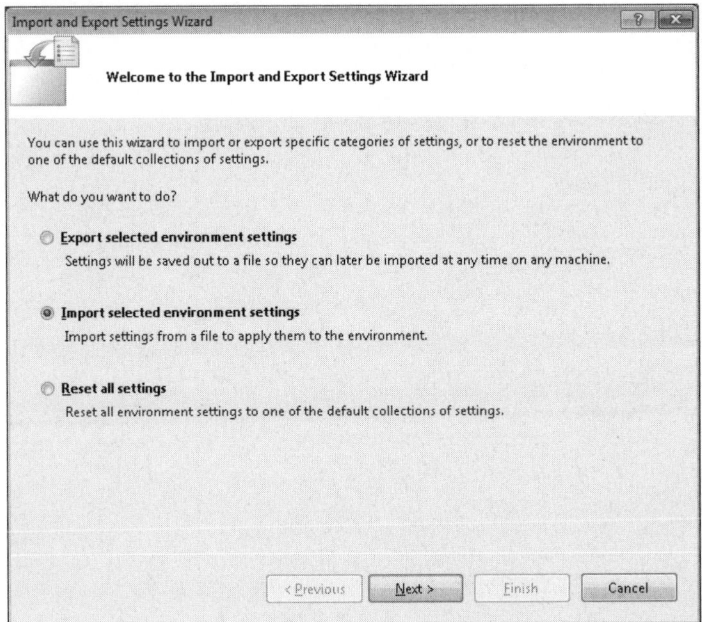

This setting enables you to import a previously exported .vssettings file.

After you click Next on the Welcome page shown in the preceding illustration, you have the option to save your existing settings (recommended) before overwriting or to just overwrite them:

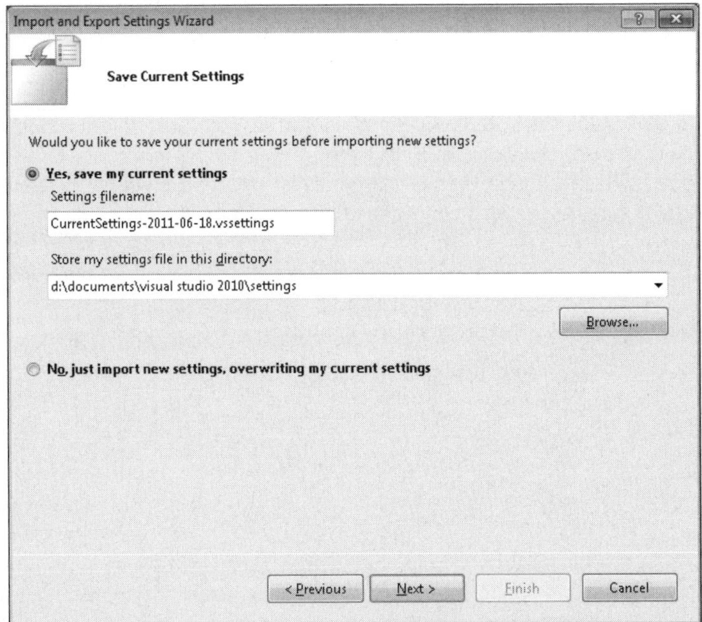

Click Next, and you can choose from the default settings, settings that have been saved previously, or you can browse for your own .vssettings file:

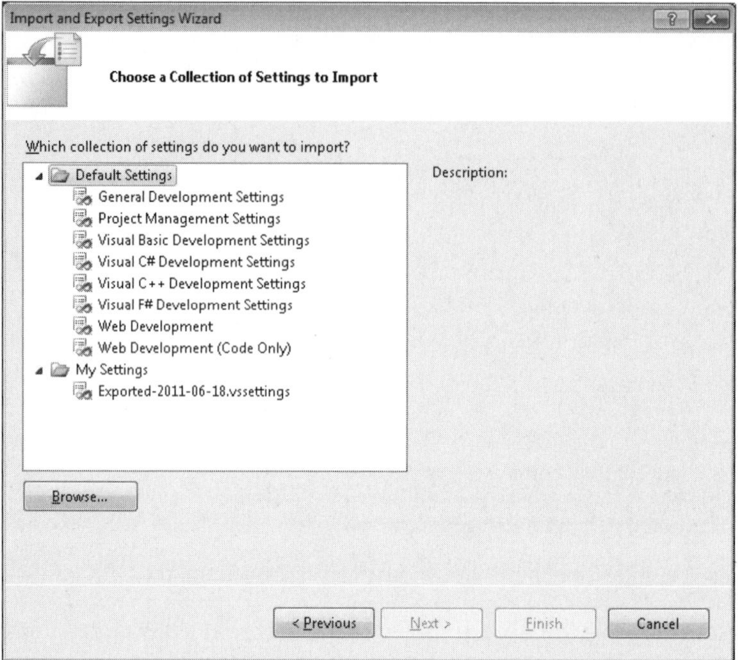

Now click Next again to choose what settings you want to import. All the previously exported settings are selected by default except for Command Window Aliases, External Tools List, and Import and Export Settings, which are considered potentially dangerous.

Warning You have to determine the potentially dangerous areas for yourself, but if doing a full export or import, you would most likely check all the items in this dialog. It is not recommended that you share full exports with team members as there may be information in the file you don't want to share. Instead, just export the items you want to share with team members in a separate file.

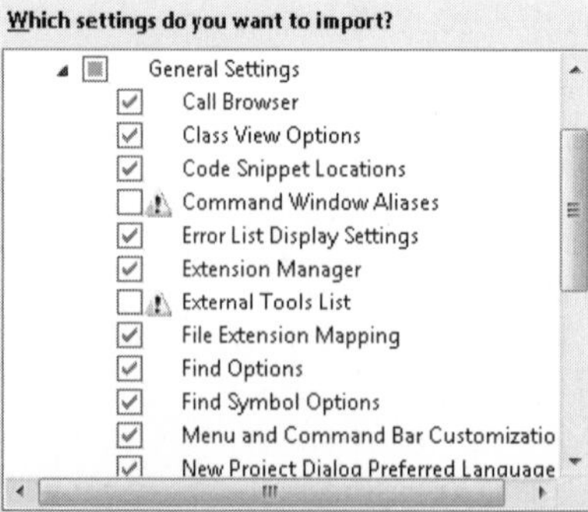

After you have checked (or unchecked) the items you want, click Finish to import the settings and to see the final page of the wizard:

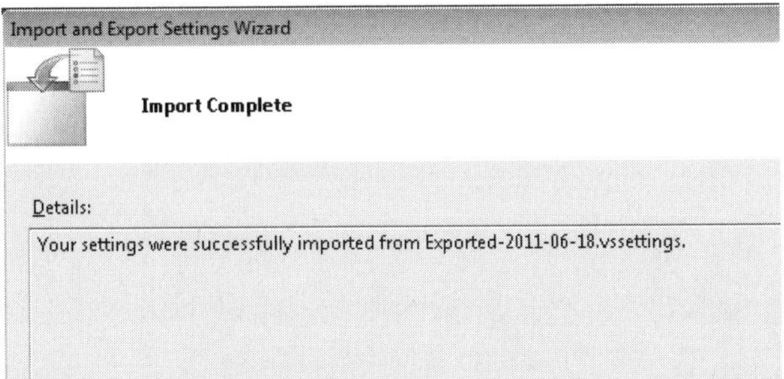

Now, just click Finish and you are done.

01.09 Change Your Visual Studio Color Scheme

WINDOWS	Alt,T, I
MENU	Tools | Import and Export Settings
COMMAND	Tools.ImportandExportSettings
VERSIONS	2005, 2008, 2010
CODE	vstipEnv0034

Ever see a set of colors your friend or coworker has and wish you could get it too? Ever go to *http://studiostyles.info* and want some of those cool color schemes?

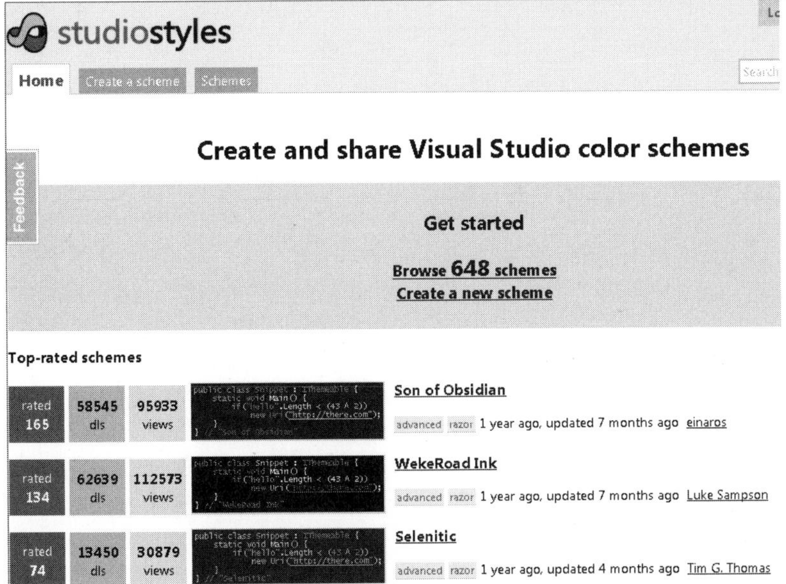

Well you can get the colors you want! Let's walk through how it's done.

Seeing What You Like

First, you see a seriously cool color scheme on someone's screen or at the Studio Styles site:

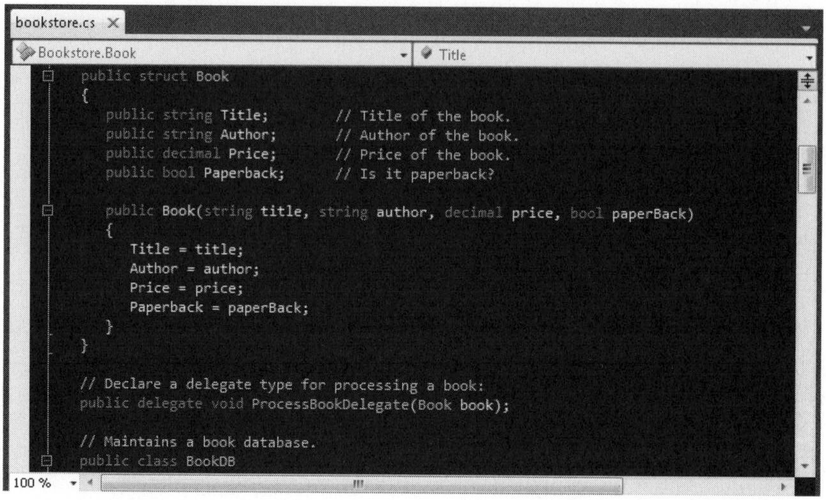

```
bookstore.cs
Bookstore.Book                    Title
public struct Book
{
    public string Title;        // Title of the book.
    public string Author;       // Author of the book.
    public decimal Price;       // Price of the book.
    public bool Paperback;      // Is it paperback?

    public Book(string title, string author, decimal price, bool paperBack)
    {
        Title = title;
        Author = author;
        Price = price;
        Paperback = paperBack;
    }
}

// Declare a delegate type for processing a book:
public delegate void ProcessBookDelegate(Book book);

// Maintains a book database.
public class BookDB
100 %
```

Getting the Goods

On someone's computer

Now that you see what you like, get them to export their fonts and colors. Go to Tools | Import And Export Settings:

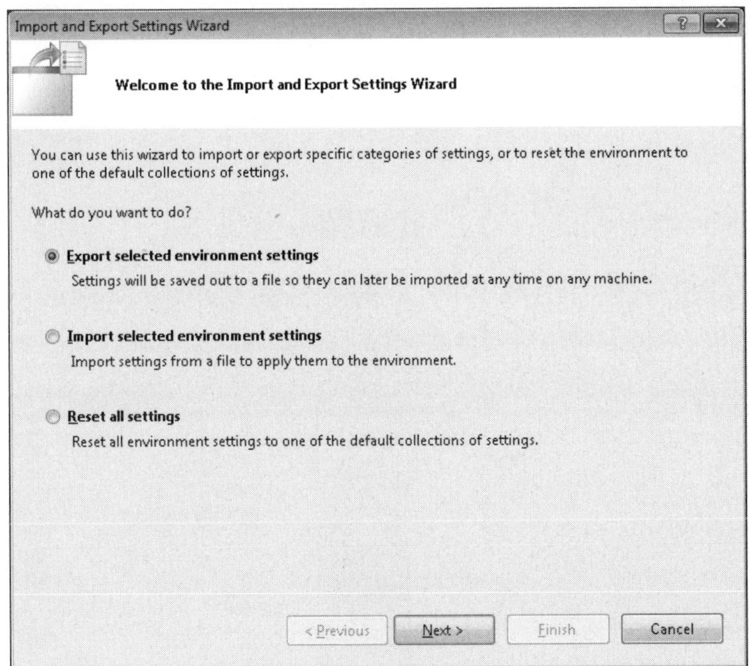

Click Next, and export *only* the fonts and colors—*nothing else*:

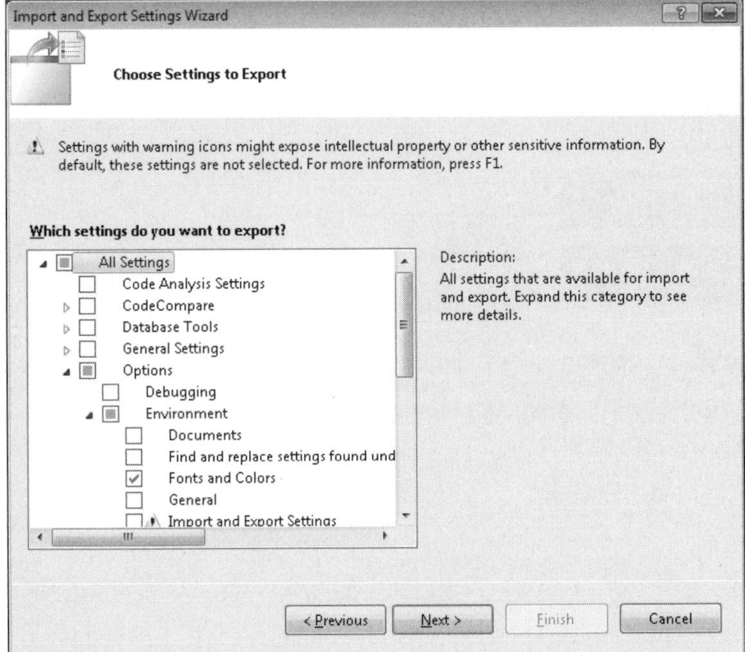

Click Next, give the settings a cool name, and click Finish:

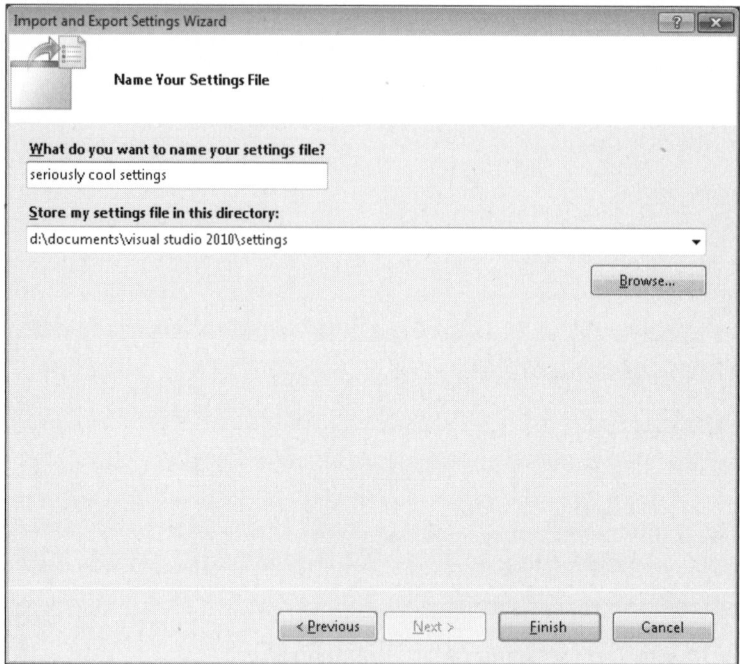

On the Studio Styles site

Click the style you want:

Choose your Visual Studio version, click Download This Scheme, and follow the instructions in the next section:

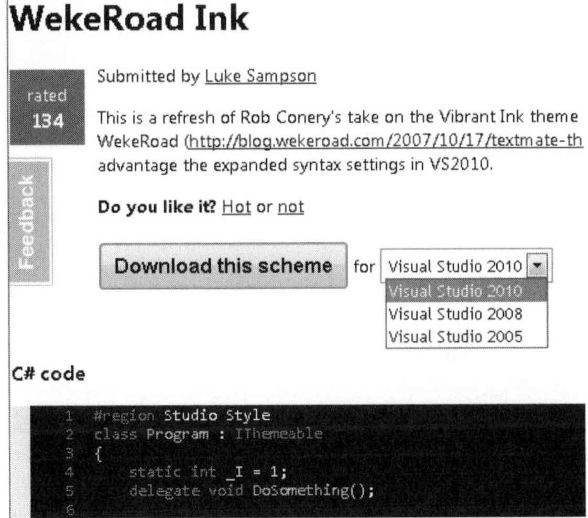

Changing Your Colors

When you have a .vssettings file you want to import, copy or move the file to your computer. While you can put the file anywhere you want on your system, I prefer to put it with the other settings files located at C:\Users\<user>\Documents\Visual Studio <version>\Settings:

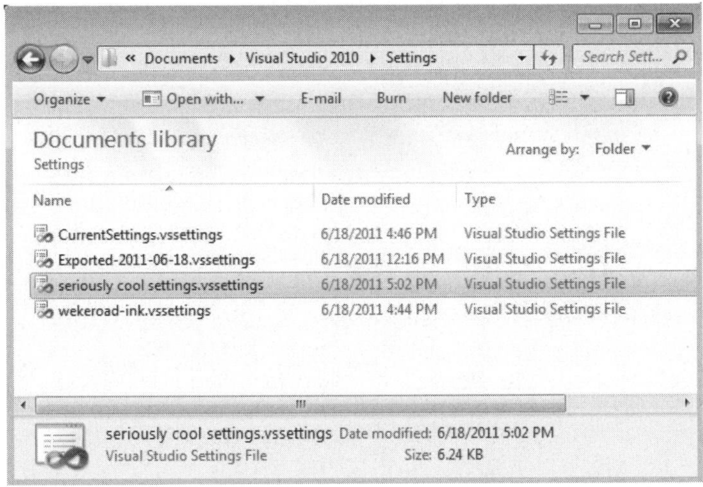

Now just go to Tools | Import And Export Settings on your computer:

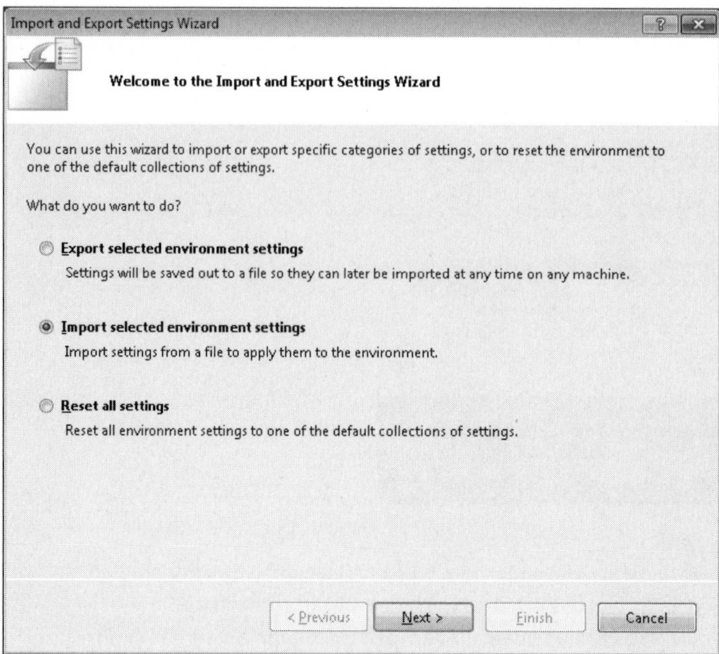

Make sure that Import Selected Environment Settings is selected, as shown in the preceding illustration, and click Next. If you haven't backed up your settings in a while, feel free to do so. Check out vstipEnv0034 ("Change Your Visual Studio Color Scheme", page 17) if you want more information on exporting your settings:

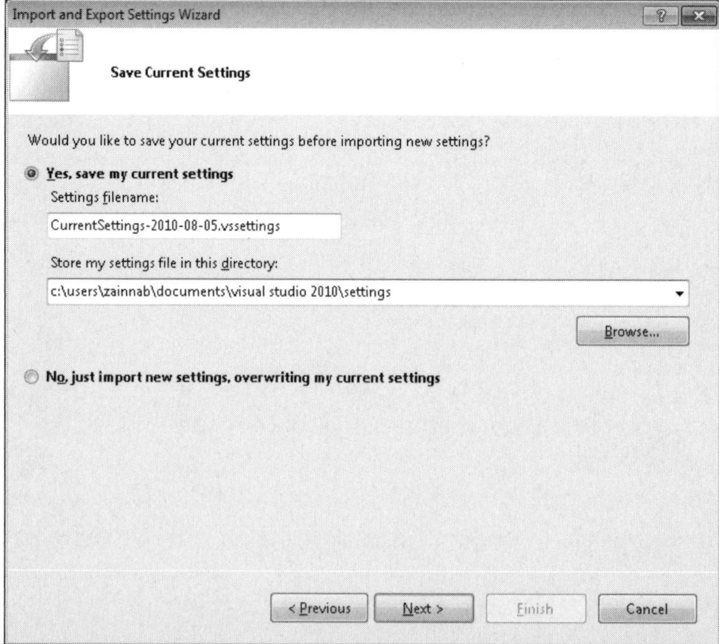

Choose the settings file that has the color scheme you want:

Note Click Browse to find your file if you didn't put it in your Settings folder.

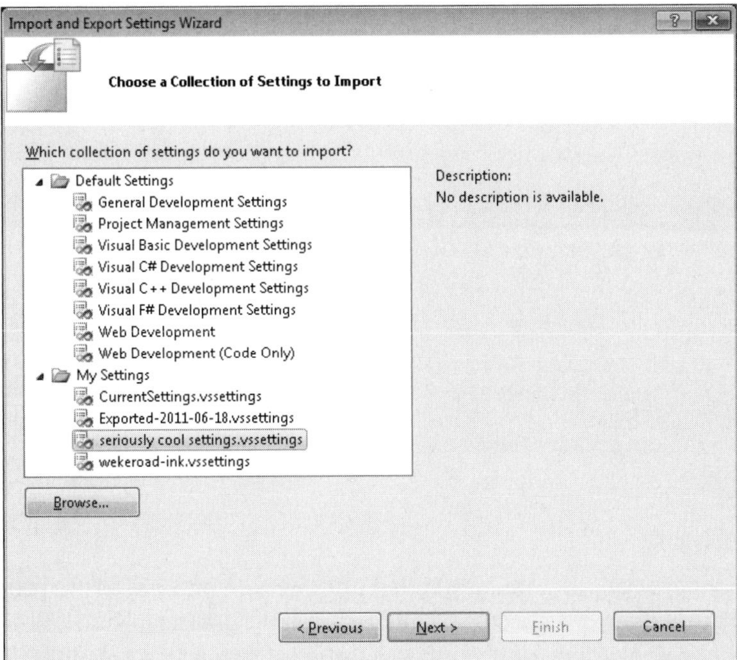

Click Next. Verify that the file is importing *only* fonts and colors, and then click Finish:

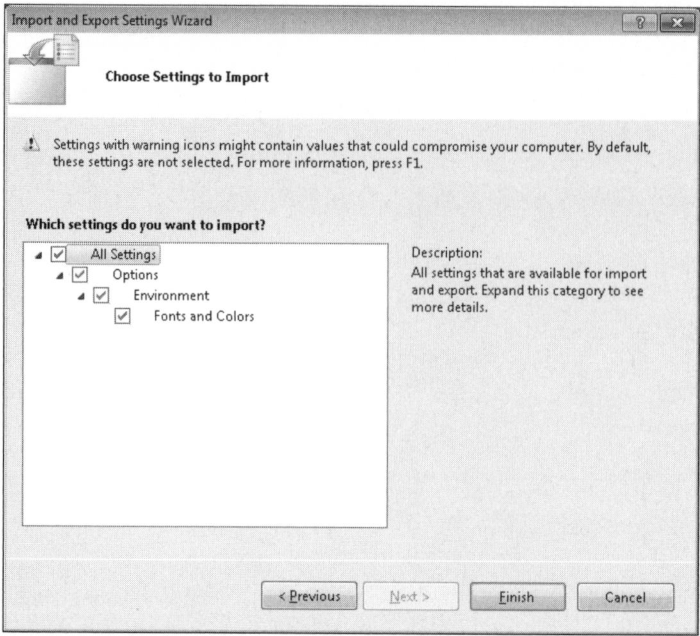

Resetting the Colors

You should have your new colors. If things get bad (for example, you get colors you don't like and didn't make a backup of your old colors) and you need to get the default colors back, all you have to do is go to Tools | Options | Fonts And Colors and click Use Defaults.

Warning Clicking Use Defaults is an option that wipes out any custom colors used previously.

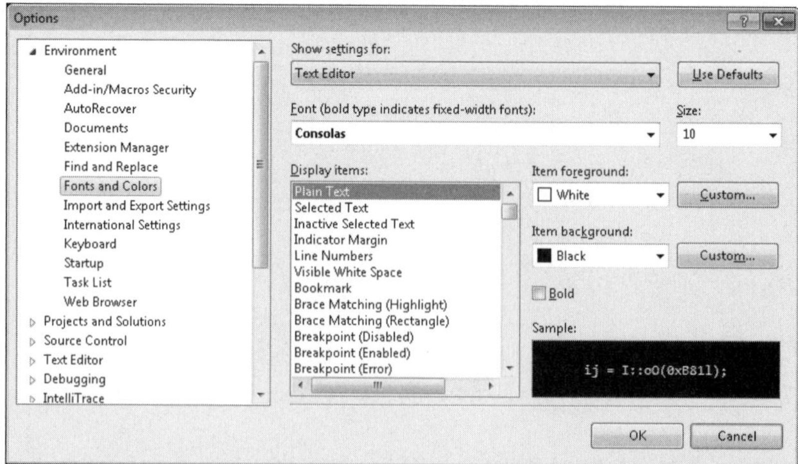

01.10 Reset All Your Development Settings

WINDOWS	Alt,T, I
MENU	Tools | Import and ExportSettings
COMMAND	Tools.ImportandExport Settings
VERSIONS	2005, 2008, 2010
CODE	vstipEnv0023

Sometimes you need to get all your settings back to their original state. You can do this with the Reset All Settings option found under Tools | Import And Export Settings:

Warning Use the Reset All Settings option at your own risk. It *will* reset your settings, including a reset of your Toolbox, getting rid of any custom items you have put in there.

After you click Next on the Welcome page shown in the preceding illustration, you see the option to save your current settings. *You should absolutely do this.*

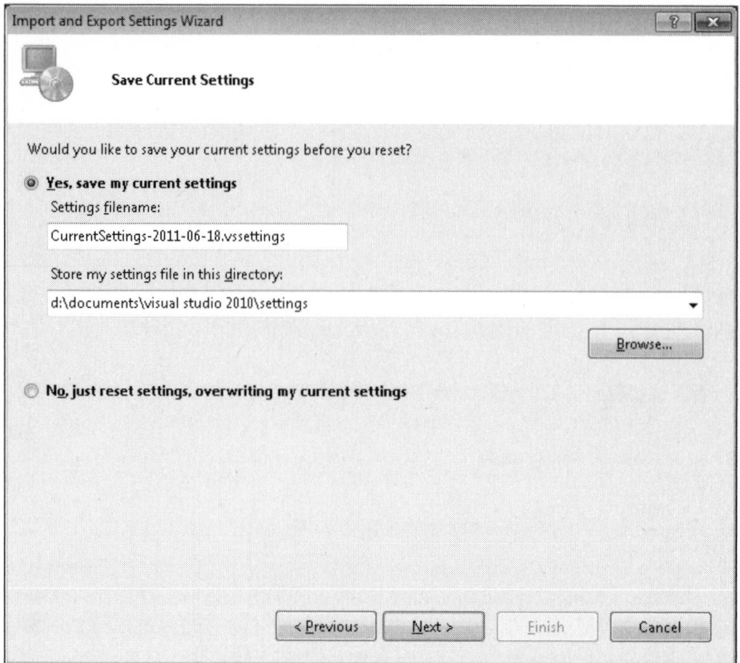

The next screen lets you choose from the list of default settings:

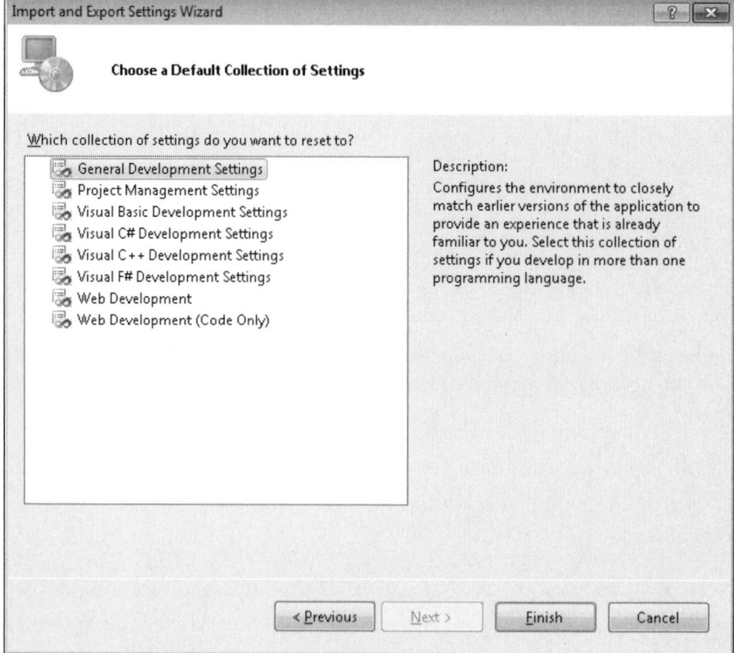

Choose your default settings, and click Finish. After the reset operation runs, it resets all your settings. This is definitely something you would do as a last resort, and remember, you can always bring back your old settings by importing settings you saved earlier (see vstipEnv0021, "Exporting Your Environment Settings", page 6).

01.11 Customize Your Toolbars in Visual Studio 2010: Toolbars Tab

WINDOWS	Alt,T, C
MENU	Tools | Customize
COMMAND	Tools.Customize
VERSIONS	2010
CODE	vstipEnv0030

You can customize any toolbar in Visual Studio 2010. Just click the drop-down arrow to the right of any toolbar, and then click Add Or Remove Buttons:

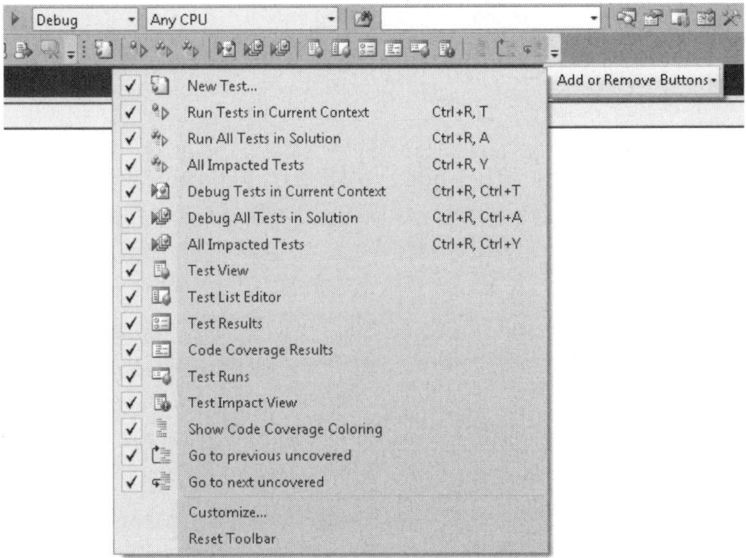

Then click Customize:

Alternatively, you can go to Tools | Customize on the menu bar. Whichever option you choose opens the Customize dialog box:

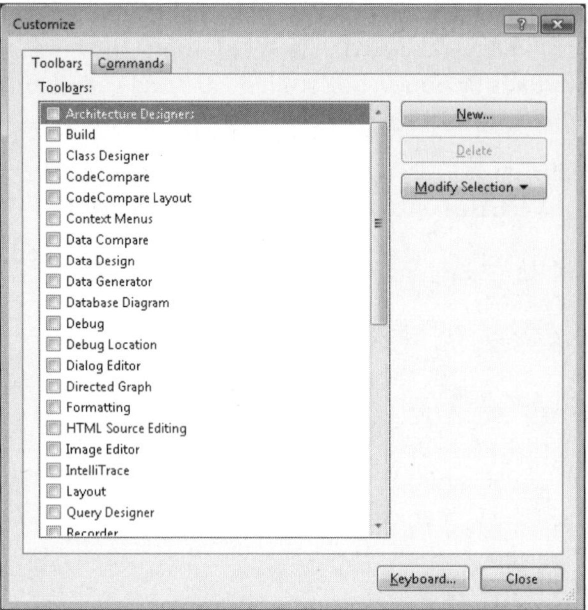

Custom Toolbars

As shown in the preceding illustration, the Toolbars tab lists all the available toolbars. After you click New to create a customized toolbar, you are prompted to give the new toolbar a name:

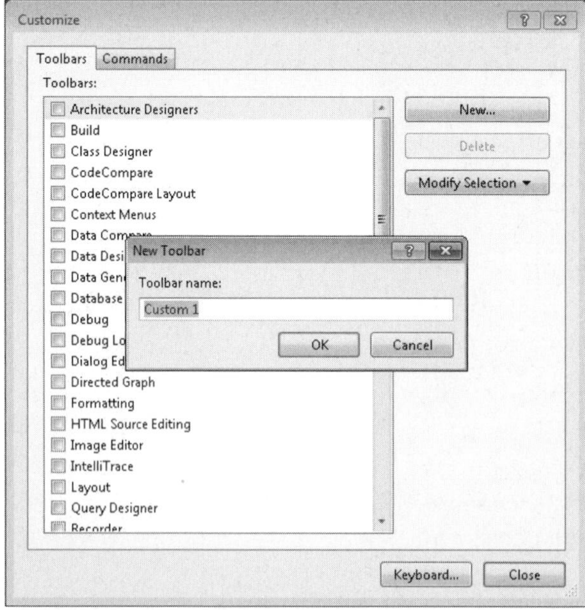

After you name it, you can delete the custom toolbar by clicking Delete, or you can change it by clicking Modify Selection to rename or relocate the toolbar:

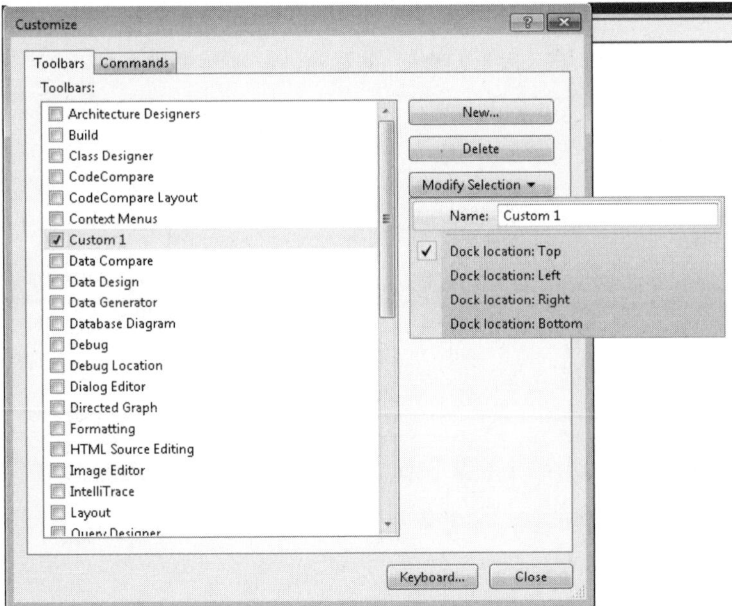

Although you can rename custom toolbars by clicking Modify Selection, default toolbars can't be changed in this way:

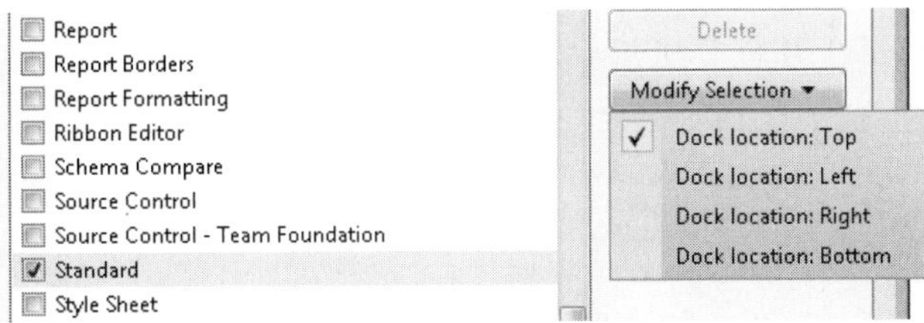

Clicking Keyboard at the bottom of the Customize dialog box takes you to the Tools | Options | Keyboard area, where you can add keyboard shortcuts for selected commands. (See vstipTool0063, "Keyboard Shortcuts: Creating New Shortcuts", page 127, for details.)

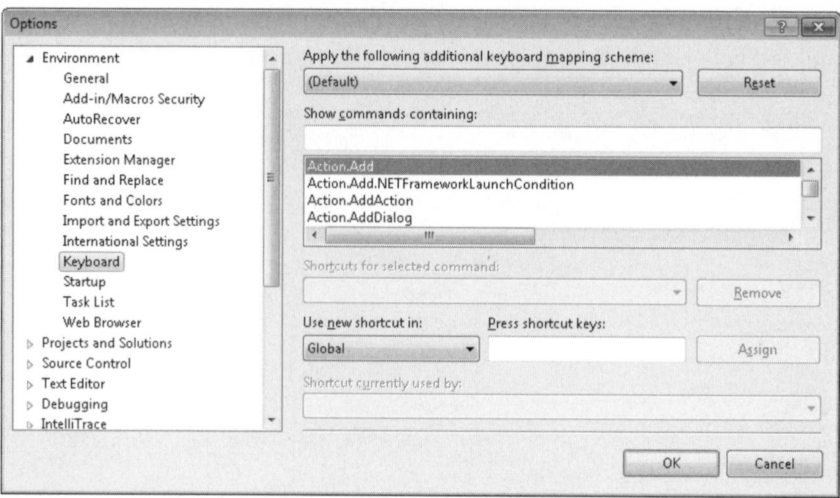

01.12 Customize Your Toolbars in Visual Studio 2010: Commands Tab

WINDOWS	Alt,T, C
MENU	Tools | Customize
COMMAND	Tools.Customize
VERSIONS	2010
CODE	vstipEnv0031

You can customize any toolbar in Visual Studio 2010. Just click the drop-down arrow to the right of any toolbar, and then click Add Or Remove Buttons:

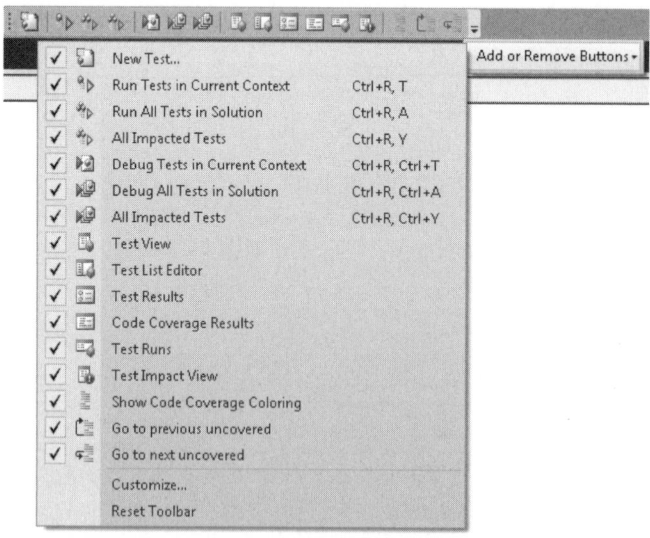

Then click Customize:

Alternatively, you can go to Tools | Customize on the menu bar.

Either option you choose opens the Customize dialog box:

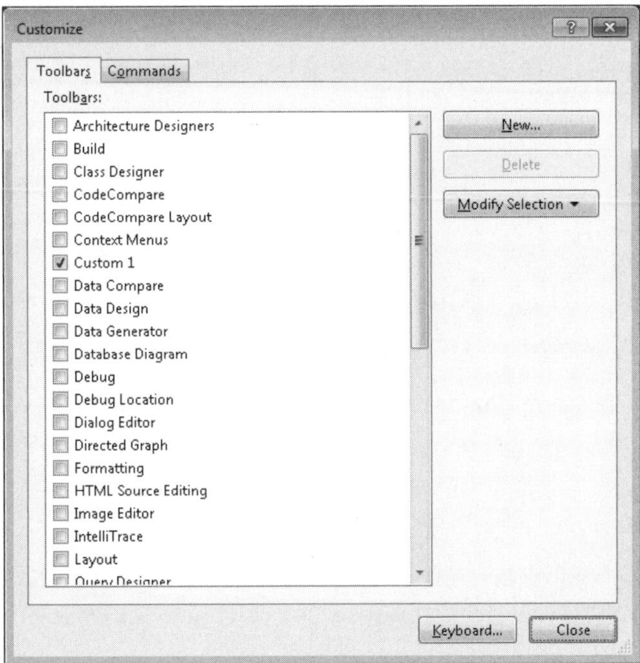

Click the Commands tab:

Note For information about the Toolbars tab, see vstipEnv0030, "Customize Your Toolbars in Visual Studio 2010 Toolbars Tab", page 27.

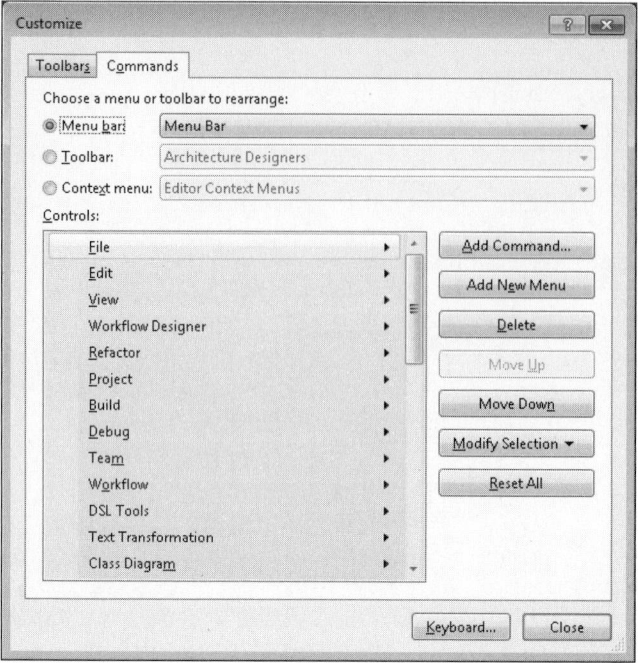

As you can see, the Customize dialog box is fairly complex, so let's break it down into its parts as we look at an example.

Rearrange

First is the choice of menu or toolbar to modify. In this case, choose the Editor Context Menus | Code Window option, which is what you see when you right-click while writing code:

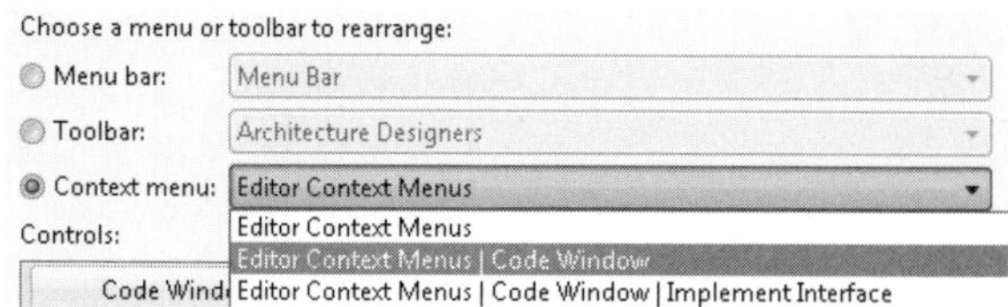

Controls

Next is the Controls area that shows the items on the menu or toolbar you have chosen to modify. For this example, it shows the items available when you right-click in a code window:

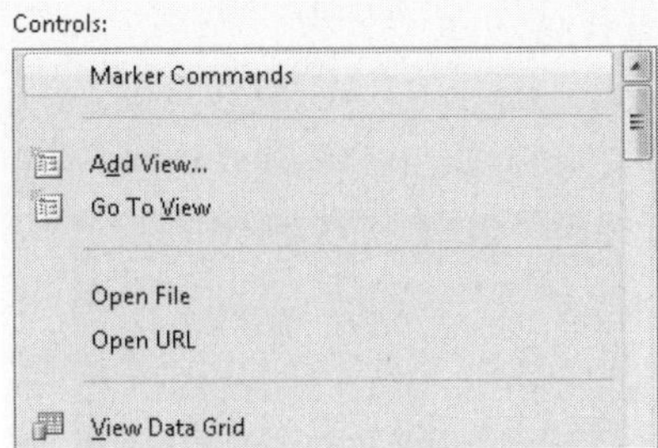

Remember that not all the items you see are available all the time because these items show up only in the proper context. So while it seems you have a large number of buttons currently available, when you right-click in your code window, this is an example of what you will currently see:

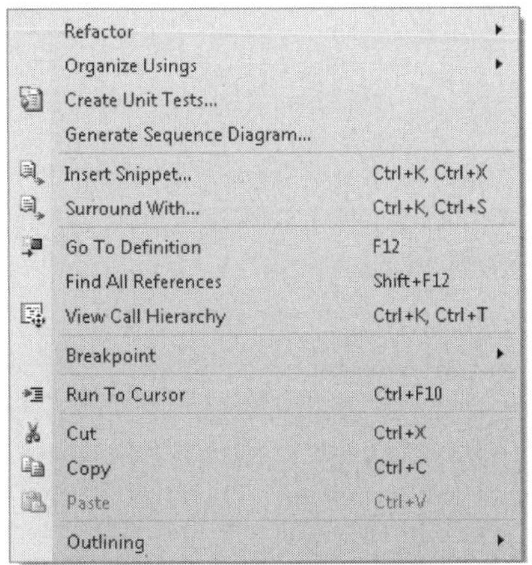

Buttons

Finally, let's look at the area of the dialog box that has all the buttons that actually *perform* actions:

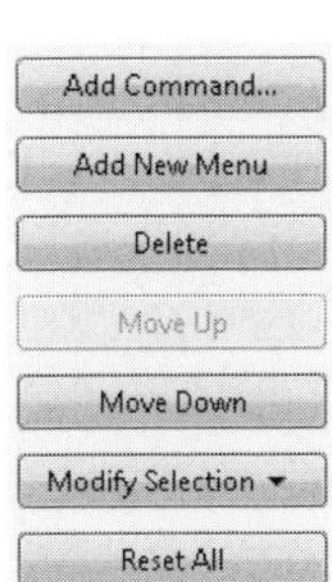

- **Add Command**
  Lets you add a new item to the existing menu or toolbar.
- **Add New Menu**
  Creates a new menu in the existing menu or toolbar.
- **Delete**
  Removes the current item from the Controls area.
- **Move [Up or Down]**
  Changes the location of the item in the Controls area.

Modify Selection

Choosing Modify Selection enables you to make changes to the existing item in the Controls area, such as resetting it to the default settings, changing the name, and modifying text visibility options. Modify Selection also enables you to make a new group on the menu or toolbar:

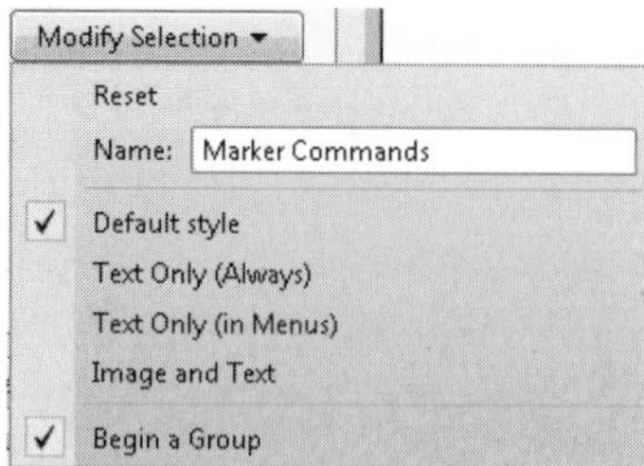

Finally, the Reset All option resets every item in the Controls area to its default settings. This capability is particularly useful if you have made a lot of changes.

Getting back to our example: Let's assume you want to add the comment and uncomment items to the context menu so that you can use them when you select some code. First, click Add Command to bring up the Add Command dialog box:

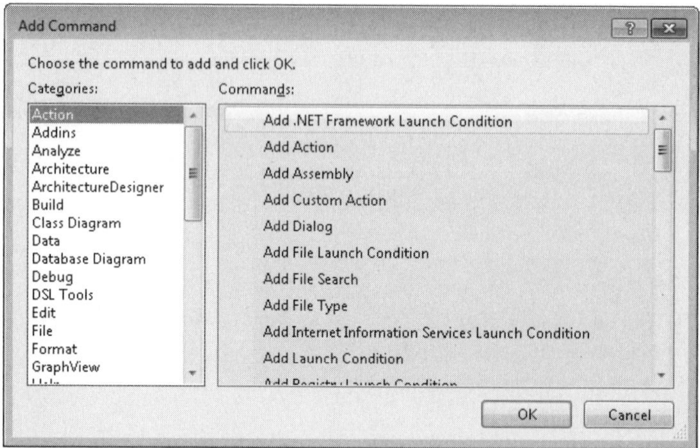

Now you need to figure out where the comment and uncomment items are located. How would you do this? Well, the best path is usually to see whether the item can be found on a menu somewhere and then use that as a clue:

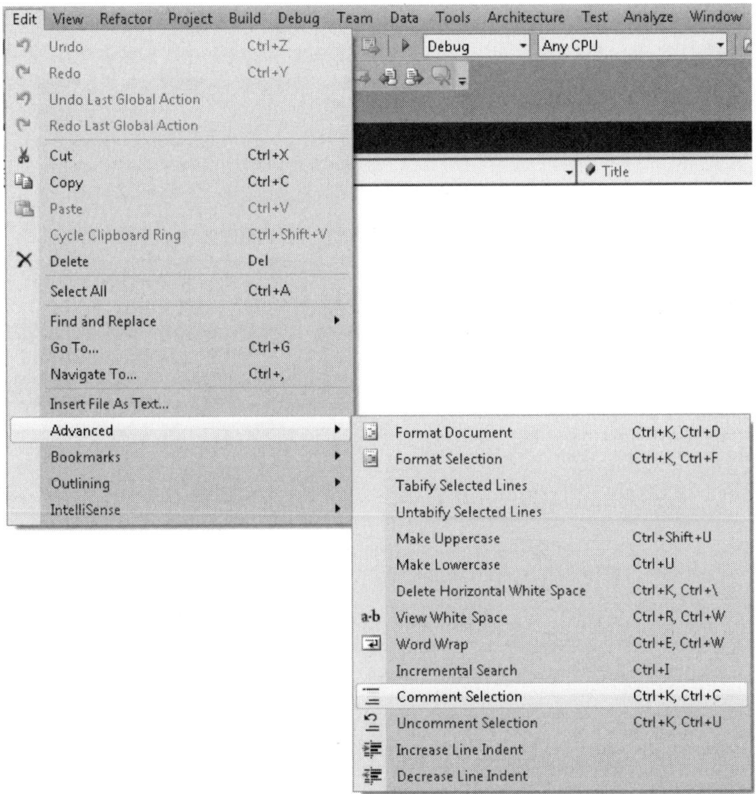

Because the items you want are off the Edit menu, you can search there first. It turns out the items you want are called Selection Comment and Selection Uncomment:

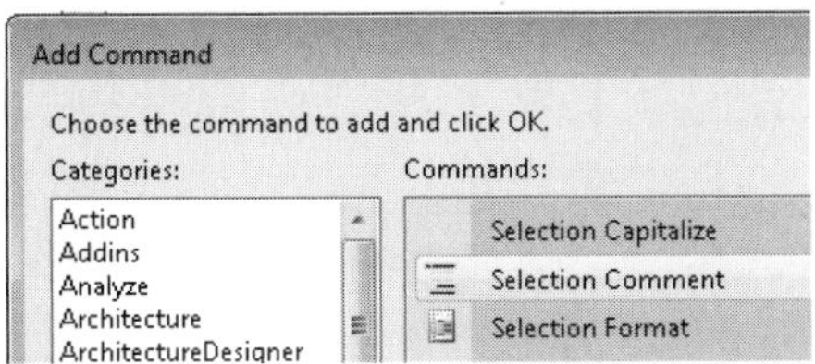

Find each one of these items, and click OK to add them to the Controls list:

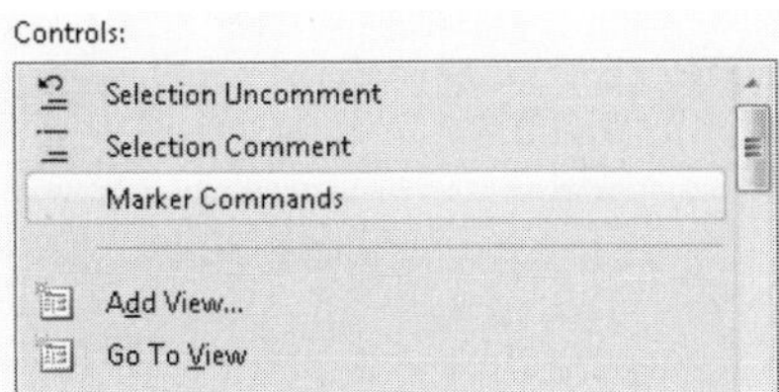

It would be nice to have these buttons in their own group, so select the item in the Controls dialog box, shown in the preceding illustration, where you would like the group line to be (Marker Commands, in this case), and then click Modify Selection and choose Begin A Group:

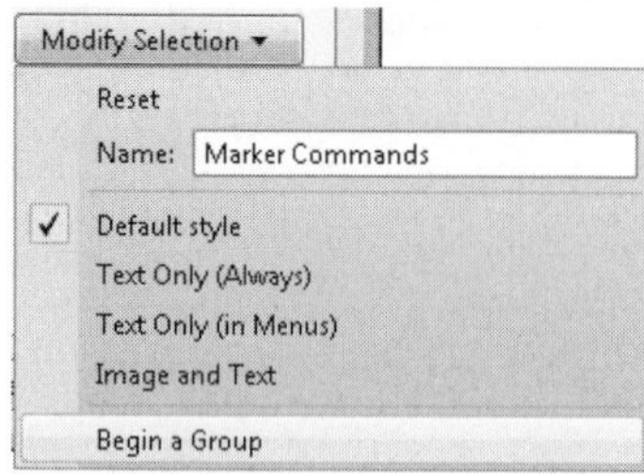

This creates a new group line, and your commands are in their own group:

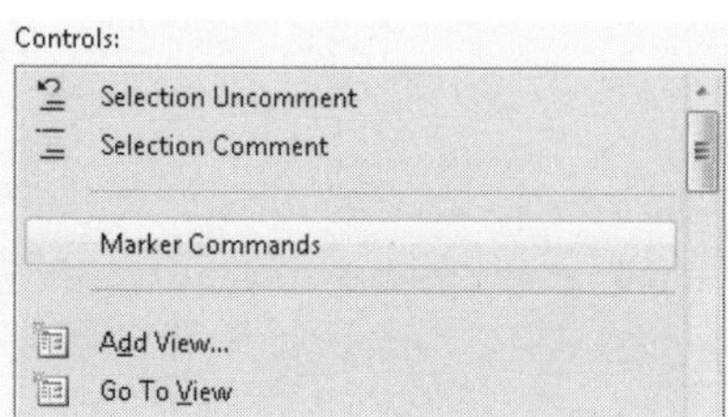

Click Close and go to any code area. Select some code, right-click, and select Comment Selection:

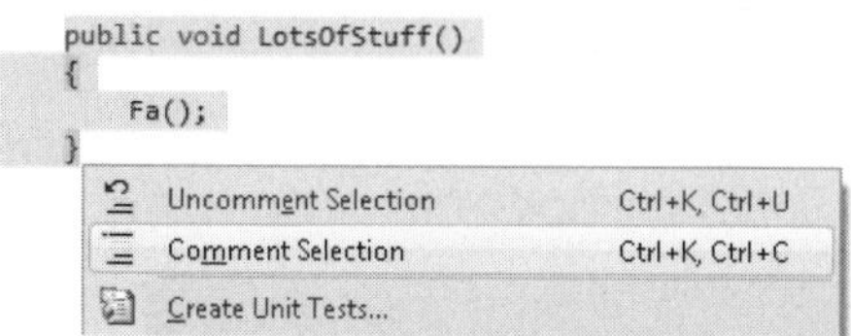

It works perfectly, and you are all set to begin making your own modifications to your environment:

```
//public void LotsOfStuff()
//{
//    Fa();
//}
```

01.13 Visual Studio Logging

VERSIONS	2005, 2008, 2010
CODE	vstipEnv0048

There's no doubt Visual Studio is an awesome piece of software, but occasionally you might run into a problem loading it. Did you know that it comes with a logging switch? While the documentation (*http://msdn.microsoft.com/en-us/library/ms241272.aspx*) is lacking, the community comment contributed by Paul Harrington on the Visual Studio team helps a great deal.

Essentially, the syntax is as follows:

```
devenv.exe /log [filename]
```

The [filename] is optional and, if not specified, the ActivityLog.xml file is called by default. The path is to the log file is:

```
%APPDATA%\Microsoft\VisualStudio\<version>\ActivityLog.xml
```

Give it a try. Go to the Visual Studio command prompt, and enter **devenv.exe /log**:

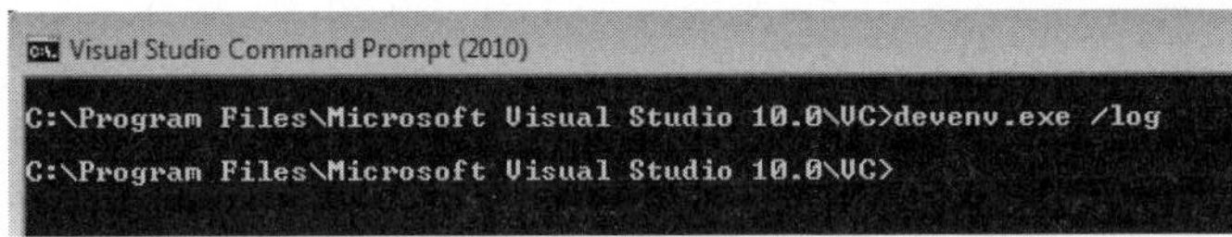

You can then navigate to the file location:

When you open the log file, the following illustration provides an example of what you might see:

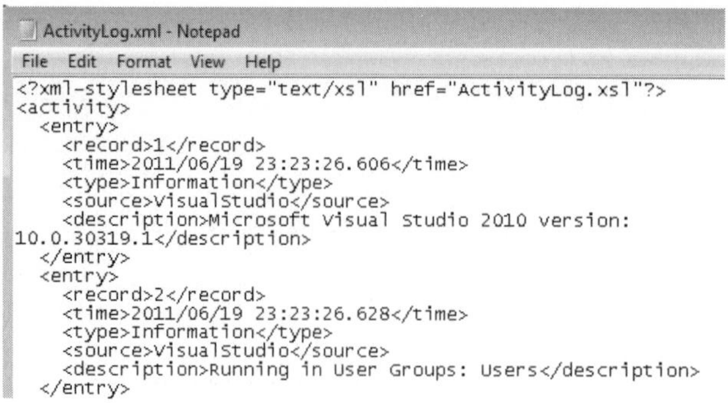

ActivityLog.xml - Notepad

File Edit Format View Help

```
<?xml-stylesheet type="text/xsl" href="ActivityLog.xsl"?>
<activity>
  <entry>
    <record>1</record>
    <time>2011/06/19 23:23:26.606</time>
    <type>Information</type>
    <source>VisualStudio</source>
    <description>Microsoft Visual Studio 2010 version:
10.0.30319.1</description>
  </entry>
  <entry>
    <record>2</record>
    <time>2011/06/19 23:23:26.628</time>
    <type>Information</type>
    <source>VisualStudio</source>
    <description>Running in User Groups: Users</description>
  </entry>
```

Fortunately, an XML style sheet (XSL) comes with the data, so if you view the XML file in your browser, you can see a much cleaner view:

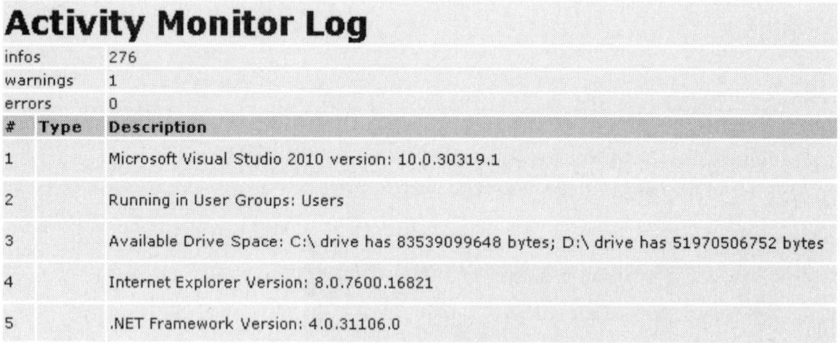

Activity Monitor Log

infos	276
warnings	1
errors	0

#	Type	Description
1		Microsoft Visual Studio 2010 version: 10.0.30319.1
2		Running in User Groups: Users
3		Available Drive Space: C:\ drive has 83539099648 bytes; D:\ drive has 51970506752 bytes
4		Internet Explorer Version: 8.0.7600.16821
5		.NET Framework Version: 4.0.31106.0

Now you can easily see the logging information and look for any issues.

01.14 Visual Studio Safe Mode

VERSIONS	2005, 2008, 2010
CODE	vstipEnv0050

Occasionally you have a situation where Visual Studio might not start up correctly or at all. Using Visual Studio in safe mode, you can load only the default environment, services, and shipped versions of third-party packages to see whether the problem is caused by one or more third-party add-ins. Just go to the Visual Studio command prompt, and type **devenv.exe /safemode**:

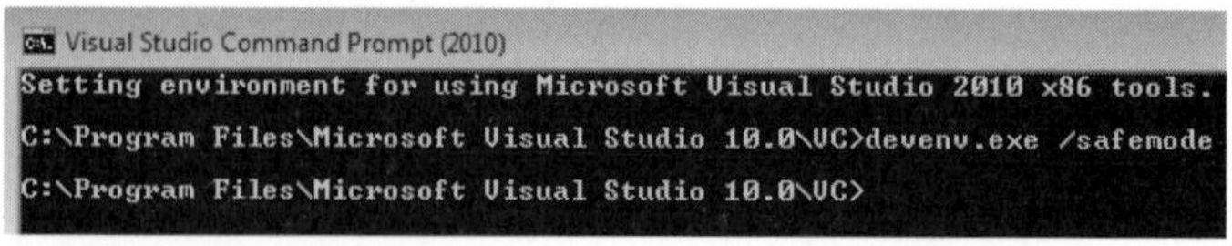

Visual Studio Command Prompt (2010)

```
Setting environment for using Microsoft Visual Studio 2010 x86 tools.
C:\Program Files\Microsoft Visual Studio 10.0\VC>devenv.exe /safemode
C:\Program Files\Microsoft Visual Studio 10.0\VC>
```

Note Although I don't show it here, I suggest using the Visual Studio logging feature before running safe mode to see whether it can help you determine the source of the problem. For more information, see vstipEnv0048, "Visual Studio Logging", page 37.

When Visual Studio starts up, it indicates it is running in safe mode in the title bar:

From here, you can start determining what might have caused Visual Studio to fail and remedy the issue.

01.15 The ResetSettings Switch

VERSIONS	2005, 2008, 2010
CODE	vstipEnv0047

Visual Studio supports several switches. One of these is the /ResetSettings switch. When used by itself, it resets Visual Studio to the default settings you initially chose during install. That's nice, but an even better option is available that can be particularly useful for people in other scenarios.

Let's take a classic example: You might have two (or more) monitors at work, but when you get home, you work with just one monitor. Your window layouts (among other things) could be very different in each place. In vstipEnv0040, "Export Your Window Layouts" (page 134), I showed you how to export just your window layouts. Using the exported information, you could create and use two different window layouts: one for work and one for home. This tip shows you how to do this when using two different machines or the same machine at work and home.

Two Different Machines

The question is: What do you do once you have exported the window layouts? Well, now you put the .vssettings files where you can easily get to them on your machines and then you go to the Properties dialog box of the Visual Studio program icon:

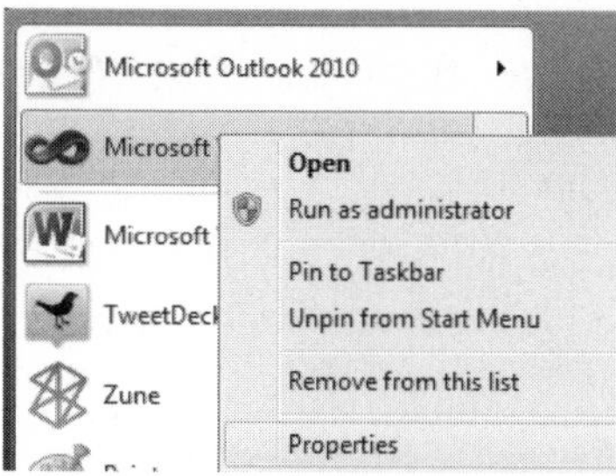

Click the Shortcut tab:

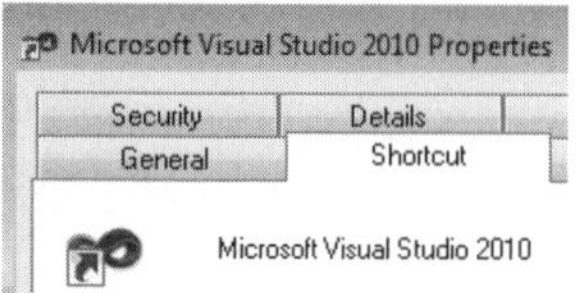

In the Target area, type **/ResetSettings [settings file]**, where [settings file] is the path to the settings file for one of your layouts:

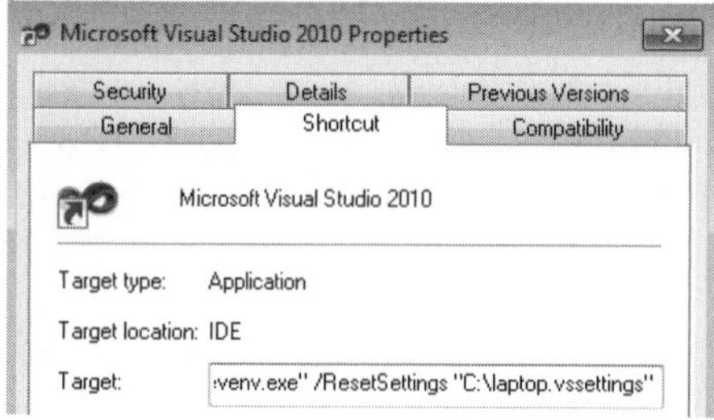

Now Visual Studio loads up with the settings appropriate for your machine.

Same Machine

What if you use the same machine for home and work, like a laptop? Just make two copies of the Visual Studio program icon, put them somewhere (on your Desktop, most likely), and give them names:

Now just follow the steps for the different machines for each icon, and you can use one icon when you are at work to get the work window layouts and the other for home with the home window layout.

Chapter 2

Projects and Items

"He recalled his exertions and solicitations, and the history of his project [...], which had been accepted for consideration [...]"

—Leo Tolstoy, "War and Peace"

After you get past your initial customization of Visual Studio, you will start creating projects and items to get your work done. This section contains a group of resources that you will find useful early on. Some will definitely be more useful to beginners (for example, searching templates), and others will apply to more advanced users (such as creating custom templates).

On the subject of custom templates, make sure you read though (and practice) how to create them. Of all the topics in this chapter, I feel that creating custom project and item templates will save you the greatest amount of time. That's a pretty bold statement—but I have seen properly set up templates save untold hours for developers.

02.01 Search for Project Templates in the New Project Dialog Box

DEFAULT	Ctrl+Shift+N (new project dialog box); Ctrl+E (puts cursor in search box)
VISUAL BASIC 6	Ctrl+Shift+N (new project dialog box); Ctrl+N (new project); Ctrl+E (puts cursor in search box)
VISUAL C# 2005	Ctrl+Shift+N (new project dialog box); Ctrl+E (puts cursor in search box)
VISUAL C++ 2	Ctrl+Shift+N (new project dialog box); Ctrl+E (puts cursor in search box)
VISUAL C++ 6	Ctrl+Shift+N (new project dialog box); Ctrl+E (puts cursor in search box)
VISUAL STUDIO 6	Ctrl+N (new project dialog box); Ctrl+E (puts cursor in search box)
WINDOWS	Alt,F, N, P (new project dialog box); Alt,F, D, N (add new project)
MENU	File | New Project; File | Add New Project
COMMAND	File.NewProject; File.AddNewProject
VERSIONS	2010
CODE	vstipProj0001

Did you know that you can search for templates in the New Project dialog box? Look in the upper-right corner, and notice the new search area.

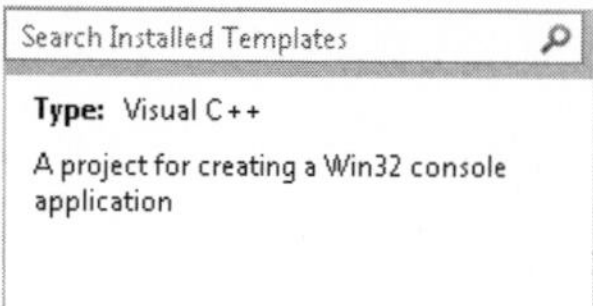

Click there or press Ctrl+E, and type the word web into the search box. The following illustration shows what you should expect to see.

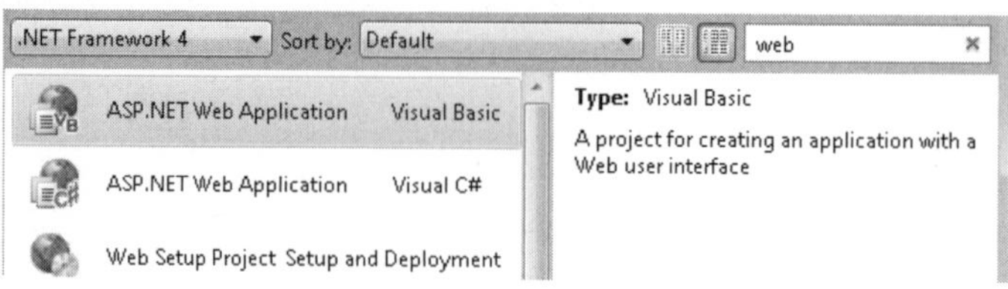

Good News

The search populates the middle pane with results from the recent, installed, or online lists, depending on which category you select.

Bad News

The search doesn't automatically filter the results according to your preferred language, and it doesn't support any advanced search options, such as Boolean searches, regular expressions, and so on.

More Good News

In most cases, you can easily filter on your language by simply typing in an abbreviation of your language (C#, VB, F#, or C++).

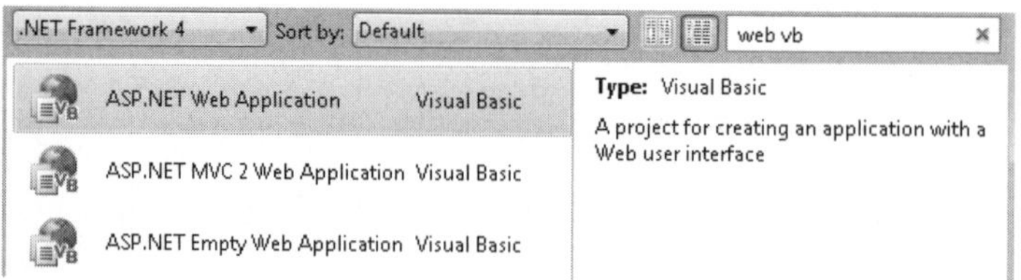

02.02 Recent Project Templates in the New Project Dialog Box

DEFAULT	Ctrl+Shift+N (new project dialog box)
VISUAL BASIC 6	Ctrl+Shift+N (new project dialog box); Ctrl+N (new project)
VISUAL C# 2005	Ctrl+Shift+N (new project dialog box)
VISUAL C++ 2	Ctrl+Shift+N (new project dialog box)
VISUAL C++ 6	Ctrl+Shift+N (new project dialog box)
VISUAL STUDIO 6	Ctrl+N (new project dialog box)
WINDOWS	Alt,F, N, P (new project); Alt,F, D, N (add new project)
MENU	File | New Project; File | Add New Project
COMMAND	File.NewProject; File.AddNewProject
VERSIONS	2010
CODE	vstipProj0002

In the Visual Studio 2010 New Project dialog box, you can get a list of your five most recently used templates. Just click Recent Templates to see a list of the templates you have used.

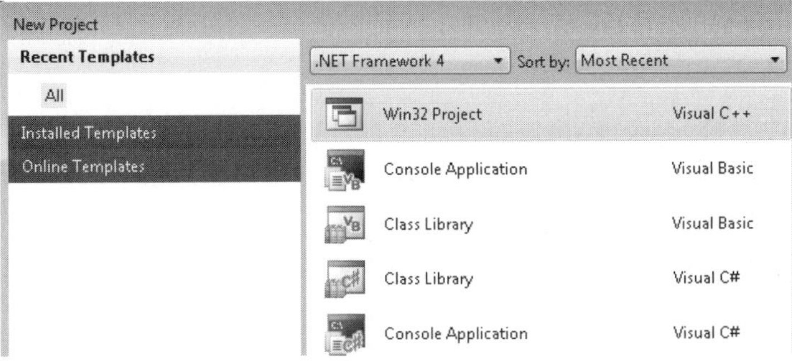

02.03 Using Older Frameworks with Multi-Targeting

DEFAULT	Ctrl+Shift+N (new project dialog box)
VISUAL BASIC 6	Ctrl+Shift+N (new project dialog box); Ctrl+N (new project)
VISUAL C# 2005	Ctrl+Shift+N (new project dialog box)
VISUAL C++ 2	Ctrl+Shift+N (new project dialog box)
VISUAL C++ 6	Ctrl+Shift+N (new project dialog box)
VISUAL STUDIO 6	Ctrl+N (new project dialog box)
WINDOWS	Alt,F, N, P (new project); Alt,F, D, N (add new project)
MENU	File | New Project; File | Add New Project
COMMAND	File.NewProject; File.AddNewProject
VERSIONS	2008, 2010
CODE	vstipProj0005

Even if you use an older version of the Microsoft .NET Framework, you can still use all the great features in Visual Studio 2008 and Visual Studio 2010 through multi-targeting.

When you create a new project, locate the drop-down list of supported .NET Framework versions and simply choose the one you prefer. You get to use most of the great features in the new IDE but still keep your older version of the .NET Framework. The following graphic shows the New Project dialog box in Visual Studio 2010.

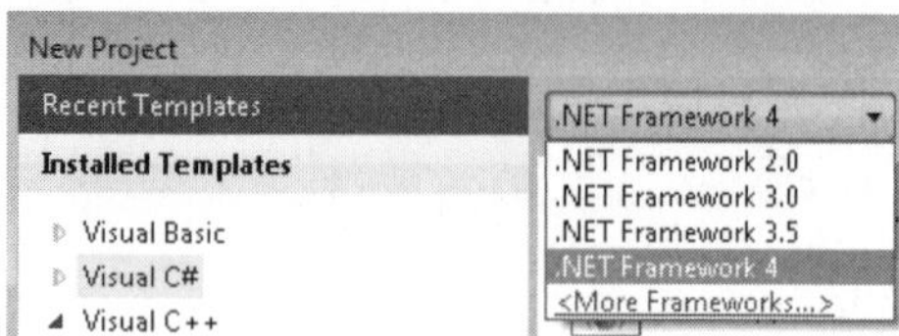

02.04 Create Web Application or Virtual Directory in IIS

DEFAULT	Shift+Alt+N
VISUAL BASIC 6	Shift+Alt+N
VISUAL C# 2005	Shift+Alt+N
VISUAL C++ 2	Shift+Alt+N
VISUAL C++ 6	Shift+Alt+N
VISUAL STUDIO 6	Shift+Alt+N
WINDOWS	Alt,F, N, W
MENU	File | New Web Site
COMMAND	File.NewWebSite
VERSIONS	2008, 2010
CODE	vstipEnv0058

How can you create Web Applications and Virtual Directories in Internet Information Server from inside Visual Studio? Just select File | New Web Site, and click Browse in the lower-right corner.

In the Choose Location dialog box, select Local IIS, and pick the website in which you want to create the new item.

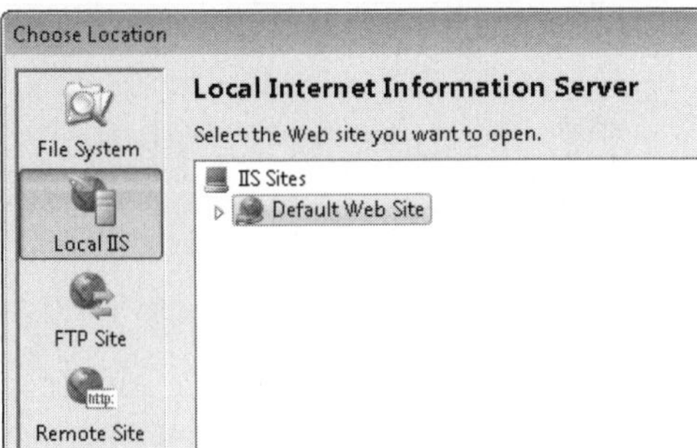

In the upper-right corner of the dialog box, notice the three buttons, as shown in the following illustration.

The button to the far left creates a new Web Application.

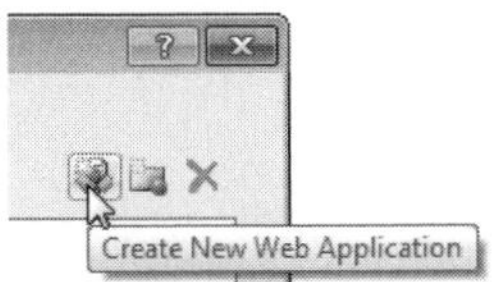

The middle button creates a new Virtual Directory.

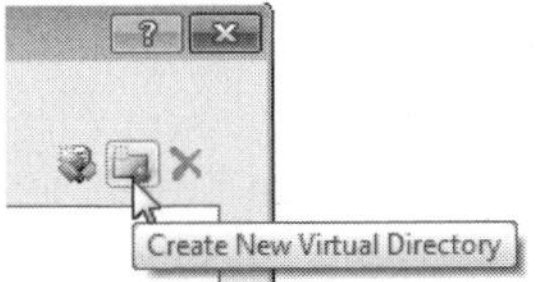

You can pick whichever one you want to create, without ever leaving Visual Studio.

02.05 Multiple Startup Projects

DEFAULT	Alt+Enter (in Solution Explorer)
VISUAL BASIC 6	Alt+Enter (in Solution Explorer)
VISUAL C# 2005	Alt+Enter (in Solution Explorer)
VISUAL C++ 2	Alt+Enter (in Solution Explorer)
VISUAL C++ 6	Alt+Enter (in Solution Explorer)
VISUAL STUDIO 6	Alt+Enter (in Solution Explorer)
WINDOWS	Alt, P, P
MENU	Project | Properties [with Solution Selected in Solution Explorer]; [Right-Click the solution in Solution Explorer] | Properties
COMMAND	Project.Properties
VERSIONS	2005, 2008, 2010
LANGUAGES	C#, VB
CODE	vstipEnv0015

It's common for developers to work with multiple projects. For example, consider a classic Client/Server scenario: One project includes all the elements shown here:

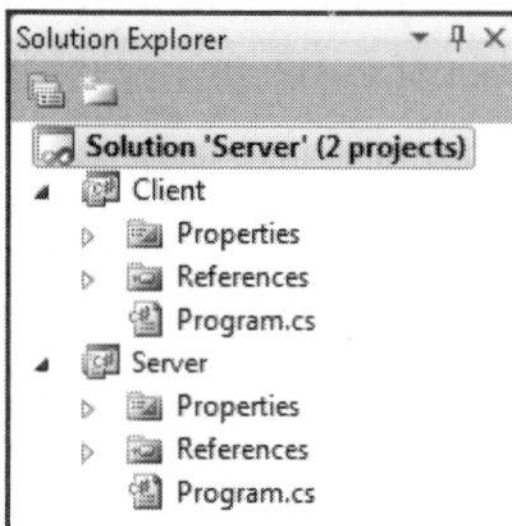

In this case, setting a single Startup Project isn't sufficient; you want both these projects to start up when you press F5. Just click the solution in Solution Explorer, and then click the Properties button (Alt+Enter) at the top.

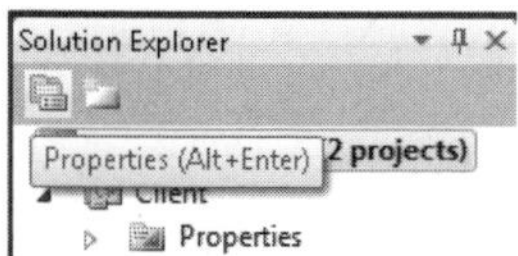

Make sure you are in the Common Properties | Startup Project area, and you should see a dialog box similar to the following.

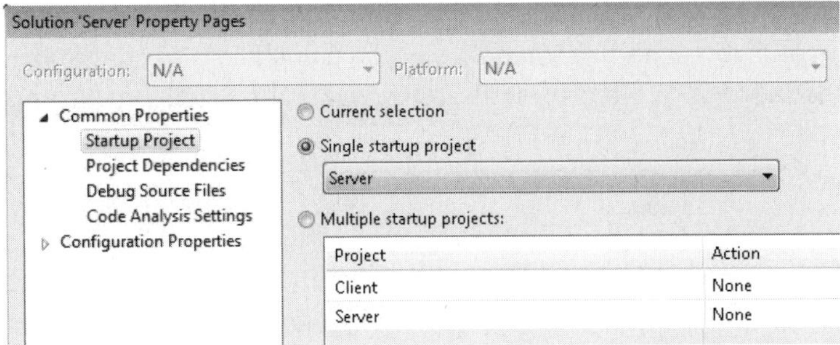

Notice that, currently, Single Startup Project is selected, but that isn't what you need. Instead, select Multiple Startup Projects.

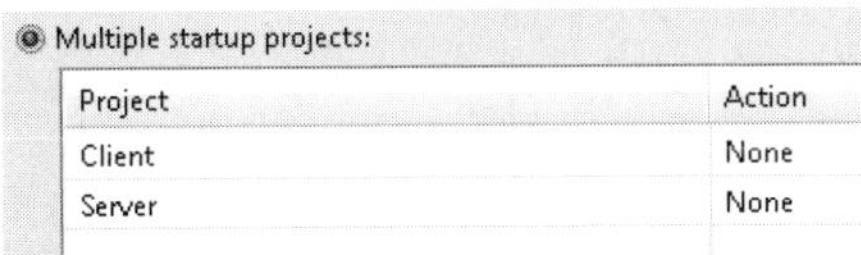

Now you need to indicate which action each project should take when you press F5. Click the drop-down in the Action field.

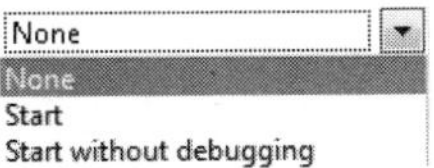

As shown in the preceding illustration, you see the following choices:

- **None**
  Don't start this project.
- **Start**
  Start with debugging.
- **Start without debugging**
  Start without attaching the debugger.

For this example, you would choose Start for both projects.

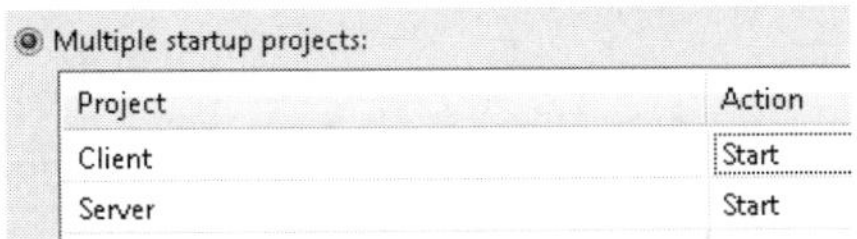

Now both projects start when you press F5. But there's just one little problem: The Client project launches first, and you need the Server project to launch first. To set the launch order, use the buttons to the far right of the project list, as shown in the following illustration.

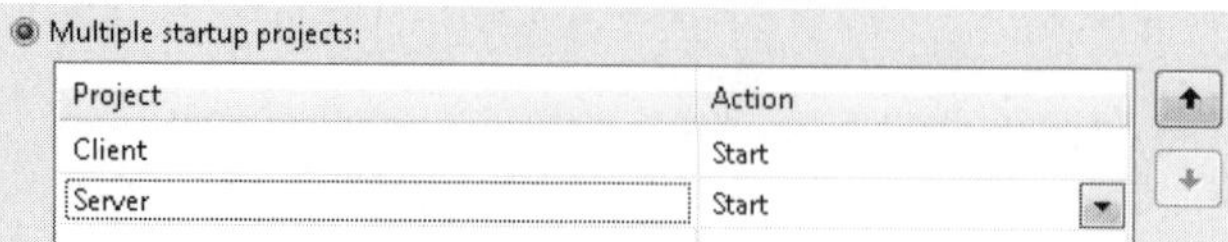

These buttons move the selected project up or down in the list so that you can arrange them to start in the order you would like. In this case, as shown in the following illustration, I've selected the Server project and then clicked the Move button to move it up in the startup order.

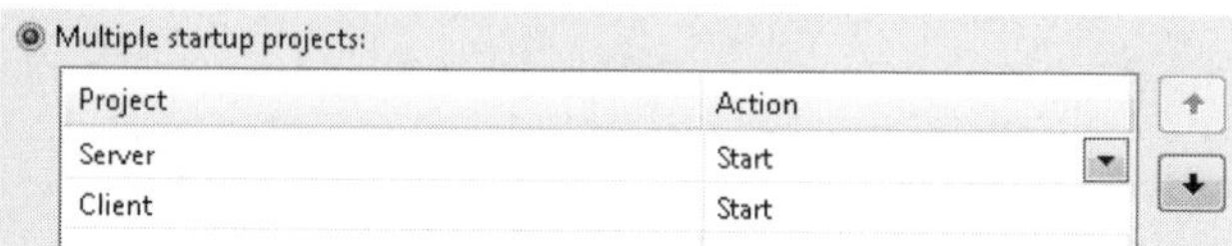

With the Server first in the list, you're all set. When you press F5, you can see the server start and then the client.

One interesting side effect of setting multiple startup projects is that the bold project name you normally see in Solution Explorer isn't there—because there is more than one startup project.

02.06 Change the Default New Project Location

WINDOWS	Alt,T, O
MENU	Tools | Options | Projects And Solutions | General
COMMAND	Tools.Options
VERSIONS	2005, 2008, 2010
CODE	vstipProj0006

You probably know that you can change the location for a new project in the New Project dialog box by entering a different location in the Location field.

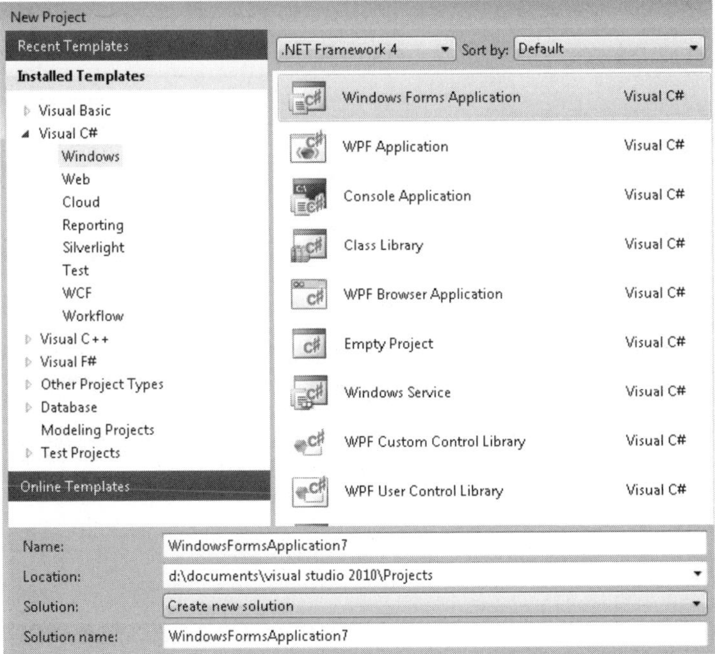

But if you do this often, did you know that you can change the default location so that you don't have to keep typing in custom paths? To change the default, select Tools | Options | Projects And Solutions | General from the menu bar. You'll see an Options dialog box, shown below, where you can change several default paths to suit your needs.

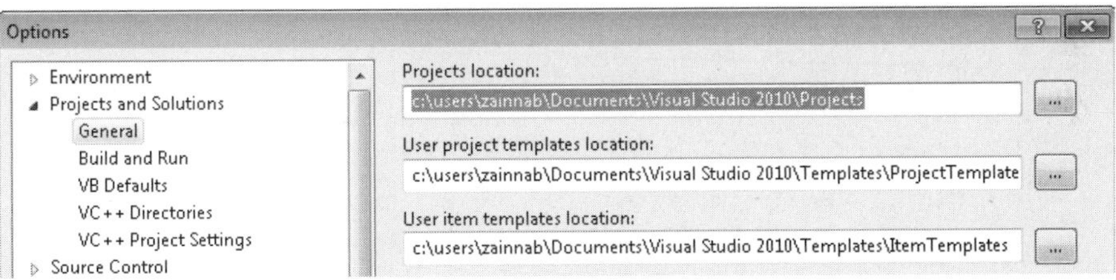

02.07 Track Active Item in Solution Explorer

WINDOWS	Alt,T, O
MENU	Tools | Options | Projects and Solutions | General
COMMAND	View.TrackActivityinSolutionExplorer
VERSIONS	2005, 2008, 2010
CODE	vstipProj0011

By default, Visual Studio tracks the file you are currently editing in Solution Explorer. The Solution Explorer tool window highlights the current file.

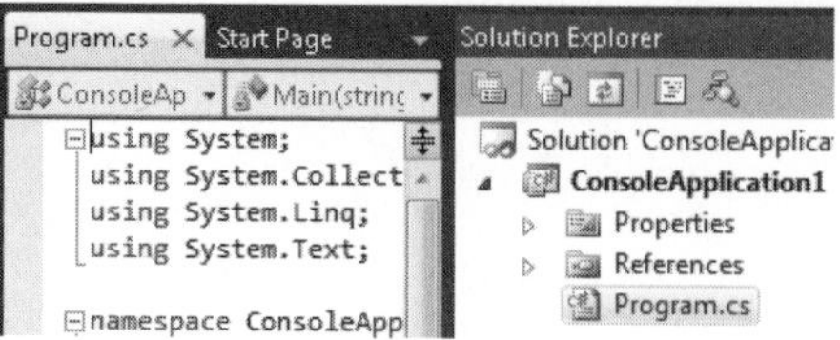

As you switch between files in the editor, notice that Solution Explorer automatically highlights the file you're currently editing. This is a great way to keep track of where you are in the solution when you are working with a lot of files.

If you don't like the feature, you can turn it off. Just select Tools | Options | Projects And Solutions | General, and clear the Track Active Item In Solution Explorer check box shown in the following illustration.

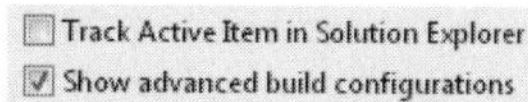

02.08 Type-Ahead Selection Support in Solution Explorer

DEFAULT	Ctrl+Alt+L
VISUAL BASIC 6	Ctrl+R; Ctrl+Alt+L
VISUAL C# 2005	Ctrl+W, S; Ctrl+W, Ctrl+S; Ctrl+Alt+L
VISUAL C++ 2	Alt+0; Ctrl+Alt+L
VISUAL C++ 6	Ctrl+Alt+L
VISUAL STUDIO 6	Ctrl+Alt+J
WINDOWS	Alt,V, P
MENU	View | Solution Explorer
COMMAND	View.SolutionExplorer
VERSIONS	2005, 2008, 2010
CODE	vstipTool0010

Have you ever had a big list of files in Solution Explorer and wanted to jump to a specific file very quickly? Just click anywhere in Solution Explorer, and start typing the name of the file you want. For example, suppose you have a solution with multiple projects:

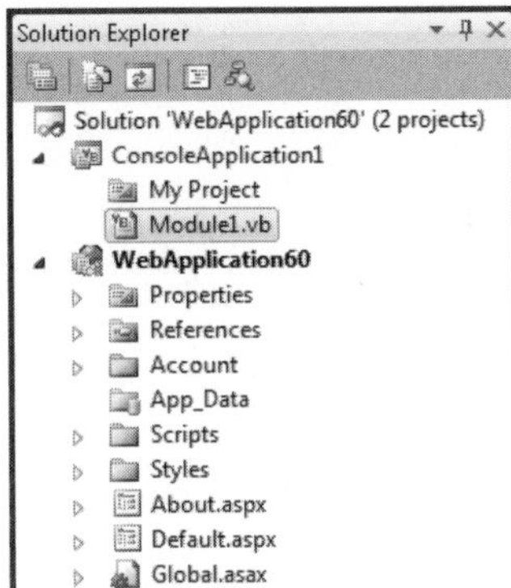

Assume you need to find a file called SeriousCoolness. To find it, click in Solution Explorer and then just start typing the name. Solution Explorer finds the file for you as you type.

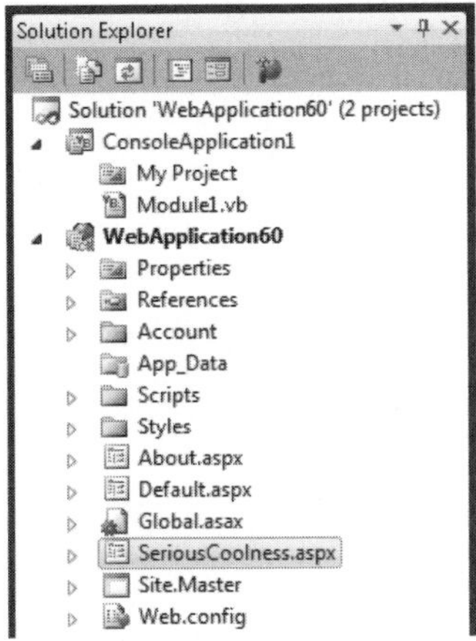

What if you don't know the whole name—just that it starts with an "S"? No worries! Just type **S** several times, and the selection cycles though all the files that begin with that letter.

Note The type-ahead feature works only with items that have been expanded, so if you have collapsed folders or projects in Solution Explorer, the tool cannot search within those areas.

02.09 Using Solution Folders

WINDOWS	(with Solution selected) Alt,P, D
MENU	(with Solution selected) Project | Add New Solution Folder; [Right-Click Solution] | Add | New Solution Folder
COMMAND	(with Solution selected) Project.AddNewSolutionFolder
VERSIONS	2005, 2008, 2010
CODE	vstipProj0009

Did you know that Visual Studio provides special folders that can help you organize large solutions? They are called, appropriately enough, "Solution Folders."

Note Solution Folders are an organizational tool in Solution Explorer; creating one doesn't create a corresponding Windows file system folder. Microsoft recommends that you organize your projects on disk in the same way that you organize them in the Solution Folder. But of course, you're free to organize them as you like.

Adding Solution Folders

To create a Solution Folder, right-click your solution (or, with the solution selected, go to Project | Add New Solution Folder). Solution Explorer adds a new folder, which you can type a name for.

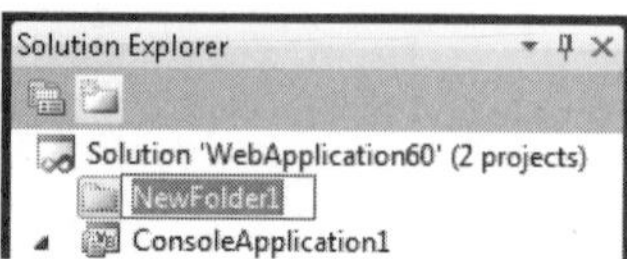

After you enter a name for the new folder, press Enter, and you're done. So what can you actually do with these things? It turns out, quite a lot:

- Move or add projects to them. Solution Folders can be nested to create greater organizational structure.
- Add, delete, or rename Solution Folders at any time, if the organizational requirements of your solution change.
- Unload all projects in a Solution Folder to make them temporarily unavailable for building.
- Collapse or hide entire Solution Folders so that you can work more easily in Solution Explorer. Hidden projects are built when you build the solution.
- Build or rebuild all the projects. The projects are built in the order specified by the project dependencies.

Removing Solution Folders

If you want to get rid of a folder, just right-click it and choose Remove to delete it, or alternatively, select it and press the Delete key.

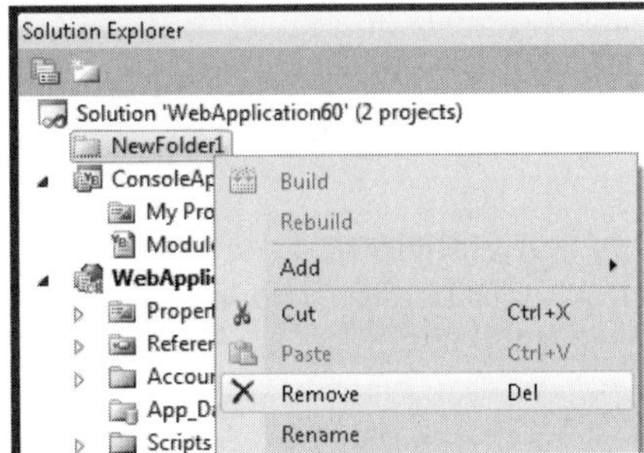

02.10 Navigating Property Tabs in the Project Properties

DEFAULT	Ctrl+PgUp; Ctrl+PgDn
VISUAL BASIC 6	Ctrl+PgUp; Ctrl+PgDn
VISUAL C# 2005	Ctrl+PgUp; Ctrl+PgDn
VISUAL C++ 2	Ctrl+PgUp; Ctrl+PgDn
VISUAL C++ 6	Ctrl+PgUp; Ctrl+PgDn
VISUAL STUDIO 6	Ctrl+PgUp; Ctrl+PgDn
WINDOWS	[no shortcut]
COMMAND	Window.PreviousTab; Window.NextTab
VERSIONS	2005, 2008, 2010
CODE	vstipProj0023

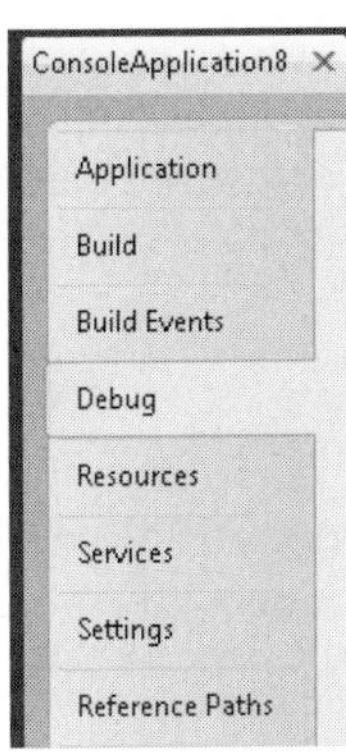

When you are looking at your project's properties, you might have wondered whether you can navigate among the property tabs by using the keyboard.

It turns out that you can. Just use Ctrl+PgUp or Ctrl+PgDn to move between the property tabs. This also works for properties in C++ projects if you want to quickly navigate among the categories.

02.11 Pin a Project to the Recent Projects List

VERSIONS	2010
CODE	vstipTool0003

Tired of your projects getting pushed out of the Recent Projects list on the Start Page? You can pin projects to the Recent Projects list in Visual Studio 2010 so that they stay around until you unpin them.

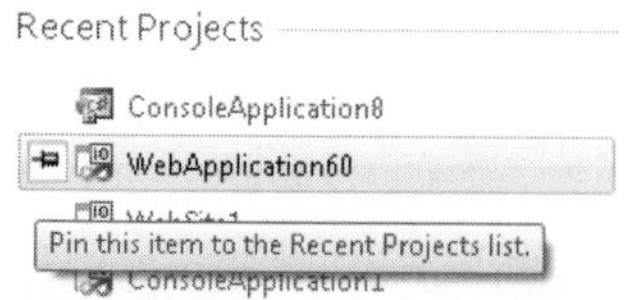

Pinned projects do not stay at the top of the list; instead, they're sorted according to when you use them. In other words, the most recent project is on top—pinned or not. Pinning guarantees only that the project will not be pushed out of the list.

02.12 Creating Temporary Projects

WINDOWS	Alt,T, O
MENU	Tools | Options | Projects and Solutions | General
COMMAND	Tools.Options
VERSIONS	2005, 2008, 2010
CODE	vstipProj0010

Temporary projects are particularly useful for showing a colleague some trick or technique quickly, or for performing ad hoc demos. To create temporary projects, select Tools | Options | Projects And Solutions | General and clear the Save New Projects When Created check box, as shown in the following illustration.

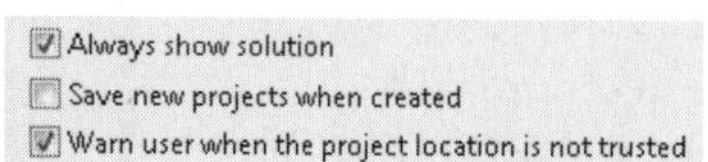

While convenient, the option has some side effects. For example, when you subsequently create a new project, the New Project dialog box does not show the usual "save" fields at the bottom of the dialog box.

Before:

Name:	WindowsApplication6
Location:	c:\users\zainnab\documents\visual studio 2010\Projects
Solution name:	WindowsApplication6

After:

The good news is that now you can create projects all day long but can choose to either save or discard the changes when the solution is closed.

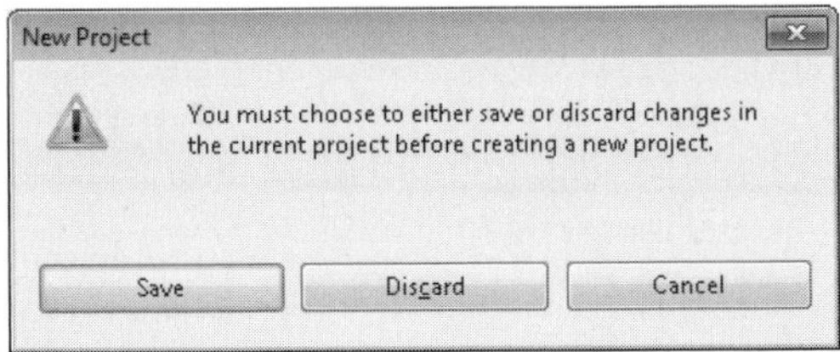

Note You can still save changes to a project—even a temporary project—anytime you like if you decide you want to keep the code around. When you decide to save, your AutoRecover settings take over. For more information, see vstipEnv0019 ("Autorecover", page 10).

02.13 Create Your Own Item Template

WINDOWS	Alt,F, E
MENU	File | Export Template
COMMAND	File.ExportTemplate
VERSIONS	2005, 2008, 2010
LANGUAGES	C#, VB
CODE	vstipProj0013

Have you ever used or created a template in Microsoft Word, Excel, or PowerPoint? Unless you live in a cave, the answer is most likely "yes." Just as with the Microsoft Office products, you can create and use your own templates in Visual Studio. This tip shows you how to make your own item template. Sometimes you just want to customize an individual item that you use frequently in projects. Class files are a perfect example of this type of scenario. Here's an example.

Create a new project, and then add a class to it (Ctrl+Shift+A).

Note The process is the same regardless of which language you're using.

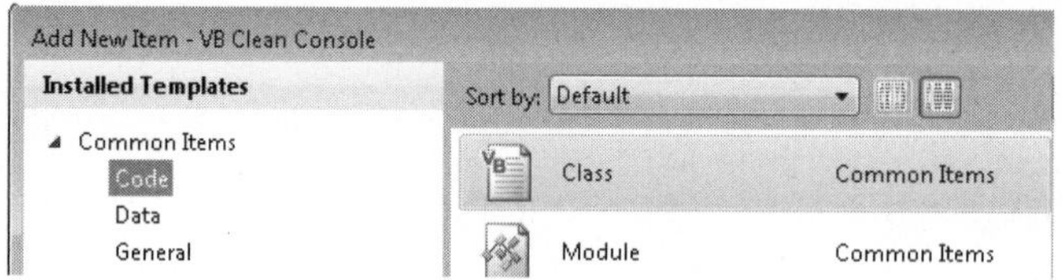

Now modify the class code so that it looks the way you would like your item template to look, and save your changes to the file.

```
Imports System.DirectoryServices

' company required comments here
Friend Class Class1
    ' todo put your connection string here

End Class
```

At this point, you can export the item template so that you can use it in future projects. Select File | Export Template to start the Export Template Wizard.

> **Note** You are prompted to save changes to your project if you haven't already done so.

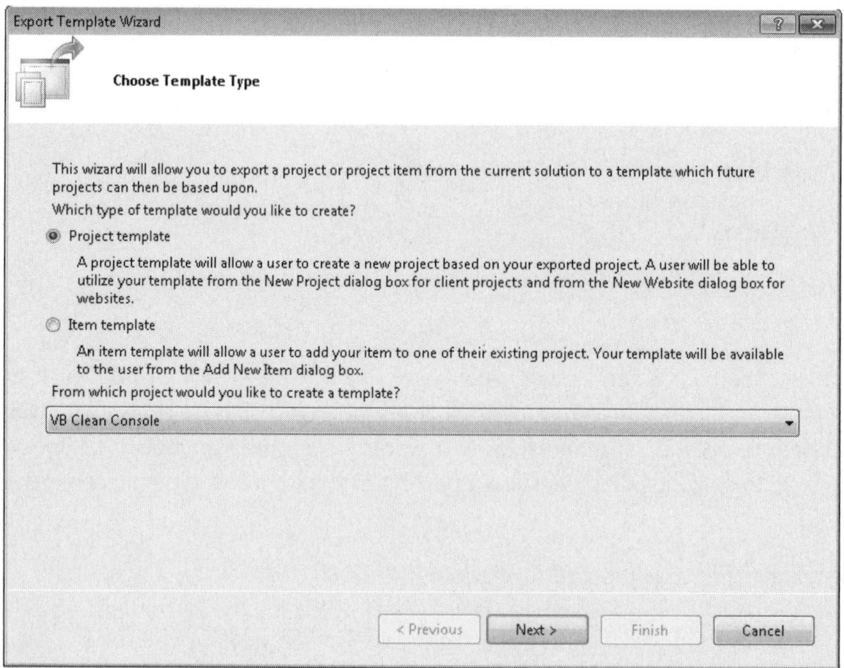

Select Item Template, and select the project that currently contains the item you want to export (if you have more than one project in your solution).

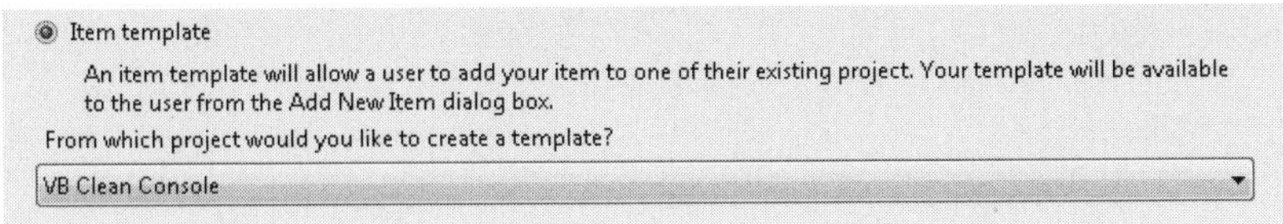

Click Next and then select the item to export as a template.

Note The wizard automatically selects any dependent files as needed based on your selection. Also, even though it looks like you can select more than one item here, you can only select a single item in this list.

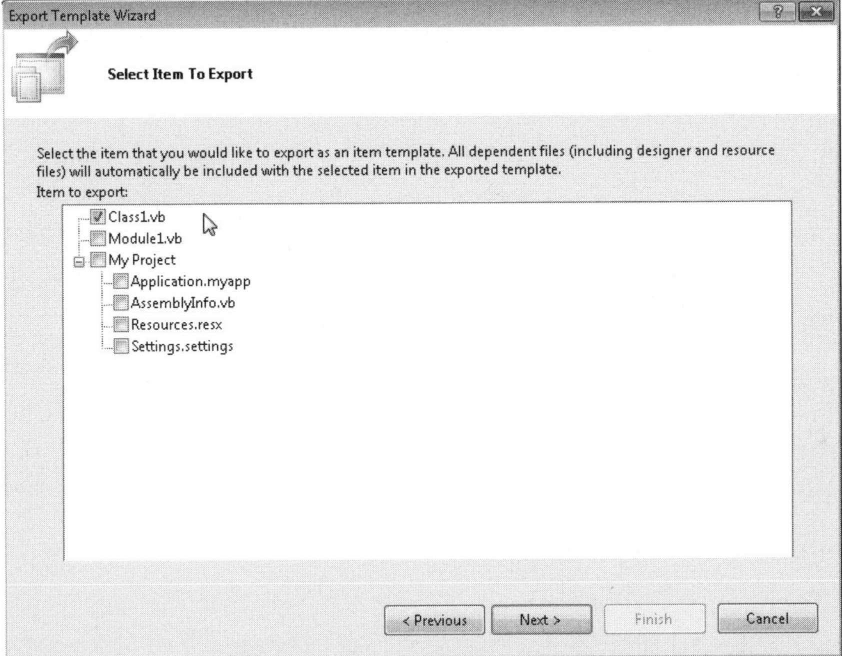

Click Next again. Now you can select any references that you want included with the item. If you have any Using or Imports statements, you need to pick the references here or the template will not work correctly.

Note The wizard generates this list of assemblies from the assembly references in the current project. If the assembly you want to reference does not appear in the list, exit the wizard and add the reference to your project, and then run the wizard again.

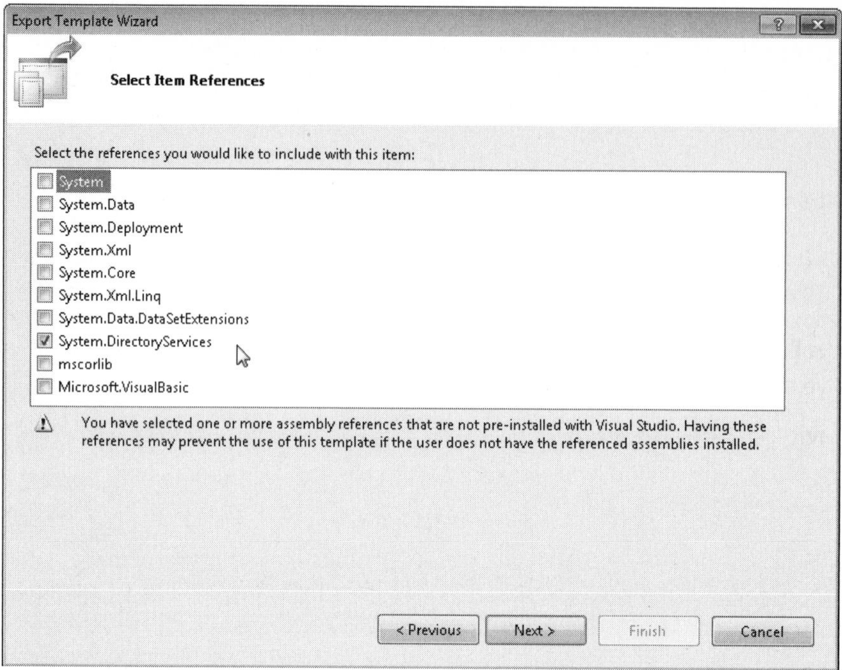

Click Next. As you can see from the following illustration, you can add quite a bit of information.

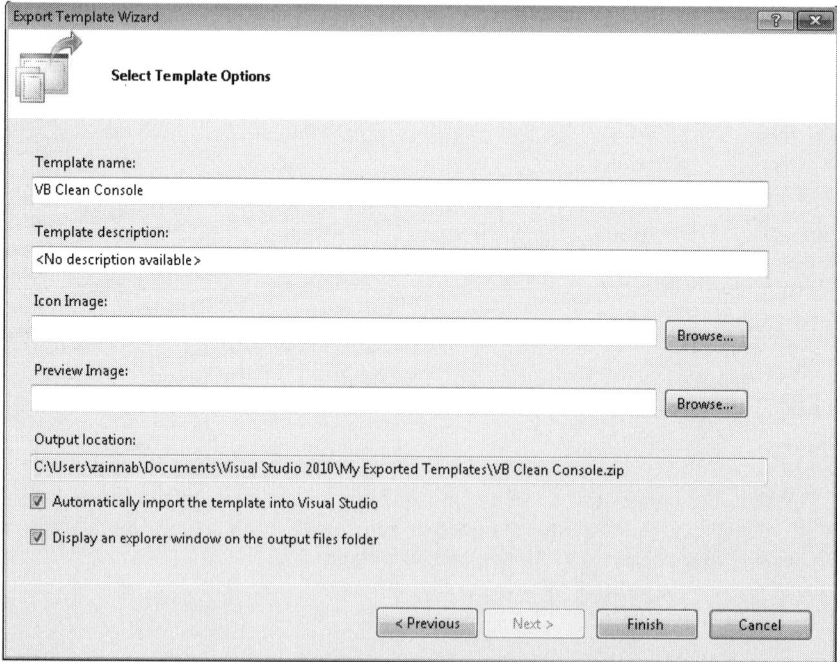

Here's a description of the information you can add:

- **Template Name** The friendly name for the template that Visual Studio displays in the list of templates. I suggest keeping this to around 50–60 characters. Don't get too verbose here.
- **Template Description** A short description that provides a little more detail about the template's purpose. In this text box, I want you to get very descriptive. This is your one and only chance to make it perfectly clear what this template should be used for, so don't skimp on detail.
- **Icon Image** A small image that represents the icon for the item. I suggest you just leave this blank.
- **Preview Image** A larger image that provides a preview of what the template looks like. As with the Icon Image field, I suggest you leave this blank.
- **Output Location** The location where the wizard stores exported items. This is the initial storage location of your templates. To be clear, they are not usable in Visual Studio when they are just created. To make them useable in Visual Studio, you need to check Automatically Import The Template Into Visual Studio. Leave this as-is unless you are storing your templates on a network share somewhere. If you do change this value, make sure you use the new location consistently when you create templates or you will wind up forgetting where you put them.
- **Automatically Import The Template Into Visual Studio** Lets you decide whether you want to import the template right away or want to do it manually later. This "import" is just a copy of the .zip file created in the appropriate location in My Documents\Visual Studio <version>\Templates\ItemTemplates. By doing this, the template immediately becomes usable in Visual Studio.
- **Display An Explorer Window On The Output Files Folder** Opens up the location where the template files are stored after they are created. This is useful when you want to see the .zip file that is created. It's interesting the first few times you do it, but then it's pretty much a waste of time. You will wind up turning off this option most of the time.

The following illustration shows the settings I used for this example.

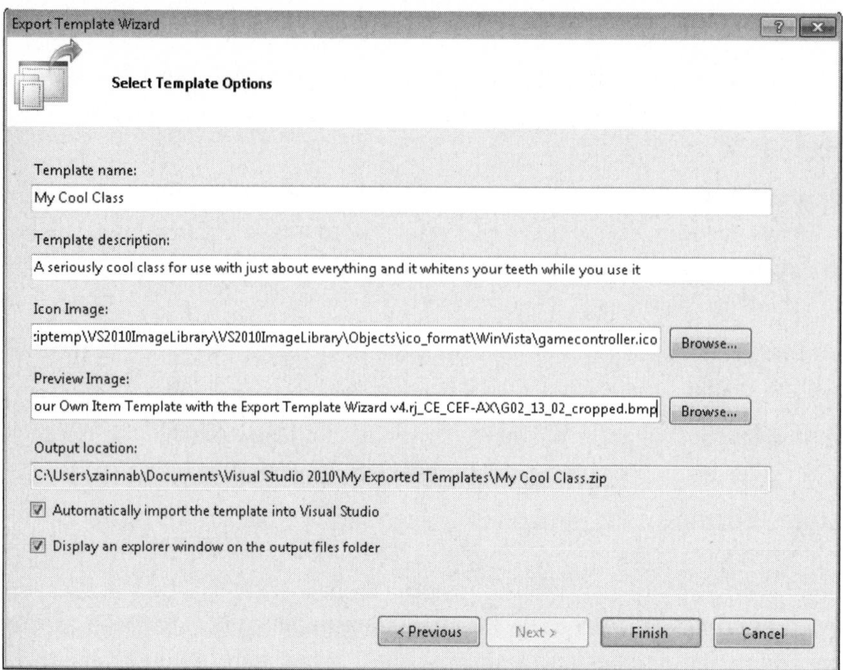

To complete the wizard, click Finish. The wizard closes and opens up the output file location, showing the .zip file that contains the exported templates.

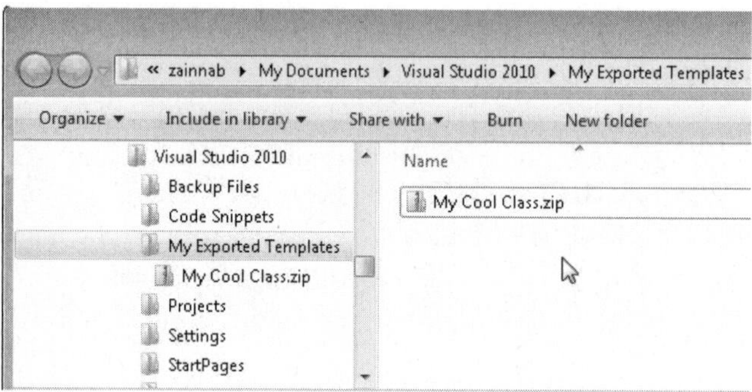

Although you aren't interested in the details right now, if you explore inside the .zip file, you can see the files that make up an item template.

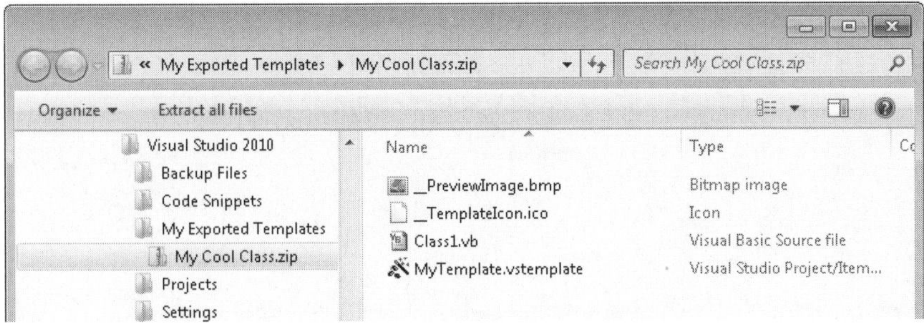

Finally, test your new template. Create a new item (Ctrl+Shift+A), and you should see the new template. Notice the Icon Image next to the name of the item and the Preview Image (the Visual Studio 2010 logo in the lower-right) that is below the description. I feel that the names and descriptions are critical but really don't see a lot of value in the icons.

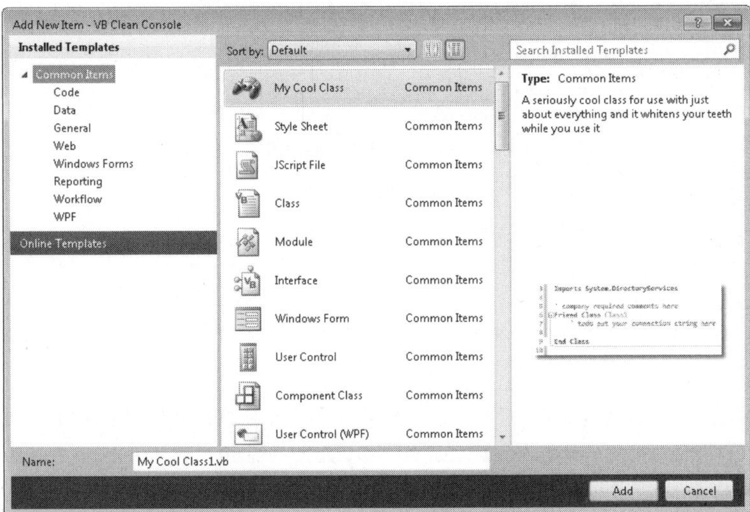

You can also see the template in the My Documents\Visual Studio <version>\Templates\ItemTemplates\ folder.

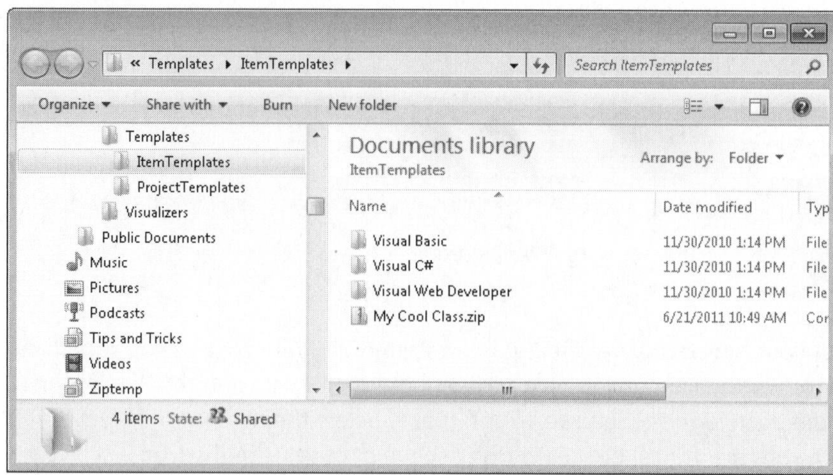

If you aren't happy with your new template, just delete the .zip file from this directory; it no longer shows up in the Add New Item dialog box.

02.14 Roll Your Own Project Template with the Export Template Wizard

WINDOWS	Alt,F, E
MENU	File | Export Template
COMMAND	File.ExportTemplate
VERSIONS	2005, 2008, 2010
CODE	vstipProj0004

Are you always adding the same extra files to projects when you create them? Ever wish you could have it all just "be there"? Well, you can when you become familiar with the Export Template Wizard.

First, set up an existing project template the way you want it. All changes (new files, code, interfaces, and so on) will be used in the template you create. In this simple example, I always want to include larry, curly, and moe C# class files with my console applications.

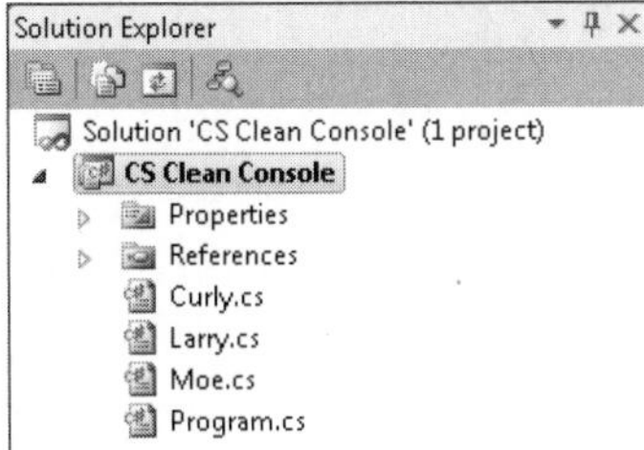

Now select File | Export Template from the menu bar.

Note Choosing Export Template prompts you to save any pending changes if you haven't already.

You'll see the Export Template Wizard. From this first screen, you can choose to make either a Project template or an Item template.

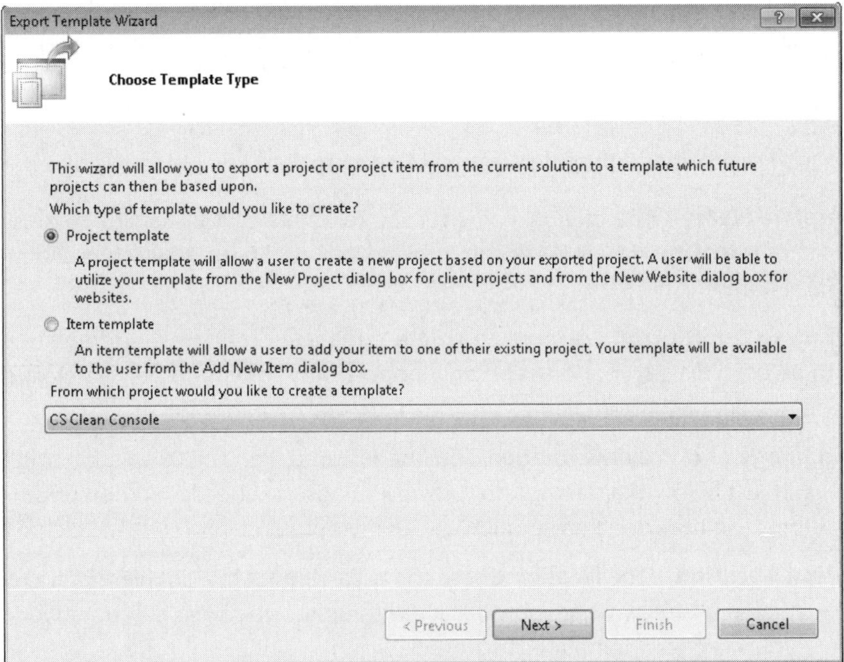

For this example, I selected Project Template and then clicked Next to continue to the Select Template Options screen, shown in the following illustration.

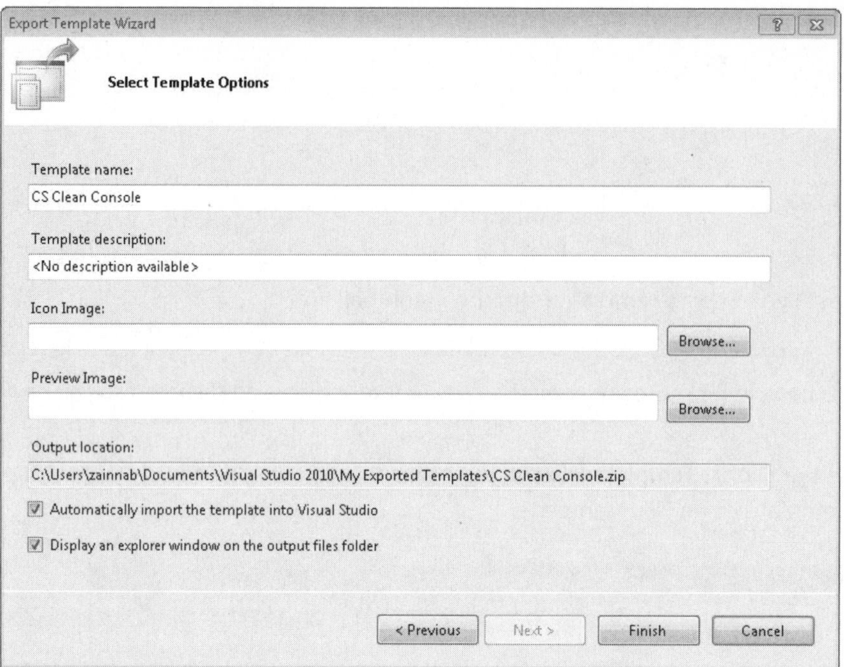

The following list provides a brief description of each option:

- **Template Name** The friendly name for the template that Visual Studio displays in the list of templates. I suggest keeping this to around 50–60 characters. Don't get too verbose here.
- **Template Description** A more complete explanation of how this template is intended to be used. This is your one and only opportunity for you to be very clear on the proper usage for this template.
- **Icon Image and Preview Image** The images used with the template name (icon image) and just below the description (preview image). I suggest you don't bother setting these because they don't have much use, in my opinion.
- **Output Location** The location where the wizard saves the .zip file that it creates. The default value is usually what you will stick with unless you have, say, a network share where you want your templates to stored.
- **Automatically Import The Template Into Visual Studio** Controls whether the wizard puts a copy of the new template to your templates directory: My Documents\Visual Studio <version>\Templates\ProjectTemplates. If you want the template to be available the next time you create a new project, select this option. Most of the time you should leave this option selected.

- **Display An Explorer Window On The Output Files Folder** Controls what happens when you complete the wizard. When selected, it displays the folder containing the .zip file that the wizard saves. After the first few times you create templates, this option can get tiresome, so I usually turn it off. I suggest you leave it on the first few times you create templates to see the template that is created.

After filling out the wizard and clicking Finish, the wizard closes and opens up my Exported Templates (output) folder, where I can see the new .zip file containing the template files.

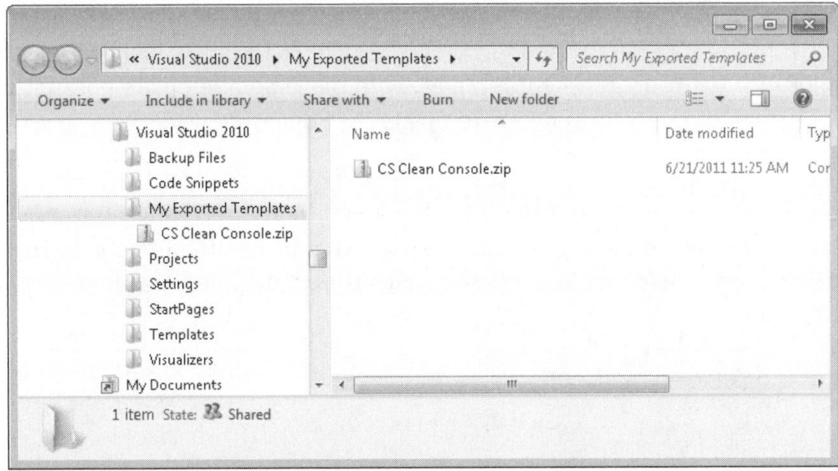

Now, when I create a new application, the new template appears, visible in the New Project dialog box.

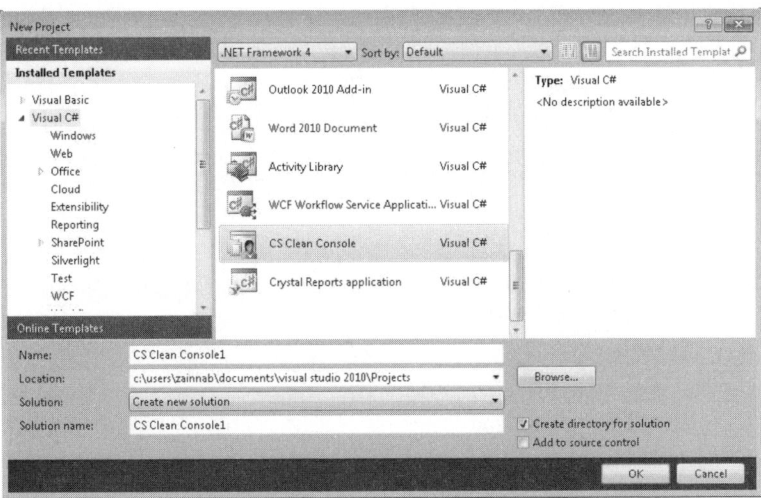

Obviously, this is a simple example; you can do a lot more with templates, and I suggest you visit the "Export Template Wizard" documentation, at *http://msdn.microsoft.com/en-us/library/ms185318.aspx*, for more detailed information about how to make good use of this feature.

02.15 Organizing Your Custom Item Templates

VERSIONS	2005, 2008, 2010
CODE	vstipProj0020

In vstipProj0013 ("Roll Your Own Item Template with the Export Template Wizard", page 57), I showed you how to create custom item templates but didn't show you how to organize them.

Fortunately, organizing them is pretty easy. After you have created your template(s), navigate to the folder My Documents\Visual Studio <version>\Templates\ItemTemplates. For example, on my machine, the path is My Documents\Visual Studio 2010\Templates\ItemTemplates.

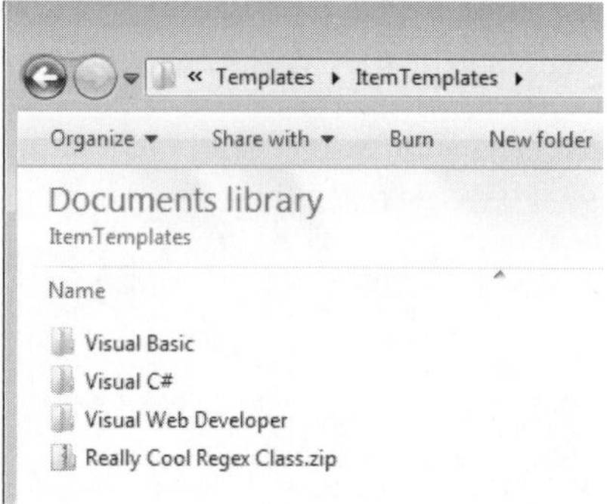

As you can see in the preceding illustration, I have a custom item—a class called "Really Cool Regex Class." Unfortunately, when I want to use it and I bring up the Add New Item (Ctrl+Shift+A) dialog box, that class shows up in the root list.

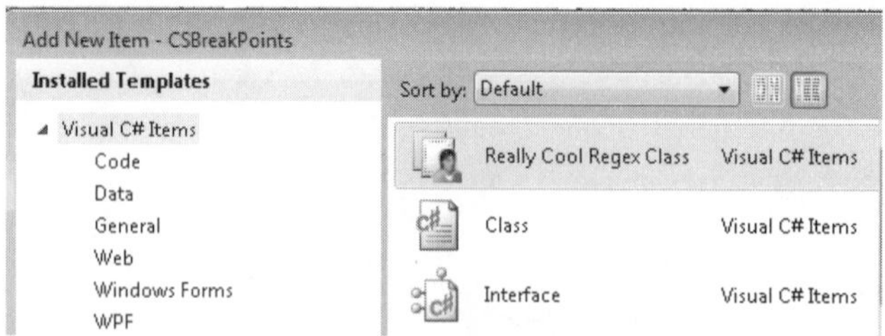

I want it to show up in the Code area, but it doesn't.

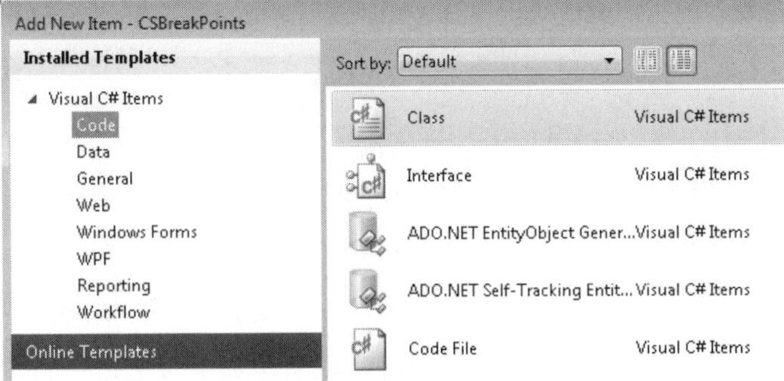

To get the custom template to show up in the Code area, you need to go back to the ItemTemplates directory and create a new folder named Code.

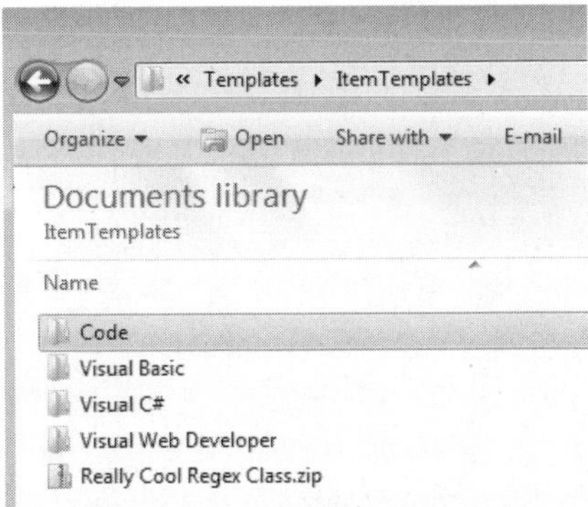

Then move the custom template into the Code folder.

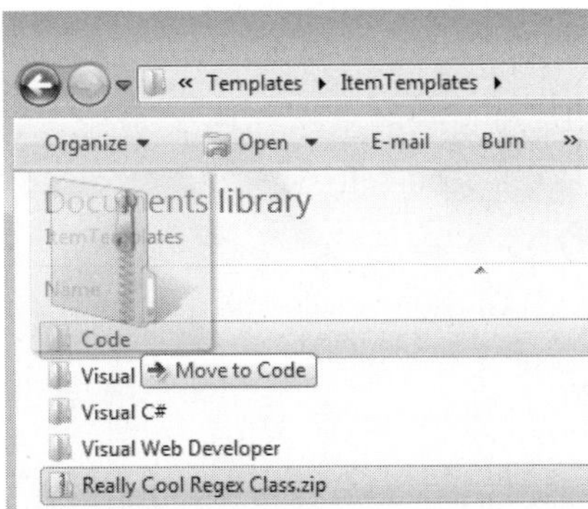

Now whenever I press Ctrl+Shift+A to add a new item, my custom template appears in the Code section.

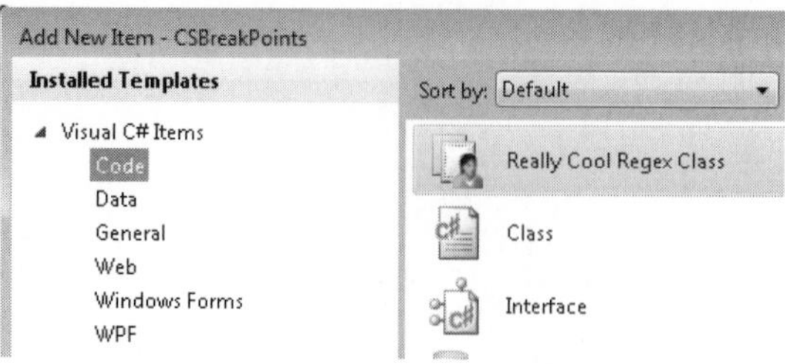

In addition to working with existing folder names, you can create custom names as well. If, for example, you wanted an XYZ Company folder for your templates you would just create one and put your templates in there:

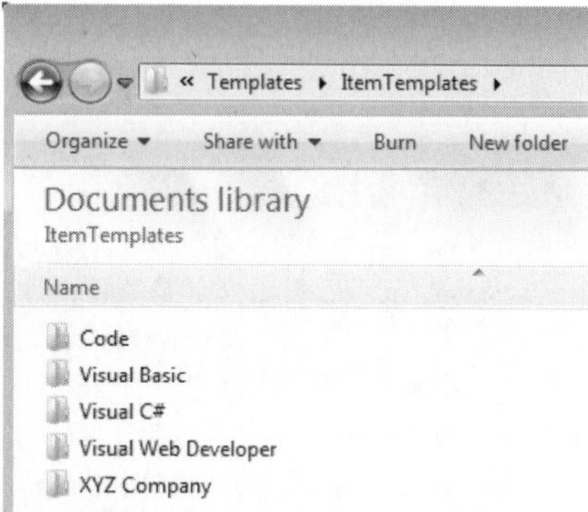

Now, when you go to add a new item, you will see your new folder in the dialog box:

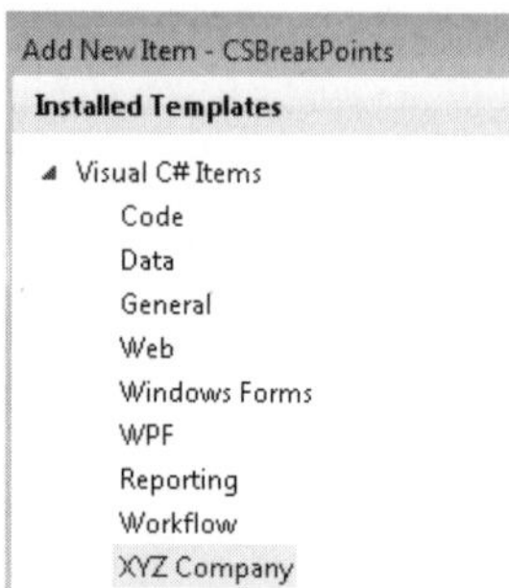

02.16 Organizing Your Custom Project Templates

VERSIONS	2005, 2008, 2010
CODE	vstipProj0019

In vstipProj0004 ("Roll Your Own Project Template with the Export Template Wizard", page 64), we discussed how to create custom project templates, but it doesn't show you how to organize them. Fortunately, that's pretty easy. After you have created one or more custom project templates, browse to My Documents\Visual Studio <version>\Templates\ProjectTemplates. For example, on my machine, the full path is My Documents\Visual Studio 2010\Templates\ProjectTemplates.

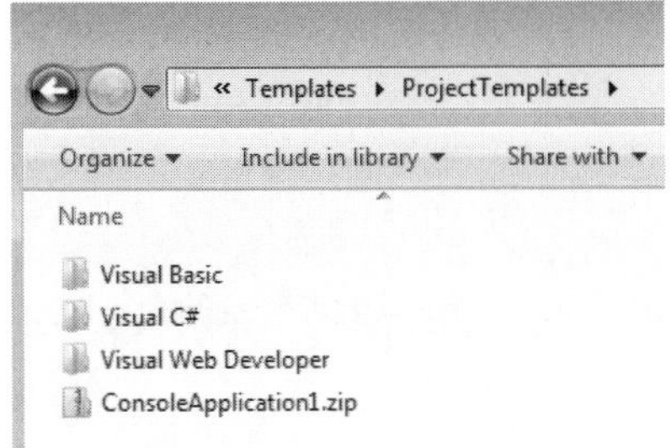

As the preceding illustration shows, I created a custom Console application project type for this example with the name ConsoleApplication1. By default, custom project templates don't show up in the project subfolders.

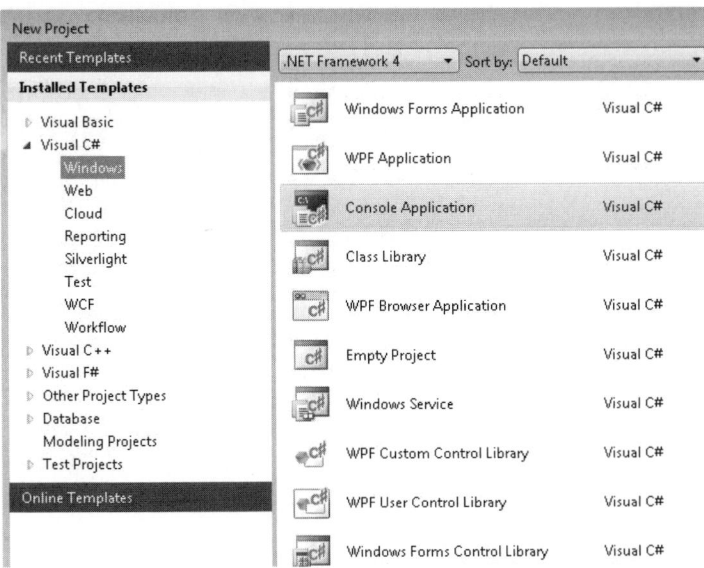

To get the custom templates to appear, the trick is to create a new folder in that directory with a name that matches where you want the template(s) to show up. You place custom templates in this new folder—and then they show up in the appropriate areas.

To do this, return to the My Documents\Visual Studio <version>\Templates\ProjectTemplates directory and create a new folder called Windows—to match the Windows area in the New Project dialog box, which is where we want the new Console template to appear.

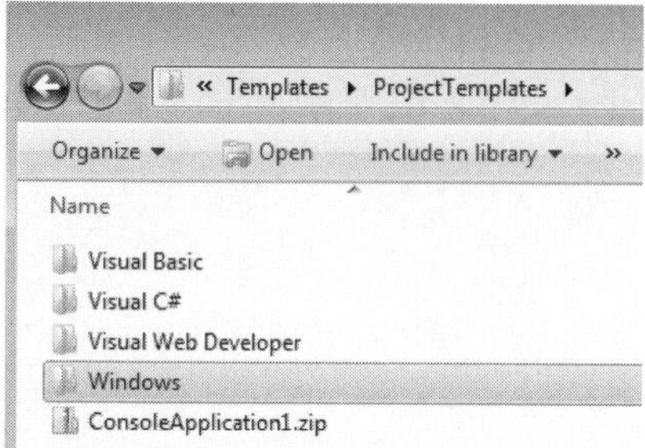

Move your template into the new folder. For this example, I moved ConsoleApplication1.zip into the Windows folder.

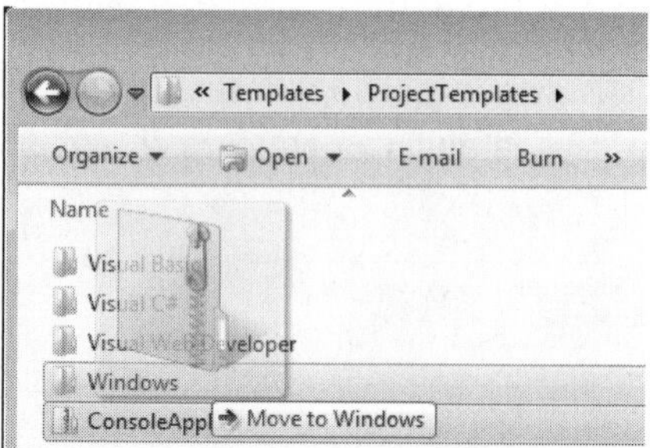

The next time you open up the New Project dialog box (Ctrl+Shift+N), it shows the project template in the proper area.

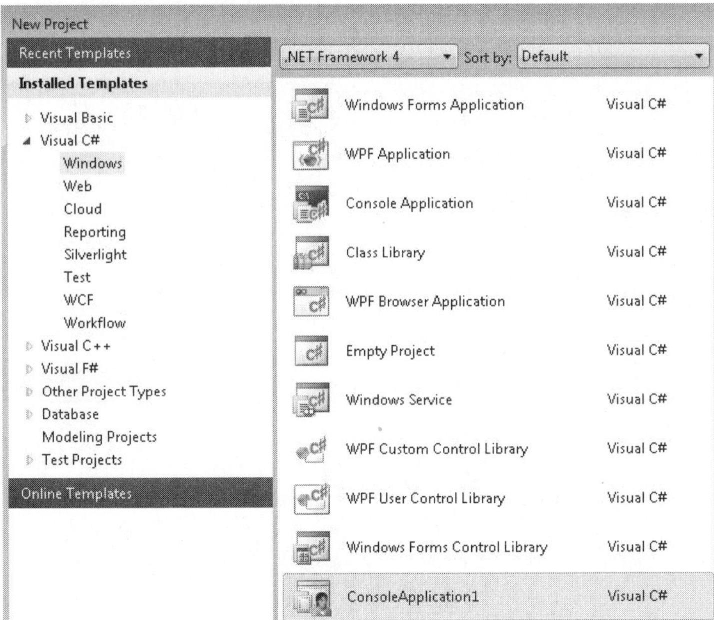

In addition to matching the existing folder names, you can create new ones. If you want a custom area for your company templates, for example, you would just create a folder with your company name and put at least one template in the folder:

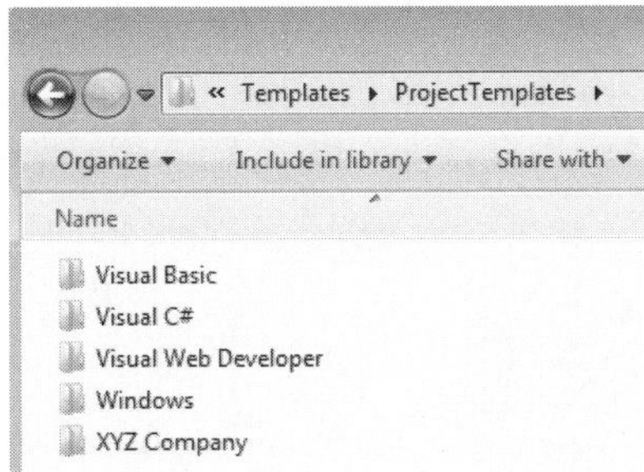

The next time you bring up the New Project dialog box, it will show your new subfolder in the list:

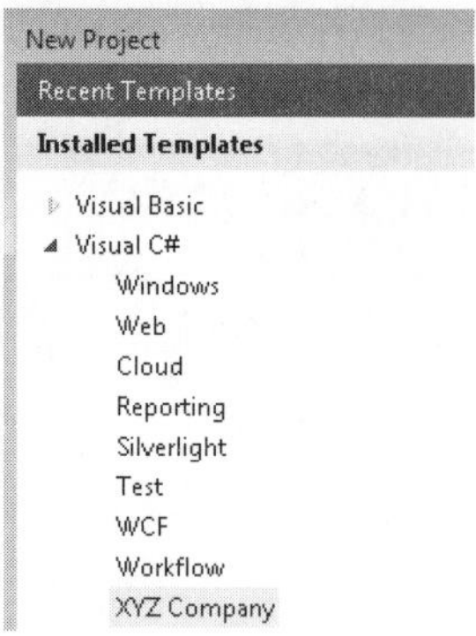

02.17 Reorganize the Default Item Templates

VERSIONS	2005, 2008, 2010
CODE	vstipProj0021

Warning The procedures in this tip could cause your templates to disappear if you don't follow the instructions carefully. So do this at your own risk. You might want to back up your ItemTemplates folder just to be safe.

You've probably noticed that General section of the New Item dialog box contains a large number of items. If you want to organize those a bit more, this tip shows you how to create custom areas in which you can store the default item templates that ship with Visual Studio. This example creates a Diagram area for the diagram items that—by default—appear in the General section.

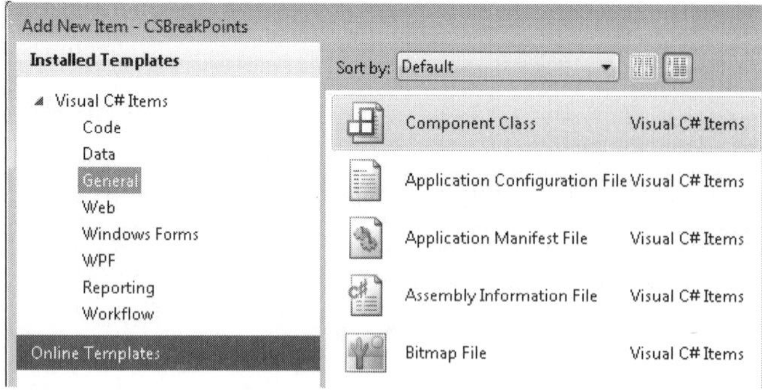

To get started, find where Visual Studio stores item templates on your machine. Typically, this is in C:\Program Files\Microsoft Visual Studio <version>\Common7\IDE\ItemTemplates\<language>. You might have to drill down into the file structure, depending on what items you're looking for, and the path might be slightly different on your machine, based on your Visual Studio version. In this case, the actual full path on my machine is C:\Program Files (x86)\Microsoft Visual Studio 10.0\Common7\IDE\ItemTemplates\CSharp.

When you've found the template location for your language, create a new folder. For this example, I created a folder called Diagrams.

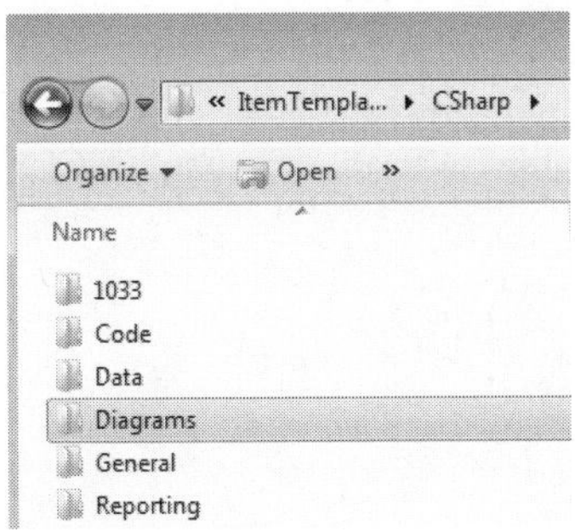

Now go into the General\1033 folder, and locate the diagram .zip files you want, as shown in the following illustration.

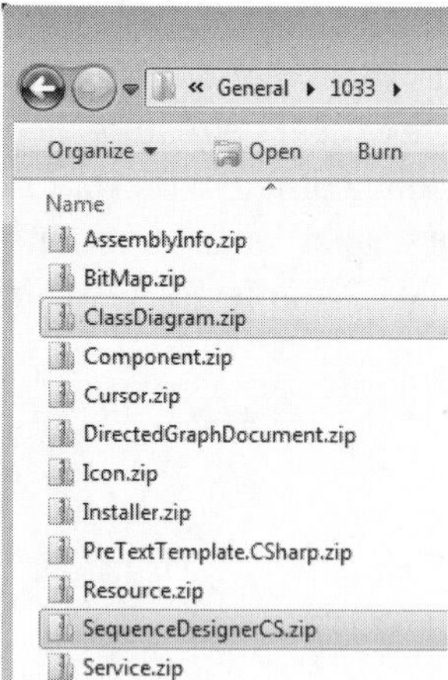

Now carefully move them to the new Diagrams folder.

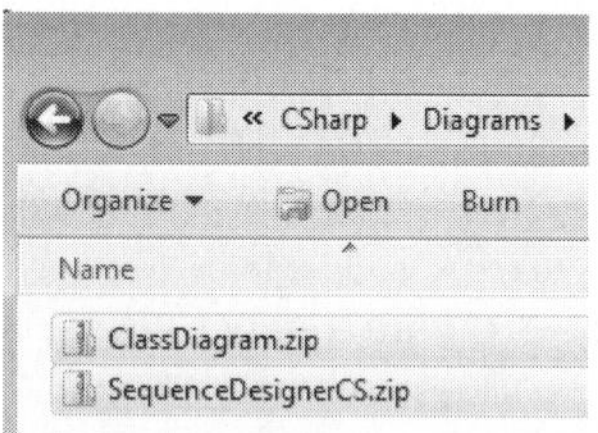

Close all instances of Visual Studio, and then run the following command from the Visual Studio command prompt (must be run with administrative privileges) :

devenv.com /installvstemplates

Warning Let this process complete without interfering. It is extremely important that you let the process finish. The devenv.com command runs without any user interface. You know it is done when another cursor shows up:

When the process completes, open up Visual Studio, and then open any project. Bring up the Add New Item dialog box (Ctrl+Shift+A). Notice your brand new Diagrams area, with the templates you moved there inside it.

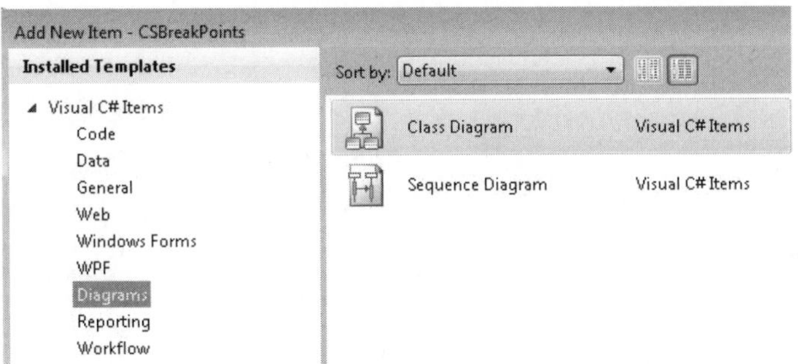

02.18 Reorganize the Default Project Templates

VERSIONS	2005, 2008, 2010
CODE	vstipProj0018

Warning The procedures in this tip could cause some of your templates to disappear unless you follow the instructions carefully. So do this at your own risk. You might want to back up your ProjectTemplates folder just to be safe.

Maybe it's just me, but I get really annoyed that, for example, my WCF project templates are in a WCF section when I go to create a new project—but my WPF projects are under "Windows." That just doesn't seem intuitive. So this example shows you how you can create custom areas for the default project templates that ship with Visual Studio. In this example, you create a WPF area for your WPF project templates.

You need to find the location where your version of Visual Studio stores project templates. Typically, that's in C:\Program Files\Microsoft Visual Studio <version>\Common7\IDE\ProjectTemplates\<language>. You might need to explore the file system to find the templates, and your path might be slightly different, based on which Visual Studio version you're running. For example, the actual full path on my machine for C# templates is C:\Program Files (x86)\Microsoft Visual Studio 10.0\Common7\IDE\ProjectTemplates\CSharp.

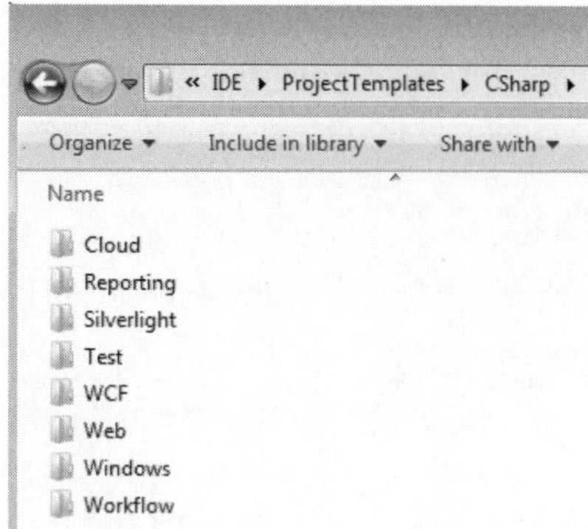

Now create a new folder, and name it "WPF."

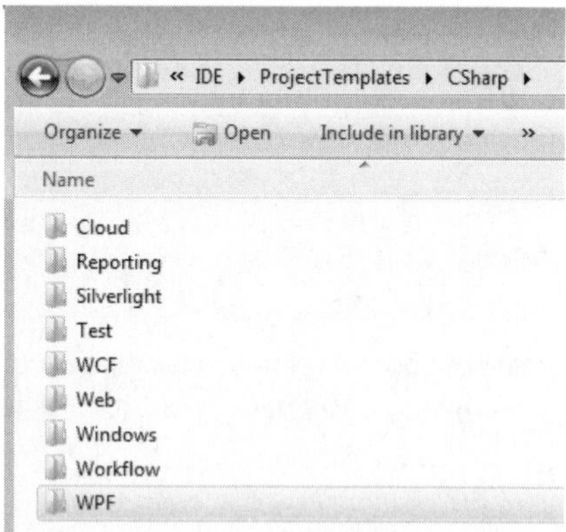

These next steps are potentially dangerous, so be careful. Navigate to the Windows folder (actually Windows\1033\), and locate the WPF templates.

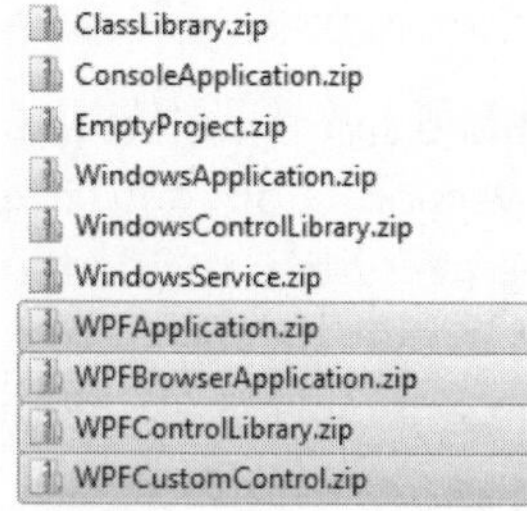

Move these .zip files into the new folder you just created.

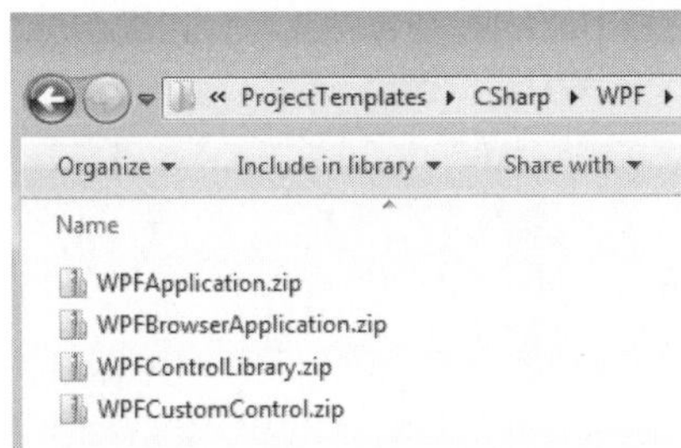

Close all instances of Visual Studio, and then run the following command from the Visual Studio command prompt, which you can find on your Start menu:

```
devenv.com /installvstemplates
```

Warning It is very important that you let this process finish without interruption. The devenv.com command runs without any user interface. You know it is done when the command prompt shows up again:

When the process completes, open up Visual Studio, and open the New Project dialog box (Ctrl+Shift+N) to see your brand-new WPF area containing the WPF templates, as shown in the following illustration.

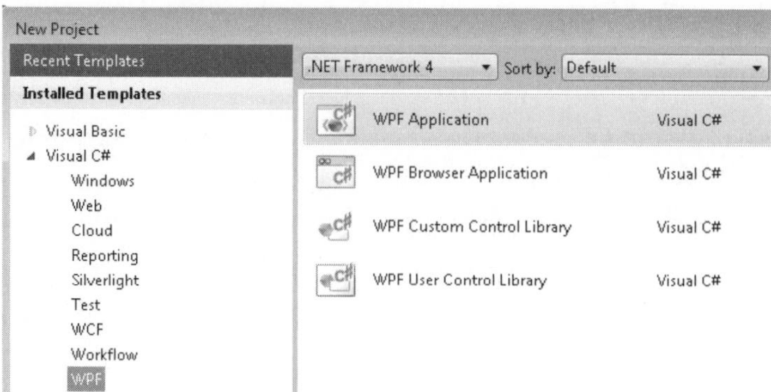

Note While researching how to do this, I experimented with copying the templates instead of moving them. However, Visual Studio apparently detects duplicate template names and doesn't allow you to have multiple copies in different locations. So I wound up with an empty WPF section; the templates stayed in their original Windows section. I suspect this is dependent on load order—and my tests indicate Visual Studio loads the known default directories first, so having a folder called "Abacus" to beat the sort order doesn't work.

02.19 Change the Templates that Appear in the New Project or Item Dialog Boxes

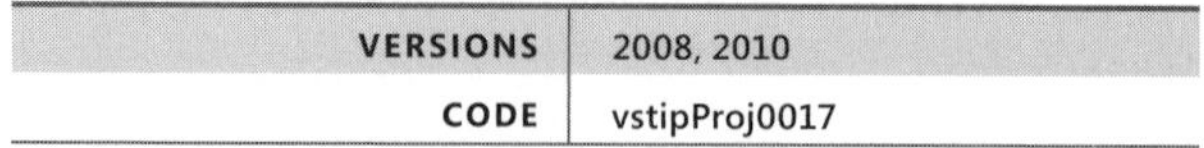

VERSIONS	2008, 2010
CODE	vstipProj0017

Warning: Manipulating templates as discussed here can cause serious problems if you don't know what you are doing. Use this information at your own risk. You should consider backing up your ProjectTemplates or ItemTemplates folders.

With all the great changes to the New Project and New Item dialog boxes, you might be perfectly happy with the list of things that Visual Studio presents by default. But for argument's sake, suppose you want to get rid of some of the entries. This example removes the C# Windows Forms Control Library from the New Project dialog box (Ctrl+Shift+N), but you can follow the same steps to remove or change items in the New Item dialog box.

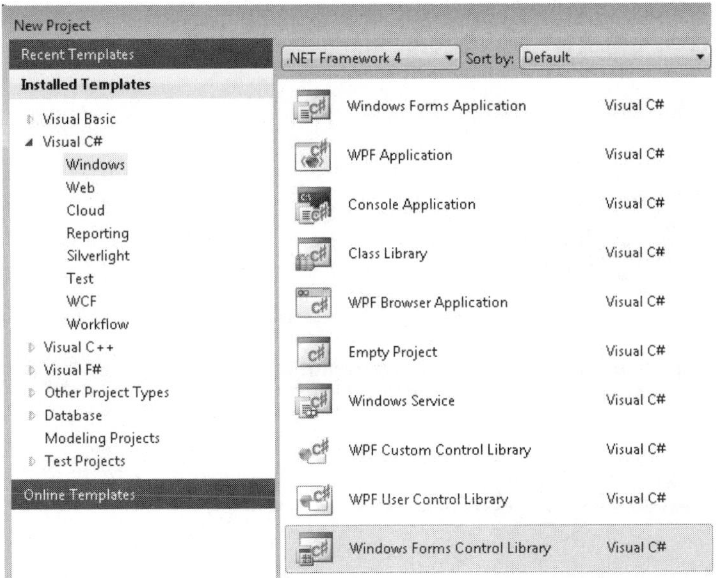

Navigate to the location where your version of Visual Studio stores templates for your selected language. Typically, that's C:\Program Files\Microsoft Visual Studio <version>\Common7\IDE\<Project or Item>Templates\<language>\<project category>. You might have to explore a little; your path might be slightly different, based on which Visual Studio version you're running. On my machine, the path to the Windows Forms Control Library .zip file is C:\Program Files (x86)\Microsoft Visual Studio 10.0\Common7\IDE\ProjectTemplates\CSharp\Windows.

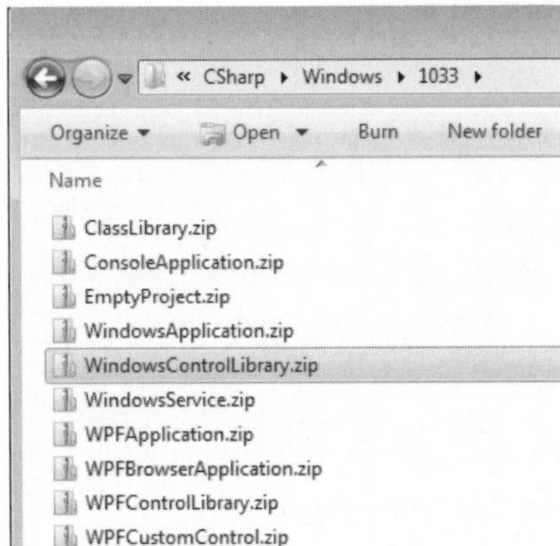

You don't want to simply delete the file—you might need it in the future. Instead, just move the .zip file to another directory. That way, you can always retrieve it from that location if you need it again.

Close all instances of Visual Studio, and then run the following command from the Visual Studio command prompt, which you can find on your Start menu:

```
devenv.com /installvstemplates
```

Warning It is very important that you let this process finish without interruption. The devenv.com command runs without any user interface. You know it is done when the cursor shows up again:

After the process completes, start Visual Studio again, and then create a new project (Ctrl+Shift+N). You should see that the moved template is no longer in the list.

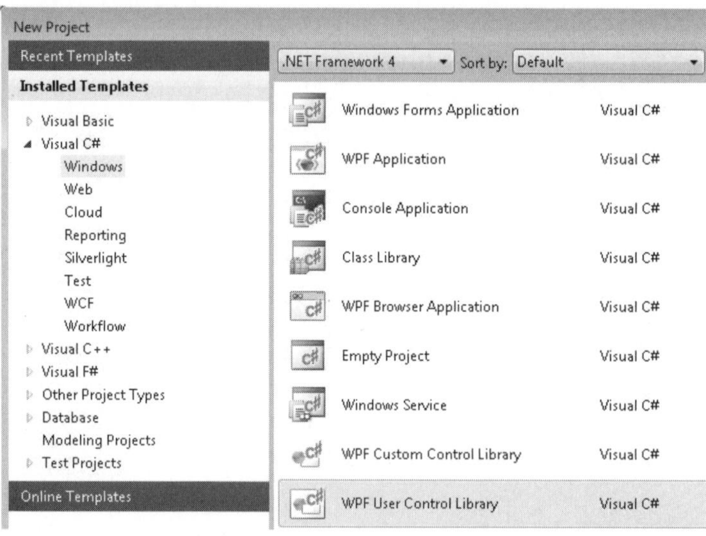

Chapter 3

Getting to Know the Environment

"A mobile robot has to devote a tremendous amount of processing time simply to avoid obstacles in the environment. Human beings do, too, but they're never aware of it—until the lights go out. Then they learn painfully just how much processing is really required."

—Michael Crichton, "Prey"

Too often we take our environment for granted—the little things that we see every day and, yet, fail to notice. This section is meant to awaken you to the possibilities in your Visual Studio environment.

Most notably, the purpose is to highlight how best to work with your window layouts, how to use the toolbox to your advantage, and how to work with commands properly, among other things. Take time to really explore the Visual Studio environment, and you can unlock the secrets to navigating that same environment successfully.

03.01 Rearrange Windows in Visual Studio 2010 Using the Guide Diamond

DEFAULT	[no shortcut]
VISUAL BASIC 6	[no shortcut]
VISUAL C# 2005	[no shortcut]
VISUAL C++ 2	Alt+F6 (dock)
VISUAL C++ 6	[no shortcut]
VISUAL STUDIO 6	[no shortcut]
WINDOWS	Alt,W, F (Float); Alt,W, K (Dock); Alt,W, T (Dock as Tabbed Document)
MENU	Window | Float; Window | Dock; Window | Dock as Tabbed Document
COMMAND	Window.Float; Window.Dock; Window.DockasTabbedDocument
VERSIONS	2010
CODE	vstipTool0008

Docking and undocking windows in the IDE has always been interesting. In Visual Studio, we have a tool called the Guide Diamond that is used to assist our efforts. The following illustration shows the Guide Diamond in Visual Studio 2008.

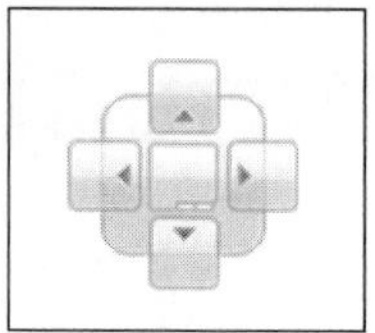

Unfortunately, this doesn't really provide good visual cues to help determine the final position of a window. Visual Studio 2010 provides a new and improved Guide Diamond that makes docking much easier, as shown in the following illustration.

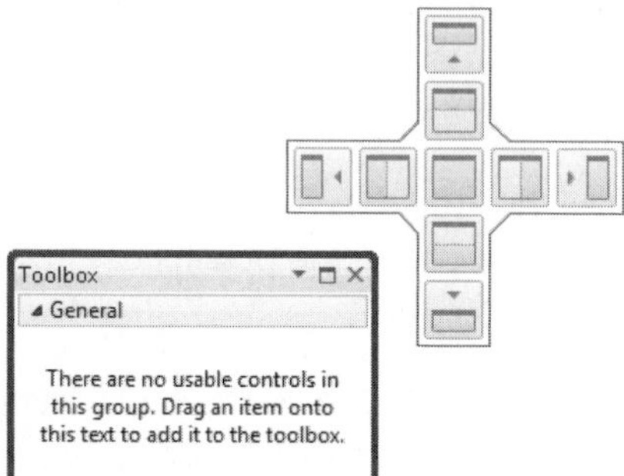

Now you can clearly see how your docked window will look based on the image in the diamond. Just drag the title bar of your window over one of the previews in the Guide Diamond.

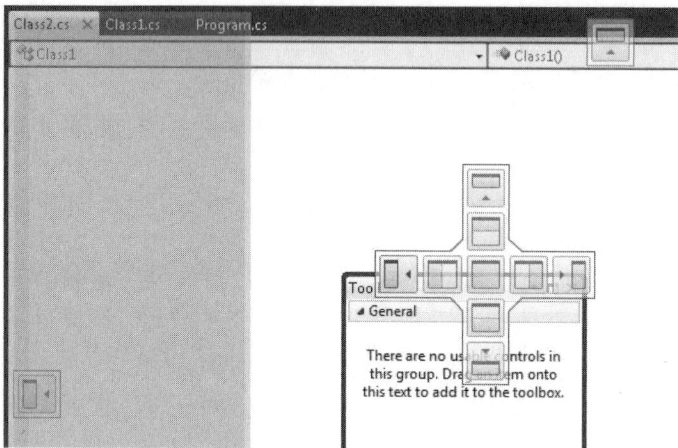

When the preview matches where you want your window to go, just release the mouse and the window docks at that location.

03.02 Dock a Floating Tool Window Back to Its Previous Location

DEFAULT	[no shortcut]
VISUAL BASIC 6	[no shortcut]
VISUAL C# 2005	[no shortcut]
VISUAL C++ 2	Alt+F6
VISUAL C++ 6	[no shortcut]
VISUAL STUDIO 6	[no shortcut]
WINDOWS	Alt,W, K
MENU	Window | Dock
COMMAND	Window.Dock
VERSIONS	2005, 2008, 2010
CODE	vstipTool0036

You can easily dock a floating tool window back to its previous docked location.

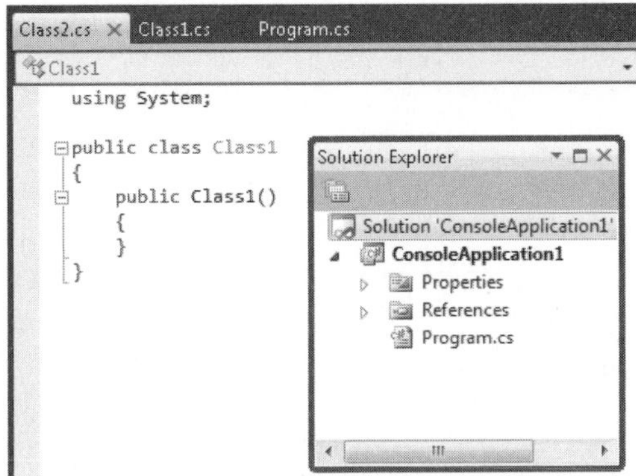

Just right-click the Title Bar, and choose Dock, as shown in the following illustration.

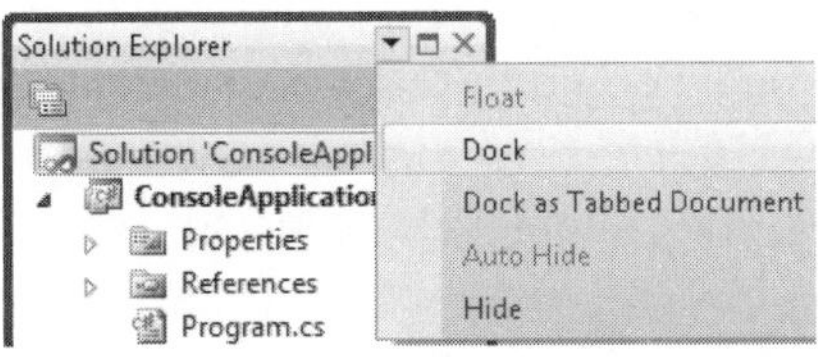

Note In Visual Studio 2008, you can also double-click the title bar to dock the window back to its previous location.

In Visual Studio 2005, to place a tool window back to its previous docking location without using the docking guides, you must double-click the title bar. Additionally, the title bar menu is slightly different for 2005. The word "Dockable" is used in place of the word "Dock."

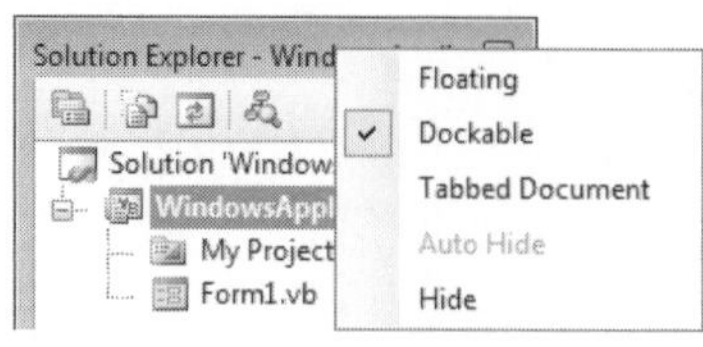

03.03 Cycle Through Your Open Tool Windows

DEFAULT	Alt+F6 (next); Alt+Shift+F6 (previous)
VISUAL BASIC 6	Alt+F6 (next); Alt+Shift+F6 (previous)
VISUAL C# 2005	Alt+F6 (next); Alt+Shift+F6 (previous)
VISUAL C++ 2	F6 (next); Shift+F6 (previous)
VISUAL C++ 6	Alt+F6 (next); Alt+Shift+F6 (previous)
VISUAL STUDIO 6	Alt+F6 (next); Alt+Shift+F6 (previous)
WINDOWS	[no shortcut]
COMMAND	Window.NextPane; Window.PreviousPane
VERSIONS	2005, 2008, 2010
CODE	vstipTool0038

In vstipTool0023, "Using the IDE Navigator," page 160, you saw how to get around among your open tool windows. Here's how to get around among your open tool windows without using the IDE Navigator.

Press Alt+F6 (next) or Alt+Shift+F6 (previous) to begin going through your open tool windows. It's important to understand what the word "open" means in this context. An "open" tool window is one whose tab appears in the IDE. For example, suppose you have the following view:

The Error List, Command Window, and Breakpoints are "open" tool windows—even though the tool windows are hidden. This is an important distinction as you use this tip, because it explains why you cycle through all the open tool windows—whether or not they are hidden.

03.04 Closing Tool Windows

DEFAULT	Shift+Esc
VISUAL BASIC 6	Shift+Esc
VISUAL C# 2005	Shift+Esc
VISUAL C++ 2	Shift+Esc
VISUAL C++ 6	Shift+Esc
VISUAL STUDIO 6	Shift+Esc
WINDOWS	[no shortcut]
COMMAND	Window.CloseToolWindow
VERSIONS	2005, 2008, 2010
CODE	vstipTool0039

Eventually, after using your tool windows, you will want to close one or more of them. You can always do this by clicking the Close button (the "X" in the upper-right corner).

Using the keyboard, you can simply press Shift+Esc to close the current tool window.

03.05 Expand and Collapse All in the Toolbox

WINDOWS	* (expand all); / (collapse all)
VERSIONS	2005, 2008, 2010
CODE	vstipTool0050

You can quickly expand the entire Toolbox by pressing the asterisk (*) when the Toolbox is active.

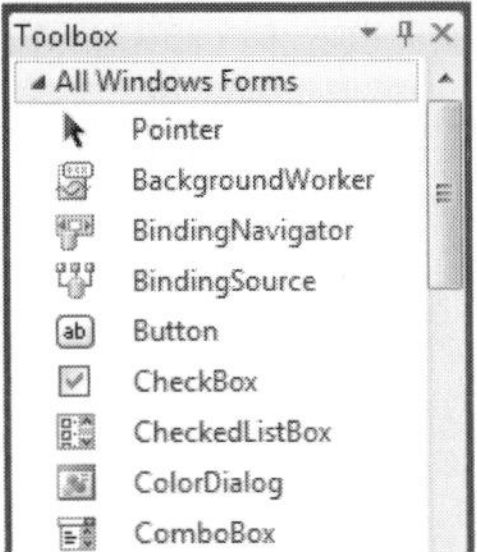

You can also collapse the entire Toolbox by pressing the forward slash (/) when the Toolbox is active.

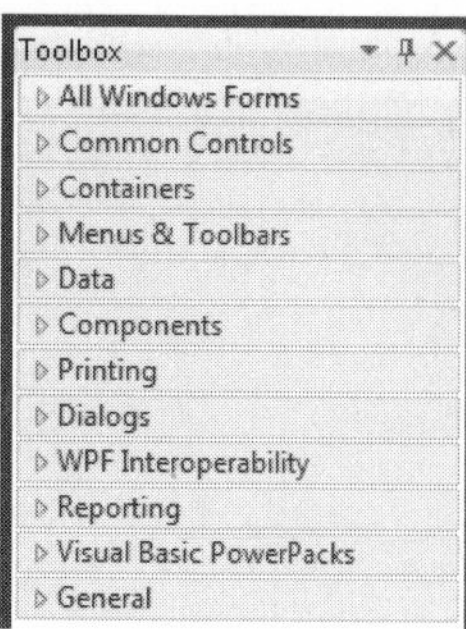

03.06 Searching in the Toolbox

DEFAULT	Ctrl+Alt+X (view toolbox)
VISUAL BASIC 6	Ctrl+Alt+X (view toolbox)
VISUAL C# 2005	Ctrl+Alt+X (view toolbox); Ctrl+W, X (view toolbox); Ctrl+W, Ctrl+X (view toolbox)
VISUAL C++ 2	Ctrl+Alt+X (view toolbox)
VISUAL C++ 6	Ctrl+Alt+X (view toolbox)
VISUAL STUDIO 6	Ctrl+Alt+X (view toolbox)
WINDOWS	Alt,V, X (view toolbox); TAB (next result); ESC (cancel)
MENU	View | Toolbox
COMMAND	View.Toolbox
VERSIONS	2010
CODE	vstipTool0114

This tip provides a much-requested and much-anticipated feature: searching the Toolbox.

Simply switch focus to the Toolbox (Ctrl+Alt+X), as shown in the following illustration.

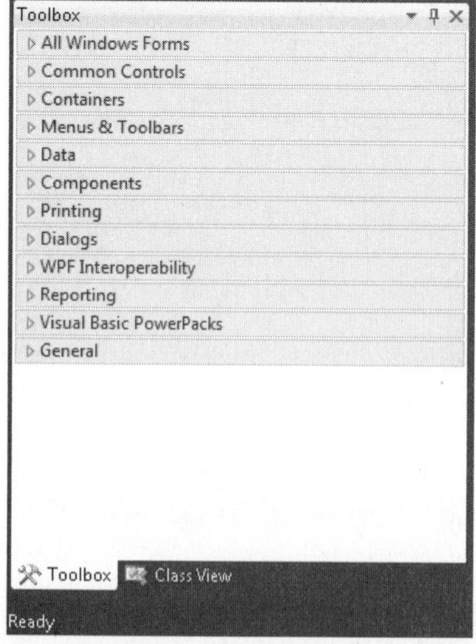

Now start typing the name of the control you are looking for. In the following example, I'm looking for the TextBox control by typing **tex**:

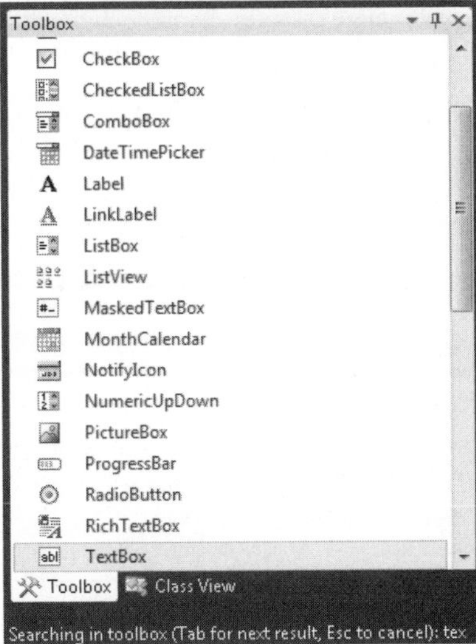

The letters you are typing appear in the Status Bar, and you are even provided instructions either for looking for the next item or for cancelling the search.

Press Tab to go the next result, or press Esc to cancel. Also, you can actively use the Backspace key to delete letters from the search when you want to quickly retype new characters.

03.07 Navigate Among Tabs in the Toolbox

KEYBOARD	Ctrl+[Up, Down] Arrow
VERSIONS	2005, 2008, 2010
CODE	vstipTool0051

You can jump between tabs in the Toolbox.

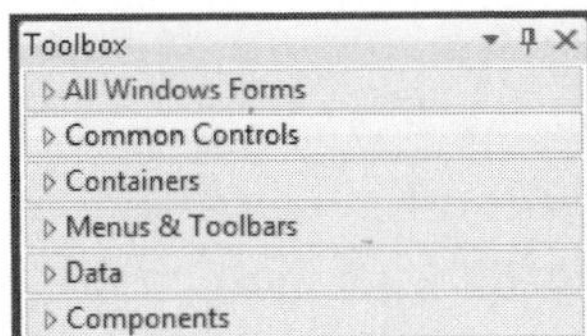

Just press Ctrl+[Up, Down] Arrow to navigate. When you use Ctrl+Down Arrow, it expands the next tab and jumps to the first item in that group, as shown in the following illustration.

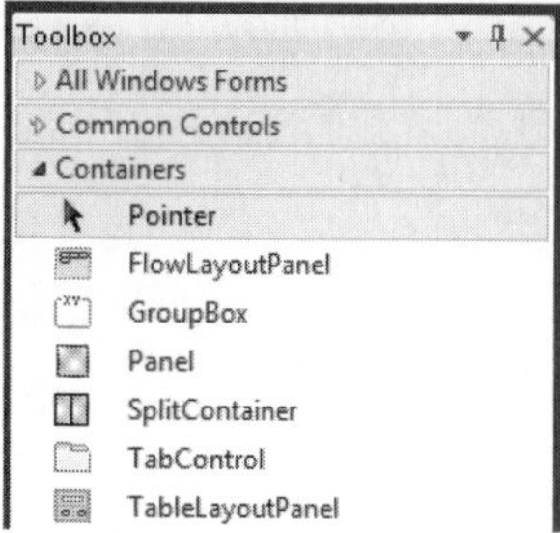

When you press Ctrl+Up Arrow it jumps to the last item in the previous control group:

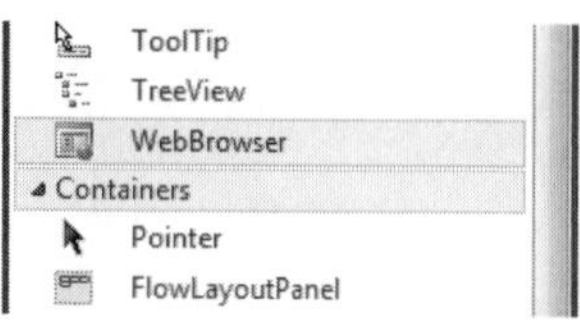

03.08 Window Layouts: The Four Modes

VERSIONS	2005, 2008, 2010
CODE	vstipEnv0051

Ever wonder why the windows seem to shift around when you go from Design to Debug Mode? The answer is simple: window layouts.

You might have seen them if you have ever tried to export your window layouts. You can find it under General Settings | Window Layouts, as shown in the following illustration.

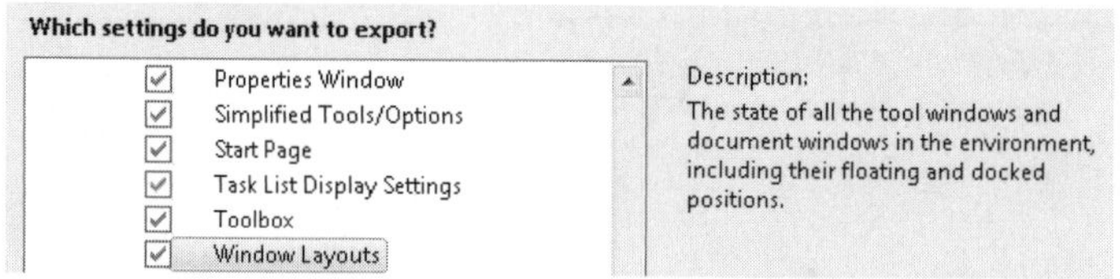

The four window layout modes in Visual Studio are as follows.

Design View

This view is the one you see when you start up Visual Studio. It's what most people refer to as the "normal" view.

Debugging View

This is the view that you get when you enter Debug Mode as you are stepping through your code.

Full Screen

This is the view that you get when you go to View | Full Screen (Shift+Alt+Enter).

File View

This is the lesser-known view that you can get when you open up a file via devenv.exe [filename].

```
\ConsoleApplication1>devenv.exe class1.cs_
```

The thing to remember here is that your tool windows and your command bar customizations are saved separately for each state. There is no way to tell Visual Studio to use one state for all modes at this time. Additionally, when you shut down Visual Studio in any state, all four states are saved.

03.09 Window Layouts: Design, Debug, and Full Screen

VERSIONS	2005, 2008, 2010
CODE	vstipEnv0052

In vstipEnv0051, "Window Layouts: The Four Modes," page 90, I discussed the four layout modes in Visual Studio. I thought it would be instructive to demonstrate the three most common modes together here.

As we discuss these modes, keep in mind that each has its own layout that can be customized to your needs. For example, you might clearly need some windows in Design Mode (for example, the Pending Changes window) that perhaps aren't necessary in Debug Mode.

Design Mode

This is the mode you see when you first start up Visual Studio. It is one of the two most common modes you will find yourself in. The following illustration shows a view of my Design Window Layout for a website.

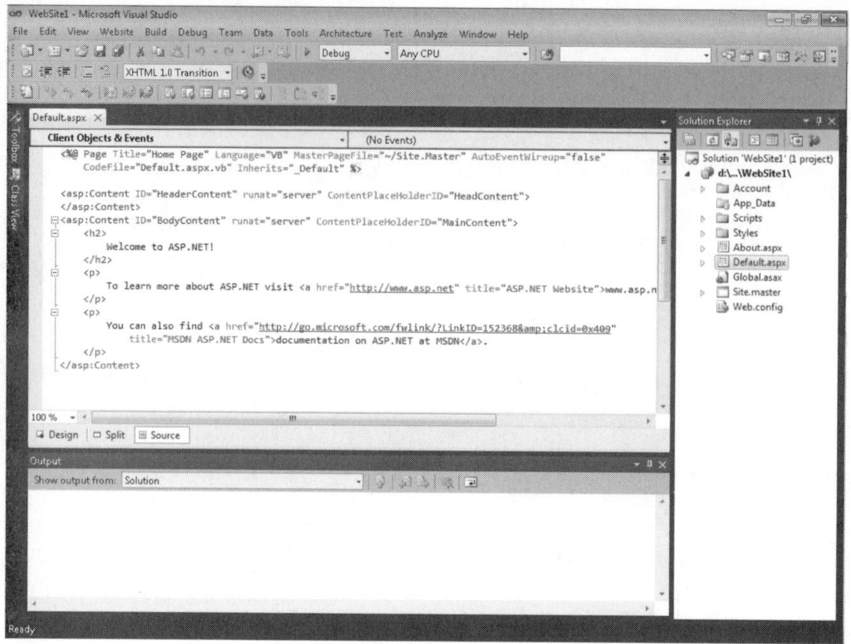

Debug Mode

When I enter Debug Mode, the second most common mode, I see my Debug Window Layout, as shown in the following console application.

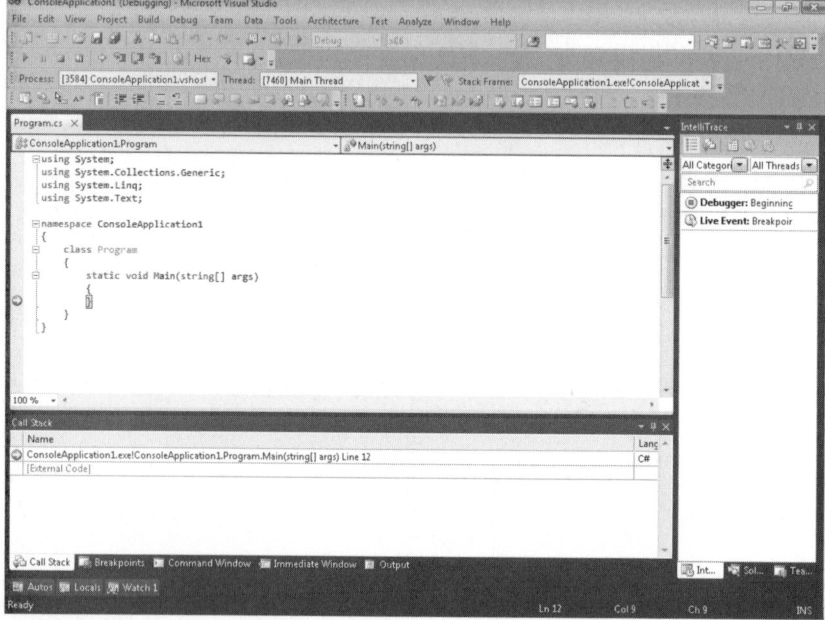

Full Screen Mode

I addressed this mode in vstipEnv0024, "Full Screen Mode," in Appendix B (*http://go.microsoft.com/FWLink/?Linkid=223758*). You can get here by pressing Shift+Alt+Enter. An example of what it looks like is shown in the following illustration.

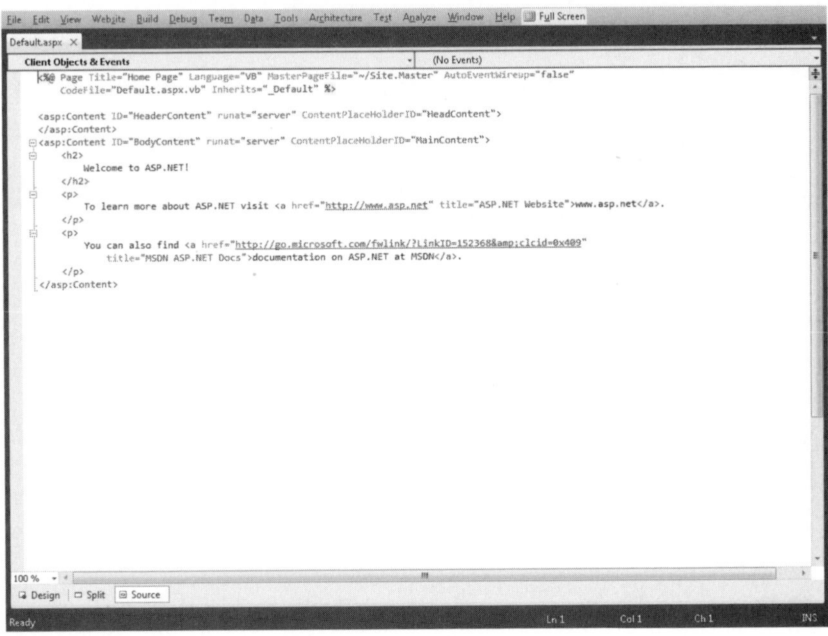

03.10 Working with Tabs in the Toolbox

WINDOWS	Shift+F10, A (with the Toolbox selected)
MENU	[Right-click the Toolbox] | Add Tab
COMMAND	Tools.AddTab
VERSIONS	2005, 2008, 2010
CODE	vstipTool0054

The Toolbox is a pretty cool place, and one of its best features is the ability to organize items by using tabs.

Creating Tabs

To create a custom tab, right-click inside the Toolbox and choose Add Tab, as shown in the following illustration.

Just type in a name for your new tab, and press Enter.

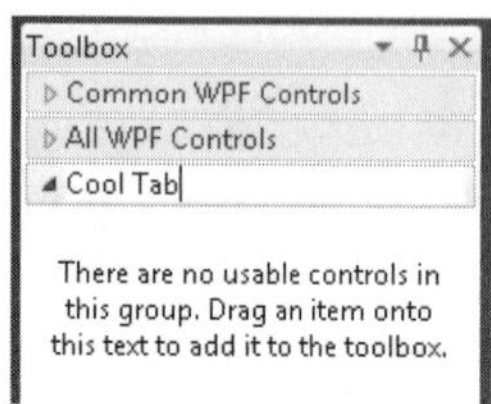

Adding Items

You can add items to your custom tab as you see fit. For example, to add controls to this new tab from existing tabs, just pick the control you want and copy it.

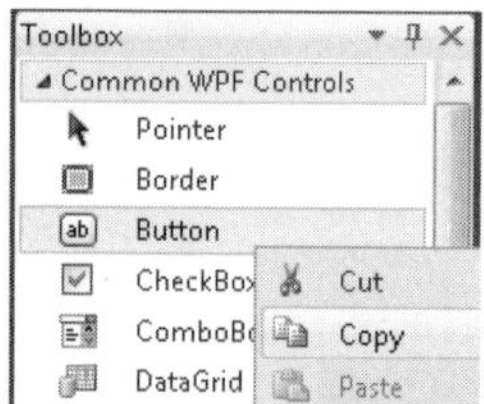

Then go to your customized tab, and paste inside it to get a copy of that control for your use.

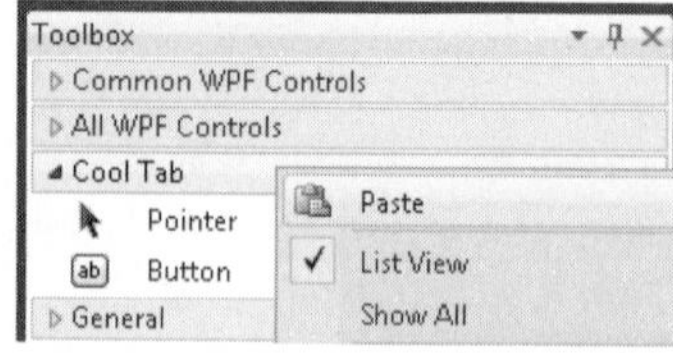

You can also click and drag items onto new tabs.

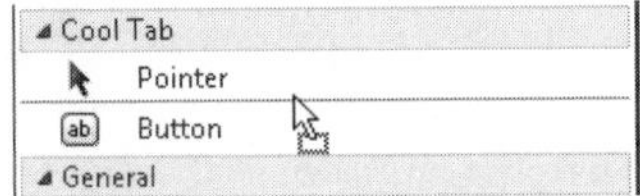

Custom Controls

Of course, if you want custom controls, you can always right-click in the custom tab and select Choose Items, as shown in the following illustration.

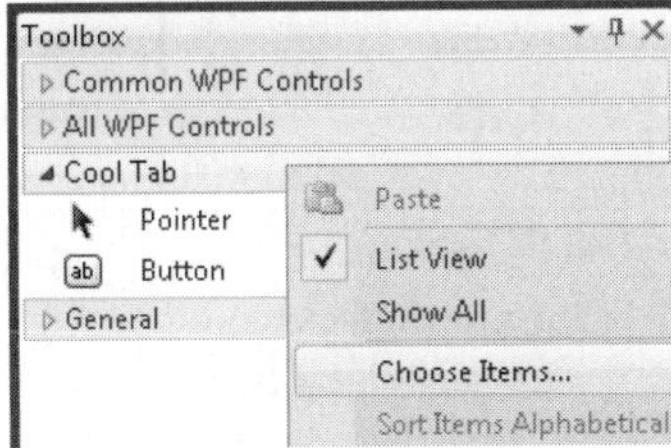

Renaming Tabs

If you don't like a tab name, you can always rename it:

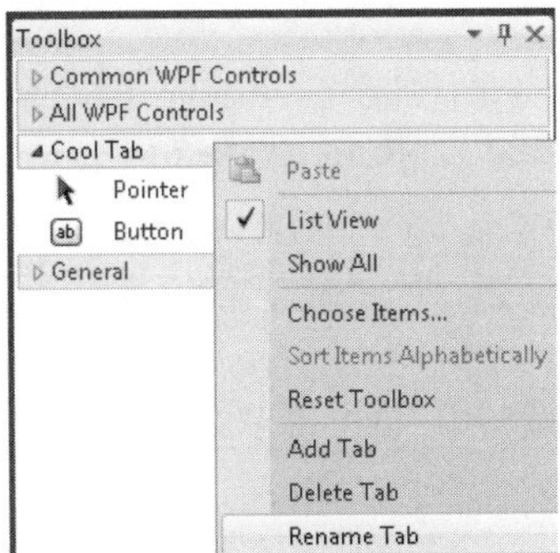

Deleting Tabs

Also notice the option to delete the tab, shown in the preceding illustration. If you choose this option, the following dialog box appears. When you click OK in this dialog box, you lose the tab as well as all the items on it.

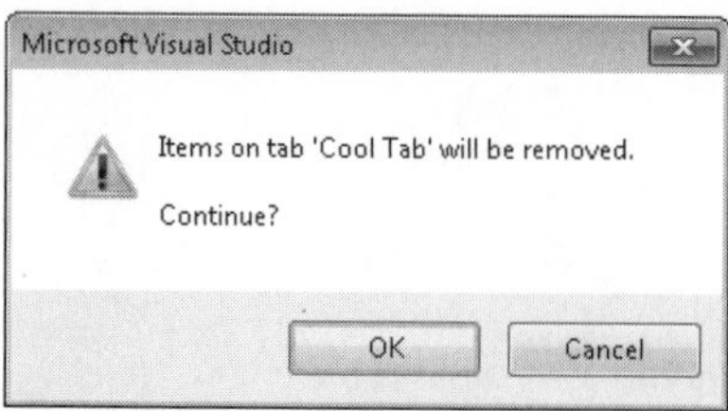

This action is just an organizational mechanism and doesn't permanently delete any controls from your system, so you can add them as needed to any future tabs.

03.11 Using Additional Browsers for Web Development

WINDOWS	Alt,F, H (with file selected in Solution Explorer)
MENU	File | Browse With (with file selected in Solution Explorer)
COMMAND	File.BrowseWith (with file selected in Solution Explorer)
VERSIONS	2005, 2008, 2010
CODE	vstipEnv0057

When you are doing web development in Visual Studio, you might want to use a different default browser than you are currently using. You can do this by using the Browse With dialog box.

Getting to this dialog box is a little interesting because it is context sensitive. It is best to have either your web project or a webpage selected in Solution Explorer to see the Browse With option on the File Menu or when you right-click:

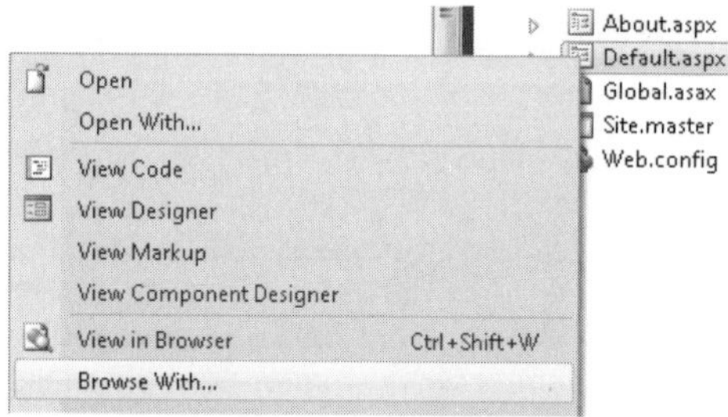

The Browse With dialog box appears as shown in the following illustration.

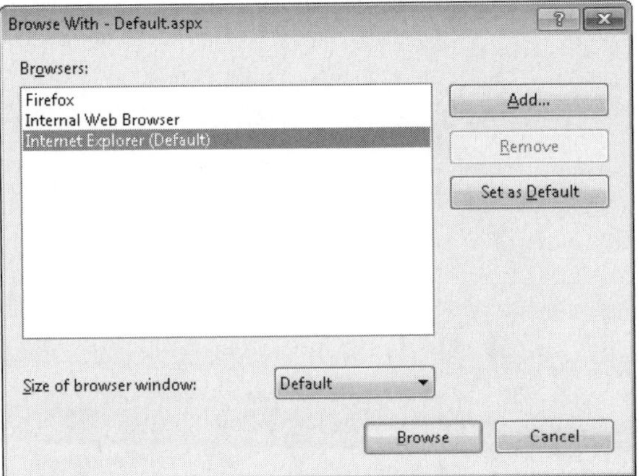

Adding New Browsers

Visual Studio automatically detects some browsers. For example, I installed Firefox and the preceding dialog box automatically detected it. However, if you don't see your browser in the Browse With dialog box, you can click Add, enter the path to the executable in the Program Name field, and enter a friendly name for your browser in the Friendly Name field, as shown in the following illustration.

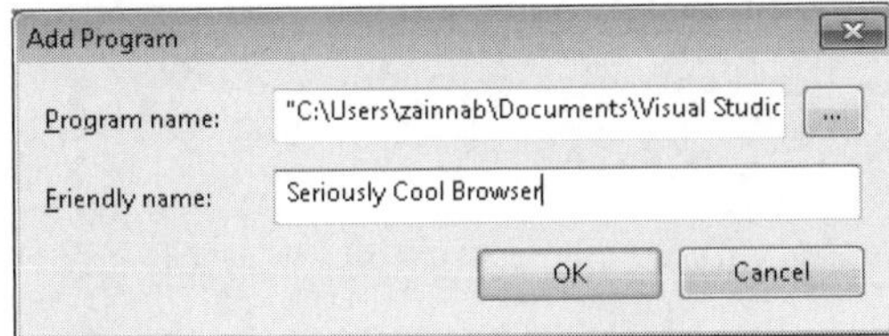

Changing the Default Browser

You can also change the default browser by choosing a browser in the list and then clicking Set As Default:

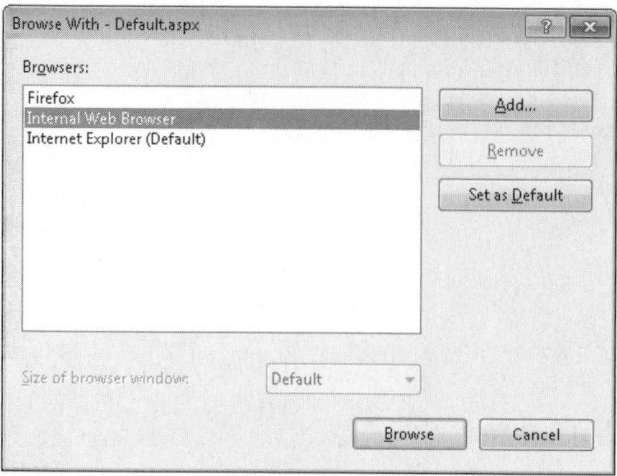

Browser Window Size

Choose the window size you want for your browser by using the Size Of Browser Window drop-down list:

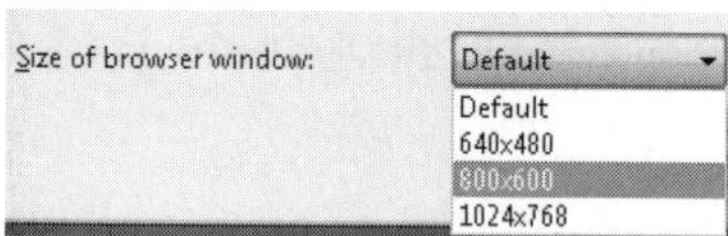

Removing Browsers

Eventually, you might want to get rid of some of your browser choices. Simply select the browser in the list, and click Remove:

03.12 Auto-Hide All Tool Windows

WINDOWS	Alt,W, U
MENU	Window | Auto Hide All
COMMAND	Window.AutoHideAll
VERSIONS	2005, 2008, 2010
CODE	vstipTool0034

Warning While this is a great tip, there is no way to "un-auto-hide" all tool windows, so you have to bring your tool windows back individually.

So let's say you have a crowded space with lots of tool windows open, as shown in the following illustration.

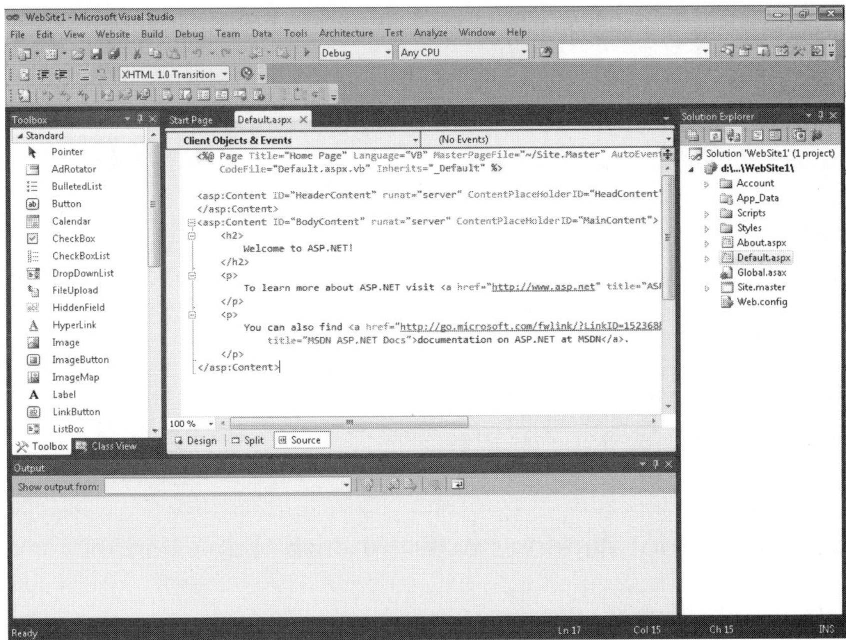

You can make all the tool windows go away quickly—just go to Window | Auto Hide All:

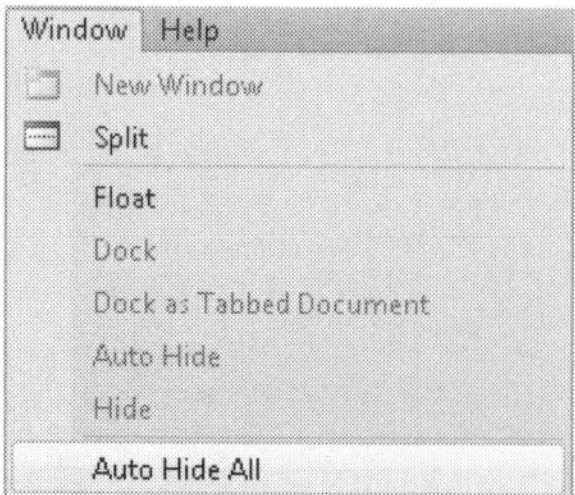

All the tool windows are automatically hidden.

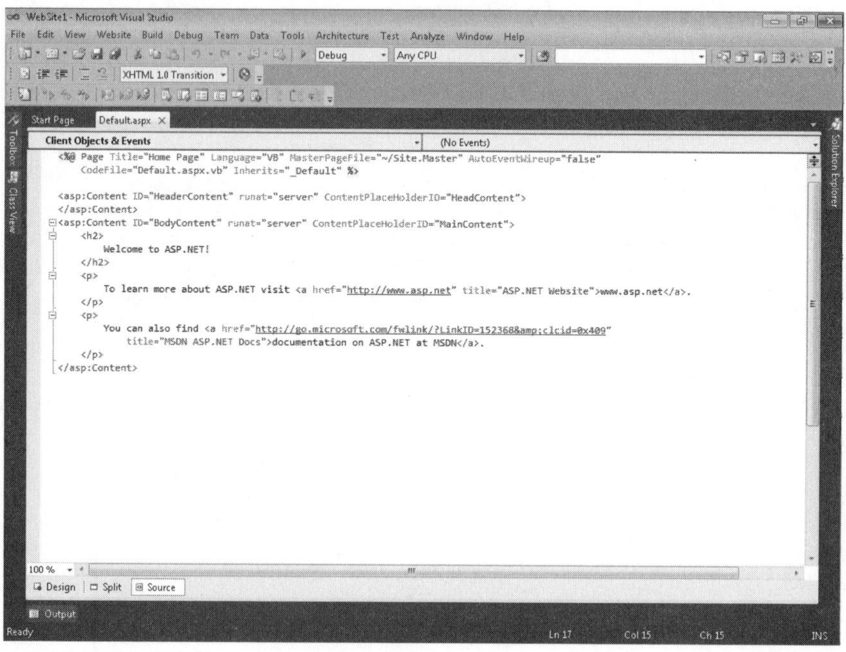

03.13 Showing Hidden Tool Windows with the Auto Hide Channel

VERSIONS	2005, 2008, 2010
CODE	vstipTool0037

You can use a special place called the Auto Hide Channel to see what tool windows are hidden. Just go to any area that has hidden tool windows, and then right-click the bar where the tabs are to see a list of the hidden tool windows.

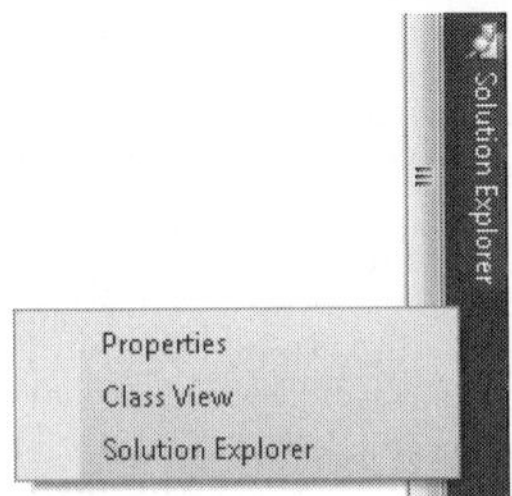

The best part is that this works on the bottom channel.

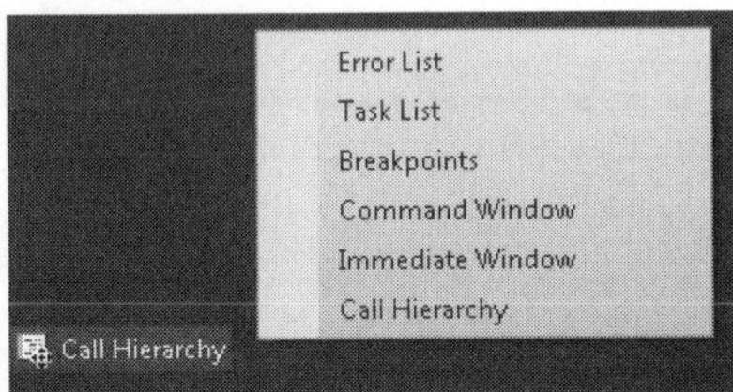

And it works on the channel to the left as well.

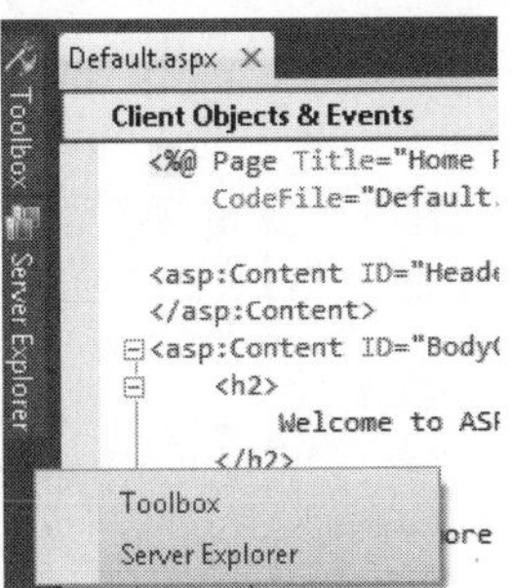

For best results, click in the empty space in the channel, beyond any tabs, as shown in the following illustration.

And, of course, to show any hidden window, just select it from the list.

03.14 Moving Tool Windows Around with Your Keyboard

DEFAULT	Alt+- (dock menu)
VISUAL BASIC 6	[no shortcut]
VISUAL C# 2005	Alt+- (dock menu)
VISUAL C++ 2	Alt+- (dock menu)
VISUAL C++ 6	Alt+- (dock menu)
VISUAL STUDIO 6	Alt+- (dock menu)
WINDOWS	Alt,Space (floating tool windows)
MENU	Window | [Float, Dock, etc.] (dock menu)
COMMAND	Window.ShowDockMenu
VERSIONS	2010
CODE	vstipTool0041

Note The minus sign (-) used in the keyboard shortcut is from the top row of numeric keys on your keyboard, not the minus sign on the numeric keypad.

With the rewrite of the IDE for Visual Studio 2010, you'll find some changes in how you control the tool windows. When an active tool window is docked, you can use Alt+minus (-) to bring up the Dock menu and then use your arrow keys to pick an item from the menu.

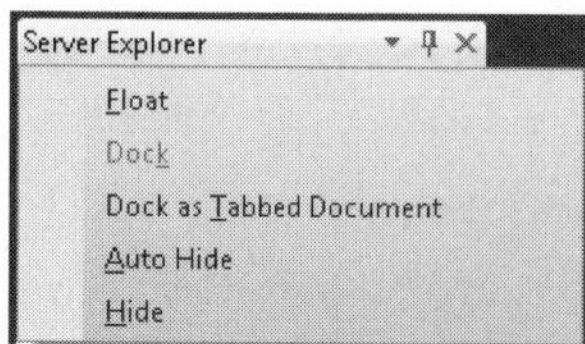

This works for floating tool windows as well.

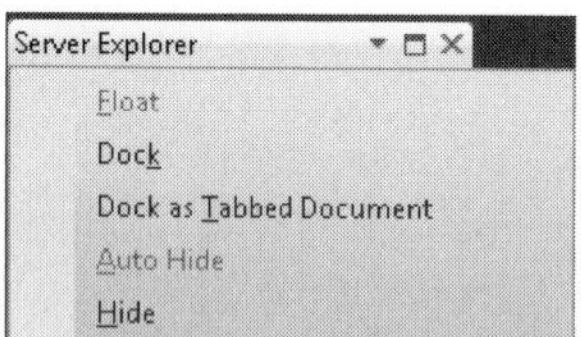

But active floating tool windows have a System menu that you can access *only* by pressing Alt+Space.

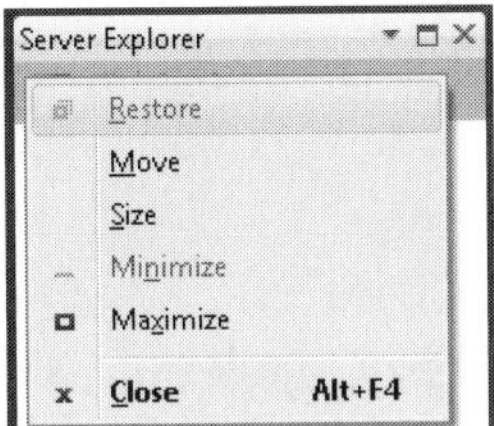

These commands should be familiar to just about everyone, and they give you full control over moving, resizing, and other window manipulations.

03.15 Keyboard Access to a Tool Window's Toolbar

WINDOWS	Shift+Alt; Tab
VERSIONS	2005, 2008, 2010
CODE	vstipTool0042

Sometimes, when you have an active tool window, you just want access to the toolbar in the window without having to reach over and use your mouse.

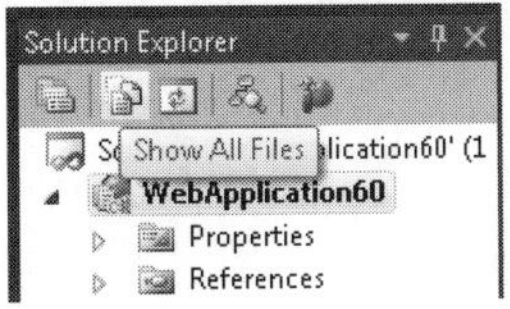

A little-known fact is that you can do this very easily for any active tool window by pressing Shift+Alt for some or by pressing Tab for others. For example, to get access to the Solution Explorer Toolbar, just press Shift+Alt.

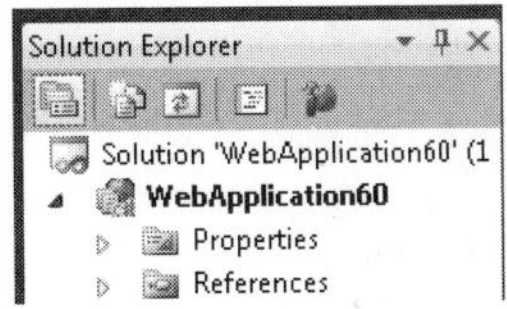

In the Properties Tool Window, you would use press the Tab key to gain access to the toolbar.

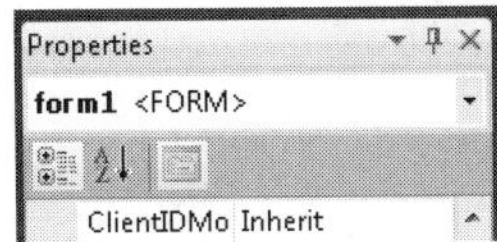

Now you can use your arrow keys to move between toolbar items, and use the Enter key to "press" the button you choose.

03.16 Command Prompt History

WINDOWS	F7 (history window); [Up / Down] Arrow (history)
CODE	vstipTool0055

Many people like to use the command prompt; I thought we might explore one of the oldest features around: command history.

Note The following examples will not work unless you have typed some commands into the Command Window already, so type a few commands and then clear the screen by typing **cls** and pressing Enter.

There are two main ways to get commands you've typed in previously. First, you can just press the Up Arrow key to start going through your history at the prompt itself.

The advantage here is that you can quickly edit the command to change it if needed. However, if you just want to run a command from your history, you can use a very old trick by pressing F7.

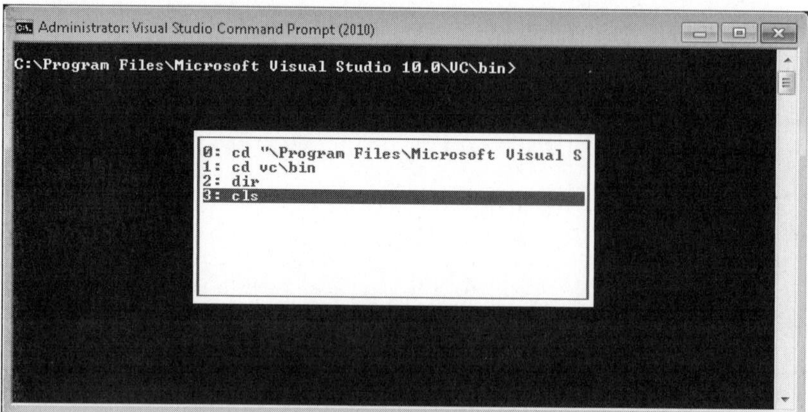

Pressing F7 runs the command you selected from the list by using your Up or Down Arrow keys.

03.17 Command Prompt Tab Completion

WINDOWS	Tab
CODE	vstipTool0056

When using the Visual Studio command prompt (or any command prompt), you have several ways to use tab completion.

Simple Search

You can type the first letter of a file, as shown in the following illustration.

Then press Tab one or more times to see all the files that begin with that letter.

Wildcard Search

Not as well-known is the ability to use wildcards to match characters. You can use an asterisk (*) to represent any number of characters and a question mark (?) to represent a single character.

So if you want to find a file name that has the letter "a" anywhere in it, you would use ***a*** as shown in the following illustration.

Visual Studio Command Prompt (2010)

```
C:\Program Files\Microsoft Visual Studio 10.0\VC\bin>*a*_
```

Then press Tab to get the first result.

Visual Studio Command Prompt (2010)

```
C:\Program Files\Microsoft Visual Studio 10.0\VC\bin>amd64_
```

Press Tab several times, and notice that each file name listed contains the letter "a" somewhere in it.

What about a two-letter file that begins with a "c" but can have any other character and any extension? Use **c?.*** and press Tab.

Visual Studio Command Prompt (2010)

```
C:\Program Files\Microsoft Visual Studio 10.0\VC\bin>c?.*_
```

Press Tab again.

Visual Studio Command Prompt (2010)

```
C:\Program Files\Microsoft Visual Studio 10.0\VC\bin>c1.dll_
```

This feature extends to any commands you want to use as well. You can type something like **edit *a***, as shown in the following illustration.

Visual Studio Command Prompt (2010)

```
C:\Program Files\Microsoft Visual Studio 10.0\VC\bin>edit *a*_
```

Then press Tab to see the following result:

Visual Studio Command Prompt (2010)

```
C:\Program Files\Microsoft Visual Studio 10.0\VC\bin>edit amd64_
```

If I keep pressing tab, it continues to cycle through all file names that contain an "a".

Finally

As you can see, tab completion is a very useful and powerful feature with the command prompt. You definitely want this skill in your tool belt.

03.18 Undock and Dock a Single Tool Window in a Group

DEFAULT	[no shortcut]
VISUAL BASIC 6	[no shortcut]
VISUAL C# 2005	[no shortcut]
VISUAL C++ 2	Alt+F6 (dock)
VISUAL C++ 6	[no shortcut]
VISUAL STUDIO 6	[no shortcut]
WINDOWS	Alt,–, F (float, VS2010 Only); Alt,–, K (dock, VS2010 Only); Alt, W, F (float); Alt, W, K (dock)
MENU	Window | Float; Window | Dock
COMMAND	Window.Float; Window.Dock
VERSIONS	2005, 2008, 2010
CODE	vstipTool0099

Docking and undocking tool windows is a common activity. In this tip, we look at the different techniques you can use to accomplish these tasks.

Undock

You have multiple ways to undock a single tool window in a group.

Click and drag

With the mouse, you can click and drag the tab out of the group.

Menu

With the tool window active, you can select Window | Float from the menu bar, as shown in the following illustration.

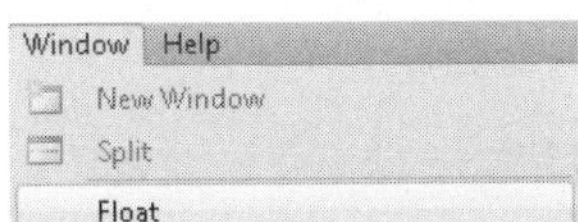

Control box (Visual Studio 2010 only)

Press Alt+minus (–) to get the tool window menu.

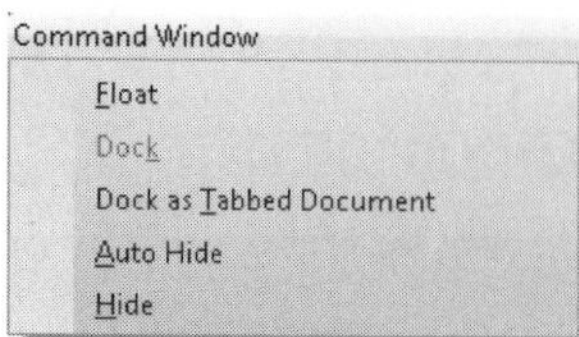

Then press "F" to make the tool window float.

Result

Whichever method you use, the result is the same: You wind up with an undocked tool window.

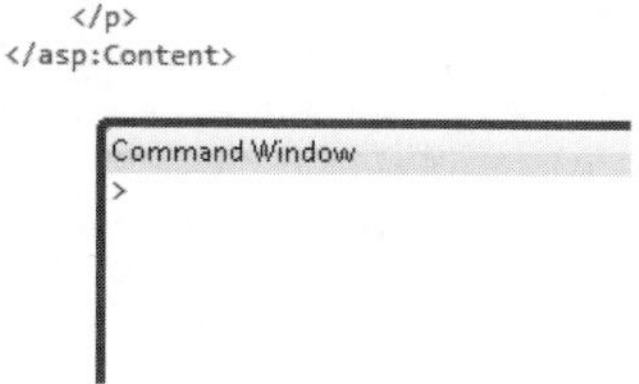

Dock

To dock a floating tool window back into a group (assuming it came from a group), you also have multiple options.

Click and drag

By far, the hardest option is to click and drag the tool window back into the group. The best way to do this is to drag the tool window title bar over the title bar of another tool window in the group you want it to join, as shown in the following illustration.

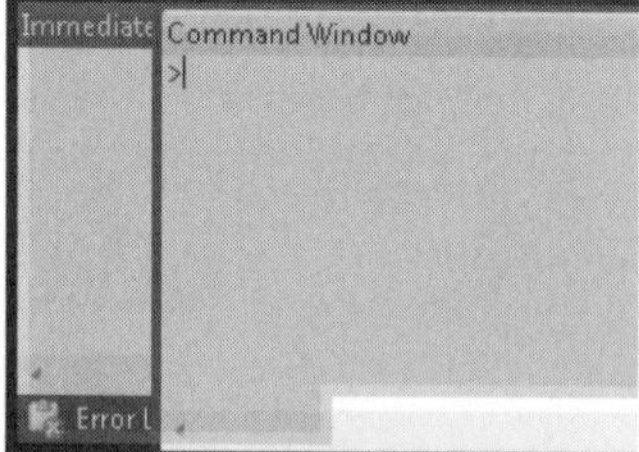

Notice how the target shading looks like a tab being put onto the existing group? That is what you look for when doing it this way. Of course, I would do it this way only if I were taking a tab from one group to another, *not* if I were returning a floating tool window back to its original group.

Menu

The menu option is pretty easy: Just go to Window | Dock, as shown in the following illustration.

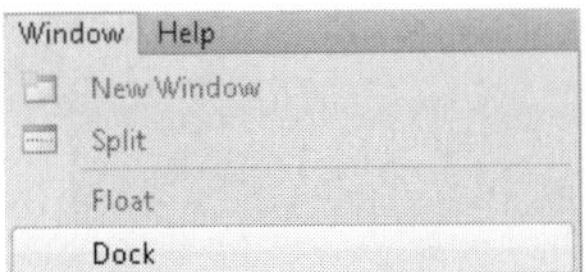

Control box (Visual Studio 2010 only)

And then there is the Control menu. Press Alt+minus (–) to get the menu.

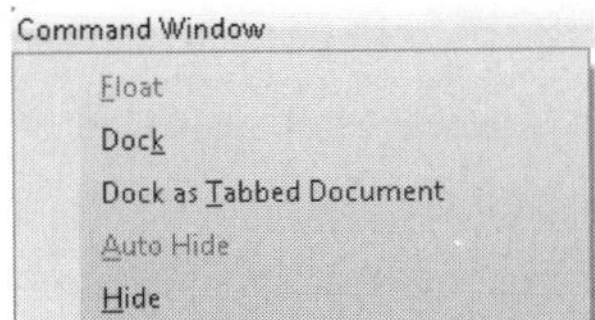

Then press "K" to make the tool window dock back to its original location.

Result

You can use any of these methods to put the tool window back into the group it came from, with the notable exception of the click and drag method, which can be used to put the tool window anywhere.

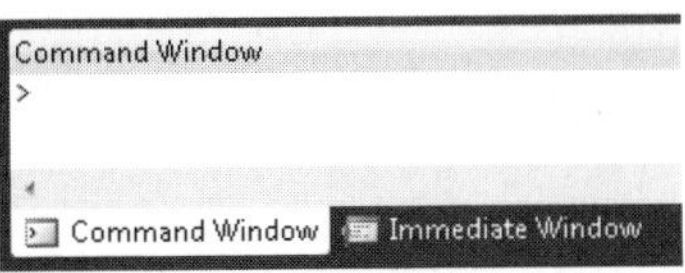

03.19 Understanding Commands: Simple Commands

VERSIONS	2005, 2008, 2010
CODE	vstipTool0067

Just about everything you do in Visual Studio comes with an associated command. But what exactly is a command?

According to the MSDN documentation (*http://msdn.microsoft.com/en-us/library/kcc7tke7.aspx*), commands "allow direct interaction with the integrated development environment (IDE) from the keyboard. Dialog boxes, windows, and other items within the IDE have a command equivalent that you can type into the Command window or Find/Command box to display and, in some cases, execute the item."

In plain English, commands allow you to perform actions in Visual Studio. Let's take adding a class as an example.

First, let's examine the typical way you add a class. Normally, you would just go to Project | Add Class.

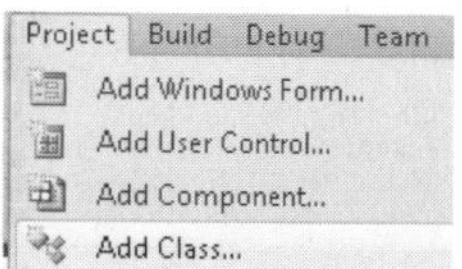

Obviously, this command is used to add a new class to your project and shows the Add New Item dialog box.

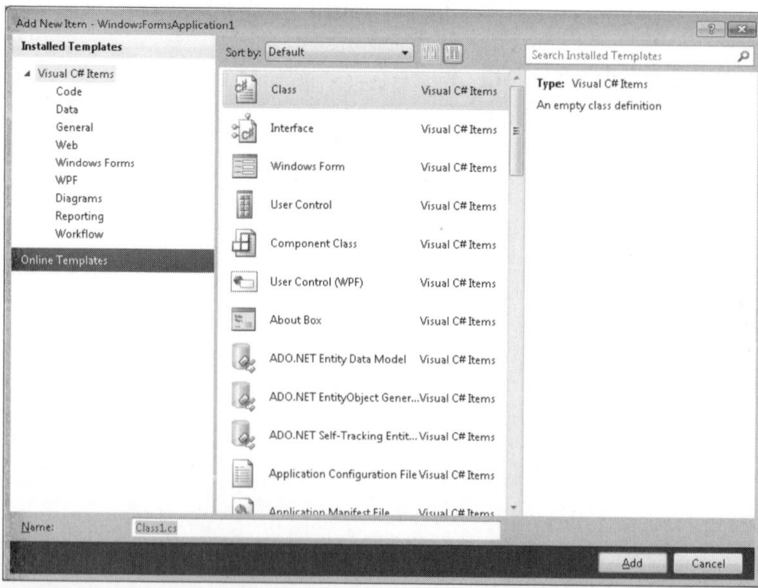

That's too much extra work for something I like to use all the time. I want to search and see whether a specific command is associated with this action. To do this, I'll use what most people refer to as the "command well," because it is a deep "well" of commands. It's where all the commands that you can use are located. To get there, go to Tools | Options | Environment | Keyboard, as shown in the following illustration

Note For this example, I'm using the General keyboard settings, so your settings might have a shortcut key assigned already. You can still follow this tip to create a new shortcut.

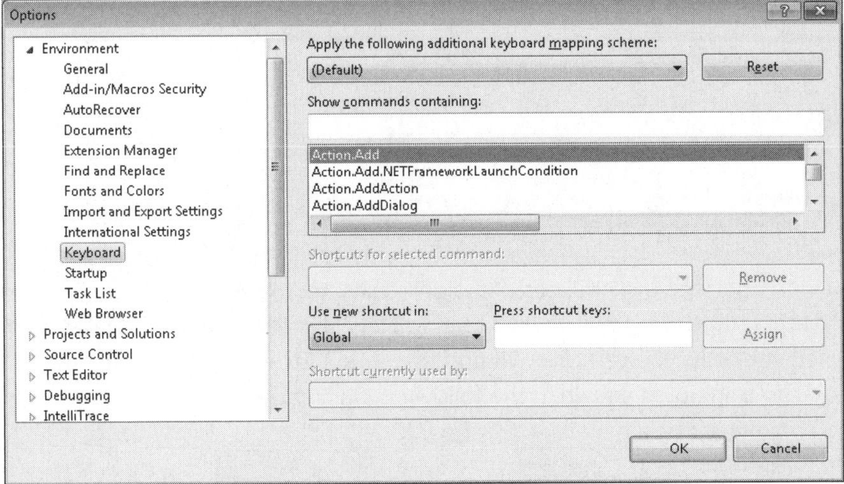

I'll type a keyword in the Show Commands Containing area to narrow down the command list. In this case, the keywords Add Class are used in the menu item, so I will use them here. In the following illustration, you can see how I have removed the spaces for the command.

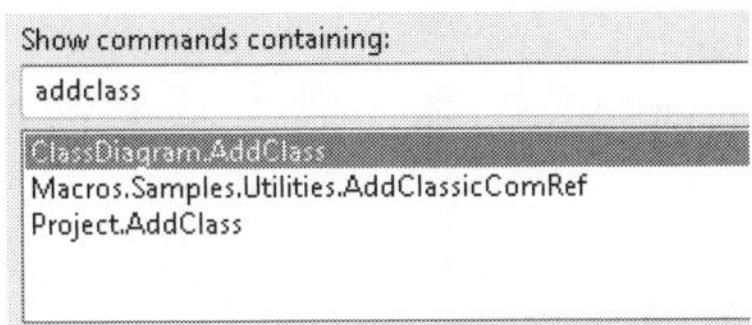

Notice that among the available commands is the Project.AddClass command. It's common to find a command that follows the menu structure, and this one is no exception.

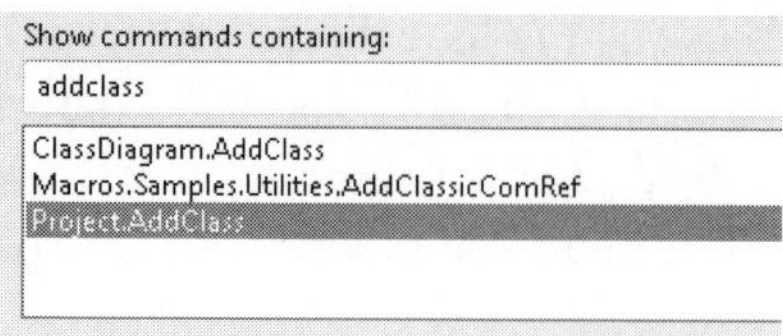

Also notice that no shortcuts are associated with the command. We can now add one. For this example, let's use Ctrl+M, Ctrl+7 as the shortcut key to be assigned.

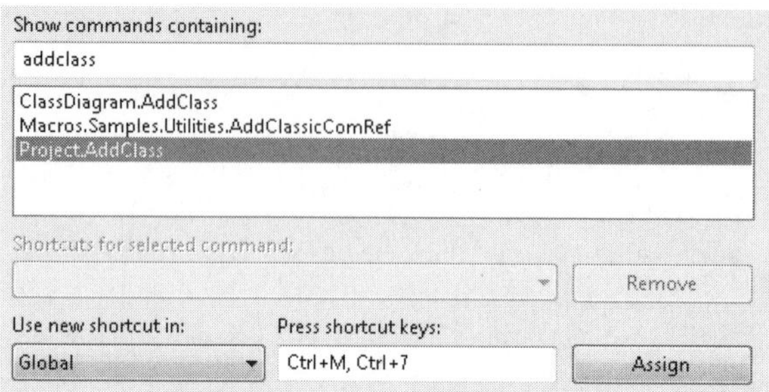

For now, I won't get into the nuances of assigning shortcut keys, but you can get the details at vstipTool0063, "Keyboard Shortcuts: Creating New Shortcuts," page 127. Assuming the key was assigned correctly, you can click OK and then press Ctrl+M, Ctrl+7 to see the Add New Item dialog box pop up, as shown in the following illustration.

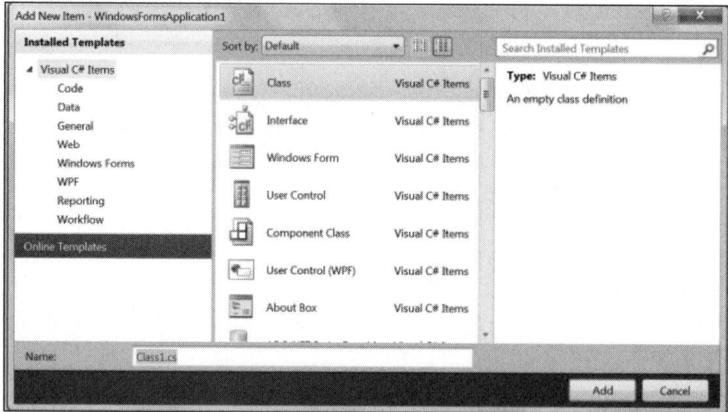

Now you understand the power of commands. They can be quite useful, and after you assign a shortcut key, you can see it in the menu as well (if applicable).

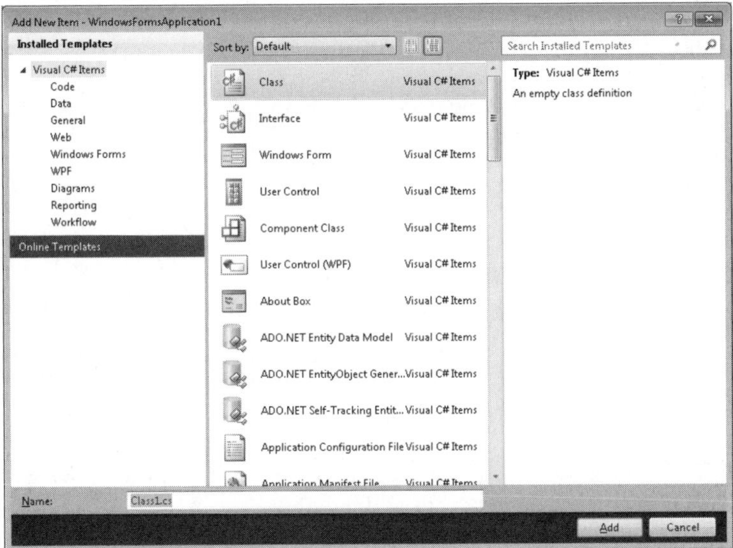

03.20 Understanding Commands: Aliases

DEFAULT	Ctrl+Alt+A
VISUAL BASIC 6	Ctrl+Alt+A
VISUAL C# 2005	Ctrl+Alt+A; Ctrl+W, A; Ctrl+W, Ctrl+A
VISUAL C++ 2	Ctrl+Alt+A
VISUAL C++ 6	Ctrl+Alt+A
VISUAL STUDIO 6	Ctrl+Alt+A
WINDOWS	Alt,V, E, C
MENU	View | Other Windows | Command Window
COMMAND	View.CommandWindow
VERSIONS	2005, 2008, 2010
CODE	vstipTool0068

It is sometimes cumbersome to type in a full command. You can use aliases to quickly use a command without having to type in the full command syntax. If you want a list of the current aliases, just open the Command Window (Ctrl+Alt+A) and type **alias**.

```
Command Window
>alias
alias ? Debug.Print
alias ?? Debug.QuickWatch
alias AddProj File.AddNewProject
alias alias Tools.Alias
alias autos Debug.Autos
alias bl Debug.Breakpoints
alias bp Debug.ToggleBreakpoint
alias callstack Debug.CallStack
alias ClearBook Edit.ClearBookmarks
alias close File.Close
alias CloseAll Window.CloseAllDocuments
```

By the way, you can clear the Command Window out at any time by typing **cls**, just in case you get a lot of clutter in the window.

Let's take a simple alias as an example. How about the "Debug.ToggleBreakpoint" command? Notice in the preceding list that the alias is "bp". Let's find a line of code.

```
            Console.WriteLine("Blah");
```

Now we can go to the Command Window and type **bp**, as shown in the following illustration.

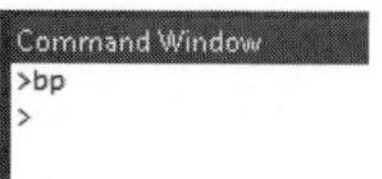

It puts a breakpoint on the line.

Create a New Alias

In addition to the aliases that are already there, you can create new ones. Let's create one for the Project.AddClass command. Simply type **alias [alias to use] [command]**. In our case, let's put in **alias ac Project.AddClass**, as shown in the following illustration.

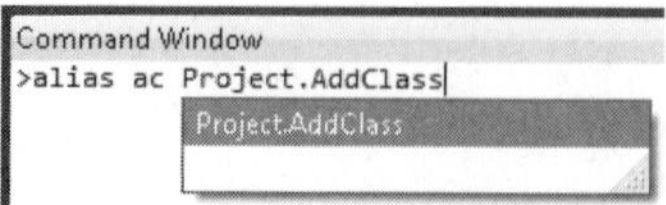

Anytime we want to add a class, we can type the command alias **ac** and get the Add New Item dialog box.

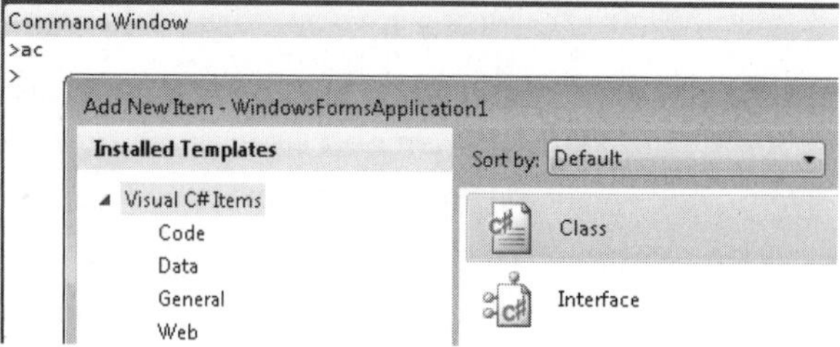

Viewing Assigned Aliases

To show what command an alias is assigned to, just type **alias [alias]**. So, in this case, I would put in **alias ac** to see what command "ac" is bound to.

```
Command Window
>alias ac
alias ac Project.AddClass
>
```

Delete an Alias

To get rid of an alias, type **alias [alias] /d[elete]**. To get rid of the alias we just made, we would type **alias ac /d**.

```
Command Window
>alias ac /d
>
```

You can confirm the alias is gone by typing **alias ac**. You should see the result shown in the following illustration.

```
Command Window
>alias ac /d
>alias ac
No alias 'ac' is defined
>
```

03.21 Understanding Commands: Arguments and Switches

DEFAULT	Ctrl+Alt+A
VISUAL BASIC 6	Ctrl+Alt+A
VISUAL C# 2005	Ctrl+Alt+A; Ctrl+W, A; Ctrl+W, Ctrl+A
VISUAL C++ 2	Ctrl+Alt+A
VISUAL C++ 6	Ctrl+Alt+A
VISUAL STUDIO 6	Ctrl+Alt+A
WINDOWS	Alt,V, E, C
MENU	View | Other Windows | Command Window
COMMAND	View.CommandWindow
VERSIONS	2005, 2008, 2010
CODE	vstipTool0069

Some commands take arguments and switches so that you can quickly execute them without having to deal with user interface elements. You can get a list of commands that take arguments by going to the MSDN Documentation article entitled "Visual Studio Commands with Arguments," at *http://msdn.microsoft.com/en-us/library/c338aexd.aspx*.

The best way to learn is by doing, so let's use the Edit.Find command. If you want to know more about what Find can do, take a look at vstipFind0007, "Using Quick Find," on page 172.

Basic Use

First, open up the Command Window (Ctrl+Alt+A) and run the command without any arguments, as shown in the following illustration.

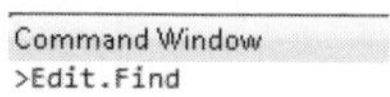

The preceding command opens the Find And Replace dialog box, shown in the following illustration.

Arguments and Switches

According to the "Find Command" documentation at *http://msdn.microsoft.com/en-us/library/295dhke9.aspx*, the Edit.Find command takes one argument and 12 possible switches. The general syntax for the command is as follows:

```
Edit.Find findwhat [/case] [/doc | /proc | /open | /sel] [/markall] [/options] [/reset] [/
up] [/wild | /regex] [/word]
```

I'll resist the urge to copy and paste from the documentation here and just focus on the items we are going to use.

Argument

- **findwhat**—Required. The text to match.

Switches

- **/doc** or **/d**—Optional. Searches the current document only. You can use only one of the available search scopes: /doc, /proc (procedure), /open (all open documents), or /sel (current selection).
- **/markall** or **/m**—Optional. Places a [bookmark] on each line that contains a search match within the current document.
- **/wild** or **/l**—Optional. Uses predefined special characters in the findwhat argument as notations to represent a character or sequence of characters.

List Current Options

You can list out the current options that are set for the Edit.Find command by typing **Edit.Find /options**, as shown in the following illustration.

```
Command Window
>Edit.Find /options
/wild /doc
>
```

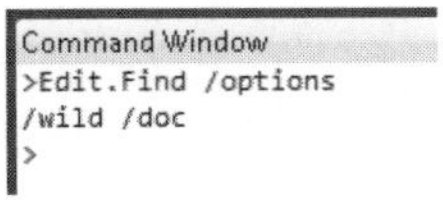

Reset Options

You can reset the options to the default values by typing **Edit.Find /reset**.

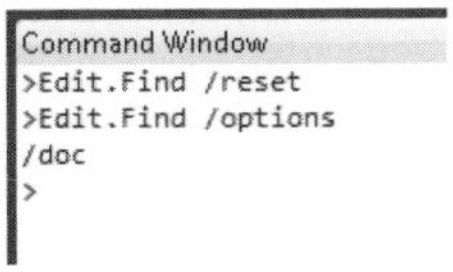

```
Command Window
>Edit.Find /reset
>Edit.Find /options
/doc
>
```

Using the Arguments and Switches

Let's put this command to the test. We want to bypass the Quick Find dialog box and just find things. We will use the following command:

```
Edit.Find *c* /wild /doc /markall
```

This command finds any line in the current document (/doc) that has the letter "c" anywhere in it, using wildcards (/wild) and placing a bookmark (/markall) on each line.

The following illustration shows the code we are going to use before we run the command.

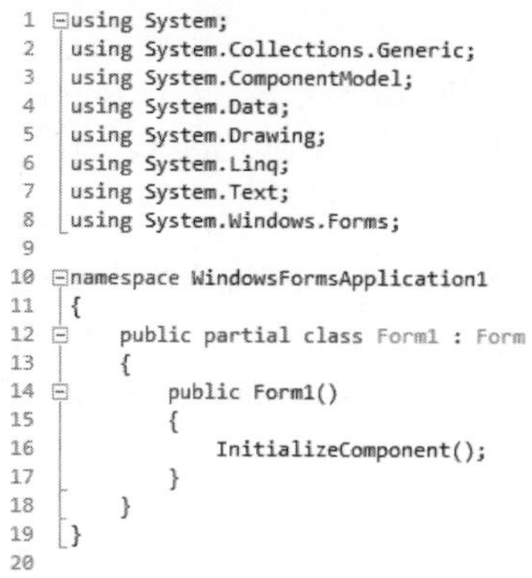

```
using System;
using System.Collections.Generic;
using System.ComponentModel;
using System.Data;
using System.Drawing;
using System.Linq;
using System.Text;
using System.Windows.Forms;

namespace WindowsFormsApplication1
{
    public partial class Form1 : Form
    {
        public Form1()
        {
            InitializeComponent();
        }
    }
}
```

We run our command.

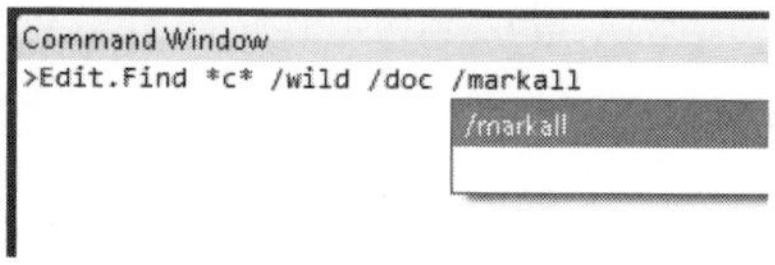

```
Command Window
>Edit.Find *c* /wild /doc /markall
                          /markall
```

The result is shown in the following illustration.

```
using System;
using System.Collections.Generic;
using System.ComponentModel;
using System.Data;
using System.Drawing;
using System.Linq;
using System.Text;
using System.Windows.Forms;

namespace WindowsFormsApplication1
{
    public partial class Form1 : Form
    {
        public Form1()
        {
            InitializeComponent();
        }
    }
}
```

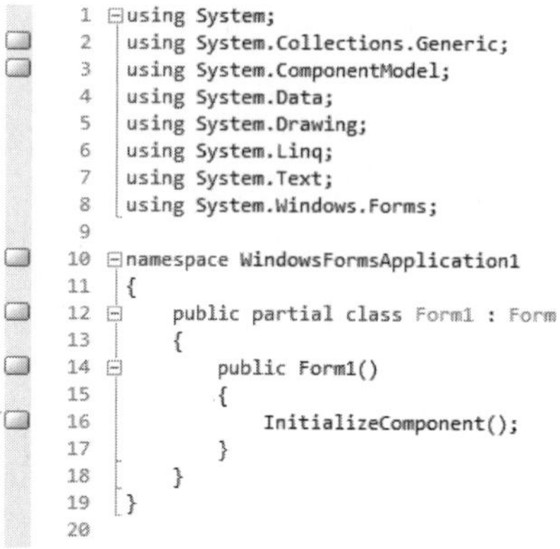

And now we have a working command that bypasses the Quick Find dialog box and just finds things.

Make an Alias

What if we want to use this all the time? We can make an alias out of the command. In this case, we type **alias findc Edit.Find *c* /wild /doc /markall**, as shown in the following illustration.

```
Command Window
>alias findc Edit.Find *c* /wild /doc /markall
```

More information on aliases can be found in vstipTool0068 ("Understanding Commands: Aliases," page 113). You can double-check the alias assignment by typing **alias findc**.

```
Command Window
>alias findc
alias findc Edit.Find *c* /wild /doc /markall
>
```

From now on, you just type **findc** in the Command Window, and it performs the predefined search.

03.22 Testing a Command

DEFAULT	Ctrl+Alt+A
VISUAL BASIC 6	Ctrl+Alt+A
VISUAL C# 2005	Ctrl+Alt+A; Ctrl+W, A; Ctrl+W, Ctrl+A
VISUAL C++ 2	Ctrl+Alt+A
VISUAL C++ 6	Ctrl+Alt+A
VISUAL STUDIO 6	Ctrl+Alt+A
WINDOWS	Alt,V, E, C
MENU	View | Other Windows | Command Window
COMMAND	View.CommandWindow
VERSIONS	2005, 2008, 2010
CODE	vstipTool0065

Throughout these tips, I include the command when available. But you might be wondering how to test a command to see how it works. Let's take a look at one quick way.

First, figure out what command you want to test. In our case, let's test "View.ViewCode".

Press Ctrl+Alt+A to bring up the Command Window.

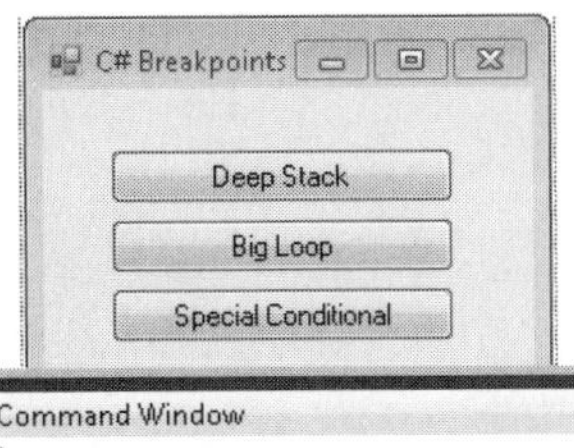

Because we're testing "ViewCode", we have a Design window open so that it can switch to the code. Now start typing the command we want to test (case doesn't matter).

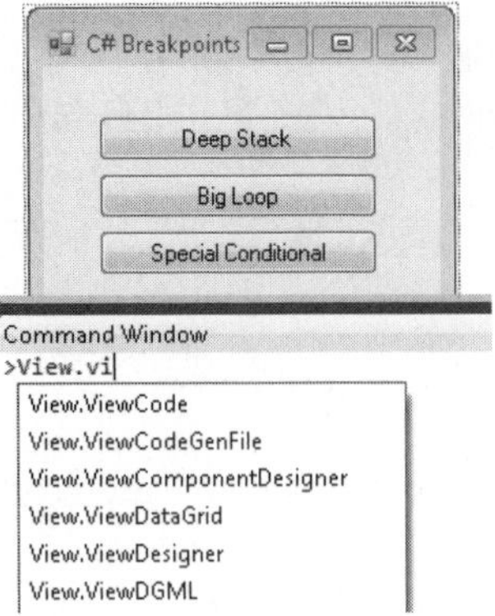

As you can see in the preceding illustration, we have IntelliSense helping us with the command. Now we just press Enter to see the command in action.

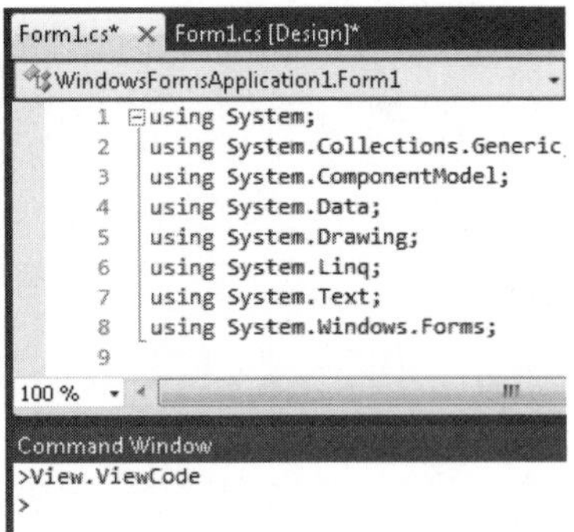

Now you have tested a command. Feel free to try various commands to see what they do, but make sure to set up the context as we did in this example to ensure that the command works properly. Some commands can't be run from the Command Window and might require that you assign a shortcut key or use the Find Combo box.

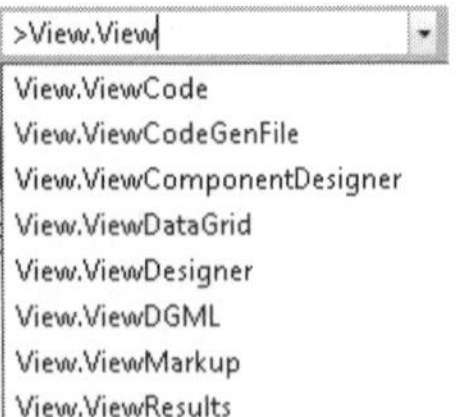

Refer to vstipTool0070 ("Understanding Commands: Running Commands," on the next page) for more information.

03.23 Understanding Commands: Running Commands

DEFAULT	Ctrl+Alt+A (command window); Ctrl+Alt+I (immediate window); Ctrl+/ (find combo box with command symbol)
VISUAL BASIC 6	Ctrl+Alt+A (command window); Ctrl+Alt+I; Ctrl+G (immediate window); (no shortcut for find combo box)
VISUAL C# 2005	Ctrl+Alt+A; Ctrl+W, A; Ctrl+W, Ctrl+A (command window) Ctrl+Alt+I; Ctrl+D, I; Ctrl+D, Ctrl+I (immediate window) Ctrl+/ (find combo box)
VISUAL C++ 2	Ctrl+Alt+A (command window); Ctrl+Alt+I (immediate window); Ctrl+/ (find combo box with command symbol)
VISUAL C++ 6	Ctrl+Alt+A (command window); Ctrl+Alt+I (immediate window); Ctrl+/ (find combo box with command symbol)
VISUAL STUDIO 6	Ctrl+Alt+A (command window); Ctrl+Alt+I (immediate window); Ctrl+/ (find combo box with command symbol)
WINDOWS	Alt,V, E, C
MENU	View | Other Windows | Command Window; Debug | Windows | Immediate Window
COMMAND	View.CommandWindow; Debug.Immediate; Edit.GoToFindCombo; Tools.GoToCommandLine
VERSIONS	2005, 2008, 2010
CODE	vstipTool0070

Whenever you work with commands, you have four main ways you can run them. For example, not all commands will run from the Command Window, so it is a good idea to familiarize yourself with the other options. Let's take a look at each way.

Shortcuts

The easiest way to run a command is when a shortcut is attached to it. For example, View.Code has a couple of shortcut keys attached to it.

Note For more information about shortcut keys, see vstipTool0061 ("Find Keyboard Shortcuts," on the next page).

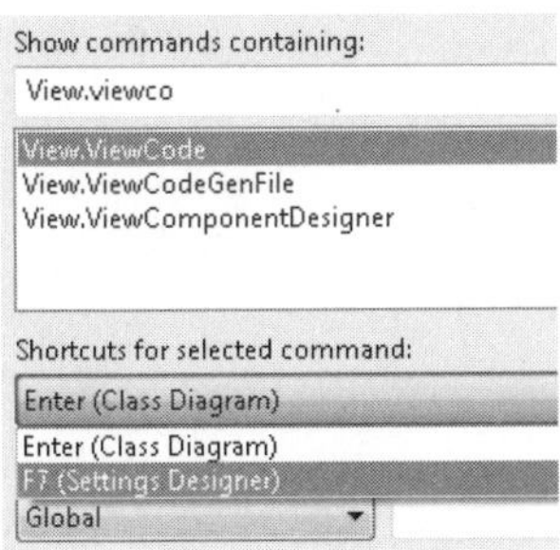

Command Window

The Command Window (Ctrl+Alt+A) is specifically designed to run commands. Just type in the command, and press Enter.

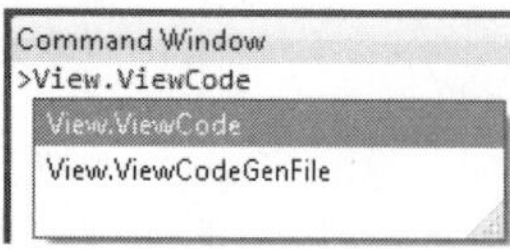

Immediate Window

You can run many commands from the Immediate Window (Ctrl+Alt+I) by typing a greater-than sign (>). Then type any command and press Enter.

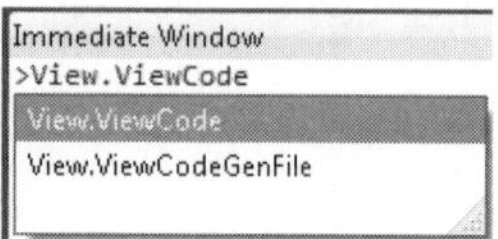

Find Combo Box

A little-known feature enables you to run commands from the Find Combo Box (Ctrl+D) on the standard toolbar. Just type a greater-than sign (>), then type any command, and press Enter.

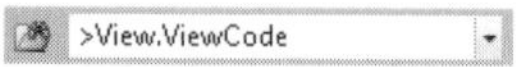

For most language settings, you can bypass the typing of the greater-than sign by using Ctrl+Forward Slash (/), which takes you to the Find Combo Box and automatically inserts the sign for you.

03.24 Find Keyboard Shortcuts

WINDOWS	Alt,T, O
MENU	Tools | Options | Environment | Keyboard
COMMAND	Tools.CustomizeKeyboard
VERSIONS	2005, 2008, 2010
CODE	vstipTool0061

Ever just want to see the keyboard shortcuts available in Visual Studio? Let's say, for example, that you want to see if View | Code has any keyboard shortcuts. A quick look at the menu doesn't reveal anything.

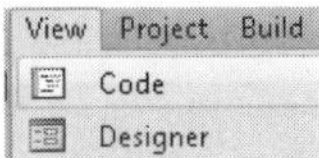

But that's not the end of the story. If we go to Tools | Options | Environment | Keyboard, we get the following dialog box.

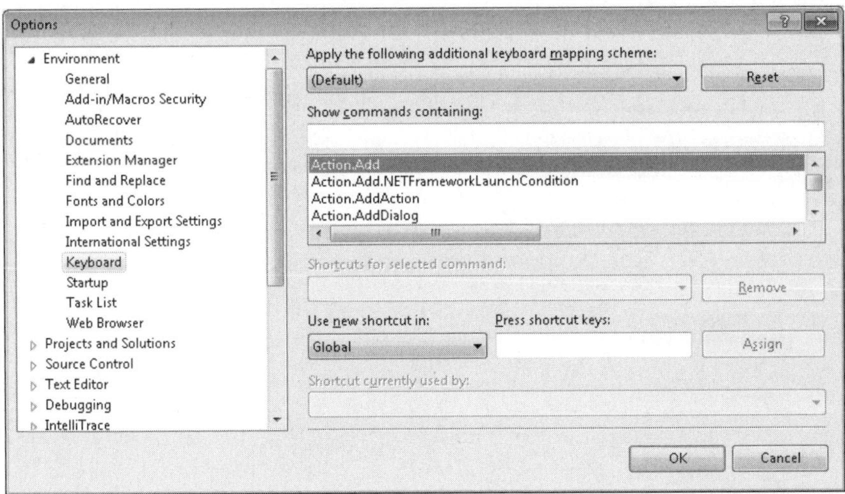

Pretty much everything you do in Visual Studio has a command that runs to execute that action. In our case, we know that View | Code is the path to the command we want, so let's start by trying to see whether we have a "View.Code" command. Notice that commands use dot notation between items:

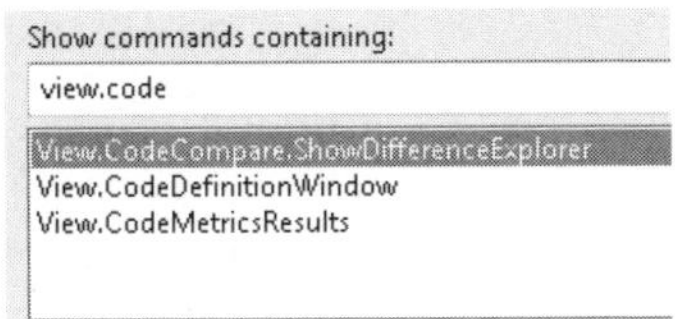

Sadly, what we want isn't there. OK, so either it isn't there or it's called something else. We still know it's off the View menu, so let's type in **View.** and browse to see whether anything pops up.

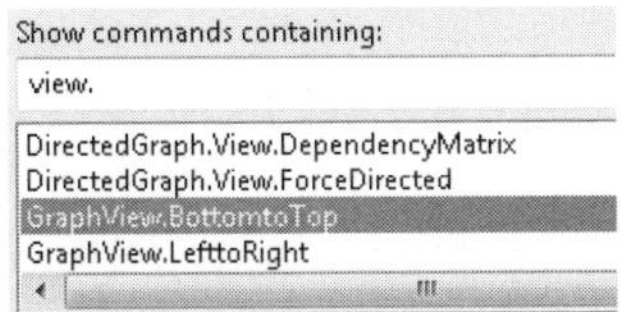

If we scroll down far enough, we actually find an entry for "View.ViewCode". If we look under Shortcuts For Selected Command, we see a couple of shortcut entries, as shown in the following illustration.

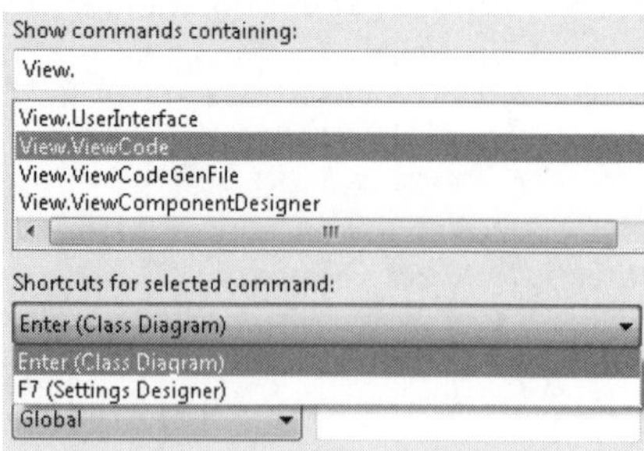

It looks like pressing F7 in the Designer does the trick, so let's try it.

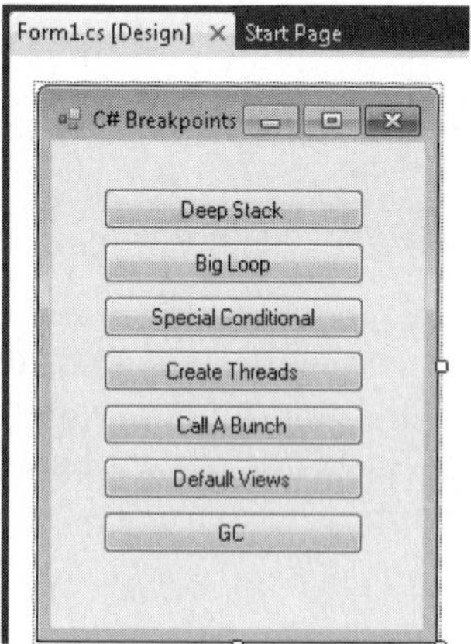

Go to the Designer and press F7.

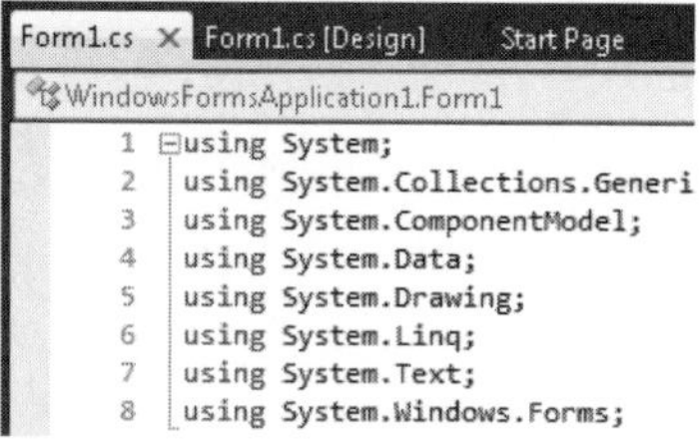

As we can see in the preceding illustration, we have discovered the shortcut key for viewing code in the Designer.

There is also another entry for the Class Diagram that uses Enter to show us code. Let's open up a Class Diagram and select a class.

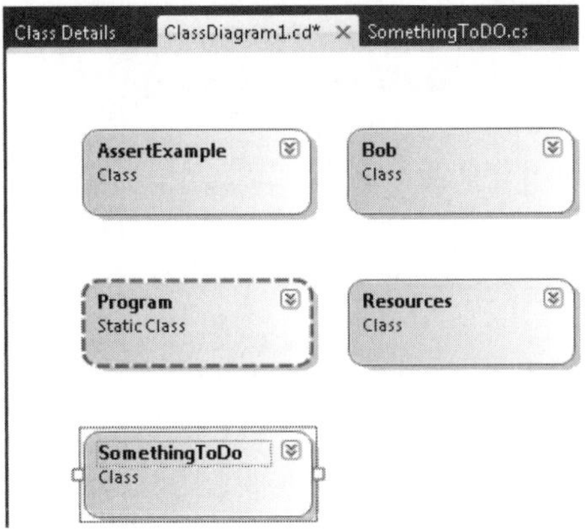

Then press Enter.

```
using System;
using System.Collections.Generic;
using System.Linq;
using System.Text;

namespace WindowsFormsApplication1
{
    class SomethingToDo
    {
```

It takes us to the code as well. So now you know how to find shortcut keys (if they exist) for a command.

03.25 Keyboard Shortcuts: Additional Mapping Schemes

WINDOWS	Alt,T, O
MENU	Tools | Options | Environment | Keyboard
COMMAND	Tools.CustomizeKeyboard
VERSIONS	2005, 2008, 2010
CODE	vstipTool0062

One of the most important places you can go in Visual Studio is the Tools | Options | Environment | Keyboard area, shown in the following illustration.

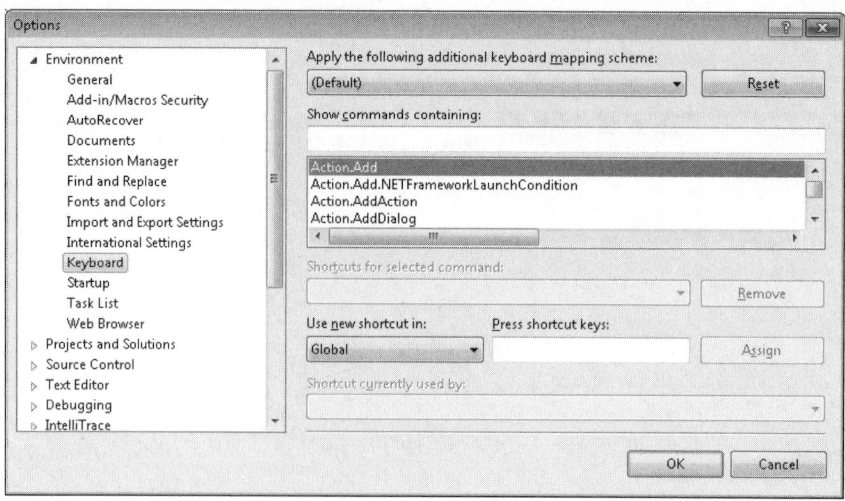

In vstipTool0061, "Find Keyboard Shortcuts," page 122, we looked at how to find shortcut keys for given commands. Now let's focus on the Apply The Following Additional Keyboard Mapping Scheme drop-down list.

This list allows you to apply additional keyboard shortcuts that were common in certain previous versions.

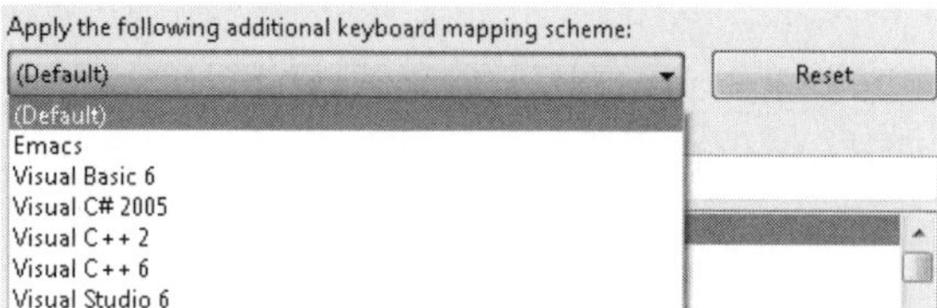

Let's take an example. If we have the default mapping scheme and want to see the shortcuts for View.ViewCode, we see the options presented in the following illustration.

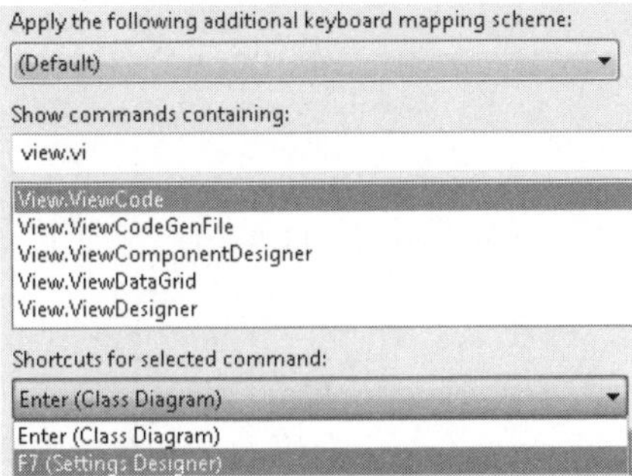

However, if we add an additional mapping scheme (Visual C++ 6 in this example), this gets the following result:

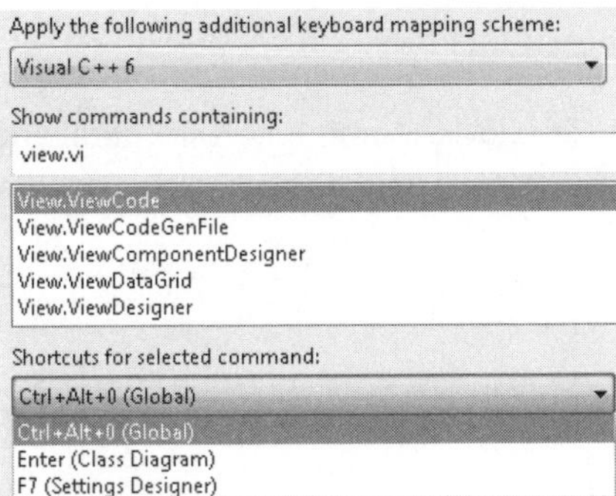

Notice that we have a new shortcut that wasn't there before. This is how adding additional mapping schemes work. If you don't want these additional keys, just set Apply The Following Additional Keyboard Mapping Scheme to Default (or General, if it is available in the list).

03.26 Keyboard Shortcuts: Creating New Shortcuts

WINDOWS	Alt,T, O
MENU	Tools | Options | Environment | Keyboard
COMMAND	Tools.CustomizeKeyboard
VERSIONS	2005, 2008, 2010
CODE	vstipTool0063

Creating keyboard shortcuts is easy. Let's walk through an example to show you how. First, go to Tools | Options | Environment | Keyboard.

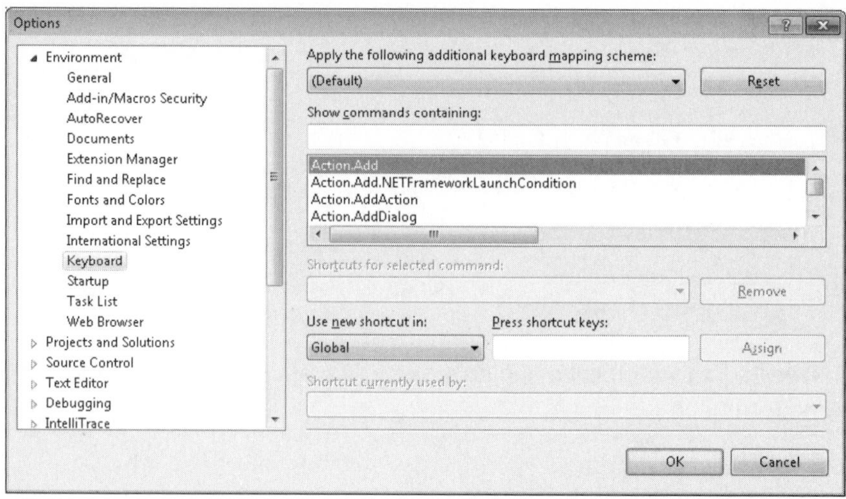

Now let's assume we want to modify the "View.ViewCode" command to include a new short-cut. Notice the existing shortcuts (assuming no additional keyboard mapping schemes).

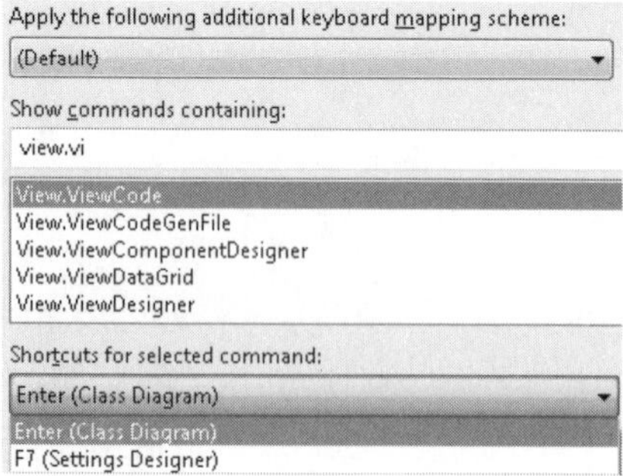

We want to add Ctrl+Z as the shortcut, so click in the Press Shortcut Keys area and press Ctrl+Z.

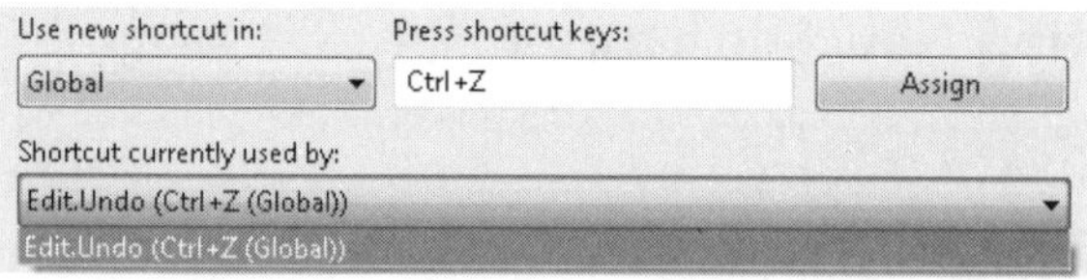

There is a problem. Looking down at the Shortcut Currently Used By area, we see that Ctrl+Z is already mapped to the Edit.Undo command. Because that is an important key combination to us, let's try a new set of shortcut keys. How about Ctrl+Alt+4? Just use backspace to get rid of the current entry, and press Ctrl+Alt+4.

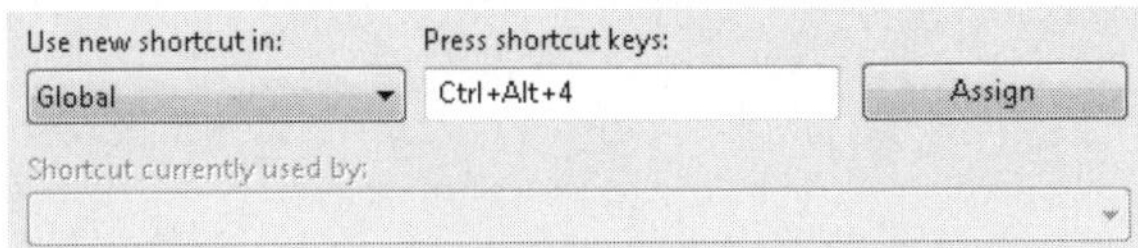

Perfect. It isn't being used by anything currently—but we aren't done yet. We have to decide what scope we want this shortcut to be available in. Notice the drop-down to the left of the new shortcut under Use New Shortcut In? The default scope is global, so you can use it at any time. However, you can narrow the scope down to a specific area.

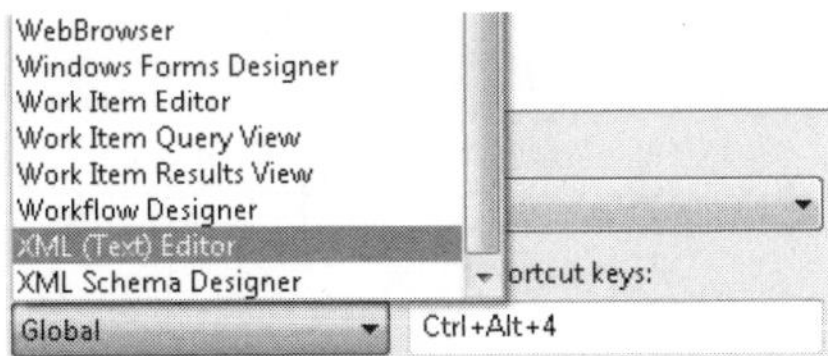

For example, if we wanted to have this shortcut available only when we're editing XML, we would change Global to XML (Text) Editor. For now, let's keep the Global setting.

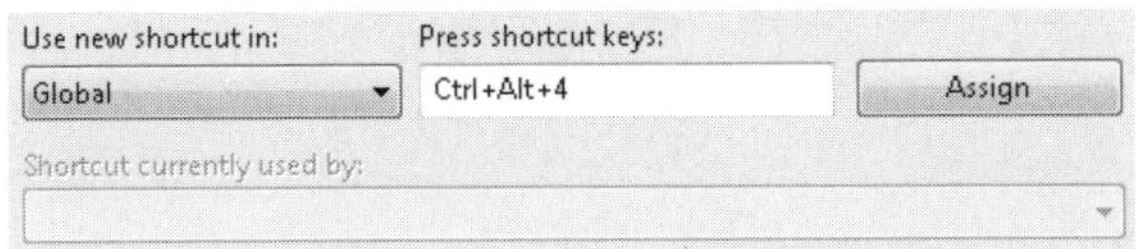

After we've decided on the scope and the shortcut keys, all we have to do is click Assign, as shown in the preceding illustration, to make the shortcut available.

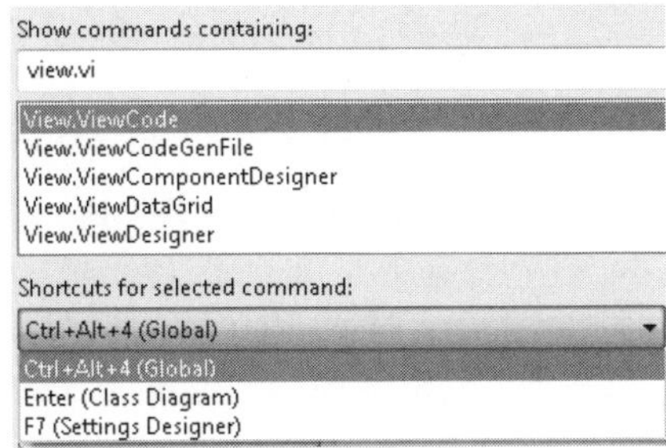

If you mess up here, you can choose the shortcut key and click Remove to start over.

Warning You can remove *any* shortcut, so be careful to remove only the shortcuts you actually want to eliminate.

Click OK, and let's go test our new shortcut. Go to Design View in any project.

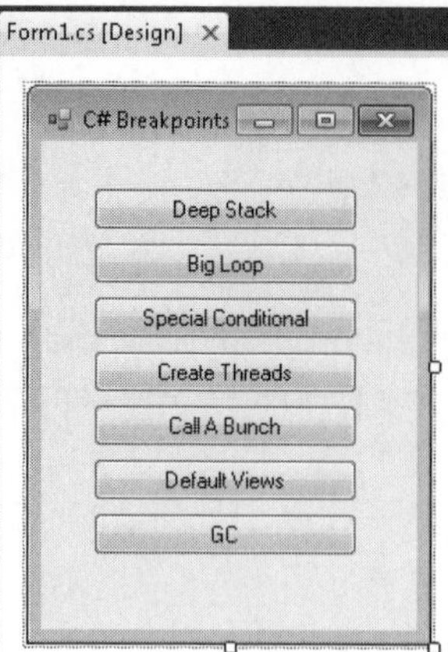

Press Ctrl+Alt+4 to see the following result:

Form1.cs | Form1.cs [Design]

WindowsFormsApplication1.Form1 | Form1()

```
using System;
using System.Collections.Generic;
using System.ComponentModel;
using System.Data;
using System.Drawing;
using System.Linq;
using System.Text;
using System.Windows.Forms;

namespace WindowsFormsApplication1
{
    public partial class Form1 : Form
    {
        public Form1()
        {
            InitializeComponent();
        }
    }
```

It should take you to the code. You now know how to map new keyboard shortcuts.

Reset

If you make a mistake with your shortcut keys, you can always click the Reset button in Tools | Options | Environment | Keyboard.

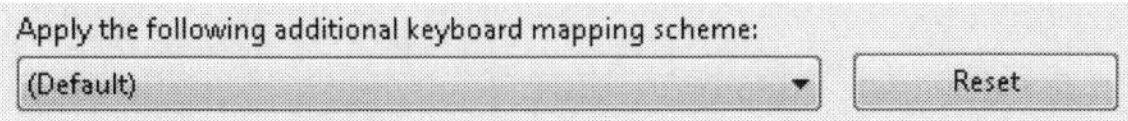

Don't take this option lightly. Refer to vstipTool0064 ("Keyboard Shortcuts Reset All Your Shortcuts," page 131).

03.27 Keyboard Shortcuts: Reset All Your Shortcuts

WINDOWS	Alt,T, O
MENU	Tools | Options | Environment | Keyboard
COMMAND	Tools.CustomizeKeyboard
VERSIONS	2005, 2008, 2010
CODE	vstipTool0064

On rare occasions, you might lose track of all the custom shortcuts you have made, or maybe you just want to reset all your shortcuts back to their default settings. You can reset all your keyboard shortcuts by clicking the Reset button in Tools | Options | Environment | Keyboard.

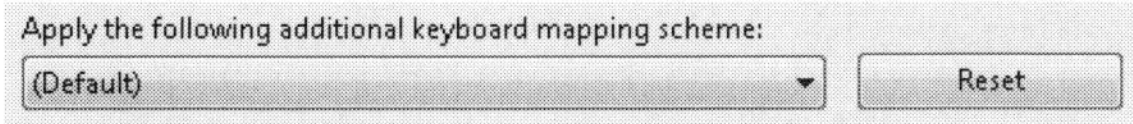

When you click this button, you get the following warning message:

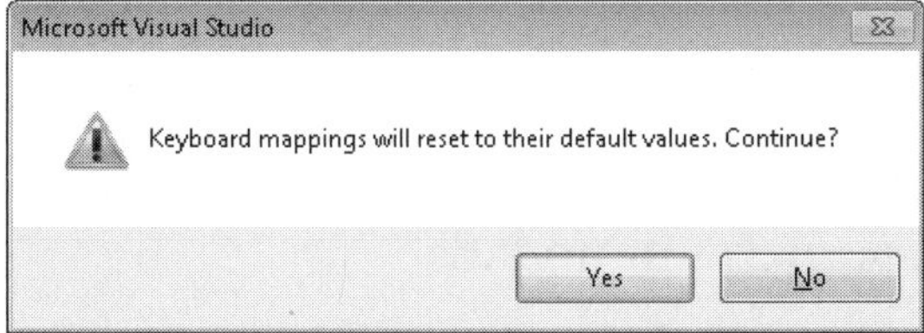

Note Take this warning seriously! It *resets all keyboard mappings to their default values* if you click Yes, so you should use this only if you are sure of the consequences.

The following before-and-after illustrations show what happens after you click Yes in the preceding Warning message.

Before:

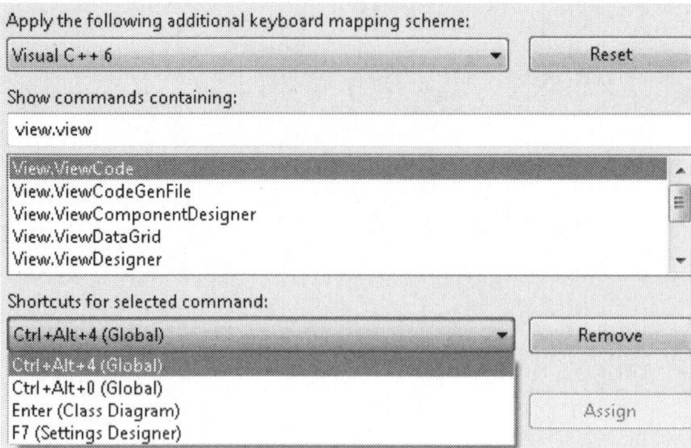

After:

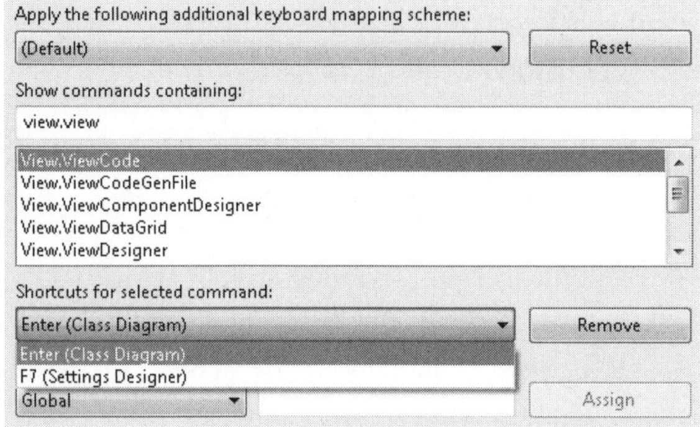

03.28 Understanding Commands: Logging Commands

COMMAND	log; Tools.LogCommandWindowOutput
VERSIONS	2005, 2008, 2010
CODE	vstipTool0071

When using commands, sometimes you want to keep a log of the ones you used. This is especially useful when you are experimenting with commands to see what iterations you went through. The syntax for logging is as follows:

```
log [filename] [/on|/off] [/overwrite]
```

Or you can use the following:

```
Tools.LogCommandWindowOutput [filename] [/on|/off] [/overwrite]
```

Arguments

The following sections describe what the preceding arguments do.

Filename

It's highly recommended that you use a path and file name; otherwise, the default file name is cmdline.log and the log file is stored at C:\Users\<user>\AppData\Roaming\Microsoft\VisualStudio\<version>.

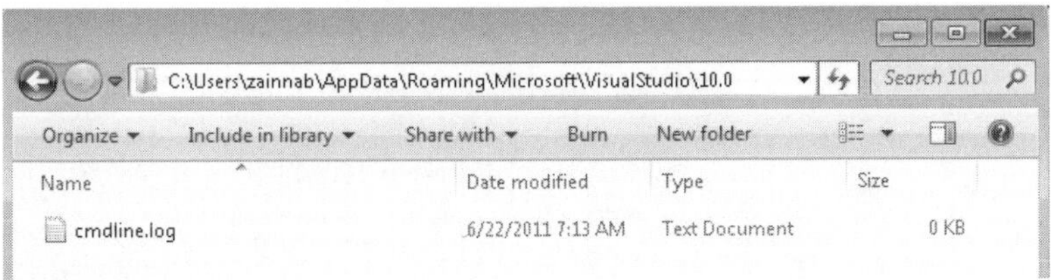

/on /off

This argument turns logging on or off.

/overwrite

By default, all logging operations append to your log file. The /overwrite switch changes this behavior and erases any previous commands from the log when a new log session starts.

Example

First, type the "log" command in the Command Window (Ctrl+Alt+A) and specify a file name by typing **log C:\Users\<user>\Documents\vslog.txt /on**, as shown in the following illustration.

```
Command Window
>log C:\Users\zainnab\Documents\vslog.txt /on
>
```

Now type in a couple of commands. The specific commands don't matter here, so feel free to substitute your own commands instead of using mine if you like. I used the commands View.ViewCode to get a code window, and I used Edit.Find sys to find some text.

```
Command Window
>log C:\Users\zainnab\Documents\vslog.txt /on
>View.ViewCode
>Edit.Find sys
>
```

At this point, you're done typing comments. Turn logging off by using the **log /off** command.

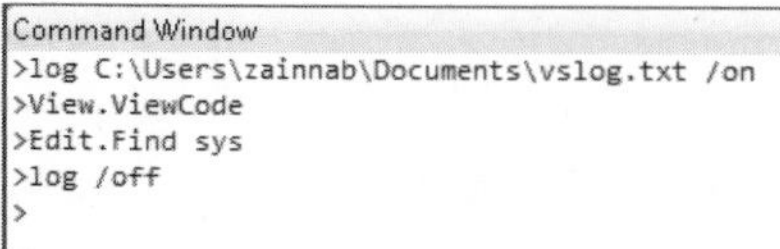

Now browse to the My Documents folder to see the file.

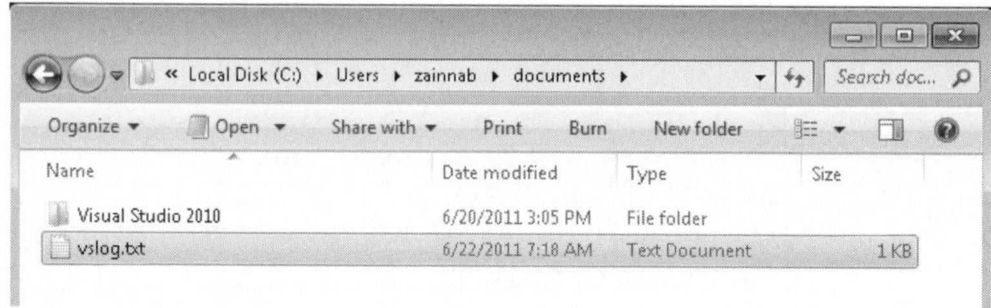

If you open the file, you should see something similar to the following:

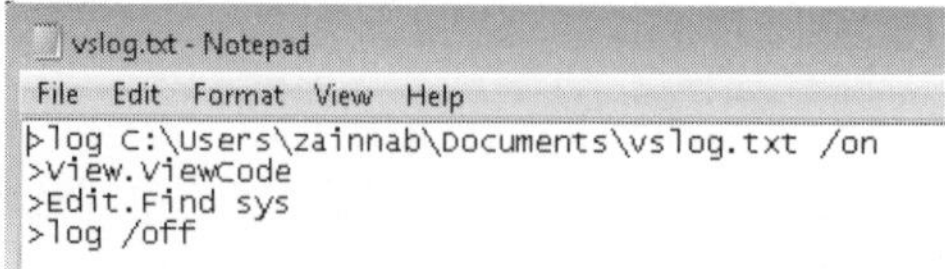

As you can see, the file contains a running log of the commands you entered, including the last command to turn logging off.

03.29 Export Your Window Layouts

WINDOWS	Alt,T, I
MENU	Tools | Import and Export Settings
COMMAND	Tools.ImportandExportSettings
VERSIONS	2005, 2008, 2010
CODE	vstipEnv0040

After you get your tool and document windows just the way you want them inside Visual Studio, you want to be able to get those settings back if anything goes wrong.

You can export just your window layouts by going to Tools | Import And Export Settings and choosing Export Selected Environment Settings, and then click Next.

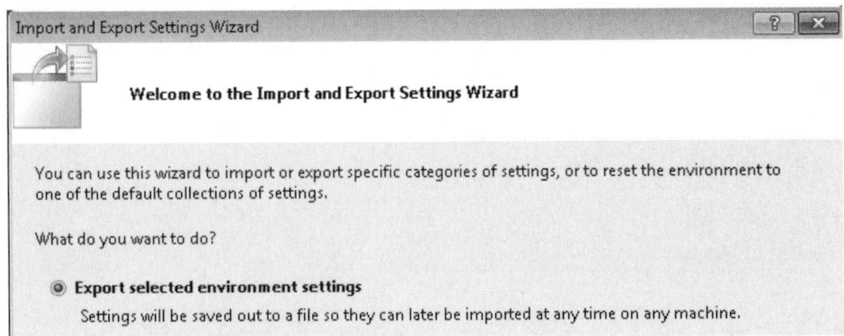

Now clear the All Settings check box.

Which settings do you want to export?

- All Settings
  - Code Analysis Settings
  - CodeCompare
  - Database Tools
  - General Settings
  - Options
  - Visual Studio Team Foundation Server

Go to General Settings, select Window Layouts, and then click Next.

Which settings do you want to export?

- Menu and Command Bar Customizatio
- New Project Dialog Preferred Language
- Object Browser Options
- Output Window Options
- Properties Window
- Simplified Tools/Options
- Start Page
- Task List Display Settings
- Toolbox
- Window Layouts

Give the .vssettings file a name and a location to be saved into, click Finish, and then click Close.

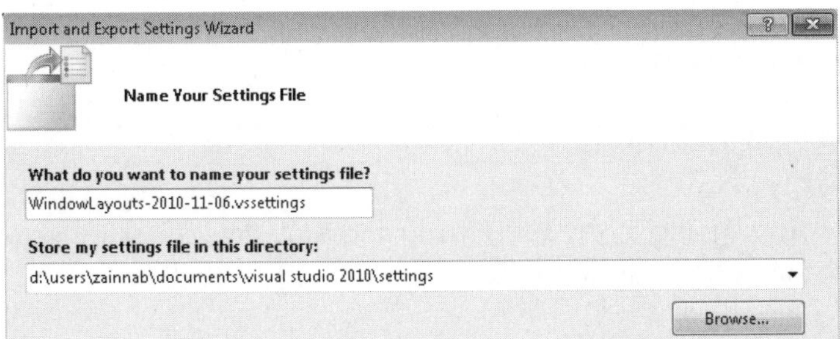

You now can import these settings (see vstipEnv0022, "Importing or Changing Your Environment Settings," in Appendix B [*http://go.microsoft.com/FWLink/?Linkid=223758*]) whenever you want to get your preferred layouts.

03.30 Stop the Toolbox from Auto-Populating from the Solution

WINDOWS	Alt,T, O
MENU	Tools | Options | Windows Forms Designer
COMMAND	Tools.Options
VERSIONS	2005, 2008, 2010
CODE	vstipTool0090

If you find that the Toolbox is taking a long time scanning a solution with a lot of projects in it, you can keep it from doing this.

Just go to Tools | Options | Windows Forms Designer, and set AutoToolboxPopulate to False.

To display custom items when AutoToolboxPopulate is set to False, you can select Choose Items from the Toolbox context menu and add the items manually to the Toolbox.

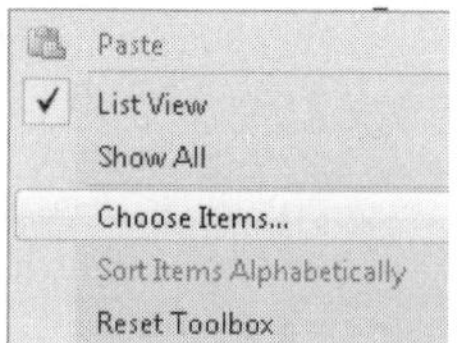

People often set this to False accidentally. If you find your controls are not automatically showing up in the Toolbox, setting this to True might solve the problem.

03.31 Using External Tools

WINDOWS	Alt,T, E
MENU	Tools | External Tools; Tools | [external tool of choice]
COMMAND	Tools.ExternalTools
VERSIONS	2005, 2008, 2010
CODE	vstipTool0059

You can run external tools by going to the Tools menu and running your external tool of choice, as shown in the following illustration.

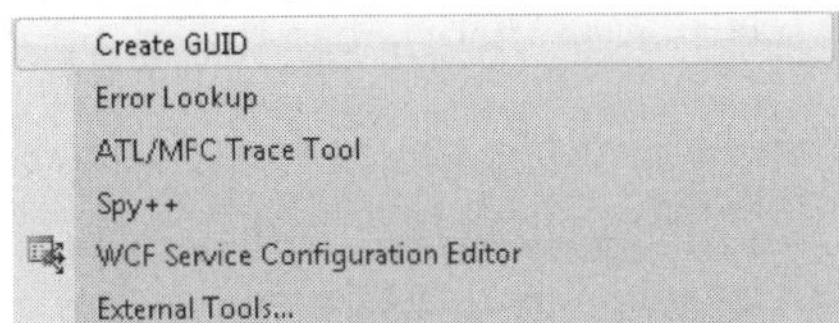

If you want to add additional external tools, you can go to Tools | External Tools.

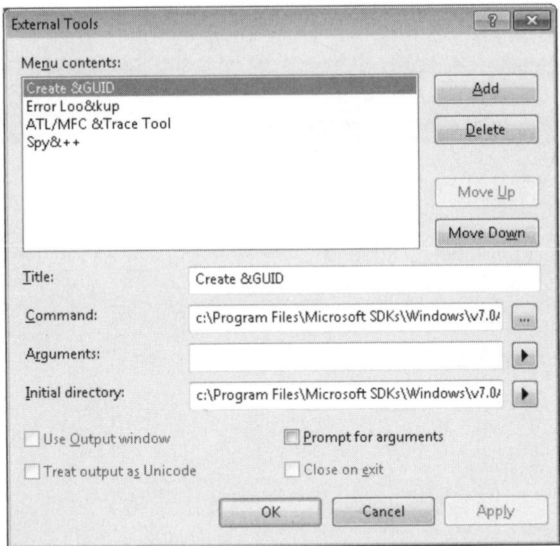

As an example, let's add the Visual Studio command prompt to our external tools list. First, click Add and put in a Title of **Visual Studio Command Prompt**.

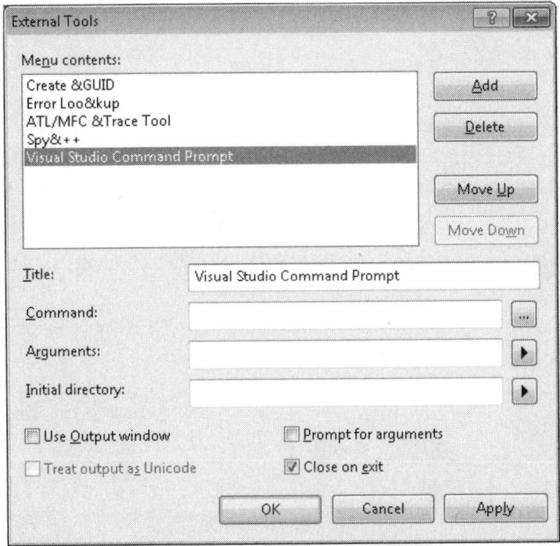

In this case, the Visual Studio command prompt has an icon that we can use to get the information we need. Let's go to its properties.

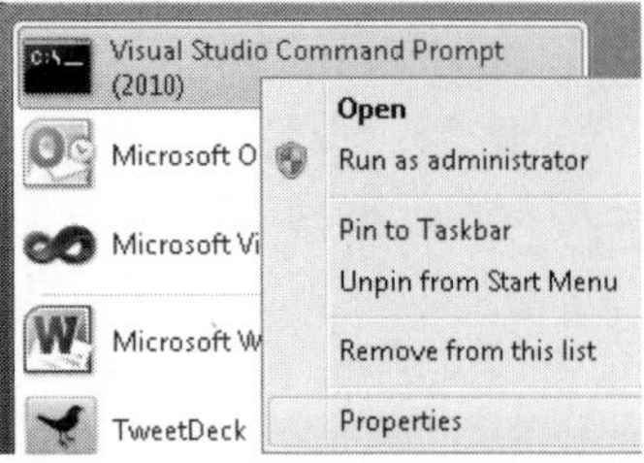

After you click Properties, you see the following dialog box.

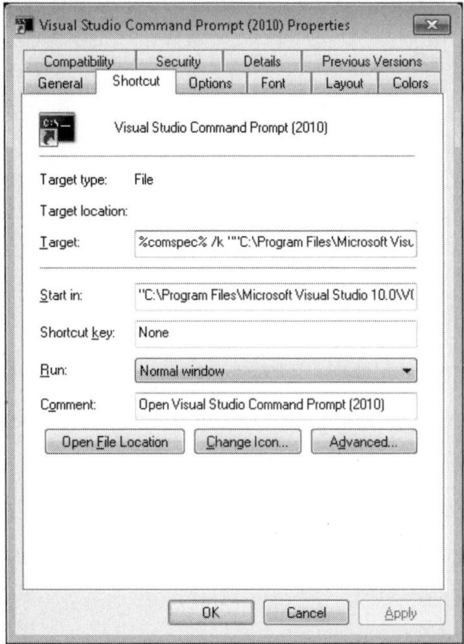

As you can see, the Target field points to %comspec%, with some arguments after it. The variable %comspec% points to the command prompt on the current Windows system and can be used on just about any version of Windows. Let's put that into the Command field for our purposes.

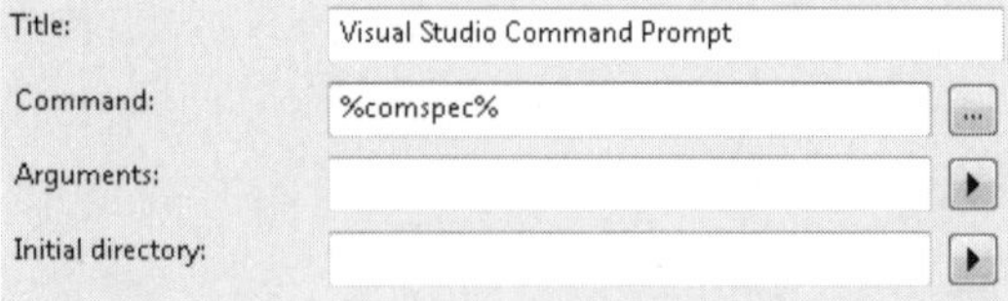

If you weren't using a system variable like this, you could type in the path to the command or use the ellipsis and browse.

For the Arguments field, again, let's just take from the Visual Studio command prompt properties and enter the path shown in the following illustration.

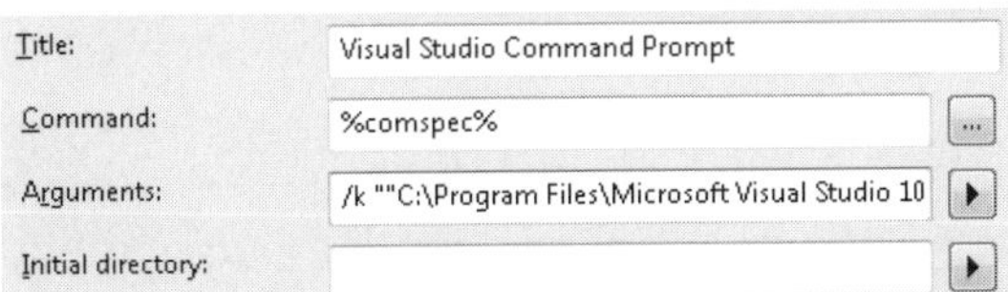

If you want to add items specific to Visual Studio, you can click the arrow to the right and get a large list of variables you can insert as arguments.

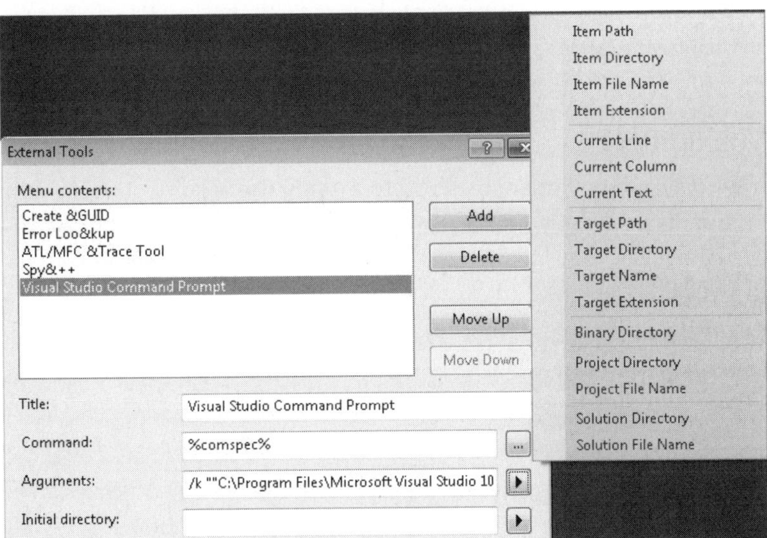

The Initial Directory lets you define where you want to start up. I don't have a preference here, so I will leave it blank, but I could type in a path or use one of the variables available to me by clicking on the arrow to the right of the Initial Directory field.

Finally, you can choose from several options at the bottom.

Use Output Window

Selecting this option runs the command and puts any output into the Output window. This is useful for commands that just return some data you want to look at. For our command prompt, this wouldn't be a good choice because we want to type in commands.

Treat Output As Unicode

If your tool returns Unicode output, you would select this check box.

Prompt For Arguments

This option shows a dialog box that enables you to modify the arguments before the command is run or to put in completely new arguments.

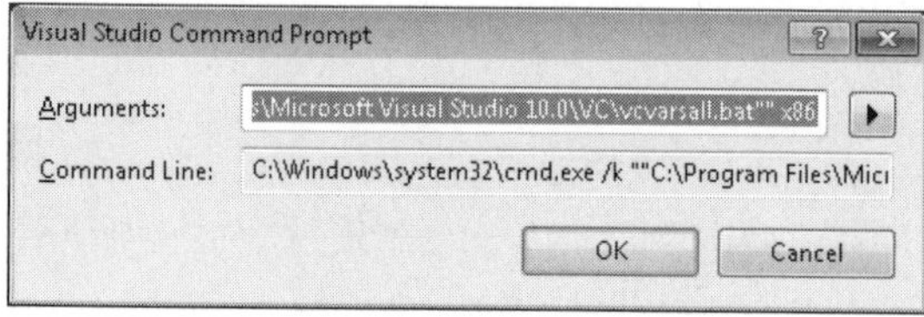

Close On Exit

Selecting this option determines whether the window should close when the tool closes. In the case of our command prompt, with this option checked when we type **exit** and press Enter, the window closes. However, if this option is *not* checked and we do the same thing, we get the result shown in the following illustration.

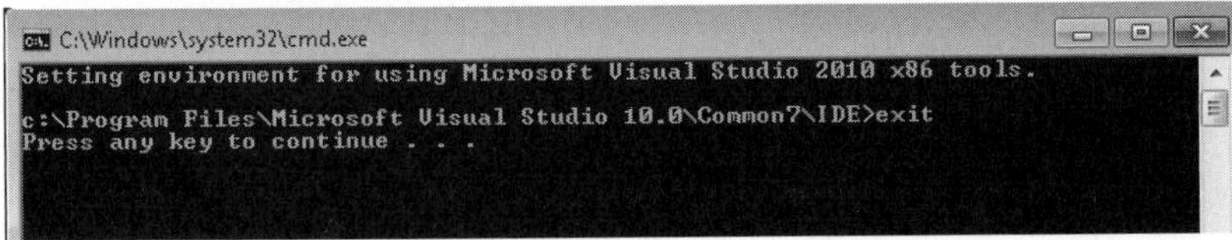

When you are all done, just click OK, and you now have your command showing up in the external tools list off the Tools menu.

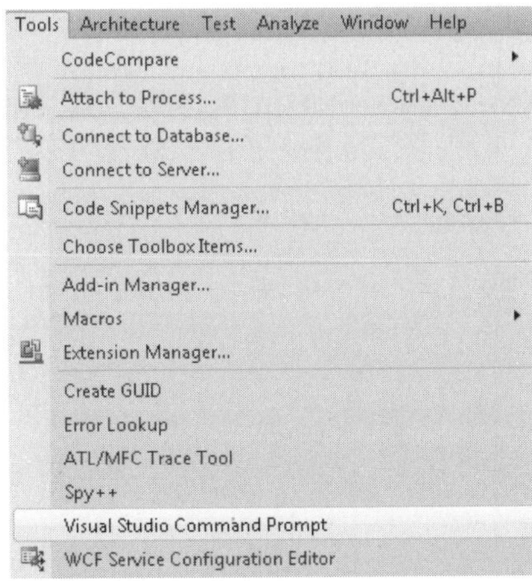

03.32 Create Keyboard Accelerators for External Tools

WINDOWS	Alt,T, E
MENU	Tools | External Tools
COMMAND	Tools.ExternalTools
VERSIONS	2005, 2008, 2010
CODE	vstipTool0093

In vstipTool0059 ("Using External Tools," page 136), I showed you how to add external tools to the Visual Studio Tools menu).

After you create an entry, you probably want to have an accelerator key assigned so that you can use your keyboard to activate the new tool. First, you can see what these keys look like by going to the Tools menu, using your keyboard (Alt+T).

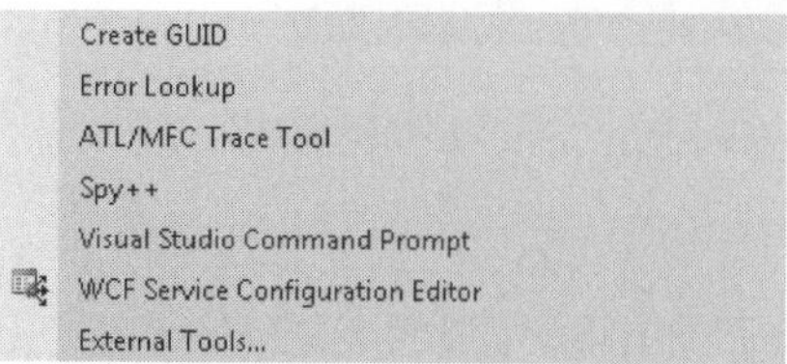

Now you can press any letter that is underlined to access that item. For example, if the letter "G" if pressed, it opens up the Create GUID tool. You can see how this is created by going to Tools | External Tools on the menu bar.

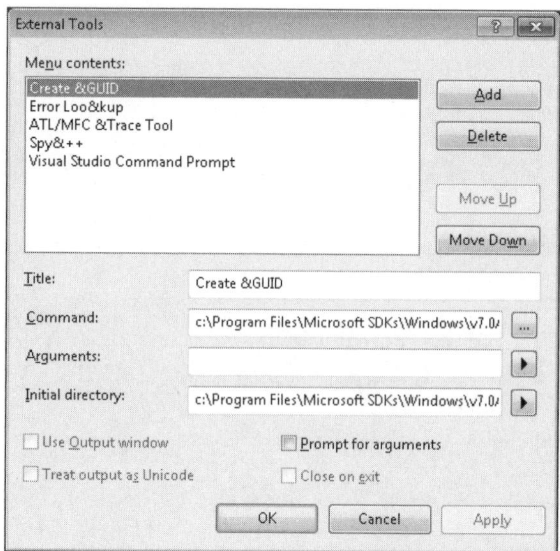

Notice the ampersand (&) before the "G" in "GUID"? Anytime you put an ampersand before any character in your title, the next character after it becomes the accelerator key. As you can see, all these entries have accelerator keys assigned to them. Now you can create special keys for your external tools access.

03.33 Exporting Your Command Window Aliases and External Tools List

WINDOWS	Alt,T, I
MENU	Tools | Import and Export Settings
COMMAND	Tools.ImportandExportSettings
VERSIONS	2005, 2008, 2010
CODE	vstipEnv0043

As you probably know, you can export just about any setting you want. Usually, you export several settings together. However, when it comes time to import settings, the following two settings do not get imported by default: Command Window Aliases and External Tools List:

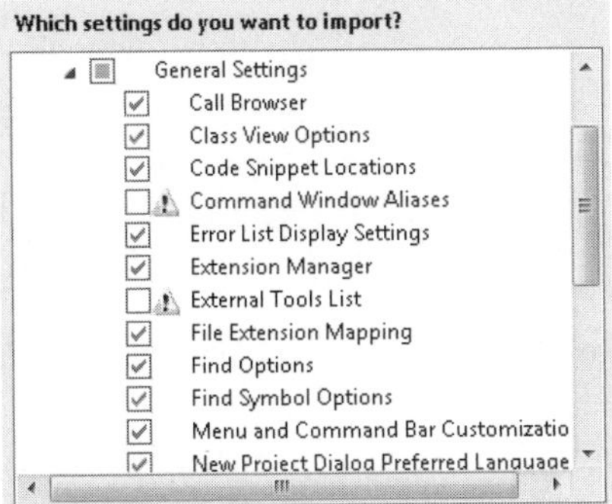

Sometimes, when importing, users just click through the wizard and forget this is the case. For this reason, it might be a good idea to make sure that you have these two settings exported separately as an extra copy. Then you can just import these settings as needed.

To do this, just go to Tools | Import And Export Settings and select Export Selected Environment Settings:

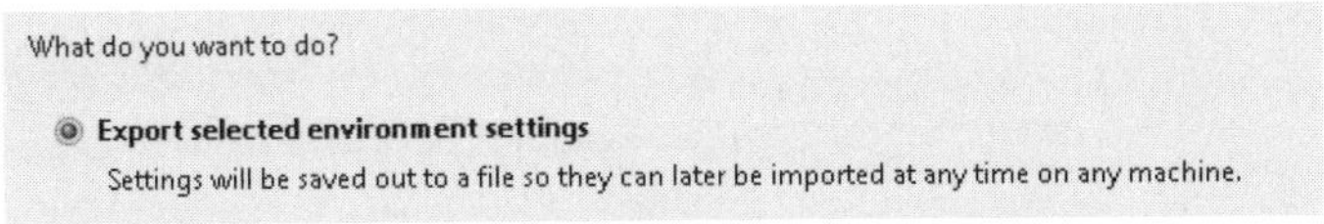

Click Next, clear the All Settings check box, and then select the Command Window Aliases and External Tools List check boxes:

Which settings do you want to export?

- General Settings
  - [ ] Call Browser
  - [ ] Class View Options
  - [ ] Code Snippet Locations
  - [x] Command Window Aliases
  - [ ] Error List Display Settings
  - [ ] Extension Manager
  - [x] External Tools List
  - [ ] File Extension Mapping
  - [ ] Find Options
  - [ ] Find Symbol Options

From here, just complete the wizard normally and make sure to give your exported file a logical name, such as Command Aliases and External Tools List.

03.34 Creating and Using a Macro

DEFAULT	Ctrl+Shift+R (record/stop recording); Ctrl+Shift+P (run)
VISUAL BASIC 6	[no shortcut] (record/stop recording); [no shortcut] (run)
VISUAL C# 2005	Ctrl+Shift+R (record/stop recording); Ctrl+Shift+P (run)
VISUAL C++ 2	Ctrl+Shift+R (record/stop recording); Ctrl+Shift+P (run)
VISUAL C++ 6	Ctrl+Shift+R (record/stop recording); Ctrl+Shift+P (run)
VISUAL STUDIO 6	[no shortcut] (record/stop recording)
WINDOWS	Alt,T, M, C (record / stop recording); Alt,T, M, R (run)
MENU	Tools | Macros | Record Temporary Macro; Tools | Macros | Run Temporary Macro; Tools | Macros | Save Temporary Macro
COMMAND	Tools.RecordTemporaryMacro; Tools.RunTemporaryMacro; Tools.SaveTemporaryMacro
VERSIONS	2005, 2008, 2010
CODE	vstipEnv0055

You can record macros to do just about anything in Visual Studio. In this example, we create a macro that adds a new class to our project. First, create a new project. For this example, create a Console Application:

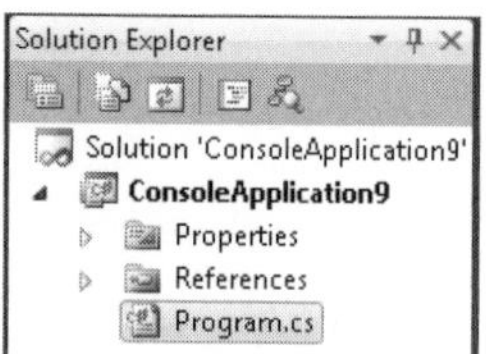

Now we are going to add a class to the project and give the class a name. When we do this, we will record the actions into a temporary macro by pressing Ctrl+Shift+R. You should see the following status in the lower-left corner:

Add a new class (Ctrl+Shift+A) called **Bubba.cs**:

Warning You can run into numerous little "gotchas" when creating macros. One that took me a little while to figure out was leaving off the ".cs" at the end of the file name. For some reason, Visual Studio doesn't like that at all. Keep an eye out for little things like that as you use this feature.

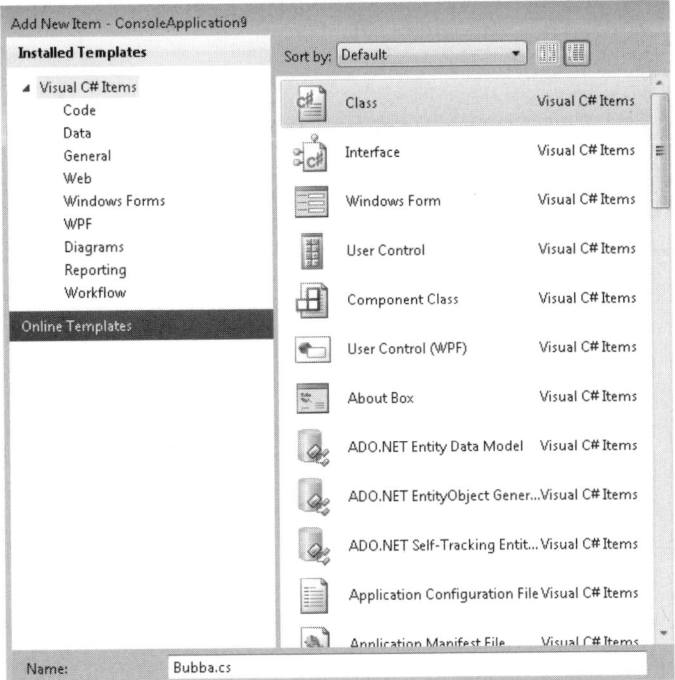

Add a comment to the class:

```
namespace ConsoleApplication1
{
    class Bubba
    {
        // this is the bubba class
    }
}
```

Stop recording (Ctrl+Shift+R), and then go to Tools | Macros | Save Temporary Macro. Name the macro **MakeBubba** in the Macro Explorer:

Now we can test out our new macro by creating a new project and going to the Macro Explorer (Alt+F8). Right-click the MakeBubba macro, and choose Run:

It should make the new class and put your comment in:

```
namespace ConsoleApplication1
{
    class Bubba
    {
        // this is the bubba class
    }
}
```

After you have created your macro, you might want to see the code behind it. You can go to the Macro Explorer (Alt+F8), right-click any macro, and then choose Edit to see the code. Here is what my code (cleaned up a bit) looks like for the macro we just made:

```
Sub MakeBubba()
    DTE.ItemOperations.AddNewItem _
    ("Visual C# Items\Code\Class", "Bubba.cs")

    DTE.ActiveDocument.Selection.LineDown(False, 8)
    DTE.ActiveDocument.Selection.CharRight(False, 5)
    DTE.ActiveDocument.Selection.NewLine()

    DTE.ActiveDocument.Selection.Text = "// bubba class"
End Sub
```

Notice that it is fairly easy to read and understand, which makes it easy to edit as well. Now that you have a working macro, you should visit vstipTool0066 ("Create a Shortcut Key for a Macro," in Appendix B [*http://go.microsoft.com/FWLink/?Linkid=223758*]) and create a shortcut key for it.

03.35 Visual Studio Image Library

VERSIONS	2005, 2008, 2010
CODE	vstipEnv0049

As a developer, you are always looking for images that can be used in your applications. Visual Studio comes with a set of images to help you out. In fact, it comes with over 2000 output files, images ready for immediate use, as well as a variety of source files that you can use to create your own images if needed. These images come from Microsoft Windows, the Office system, Microsoft Visual Studio, and other Microsoft software.

You can find them in a .zip file located at "C:\Program Files\Microsoft Visual Studio <version>\Common7\VS<version>ImageLibrary\1033." For example, I found my images at "C:\Program Files (x86)\Microsoft Visual Studio 10.0\Common7\VS2010ImageLibrary\1033":

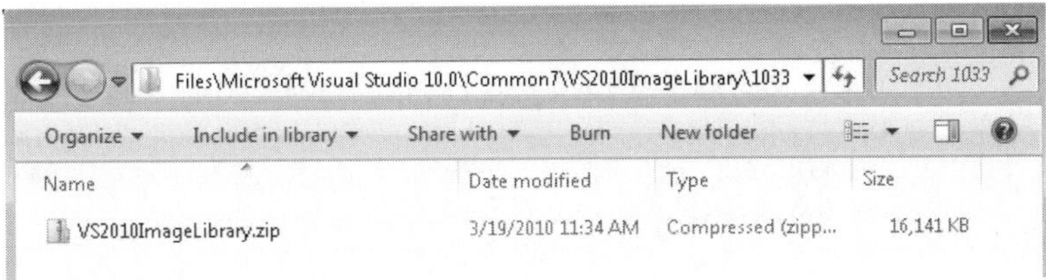

Types of Files

The Visual Studio Image Library folders contain source files and output files.

Source files

Source files contain building blocks intended for use with an image editor to generate new or to customize existing icons.

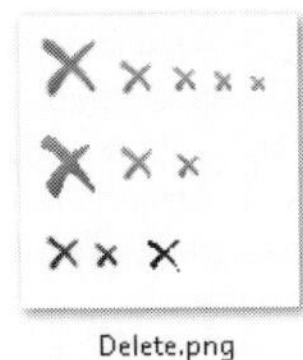

Delete.png

Output files

Typically, output files are composite images made up of a base concept with 1–3 adorners, ready for immediate use by developers.

lan
disconnect.ico

Image Library Contents

The following illustration provides an idea of what is included in the Visual Studio Image Library and what each group of images is used for:

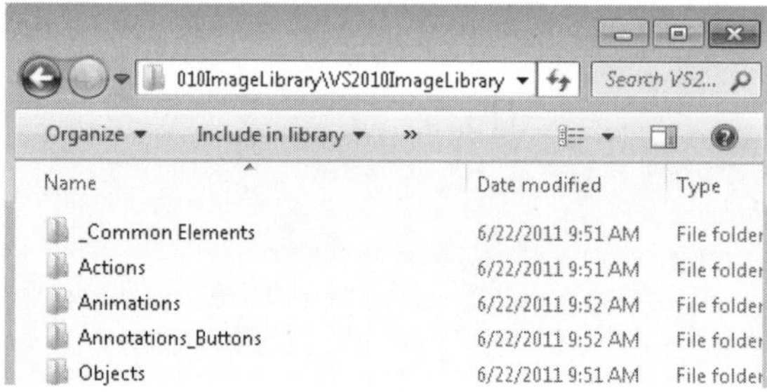

_Common Elements

Have you ever tried to edit an existing image that is made up of several overlapping elements? Then you know how hard it is to make simple changes in an output file. In this section, each source file is made up of various sizes of each element on a transparent background. When used with an image editor that utilizes layers, such as Adobe Photoshop or Paint.NET, you can choose the size of an element that fits best with what you're trying to do and then make adjustments by layering the pieces, moving them around without editing the bits that are in the lower layers.

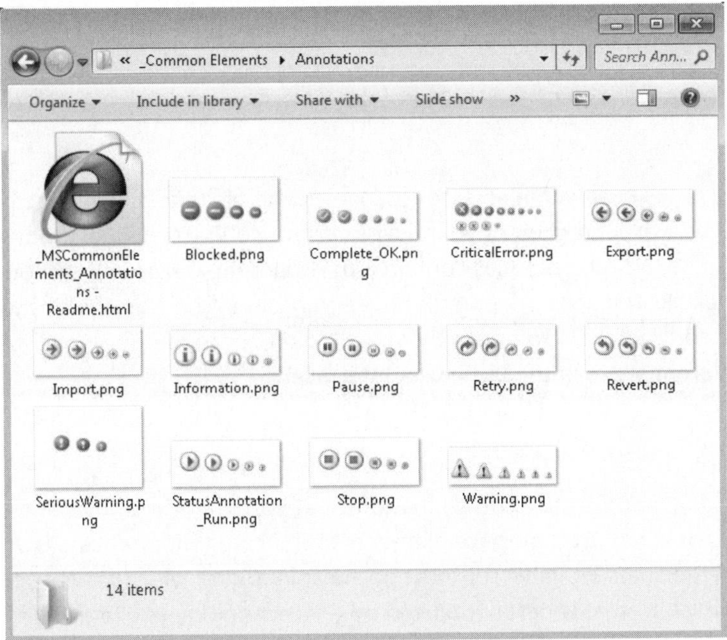

When the final image is composed just the way you like it, you can then flatten and save the file in a usable format such as .ico, .bmp, or .png. A typical use of source files would be to take an existing image and add an adorner from the _Common Elements source files, such as adding a "new" star to the upper left to indicate a command that creates a new item of that base type:

Actions

The Actions folder set contains output file images that represent verbs. Most commands are verbs, so if you are building a toolbar or ribbon, you would find most of those images in the Actions folder. In the Visual Studio Image Library, the Actions images are separated by format (24-bit, 32-bit, .ico, and .png), size (16x16, 24x24, 32x32), and style (Office/Visual Studio, DataTools, Windows Vista, and Windows XP).

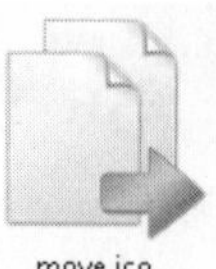

Use the format that works best within your code; 24-bit .bmp files use a fuchsia color that you can map to the background color of your user interface so that it appears to have a transparent background; 32-bit .bmp files contain a transparent background, although in File Explorer it appears black, and .ico and .png files have transparent backgrounds as well. Also, each style is illustrated differently, so generally, you should choose one style and stay consistent, not mixing different styles in the same user interface.

Animations

This folder contains a few of the common animations that you see in Windows and that are used in dialog boxes or other user interface elements to indicate that a process is underway. You have .avi and .gif formats available for most of the animations; which format you use will be determined by which format is best supported by the technology you're using for your user interface.

Annotations_Buttons

The Annotations_Buttons folder contains images for notifications, simple actions such as expand/collapse, or to describe the state of an object or process—for example, running, paused, or offline. This group of files is also separated out by format (24-bit .bmp, .ico, and .png) as well as style. Notice that the Windows Vista .ico annotations contain the full range of sizes that can be viewed in the File Explorer and appear correctly in accordance with the size required by your user interface.

Objects

Objects are output image files representing nouns. Because they represent objects, the most common usage for these files is in tree views, list views, or containers such as toolboxes. When used in this way, these images enable the user to scan a list of elements and to identify types of objects without needing to read the name of the item. Sometimes objects can also represent commands, such as a command to create a new object of that type (New File) or to launch a user interface element related to that object (for example, a stopwatch image used to indicate Start Timer).

In the png_format Windows Vista folder, you can find a wide variety of sizes and colors of various flags, arrows, +/- signs, and so forth, which can be used to indicate a variety of meanings. Generally, Object images are used as base elements when creating a new compound icon. Base elements augmented by annotations or other actions/object images can indicate the state or type of the base image and form a visual language when used with variations of similar icons:

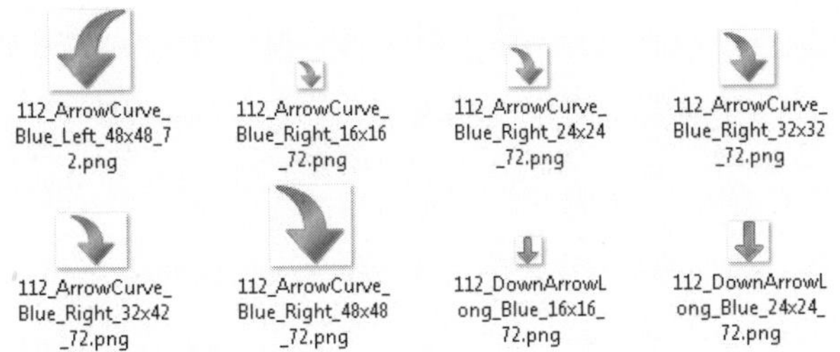

Using the Images

The images are meant to be used for their original intent. So, for example, you can't use the Paste image for something other than a paste operation. When you are using or creating these images, it is important that you make sure to use the images in a manner that is consistent with the description of the respective image in the readme document found in its respective folder:

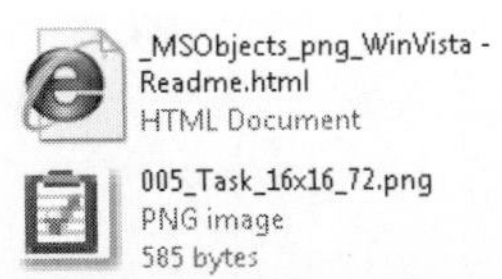

Chapter 4

Working with Documents

"He turned off the word processor, realizing just a second after he'd flicked the switch that he'd forgotten to save the document. Well, that was all right. Maybe it had even been the critic in his subconscious, telling him the document wasn't worth saving."

—Stephen King, "Secret Window, Secret Garden" in "Four Past Midnight"

Documents serve as the cornerstone of your activities in Visual Studio. Writing code, debugging code, creating interfaces, or just about anything else you do is done with documents. Yet we still seem to take our documents for granted. This chapter focuses on working with documents in the File Tab Channel as well as ways to navigate better. Several advanced topics, such as creating custom file extensions and working with previous versions are covered as well.

04.01 Insert Documents to the Right of Existing Tabs

WINDOWS	Alt,T, O
MENU	Tools | Options | Environment | Documents
VERSIONS	2010
CODE	vstipEnv0001

By default, Visual Studio 2010 opens up new tabs to the left of existing ones, as shown in the following illustration.

You now have an option to put newly opened documents in the file channel to the right of existing tabs.

Just go to Tools | Options | Environment | Documents, and select the Insert Documents To The Right Of Existing Tabs option.

You should see new tabs show up to the right of existing tabs.

04.02 Recent Files

WINDOWS	Alt,W, [1,2,3, etc] (windows); Alt,F, F, [1,2,3, etc] (files); Alt,F, J, [1,2,3, etc] (projects and solutions)
MENU	Tools | Options | General | Recent files; Window | [1,2,3, etc]; File | Recent Files | [1,2,3, etc]; File | Recent Projects and Solutions | [1,2,3, etc]
COMMAND	Tools.Options
VERSIONS	2005, 2008, 2010
CODE	vstipEnv0013

By default, the Window menu shows the 10 most recent files you had open, as shown in the illustration to the right.

Likewise, the Recent Files and Recent Projects And Solutions items on the File menu show only the last 20 entries.

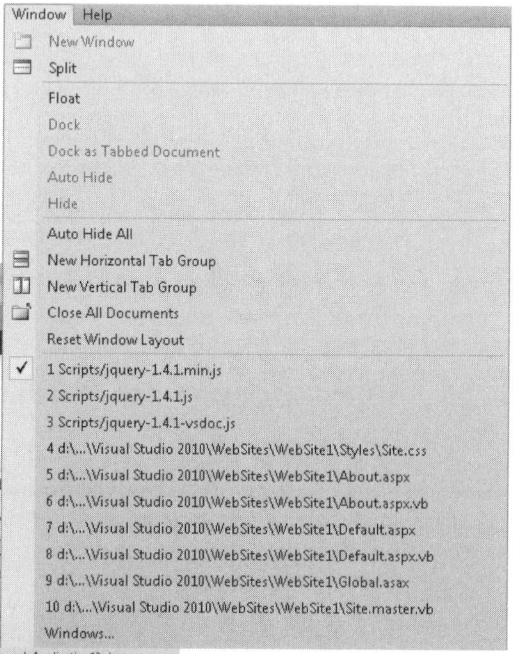

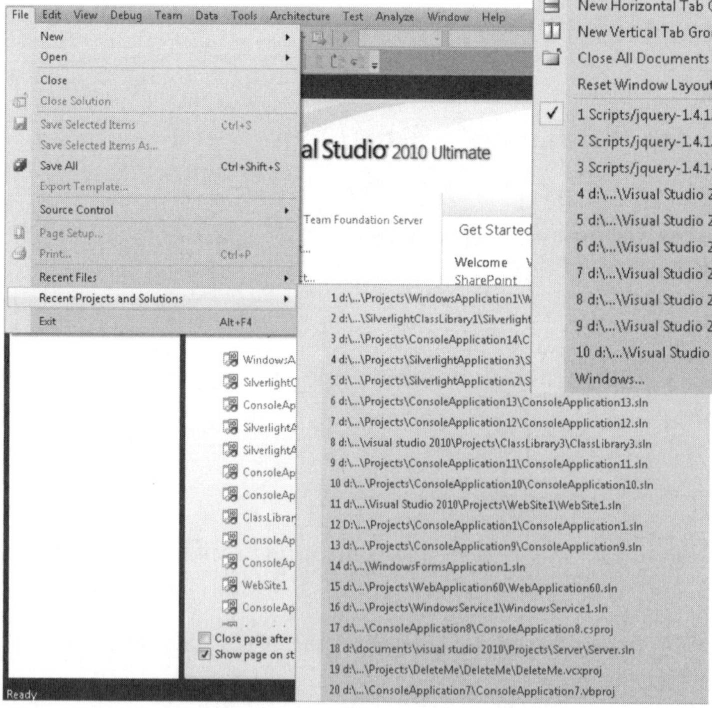

You can easily modify these numbers (up or down) by going to Tools | Options | General | Recent files.

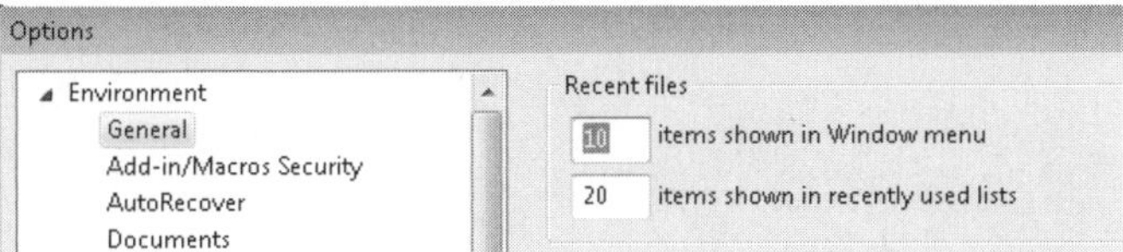

For each of these options, the minimum value is 1 and the maximum value is 24. Experiment with numbers that suit your taste.

04.03 Working with Documents on Multiple Monitors

WINDOWS	Alt,W, F (float); Alt,W,T (dock)
MENU	Window | Float; Window | Dock as Tabbed Document
COMMAND	Window.Float; Window.DockasTabbedDocument
VERSIONS	2010
CODE	vstipTool0004

This is one we have all been wanting for a long time: detachable document windows. You can now detach document windows and put them on another monitor! You have a couple of ways to do this.

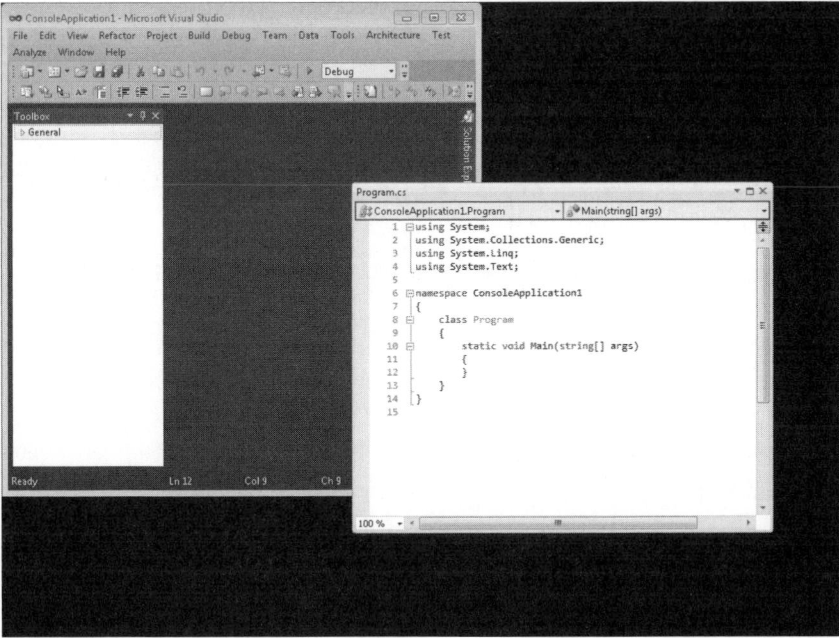

The first way is to simply click and drag the tab for the document window out of the IDE.

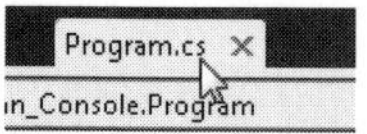

The second way is to go to Window | Float on the menu bar, as shown in the following illustration.

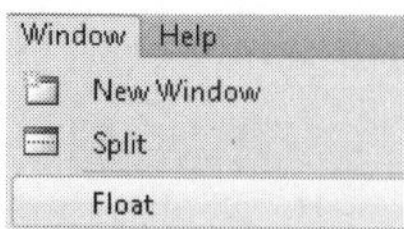

What if you want to put the window back? No worries; just right-click the title bar of the document and choose Dock As Tabbed Document.

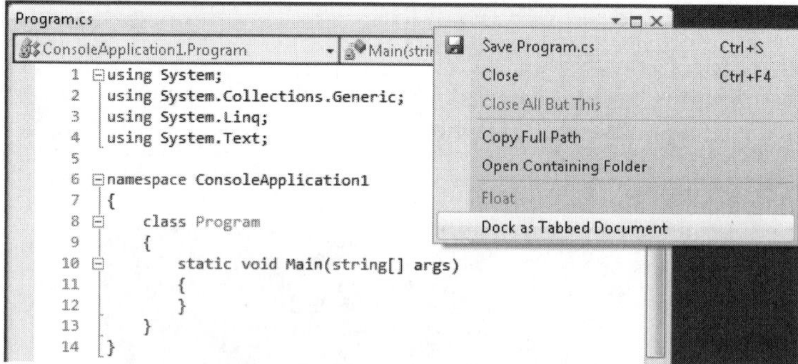

If you want an alternative method, you can go the following route: Click and drag the document window by its title bar into the IDE.

The guide diamond appears in the IDE, as shown in the following illustration.

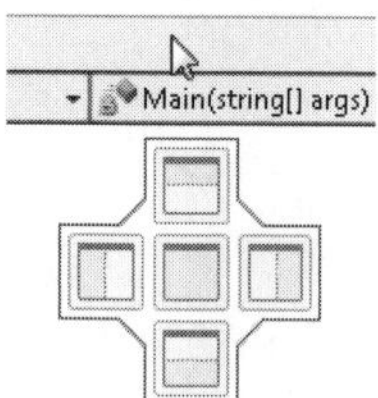

Hold down the left mouse button, and move your cursor over the middle item in the guide diamond. You should see an outline of where the window will be docked.

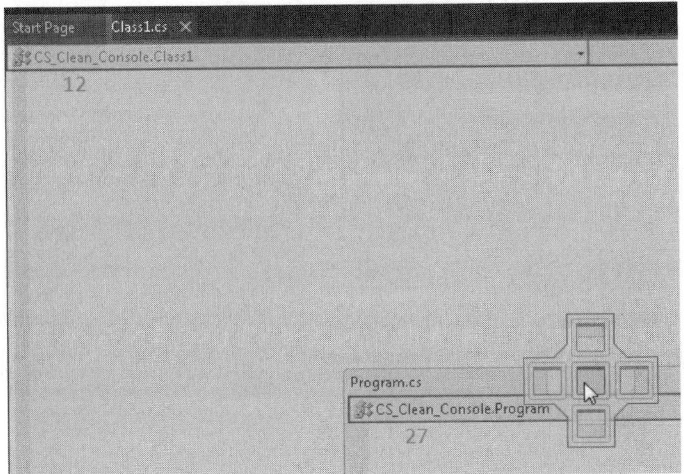

Release the mouse button, and it should dock where you want it to go.

04.04 Navigate Open Document Windows

DEFAULT	Ctrl+F6 (next); Ctrl+Shift+F6 (previous)
VISUAL C++ 2	Ctrl+F6; Ctrl+Tab (next) Ctrl+Shift+F6; Ctrl+Shift+Tab (previous)
VISUAL STUDIO 6	Ctrl+F6; Ctrl+Tab (next) Ctrl+Shift+F6; Ctrl+Shift+Tab (previous)
COMMAND	Window.NextDocumentWindow; Window.PreviousDocumentWindow
VERSIONS	2005, 2008, 2010
CODE	vstipTool0013

OK, so you have a lot of files open in the file channel:

And you don't want to use your mouse to switch between tabs. Just press Ctrl+F6 to go forward.

Or press Ctrl+Shift+F6 to go backward.

04.05 Close the Current Document Window

DEFAULT	Ctrl+F4
VISUAL BASIC 6	Ctrl+F4
VISUAL C# 2005	Ctrl+F4
VISUAL C++ 2	Ctrl+F4
VISUAL C++ 6	Ctrl+F4
VISUAL STUDIO 6	Ctrl+F4
WINDOWS	Alt,F, C
MENU	File | Close
COMMAND	Window.CloseDocumentWindow; File.Close
VERSIONS	2005, 2008, 2010
CODE	vstipTool0014

You can close the current document window from the keyboard. Just make sure you are in the document you want to close.

Then press Ctrl+F4. The current document closes, and it prompts you to save changes if you haven't already.

04.06 Open a File Location from the File Tab

DEFAULT	Alt+- (minus sign), O (VS2010 Only)
VISUAL BASIC 6	[no shortcut]
WINDOWS	Alt+- (minus sign), O (VS2010 Only)
COMMAND	File.OpenContainingFolder; Window.ShowDockMenu
VERSIONS	2005, 2008, 2010
CODE	vstipEdit0014

Do you often find yourself needing to go to your project location in Windows Explorer? Just right-click the file's tab, and choose Open Containing Folder.

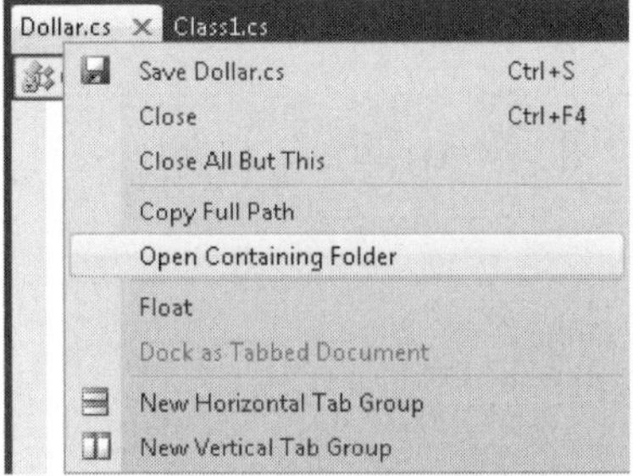

The file location opens in Windows Explorer, and you can manipulate the files from there.

04.07 Open the File Menu Drop-Down List from Your Keyboard

DEFAULT	Ctrl+Alt+Down Arrow
VISUAL BASIC 6	Ctrl+Alt+Down Arrow
VISUAL C# 2005	Ctrl+Alt+Down Arrow
VISUAL C++ 2	Ctrl+Alt+Down Arrow
VISUAL C++ 6	Ctrl+Alt+Down Arrow
VISUAL STUDIO 6	Ctrl+Alt+Down Arrow
WINDOWS	[no shortcut]
COMMAND	Window.ShowEzMDIFileList
VERSIONS	2005, 2008, 2010
CODE	vstipEnv0003

When you have a lot of files open, it is sometimes easier to view them as a list instead of tabs. The File menu drop-down list does that for you. You can click the drop-down button to the far right on the file tab, or you can simply use Ctrl+Alt+Down Arrow to activate it.

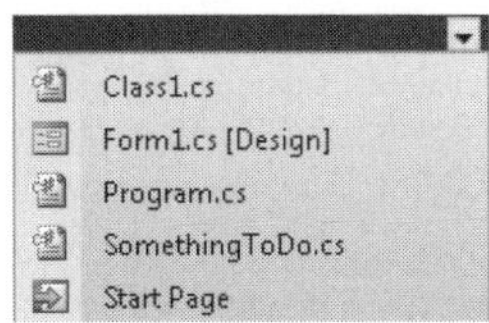

An interesting thing about this list is that it has type-ahead functionality. So, in this example, if you type the letter **S**, it automatically selects SomethingToDo.cs. Hitting **S** again results in Start Page being selected. If you have a lot of files, you can type more characters to narrow down the selection. For example, typing **ST** jumps straight to Start Page.

04.08 Using the IDE Navigator

DEFAULT	Ctrl+Tab (forward in Active Files); Ctrl+Shift+Tab (backward in Active Files); Alt+F7 (forward in Active Tool Windows); Alt+Shift+F7 (backward in Active Tool Windows)
VISUAL BASIC 6	[no shortcuts]
VISUAL C# 2005	Ctrl+Tab (forward in Active Files); Ctrl+Shift+Tab (backward in Active Files); Alt+F7 (forward in Active Tool Windows); Alt+Shift+F7 (backward in Active Tool Windows)
VISUAL C++ 2	[no shortcuts]
VISUAL C++ 6	Ctrl+Tab (forward in Active Files); Ctrl+Shift+Tab (backward in Active Files); Alt+F7 (forward in Active Tool Windows); Alt+Shift+F7 (backward in Active Tool Windows)
VISUAL STUDIO 6	Ctrl+Tab (forward in Active Files); Ctrl+Shift+Tab (backward in Active Files); Alt+F7 (forward in Active Tool Windows); Alt+Shift+F7 (backward in Active Tool Windows)
WINDOWS	[no shortcuts]
COMMAND	Window.NextDocumentWindowNav; Window.PreviousDocumentWindowNav; Window.NextToolWindowNav; Window.PreviousToolWindowNav
VERSIONS	2005, 2008, 2010
CODE	vstipTool0023

Navigating documents and tool windows in the IDE is a critical part of your development experience. You can easily move among active file and tool windows by pressing Ctrl+Tab.

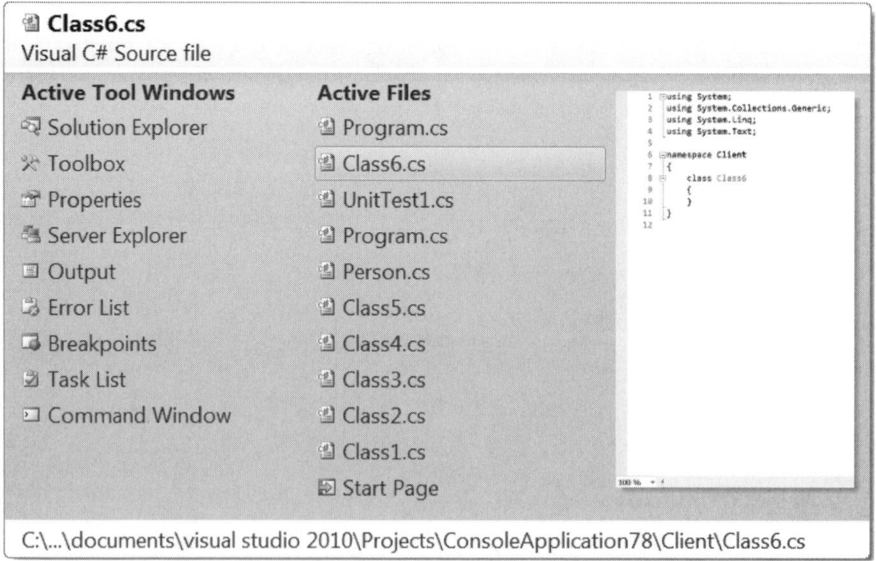

Note The images in this tip show the IDE Navigator with document preview (image to the right of the lists). This feature is off by default in Visual Studio 2010, but can be turned on as shown in vstipTool0113, "Thumbnail Previews in the IDE Navigator", in Appendix B (*http://go.microsoft.com/FWLink/?Linkid=223758*).

Some interesting things come with using this feature. For example, holding down the Ctrl key keeps the IDE Navigator showing once it is up. Also, you can select any item in this dialog box, while it is showing, by using your mouse or arrow keys.

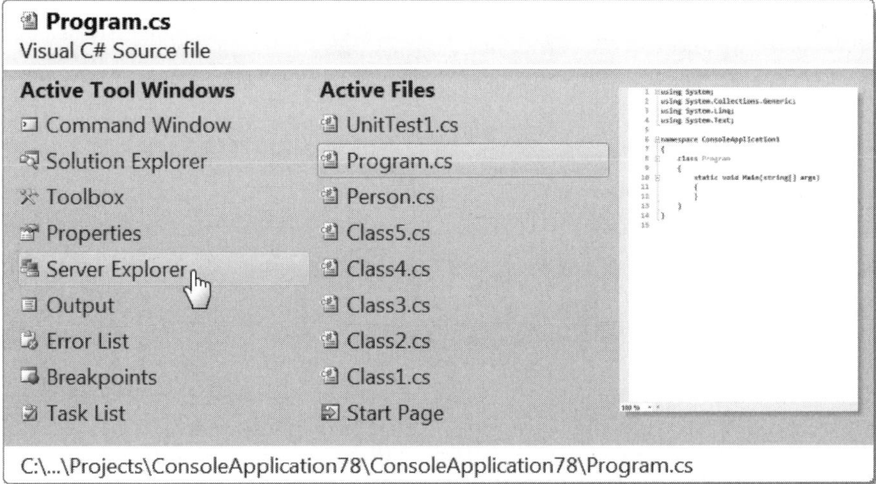

Navigator Areas

Let's take a look at the two major areas in the navigator: Active Files and Active Tool Windows.

Active files

To navigate active files, press Ctrl+Tab to go forward and Ctrl+Shift+Tab to go backward though the list. The currently selected file is highlighted, and its name is displayed at the top of the dialog box. Also, notice that the full file path is shown at the bottom of the IDE navigator.

Active tool windows

This part of the dialog box shows all your tool windows that are currently open. To get to this area, you can use Alt+F7 or Alt+Shift+F7. The interesting part is that this list changes depending on when you use it. The following illustration shows what mine looks like while I am writing code.

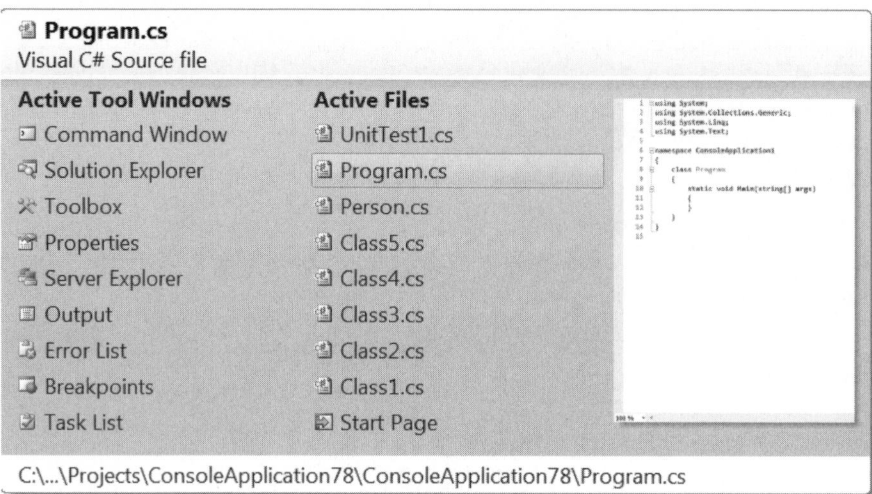

And here's what it looks like when I'm debugging:

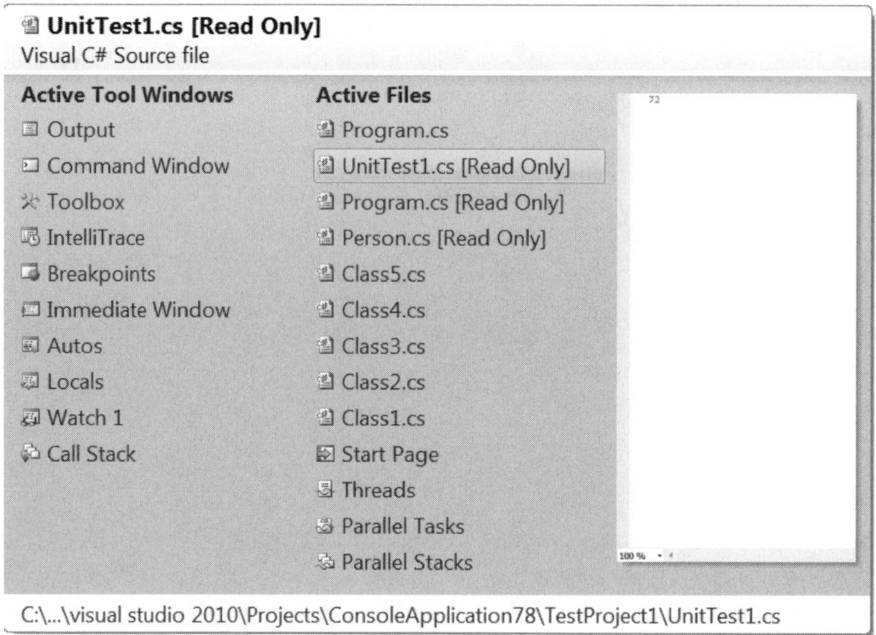

04.09 Multiple Views of the Same Document

WINDOWS	Alt,W, N
MENU	Window | New Window
COMMAND	Window.NewWindow
VERSIONS	2005, 2008, 2010
CODE	vstipEnv0016

Sometimes you might want to look at a particularly large document in several different areas at the same time. For example, you might want to look at the same document on multiple monitors. This tip shows you how to make this happen.

Special Note for VB Users in Visual Studio 2010

This feature is turned off by default in VB. A lot of history and reasoning is behind this, but the long and short of it is that this was fixed for 2010 but time ran out and it wasn't tested. So you can turn this on for VB, but you do so at your own risk. Special thanks to my friend Dustin Campbell for supplying the history and the fix.

To to fix this, go to "HKEY_LOCAL_MACHINE\SOFTWARE\Microsoft\VisualStudio\10.0\Languages\Language Services\Basic\" and rename the Single Code Window Only registry key to something like **[your initials here] Single Code Window Only**. The following illustration shows what I did:

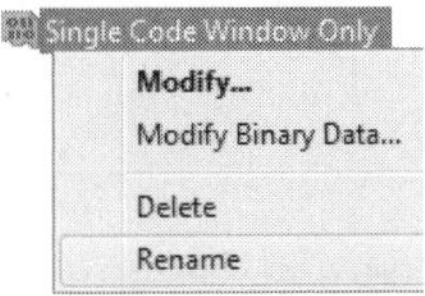

zn Single Code Window Only

Now restart Visual Studio, and you are good to go for the rest of this tip.

Multiple Views

I came across this while I was checking my email one day and noticed a thread started by the legendary Deborah Kurata concerning the Window | New Window menu item. The following example describes how it works.

Open a document window.

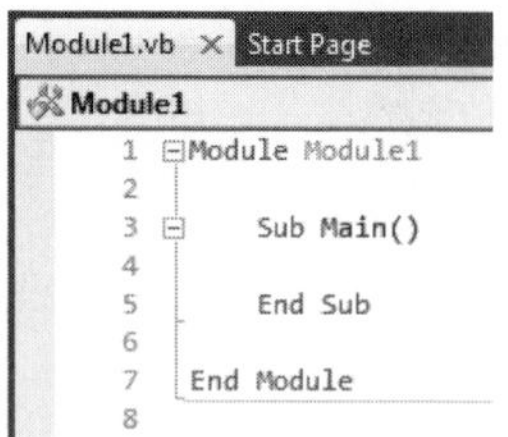

Now go to Window | New Window on the menu bar to open a duplicate window of the current document.

Notice that ":1" is added to the existing document tab text and that ":2" is appended to the name on the new document tab. You can apparently do this *forever* (or at least up to 150, which is as high as I have tested this feature).

04.10 Closing Just the Selected Files You Want

WINDOWS	Alt,W, W
MENU	Window | Windows
COMMAND	Window.Windows
VERSIONS	2005, 2008, 2010
CODE	vstipEnv0010

What do you do when you have a lot of files open and want to close only a few of them? Just go to Window | Windows on the menu bar, as shown in the following illustration.

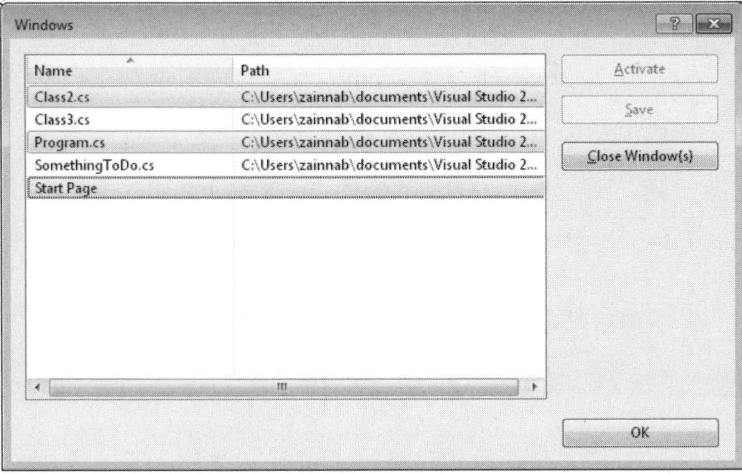

Select the files you want to close (Ctrl+Left-click), and then click Close Window(s). It closes the windows you selected and leaves the rest open.

04.11 Understanding the File Open Location

MENU	Tools | Options | Environment | Documents
VERSIONS	2005, 2008, 2010
CODE	vstipEnv0035

Have you ever noticed that when you go to open a file in Visual Studio (Ctrl+O) it automatically uses the directory of the current active document?

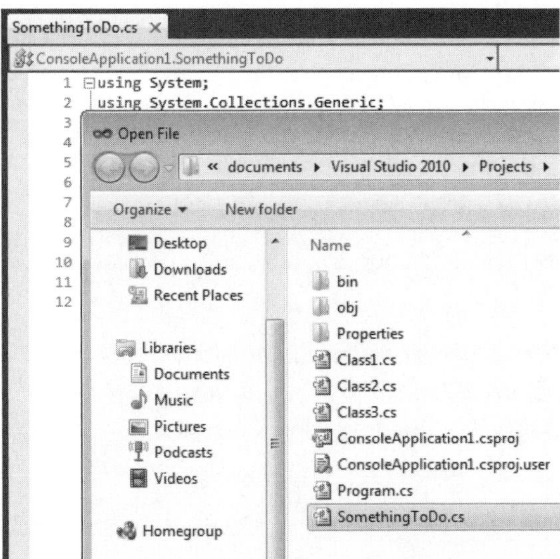

This is controlled by the Open File Using Directory Of Currently Active Document option. You can find this at Tools | Options | Environment | Documents.

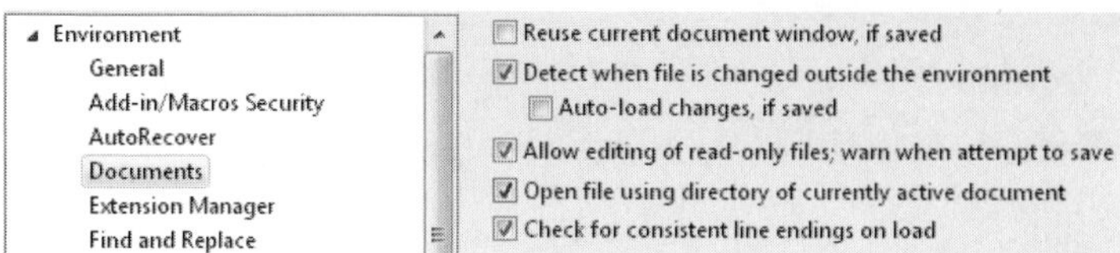

You can turn this feature off by clearing its check box, and Visual Studio then uses the DefaultFileOpenLocation from HKEY_CURRENT_USER\Software\Microsoft\VisualStudio\<version> in the registry instead.

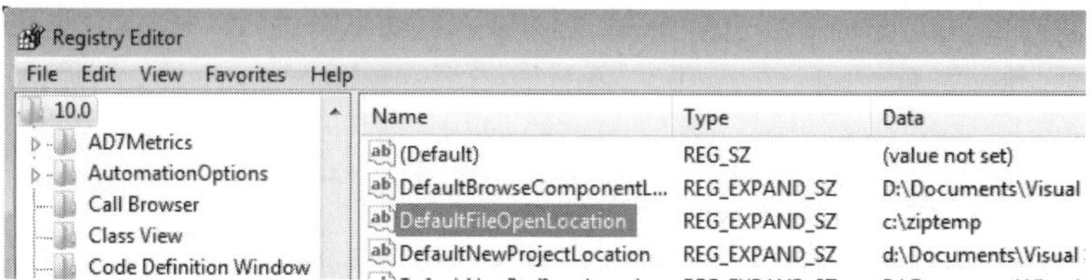

Be aware that the DefaultFileOpenLocation changes every time you successfully open a file in the Open File dialog box. However, the update is not written to the registry until you close Visual Studio.

04.12 Show Previous Versions

VERSIONS	2008, 2010
CODE	vstipEnv0036

Note For more information about previous versions including how to activate it if you don't currently have it turned on, go to *http://windows.microsoft.com/en-US/windows-vista/Previous-versions-of-files-frequently-asked-questions*.

Ever want to go back in time when you save a change to your code that you didn't want saved? If you use source control, you are usually OK, but if you don't, this tip is for you.

If you run a Windows Vista or later operating system (excluding Home Editions), you have an option you might not have noticed before called Show Previous Versions. It shows up in various applications, such as Notepad, as shown in the following illustration.

You can also see this option in the Open Project dialog box as well.

When you click Show Previous Versions, you can see prior versions of the current directory you are in, as shown in the following illustration.

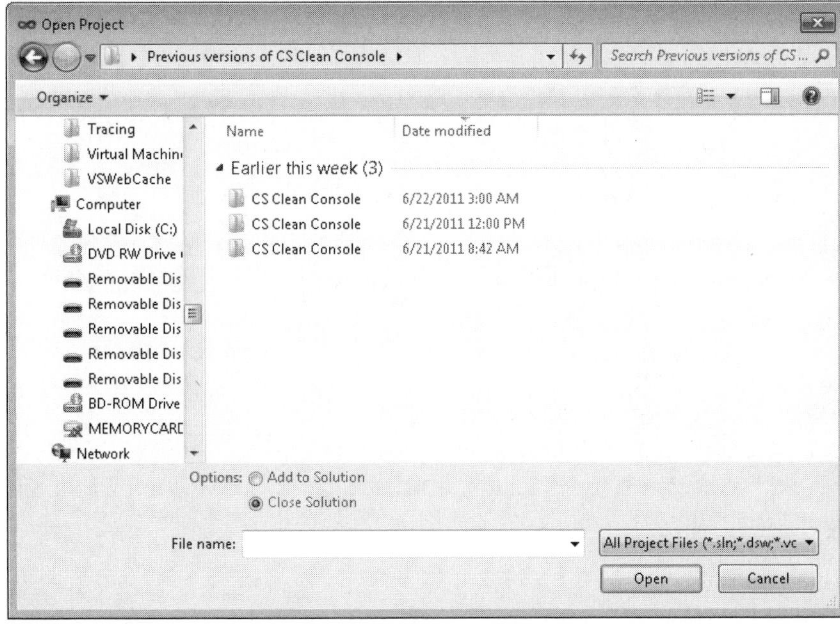

Now you can open previous versions of solutions, projects, files, and so forth, and do what you like.

04.13 Using Custom File Extension Associations

WINDOWS	Alt,T, O
MENU	Tools | Options | Text Editor | File Extension
COMMAND	Tools.Options
VERSIONS	2005, 2008, 2010
CODE	vstipEnv0038

If you have a custom file extension that you would like to associate with an editing experience, just go to Tools | Options | Text Editor | File Extension to see the options shown in the following illustration.

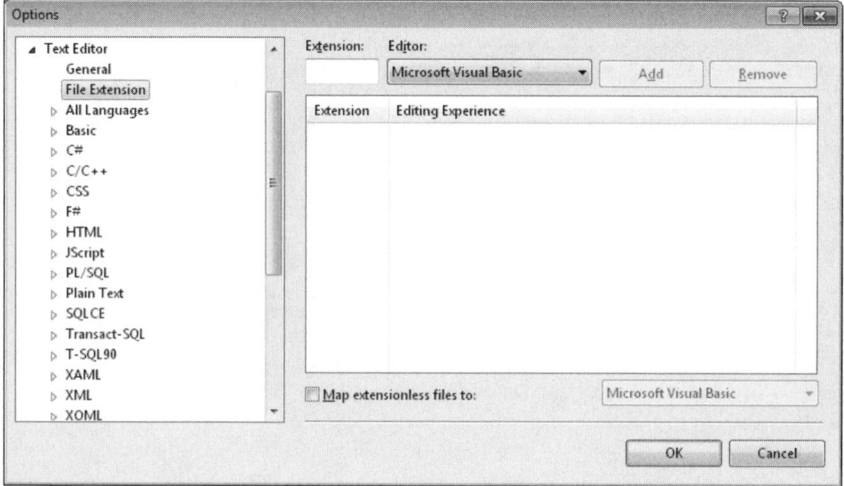

Simply type in your extension and the editing experience you want to have when it is opened. In the following example, I have a .cool extension that is associated with the Script Editor:

When I click Add, as shown in the preceding illustration, the following information is added to the overall list:

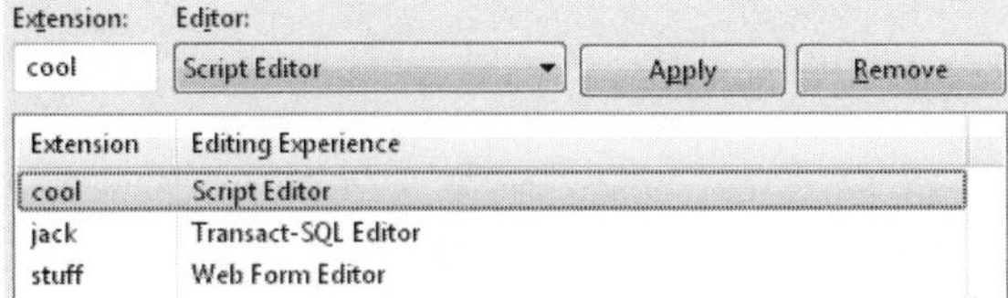

Notice that you can select any item in the list, modify the extension and/or editor, and then click Apply to save the changes. Additionally, you can click Remove to take any entry out of the list.

Chapter 5
Finding Things

"I am in hopes, then, that we may find the object of our search thus. I imagine that our state, being rightly organized, is a perfectly good state."

—Plato, "The Republic"

It's very frustrating when you are looking for something in your code and can't find it. This can range from a simple method definition to a complex set of classes in the .NET Framework, and everything in between. This chapter explores how to use the various search features in Visual Studio.

The ability to find information and then act on that information in some way is one of the central keys to creating good code. When we search for or replace code with complex criteria, our mastery of the various Find dialog boxes becomes the difference between a few minutes or several hours of work.

05.01 Repeat Your Last Search

DEFAULT	F3 (next); Shift+F3 (previous)
VISUAL BASIC 6	F3 (next); Shift+F3 (previous)
VISUAL C# 2005	F3 (next); Shift+F3 (previous)
VISUAL C++ 2	F3 (next); Shift+F3 (previous)
VISUAL C++ 6	F3 (next); Shift+F3 (previous)
VISUAL STUDIO 6	F3 (next); Shift+F3 (previous)
WINDOWS	[no shortcut]
COMMAND	Edit.FindNext; Edit.FindPrevious
VERSIONS	2005, 2008, 2010
CODE	vstipFind0004

After you perform a Find operation, you can quickly repeat that find. The following steps show you how.

Verify that your last Find shows up in the Find combo box on the Standard toolbar (usually located toward the upper right of your screen).

Press F3 (next) or Shift+F3 (previous) to move through the results.

Continue pressing F3 (next) or Shift+F3 (previous) as needed to find what you are looking for.

05.02 Using Quick Find

DEFAULT	Ctrl+F
VISUAL BASIC 6	Ctrl+F
VISUAL C# 2005	Ctrl+F
VISUAL C++ 2	Alt+F3
VISUAL C++ 6	Ctrl+F
VISUAL STUDIO 6	Ctrl+F
WINDOWS	Alt, E, F, F
MENU	Edit | Find and Replace | Quick Find
COMMAND	Edit.Find
VERSIONS	2005, 2008, 2010
CODE	vstipFind0007

There's more to Quick Find than meets the eye. The first thing to understand is that this is a tool window, so it can be moved and docked like any other tool window. Press Ctrl+F to bring up Quick Find.

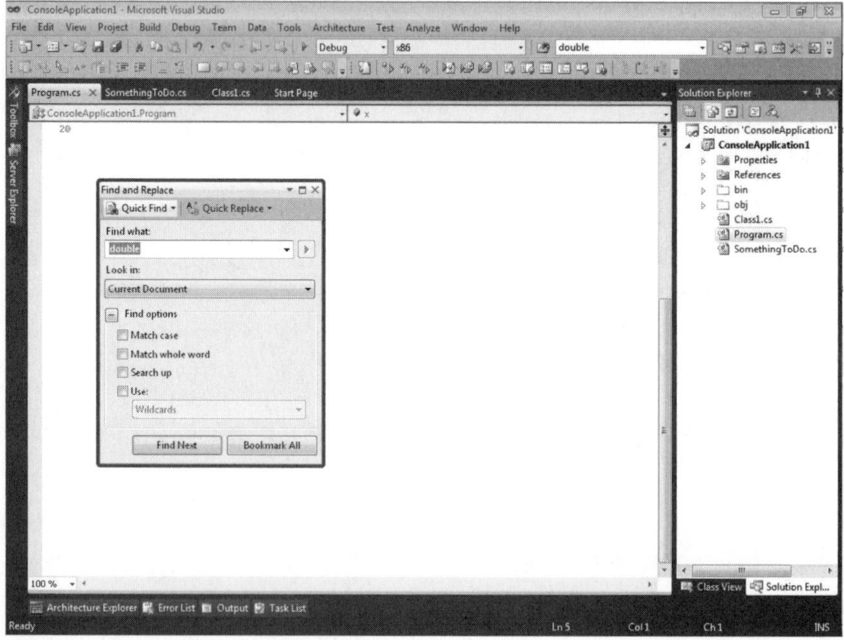

The Quick Find drop-down menu lets you choose what type of find you want to do:

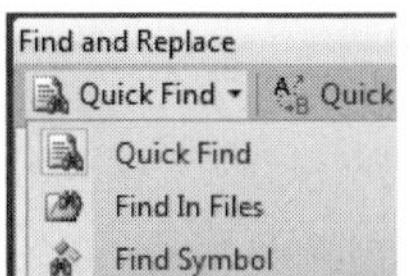

Find What

For this discussion, we want to focus only on Quick Find, but each of these items comes with its own set of options. The Find What area is used to determine what you want to find:

You can type what to look for in the drop-down combo box, or you can choose from the list of previous searches:

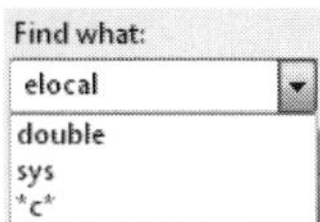

Don't worry about the arrow button to the right of the drop-down combo box (not shown here)—we will get to that later.

Look In

Next is the Look In area. It's used to determine the scope of your search:

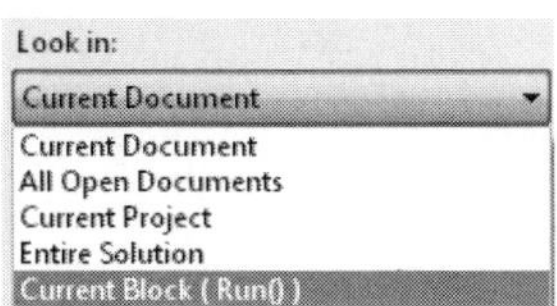

Most of the options are pretty self-explanatory, but we have a couple of key things to know, as follows:

1. The Current Project and Entire Solution actions search files whether they are open or closed.
2. Current Block is a little misleading because it doesn't search the current block but the entire method you are currently in.

Find Options

The Find Options area is where the fun really happens:

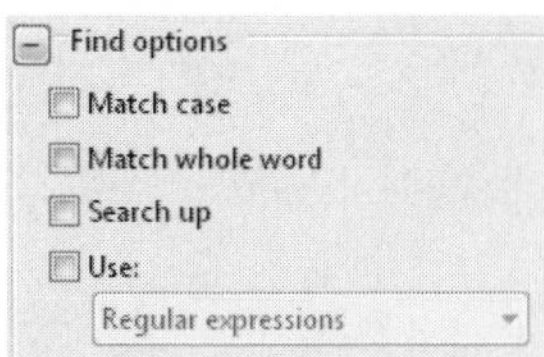

Following is a run-down of these options:

Match case

This option makes your search case-specific. Searching for elocal would show "elocal" but not "eLocal" or any other variant.

Match whole word

By default, your search is a "contains" operation and therefore finds a result anywhere the word exists. For example, searching for "elocal" finds "elocal" and "elocalstuff", and so on. This option restricts the search to only the word by itself. So, in this example, it finds "elocal" but *not* "elocalstuff."

Search up

Ordinarily, the search starts from the current cursor location and searches down in the current document. You can use this option to search up from the current cursor location instead.

Use

This option is a *lot* more interesting and requires a bit of explanation. When you select this, you get to choose between Regular Expressions and Wildcards:

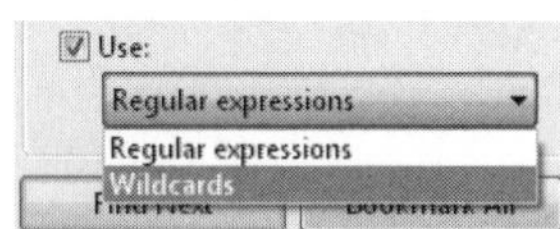

When you use this option, it automatically enables the Expression Builder button to the right of the Find What combo box:

Regular expressions

Whether or not you are familiar with regular expressions, Visual Studio has its own syntax, so be aware of the differences. The following illustration shows what options the Expression Builder button provides you when Regular Expressions is selected.

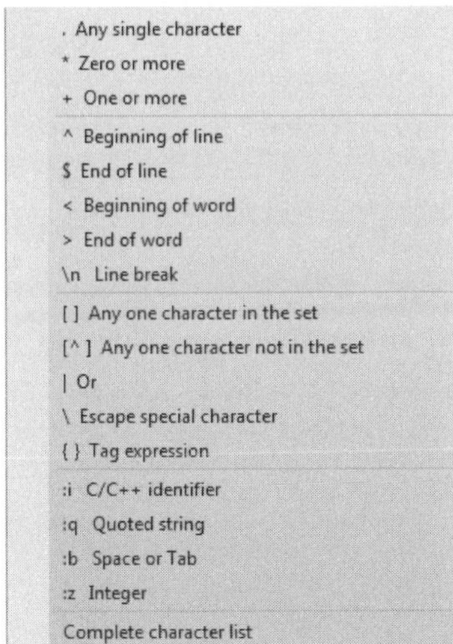

Note To see the details of the regular expression syntax available in Visual Studio, see the topic "Regular Expressions (Visual Studio)" at *http://msdn.microsoft.com/en-us/library/2k3te2cs.aspx*.

Wildcards

These aren't as advanced as regular expressions but are more familiar to people. They allow you to use special characters to represent one or more letters. More information about wildcard searches can be found at *http://msdn.microsoft.com/en-us/library/afy96z92.aspx*. The following illustration shows what options the Expression Builder button provides when Wildcards is selected.

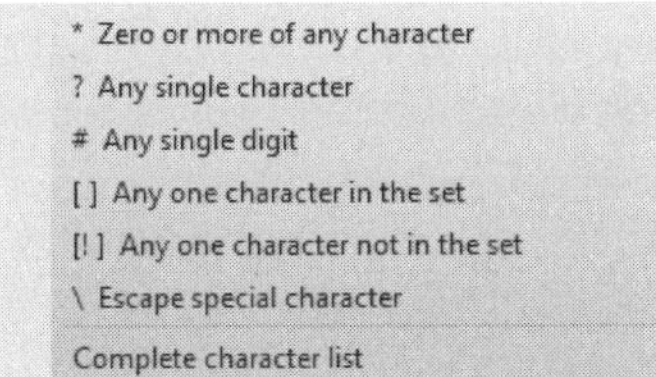

Buttons

Finally, we have the two buttons at the bottom of the Quick Find tool window:

Find Next

Keeps going to the next instance of the search term you are looking for until it reaches your original starting point.

Bookmark All

Automatically places a bookmark at every location where the search term is found. Use this with caution because it can definitely cause a large number of bookmarks to be created.

05.03 Using a Simple Quick Replace

DEFAULT	Ctrl+H
VISUAL BASIC 6	Ctrl+H
VISUAL C# 2005	Ctrl+H
VISUAL C++ 2	Ctrl+H
VISUAL C++ 6	Ctrl+H
VISUAL STUDIO 6	Ctrl+H
WINDOWS	Alt, E, F, R
MENU	Edit | Find and Replace | Quick Replace
COMMAND	Edit.Replace
VERSIONS	2005, 2008, 2010
CODE	vstipFind0008

Previously, we looked at Quick Find, and now we will look at Quick Replace. They are almost exactly the same except for the replace operation itself. For that reason, I will not repeat all the options here but refer you back to vstipFind0007 ("Using Quick Find," page 172), for most of the details.

Press Ctrl+H to bring up Quick Replace:

This is a tool window, so it can be docked like any other tool window, pretty much anywhere you want. Notice that the Quick Replace drop-down menu lets you choose what type of replace you want to do:

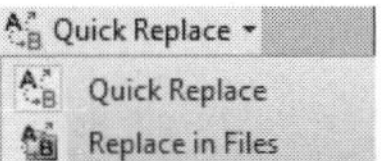

For this discussion, let's focus only on Quick Replace. The Find What area is used to determine what you want to find:

The Replace With area functions exactly the same way, but it takes the text that you want to be used to replace the Find What text with:

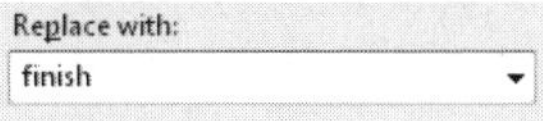

The Look In and Find Options function the same way as using Quick Find and are explained in vstipFind0007 ("Using Quick Find," page 172).

Finally, we have the three buttons at the bottom of the Quick Replace tool window:

- **Find Next**—Selects the next instance of the search term you are looking for until it reaches your original starting point.
- **Replace**—Replaces the currently selected item from Find What by using the text in Replace With.
- **Replace All**—Replaces all instances of Find What by using the text in Replace With. This produces a dialog box that shows how many replacements were made:

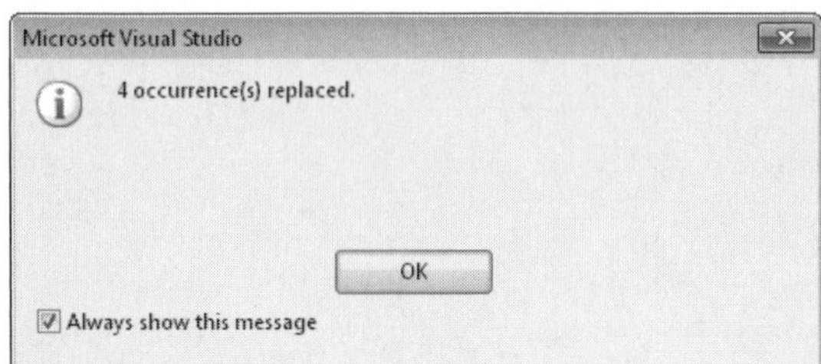

Make sure to pay attention to this value because it might be higher (or lower) than expected and might require further investigation. If you make a mistake, you can always undo a Replace All:

05.04 Hide the Quick Find and Quick Replace Tool Window After the First Match

WINDOWS	Alt, T, O
MENU	Tools | Options | Environment | Find and Replace
VERSIONS	2005, 2008, 2010
CODE	vstipFind0010

When using the Quick Find or the Quick Replace tool window, you have an option to make the window disappear after the first match. This can be useful when you want to use your shortcut keys after the first match is found.

Just go to Tools | Options | Environment | Find And Replace, and then select the Hide Find And Replace Window After A Match Is Located For Quick Find Or Quick Replace check box.

05.05 Undo Quick Replace and Replace in Files

DEFAULT	Ctrl+Z; Alt+Backspace
VISUAL BASIC 6	Ctrl+Z; Alt+Backspace
VISUAL C# 2005	Ctrl+Z; Alt+Backspace
VISUAL C++ 2	Ctrl+Z; Alt+Backspace
VISUAL C++ 6	Ctrl+Z; Alt+Backspace
VISUAL STUDIO 6	Ctrl+Z; Alt+Backspace
WINDOWS	Alt,E, U
MENU	Edit | Undo
COMMAND	Edit.Undo
VERSIONS	2005, 2008, 2010
CODE	vstipFind0020

When using Find And Replace, people often wonder under what conditions you can undo the changes. Because performing a Find Next and Replace operation is very straightforward and easy to undo, let's focus on how to undo the "Replace All" operations. Following is a summary of the conditions that allow undo to happen.

Quick Replace (Ctrl+H)

Let's assume we're choosing the Quick Replace option with the Look In option set to Current Project or Entire Solution:

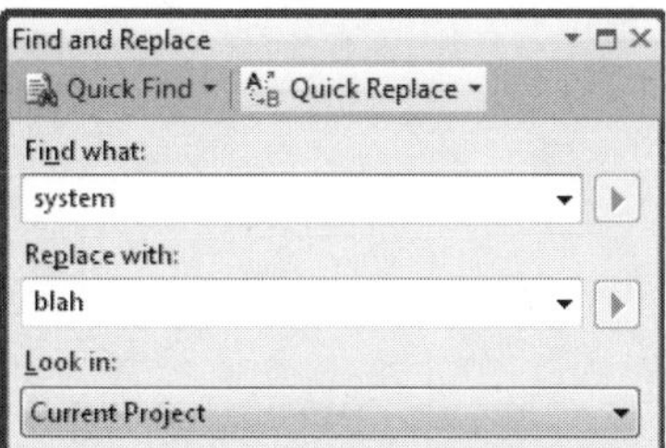

A Replace All operation, by default, opens documents and marks them by putting an asterisk in the file name tab so that you can undo the changes:

When we undo (Ctrl+Z), it reverses *all* the changes made. In this case, it undoes all eleven changes:

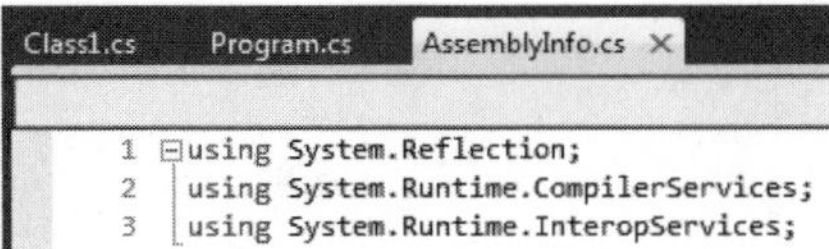

From the toolbar, the following entry appears in the undo stack:

Replace in Files (Ctrl+Shift+H)

If we perform a Replace in Files operation with Look In set to Current Project, Entire Solution, or Visual C++ Include Directories, we see the following dialog box:

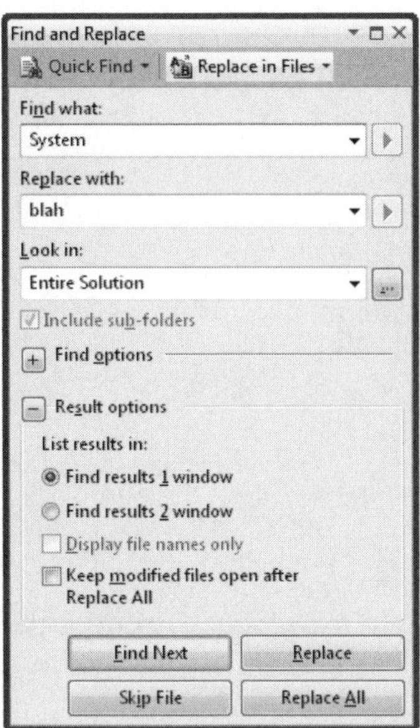

As shown in the preceding illustration, notice the option called Keep Modified Files Open After Replace All. If we do not select this option and click Replace All, we get the following message:

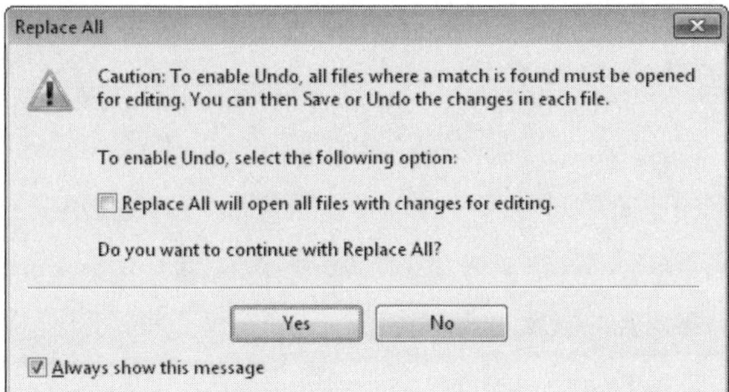

Checking the Replace All Will Open All Files With Changes For Editing makes it possible to undo *all* the changes made:

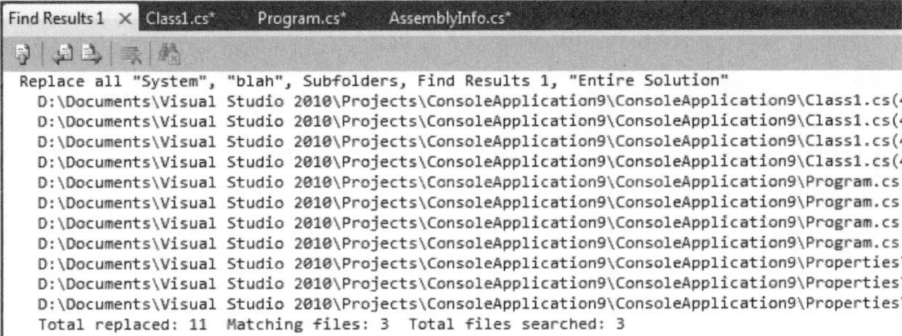

The entry in the undo stack on the toolbar looks like this:

So, as you can see, it is quite easy to undo the changes made by Quick Replace and Replace in Files.

05.06 Using the Find Combo Box Keyboard Shortcuts

DEFAULT	Ctrl+D (find); Ctrl+/ (run command); Ctrl+G (go to line); Ctrl+Shift+G (go to file); F9 (set breakpoint)
VISUAL BASIC 6	[no shortcut] (find); [no shortcut] (run command); [no shortcut] (go to line); Ctrl+Shift+G (go to file); F9 (set breakpoint)
VISUAL C# 2005	Ctrl+/ (find); [no shortcut] (run command); Ctrl+G (go to line); Ctrl+Shift+G (go to file); F9 (set breakpoint)
VISUAL C++ 2	Ctrl+F (find); ALT+A (find); Ctrl+D (find); Ctrl+/ (run command); Ctrl+G (go to line); Ctrl+Shift+G (go to file); F9 (set breakpoint); Ctrl+Shift+F9 (set breakpoint)
VISUAL C++ 6	Ctrl+D (find); Ctrl+/ (run command); Ctrl+G (go to line); Ctrl+Shift+G (go to file); F9 (set breakpoint)
VISUAL STUDIO 6	Ctrl+Shift+F (find); Ctrl+/ (run command); Ctrl+G (go to line); Ctrl+Shift+G (go to file); F9 (set breakpoint)
COMMAND	Edit.GoToFindCombo; Tools.GoToCommandLine; Edit.GoTo; Edit.OpenFile; Debug.ToggleBreakpoint
VERSIONS	2005, 2008, 2010
CODE	vstipFind0019

We have looked at the Find Combo box in a variety of places. Recall that this toolbar item is located on the standard toolbar by default:

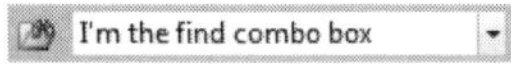

I thought it would be a good idea to consolidate the keyboard shortcuts of this wonderful tool into one place.

Find (Ctrl+D)

First and foremost, the Find / Command box is used to find strings. Just press Ctrl+D to go to the box and type in your search term:

When you press Enter, it searches for your string by using the settings from Quick Find (Ctrl+F) as it searches. Pressing Enter again finds the next instance, and so on.

Run Command (Ctrl+/)

The Find / Command box is also used to run commands. For more information about commands, see vstipTool0067 ("Understanding Commands: Simple Commands," page 110). Just press Ctrl+/ to go to the box, and type in your command:

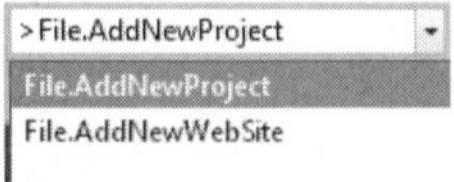

When you press Enter, it runs the command you typed.

Go To Line (Ctrl+G)

When in the Find / Command box, you can type any line number:

Then press Ctrl+G, and you are taken to the line number that you entered.

Go To File (Ctrl+Shift+G)

Type in any file name that is in your solution or in the INCLUDE path:

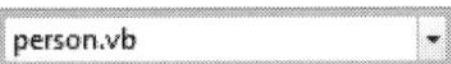

Use Ctrl+Shift+G to go to the file. If the file isn't already open, this command opens the file first.

Set a Breakpoint (F9)

Enter any function name:

Then press F9, and Visual Studio sets a breakpoint on the function:

```
class Class1
{
    public void DoStuff()
    {

```

A couple of things to note:

- Pressing F9 again does *not* turn off the breakpoint—that is, it's not a toggle.
- This feature works only with open documents.

05.07 Using Incremental Search

DEFAULT	Ctrl+I
VISUAL BASIC 6	Alt+I
VISUAL C# 2005	Ctrl+I
VISUAL C++ 2	Ctrl+I
VISUAL C++ 6	Ctrl+I
VISUAL STUDIO 6	[no shortcut]
WINDOWS	Alt,E, V, S
MENU	Edit | Advanced | Incremental Search
COMMAND	Edit.IncrementalSearch
VERSIONS	2005, 2008, 2010
CODE	vstipFind0001

Incremental search is a powerful feature to use when you want to keep your cursor in the editor while searching in the current document. It allows you to keep your hands on the keyboard without having to use the mouse for any dialog boxes.

To conduct an incremental search, press Ctrl+I and start typing the text you are searching for. You'll see the cursor in the editor jump to the first match, highlighting the current search string, and your mouse cursor turns into a pair of binoculars with an arrow pointing in the direction (up or down) you are searching:

```
// i love public tips
private int x = 10;
public int y = 0;
```

If you look at the status bar, you can see the details of your incremental search:

Press Ctrl+I again to jump to the next occurrence of the search string:

```
// i love public tips
private int x = 10;
public int y = 0;
```

The following table lists all the options you can leverage while in this mode:

ACTION	SHORTCUT
Move to the next match in the file	Ctrl+I
Reverse the direction of the search	Ctrl+Shift+I
Remove a character from the search string	Backspace
Stop the incremental search	Esc

05.08 Search the Currently Selected String Without the Find Window

DEFAULT	Ctrl+F3 (next); Ctrl+Shift+F3 (previous)
VISUAL BASIC 6	Ctrl+F3 (next); Ctrl+Shift+F3 (previous)
VISUAL C# 2005	Ctrl+F3 (next); Ctrl+Shift+F3 (previous)
VISUAL C++ 2	Ctrl+F3 (next); Ctrl+Shift+F3 (previous)
VISUAL C++ 6	Ctrl+F3 (next); Ctrl+Shift+F3 (previous)
VISUAL STUDIO 6	Ctrl+F3 (next); Ctrl+Shift+F3 (previous)
WINDOWS	[no shortcut]
COMMAND	Edit.FindNextSelected; Edit.FindPreviousSelected
VERSIONS	2005, 2008, 2010
CODE	vstipFind0003

Ever just want to find the next (or previous) instance of a word quickly without using the Quick Find dialog box? Well, it's easy.

Put the cursor in any word you want to look for:

```
public double x = 10;
public double y = 30;
public double z = 50;
public double a = 30;
```

Press Ctrl+F3 (next) or Ctrl+Shift+F3 (previous) to start a find:

```
public double x = 10;
public double y = 30;
public double z = 50;
public double a = 30;
```

You can also see a message in the status bar showing you the parameters of the search:

Note As you can see, the find has certain settings already in place. These settings can be changed in the Find dialog box (Ctrl+F).

After the Find has started, just press F3 (next) or Shift+F3 (previous) to continue searching as you normally would with a Quick Find.

05.09 Find In Files: Find Options

DEFAULT	Ctrl+Shift+F
VISUAL BASIC 6	Ctrl+Shift+F
VISUAL C# 2005	Ctrl+Shift+F
VISUAL C++ 2	Ctrl+Shift+F
VISUAL C++ 6	Ctrl+Shift+F
VISUAL STUDIO 6	[no shortcut]
WINDOWS	Alt,E, F, I
MENU	Edit | Find and Replace | Find in Files
COMMAND	Edit.FindinFiles
VERSIONS	2005, 2008, 2010
CODE	vstipFind0013

When working in Visual Studio, you often need to search for information in files. Find In Files allows you to quickly locate information you need. Let's begin by looking at the options you can set to find information in files (Ctrl+Shift+F).

Note If you have already read vstipFind0007 ("Using Quick Find," page 172), you might want to just skim this one because much of the information is repeated here for those who might not have read the prior tip.

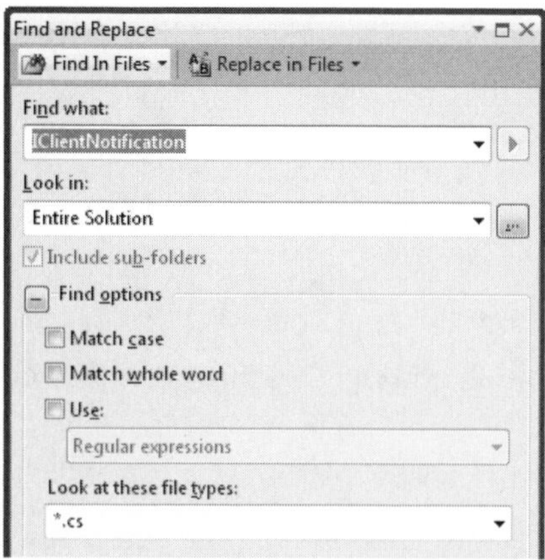

Find What

The Find What combo box lets you type in text to find or choose from previous text that has been searched:

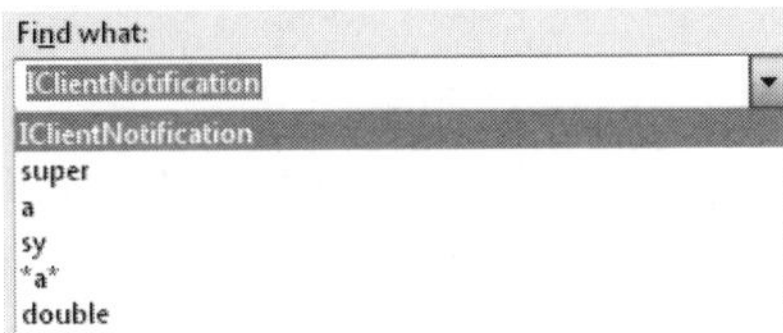

This area is very closely bound to all but one of the options under Find Options:

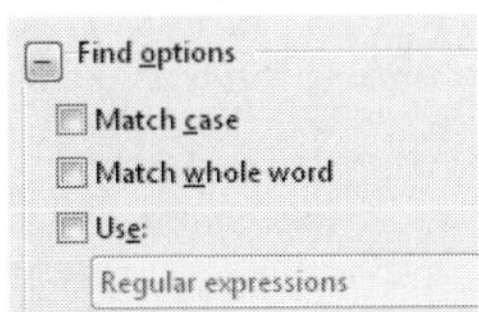

Following is an overview of these options:

Match case

This option makes your search case-specific. Searching for elocal would show "elocal" but not "eLocal" or any other variant.

Match whole word

By default, the search is a "contains" operation and finds the word anywhere it exists. For example, searching for "elocal" finds "elocal" and "elocalstuff", and so on.

Use

This is a *lot* more interesting and requires a bit of explanation. When you select this, you get to choose between Regular Expressions and Wildcards:

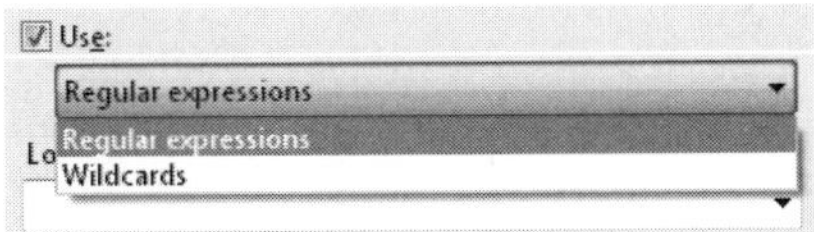

When you use this option, it automatically enables the Expression Builder button to the right of the Find What combo box:

Regular expressions

Whether or not you are familiar with regular expressions, Visual Studio has its own syntax, so be aware of the differences. The following illustration shows the options provided by the Expression Builder button when you have selected Regular Expressions:

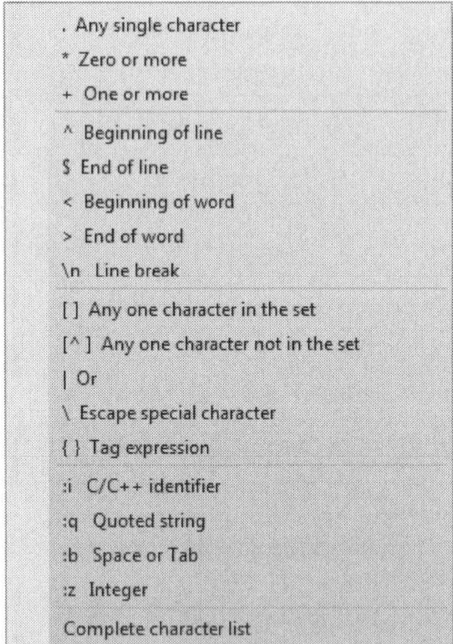

Note To see the details of the regular expression syntax available in Visual Studio, see the topic "Regular Expressions (Visual Studio)" at *http://msdn.microsoft.com/en-us/library/2k3te2cs.aspx.*

Wildcards

This option isn't as advanced as regular expressions but is more familiar to most people. It allows you to use special characters to represent one or more letters. For more information about wildcard searches, see "Wildcards (Visual Studio) at *http://msdn.microsoft.com/en-us/library/afy96z92.aspx*. The following illustration shows the options provided by the Expression Builder button when Wildcards is selected:

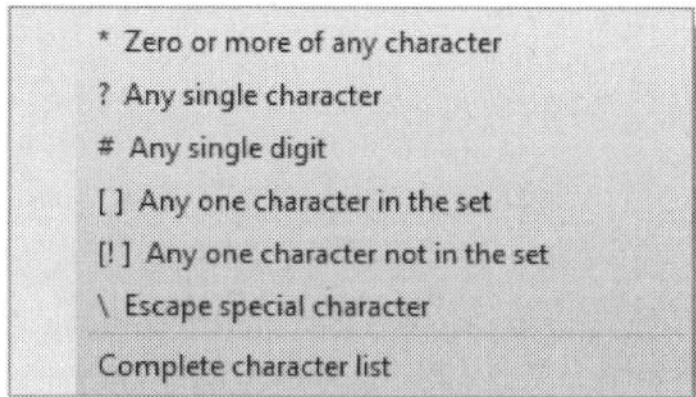

Look in

The Look in drop-down list lets you specify what areas you want to look in:

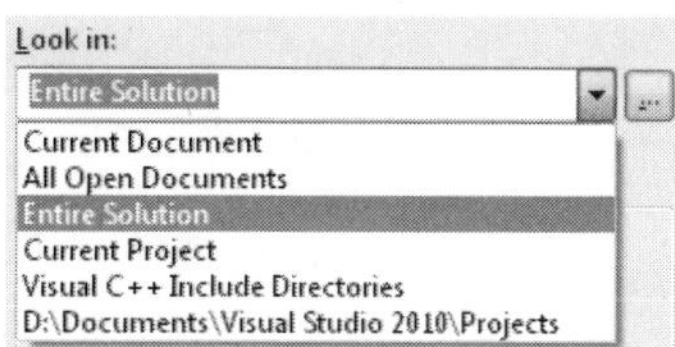

Most of the options are pretty self-explanatory. The Current Project and Entire Solution commands search files whether they are open or closed.

The Choose Search Folders and Look At These File Types options are discussed in vstipFind0005 ("How to Customize What Files to Search with Find In Files," in Appendix B [*http://go.microsoft.com/FWLink/?Linkid=223758*]):

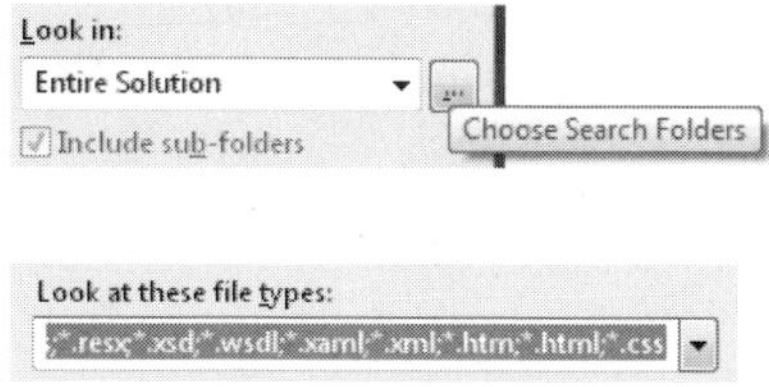

Include sub-folders

This option searches the current directory and all subdirectories and shows up only if you use the Visual C++ Include Directories or Choose Search Folders options:

05.10 Find In Files: Result Options

DEFAULT	Ctrl+Shift+F (find); F8 (next); Shift+F8 (previous);
VISUAL BASIC 6	Ctrl+Shift+F (find);[no shortcut] (next); [no shortcut] (previous);
VISUAL C# 2005	Ctrl+Shift+F (find); F8 (next); Shift+F8 (previous);
VISUAL C++ 2	Ctrl+Shift+F (find); F4 (next); Shift+F4 (previous);
VISUAL C++ 6	Ctrl+Shift+F (find); F8 (next); F4 (next); Shift+F8 (previous); Shift+F4 (previous);
VISUAL STUDIO 6	[no shortcut] (find); F8 (next); F12 (next); Shift+F8 (previous); Shift+F12 (previous);
WINDOWS	Alt,E, F, I (find)
MENU	Edit | Find and Replace | Find in Files
COMMAND	Edit.FindinFiles; Edit.GoToNextLocation; Edit.GoToPrevLocation; Edit.ClearFindResults1; Edit.ClearFindResults2
VERSIONS	2005, 2008, 2010
CODE	vstipFind0014

When working with Find In Files (Ctrl+Shift+F), you can choose several result options:

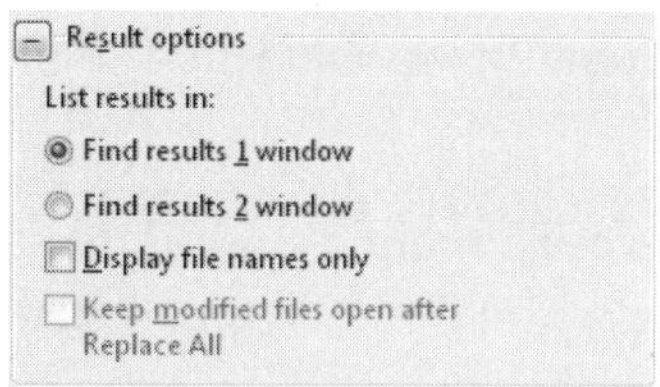

Find Results [1,2] Window

The Find Results windows allow you to view and navigate the results of a find operation. Each time you use Find, the results replace the contents of the previous find. This is why two windows are available—so that you avoid overwriting a find result you might want to keep.

Navigation

You can use F8 and Shift+F8 to go to the next and previous items in the results list. This operation also shows the line of code where the item was found, which includes opening closed files if needed:

The Find Results windows have toolbar buttons that allow you to go to the next and previous items as well:

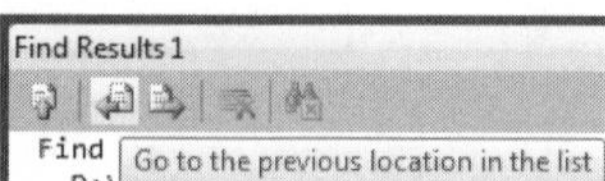

Clear All

You can manually clear the results in a Find Results window by clicking Clear All:

Display File Names Only

The operation shows only the files names in your results and not the full path and additional information. This means the result set is much smaller.

Before:

```
Find Results 1
Find all "System", Wildcards, Find Results 1, Current Document
  D:\Documents\Visual Studio 2010\Projects\ConsoleApplication18\Program.cs(1):using System;
  D:\Documents\Visual Studio 2010\Projects\ConsoleApplication18\Program.cs(2):using System.Collections.Generic;
  D:\Documents\Visual Studio 2010\Projects\ConsoleApplication18\Program.cs(3):using System.Linq;
  D:\Documents\Visual Studio 2010\Projects\ConsoleApplication18\Program.cs(4):using System.Text;
Matching lines: 4
```

After:

```
Find Results 1
Find all "System", Wildcards, Find Results 1, Current Document
  D:\Documents\Visual Studio 2010\Projects\ConsoleApplication18\Program.cs
Matching lines: 1
```

You can do much more with the displayed results than this. See vstipFind0002 ("Customize How Find In Files Results Are Displayed in the Find Results Window," page 206) for more information.

Keep Modified Files Open After Replace All

This option doesn't apply to Find In Files and is always disabled when doing a find operation. You can see this option when using the Replace In Files option.

05.11 Replace In Files: Basic Options

DEFAULT	Ctrl+Shift+H
VISUAL BASIC 6	Ctrl+Shift+H
VISUAL C# 2005	Ctrl+Shift+H
VISUAL C++ 2	Ctrl+Shift+H
VISUAL C++ 6	Ctrl+Shift+H
VISUAL STUDIO 6	Ctrl+Shift+H
WINDOWS	Alt,E, F, S
MENU	Edit | Find and Replace | Replace in Files
COMMAND	Edit.ReplaceinFiles
VERSIONS	2005, 2008, 2010
CODE	vstipFind0015

Did you know that you can replace text in files, whether or not they are open, by choosing Replace In Files (Ctrl+Shift+H)? Let's take a look at what can be done.

Find Options

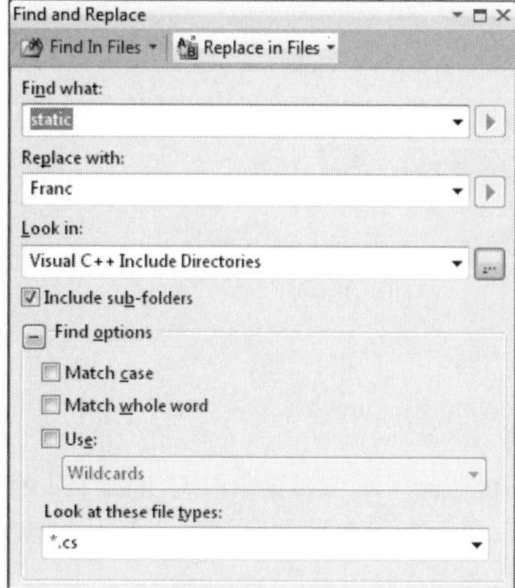

Fortunately, the majority of find options are the same for Replace In Files as they are for Find In Files (see vstipFind0013, "Find In Files: Find Options," on page 186), so you can leverage those skills again here.

Replace With

This area is the most interesting piece of the Replace In Files dialog box. It can be as simple as a literal string (replacing "static" with "Franc", for example) or very, very complex. In simple situations, you just want to use the literal text as a replacement to the Find What text.

Result Options

Again, these options are exactly like the Find In Files options (vstipTool0014, "Find In Files: Result Options," page 158) with the exception of the Keep Modified Files Open After Replace All option:

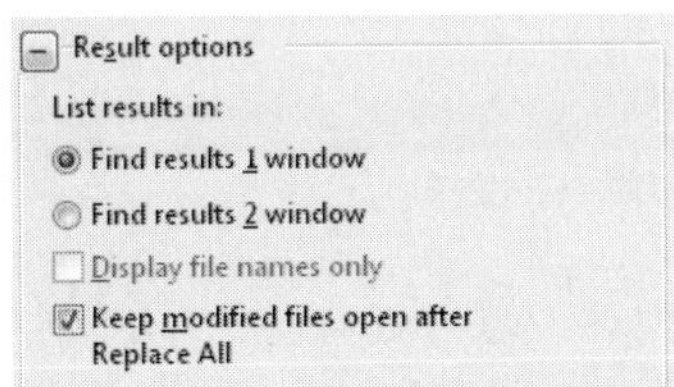

This option makes it possible to keep modified files open after they are changed so that you can review the change or make additional manual changes. This is particularly useful when you are modifying closed files and want to look inside files that were modified.

Execution

After all the options have been set, we can execute find and replace operations by using the following four buttons:

Find Next

Used to find the next instance of the Find What search string.

Replace

Used to replace the current instance of the Find What string with the Replace With string and then find the next instance.

Replace All

Used to replace all instances of the Find What string with the Replace With string, in all files within the Look In scope.

> **Warning** The Replace All option can get you into big trouble if you don't pay attention to the scope of Look In.

Skip File

Available when the Look In list includes multiple files. Choose this button if you do not want to search or modify the current file. The search continues in the next file on the Look In list.

05.12 Go To Definition for Cascading Style Sheets

DEFAULT	F12
VISUAL BASIC 6	F12; Shift+F2
VISUAL C# 2005	F12
VISUAL C++ 2	F11; Alt+F1
VISUAL C++ 6	F12
VISUAL STUDIO 6	[no shortcut]
WINDOWS	[no shortcut]
COMMAND	Edit.GoToDefinition
VERSIONS	2008, 2010
CODE	vstipFind0021

For those who are familiar with using Go To Definition in your code, you might not be aware that you can use the same technique to go to your Cascading Style Sheet (CSS) definition class for attributes. Just put your cursor inside the class name:

```
<div class="bold">
        something cool
</div>
```

Then press F12 (or right-click and choose Go To Definition). It instantly takes you to the CSS definition and highlights it:

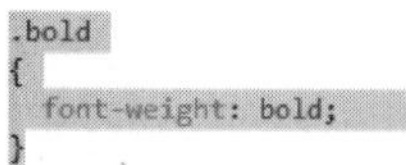

```
.bold
{
  font-weight: bold;
}
```

Now you can review the definition and make changes as you see fit.

05.13 How to Use Navigate To

DEFAULT	Ctrl+, [comma]
VISUAL BASIC 6	Ctrl+, [comma]
VISUAL C# 2005	Ctrl+, [comma]
VISUAL C++ 2	Ctrl+, [comma]
VISUAL C++ 6	Ctrl+, [comma]
VISUAL STUDIO 6	Ctrl+, [comma]
WINDOWS	Alt,E, .[period]
MENU	Edit | Navigate To
COMMAND	Edit.NavigateTo
VERSIONS	2010
CODE	vstipTool0006

The Navigate To dialog box is very useful for finding symbols. The search is an "includes" operation, so it shows you symbols that contain the letters you type. Just put in what you are looking for:

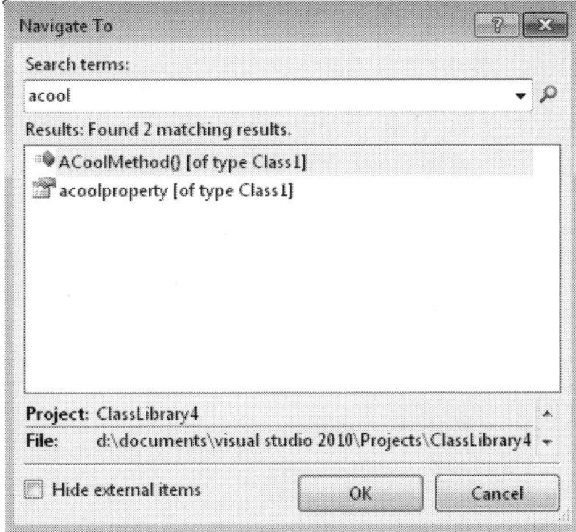

Notice that the search is *not* case-specific. However, you might notice a surprise in this dialog box. Watch what happens when you put in **ACM**:

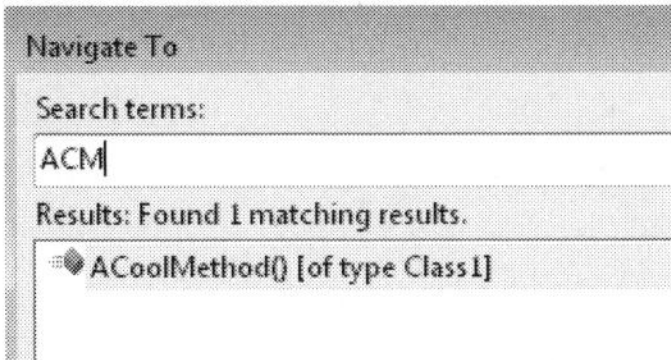

It pays attention to Pascal Case. There is also summary information at the bottom of this dialog box:

You're probably wondering about the Hide External Items option as well. When selected, only the local project is examined for symbols, instead of your project *plus* every library you reference.

Also, notice that the Navigate To syntax does not support special logic or special characters such as the following:

- Wildcard matching
- Boolean logic operators
- Regular expressions

05.14 Understanding Find Symbol

DEFAULT	Alt+F12
VISUAL BASIC 6	Alt+F12
VISUAL C# 2005	Alt+F12
VISUAL C++ 2	Alt+F12; Ctrl+F11; Ctrl+Alt+F11
VISUAL C++ 6	Alt+F12; Ctrl+Shift+Y
VISUAL STUDIO 6	Alt+F12
WINDOWS	Alt,E, F, Y
MENU	Edit | Find and Replace | Find Symbol
COMMAND	Edit.FindSymbol
VERSIONS	2005, 2008, 2010
CODE	vstipFind0011

You can quickly search for symbols (objects, definitions, and references) by using the Find Symbol dialog box (Alt+F12):

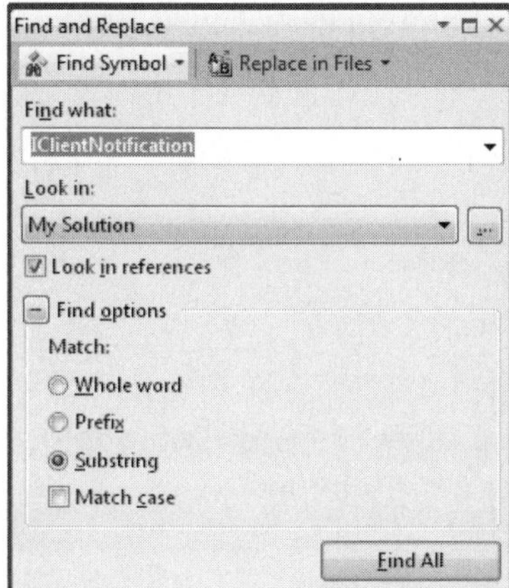

Find What

This is pretty straightforward; you just type in the search string you are looking for.

Note You can also get to Find Symbol by using any shortcut to get to the Find and Replace dialog box and selecting Find Symbol from the drop-down list in the upper-right corner.

Look In

This indicates where you want to look:

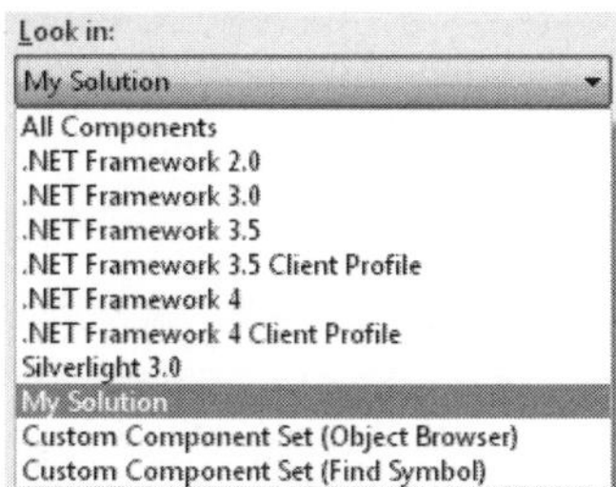

As you can see, the Look In dialog box has a number of search options.

All Components

Includes the current solution and its referenced components, all of the .NET Framework, and any components that you have added.

Framework X / Silverlight X

Searches specific versions of the Framework for a symbol.

My Solution

Searches the current open solution.

Custom Component Set (Object Browser)

Searches the predefined custom component set in the Object Browser. See vstipTool0078 ("The Object Browser: Browsing Scope," page 358) for more information.

Custom Component Set (Find Symbol)

Searches the custom component set defined in this dialog box. You edit the list of components by clicking the ellipsis in the dialog box:

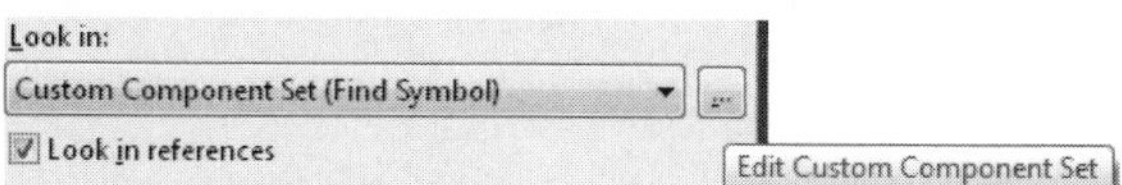

The Edit Custom Component Set dialog box allows you to pick components from a variety of areas to have a specialized search experience when looking for symbols. It allows for a very refined search capability:

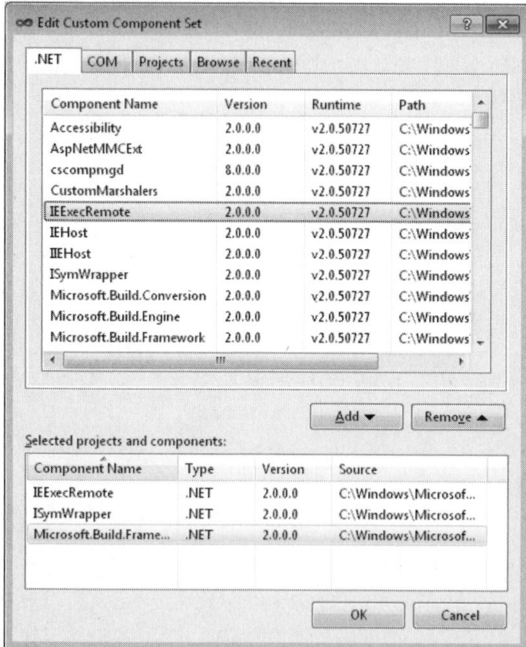

Look In References

Displays references in the projects within the current browsing scope.

Find Options

Match

Sets criteria for the search string when finding matches.

Whole Word

Finds the complete word only, not partial matches.

Prefix

Finds results where the search string is at the beginning of the result.

Substring

Finds results where the search string is anywhere in the result.

Match Case

Finds only results that exactly match the case of the search string.

Find All

Initiates the search based on the criteria that has been set.

Search Results

When you run a search, the results look something like this:

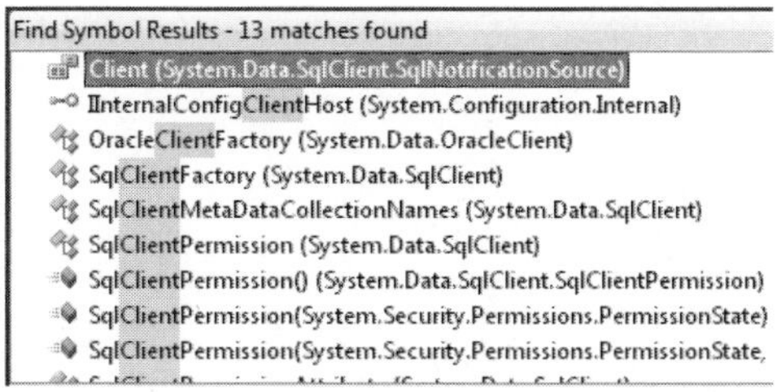

The icons to the left of each entry indicate what type of symbol you are looking at in the results. For a complete list of icons and their meanings, see vstipTool0076 ("Class View and Object Browser Icons," in Appendix B [*http://go.microsoft.com/FWLink/?Linkid=223758*]) for more information.

Additionally, you can use F8 or Shift+F8 to navigate forward or backward through the results while automatically showing the location of the result as you proceed.

05.15 Find Symbol Results Shortcuts

DEFAULT	F12 (go to definition); Ctrl+F12 (go to declaration); Shift+F12 (find all references); Ctrl+C (copy); Ctrl+Insert (copy);
VISUAL BASIC 6	F12 (go to definition); Shift+F2 (go to definition); Ctrl+F12 (go to declaration); Alt+F2 (find all references); Ctrl+C (copy); Ctrl+Insert (copy);
VISUAL C# 2005	F12 (go to definition); Ctrl+F12 (go to declaration); Shift+F12 (find all references); Ctrl+K, Ctrl+R (find all references); Ctrl+K, R (find all references); Ctrl+C (copy); Ctrl+Insert (copy);
VISUAL C++ 2	F11 (go to definition); Alt+F1 (go to definition); [no shortcut] (find all references); Ctrl+C (copy); Ctrl+Insert (copy);
VISUAL C++ 6	F12 (go to definition); Ctrl+F12 (go to declaration); Ctrl+Alt+F12 (go to declaration); [no shortcut] (find all references); Ctrl+C (copy); Ctrl+Insert (copy);
VISUAL STUDIO 6	[no shortcut] (go to definition); Ctrl+F12 (go to declaration); [no shortcut] (find all references); Ctrl+C (copy); Ctrl+Insert (copy);
WINDOWS	Alt,E, C (copy)
MENU	Edit | Copy
COMMAND	Edit.GoToDefinition; Edit.GoToDeclaration; Edit.FindAllReferences;View.BrowseDefinition;Edit.Copy;Edit.ClearAll
VERSIONS	2005, 2008, 2010
CODE	vstipFind0012

To locate any symbol, you can quickly leverage a series of commands to help you. The nice thing about these commands is that many of them work both in the Find Symbol Results window and in the code editor.

Go To Definition (F12)

This command takes you to the definition of the symbol in your code, if one is available.

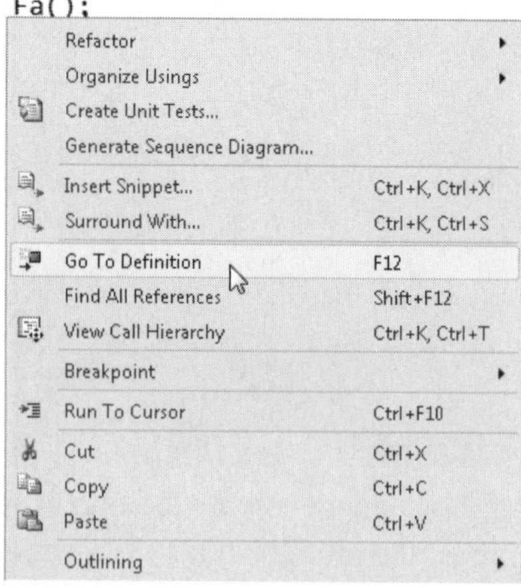

```
public void Fa()
{
    So();
}
```

Go To Declaration (Ctrl+F12)

Note The information in this section applies to C++ only.

This command takes you to the declaration of the symbol in your code, if one is available.

Go To Reference (Shift+F12)

This command works for any symbol:

This command finds all references to that symbol:

Find Symbol Results - 9 matches found

C:\Users\zainnab\Documents\Visual Studio 2010\Projects\TailSpinToys\Main\Tailspin.
C:\Users\zainnab\Documents\Visual Studio 2010\Projects\TailSpinToys\Main\Tailspin.
C:\Users\zainnab\Documents\Visual Studio 2010\Projects\TailSpinToys\Main\Tailspin.
C:\Users\zainnab\Documents\Visual Studio 2010\Projects\TailSpinToys\Main\Tailspin.
C:\Users\zainnab\Documents\Visual Studio 2010\Projects\TailSpinToys\Main\Tailspin.
C:\Users\zainnab\Documents\Visual Studio 2010\Projects\TailSpinToys\Main\Tailspin.
C:\Users\zainnab\Documents\Visual Studio 2010\Projects\TailSpinToys\Main\Tailspin.
C:\Users\zainnab\Documents\Visual Studio 2010\Projects\TailSpinToys\Main\Tailspin.
C:\Users\zainnab\Documents\Visual Studio 2010\Projects\TailSpinToys\Main\Tailspin.

If you are using the Find Symbol Results window, you can make this much easier by simply expanding a node in the window. It automatically shows all references:

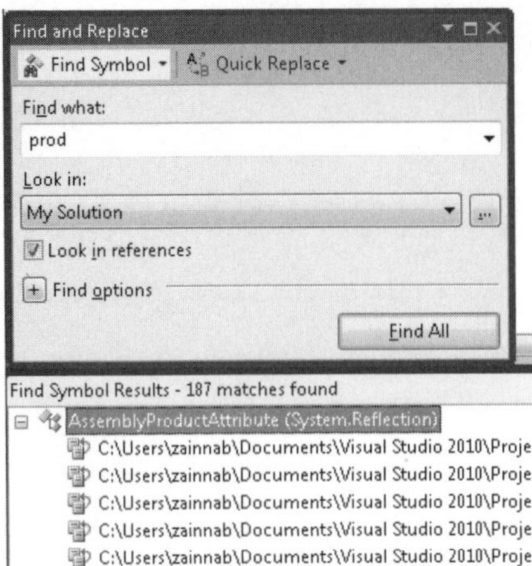

If no references are found, it tells you that also:

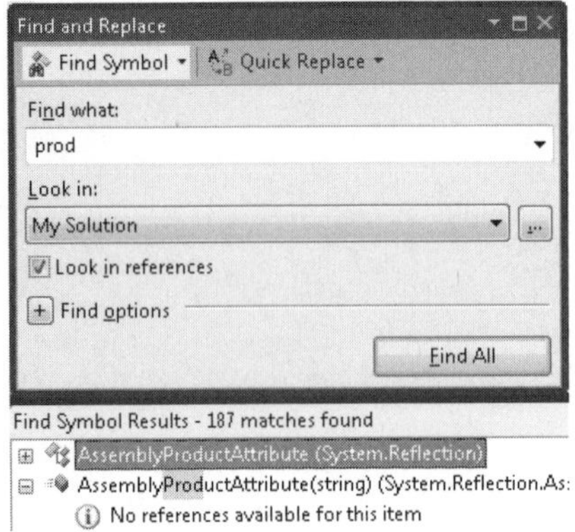

Browse Definition

For any symbol in your results, simply right-click and choose Browse Definition:

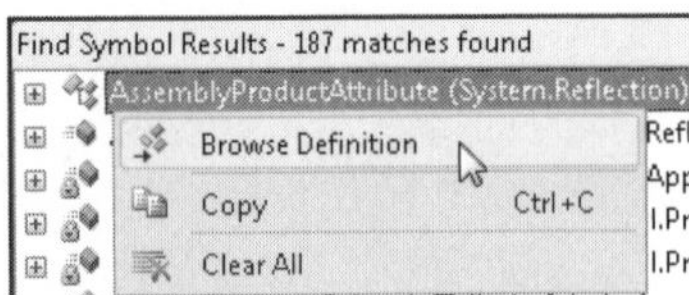

Clicking Browse Definition takes you to the primary node (typically top level) for the symbol in the Object Browser, which can be particularly useful for deeper examination:

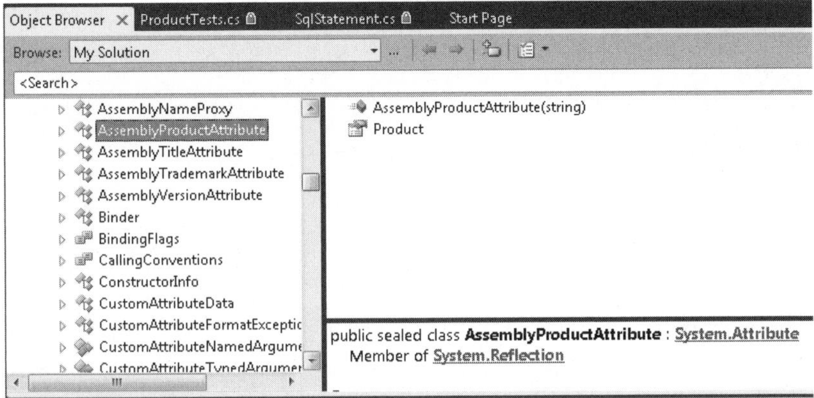

Copy (Ctrl+C)

Allows you to copy the fully qualified name for the selected symbol to the clipboard. You can then paste the code as text into the code editor.

Clear All

Clears the Find Symbol Results window.

05.16 Replace in Files: Tagged Expressions

DEFAULT	Ctrl+Shift+H
VISUAL BASIC 6	Ctrl+Shift+H
VISUAL C# 2005	Ctrl+Shift+H
VISUAL C++ 2	Ctrl+Shift+H
VISUAL C++ 6	Ctrl+Shift+H
VISUAL STUDIO 6	Ctrl+Shift+H
WINDOWS	Alt,E, F, S
MENU	Edit | Find and Replace | Replace in Files
COMMAND	Edit.ReplaceinFiles
VERSIONS	2005, 2008, 2010
CODE	vstipFind0016

As mentioned in vstipFind0015 ("Replace In Files: Basic Options," page 192), the Replace With area is the most interesting piece of the Replace In Files dialog box. It can be as simple as a literal string replacement:

Under normal situations, this is just the literal text you want to use as a replacement for the Find What text. However, suppose you choose to use regular expressions:

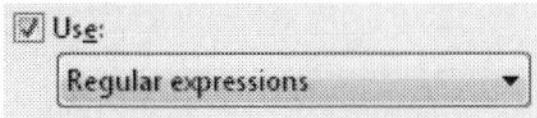

This enables the Expression Builder:

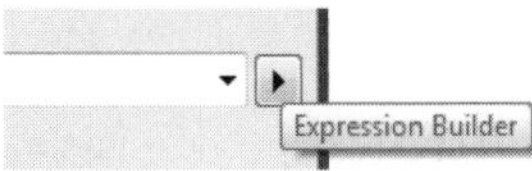

These options are *not* like the builder options you get in the Find What area:

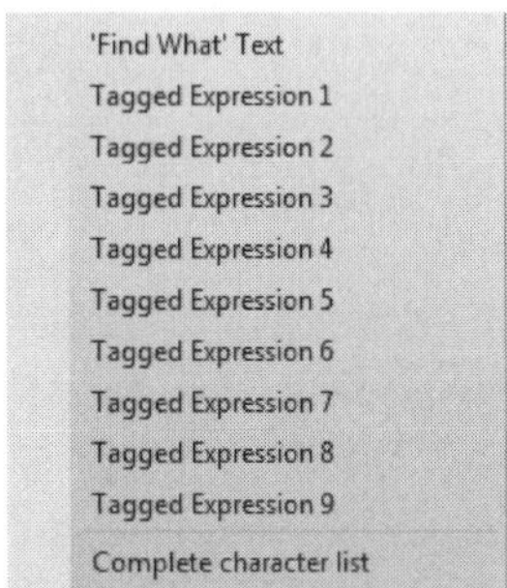

In addition to being able to use any of the regular expression characters, you can refer to the original text and any tagged expressions.

Example

The best way to show how tagged expressions work is with an example. Let's assume you have the following text:

```
static void Main(string[] args)
{
    // bubbajones
    // bubbajones
    // bubbajones
    // bubbajones
    // bubbajones
    // bubbajones
}
```

And you use the following options:

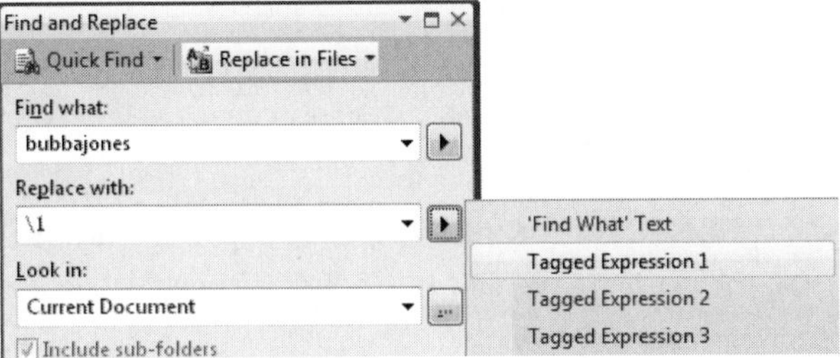

Notice the curly brackets around "jones"? That denotes a tagged expression. Every time you use the brackets, it creates a tagged expression that is numbered (beginning with 1). So, in this example, we are looking for "bubba{jones}" and replacing it with tagged expression 1 (which is just "jones"). Also, notice the notation used to refer to the tagged expression: \n, where n is the tagged expression we want.

When I do my replacements, this is the result:

```
static void Main(string[] args)
{
    // jones
    // jones
    // jones
    // jones
    // jones
    // jones
}
```

We can take this further. Now we want to turn "bubbajones" into "jonesbubba," so we can use the following settings:

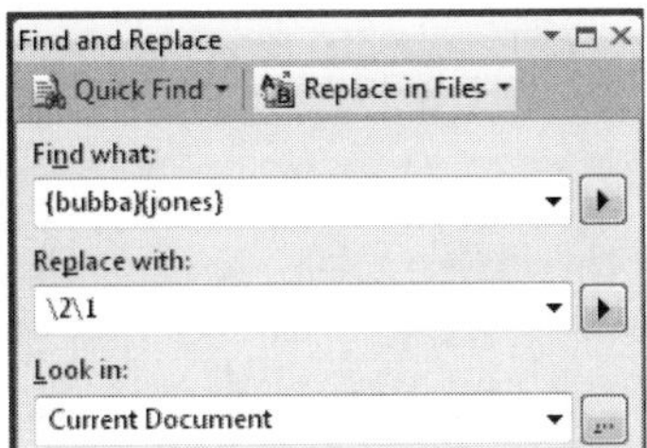

So now we are looking for "{bubba}{jones}," which creates tagged expression 1 ("bubba") and tagged expression 2 ("jones"). At this point, it's simply a matter of replacing with the expressions switched around ("\2\1"), and we get the following:

```
static void Main(string[] args)
{
    // bubbajones
    // bubbajones
    // bubbajones
    // bubbajones
    // bubbajones
    // bubbajones
}
```

Of course, this can get much more complex when using regular expressions, so you definitely need to spend some time learning how to fully leverage these features.

05.17 Customize Results in Find In Files Searches

DEFAULT	Ctrl+Shift+F
VISUAL BASIC 6	Ctrl+Shift+F
VISUAL C# 2005	Ctrl+Shift+F
VISUAL C++ 2	Ctrl+Shift+F
VISUAL C++ 6	Ctrl+Shift+F
VISUAL STUDIO 6	[no shortcut]
WINDOWS	Alt,E, F, I
MENU	Edit | Find and Replace | Find in Files
COMMAND	Edit.FindinFiles
VERSIONS	2005, 2008, 2010
CODE	vstipFind0002

You can customize your Find In Files results to just about any format you can imagine. For example, let's say you don't want to view the entire file path shown in the Find Results tool window:

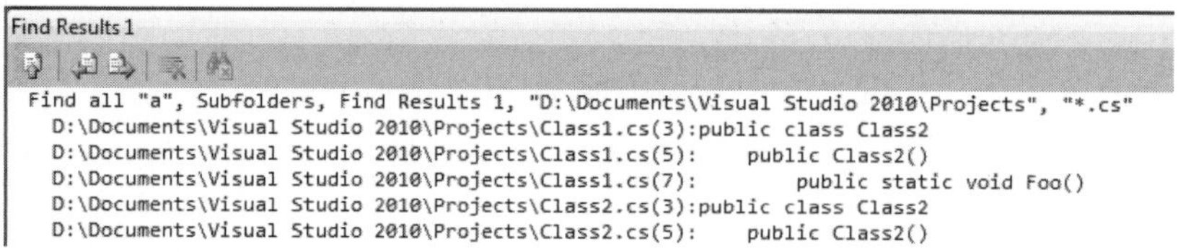

```
Find Results 1
Find all "a", Subfolders, Find Results 1, "D:\Documents\Visual Studio 2010\Projects", "*.cs"
  D:\Documents\Visual Studio 2010\Projects\Class1.cs(3):public class Class2
  D:\Documents\Visual Studio 2010\Projects\Class1.cs(5):    public Class2()
  D:\Documents\Visual Studio 2010\Projects\Class1.cs(7):        public static void Foo()
  D:\Documents\Visual Studio 2010\Projects\Class2.cs(3):public class Class2
  D:\Documents\Visual Studio 2010\Projects\Class2.cs(5):    public Class2()
```

Instead, you want this:

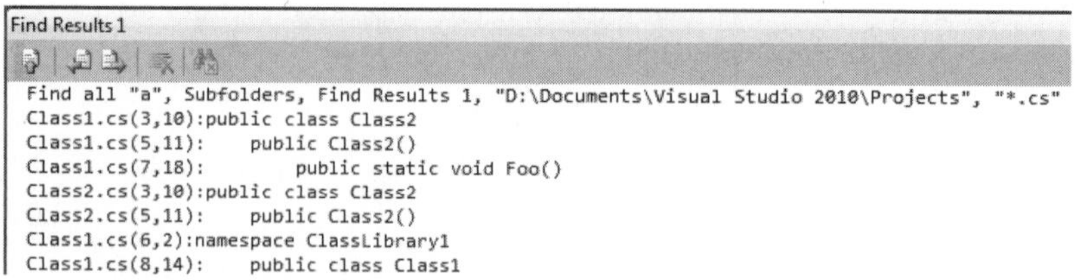

```
Find Results 1
Find all "a", Subfolders, Find Results 1, "D:\Documents\Visual Studio 2010\Projects", "*.cs"
Class1.cs(3,10):public class Class2
Class1.cs(5,11):    public Class2()
Class1.cs(7,18):        public static void Foo()
Class2.cs(3,10):public class Class2
Class2.cs(5,11):    public Class2()
Class1.cs(6,2):namespace ClassLibrary1
Class1.cs(8,14):    public class Class1
```

You can easily make this change. Just follow these instructions:

Warning This involves modifying the registry, so use this tip at your own risk.

1. Open RegEdit.exe.
2. Go to HKEY_CURRENT_USER\Software\Microsoft\VisualStudio\<version>\Find.
3. Add a new string called Find Result Format, with a value of fe($l,$c):$t\r\n.

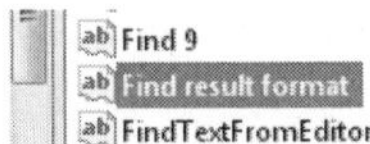

REG_SZ person.vb
REG_SZ fe($l,$c):$t\r\n
REG_SZ 1

4. In Visual Studio, run a Find In Files search.

Note You do not need to restart Visual Studio to see the changes made in the registry, which is great for testing different string combinations.

Variables

For your reference, the following are valid values you can use when creating your own custom values.

Files

- **$p** path
- **$f** filename
- **$v** drive/unc share
- **$d** directory
- **$n** name
- ***$e*** .extension

Location

- **$l** line
- **$c** col
- **$x** end col if on first line, else end of first line
- **$L** span end line
- **$C** span end col

Text

- **$0** matched text
- **$t** text of first line
- **$s** summary of hit
- **$T** text of spanned lines

Char

- **\n** newline
- **\s** space
- **\t** tab
- **** backslash
- **\$** $

Chapter 6

Writing Code

"We will never be rid of code, because code represents the details of the requirements. At some level those details cannot be ignored or abstracted; they have to be specified. And specifying requirements in such detail that a machine can execute them is programming. Such a specification is code."

—Robert C. Martin, "Clean Code: A Handbook of Agile Software Craftsmanship"

Writing code and debugging code are the two activities we tend to do more than any other as developers. It's no accident that this chapter is one of the two largest in the book. Within these pages, you'll find tips from older versions all the way through to the great new features in Visual Studio 2010. Really take your time to absorb the material here, and find those pieces that are most relevant to your situation.

As you are reading, make sure to pay particular attention to the new IntelliSense and box selection improvements. In my travels, thousands of people have found these particularly useful for daily work. Also, take some time to review the tips on code snippets and discover how they can accelerate your code writing.

06.01 Zoom In or Out of Text in the Editor Using the Mouse Wheel

WINDOWS	Ctrl,Mouse Wheel
COMMAND	View.ZoomIn; View.ZoomOut
VERSIONS	2010
CODE	vstipEdit0002

The editor has a new feature that allows you to instantly change the zoom factor of text. It's particularly useful for pair programming and doing code demos for your team. Just hold down your Ctrl key and use the wheel on your mouse to zoom in or out.

```
using System;
using System.Collec
using System.Linq;
using System.Text;
```

```
using System;
using System.Colle
using System.Linq;
using System.Text;
```

If you don't like this feature, you can disable it by installing an extension called "Disable Mouse Wheel Zoom," which you can find at *http://visualstudiogallery.msdn.microsoft.com/en-us/d088791c-150a-4834-8f28-462696a82bb8?SRC=VSIDE.*

06.02 Zoom In or Out of Text in the Editor

DEFAULT	Ctrl+Shift+> (zoom in); Ctrl+Shift+< (zoom out)
VISUAL BASIC 6	Ctrl+Shift+> (zoom in); Ctrl+Shift+< (zoom out)
VISUAL C# 2005	Ctrl+Shift+> (zoom in); Ctrl+Shift+< (zoom out)
VISUAL C++ 2	Ctrl+Shift+> (zoom in); Ctrl+Shift+< (zoom out)
VISUAL C++ 6	Ctrl+Shift+> (zoom in); Ctrl+Shift+< (zoom out)
VISUAL STUDIO 6	Ctrl+Shift+> (zoom in); Ctrl+Shift+< (zoom out)
WINDOWS	[no shortcut]
COMMAND	View.ZoomIn; View.ZoomOut
VERSIONS	2010
CODE	vstipEdit0003

In vstipEdit0002, "Zoom In or Out of Text in the Editor Using the Mouse Wheel," on page 209, I showed you how to use the mouse to zoom in and out of your text. Now I'll show you two additional ways to accomplish this goal.

Combo Box

First, you can change the zoom factor for text by using the Zoom combo box in the lower-left corner of the editor. Simply choose a pre-determined size, or type in a value of your own. To my knowledge there is no keyboard shortcut for getting to this area.

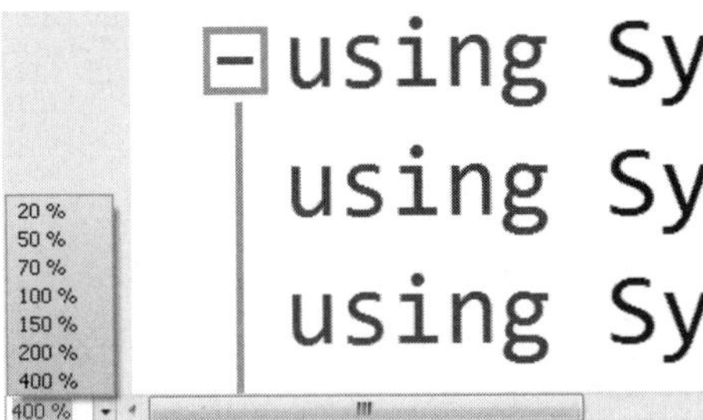

Keyboard

Second, you can use the keyboard shortcuts Ctrl+Shift+Greater Than (>), to zoom in, and Ctrl+Shift+Less Than (<), to zoom out.

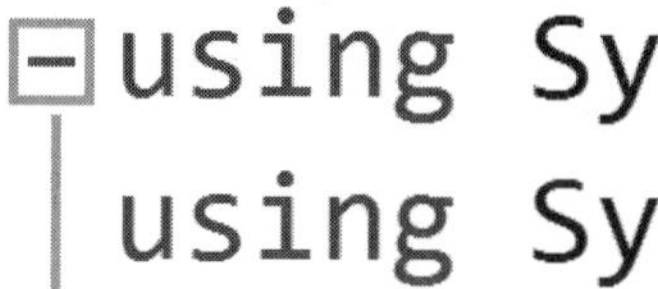

Universal Zoom

The zoom factor is per tab and doesn't apply across each file, so you need to manually set it on each tab. Alternatively, you can use an extension called "Presentation Zoom," located at *http://visualstudiogallery.msdn.microsoft.com/en-us/6a7a0b57-7059-470d-bcfa-60ceb78dc752?SRC=VSIDE*.

06.03 How to Keep from Accidentally Copying a Blank Line

WINDOWS	Alt,T, O
MENU	Tools | Options | Text Editor | All Languages | General
VERSIONS	2005, 2008, 2010
CODE	vstipEdit0004

Ever cut something and accidentally cut a blank line? I can't really think of a good reason to cut or copy just a blank line, and yet you are still allowed to do it.

The good news is that you can keep this from ever happening again by simply going to Tools | Options | Text Editor | All Languages | General and clearing the Apply Cut Or Copy Commands To Blank Lines When There Is No Selection check box.

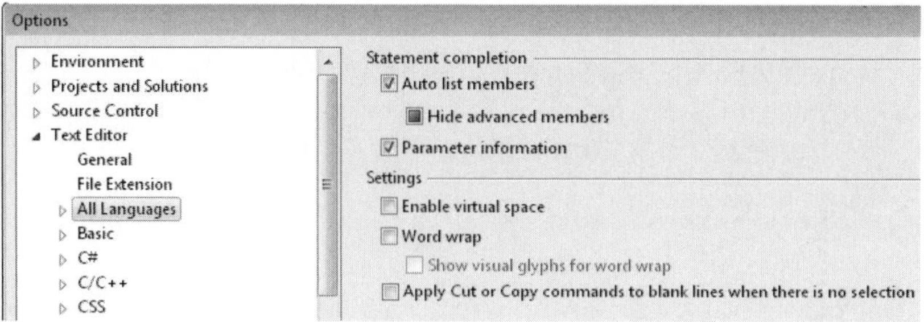

06.04 Make IntelliSense Transparent

WINDOWS	Ctrl
VERSIONS	2008, 2010
CODE	vstipEdit0077

Sometimes when you are writing code, you find yourself in a situation where IntelliSense is covering up something you want to see, as shown in the following illustration.

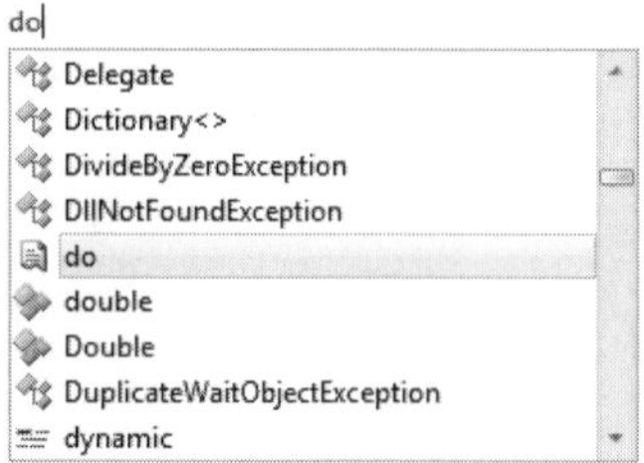

You can make it temporarily transparent simply by pressing and holding the Ctrl key.

```
do
{
    Console.WriteLine("Best Doctor");
    Console.WriteLine("David Tennant");
    Console.WriteLine("Don't blink ;-)");
} while (true);
```

Using this tip, you don't have to get rid of IntelliSense, look at the code, and then bring IntelliSense back. Just press the Ctrl key, get the information you need, and move on.

06.05 Cut or Delete the Current Line

DEFAULT	Ctrl+L (cut line); Ctrl+Shift+L (delete line); Shift+Del (cut line); Ctrl+X (cut line)
VISUAL BASIC 6	Ctrl+Y (cut line); [no shortcut] (delete line); Shift+Del (cut line); Ctrl+X (cut line)
VISUAL C# 2005	Ctrl+Y (cut line); Ctrl+Shift+L (delete line); Shift+Del (cut line); Ctrl+X (cut line)
VISUAL C++ 2	Ctrl+Y (cut line); Ctrl+L (cut line); Ctrl+Shift+L (delete line); Shift+Del (cut line); Ctrl+X (cut line); Ctrl+Alt+W (cut line)
VISUAL C++ 6	Ctrl+L (cut line); Shift+Alt+L (cut line); Ctrl+Shift+L (delete line); Shift+Del (cut line); Ctrl+X (cut line)
VISUAL STUDIO 6	Ctrl+M (cut line); Ctrl+L (cut line); Ctrl+Shift+L (delete line); Ctrl+Shift+M (delete line); Shift+Del (cut line); Ctrl+X (cut line)
WINDOWS	Alt,E, T
MENU	Edit | Cut
COMMAND	Edit.LineCut; Edit.LineDelete; Edit.Cut
VERSIONS	2005, 2008, 2010
CODE	vstipEdit0038

You will often find times when you want to cut a line to be pasted somewhere else or just delete a line entirely. Let's take a look at how you can quickly cut or delete any line.

Regardless of what you are trying to do, begin by placing your cursor inside the line anywhere:

```
throw new ArgumentException("userName");
```

Cut

If you want to cut the line for use somewhere else, perform one of the following actions:

- Press Ctrl+L to cut the line; this uses the Edit.LineCut command.
- Press Shift+Del or Ctrl+X to cut the line using the Edit.Cut command.

There is no difference in the result just two different commands for accomplishing the same task.

Delete

If you want to delete the line instead, you can use Ctrl+Shift+L to have it permanently removed from your code.

06.06 Using the New IntelliSense: Keywords

DEFAULT	Ctrl+J
VISUAL BASIC 6	Ctrl+J
VISUAL C# 2005	Ctrl+J Ctrl+K, L Ctrl+K, Ctrl+L
VISUAL C++ 2	Ctrl+J Ctrl+Alt+T
VISUAL C++ 6	Ctrl+J Ctrl+Alt+T
VISUAL STUDIO 6	Ctrl+J
WINDOWS	Alt,E, I, L
MENU	Edit | IntelliSense | List Members
COMMAND	Edit.ListMembers
VERSIONS	2010
LANGUAGES	VB, C#
CODE	vstipEdit0016

The one feature we use more than just about anything else in Visual Studio is IntelliSense. It has been our friend for many years. Well, it just got friendlier. To show you the new features, let's take a closer look at Visual Studio 2008 IntelliSense. Notice what happens when you type **Console.Key**:

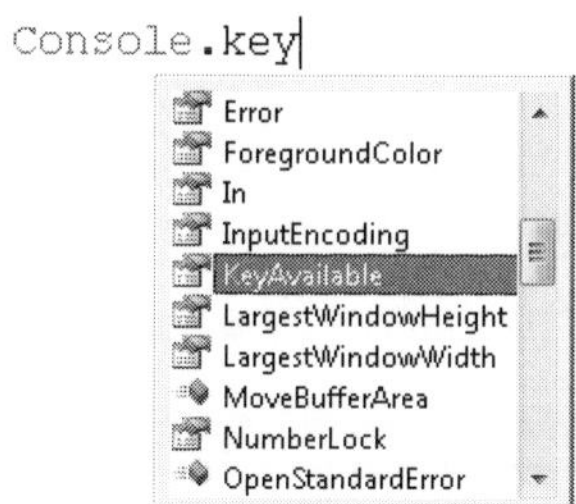

It does what you would expect it to do and highlights the first (in this case, *only*) item that *begins with* the word "Key" in a huge alphabetical list of item names. That's great, but what if you don't know what you are looking for but you do know that it has the word "Key" somewhere in it? Well, you can go search in the Object Browser, of course, or better yet, you can use the new IntelliSense in Visual Studio 2010. Look what happens when you do the same thing in Visual Studio 2010:

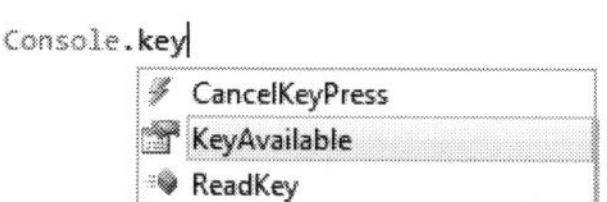

It now shows only those items that have the word "Key" in them and doesn't care where the word is in the name of the member. This results in a significantly smaller list of items in IntelliSense and an easier way to find names even if you don't know what they begin with.

06.07 Using the New IntelliSense: Pascal Case

DEFAULT	Ctrl+J
VISUAL BASIC 6	Ctrl+J
VISUAL C# 2005	Ctrl+J Ctrl+K, L Ctrl+K, Ctrl+L
VISUAL C++ 2	Ctrl+J Ctrl+Alt+T
VISUAL C++ 6	Ctrl+J Ctrl+Alt+T
VISUAL STUDIO 6	Ctrl+J
WINDOWS	Alt,E, I, L
MENU	Edit | IntelliSense | List Members
COMMAND	Edit.ListMembers
VERSIONS	2010
LANGUAGES	VB, C#
CODE	vstipEdit0017

Have you ever been in a situation where you wanted to use IntelliSense to get a method but you're faced with a *ton* of methods that start with same word, meaning that you have to type almost the entire method name?

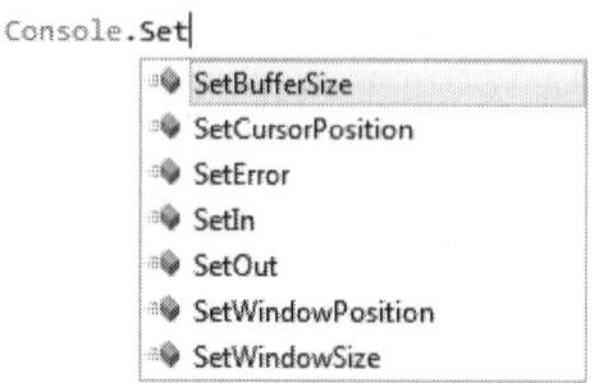

Well, those days are over. Let's say you want the SetWindowSize method, but you really, really don't want to type it out or even scroll down to get the method. IntelliSense now supports Pascal case. All you have to do is type **SWS**, and you are all set:

```
Console.SWS
```

SetWindowSize

What if you don't remember all the uppercase letters in a name? No problem. Just type what you know (they don't even have to be in the correct order), and IntelliSense narrows the list down for you:

```
Console.SW
```

SetWindowPosition
SetWindowSize

06.08 Comment and Uncomment in Web Pages

DEFAULT	Ctrl+K, Ctrl+C (comment); Ctrl+K, Ctrl+U (uncomment)
VISUAL BASIC 6	Ctrl+K, Ctrl+C (comment); Ctrl+K, Ctrl+U (uncomment)
VISUAL C# 2005	Ctrl+K, Ctrl+C (comment); Ctrl+E, Ctrl+C (comment); Ctrl +E, C (comment); Ctrl+K, Ctrl+U (uncomment)
VISUAL C++ 2	[no shortcut]
VISUAL C++ 6	Ctrl+K, Ctrl+C (comment); Ctrl+K, Ctrl+U (uncomment)
VISUAL STUDIO 6	Ctrl+K, Ctrl+C (comment); Ctrl+K, Ctrl+U (uncomment)
WINDOWS	Alt,E, V, M (comment) Alt,E, V, E (uncomment)
MENU	Edit | Advanced | Comment Selection; Edit | Advanced | Uncomment Selection
COMMAND	Edit.CommentSelection; Edit.UncommentSelection
VERSIONS	2005, 2008, 2010
CODE	vstipEdit0083

By now, you probably know that you can comment and uncomment your code, but did you know that you can do the same thing with your source during web development? Just put your cursor inside any element you want commented, as shown in the following illustration.

```
<h2>
    Welcome to ASP.NET!
</h2>
```

Comment

Now just press Ctrl+K, Ctrl+C to comment out the selection.

```
<%--<h2>
    Welcome to ASP.NET!
</h2>--%>
```

Of course, you can also select multiple elements:

```
<p>
    To learn more about 
</p>
<p>
    You can also find <a
        title="MSDN ASP.
</p>
```

And you can comment them out too:

```
<%--<p>
    To learn
</p>
<p>
    You can
        titl
</p>--%>
```

Uncomment

Naturally, you can put your cursor inside any commented area:

```
<%--<p>
    To learn
</p>
<p>
    You can
        titl
</p>--%>
```

And you can uncomment that area by pressing Ctrl+K, Ctrl+U:

```
<p>
    To learn
</p>
<p>
    You can
        titl
</p>
```

06.09 Insert a Blank Line Above or Below the Current Line

DEFAULT	Ctrl+Enter (line above); Ctrl+Shift+Enter (line below)
VISUAL BASIC 6	Ctrl+Enter (line above); Ctrl+Shift+Enter (line below)
VISUAL C# 2005	Ctrl+Enter (line above); Ctrl+Shift+Enter (line below)
VISUAL C++ 2	Ctrl+Enter (line above); Ctrl+Shift+Enter (line below)
VISUAL C++ 6	Ctrl+Enter (line above); Ctrl+Shift+Enter (line below)
VISUAL STUDIO 6	Ctrl+Enter (line above); Ctrl+Shift+Enter (line below)
WINDOWS	[no shortcut]
COMMAND	Edit.LineOpenAbove; Edit.LineOpenBelow
VERSIONS	2005, 2008, 2010
CODE	vstipEdit0005

This is a great feature for adding extra white space when you need it. Go to any line in the editor, and press Ctrl+Enter to insert a blank line above or press Ctrl+Shift+Enter to insert a blank line below the current line, as shown in the following illustration.

```
// i love public tips and tricks

public int x = 10;

public int y = 30;
```

06.10 Transpose Lines, Words, and Characters

DEFAULT	Alt+Shift+T (line); Ctrl+Shift+T (word); Ctrl+T (character)
VISUAL BASIC 6	Alt+Shift+T (line); Ctrl+Shift+T (word); [no shortcut] (character)
VISUAL C# 2005	Alt+Shift+T (line); Ctrl+Shift+T (word); Ctrl+T (character)
VISUAL C++ 2	Alt+Shift+T (line); Ctrl+Shift+T (word); Ctrl+T (character)
VISUAL C++ 6	Alt+Shift+T (line); Ctrl+Shift+T (word); Ctrl+T (character)
VISUAL STUDIO 6	Alt+Shift+T (line); Ctrl+Shift+T (word); Ctrl+T (character)
WINDOWS	[no shortcut]
COMMAND	Edit.LineTranspose; Edit.WordTranspose; Edit.CharTranspose
VERSIONS	2005, 2008, 2010
CODE	vstipEdit0042

Ever have a line you want to move down or switch with another line? Just find a couple of lines you want to switch, and put your cursor in the top line:

```
'seriously cool comment #2
'seriously cool comment #1
```

Then press Alt+Shift+T to transpose the two lines:

```
'seriously cool comment #1
'seriously cool comment #2
```

You can also do something similar with words. Place the cursor in the word you want to transpose:

```
'cool seriously comment
```

Press Ctrl+Shift+T:

```
'seriously cool comment
```

Just want to transpose a character? Just place the cursor to the right of the character you want to transpose:

```
'seriuosly
```

And then press Ctrl+T to transpose that character with the character at its immediate right:

```
'seriously
```

06.11 How to Cycle Through the Clipboard Ring

DEFAULT	Ctrl+Shift+V; Ctrl+Shift+Insert
VISUAL BASIC 6	Ctrl+Shift+V; Ctrl+Shift+Insert
VISUAL C# 2005	Ctrl+Shift+V; Ctrl+Shift+Insert
VISUAL C++ 2	Ctrl+Shift+V; Ctrl+Shift+Insert
VISUAL C++ 6	Ctrl+Shift+Insert
VISUAL STUDIO 6	Ctrl+Shift+V; Ctrl+Shift+Insert
WINDOWS	Alt,E, Y
MENU	Edit | Cycle Clipboard Ring
COMMAND	Edit.CycleClipboardRing
VERSIONS	2005, 2008, 2010
CODE	vstipEdit0001

The Clipboard Ring keeps track of the past 20 items you've either cut or copied so that you can reuse them over and over again. After you hit item 20, it goes back to the first item. This is why the feature is called the Clipboard Ring.

This is particularly useful when you move between several code windows and need to copy and paste different items. You can copy all of the code from the original window and then go to one of the other windows and, using the Clipboard Ring, paste all of your items.

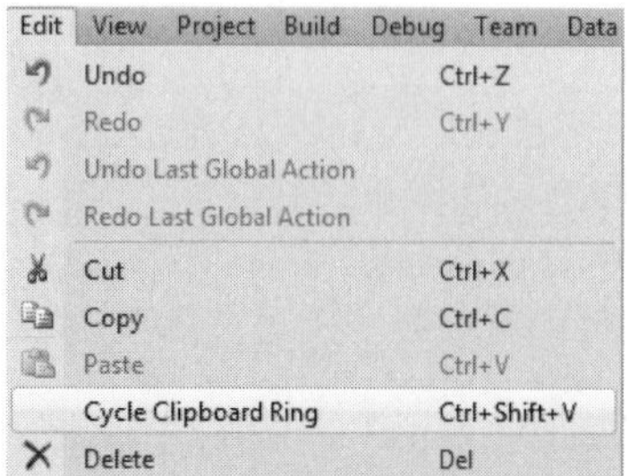

Try it out. Copy a few pieces of text into your clipboard, and then keep pressing Ctrl+Shift+V to repeat-paste them into the editor. This is one seriously cool time-saving feature. Unfortunately, there is no way to see the contents of the Clipboard Ring in Visual Studio without cycling through the list.

06.12 Using the Undo and Redo Stack

DEFAULT	Ctrl+Z (undo); Alt+Backspace (undo); Ctrl+Shift+Z (redo); Alt+Shift+Backspace (redo); Ctrl+Y (redo)
VISUAL BASIC 6	Ctrl+Shift+Z (redo); Alt+Shift+Backspace (redo)
VISUAL C# 2005	Ctrl+Z (undo); Alt+Backspace (undo); Ctrl+Shift+Z (redo); Alt+Shift+Backspace (redo); Ctrl+Y (redo)
VISUAL C++ 2	Ctrl+Shift+Z (redo); Alt+Shift+Backspace (redo); Ctrl+Y (redo); Ctrl+A
VISUAL C++ 6	Ctrl+Z (undo); Alt+Backspace (undo); Ctrl+Shift+Z (redo); Alt+Shift+Backspace (redo); Ctrl+Y (redo)
VISUAL STUDIO 6	Ctrl+Z (undo); Alt+Backspace (undo); Ctrl+Shift+Z (redo); Alt+Shift+Backspace (redo); Ctrl+Y (redo)
WINDOWS	Alt,E, U (undo); Alt,E, R (redo)
MENU	Edit | Undo; Edit | Redo
COMMAND	Edit.Undo; Edit.Redo
VERSIONS	2005, 2008, 2010
CODE	vstipEdit0045

We have all used Ctrl+Z (undo) at one time or another to fix a mistake. Did you know you don't have to press Ctrl+Z a billion times to go back to a particular action? The Undo and Redo stacks are readily available for you to use for quick, multiple undo or redo operations.

It's easy to use. Just locate the Undo and Redo section of the toolbar shown in the following illustration.

Next, click the drop-down arrow for the action you want to perform. In this case, let's look at the Undo stack:

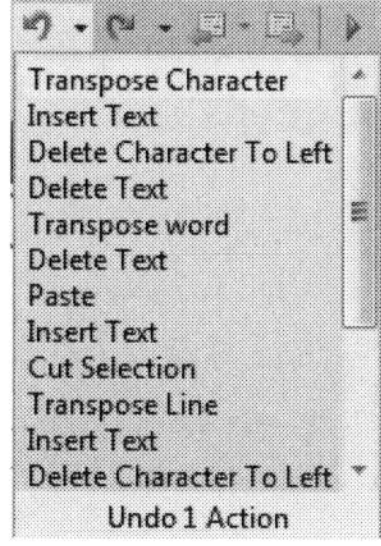

By default, it undoes only the last action. However, notice what happens when I put my mouse over the list:

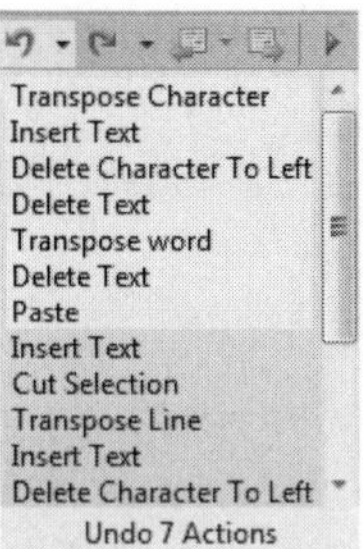

It automatically selects multiple actions to undo or redo. Also notice that it shows you at the bottom how many actions you are about to undo. When you have all the actions selected that you want to undo or redo, just click the left mouse button.

06.13 Undo and Redo Global Actions

WINDOWS	Alt,E, N (undo); Alt,E, U (redo)
MENU	Edit | Undo Last Global Action; Edit | Redo Last Global Action
COMMAND	Edit.UndoLastGlobalAction; Edit.RedoLastGlobalAction
VERSIONS	2005, 2008, 2010
CODE	vstipEdit0020

Everyone knows about undo and redo, but did you know that the Edit menu offers global versions of these actions?

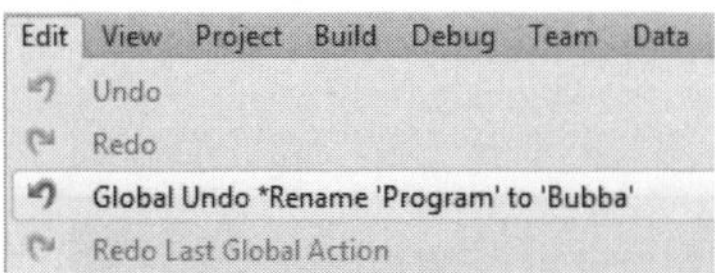

By definition, global actions impact multiple files. Global actions include renaming a class or namespace, performing a find-and-replace operation across a solution, refactoring a database, or any other action that changes multiple files.

You can apply the global undo and redo commands to actions in the current Visual Studio session, even after you close the solution that an action applies to.

06.14 How to Use Reference Highlighting

DEFAULT	Ctrl+Shift+Down Arrow (next); Ctrl+Shift+Up Arrow (previous)
VISUAL BASIC 6	Ctrl+Shift+Down Arrow (next); Ctrl+Shift+Up Arrow (previous)
VISUAL C# 2005	Ctrl+Shift+Down Arrow (next); Ctrl+Shift+Up Arrow (previous)
VISUAL C++ 2	Ctrl+Shift+Down Arrow (next); Ctrl+Shift+Up Arrow (previous)
VISUAL C++ 6	Ctrl+Shift+Down Arrow (next); Ctrl+Shift+Up Arrow (previous)
VISUAL STUDIO 6	Ctrl+Shift+Down Arrow (next); Ctrl+Shift+Up Arrow (previous)
WINDOWS	[no shortcut]
COMMAND	Edit.NextHighlightedReference; Edit.PreviousHighlightedReference
VERSIONS	2010
LANGUAGES	C#, VB
CODE	vstipEdit0010

This is absolutely one of my favorite tips because you don't have to do anything to make it work. The MSDN documentation (at *http://msdn.microsoft.com/en-us/library/ee349251.aspx*) describes reference highlighting this way:

"When you click a symbol in the Code Editor, all instances of the symbol are highlighted in the document. [...] Highlighted symbols may include declarations and references, and generally anything else that Find All References would return. This includes the names of classes, objects, variables, methods, and properties."

```
private void SomeCoolMethod()
{
    // blah
}

private void A()
{
    SomeCoolMethod();
}

private void B()
{
    SomeCoolMethod();
}

private void C()
{
    SomeCoolMethod();
}
```

Navigation

All you have to do is click in any symbol, and it automatically highlights any references in the current document. You can navigate through the highlights by using Ctrl+Shift+Down Arrow (next) or Ctrl+Shift+Up Arrow (previous).

Turning it Off

What if you don't like this feature? You can always turn it off by using following instructions, depending on whether you're working in VB or C#.

VB: Go to Tools | Options | Text Editor | Basic | VB Specific, and clear the Enable Highlighting Of References And Keywords check box.

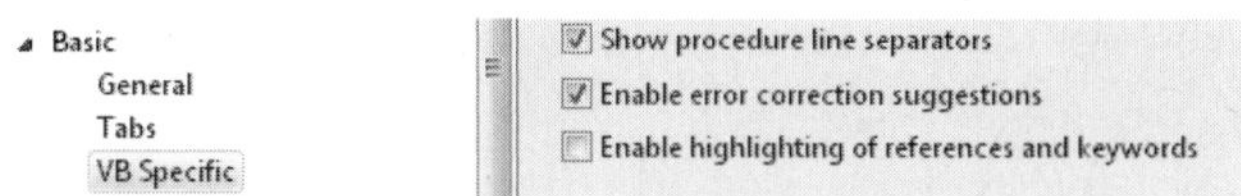

C#: Go to Tools | Options | Text Editor | C#| Advanced, and clear the Highlight References To Symbol Under Cursor check box.

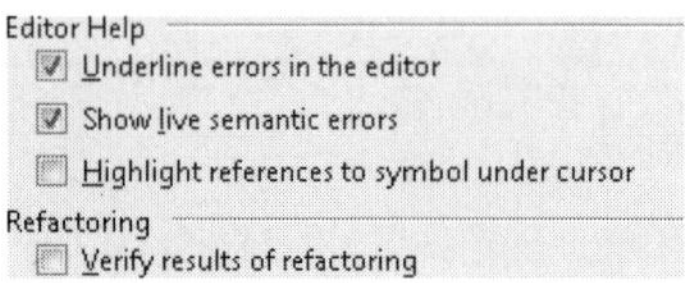

06.15 Moving or Selecting Between Matching Braces (C++, C# Only)

DEFAULT	Ctrl+] (move); Ctrl+Shift+] (select)
VISUAL BASIC 6	Ctrl+] (move); Ctrl+Shift+] (select)
VISUAL C# 2005	Ctrl+] (move); Ctrl+Shift+] (select)
VISUAL C++ 2	Ctrl+] (move); Ctrl+M (move); Ctrl+Shift+] (select); Ctrl+Shift+M (select)
VISUAL C++ 6	Ctrl+] (move); Ctrl+Shift+] (select)
VISUAL STUDIO 6	Ctrl+] (move); Ctrl+Shift+] (select)
WINDOWS	[no shortcut]
COMMAND	Edit.GotoBrace; Edit.GotoBraceExtend
VERSIONS	2005, 2008, 2010
LANGUAGES	C++, C#
CODE	vstipEdit0075

When you are working with the C* languages, you sometimes want to move to the bottom or top of a method or code block. You can quickly travel or select between matching braces by performing the following steps.

Moving

Click next to an opening or closing brace:

```
int main(array<System:
{
    Console::WriteLine
```

```
int main(array<System::String ^> ^args)
{
```

Now press Ctrl+] to go from one brace to the other one. You should find yourself easily navigating between them. This technique is very useful when you have braces far apart from each other. Also notice that the term "brace" is very loose here and applies to curly braces, square brackets, and parentheses.

Selecting

In addition to moving, you can also select everything between matching braces by pressing Ctrl+Shift+], as shown in the following illustration.

```
int main(array<System::String ^> ^args)
{
    Console::WriteLine(L"Hello World");

    DoSomething();

    return 0;
}
```

06.16 Invoke Statement Completion

DEFAULT	Ctrl+J
VISUAL BASIC 6	Ctrl+J
VISUAL C# 2005	Ctrl+J; Ctrl+K, Ctrl+L; Ctrl+K, L
VISUAL C++ 2	Ctrl+J; Ctrl+Alt+T
VISUAL C++ 6	Ctrl+J; Ctrl+Alt+T
VISUAL STUDIO 6	Ctrl+J
WINDOWS	Alt,E, I, L
MENU	Edit | IntelliSense | List Members
COMMAND	Edit.ListMembers
VERSIONS	2005, 2008, 2010
LANGUAGES	C++ (not available in VS2010), C#, VB
CODE	vstipEdit0061

This little trick is particularly useful if you lose IntelliSense and want to get it back. You can invoke statement completion from the command line by using Ctrl+J.

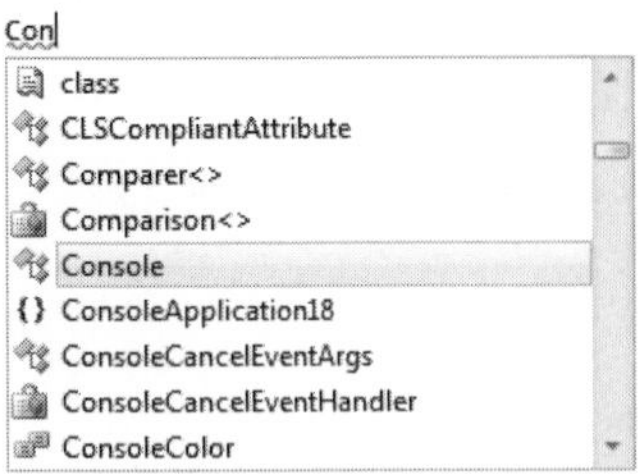

06.17 Move Between the Common Tab and All Tab in Statement Completion (VB)

DEFAULT	Alt+. (All Tab); Alt+, (Common Tab)
COMMAND	Edit.IncreaseFilterLevel; Edit.DecreaseFilterLevel
VERSIONS	2005, 2008, 2010
LANGUAGES	VB
CODE	vstipEdit0064

You don't have to take your hands off the keyboard when switching between Common and All in statement completion for Visual Basic. Just press Alt+Period (.) to go to the All tab, and press Alt+Comma (,) to go to the Common tab.

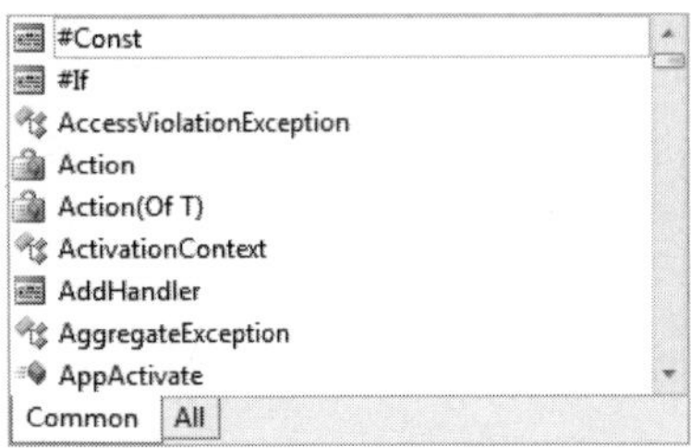

06.18 Using Parameter Information

DEFAULT	Ctrl+Shift+Space (show Parameter Info); Up or Down Arrow (move to next or previous overload)
VISUAL BASIC 6	Ctrl+Shift+Space (show Parameter Info); Ctrl+Shift+I (show Parameter Info); Up or Down Arrow (move to next or previous overload)
VISUAL C# 2005	Ctrl+Shift+Space (show Parameter Info); Ctrl+K, Ctrl+P (show Parameter Info); Ctrl+K, P (show Parameter Info); Up or Down Arrow (move to next or previous overload)
VISUAL C++ 2	Ctrl+Shift+Space (show Parameter Info); Up or Down Arrow (move to next or previous overload)
VISUAL C++ 6	Ctrl+Shift+Space (show Parameter Info); Up or Down Arrow (move to next or previous overload)
VISUAL STUDIO 6	Ctrl+Shift+Space (show Parameter Info); Ctrl+Shift+I (show Parameter Info); Up or Down Arrow (move to next or previous overload)
WINDOWS	Alt,E, I, P
MENU	Edit | IntelliSense | Parameter Info
COMMAND	Edit.ParameterInfo
VERSIONS	2005, 2008, 2010
LANGUAGES	C++ (not available in VS2010); C#, VB
CODE	vstipEdit0062

When working with a function, you automatically get parameter information, as shown in the following illustration.

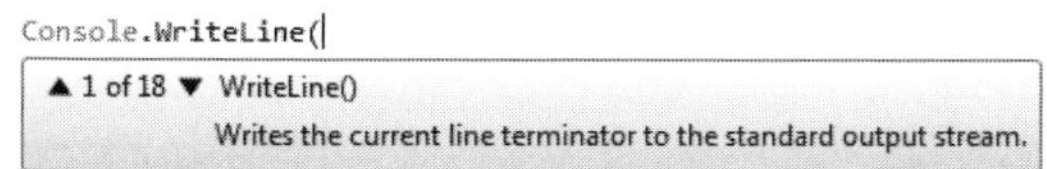

If it goes away and you want it back, you can always press Ctrl+Shift+Space.

Also notice that the function in this example has 19 overloads. You can iterate through them by pressing your Up or Down Arrow keys. If you are using your mouse, you can go forward by clicking anywhere in the parameter information area. You do not have to click the tiny up and down arrows inside the box unless you want to go backward in the list.

06.19 Using Quick Info

DEFAULT	Ctrl+K, Ctrl+I
VISUAL BASIC 6	Ctrl+K, Ctrl+I; Ctrl+I
VISUAL C# 2005	Ctrl+K, Ctrl+I; Ctrl+K, I
VISUAL C++ 2	Ctrl+T
VISUAL C++ 6	Ctrl+K, Ctrl+I
VISUAL STUDIO 6	Ctrl+K, Ctrl+I; Ctrl+I
WINDOWS	ALT,E, I, Q
MENU	Edit | IntelliSense | Quick Info
COMMAND	Edit.QuickInfo
VERSIONS	2005, 2008, 2010
LANGUAGES	C++ (not available in VS2010), C#, VB
CODE	vstipEdit0063

The Quick Info option helps you identify the details of a particular function. It comes up automatically as you type, but if it goes away, you can quickly bring it back by placing the cursor in a method and pressing Ctrl+K, Ctrl+I.

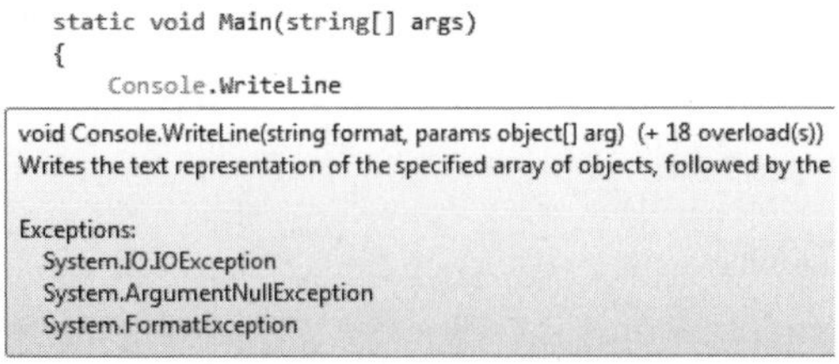

```
static void Main(string[] args)
{
    Console.WriteLine
```

void Console.WriteLine(string format, params object[] arg) (+ 18 overload(s))
Writes the text representation of the specified array of objects, followed by the

Exceptions:
System.IO.IOException
System.ArgumentNullException
System.FormatException

06.20 Word Completion

DEFAULT	Ctrl+Space; Alt+Right Arrow
VISUAL BASIC 6	Ctrl+Space; Alt+Right Arrow
VISUAL C# 2005	Ctrl+Space; Alt+Right Arrow Ctrl+K, Ctrl+W; Ctrl+K, W
VISUAL C++ 2	Ctrl+Space; Alt+Right Arrow
VISUAL C++ 6	Ctrl+Space; Alt+Right Arrow
VISUAL STUDIO 6	Ctrl+Space; Alt+Right Arrow
WINDOWS	Alt,E, I, W
MENU	Edit | IntelliSense | Complete Word
COMMAND	Edit.CompleteWord
VERSIONS	2005, 2008, 2010
LANGUAGES	C++ (not available in VS2010), C#, VB
CODE	vstipEdit0065

This one is very popular and one of the core skills to use in Visual Studio. Let's say you are typing and you have the situation shown in the following illustration.

```
Console.writel
```

You can press Ctrl+Space or Alt+Right Arrow to complete the word:

```
Console.WriteLine
```

This works only if there are no other possible matches. Suppose, for example, that you have something similar to the following:

```
Console.Wr
```

If you now press Ctrl+Space or Alt+Right Arrow to complete the word, you would just get statement completion instead.

06.21 Drag and Drop Code into the Toolbox

VERSIONS	2005, 2008, 2010
CODE	vstipTool0007

Got code you use all the time? Start using the Toolbox for more than just controls. When you are in the Editor, the Toolbox appears as shown in the following illustration.

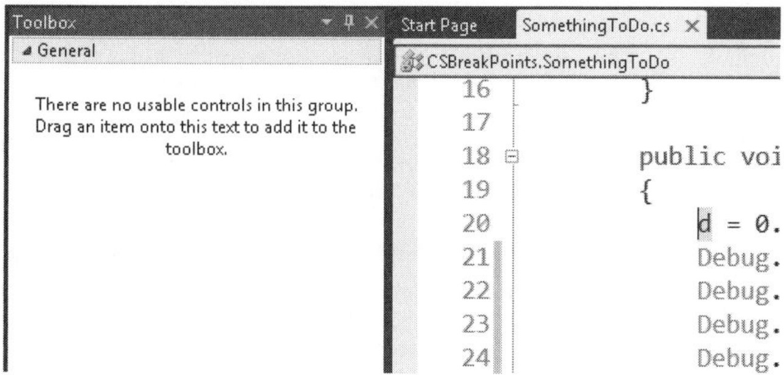

This is a vast expanse of opportunity! Just select some text from the editor, and drag it into the Toolbox and see the magic happen.

Now you have code ready to go anytime. Just place the cursor where you want the code to go, and double-click the item in your Toolbox.

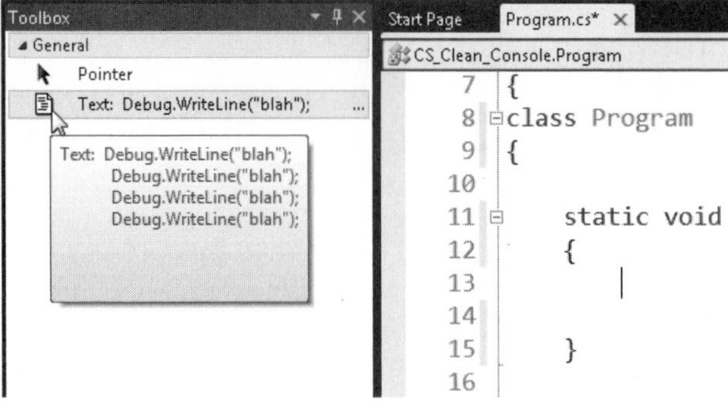

You can also click and drag where you want the code to go, as shown in the following illustration.

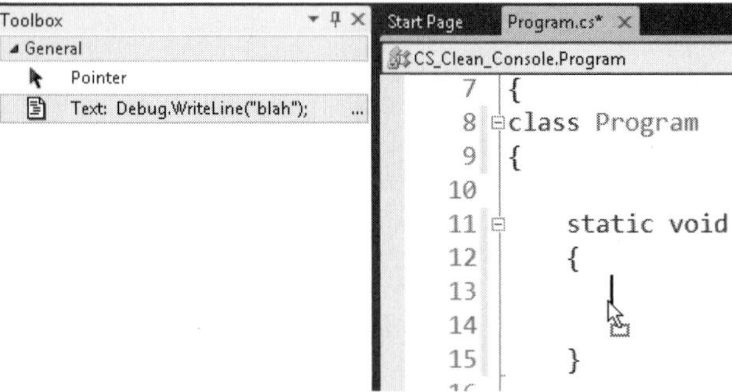

You also have a couple of extra things you can do. For example, you can rename (among other tasks) the item in the Toolbox to whatever you would like by right-clicking on it:

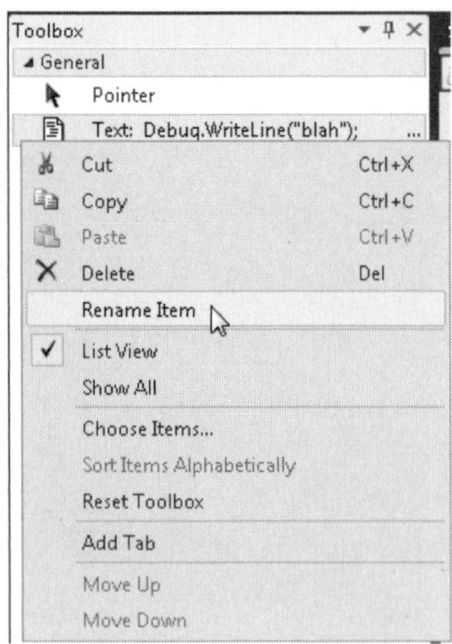

You can also create additional tabs, delete existing tabs, and rename tabs to organize the Toolbox better.

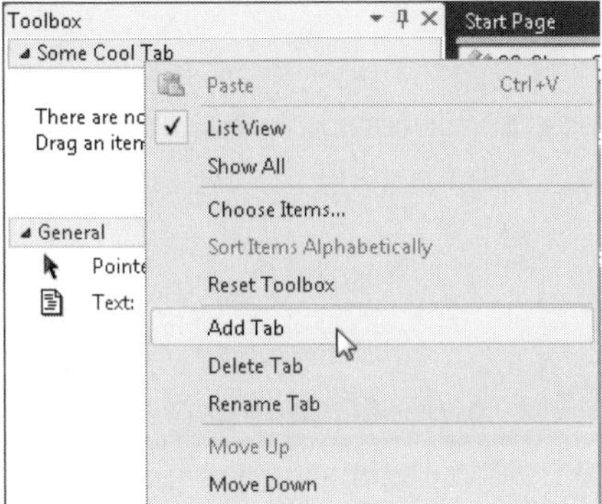

06.22 Using Smart Tags from the Keyboard

DEFAULT	Ctrl+. (period); Shift+Alt+F10
VISUAL BASIC 6	Ctrl+. (period); Shift+Alt+F10
VISUAL C# 2005	Ctrl+. (period); Shift+Alt+F10
VISUAL C++ 2	Ctrl+. (period); Shift+Alt+F10
VISUAL C++ 6	Ctrl+. (period); Shift+Alt+F10
VISUAL STUDIO 6	Ctrl+. (period); Shift+Alt+F10
WINDOWS	[no shortcut]
COMMAND	View.ShowSmartTag
VERSIONS	2008, 2010
LANGUAGES	C#, VB
CODE	vstipEdit0076

You have probably seen the smart tag indicator before. It's a blue or red bar that shows up in your code when you use certain items.

```
new Person
```

Most people just put their mouse over the line and choose the option(s) listed in the tag.

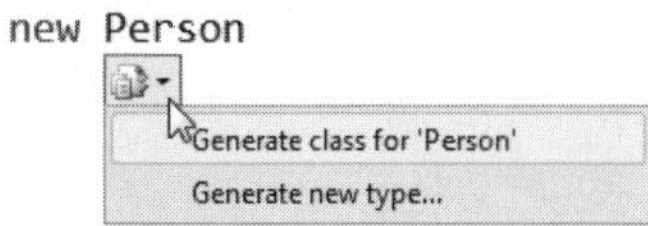

However, did you know that you can use a keyboard shortcut to bring up the options? Just press Ctrl+Period (.), and it brings up the option(s) without using the mouse.

06.23 Organize Using Statements (C# Only)

WINDOWS	Alt,E, I, [R (remove), U (sort), A (remove and sort)]
MENU	Edit | IntelliSense | Organize Usings | [Remove Unused Usings, Sort Usings, Remove and Sort]; Right Click | Organize Usings | [Remove Unused Usings, Sort Usings, Remove and Sort]
COMMAND	EditorContextMenus.CodeWindow.OrganizeUsings.[RemoveUnusedUsings, SortUsings, RemoveAndSort]
VERSIONS	2008, 2010
LANGUAGES	C#
CODE	vstipEdit0070

You can easily organize your using statements. Simply right-click anywhere in the editor to get the context menu, choose Organize Usings, and then Remove, Sort, or Remove And Sort.

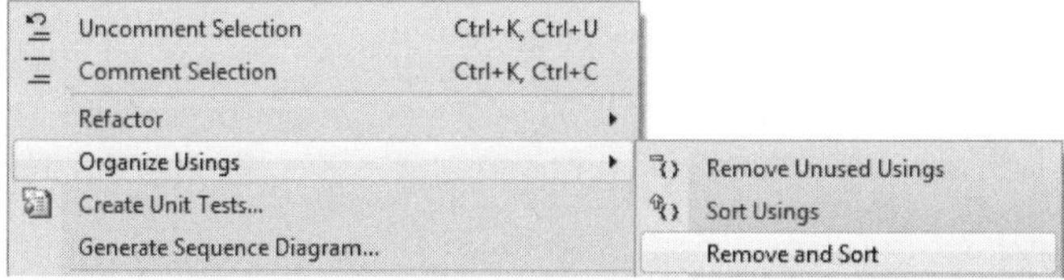

Remove Unused Usings

Before removing unused using directives, using aliases, and extern aliases, you should consider a couple things about this feature.

First, it should be used only on code that builds, because it could remove required using statements if activated on code that does not build. As shown in the following illustration, you have an option in Visual Studio 2008 (***not*** Visual Studio 2010), found at Tools | Options | Text Editor | C# | Advanced | Organize Usings, that prevents you from removing using statements if your code doesn't build.

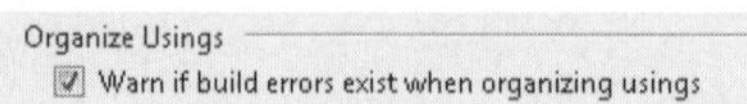

Second, it works only on the active set of code. For example, suppose you have a set of using statements such as the following:

```
using System;
using System.Collections.Generic;
using System.Linq;
using System.Text;
using Microsoft.CSharp.RuntimeBinder;
using System.Text.RegularExpressions;
using System.Collections.Concurrent;
```

If you remove the unused using statements, you see the following result:

```
using System;
```

However, suppose those using statements are organized into code that has active and inactive blocks:

```
#define DEBUG

#if DEBUG
using System;
using System.Collections.Generic;
using System.Linq;
using System.Text;

#else
using Microsoft.CSharp.RuntimeBinder;
using System.Text.RegularExpressions;
using System.Collections.Concurrent;
#endif
```

When you perform the action to remove them, only the extra using statements in the active block are removed:

```
#define DEBUG

#if DEBUG
using System;


#else
using Microsoft.CSharp.RuntimeBinder;
using System.Text.RegularExpressions;
using System.Collections.Concurrent;
#endif
```

Generally accepted reasons for removing unused using statements include the following:

- Results in cleaner code
- Significantly reduces the size of the IntelliSense list because there are fewer namespaces
- Enables potentially faster compilation because the compiler has fewer namespaces to resolve
- Avoids potential naming collisions when new types are added to the unused namespaces that might have the same name as types you are currently using

Sort Usings

When you perform a sort action on your using statements, they sort in the following order: extern aliases, using directives, using aliases. Also, by default, using statements that reference the System namespace are sorted before the other using directives. So, suppose you have some using statements such as the following:

```
using System;
using System.Collections.Generic;
using System.Linq;
using System.Text;
using Microsoft.CSharp.RuntimeBinder;
using System.Text.RegularExpressions;
using System.Collections.Concurrent;
```

When you sort them, you get the result shown in the following illustration.

```
using System;
using System.Collections.Concurrent;
using System.Collections.Generic;
using System.Linq;
using System.Text;
using System.Text.RegularExpressions;
using Microsoft.CSharp.RuntimeBinder;
```

Notice that the Microsoft namespace is below all the System namespaces. If you don't like this behavior, you can change it by going to Tools | Options | Text Editor | C# | Advanced | Organize Usings and clearing the Place 'System' Directives First When Sorting Usings check box.

Now, when you sort, you see the following result:

```
using Microsoft.CSharp.RuntimeBinder;
using System;
using System.Collections.Concurrent;
using System.Collections.Generic;
using System.Linq;
using System.Text;
using System.Text.RegularExpressions;
```

Remove and Sort

When you click the Remove And Sort command, it first performs a remove operation and then it performs a sort operation.

06.24 Switch Between Design and Source in Web Projects

DEFAULT	Shift+F7 (view designer and view markup toggle)
VISUAL BASIC 6	Shift+F7 (view designer and view markup toggle)
VISUAL C# 2005	Shift+F7 (view designer and view markup toggle)
VISUAL C++ 2	Shift+F7 (view designer and view markup toggle)
VISUAL C++ 6	Shift+F7 (view designer and view markup toggle)
VISUAL STUDIO 6	Shift+F7 (view designer and view markup toggle)
WINDOWS	Alt,V, D (view designer); Alt, V, K (view markup)
MENU	View | Designer; View | Markup
COMMAND	View.ViewDesigner; View.ViewMarkup
VERSIONS	2005, 2008, 2010
CODE	vstipEnv0045

When working with web projects, you can switch between Design and Source (Markup) views quite easily.

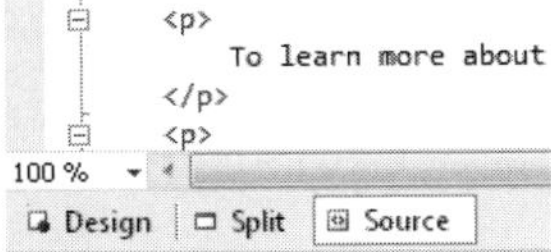

In any view, simply press Shift+F7 to switch to the other view. In other words, you can press Shift+F7 as a toggle between views.

Split View

This keyboard shortcut does not work the way you might think in Split view.

Pressing Shift+F7 takes you to either the Design or Source view (depending on which one you were in last) and does not return to Split view when you press Shift+F7 again.

06.25 Toggle Designer

DEFAULT	F7 (view designer); F7 (view code)
VISUAL BASIC 6	[no shortcut] (view designer); F7 (view code)
VISUAL C# 2005	[no shortcut] (view designer); F7 (view code)
VISUAL C++ 2	[no shortcut] (view designer); F7 (view code)
VISUAL C++ 6	[no shortcut] (view designer); F7 (view code)
VISUAL STUDIO 6	[no shortcut] (view designer); F7 (view code)
WINDOWS	Alt,V, D (view designer); Alt,V, C (view code)
MENU	View | Designer; View | Code
COMMAND	View.ToggleDesigner; View.ViewCode
VERSIONS	2005, 2008, 2010
CODE	vstipEnv0044

You often find that there is a need to switch from Design view (web, windows, or WPF) to code. You can use F7 to go from the current Source or Design view to the Code view.

To go back, just press F7 again. It's a toggle, so it jumps back and forth between the views.

In WPF applications, you can use F7 to view code but not to go back to Design view, so it isn't a full toggle operation in that scenario.

06.26 Change the Default View in the HTML Editor

WINDOWS	Alt,T, O
MENU	Tools | Options | HTML Designer | General
VERSIONS	2005, 2008, 2010
CODE	vstipEdit0088

The default view when you use the HTML Designer is Source view.

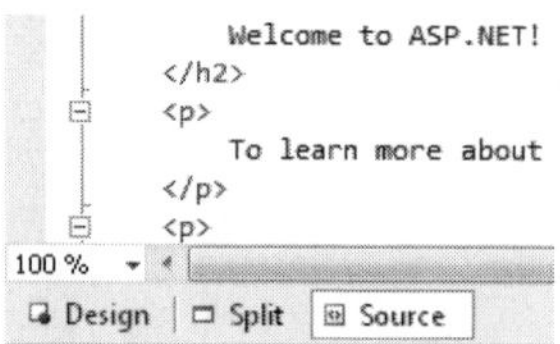

If you don't like this or just want another view to be the default, you can go to Tools | Options | HTML Designer | General and choose a new view in the Start Pages In area.

Note In Visual Studio 2005, you don't have the Split View option.

06.27 Jump Back to the Editor from Just About Anywhere

DEFAULT	Esc
VISUAL BASIC 6	Esc
VISUAL C# 2005	Esc
VISUAL C++ 2	Esc
VISUAL C++ 6	Esc; Alt+0
VISUAL STUDIO 6	Esc
WINDOWS	[no shortcut]
COMMAND	Window.ActivateDocumentWindow
VERSIONS	2005, 2008, 2010
CODE	vstipEdit0066

Did you know that you can usually get to the active document window by just pressing Esc? For example, if you are in any tool window (like the Output window) and you press Esc, you go back to the active document window.

You might have to press Esc multiple times, depending on the situation, but it should almost always wind up at the active document window.

06.28 Replacing Text with a Box Selection

DEFAULT	Shift+Alt+[Up, Down, Left, Right] Arrow
VISUAL BASIC 6	Shift+Alt+[Up, Down, Left, Right] Arrow
VISUAL C# 2005	Shift+Alt+[Up, Down, Left, Right] Arrow
VISUAL C++ 2	Shift+Alt+[Up, Down, Left, Right] Arrow
VISUAL C++ 6	Shift+Alt+[Up, Down, Left, Right] Arrow
VISUAL STUDIO 6	Shift+Alt+[Up, Down, Left, Right] Arrow
WINDOWS	[no shortcut]
COMMAND	Edit.Line[Up, Down]ExtendColumn; Edit.Char[Left, Right]ExtendColumn
VERSIONS	2010
CODE	vstipEdit0006

You have been able to select a block of text for some time in Visual Studio by holding down the Alt+Shift+Arrow keys (or Alt+Left Mouse Button) and making a selection. In Visual Studio 2010, you can now do multiline replacements of a box selection.

Simply select a block of text:

```
public int x = 10;
public int y = 30;
public int z = 50;
```

Now type your replacement text:

```
private int x = 10;
private int y = 30;
private int z = 50;
```

The Editor turns your box selection into a zero-length box selection (a multiline cursor) that you can use to type in what you like.

06.29 Pasting the Contents of One Box Selection into Another

DEFAULT	Shift+Alt+[Up, Down, Left, Right] Arrow
VISUAL BASIC 6	Shift+Alt+[Up, Down, Left, Right] Arrow
VISUAL C# 2005	Shift+Alt+[Up, Down, Left, Right] Arrow
VISUAL C++ 2	Shift+Alt+[Up, Down, Left, Right] Arrow
VISUAL C++ 6	Shift+Alt+[Up, Down, Left, Right] Arrow
VISUAL STUDIO 6	Shift+Alt+[Up, Down, Left, Right] Arrow
WINDOWS	[no shortcut]
COMMAND	Edit.Line[Up, Down]ExtendColumn; Edit.Char[Left, Right]ExtendColumn
VERSIONS	2005, 2008, 2010
CODE	vstipEdit0007

Box selection is a powerful tool that is often overlooked. One of the things you can do, for example, is paste one box selection into another of the same size. Let's assume you have the following code:

```
public int x = 10;
public int y = 30;
public int z = 50;

public double a = 30;
public Int32  b = 50;
public Int64  c = 60;
```

However, you want the first set of variables to be the same data types as the second set (and in the same order). Simply box select (Alt+Left Mouse Button) the second set of data types, and then copy the selection (Ctrl+C).

```
public int x = 10;
public int y = 30;
public int z = 50;

public double a = 30;
public Int32  b = 50;
public Int64  c = 60;
```

Next, select the first set of data types (Alt+Left Mouse Button):

```
public int x = 10;
public int y = 30;
public int z = 50;

public double a = 30;
public Int32  b = 50;
public Int64  c = 60;
```

And paste (Ctrl+V):

```
public double x = 10;
public Int32 y = 30;
public Int64 z = 50;

public double a = 30;
public Int32  b = 50;
public Int64  c = 60;
```

06.30 Pasting a Single Selection into a Box Selection

DEFAULT	Shift+Alt+[Up, Down, Left, Right] Arrow
VISUAL BASIC 6	Shift+Alt+[Up, Down, Left, Right] Arrow
VISUAL C# 2005	Shift+Alt+[Up, Down, Left, Right] Arrow
VISUAL C++ 2	Shift+Alt+[Up, Down, Left, Right] Arrow
VISUAL C++ 6	Shift+Alt+[Up, Down, Left, Right] Arrow
VISUAL STUDIO 6	Shift+Alt+[Up, Down, Left, Right] Arrow
WINDOWS	[no shortcut]
COMMAND	Edit.Line[Up, Down]ExtendColumn; Edit.Char[Left, Right]ExtendColumn
VERSIONS	2010
CODE	vstipEdit0008

In this tip, we see how to take a single selection and put it into a box selection. Let's assume you have the following code:

```
public int x = 10;
public int y = 30;
public int z = 50;

public double a = 30;
```

But you realize that you need change all the ints to doubles.

Select the double keyword and copy it (Ctrl+C):

```
public int x = 10;
public int y = 30;
public int z = 50;

public double a = 30;
```

Then box select the destination (Alt+left mouse button):

```
public int x = 10;
public int y = 30;
public int z = 50;

public double a = 30;
```

Finally, do a paste (Ctrl+V) to see the following result:

```
public double x = 10;
public double y = 30;
public double z = 50;

public double a = 30;
```

06.31 Using Zero-Length Box Selection

DEFAULT	Shift+Alt+[Up, Down, Left, Right] Arrow
VISUAL BASIC 6	Shift+Alt+[Up, Down, Left, Right] Arrow
VISUAL C# 2005	Shift+Alt+[Up, Down, Left, Right] Arrow
VISUAL C++ 2	Shift+Alt+[Up, Down, Left, Right] Arrow
VISUAL C++ 6	Shift+Alt+[Up, Down, Left, Right] Arrow
VISUAL STUDIO 6	Shift+Alt+[Up, Down, Left, Right] Arrow
WINDOWS	[no shortcut]
COMMAND	Edit.Line[Up, Down]ExtendColumn; Edit.Char[Left, Right]ExtendColumn
VERSIONS	2010
CODE	vstipEdit0009

The power of box selection is even more powerful with the new zero-length box selection. Let's assume that you have a situation with some variables, like the ones shown in the following illustration, and you want to make them all public.

```
double a = 10;
double b = 20;
double c = 30;
double d = 40;
double e = 50;
```

The answer is a zero-length box selection. Hold down your Alt key, and use your Down Arrow key to extend straight down. A line is created, as shown in the following illustration.

```
double a = 10;
double b = 20;
double c = 30;
double d = 40;
double e = 50;
```

Release the keys, and now just start typing.

```
public double a = 10;
public double b = 20;
public double c = 30;
public double d = 40;
public double e = 50;
```

This feature acts just like any cursor, so you can go forward and backward at will, plus you can put one of these anywhere you want to create or edit multiple lines of text.

06.32 View White Space

DEFAULT	Ctrl+R, Ctrl+W
VISUAL BASIC 6	[no shortcut]
VISUAL C# 2005	Ctrl+R, Ctrl+W; Ctrl+E, Ctrl+S; Ctrl+E, S
VISUAL C++ 2	Ctrl+R, Ctrl+W; Ctrl+Alt+T
VISUAL C++ 6	Ctrl+R, Ctrl+W; Ctrl+Shift+8
VISUAL STUDIO 6	Ctrl+R, Ctrl+W
WINDOWS	Alt,E, V, W
MENU	Edit | Advanced | View White Space
COMMAND	Edit.ViewWhiteSpace
VERSIONS	2005, 2008, 2010
CODE	vstipEdit0043

Ever want to see the white space you are working with? Maybe you want to know whether you have tabs or extra spaces on lines? It's easy to find out. Just go to Edit | Advanced | View White Space (Ctrl+R, Ctrl+W).

```
        // some comment
        // another comment
```

```
········//·some·comment·········
→   →   //·another·comment→ →   →
```

Spaces are represented as dots, and tabs are the arrows you see in the preceding illustration.

06.33 Collapsing Your Code with Outlining

DEFAULT	Ctrl+M, Ctrl+M
VISUAL BASIC 6	Ctrl+M, Ctrl+M
VISUAL C# 2005	Ctrl+M, Ctrl+M; Ctrl+M, M
VISUAL C++ 2	[no shortcut]
VISUAL C++ 6	[no shortcut]
VISUAL STUDIO 6	[no shortcut]
WINDOWS	Alt, E, O, T
MENU	Edit | Outlining | Toggle Outlining Expansion
COMMAND	Edit.ToggleOutliningExpansion
VERSIONS	2005, 2008, 2010
CODE	vstipEdit0029

By default, outlining is enabled in Visual Studio. It's the line you see with the boxes to indicate the status of the area (collapsed or expanded):

```
namespace CSBreakPoints
{
class SomethingToDo
{
    public void Do(Int32 iParam, Int32 iAnotherParam)
    {
        iAnotherParam = 6;
        int jLocal = iParam;
        Re(3.145 * jLocal);
    }
```

You can collapse code to get it out of your way so that you can focus on other areas. You have four ways to do it.

Minus Sign

Click the minus sign to collapse an area of code.

```
namespace CSBreakPoints
{
class SomethingToDo
{
    public void Do(Int32 iParam, Int32 iAnotherParam)
    {
        iAnotherParam = 6;
        int jLocal = iParam;
        Re(3.145 * jLocal);
    }
```

Note Visual Studio 2010, if Visual Experience is turned on in Tools | Options | Environment | General, now highlights the area that will be collapsed. If you don't like the highlighting color, you can go to Tools | Options | Environment | Fonts and Colors and change the color for the Collapsible Region setting.

Vertical Line

In Visual Studio 2010 only, click *anywhere* on the vertical line in the highlighted region.

```
namespace CSBreakPoints
{
class SomethingToDo
{
    public void Do(Int32 iParam, Int32 iAnotherParam)
    {
        iAnotherParam = 6;
        int jLocal = iParam;
        Re(3.145 * jLocal);
    }
```

Click Anywhere in Area (Keyboard Shortcut)

Click anywhere in the area to be collapsed, and press Ctrl+M, Ctrl+M.

Click Anywhere in Area (Menu Item)

Click anywhere in the area to be collapsed, and go to Edit | Outlining | Toggle Outlining Expansion on the menu bar.

After collapsing, the code area looks like this:

```
namespace CSBreakPoints
{
class SomethingToDo
{
    public void Do(Int32 iParam, Int32 iAnotherParam)...
```

06.34 Using Hide Selection

DEFAULT	Ctrl+M, Ctrl+H
VISUAL BASIC 6	Ctrl+M, Ctrl+H
VISUAL C# 2005	Ctrl+M, Ctrl+H
VISUAL C++ 2	[no shortcut]
VISUAL C++ 6	Ctrl+M, Ctrl+H
VISUAL STUDIO 6	[no shortcut]
WINDOWS	Alt, E, O, H
MENU	Edit | Outlining | Hide Selection
COMMAND	Edit.HideSelection
VERSIONS	2005 (C++ Only), 2008 (C++ Only), 2010
CODE	vstipEdit0036

Let's say you have a chunk of code such as the following:

```
public void ValidateForCheckout() {

    //Must have 1 or more items
    if (this.Items.Count <= 0)
        throw new InvalidOperationException(Messages.OrderZeroItems);

    //every order must have a shipping address - used for tax calcs
    if (this.ShippingAddress == null)
        throw new InvalidOperationException(Messages.NoAddress);


    //make sure there's a payment method
    if (this.PaymentMethod == null)
        throw new InvalidOperationException(Messages.NoPaymentMethod);


    if (this.PaymentMethod is CreditCard) {
        CreditCard cc = this.PaymentMethod as CreditCard;

        if (!cc.IsValid())
            throw new InvalidOperationException(Messages.InvalidCreditCard);

    }
```

Outlining allows you to collapse only the entire method by default (minus sign in the upper-left corner of the preceding illustration). What if you want to collapse only the if statements at the top? First, select the chunk of code you want to hide.

Note You don't have to select entire lines for this feature to work. Just select as much or as little as you want to hide.

```
public void ValidateForCheckout() {

    //Must have 1 or more items
    if (this.Items.Count <= 0)
        throw new InvalidOperationException(Messages.OrderZeroItems);

    //every order must have a shipping address - used for tax calcs
    if (this.ShippingAddress == null)
        throw new InvalidOperationException(Messages.NoAddress);


    //make sure there's a payment method
    if (this.PaymentMethod == null)
        throw new InvalidOperationException(Messages.NoPaymentMethod);


    if (this.PaymentMethod is CreditCard) {
        CreditCard cc = this.PaymentMethod as CreditCard;

        if (!cc.IsValid())
            throw new InvalidOperationException(Messages.InvalidCreditCard);

    }
```

Now either press Ctrl+M, Ctrl+H or go to Edit | Outlining | Hide Selection on your menu bar.

```
public void ValidateForCheckout() {

    ...


    //make sure there's a payment method
    if (this.PaymentMethod == null)
        throw new InvalidOperationException(Messages.NoPaymentMethod);


    if (this.PaymentMethod is CreditCard) {
        CreditCard cc = this.PaymentMethod as CreditCard;

        if (!cc.IsValid())
            throw new InvalidOperationException(Messages.InvalidCreditCard);

    }
```

You have successfully collapsed a selected region of code. Now you can expand and collapse the area as long as you like. Also, if you ever want to get rid of the new region, just press Ctrl+M, Ctrl+U or go to Edit | Outlining | Stop Hiding Current to remove the region.

06.35 Collapse to Definitions with Outlining

DEFAULT	Ctrl+M, Ctrl+O
VISUAL BASIC 6	Ctrl+M, Ctrl+O
VISUAL C# 2005	Ctrl+M, Ctrl+O; Ctrl+M, O
VISUAL C++ 2	[no shortcut]
VISUAL C++ 6	Ctrl+M, Ctrl+O
VISUAL STUDIO 6	[no shortcut]
WINDOWS	Alt, E, O, O
MENU	Edit | Outlining | Collapse to Definitions
COMMAND	Edit.CollapsetoDefinitions
VERSIONS	2005, 2008, 2010
CODE	vstipEdit0032

One of the features of outlining is the Collapse To Definitions option. This feature collapses the areas for all members. Let's suppose you have the following code:

```
public decimal TaxableGoodsSubtotal
{
    get
    {
        //one of the many reasons to love LINQ :)
        return this.Items.Where(x => x.Item.IsTaxable)
            .Sum(x => x.LineTotal);
    }
}
public decimal TotalWeightInPounds
{
    get
    {
        return this.Items.Sum(x => x.LineWeightInPounds);
    }
}

public string DiscountReason { get; set; }
public decimal DiscountAmount { get; set; }

public decimal SubTotal
{
    get
    {

        return this.Items.Sum(x => x.LineTotal)-DiscountAmount;

    }
}
```

You can press Ctrl+M, Ctrl+O, or you can go to Edit | Outlining | Collapse To Definitions on your menu bar to see the following result:

```
public decimal TaxableGoodsSubtotal...
public decimal TotalWeightInPounds...

public string DiscountReason { get; set; }
public decimal DiscountAmount { get; set; }

public decimal SubTotal...
```

06.36 Cut, Copy, and Paste Collapsed Code with Outlining

VERSIONS	2005, 2008, 2010
CODE	vstipEdit0035

When working with outlining, you can perform many timesaving operations. One of these is the ability to take a piece of code and work with it in a collapsed state.

When you collapse code using outlining (click the minus sign to the left of the signature), you get the result shown in the following illustration.

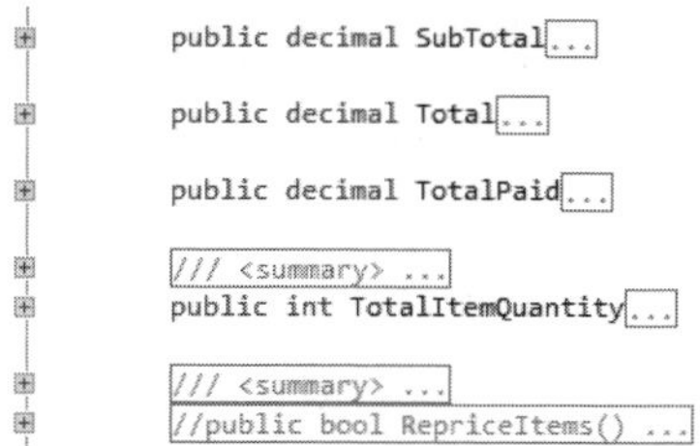

Now we can select all of that code in one compact unit:

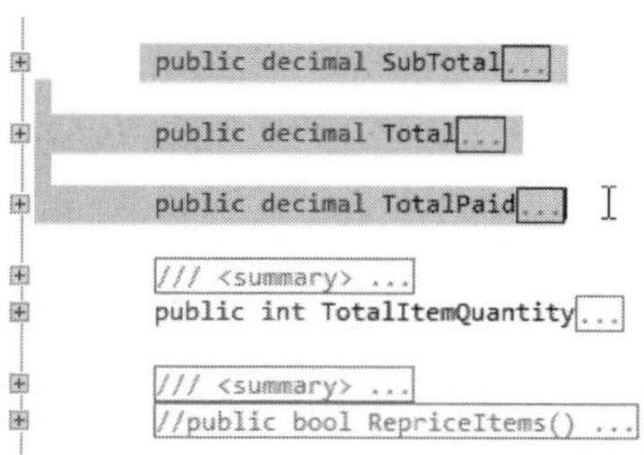

Then simply cut or copy the code, and paste it where you want.

06.37 Understanding Word Wrap

DEFAULT	Ctrl+E, Ctrl+W
VISUAL BASIC 6	[no shortcut]
VISUAL C# 2005	Ctrl+E, Ctrl+W; Ctrl+E, W
VISUAL C++ 2	Ctrl+E, Ctrl+W
VISUAL C++ 6	Ctrl+E, Ctrl+W
VISUAL STUDIO 6	Ctrl+E, Ctrl+W
WINDOWS	Alt, E, V, R
MENU	Edit | Advanced | Word Wrap; Tools | Options | Text Editor | All Languages | General
COMMAND	Edit.ToggleWordWrap
VERSIONS	2005, 2008, 2010
CODE	vstipEdit0022

You can turn on or off the word wrap feature by going to Tools | Options | Text Editor | All Languages | General and selecting or clearing the Word Wrap check box.

Word wrap automatically makes sure that your text is always in the visible space. So if you already have a lot of visible space, it probably doesn't need to wrap.

But if you have less space and wrap is turned on, it wraps automatically, as shown in the following illustration.

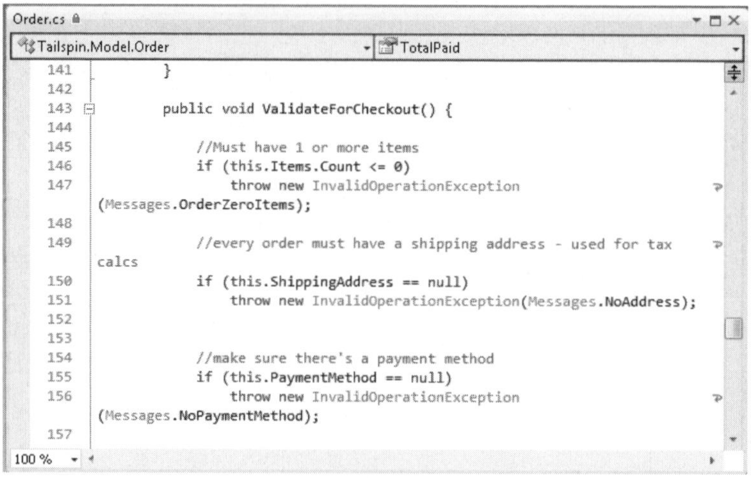

```
Order.cs
Tailspin.Model.Order                TotalPaid
        }

        public void ValidateForCheckout() {

            //Must have 1 or more items
            if (this.Items.Count <= 0)
                throw new InvalidOperationException
(Messages.OrderZeroItems);

            //every order must have a shipping address - used for tax
calcs
            if (this.ShippingAddress == null)
                throw new InvalidOperationException(Messages.NoAddress);


            //make sure there's a payment method
            if (this.PaymentMethod == null)
                throw new InvalidOperationException
(Messages.NoPaymentMethod);

100 %
```

And, naturally, if you have almost no space, it still makes sure all the text is in the visible space.

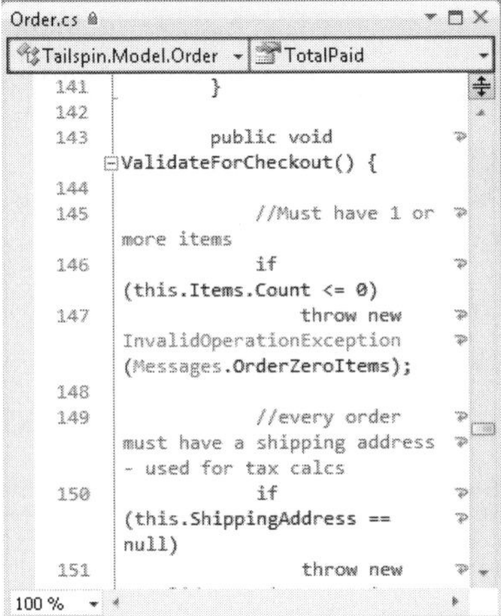

The arrows on the far right of each line (see the preceding illustration) show that the lines are being wrapped. This can be turned on or off by going to Tools | Options | Text Editor | All Languages | General and checking the Show Visual Glyphs For Word Wrap check box.

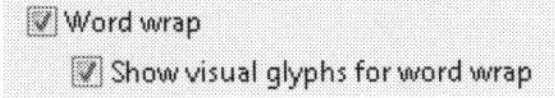

06.38 Properties Window Keyboard Shortcuts

DEFAULT	F4 (properties window); Shift+F4 (property pages)
VISUAL BASIC 6	F4 (properties window); Shift+F4 (property pages)
VISUAL C# 2005	F4 (properties window); Ctrl+W, Ctrl+P (properties window); Ctrl+W, P (properties window)
VISUAL C++ 2	Alt+Enter (properties window); Ctrl+W (properties window); [no shortcut] (property pages)
VISUAL C++ 6	Alt+Enter (properties window); [no shortcut] (property pages)
VISUAL STUDIO 6	F4 (properties window); Shift+F4 (property pages)
WINDOWS	Alt,V, W (properties window); Alt,V, Y (property pages)
MENU	View | Properties; View | Property Pages
COMMAND	View.PropertiesWindow; View.PropertyPages
VERSIONS	2005, 2008, 2010
CODE	vstipTool0111

The Properties window allows you to view and change the design-time properties and events of selected objects that are located in editors and designers. You can also use the Properties window to edit and view file, project, and solution properties. The Properties window is available from the View menu.

For more information, see "Properties Window" on MSDN at *http://msdn.microsoft.com/en-us/library/ms171352.aspx*.

Working with the Tool Window

The following table lists the keyboard shortcuts that you can use with the Properties window:

Action	Shortcut
Open / Show	F4 or Alt+Enter
Close	Shift+Esc

Working with Categories

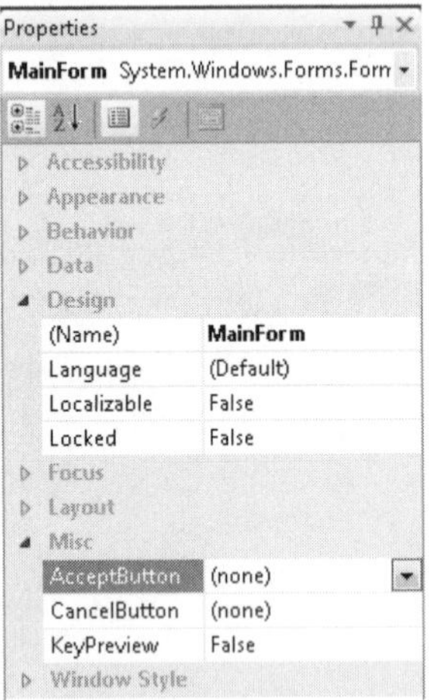

The following table lists the keyboard shortcuts that you can use when working with the categories in the Properties window:

Note The category needs to be selected as shown in the preceding illustration, using the Misc category. You can use your Arrow keys to select the node.

Action	Shortcut
Collapse	Left Arrow or - (minus)
Expand	Right Arrow or + (plus)
Show next set of properties	Page Up
Show previous set of properties	Page Down
Move to next item in list	Down or Left Arrow
Move to previous item in list	Up or Right Arrow
Move to first property	Home
Move to last property	End

Property Items

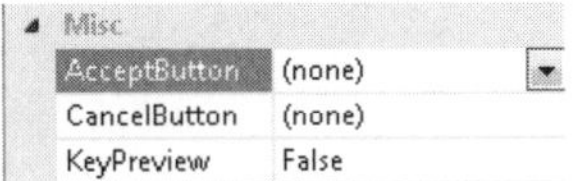

The following table lists the keyboard shortcuts that you can use when you are working with individual items in the Properties window:

ACTION	SHORTCUT
Cancel current changes	Esc
Show drop-down list	Alt+Down Arrow
Previous/next option in list	Up / Down Arrow
Cut selection	Ctrl+X
Copy selection	Ctrl+C
Paste	Ctrl+V
Undo	Ctrl+Z

06.39 Document Outline: Web Projects

DEFAULT	Ctrl+Alt+T
VISUAL BASIC 6	Ctrl+Alt+T
VISUAL C# 2005	Ctrl+Alt+T; Ctrl+W, Ctrl+U; Ctrl+W, U
VISUAL C++ 2	[no shortcut]
VISUAL C++ 6	Ctrl+Alt+D
VISUAL STUDIO 6	Ctrl+Alt+T
WINDOWS	Alt,V, E, D
MENU	View | Other Windows | Document Outline
COMMAND	View.DocumentOutline
VERSIONS	2005, 2008, 2010
LANGUAGES	C#, VB
CODE	vstipTool0116

If you are working with web projects, you need to know about the Document Outline feature (Ctrl+Alt+T). It can be used to do the following:

- View the logical structure of your document.
- Determine which elements are HTML elements and which ones are web server controls.
- Navigate to specific elements, in Design view and in Source view.

If you are working in Source view, it shows you the body element and the child elements of the head element, the page directive, and any script elements and code elements.

I created a default web application in Visual Studio 2010, added a couple of server controls, and switched to Source view. The following illustration shows what the Document Outline looks like.

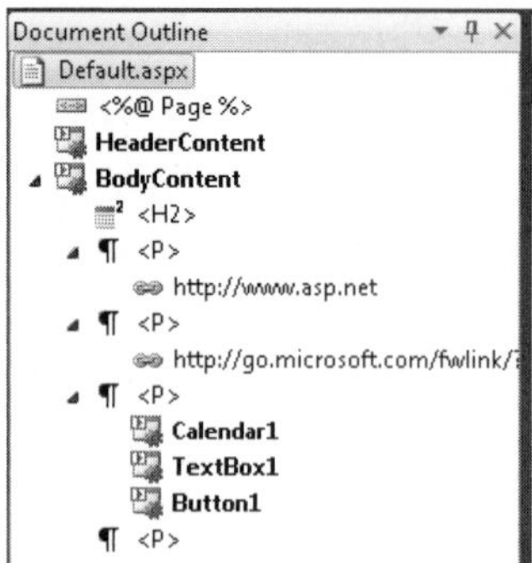

Notice that you can clearly distinguish between the HTML and server content (server content has the little gears in them). It can also be used to select items in the Source.

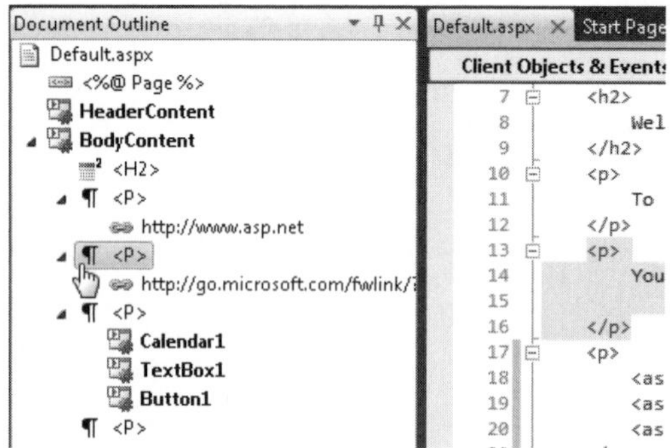

In Design view, it essentially does the same thing and allows you to get a bird's-eye view of the layout and can be used to select controls.

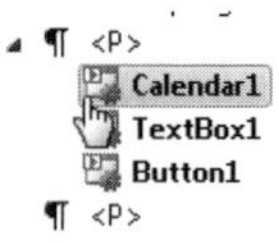

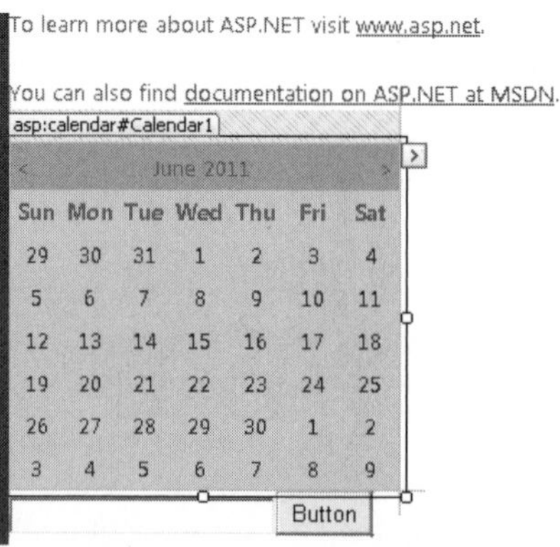

If you have a scenario with many controls, this makes getting to specific items very easy.

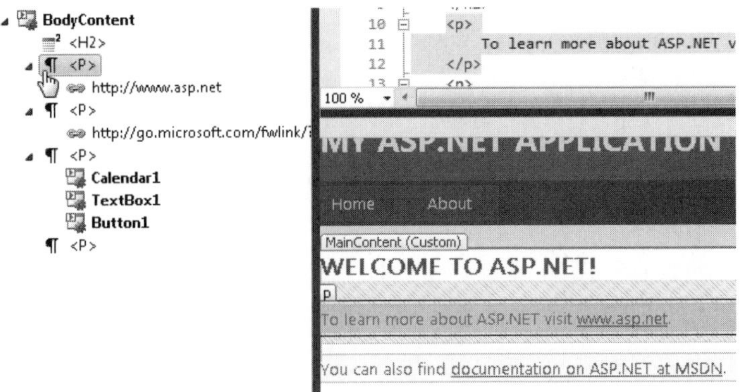

Additionally, many people like to use this feature with Split view so that it can show both Design and Source.

06.40 Inserting Code Snippets

DEFAULT	Ctrl+K, Ctrl+X
VISUAL BASIC 6	Ctrl+K, Ctrl+X
VISUAL C# 2005	Ctrl+K, Ctrl+X; Ctrl+K, X
VISUAL C++ 2	[no shortcut]
VISUAL C++ 6	Ctrl+K, Ctrl+X
VISUAL STUDIO 6	Ctrl+K, Ctrl+X
WINDOWS	Alt,E, I, I
MENU	Edit | IntelliSense | Insert Snippet
COMMAND	Edit.InsertSnippet
VERSIONS	2005, 2008, 2010
LANGUAGES	C#, VB
CODE	vstipEdit0051

Even though these have been around for a while, a lot of people still don't fully understand snippets. Let's assume you are in the editor and you want to create an if statement. You can type it out, but that would be the hard way. Why not just use a snippet? You have several ways to do this.

Tab

Just type **if**, and press the Tab key twice.

C#

The paper-like icon, shown in the following illustration, indicates that this is a snippet in C#.

VB

In VB, you don't have the paper icon, but you do have a note in the tooltip that indicates this is a snippet.

Warning Don't be fooled by the `#if` directive. You want the if statement for this example.

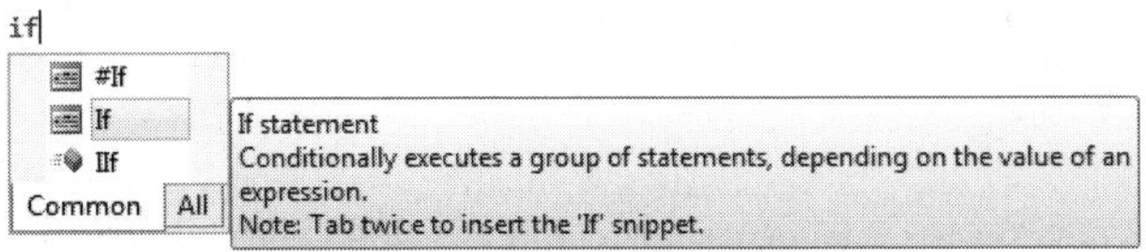

Keyboard Shortcut and Context Menu

Press Ctrl+K, Ctrl+X or right-click and choose Insert Snippet, or go to Edit | IntelliSense | Insert Snippet on the menu bar.

C#

First you see a prompt to insert the snippet, as shown in the following illustration.

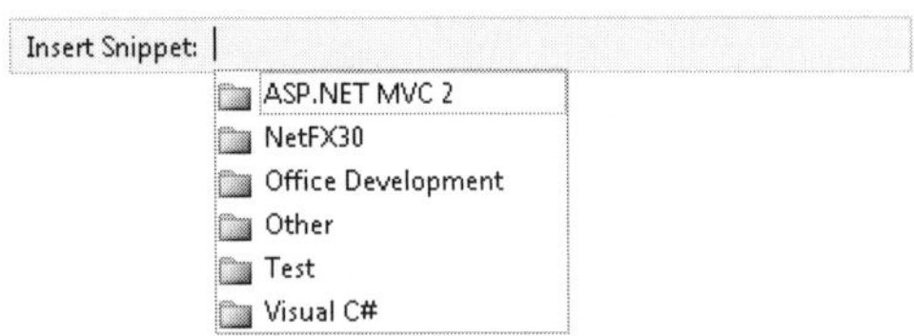

Choose Visual C# from the list, and then press Enter.

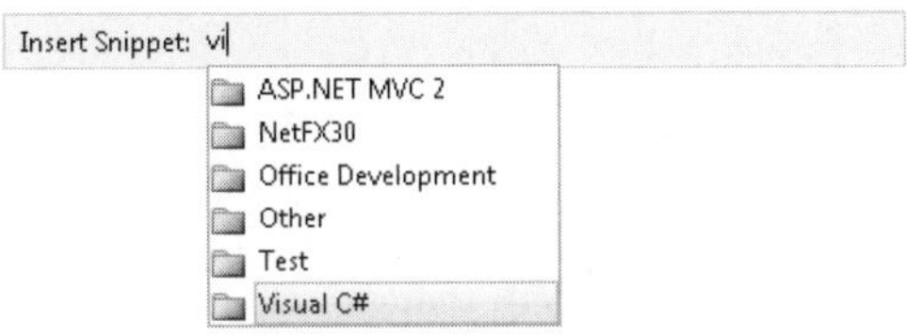

Then type **if**, and press Enter.

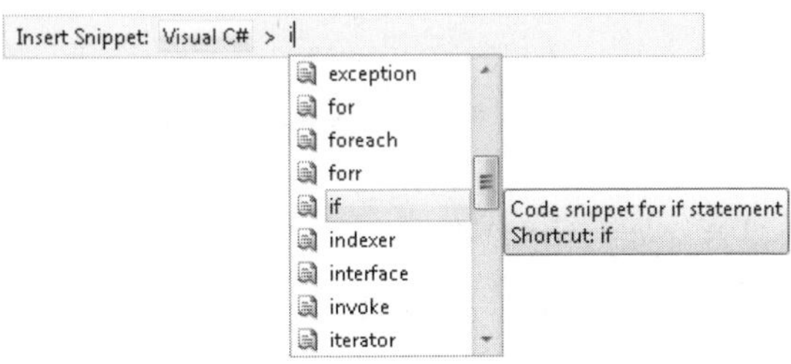

VB

Similar to C#, you see a prompt to insert the snippet, but the path is different. From the list, choose Code Patterns – If, For Each, Try Catch, Property, Etc, and then press Enter:

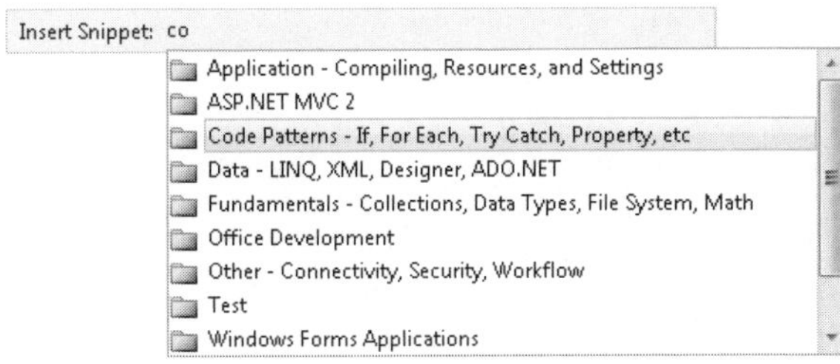

Then choose Conditionals And Loops, and press Enter:

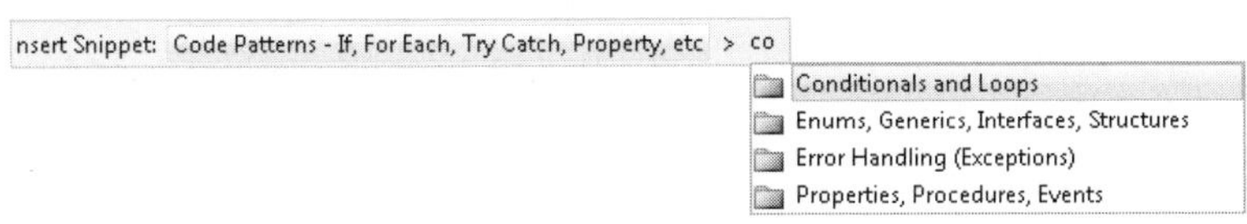

Finally, pick the if statement you want from the list:

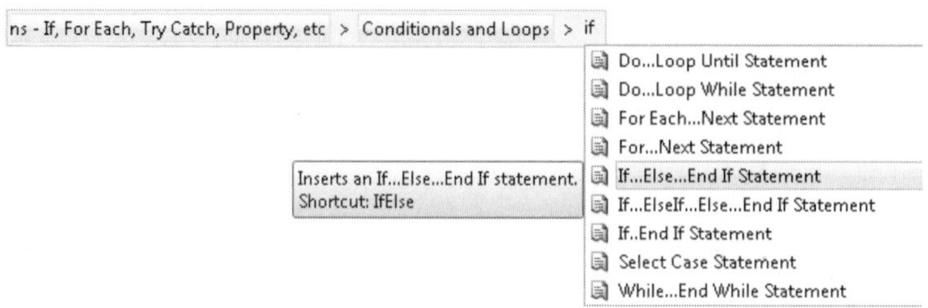

Result

No matter which option you choose, the result is essentially the same. You can now type in your condition and the rest of your logic.

06.41 Surround with a Code Snippet

DEFAULT	Ctrl+K, Ctrl+S
VISUAL BASIC 6	Ctrl+K, Ctrl+S
VISUAL C# 2005	Ctrl+K, Ctrl+S; Ctrl+K, S
VISUAL C++ 2	[no shortcut]
VISUAL C++ 6	Ctrl+K, Ctrl+S
VISUAL STUDIO 6	Ctrl+K, Ctrl+S
WINDOWS	Alt,E, I, S
MENU	Edit | IntelliSense | Surround With
COMMAND	Edit.SurroundWith
VERSIONS	2005, 2008, 2010
LANGUAGES	C#
CODE	vstipEdit0052

This is one that even people who know about snippets tend to forget. You can actually put a snippet around existing code, assuming you have some code selected.

Just press Ctrl+K, Ctrl+S:

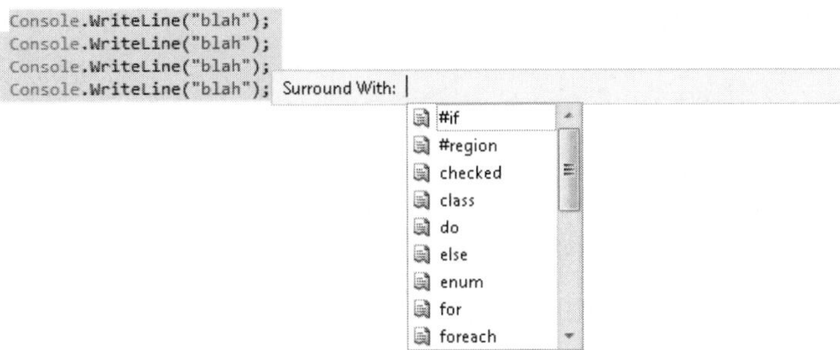

Then type the statement you want to surround the code with. In this case, let's use an if statement:

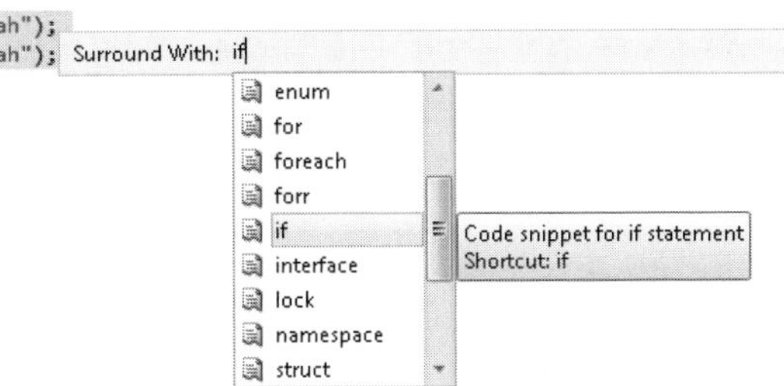

Press your Tab key once, and you see the result shown in the following illustration.

```
if (true)
{
    Console.WriteLine("blah");
    Console.WriteLine("blah");
    Console.WriteLine("blah");
    Console.WriteLine("blah");
}
```

Now you can put in your condition and any additional logic you want.

06.42 Using Code Snippets

DEFAULT	Ctrl+K, Ctrl+X
VISUAL BASIC 6	Ctrl+K, Ctrl+X
VISUAL C# 2005	Ctrl+K, Ctrl+X; Ctrl+K, X
VISUAL C++ 2	[no shortcut]
VISUAL C++ 6	Ctrl+K, Ctrl+X
VISUAL STUDIO 6	Ctrl+K, Ctrl+X
WINDOWS	Alt,E, I, I
MENU	Edit | IntelliSense | Insert Snippet
COMMAND	Edit.InsertSnippet
VERSIONS	2005, 2008, 2010
LANGUAGES	C#, VB
CODE	vstipEdit0053

I thought it would be a good idea to review how to use snippets. This example uses tags in ASP.NET, but the concepts apply across the board to all snippets.

Let's say you are in an ASP.NET application and you start to type an anchor tag, as shown in the following illustration.

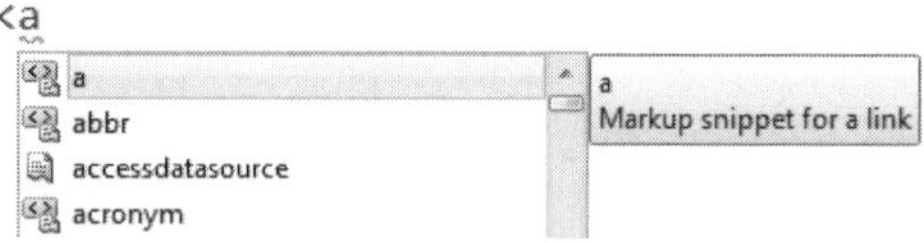

You press Tab twice to insert a snippet and see the following result:

```
<a href="#">content</a>
```

Snippets have special areas that you can change the values in by pressing Tab to cycle through them. For example, the following snippet has two special areas. Let's put in a URL:

```
<a href="http://blah.com">content</a>
```

Now press Tab to go to the next area, and type in some text as shown in the following illustration.

```
<a href="http://blah.com">this is cool</a>
```

You can keep pressing Tab to toggle between these two locations as much as you want. When you are done, you can press Enter to put the cursor at the end of the element and continue typing more code.

So, in a nutshell, that's how to work with snippets. They take a little getting used to, but they are great timesavers.

06.43 HTML Code Snippets

DEFAULT	Ctrl+K, Ctrl+X
VISUAL BASIC 6	Ctrl+K, Ctrl+X
VISUAL C# 2005	Ctrl+K, Ctrl+X; Ctrl+K, X
VISUAL C++ 2	[no shortcut]
VISUAL C++ 6	Ctrl+K, Ctrl+X
VISUAL STUDIO 6	Ctrl+K, Ctrl+X
WINDOWS	Alt,E, I, I
MENU	Edit | IntelliSense | Insert Snippet
COMMAND	Edit.InsertSnippet
VERSIONS	2010
CODE	vstipEdit0018

You might have used code snippets for a while now, but did you know that Visual Studio 2010 has added support for HTML snippets?

From any webpage, go to Edit | IntelliSense | Insert Snippet on the menu bar (Ctrl+K, Ctrl+X). You should see the Insert Snippet prompt:

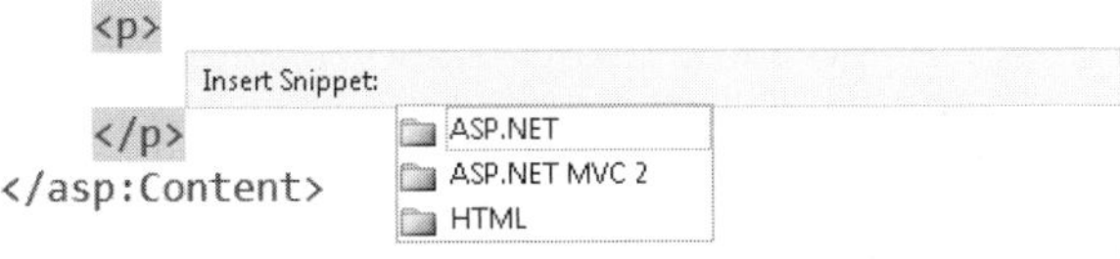

Next, choose your category and the specific snippet you want:

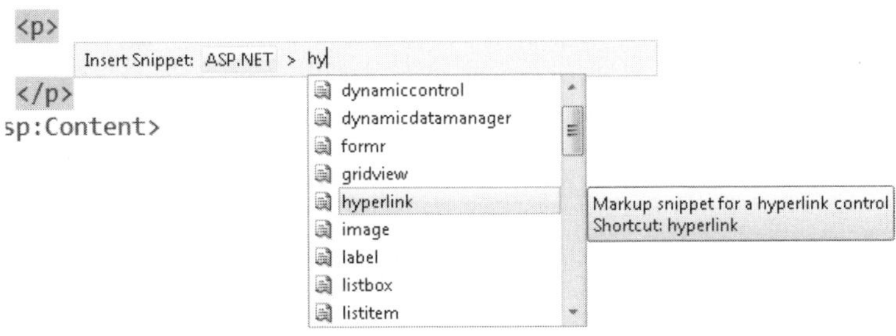

Type in the details, pressing Tab if there are multiple areas where you need to put in details.

```
    <p>
        <a href="http://blah.com">content</a>
    </p>
</asp:Content>
```

Press Enter when you are done, and continue putting in your code.

Note This is the long way to insert a snippet the quicker way, in most cases, is to just start typing an element and hit tab twice to insert the snippet for that element.

06.44 JavaScript Code Snippets

DEFAULT	Ctrl+K, Ctrl+B
VISUAL BASIC 6	Ctrl+K, Ctrl+B
VISUAL C# 2005	Ctrl+K, Ctrl+B
VISUAL C++ 2	[no shortcut]
VISUAL C++ 6	Ctrl+K, Ctrl+B
VISUAL STUDIO 6	Ctrl+K, Ctrl+B
WINDOWS	Alt,E, I, I
MENU	Edit | IntelliSense | Insert Snippet
COMMAND	Edit.InsertSnippet
VERSIONS	2010
CODE	vstipEdit19

Want to get that JavaScript code created more quickly? Use JavaScript snippets.

When you are inside any script block, go to Edit | IntelliSense | Insert Snippet on the menu bar (Ctrl+K, Ctrl+X), choose the JScript category, as shown in the following illustration, and then press Tab.

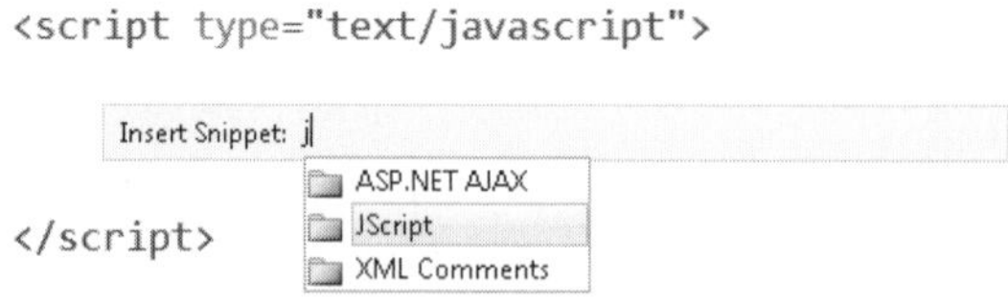

Now pick what you want to do, and then press Tab again.

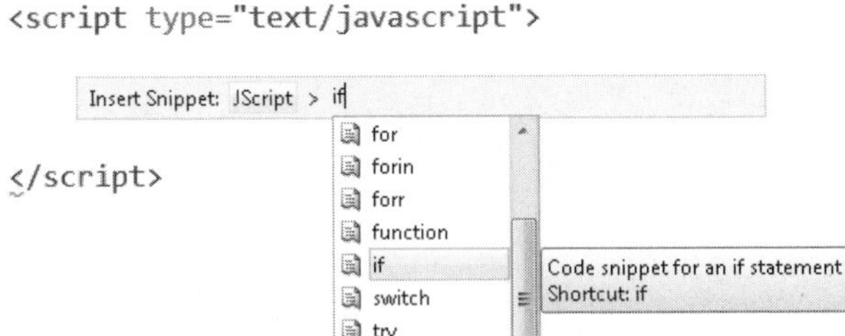

Now fill in any details, pressing Tab to cycle between details if needed.

```
<script type="text/javascript">

    if (true) {

    }

</script>
```

Then press Enter when you are done, and keep typing your code.

06.45 Using the Code Snippets Manager

DEFAULT	Ctrl+K, Ctrl+B
VISUAL C++ 2	[no shortcut]
WINDOWS	Alt,T, T
MENU	Tools | Code Snippets Manager
COMMAND	Tools.CodeSnippetsManager
VERSIONS	2005, 2008, 2010
CODE	vstipTool0015

Ever wonder where you can get a list of code snippets just to browse? The Code Snippets Manager is your friend. Start by pressing Ctrl+K, Ctrl+B to see the following dialog box.

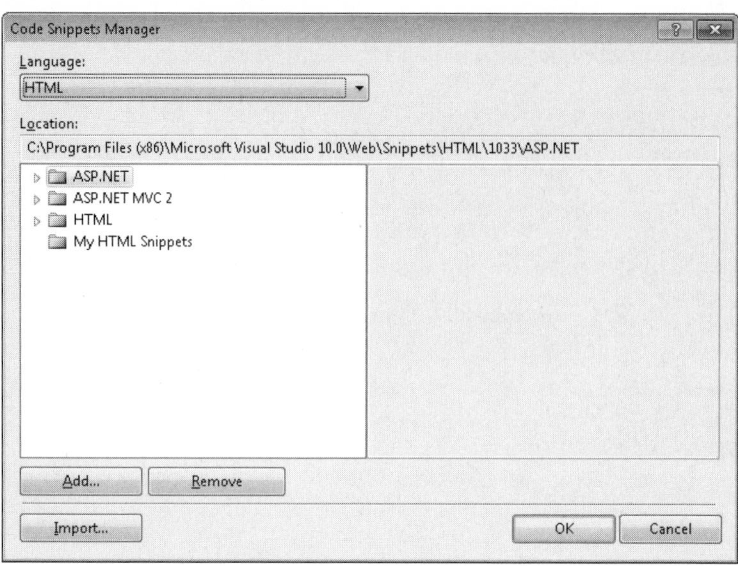

The first thing you need to do is pick the language you want to browse through. Go ahead and choose Visual Basic for this example. This action gives you several folders (categories) to choose from. Let's choose the Application – Compiling, Resources, And Settings folder, as shown in the following illustration.

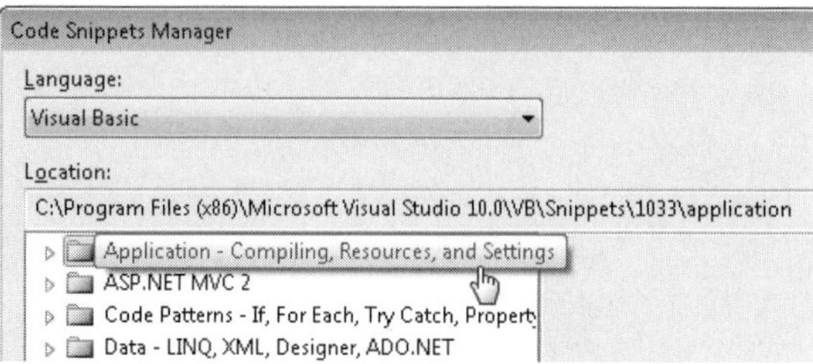

From here, you can browse individual snippets and put your mouse over each of them to get the full description:

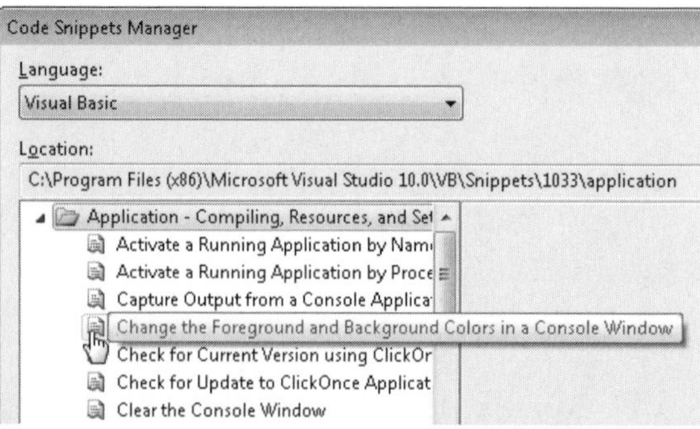

Click the Change The Foreground And Background Colors In A Console Window snippet. Notice that summary information about the snippet is provided:

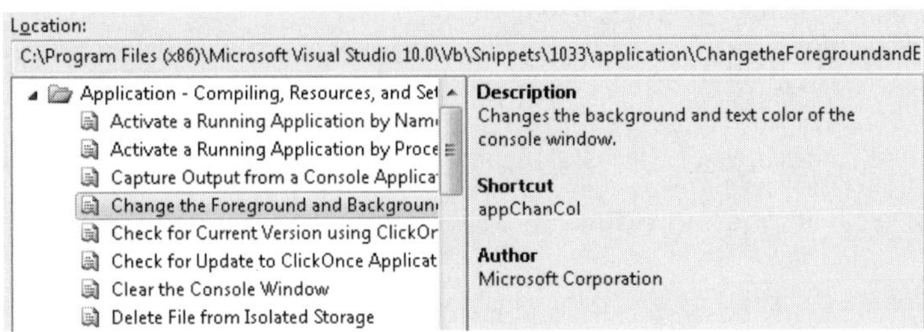

To use this snippet, you have to copy the shortcut name, "appChanCol" in this case. Now click OK or Cancel to close the dialog box, and paste your shortcut name into the editor.

```
Sub Main()

    appChanCol

End Sub
```

Finally, press Tab twice to get the results shown in the following illustration.

Note Technically, you have to press Tab only once in this case, but pressing it twice preserves muscle memory for the snippets and has no downside.

```
Sub Main()

    Console.BackgroundColor = ConsoleColor.DarkRed
    Console.ForegroundColor = ConsoleColor.Gray
    Console.Clear()


End Sub
```

But what about the buttons in the Code Snippet Manager we didn't talk about?

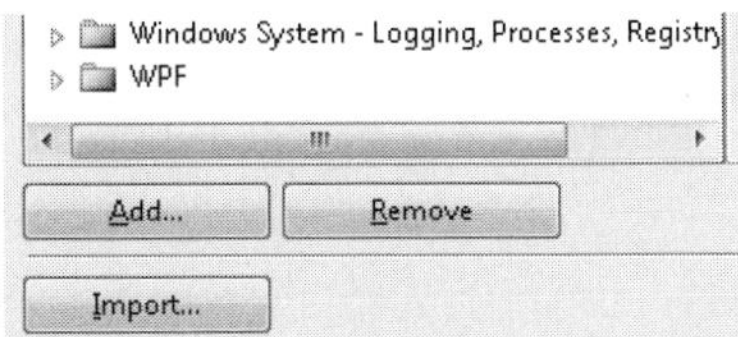

Following are quick descriptions of what they do.

- **Add**—Lets you pick a folder to add to the current list of folders for snippets. The folder can be any accessible location, including network drives. This is useful for shared snippets among team members where everyone uses snippets on a shared drive.
- **Remove**—Takes a folder out of the list but does not physically delete the folder.
- **Import**—Used for including individual .snippet files in the folder you are currently viewing.

06.46 Insert Quotes When Typing Attribute Values

WINDOWS	Alt,T, O
MENU	Tools | Options
VERSIONS	2005, 2008, 2010
CODE	vstipEdit0082

One of the more annoying things about web development in Visual Studio is that when you type in attributes it doesn't include the quotes automatically.

You can have quotes included automatically when you type in attributes if you go to Tools | Options | Text Editor | HTML | Formatting and select Insert Attribute Value Quotes When Typing:

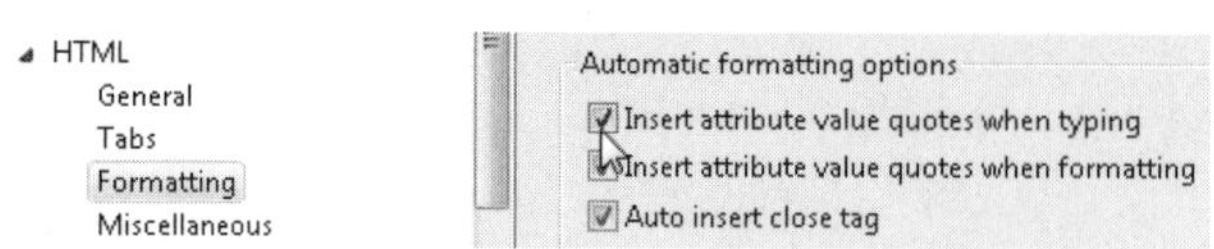

From now on, you will see the quotes when you type in the attributes:

06.47 Format the Current Document or Selection (Web)

DEFAULT	Ctrl+K, Ctrl+D (document); Ctrl+K, Ctrl+F (selection)
VISUAL BASIC 6	Ctrl+K, Ctrl+D (document); Ctrl+K, Ctrl+F (selection)
VISUAL C# 2005	Ctrl+K, Ctrl+D (document); Ctrl+K, Ctrl+E (document); Ctrl+K, E (document); Ctrl+K, Ctrl+F (selection); Ctrl+E, Ctrl+F (selection); Ctrl+E, F (selection)
VISUAL C++ 2	[no shortcut] (document); Ctrl+Shift+F (selection); Ctrl+Alt+I (selection)
VISUAL C++ 6	Ctrl+K, Ctrl+D (document); Ctrl+K, Ctrl+F (selection); Alt+F8 (selection)
VISUAL STUDIO 6	Ctrl+K, Ctrl+D (document); Ctrl+K, Ctrl+F (selection); Alt+F8 (selection)
WINDOWS	Alt,E, V, A (document); Alt,E, V, F (selection)
MENU	Edit | Advanced | Format Document; Edit | Advanced | Format Selection
COMMAND	Edit.FormatDocument; Edit.FormatSelection
VERSIONS	2008, 2010
CODE	vstipEdit0089

In vstipEdit0057 ("Format the Current Document or Selection," in Appendix B [*http://go.microsoft.com/FWLink/?Linkid=223758*]), I showed you how to format code. I thought it would be a good idea to look at the same task from a web project perspective. Let's say you have the following HTML:

```
<div> something cool here </div>
```

Warning You need to have spaces around the <DIV> tags, as I have shown here, or the formatting will not work correctly.

But you want to clean it up a bit. Just select everything you want formatted, right-click, and choose Format Selection (Ctrl+K, Ctrl+F), as shown in the following illustration.

You see the following result:

```
<div>
    something cool here
</div>
```

The formatting rules that govern this operation can be found at Tools | Options | Text Editor | HTML | Formatting. You can also format the entire document by going to Edit | Advanced | Format Document or using the shortcut Ctrl+K, Ctrl+D.

06.48 Using the Navigation Bar

DEFAULT	Ctrl+F2 (navigation bar); Tab (move between Objects and Members drop-down lists)
VISUAL BASIC 6	Ctrl+F2 (navigation bar); Tab (move between Objects and Members drop-down lists)
VISUAL C# 2005	Ctrl+F2 (navigation bar); Tab (move between Objects and Members drop-down lists)
VISUAL C++ 2	Ctrl+F2 (navigation bar); Tab (move between Objects and Members drop-down lists)
VISUAL C++ 6	Ctrl+F8 (navigation bar);Tab (move between Objects and Members drop-down lists)
VISUAL STUDIO 6	Ctrl+F2 (navigation bar); Tab (move between Objects and Members drop-down lists)
WINDOWS	[no shortcut]
COMMAND	Window.MovetoNavigationBar
VERSIONS	2005, 2008, 2010
CODE	vstipTool0026

Ever notice the two drop-down lists just below the file tab channel? The one on the left is the Objects list (classes and objects), and the one on the right is the Members list.

You probably don't have much use for the Objects list unless you have a lot of classes in one file. The Members list is extremely useful when you want to jump around in your code. If you have a class with several functions, you can click the Members list to see them all:

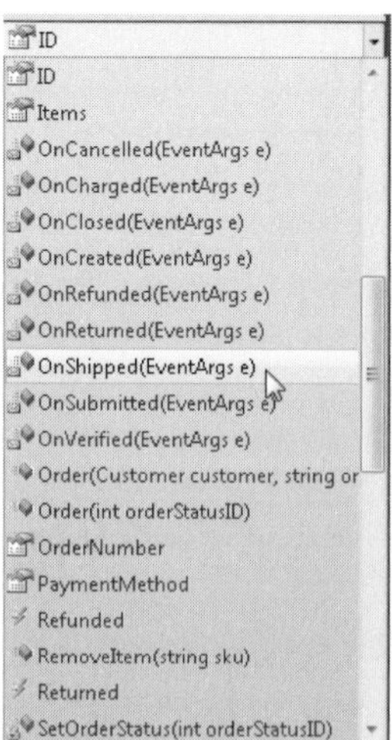

Now you can just click a member to instantly go to that section in your code.

06.49 HTML Editor Tag Navigation

VERSIONS	2005, 2008, 2010
CODE	vstipEdit0091

According to the documentation, "the tag navigator is a representation of the element that is currently selected in the document, along with the hierarchy of parent tags to which it belongs."

For more detailed information, see the topic "HTML Editor Tag Navigation in Visual Web Developer" at *http://msdn.microsoft.com/en-us/library/b53y76zk.aspx*.

The tag navigator is particularly useful for working with deeply nested structures such as tables within tables. You can use the tag navigator to determine which element in the document has the focus.

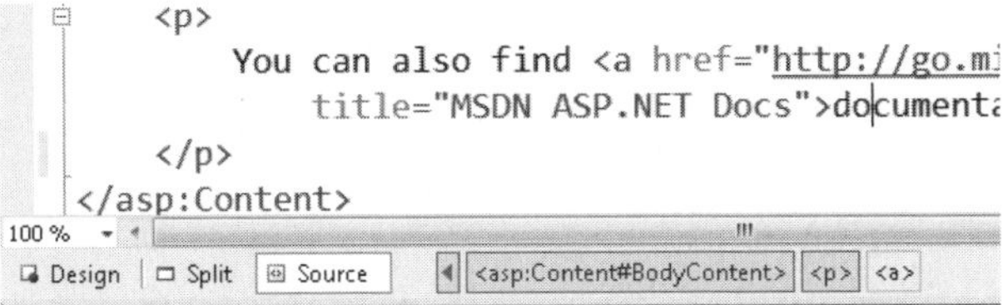

In addition, you can use the tag navigator to move from the current element to an element that is located higher in the current hierarchy:

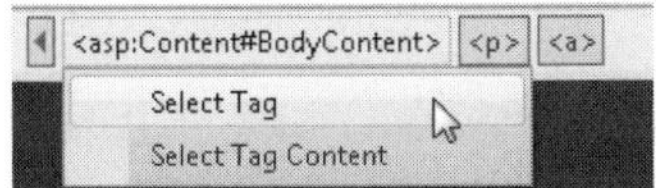

Note The tag navigator does not display all of the elements in the current document. Instead, it shows the path from the current element to the outermost parent. For information about how to see all of the elements in the document, see vstipTool0116 ("Document Outline: Web Projects," page 251).

06.50 Format HTML on Paste

WINDOWS	Alt,T, O
MENU	Tools | Options Text Editor | HTML | Miscellaneous
COMMAND	Tools.Options
VERSIONS	2005, 2008, 2010
CODE	vstipEdit0092

If you find yourself copying and pasting unformatted HTML a lot, this tip is for you. Just go to Tools | Options | Text Editor | HTML | Miscellaneous, and select Format HTML On Paste.

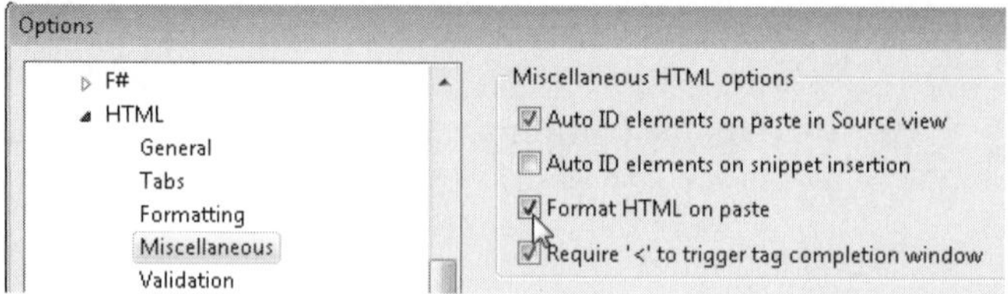

From now on, when you paste it, your HTML is formatted according to the rules set up in Tools | Options | Text Editor | HTML | Formatting.

06.51 Display HTML/CSS Warnings as Errors

WINDOWS	Alt,T, O
MENU	Tools | Options Text Editor | HTML | Validation
VERSIONS	2005, 2008, 2010
CODE	vstipEdit0084

Normally, HTML and CSS syntax problems show up as warnings (green squiggles):

```
<a href=this is cool.aspx></a>
```

These syntax problems also show up as warnings in the Error List window:

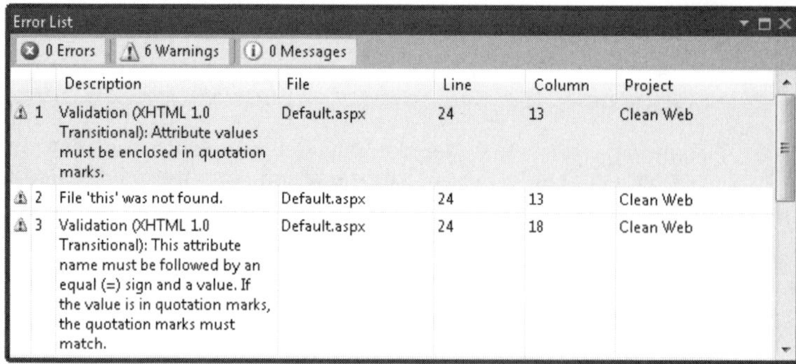

This means that you can build and run the application if you choose to ignore the warnings. Or you can have them show up as errors instead, by going to Tools | Options | Text Editor | HTML | Validation and clearing the As Warnings check box.

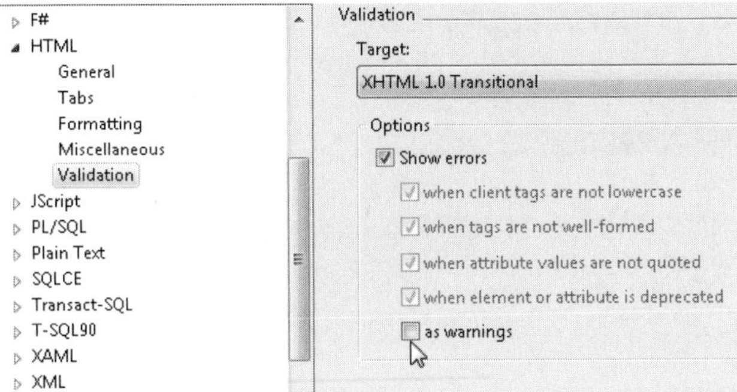

Now the green squiggles will be red:

```
<a href=this is cool.aspx></a>
```

The previous warnings now show up as errors in the Error List window and you are notified when you try to build that a problem exists.

06.52 Updating JScript IntelliSense

DEFAULT	Ctrl+Shift+J
WINDOWS	Alt,E, I, J
MENU	Edit | IntelliSense | Update JScript IntelliSense
COMMAND	Edit.UpdateJScriptIntellisense
VERSIONS	2008, 2010
CODE	vstipEdit0086

If you find that your IntelliSense isn't showing for JScript items you recently put in, you can update the JScript IntelliSense by going to Edit | IntelliSense | Update JScript IntelliSense or pressing Ctrl+Shift+J.

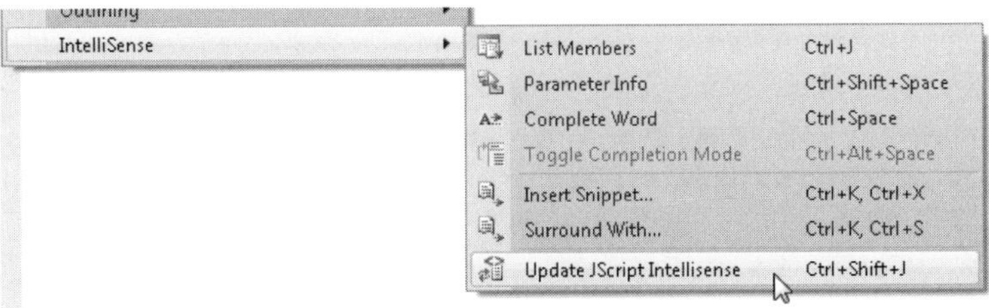

It goes by quickly, but you might see the "Updating JScript IntelliSense" message in the Status Bar at the lower-left corner of your screen.

When it is done, you should be able to see the newly added items.

06.53 Using JScript Libraries in Other JScript Files

VERSIONS	2008, 2010
CODE	vstipProj0025

When you want to use your own custom JScript library, it's a very straightforward process. You just click and drag the file from Solution Explorer into your web page.

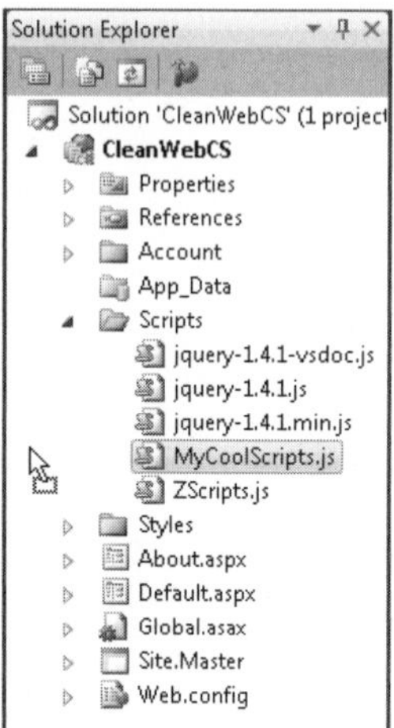

Then start using the library:

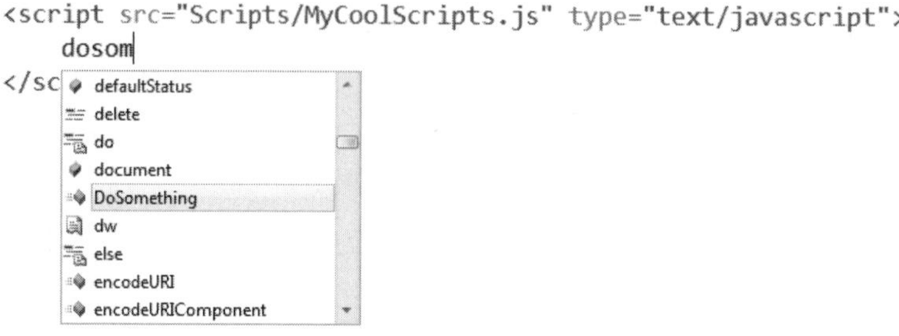

But what if you want to use the library in another JScript file? No problem. To have one file used by another, just click and drag the file name from the resource file into the consuming file.

When you do, it makes a reference automatically:

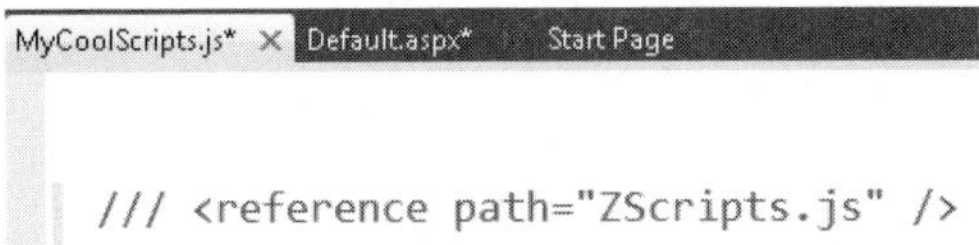

And you can start using it right away with IntelliSense now aware of the resource contents:

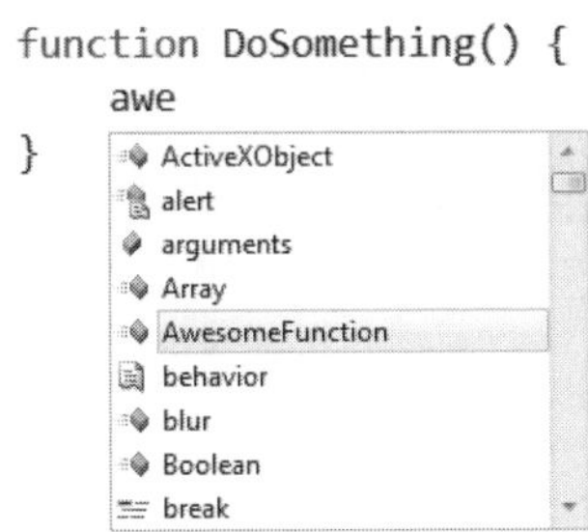

06.54 Create New Code Snippets from Existing Ones

DEFAULT	Ctrl+K, Ctrl+B
VISUAL BASIC 6	Ctrl+K, Ctrl+B
VISUAL C# 2005	Ctrl+K, Ctrl+B
VISUAL C++ 2	[no shortcut]
VISUAL C++ 6	Ctrl+K, Ctrl+B
VISUAL STUDIO 6	Ctrl+K, Ctrl+B
WINDOWS	Alt,T, T
MENU	Tools | Code Snippets Manager
COMMAND	Tools.CodeSnippetsManager
VERSIONS	2005, 2008, 2010
CODE	vstipTool0016

When you use snippets, you often need to change the default values. Naturally, you can modify the values after the snippet is used. But what if you want to permanently change the value and make a new snippet out of it?

First, figure out which snippet you want to modify by finding it in the Code Snippets Manager (see vstipTool0015, "Using the Code Snippets Manager," in Appendix B [*http://go.microsoft.com/FWLink/?Linkid=223758*]). In this case, let's modify the If..End If snippet for Visual Basic.

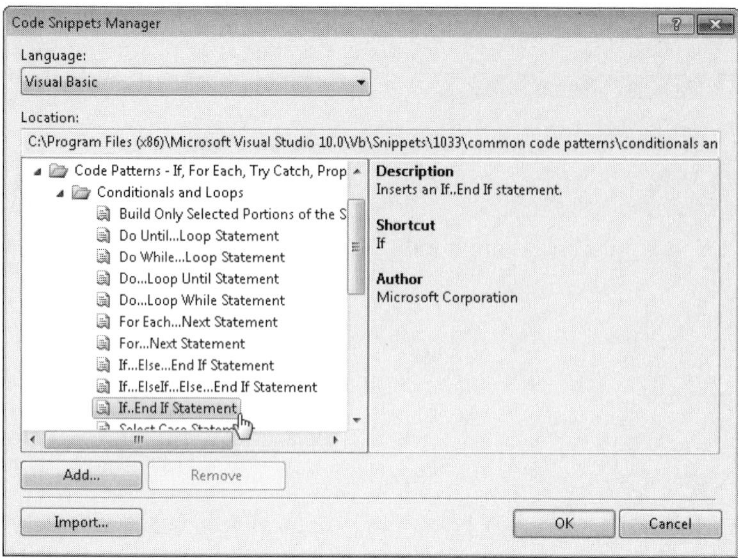

What you are after is the location of the snippet. See the path under Location in the following illustration. Select the path in the dialog box and Copy it (Ctrl+C).

Now, go to File | Open | File, paste in the file path, and click Open.

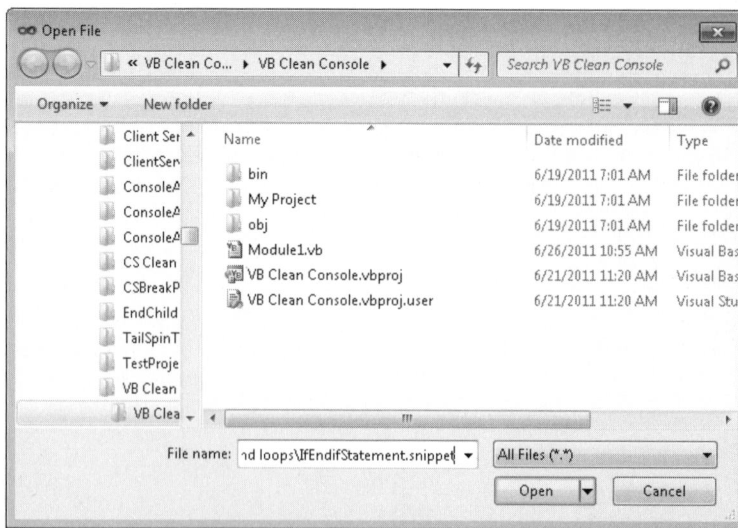

This next part is really just to make sure we don't modify the original snippet. As you gain more experience doing modifications, you might choose to change the original, but for now, you want to make sure you can keep your existing set of snippets intact. Go to File | Save IfEndifStatement.snippet As:

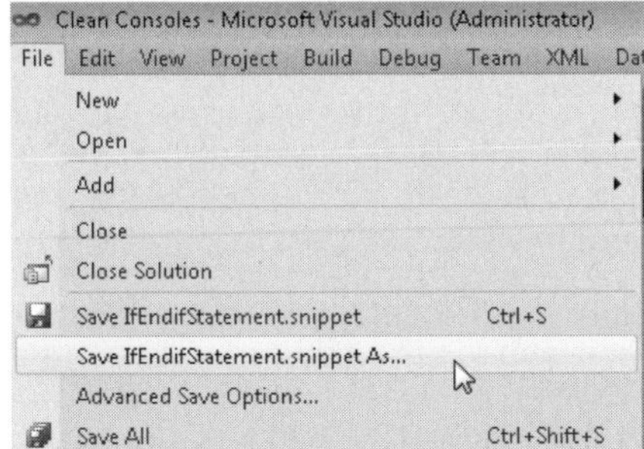

Now just save the file with the original file name and your initials appended to the end.

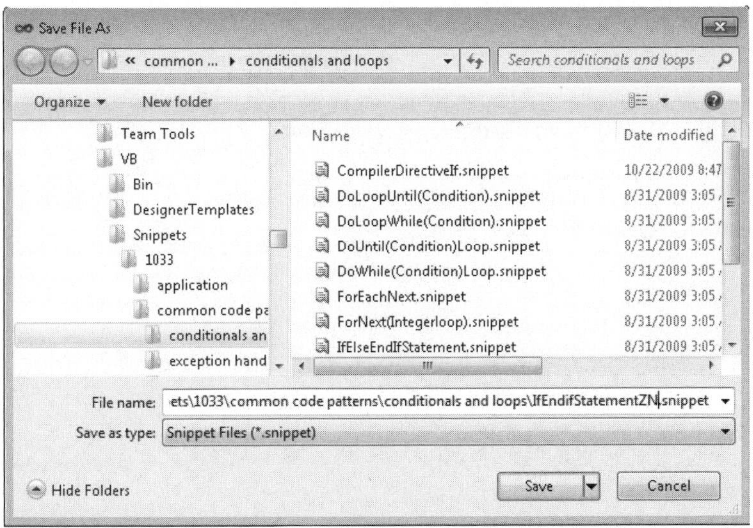

You are ready to modify the snippet. Start with the header information:

```
<Header>
  <Title>If..End If Statement</Title>
  <Author>Microsoft Corporation</Author>
  <Description>Inserts an If..End If statement.</Description>
  <Shortcut>If</Shortcut>
</Header>
```

For now, just change the Title and Shortcut to include your initials:

```
<Title>If..End If Statement (ZN)</Title>
```

```
<Shortcut>Ifzn</Shortcut>
```

Note The key here is the shortcut name. It is the name you will use most often to invoke this snippet so make it something that makes sense.

Because you are here to change the default value as well, locate the Default tag:

```
<Declarations>
  <Literal>
    <ID>Condition</ID>
    <Type>Boolean</Type>
    <ToolTip>Replace with an
    <Default>True</Default>
  </Literal>
</Declarations>
```

Change "True" to "False," and then save the file and close it.

You are ready to use your new snippet. Go into your code, type in your new snippet shortcut, and press Tab (once or twice, both work the same).

```
Sub Main()

    ifzn

End Sub
```

And you get the following result:

```
Sub Main()

    If False Then

    End If


End Sub
```

You now have a new snippet you can use. You can verify this by going back into the Code Snippets Manager (Ctrl+K, Ctrl+B) and finding your snippet in the list.

06.55 Understanding the Navigation Stack

DEFAULT	Ctrl+Shift+8 (back); Ctrl+Shift+7 (forward)
VISUAL BASIC 6	[no shortcut] (back); Ctrl+Shift+7 (forward)
VISUAL C# 2005	Ctrl+Shift+8 (back); Ctrl+Shift+7 (forward)
VISUAL C++ 2	Ctrl+Shift+8 (back); Ctrl+Num * (back); Ctrl+Shift+7 (forward)
VISUAL C++ 6	Ctrl+Num * (back); Ctrl+Shift+7 (forward)
VISUAL STUDIO 6	Ctrl+Shift+8 (back); Ctrl+Shift+7 (forward)
WINDOWS	[no shortcut]
COMMAND	View.PopBrowseContext; View.ForwardBrowseContext
VERSIONS	2005, 2008, 2010
LANGUAGES	C++, C#
CODE	vstipEdit0078

Did you know that a dedicated stack is available to you, just for going to definitions? Let's look at a couple of examples.

Suppose you are looking at a method call, as shown in the following illustration.

```
Re(3.145 * jLocal);
Doh();
```

You can press F12 to go to its definition:

```
public void Doh()
{
    Console.WriteLine("Hit da Doh!");
}
```

How do you go back? Just press Ctrl+Shift+8, and it takes you back:

```
Re(3.145 * jLocal);
Doh();
```

Pressing Ctrl+Shift+7 moves you to the definition again.

```
public void Doh()
{
    Console.WriteLine("Hit da Doh!");
}
```

So what's going on? Well, every time you go to a definition it keeps track of where you come from. This works every time you go to definition so that you can always find your way back. The following illustrations show another example.

```
Mi("A me so la ti do");
AddStuff(5, 3);
```

Press F12 (go to definition):

```
public int AddStuff(int a, int b)
{
    a += GetNumber();
    return a + b;
}
```

From here, you could press Ctrl+Shift+8 to go back. But what if you want to keep digging into definitions? In this example, let's say you've clicked in the GetNumber method:

```
public int AddStuff(int a, int b)
{
    a += GetNumber();
    return a + b;
}
```

Now press F12:

```
public int GetNumber()
{
    return 5;
}
```

Now, if you want to go back, press Ctrl+Shift+8:

```
public int AddStuff(int a, int b)
{
    a += GetNumber();
    return a + b;
}
```

Then press Ctrl+Shift+8 again:

```
Mi("A me so la ti do");
AddStuff(5, 3);
```

06.56 Navigate Backward and Navigate Forward Using Go Back Markers

DEFAULT	Ctrl+- (back); Ctrl+Shift+- (forward)
VISUAL BASIC 6	Ctrl+- (back); Ctrl+Shift+F2 (back); Ctrl+Shift+- (forward)
VISUAL C# 2005	Ctrl+- (back); Ctrl+Shift+- (forward)
VISUAL C++ 2	Ctrl+- (back); Ctrl+Shift+- (forward)
VISUAL C++ 6	Ctrl+- (back); Ctrl+Shift+- (forward)
VISUAL STUDIO 6	Ctrl+- (back); Ctrl+Shift+- (forward)
WINDOWS	Alt,V, B (back); Alt,V, F (forward)
MENU	View | Navigate Backward; View | Navigate Forward
COMMAND	View.NavigateBackward; View.NavigateForward
VERSIONS	2005, 2008, 2010
CODE	vstipEdit0024

If you move in a single command more than several lines away from where you are currently working or if you edit in a particular location that is not adjacent to the last place you edited, the editor remembers locations. It does this by creating Go Back markers based on specific conditions. The goal is to remember interesting locations so that you can recall where you have been working without remembering so many locations that the feature is not useful (such as every character typed, or every line entering several new lines of code one right after the other).

A Go Back marker is dropped under the following conditions:

- An incremental search (including reverse) leaves a Go Back marker at the beginning of the search and another one at the end.
- A Go To Line action, like Ctrl+G, or a mouse-click that moves the cursor 11 lines or more from the current position drops a Go Back marker at the new location.
- A destructive action (like pressing backspace) after having moved the cursor to a new location drops a Go Back marker.
- Doing a search, like Ctrl+F, drops a Go Back marker at the found location.
- Opening a file drops a Go Back marker wherever the cursor was on the old file and drops another on the opened file.

That now brings us to the navigation buttons on the Standard Toolbar (and keyboard shortcuts, too). These gems make travelling around your code much, much easier:

You can use the buttons to quickly navigate among the Go Back markers that have been dropped throughout Visual Studio. To quickly look at the list of places you can go, just click the drop-down arrow for the back button.

Note The navigation buttons in the Standard Toolbar are on the upper-left of the image below.

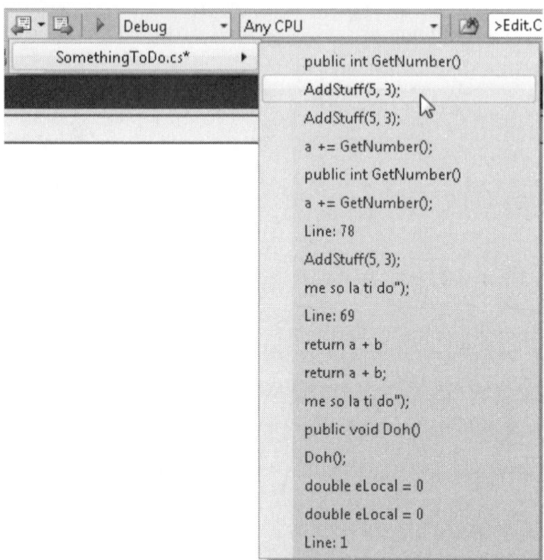

06.57 Select from the Current Cursor Location to the Last Go Back Marker

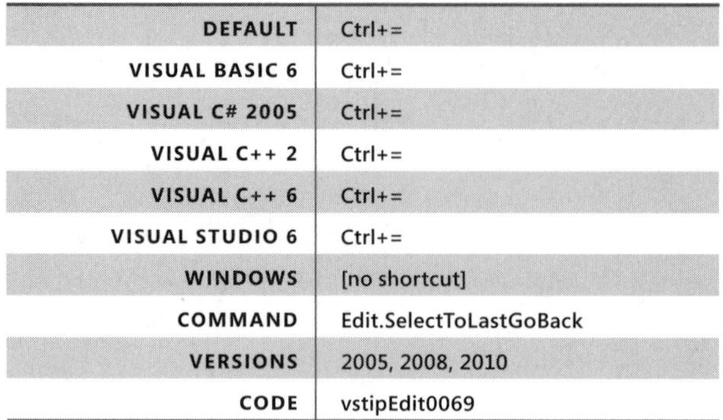

DEFAULT	Ctrl+=
VISUAL BASIC 6	Ctrl+=
VISUAL C# 2005	Ctrl+=
VISUAL C++ 2	Ctrl+=
VISUAL C++ 6	Ctrl+=
VISUAL STUDIO 6	Ctrl+=
WINDOWS	[no shortcut]
COMMAND	Edit.SelectToLastGoBack
VERSIONS	2005, 2008, 2010
CODE	vstipEdit0069

In vstipEdit0024 ("Navigate Backward and Navigate Forward Using Go Back Markers," on page 277), we defined Go Back markers. In this tip, we look at how they can be useful for selecting text. Let's say you are writing some code and want to quickly select a chunk of text. In the following illustration, the cursor is at your starting location (line 15).

```
15 Console.WriteLine("Blah");
16 Console.WriteLine("Blah");
17 Console.WriteLine("Blah");
18 Console.WriteLine("Blah");
19 Console.WriteLine("Blah");
20 Console.WriteLine("Blah");
21 Console.WriteLine("Blah");
22 Console.WriteLine("Blah");
23 Console.WriteLine("Blah");
24 Console.WriteLine("Blah");
25 Console.WriteLine("Blah");
26 Console.WriteLine("Blah");
27 Console.WriteLine("Blah");
28 Console.WriteLine("Blah");
29 Console.WriteLine("Blah");
30 Console.WriteLine("Blah");
31
```

You click on a new location (line 27), which results in a Go Back marker (which you can't see) being placed at the starting location (line 15).

```
15 Console.WriteLine("Blah");
16 Console.WriteLine("Blah");
17 Console.WriteLine("Blah");
18 Console.WriteLine("Blah");
19 Console.WriteLine("Blah");
20 Console.WriteLine("Blah");
21 Console.WriteLine("Blah");
22 Console.WriteLine("Blah");
23 Console.WriteLine("Blah");
24 Console.WriteLine("Blah");
25 Console.WriteLine("Blah");
26 Console.WriteLine("Blah");
27 Console.WriteLine("Blah");
28 Console.WriteLine("Blah");
29 Console.WriteLine("Blah");
30 Console.WriteLine("Blah");
31
```

Now we have the Go Back marker at the beginning of line 15 and the current cursor location at the end of line 27. In this case, you had to jump at least 11 lines to get your Go Back marker. To select from the current cursor location to the last Go Back marker, just press Ctrl+= and watch the magic happen.

```
Console.WriteLine("Blah");
Console.WriteLine("Blah");
Console.WriteLine("Blah");
Console.WriteLine("Blah");
Console.WriteLine("Blah");
Console.WriteLine("Blah");
Console.WriteLine("Blah");
Console.WriteLine("Blah");
Console.WriteLine("Blah");
Console.WriteLine("Blah");
Console.WriteLine("Blah");
Console.WriteLine("Blah");
Console.WriteLine("Blah");
Console.WriteLine("Blah");
Console.WriteLine("Blah");
Console.WriteLine("Blah");

```

06.58 Track Changes in the Editor

WINDOWS	Alt,T, O
MENU	Tools | Options | Text Editor | General
COMMAND	Tools.Options
VERSIONS	2005, 2008, 2010
CODE	vstipEdit0048

To use this feature, you need to go to Tools | Options | Text Editor | General and have Track Changes and Selection Margin checked.

Ever wonder how the colored lines to the left of your code (by the line numbers) actually work?

Let's begin with a clean slate.

```
11 static void Main(string[] args)
12 {
13
14
15
16
17 }
```

Let's add a couple of lines of code, and now we see two vertical yellow (you'll have to trust me on the colors) lines to the left of lines 14 and 15:

```
static void Main(string[] args)
{

Console.WriteLine("blah");
Console.WriteLine("blah");

}
```

All new code will have a yellow line to show you what part of the document is unsaved. If we save the code, the yellow lines turn green to indicate code that has been saved.

The saved indicator remains as long as you have the file open. When you close and reopen the file, the line goes away:

```
static void Main(string[] args)
{

Console.WriteLine("blah");
Console.WriteLine("blah");

}
```

In Visual Studio 2010, an orange indicator shows a change that is different from the saved version. This was added for the scenario where a user does an undo after saving the changes.

You can use the following grid to help keep the colors straight.

Marker	Different from file saved on disk?	Different from file that was opened?
Nothing	No	No
Yellow	Yes	Yes
Green	No	Yes
Orange	Yes	No

06.59 Edit Read-Only Files

WINDOWS	Alt,T, O
MENU	Tools | Options | Environment | Documents
COMMAND	Tools.Options
VERSIONS	2008, 2010
CODE	vstipEdit0074

When you open a read-only document, you get an indicator that looks like a tiny lock on the file tab:

If you make changes and try to save them, you are (by default) met with the Save Of Read-Only File dialog box.

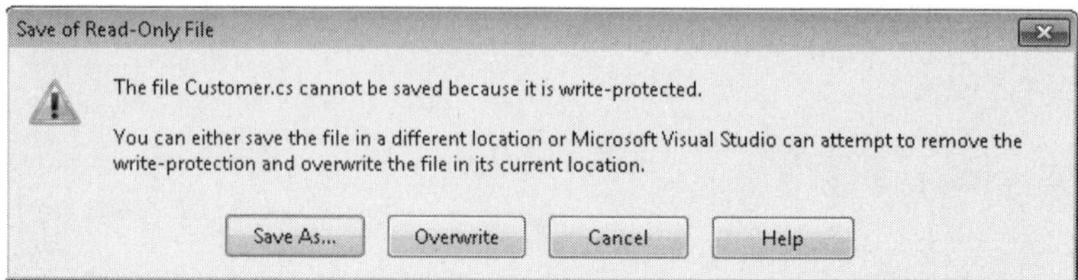

At this point, you can save your changes as another copy of the file, overwrite the existing file, or cancel. If you don't like these options, you can turn this feature off by going to Tools | Options | Environment | Documents and clear the Allow Editing Of Read-Only Files; Warn When Attempt To Save check box.

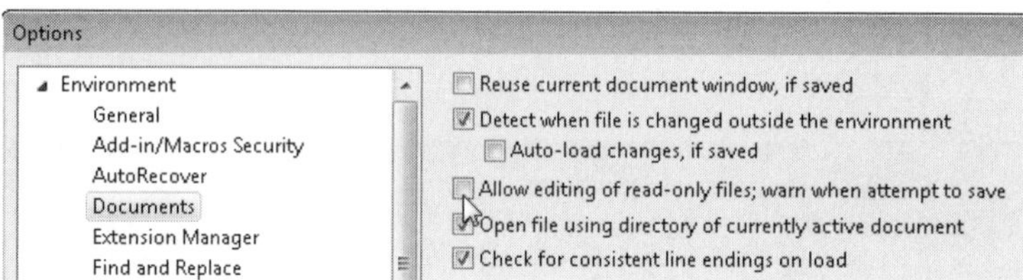

Now if you attempt to make any changes to a read-only file, you see the Edit of Read-Only File dialog box.

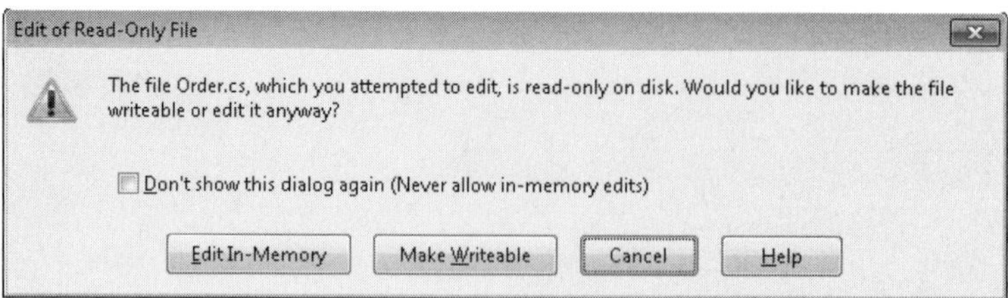

Edit In-Memory

Allows you to make edits and then display the Save Of Read-Only File dialog box when you save changes.

Make Writable

If possible, turns off the read-only attribute of the file so that it can be edited.

06.60 Choosing CSS Versions

WINDOWS	Alt,T, O
MENU	Tools | Options Text Editor | HTML | Validation (HTML Schema)
COMMAND	Tools.Options
VERSIONS	2005, 2008, 2010, 2010 SP1
CODE	vstipEdit0093

When working with Cascading Style Sheets (CSS), you often find yourself working with specific versions. In this tip, we look at how to set your CSS version for dedicated and embedded styles.

Note Visual Studio 2010 Service Pack 1 added limited support for HTML5 and CSS3. For more information, see *http://blogs.msdn.com/b/zainnab/archive/2011/04/12/vs2010-sp1-new-features-html-5-and-css-3-support.aspx*.

Dedicated Style Sheets

When you create a CSS file in Visual Studio, you can choose the version you want by selecting it from the Cascading Style Sheet Version For Validation drop-down list on the Style Sheet Toolbar:

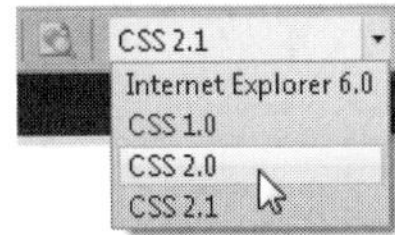

Note CSS3 doesn't show up in this list even after you install Visual Studio 2010 Service Pack 1.

Embedded Styles

It is recommended that you use dedicated style sheets; however, you might find that you want to embed styles in your HTML source.

When you do this, it might not be clear how you select the CSS version. Most people think it is the same as the version chosen for dedicated CSS files. This is not the case. It's bound to the choice you make in the Target Schema For Validation drop-down list located on the HTML Source Editing Toolbar or at Tools | Options | Text Editor | HTML | Validation (HTML Schema).

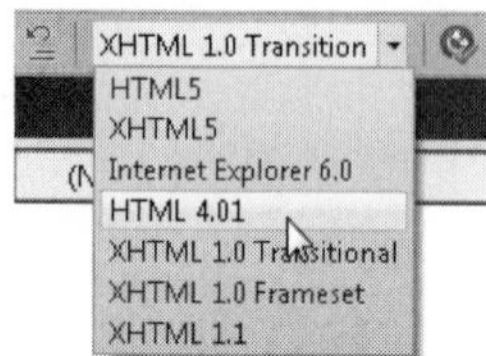

The following table shows how the CSS version relates to the choices.

HTML Schema	CSS Schema
Internet Explorer 6.0	Internet Explorer 6.0
HTML 4.01	CSS 1.0
XHTML 1.0 Transitional	CSS 2.0
XHTML 1.0 Frameset	CSS 2.0
XHTML 1.1	CSS 2.1
HTML5 (limited)	CSS 3.0 (limited)
XHTML5 (limited)	CSS 3.0 (limited)

Finally

You have many good reasons to use dedicated style sheets, but if you do find yourself doing embedded CSS, make sure you understand which schema you are using based on your HTML schema choices.

06.61 Understanding Tag Specific Options

WINDOWS	Alt,T, O
MENU	Tools | Options | Text Editor | HTML | Formatting
COMMAND	Tools.Options
VERSIONS	2005, 2008, 2010
CODE	vstipEdit0090

In vstipEdit0089 ("Format the Current Document or Selection HTML Designer," on page 265), I showed you how to use selection formatting on a sample.

Let's say you don't like the way <DIV> tags are formatted. You can go to Tools | Options | Text Editor | HTML | Formatting and click the Tag Specific Options button.

Exploring the Tag Specific Options Dialog Box

This dialog box is somewhat complicated, so let's go though it one area at a time. For reference, the following illustration provides a bird's eye view to help us stay oriented as we go along.

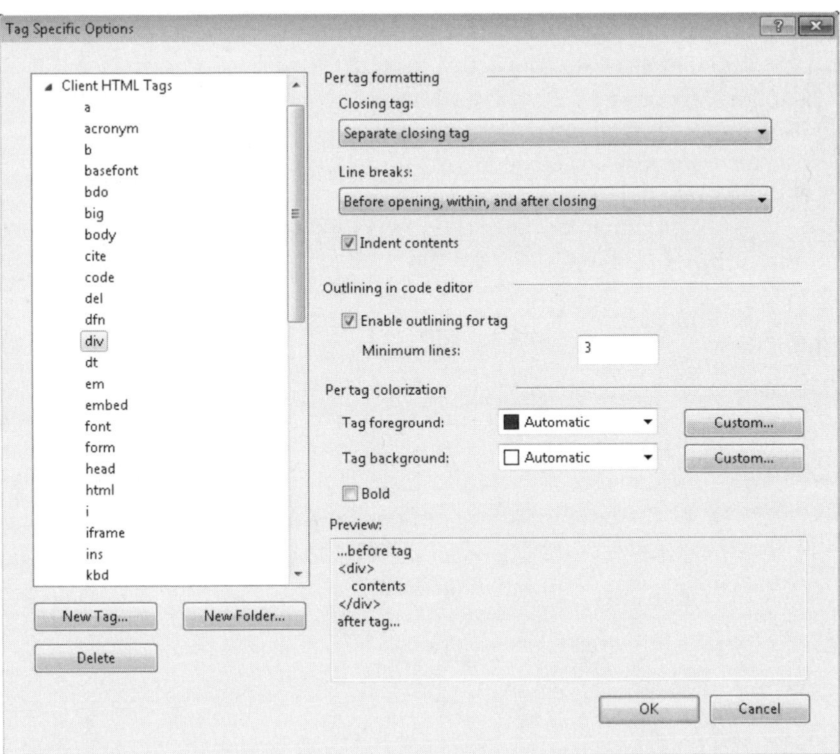

Tree view

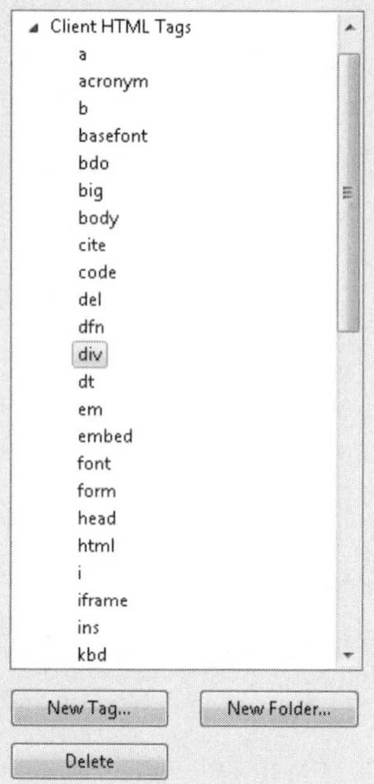

Allows you to select either the individual tag to format or a class of tags. By default, the tree contains the following nodes:

Default Settings

Expand this node to set default formatting options for a complete class of tags, such as all server tags that support contents.

Client HTML Tags

Expand this node to set custom formatting options for HTML elements.

ASP.NET Controls

Expand this node to set custom formatting options for ASP.NET server controls.

New Tag

Use to define new tags that aren't already listed.

New Folder

Create a new node on the tree for organizing custom tags.

Delete

Delete a tag or folder.

Note In the following examples, our working reference is the <DIV> tag from the Client HTML Tags section of the Tag Specific Actions dialog box.

Per tag formatting

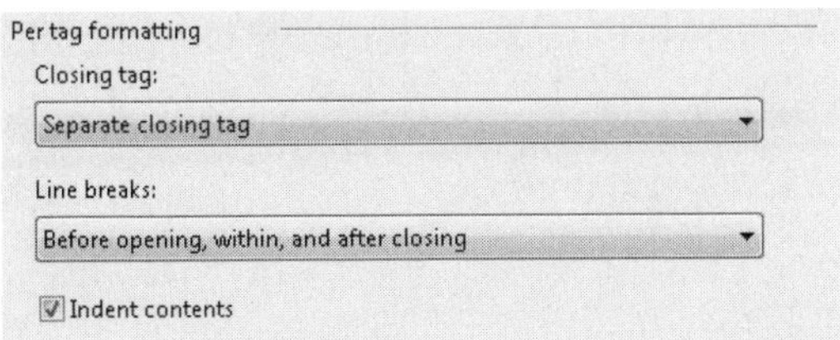

Per tag formatting works on a model with default settings for each tag. These settings provide the base rules by which the tag is formatted. The four categories of tags are as follows:

- Client tags that do not support contents, such as
- Client tags that support contents, such as <TABLE> or <H1>
- Server tags that do not support contents, such as asp:CheckBox
- Server tags that support contents, such as asp:Repeater

For each tag, the values from the appropriate category in the preceding list are used, unless an override is specified for that tag. By default, some overrides are supplied based on the common usage of the tags.

Closing tag

Indicates how the closing tag should look when automatically created.

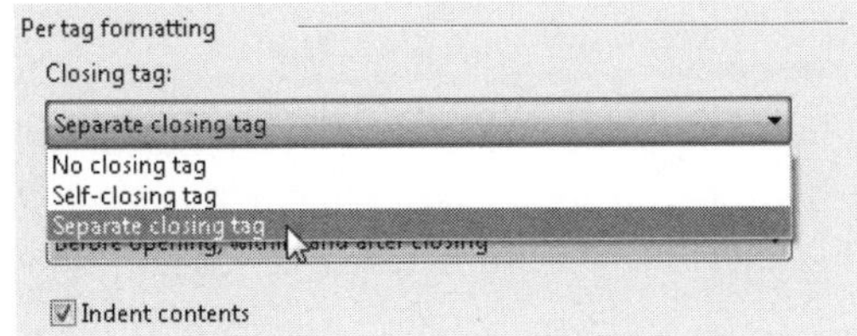

Line breaks

Directs the formatting to place line breaks as specific points in the entire element.

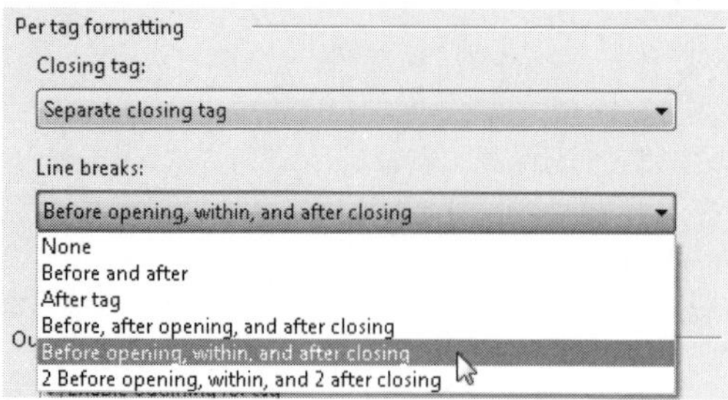

Indent contents

Indents the contents for the element, if appropriate.

Preview

The absolute *best* way to see how the per-tag formatting is going to look is to use the Preview area (bottom of the dialog box). It updates based on your choices so that you can make informed decisions on the formatting. Unfortunately it does not show color choices (described later).

Outlining in code editor

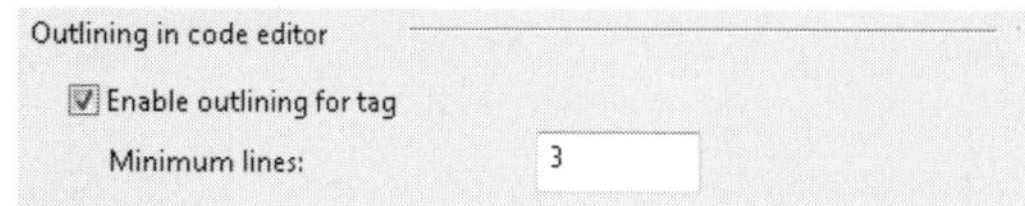

Enable outlining for tag

When outlining is enabled, the editor monitors the number of lines in the element and then applies outlining to the tag when the element exceeds the specified line threshold. (The editor does not automatically collapse the tag.) This feature is useful for collapsing long elements, such as large tables.

> **Note** If outlining doesn't show up as expected try closing and re-opening the file to make it appear.

Minimum lines

Number of lines before outlining is enabled for the element.

Example: The <DIV> has outlining enabled and minimum lines set to three. For three lines or more in an element, outlining, the minus sign to the left of the opening tag, is enabled for that element:

```
<div>
    something cool is here
</div>
```

Notice the outlining (the minus sign to the left of the opening <DIV> tag, shown in the preceding illustration) that has kicked in because we have the minimum number of lines. In this example, if the minimum lines are changed to five, outlining is not enabled and no minus sign appears:

```
<div>
    something cool is here
</div>
```

Per tag colorization

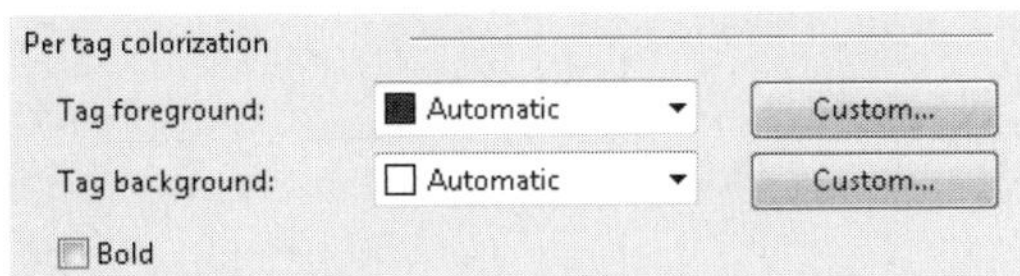

Tag foreground

The color of the text for the tags.

Tag background

The color of the text background.

Bold

Makes the tags bold.

Finally

You can see that there is much to learn about tag-specific options. Take your time as you explore the possibilities in the Tag Specific Options dialog box.

Chapter 7
Debugging

"It has been just so in all my inventions. The first step is an intuition—and comes with a burst, then difficulties arise. This thing that gives out and then that—'Bugs' as such little faults and difficulties are called show themselves and months of anxious watching, study and labor are requisite before commercial success—or failure—is certainly reached."

—Thomas Alva Edison
Letter to Theodore Puskas (18 Nov 1878)

As a developer, you spend a great deal of time debugging. Visual Studio has long provided great tools for helping find errors in your code. This chapter focuses on showing how to take full advantage of common items like the Locals and Autos windows as well as exploring more advanced techniques such as setting tracepoints in the Call Stack window.

Additionally, lots of great new features in Visual Studio 2010 can help with your trouble-shooting efforts. Major changes have been made to the Breakpoints window, and new DataTips are available to provide information when and where you need it. There is no short-age of great techniques to cut down the time you spend finding problems in your code.

07.01 Setting a Breakpoint with Code

VERSIONS	2005, 2008, 2010
CODE	vstipDebug0036

Sometimes you want to have clear breakpoints in your code that travel with the source. You can do this quite easily.

Compiler Directive

In C# and VB, you need to set a compiler option that hits the breakpoint only when debugging. If you don't, your release code continues to hit the code-based breakpoint, which is generally considered a bad thing. To do this, you set the #If DEBUG compiler option, as you can see in each of the following code samples.

C#

In C#, you set a breakpoint by using the System.Diagnostics.Debugger.Break method:

```
#if DEBUG
   System.Diagnostics.Debugger.Break();
#endif
```

VB

In VB, you set a breakpoint by using the Stop command:

```
#If DEBUG Then
        Stop
#End If
```

Now you can use code to set breakpoints. Just as an aside, breakpoints set in this way do not show up in the Breakpoints window.

C++

In C++, it's a very similar situation. Based on the type of C++ project you are creating, these commands can change slightly; but with native C++, you can use the __debugbreak command with the #if _DEBUG compiler option:

```
#if _DEBUG

    __debugbreak;

#endif
```

07.02 Using Ctrl+Alt+B to Open the Breakpoints Window

DEFAULT	Ctrl+Alt+B
VISUAL BASIC 6	Ctrl+Alt+B
VISUAL C# 2005	Ctrl+Alt+B; Ctrl+D, Ctrl+B; Ctrl+D, B
VISUAL C++ 2	Ctrl+Alt+B; Ctrl+B
VISUAL C++ 6	Ctrl+Alt+B; Alt+F9
VISUAL STUDIO 6	Ctrl+B
WINDOWS	Alt, D, W, B
MENU	Debug | Windows | Breakpoints
COMMAND	Debug.Breakpoints
VERSIONS	2005, 2008, 2010
CODE	vstipDebug0011

Use Ctrl+Alt+B to open the Breakpoints window or, if it is already open, to give it the focus.

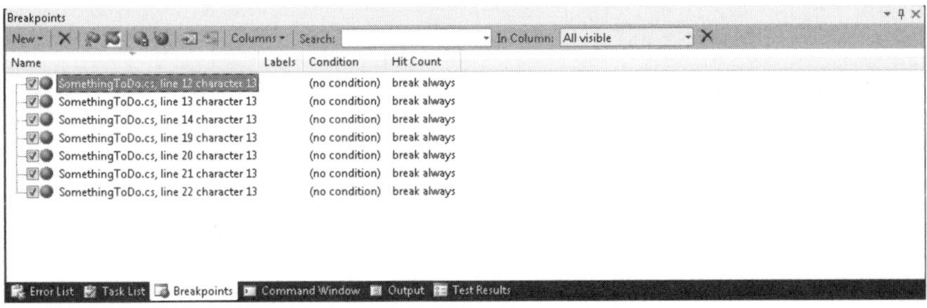

07.03 Adding Labels to Breakpoints

DEFAULT	Alt+F9, L
VISUAL BASIC 6	Alt+F9, L
VISUAL C# 2005	Alt+F9, L
VISUAL C++ 2	Alt+F9, L
VISUAL C++ 6	[no shortcut]
VISUAL STUDIO 6	Alt+F9, L
WINDOWS	Shift+F10, A (inside Breakpoints Window)
MENU	[Context Menu] | Edit Labels
COMMAND	EditorContextMenus.CodeWindow.Breakpoint.BreakpointEditlabels
VERSIONS	2010
CODE	vstipDebug0001

Did you know that breakpoints in Visual Studio 2010 support labels? This tip explains how you can use them. How do labels help you? Well, first, you can now have friendly names for breakpoints to make them easier to understand. Second, you can sort by the label names.

And, third, you can search the labels from the Breakpoints window. (See vstipDebug0002, "Searching Breakpoints," on page 312.)

After setting one or more breakpoints in your code, open the Breakpoint window (Ctrl+Alt+B). Notice the new Labels column:

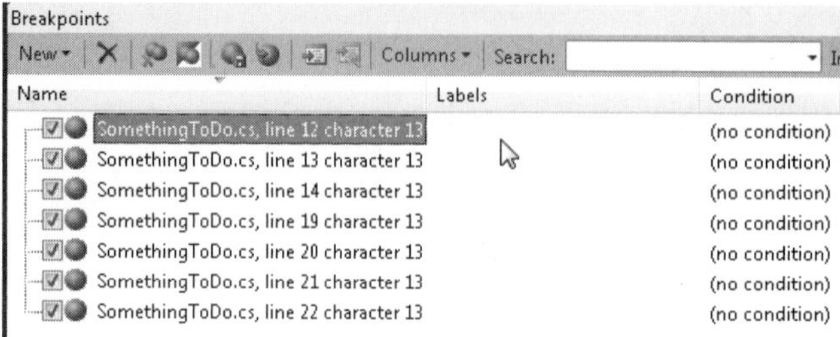

Right-click one or more selected breakpoints to bring up the context menu, and choose Edit Labels (Alt+F9, L):

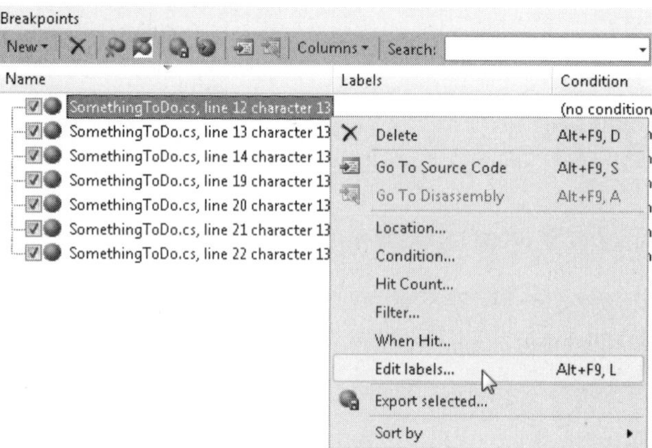

You get the following dialog box:

You can type in one (or more) labels for the breakpoint and/or select one of the labels previously used, and then click OK. You should see now your label(s):

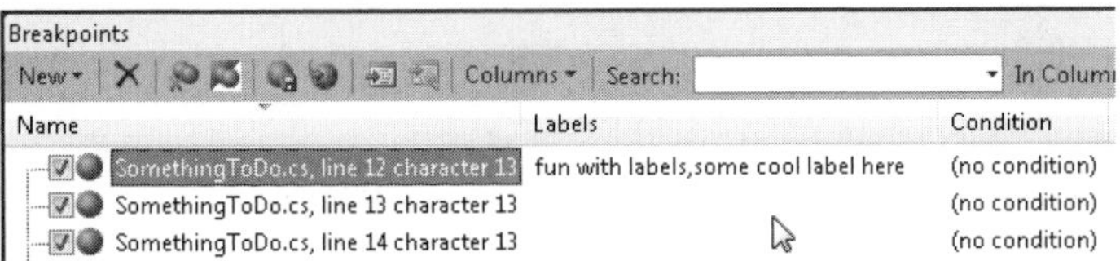

07.04 Enable or Disable All Breakpoints

WINDOWS	Alt,D, N
MENU	Debug | Disable All Breakpoints; Debug | Enable All Breakpoints
COMMAND	Debug.DisableAllBreakpoints; Debug.EnableAllBreakpoints
VERSIONS	2005, 2008, 2010
CODE	vstipDebug0018

There are times when you will want to quickly and temporarily turn off all or some of your breakpoints. This tip covers how to disable and enable your breakpoints.

You can go to Debug | Disable All Breakpoints on the menu bar, or in the Breakpoints window, you can click the Enable Or Disable All Breakpoints button:

Note In Visual Studio 2010, only the breakpoints currently visible in the window are disabled when you use this option, so it is very useful for enabling or disabling a subset of your breakpoints when used with the Search feature.

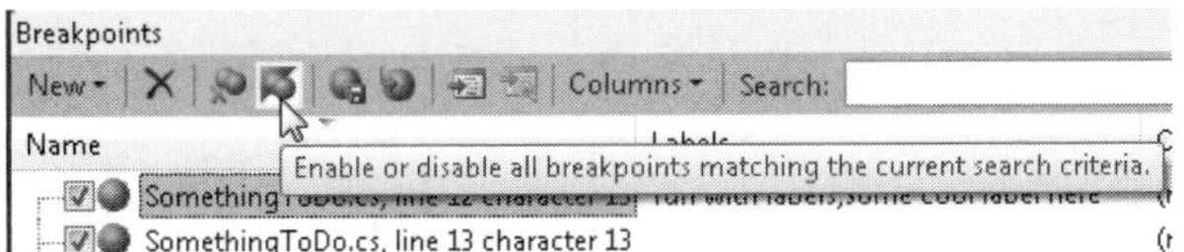

The result, in either case, is the same. One or more breakpoints in the current project are disabled:

```
public void Do ( Int32 iParam , Int32 iAnotherParam )
{
    iAnotherParam = 6;
    int jLocal = iParam;
    Re ( 3.145 * jLocal );
}
```

To enable them again, just go to Debug | Enable All Breakpoints on the menu bar, or click the Enable Or Disable All Breakpoints button in the Breakpoints window again:

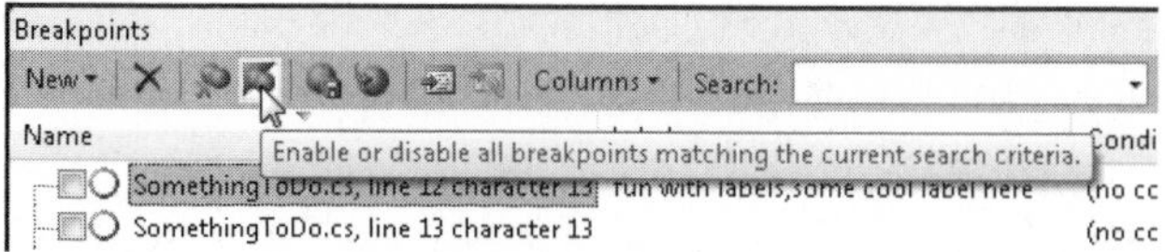

07.05 TODO Comments in the Task List

VERSIONS	2005, 2008, 2010
CODE	vstipTool0029

Have you ever written some code and want to leave a reminder to yourself to do something? Did you know about the "To Do" comment feature? It is a great feature, and because the comment goes directly in the source, everyone can have access to the information when you check in code.

So here's how it works.

VB

In VB, you just put any comment in that begins with "todo" (case doesn't matter):

```
'TODO fix this connection string
```

C#

In C#, it's the same thing (again, case doesn't matter):

```
//todo fix this connection string
```

C++

The C++ version looks just like C#, but you have to explicitly turn this feature on, and the "TODO" must be all uppercase. Go to Tools | Options | Text Editor | C/C++ | Formatting | Miscellaneous, and change Enumerate Comment Tasks to True:

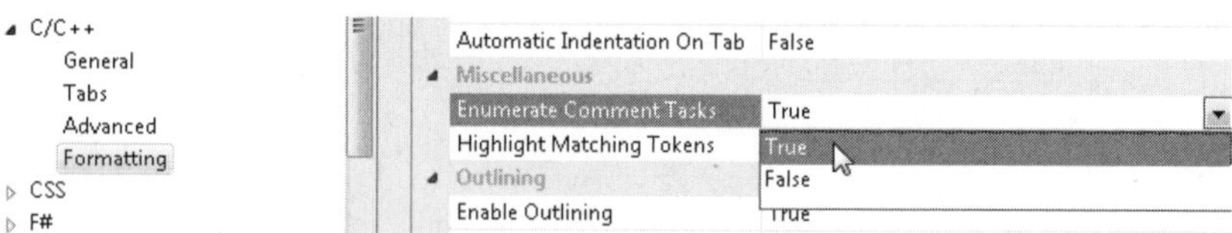

Whichever language you use, the result is a nice entry in your Task List dialog box:

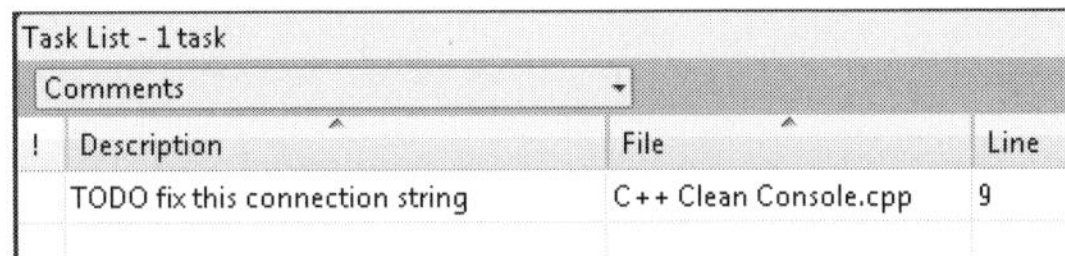

Note To see these items, you have to click the drop-down list in the Task List dialog box and choose Comments, as shown in the preceding illustration.

Like all Task List items, comments are Solution-wide in scope, so you will see all the shortcuts for the entire solution in the Task List window.

07.06 Create Custom Tokens for the Task List

WINDOWS	Alt,T, O
MENU	Tools | Options
COMMAND	Tools.Options
VERSIONS	2005, 2008, 2010
CODE	vstipTool0032

In vstipTool0029 ("TODO Comments in the Task List," page 296), I showed you how to create comments that show up in the Task List:

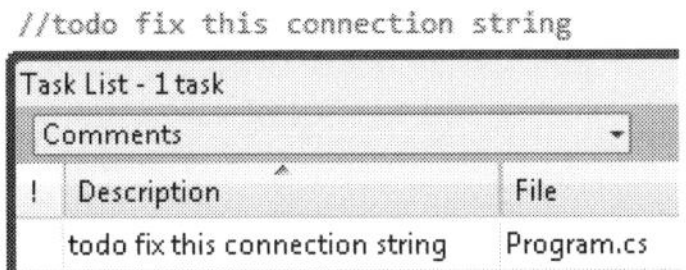

The "TODO" part is known as a token. It's a trigger to indicate that an item should be put in the Task List. Did you know you can create your own custom tokens? Go to Tools | Options | Environment | Task List | Tokens to see the following window:

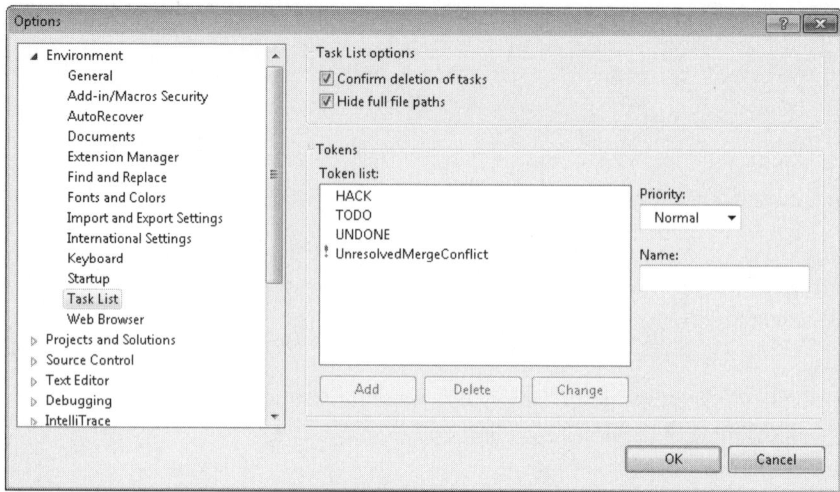

As shown in the preceding illustration, notice the following entries in this area: HACK, TODO, UNDONE, and UnresolvedMergeConflict. By the way, UnresolvedMergeConflict is not an error; it is an actual token that you can use.

For now, let's create a couple of our own. In the Name text box, type in the word **low**, set the priority to Low, and then click Add. You should see the following:

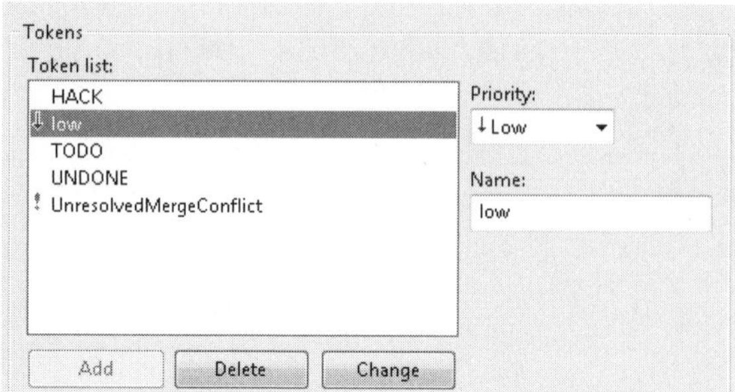

Now do the same thing again, this time using the word **high** and setting the priority to High:

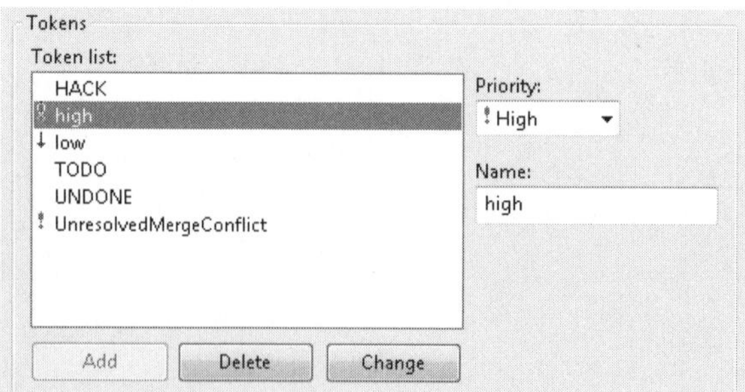

You now have a couple of custom tokens. Add two comments to your existing code, and use the new "low" and "high" tokens:

```
//todo fix this connection string
//low tell Joe to fix this part
//high tell Mary to redo this section
```

You now see the following in the Task List:

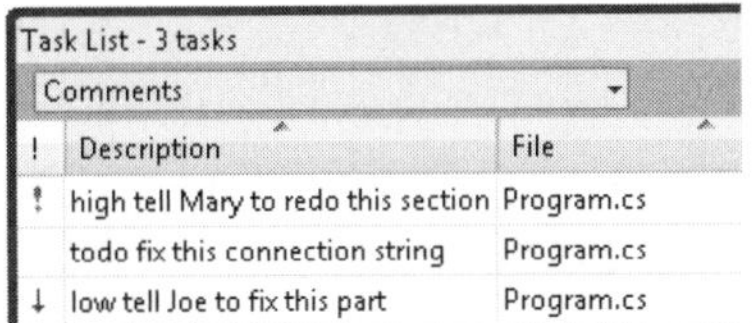

Sharing Tokens

You can create as many tokens as you want to suit your needs, so feel free to experiment with these. Unfortunately, the tokens aren't shared unless you export them and then someone else imports them. Go to Tools | Import And Export Settings, and export the Task List Options found under All Settings, Options, Environment:

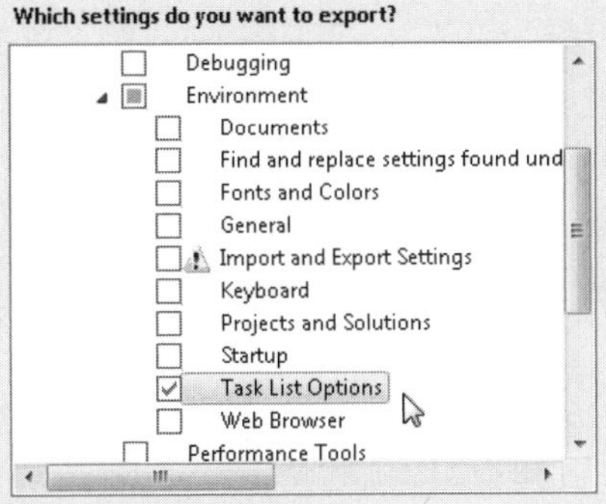

07.07 Create Code Shortcuts in the Task List

DEFAULT	Ctrl+K, Ctrl+H
VISUAL BASIC 6	Ctrl+K, Ctrl+H
VISUAL C# 2005	Ctrl+K, Ctrl+H; Ctrl+E, Ctrl+T; Ctrl+E, T
VISUAL C++ 2	[no shortcut]
VISUAL C++ 6	Ctrl+K, Ctrl+H
VISUAL STUDIO 6	Ctrl+K, Ctrl+H
WINDOWS	Alt,E, K, H
MENU	Edit | Bookmarks | Add Task List Shortcut
COMMAND	Command Edit.ToggleTaskListShortcut
VERSIONS	2005, 2008, 2010
CODE	vstipTool0030

In vstipTool0029 ("TODO Comments in the Task List," page 296), I showed you how to create comments that show up in your Task List window. However, sometimes all you want is a shortcut to a line of code that you visit often. You can create shortcuts to any line of code. Just place the cursor on the line, and press Ctrl+K, Ctrl+H (toggles the shortcut on or off). This creates the shortcut glyph in the margin:

```
        iAnotherParam = 6;
        int jLocal = iParam;
        Re ( 3.145 * jLocal );
```

To see all your shortcuts, go to the Task List dialog (Ctrl+\, T), and choose Shortcuts from the drop-down list:

Now you should see all the shortcuts you created:

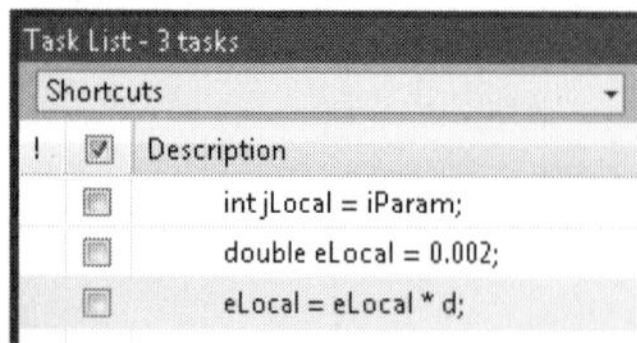

You can treat them like any other task, and you can set priority levels as well as mark them complete:

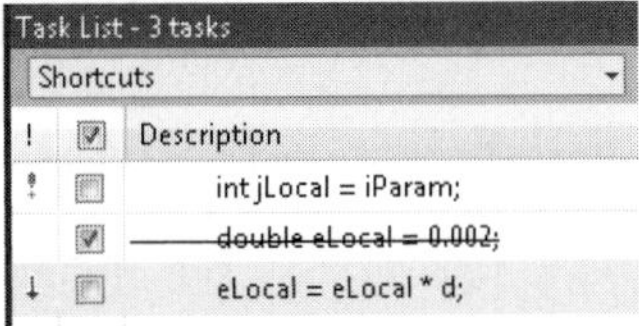

You can double-click any item to go to the line of code referenced in the shortcut, right-click, and then choose Delete to remove it from the list.

Like all Task List items, these are Solution-wide in scope, so you will see all the shortcuts for the entire solution in the Task List window.

07.08 Code Definition Window

DEFAULT	Ctrl+\, Ctrl+D; Ctrl+\, D
VISUAL BASIC 6	Ctrl+\, Ctrl+D; Ctrl+\, D
VISUAL C# 2005	Ctrl+\, Ctrl+D; Ctrl+\, D; Ctrl+W, Ctrl+D; Ctrl+W, D
VISUAL C++ 2	Ctrl+\, Ctrl+D; Ctrl+\, D
VISUAL C++ 6	Ctrl+\, Ctrl+D; Ctrl+\, D; Ctrl+Shift+V
VISUAL STUDIO 6	Ctrl+\, Ctrl+D; Ctrl+\, D
WINDOWS	Alt,V, D
MENU	View | Code Definition Window
COMMAND	View.CodeDefinitionWindow
VERSIONS	2005, 2008, 2010
LANGUAGES	C++, C#
CODE	vstipTool0012

Ever want to just click on a reference and see the definition as you go without having to use Go To Definition (F12)? For quite some time, the Code Definition window has been available to use just for this purpose. Go to View | Code Definition Window, and you see the following:

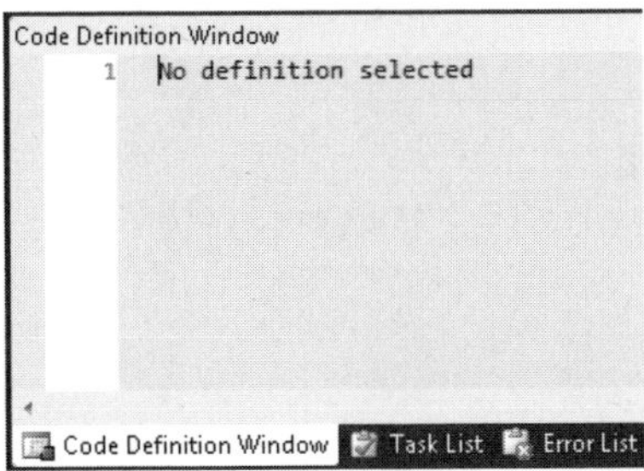

Now click on any symbol you would like to get a definition for, and you should get something like this:

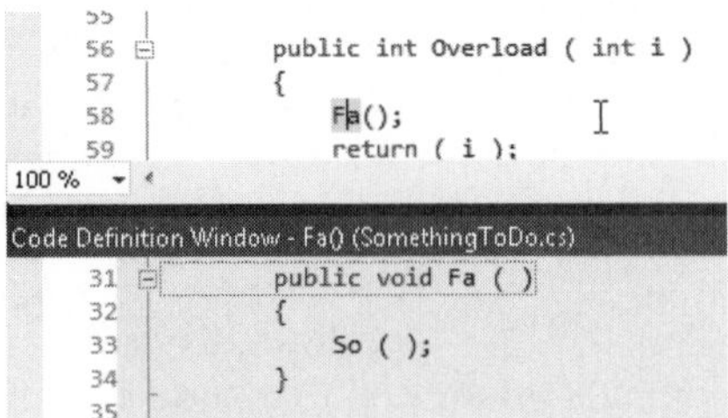

The Code Definition window provides you with an instant, read-only view of your definition so that you don't have to look for it when you are looking at a symbol.

07.09 Save Changes Before Building

WINDOWS	Alt,T, O
MENU	Tools | Options | Projects and Solutions | Build and Run
COMMAND	Tools.Options
VERSIONS	2005, 2008, 2010
CODE	vstipProj0015

In Tools | Options | Projects and Solutions | Build And Run, notice the Before Building option:

The default setting is to save all changes to the solution file and to save all project files that changed since the last build, but other options are also available:

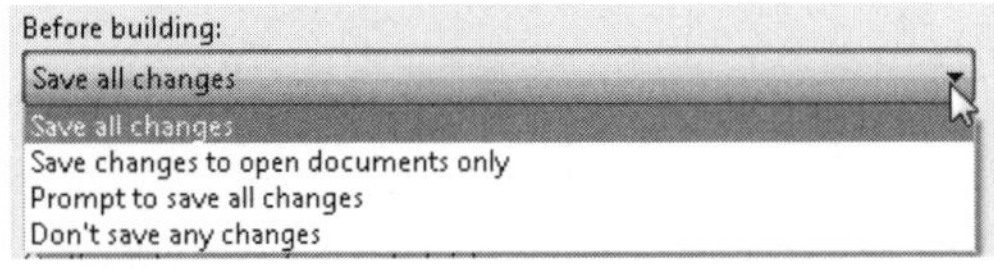

Save Changes To Open Documents Only

This option does what it says and saves changes to all open documents without any prompt.

Prompt To Save All Changes

This option prompts you with a choice about saving changes:

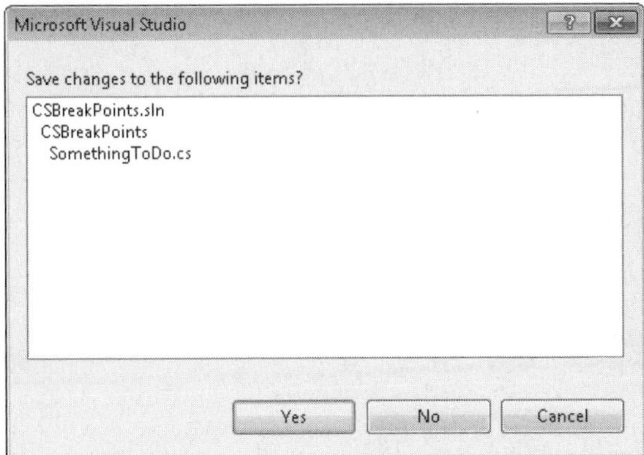

Don't Save Any Changes

This runs the code but does not save any of the changes you have made. Usually this is not a good idea, but it might be useful in some situations where you are testing many different code scenarios quickly.

07.10 Navigate Errors in the Error List

DEFAULT	F8 (next); Shift+F8 (previous)
VISUAL BASIC 6	[no shortcut]
VISUAL C# 2005	F8 (next); Shift+F8 (previous)
VISUAL C++ 2	F4 (next); Shift+F4 (previous)
VISUAL C++ 6	F8 (next); F4 (next)
VISUAL STUDIO 6	F8 (next); F12 (next); Shift+F8 (previous); Shift+F12 (previous)
WINDOWS	[no shortcut]
COMMAND	Edit.GoToNextLocation; Edit.GoToPrevLocation
VERSIONS	2005, 2008, 2010
CODE	vstipTool0019

When checking out errors in the Errors window, you can easily navigate to the next error by pressing F8 or to the previous error by pressing Shift+F8. These actions rotate through all the errors in the direction of choice:

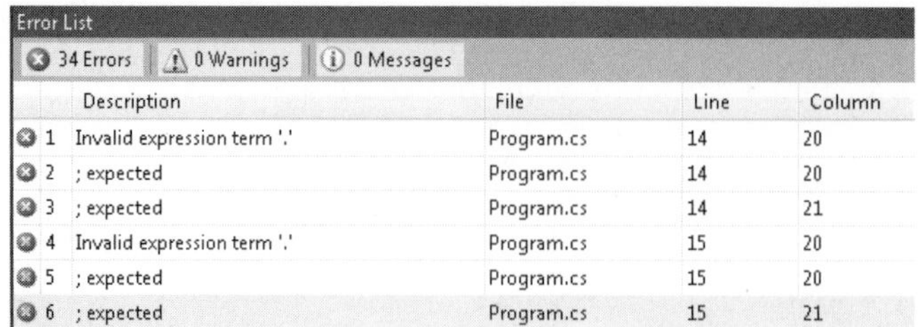

Error List

34 Errors | 0 Warnings | 0 Messages

	Description	File	Line	Column
1	Invalid expression term '.'	Program.cs	14	20
2	; expected	Program.cs	14	20
3	; expected	Program.cs	14	21
4	Invalid expression term '.'	Program.cs	15	20
5	; expected	Program.cs	15	20
6	; expected	Program.cs	15	21

Additionally, as you cycle through, the location of each error in your code is selected:

```
            Console.WriteLine
            Console.WriteLine
            Console.WriteLine
            Console.WriteLine
            Console.WriteLine
```

07.11 Ordering and Multicolumn Sorting in Tool Windows

VERSIONS	2005, 2008, 2010
CODE	vstipTool0021

When working with the various tool windows, you often need the ability to rearrange the information in different ways. With column ordering and column sorting, you have this ability.

Column Ordering

This technique can be used in a variety of tool windows, most notably the Task List window. Let's begin with reordering the columns. In tool windows where this is supported, you can drag the columns around to put them in the order you want:

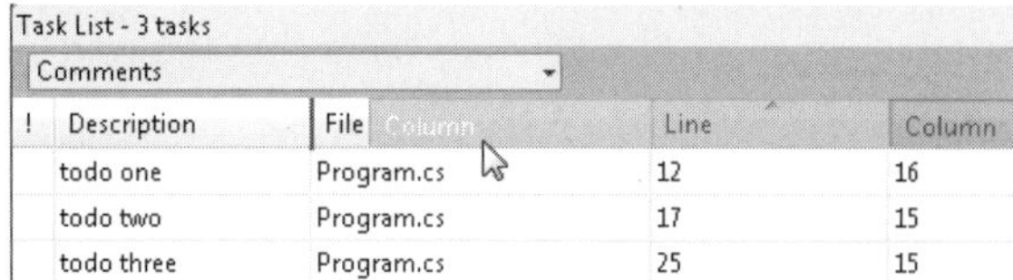

Task List - 3 tasks

Comments

!	Description	File	Line	Column
	todo one	Program.cs	12	16
	todo two	Program.cs	17	15
	todo three	Program.cs	25	15

Additionally, you can sort by clicking on a column to make it sort ascending or descending, as shown in the following illustrations:

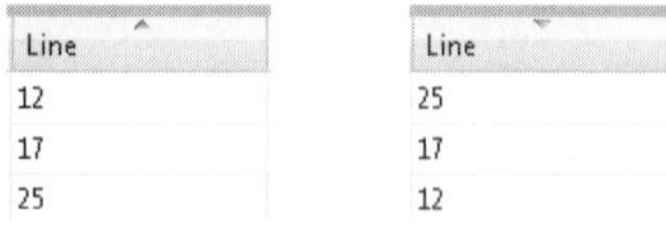

Line
12
17
25

Line
25
17
12

Multicolumn Sorting

But the best part is that you can have multicolumn sorting. So you can sort first by one column:

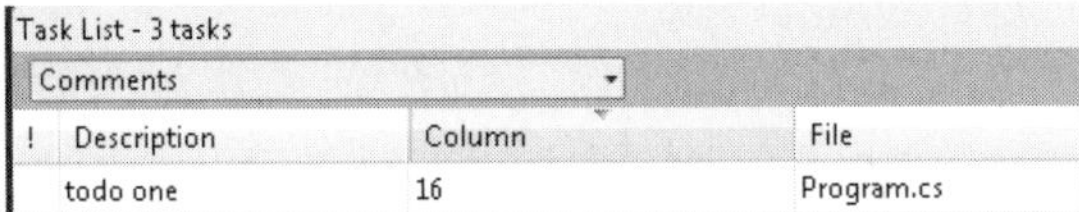

Then just press Shift, and click on the next column you would like to sort by:

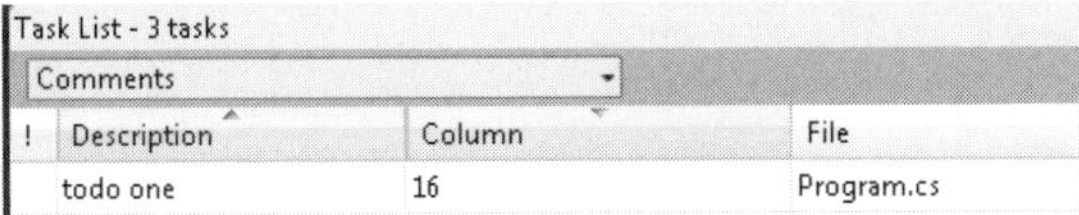

If you want, you can continue to hold Shift and sort by more columns:

Task List - 3 tasks

Comments

!	Description	Column	File
	todo one	16	Program.cs

07.12 Pin a DataTip to Source Code

COMMAND	EditorContextMenus.CodeWindow.PinToSource
VERSIONS	2010
CODE	vstipDebug0005

In Visual Studio 2010, you can now pin DataTips to source code. The purpose of pinned DataTips is to have the information stay with the line of code at all times, even after you scroll away from that line. To create one, just put your mouse pointer over any variable while debugging:

```
x = x + 1;
    x | 11
```

Notice the little pin at the end of the DataTip shown in the preceding illustration? If you click the pin, you have a pinned DataTip. The most obvious indicator of this is the pushpin that now shows up in the far left margin:

```
15
16      x = x + 1;   x 11
17
```

It is now, quite literally, pinned to a certain line of code. If you click the DataTip and drag it, you can change the line that the DataTip is pinned to:

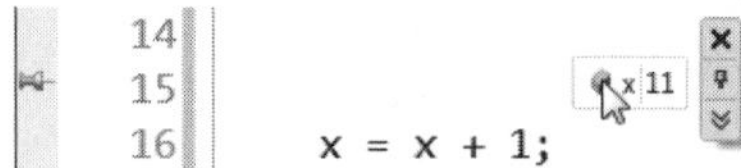

You can also drill down into objects and pin properties as well:

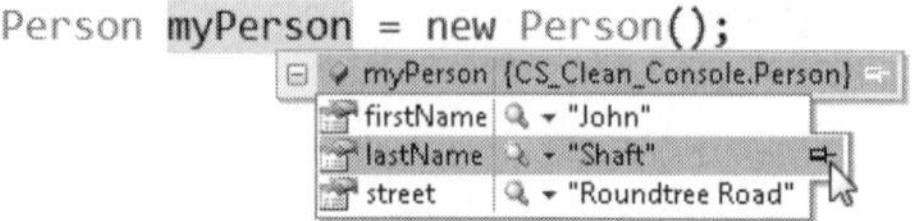

07.13 Create a Floating DataTip

VERSIONS	2010
CODE	vstipDebug0006

Floating DataTips are great for having information available where you want it. This tip shows how you use them. First, enter Break Mode, and pause your mouse pointer over a variable in the current scope; you should see something like the following:

```
int x = 10;
```

Click the pin to create a pinned DataTip (see vstipDebug0005, "Pin a DataTip to Source Code," on page 305). Now, to make it a floating tip, put your mouse over the pinned tip until you see the control panel shown in the following illustration.

Note The control panel might not come up exactly where the pinned tip is, so you might have to look around a bit to find it.

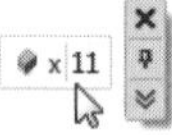

For this tip, our focus is on the pin in the middle:

Click it, and you should get a floating DataTip. (Notice the yellow color for floating DataTips.)

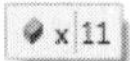

OK, so why should you care? Well, unlike pinned DataTips, floating DataTips don't follow the source code as you step through it. This is useful if you want to step through code and have one or more pieces of information. The control panel might not come up exactly where the pinned tip is, so you might have to look around a bit to find it.

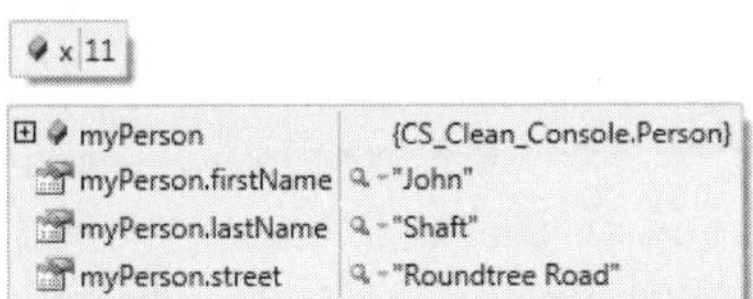

07.14 Adding Comments to a DataTip

VERSIONS	2010
CODE	vstipDebug0007

You might want to make a comment to remind yourself about something in a DataTip (pinned or floating), and now you can. First, enter Debug Mode, and then pause your mouse over a pinned (see vstipDebug0005, "Pin a DataTip to Source Code," on page 305) or floating tip (see vstipDebug0006, "Create a Floating DataTip," page 306) until you see the control panel shown in the following illustration.

Note The control panel might not come up exactly where the pinned tip is, so you might have to look around a bit to find it.

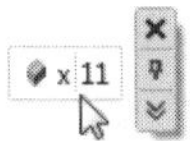

Click the chevron at the bottom:

You should see something like the following illustration on your DataTip:

Now you can put in comments that travel with the DataTip at all times:

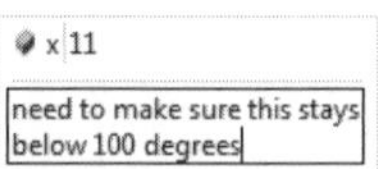

At the time of this writing, no upper limit is assigned to the amount of text you can put into this area. I was able to successfully paste the entire text of "War and Peace" in here. While I don't suggest you do the same, the point is that you can be quite verbose with your comments if you need to be.

07.15 Use a DataTip to Edit a Value

VERSIONS	2008, 2010
CODE	vstipDebug0026

You can change a variable value on the fly in a variety of ways. One of them is through the DataTip. Just click the value for a simple variable to change it:

```
x = x + 1;
        x 1337
```

For more complex types, you might need to expand the variables and edit individual items:

07.16 DataTip Value from the Last Debug Session

VERSIONS	2010
CODE	vstipDebug0012

Ever forget the values of variables you were just debugging? This is one of the coolest features of the DataTips in Visual Studio 2010. Let's assume that you have a pinned DataTip in your code (see vstipDebug0005, "Pin a DataTip to Source Code," on page 305):

```
x = x + 1;   x 11
```

Now you stop debugging. Even though you are not debugging, you can still view the value from the last debug session by simply resting your mouse pointer over the pin in the margin:

```
             Value from last debug session
x = x + 1;   x 11
```

07.17 Import and Export DataTips

WINDOWS	Alt,D, X,X, Enter; Alt,D, P, P, Enter
MENU	Debug | Export DataTips; Debug | Import DataTips
COMMAND	Debug.ExportDataTips; Debug.ImportDataTips
VERSIONS	2005, 2008, 2010
CODE	vstipDebug0013

Just as with breakpoints (see vstipDebug0003, "How to Import and Export Breakpoints," on page 329), you now have the ability to share your DataTips with team members by using the Export / Import features. Just go to Debug | Import (or Export) DataTips:

When you export the DataTips, they are exported as XML. You can version these files along with your source code so that other team members can have a copy of your DataTips.

07.18 Using the Call Hierarchy

DEFAULT	Ctrl+K, Ctrl+T; Ctrl+K, T
VISUAL C++ 2	[no shortcut]
MENU	[Context Menu] | View Call Hierarchy
COMMAND	EditorContextMenus.CodeWindow.ViewCallHierarchy
VERSIONS	2010
LANGUAGES	C++, C#
CODE	vstipTool0005

The Call Hierarchy window allows you to visualize calls to and from a selected method, property, or constructor. To see how it works, just right-click any method, property, or constructor in the editor and select View Call Hierarchy:

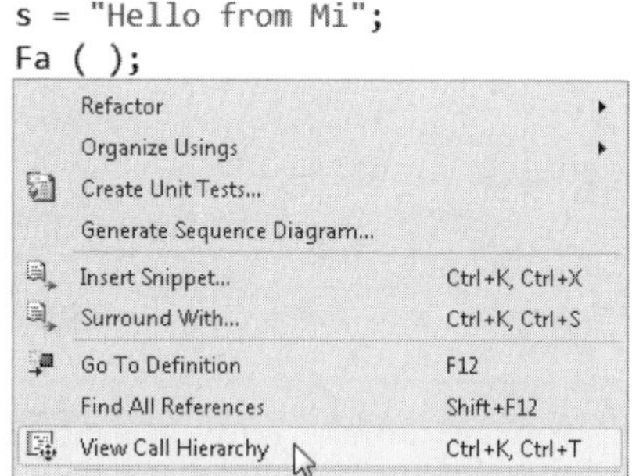

You should get a window similar to the following:

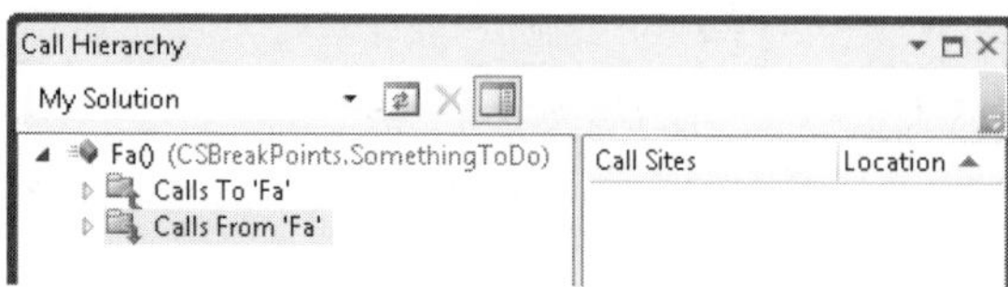

Notice the Calls To and Calls From areas related to your selection. You can expand them:

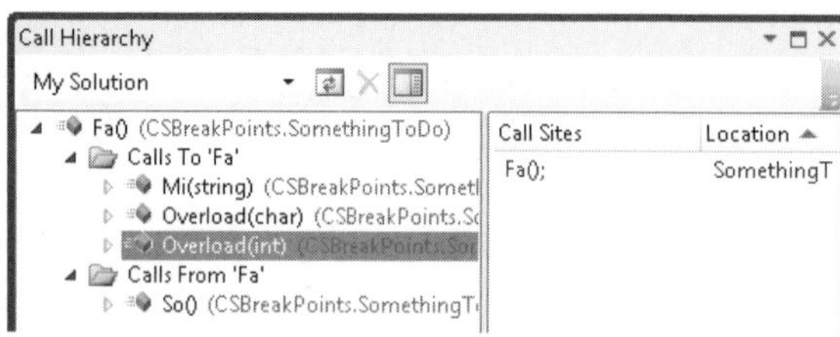

When you click on a node in the tree, the Call Sites pane updates so that you can visit the call if you want to:

Note You can double-click on the call site to have it automatically take you to the reference.

You can continue expanding the hierarchy to see further Calls To and Calls From information:

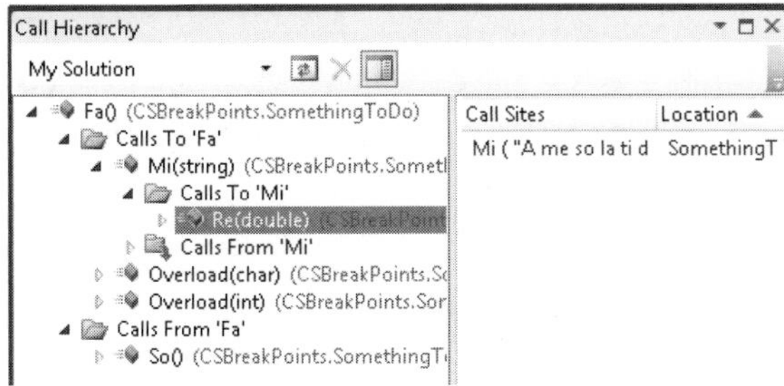

The best part is that you can right-click a symbol and get several options:

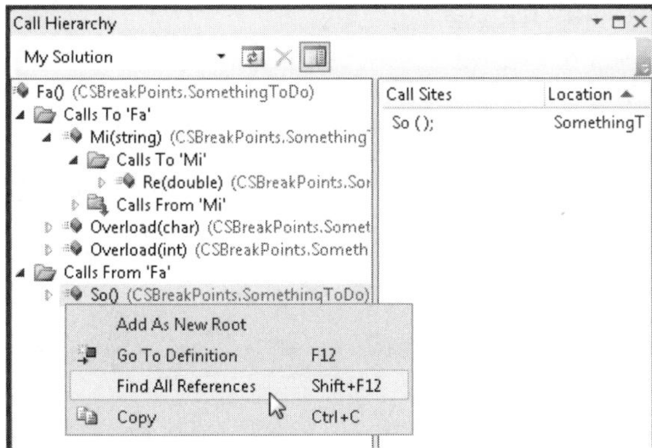

The following table describes some options you will come across as you use this feature:

Context Menu Item	Description
Add As New Root	Adds the selected node to the tree view pane as a new root node.
Remove Root	Removes the selected root node from the tree view pane. This option is available only from a root node. You can also use the Remove Root toolbar button to remove the selected root node.
Go To Definition	Runs the Go To Definition command on the selected node. This navigates to the original definition for a method call or variable definition. You can also press F12 to run the Go To Definition command on the selected node.
Find All References	Runs the Find All References command on the selected node. This finds all the lines of code in your project that reference a class or member. You can also use Shift+F12 to run the Find All References command on the selected node.
Copy	Copies the contents of the selected node (but not its subnodes).
Refresh	Collapses the selected node so that re-expanding it displays current information.

07.19 Searching Breakpoints

VERSIONS	2010
CODE	vstipDebug0002

When working with larger sets of breakpoints, it is useful to be able to search and filter based on criteria you choose. In Visual Studio 2010, you finally have the ability to search breakpoints the way you want. The ability to search your breakpoints is critical to being able to take actions on groups of breakpoints because the Breakpoints window commands now act on breakpoints that match the current search criteria. First, set some sample breakpoints in your code, and then open the Breakpoints window (Ctrl+Alt+B):

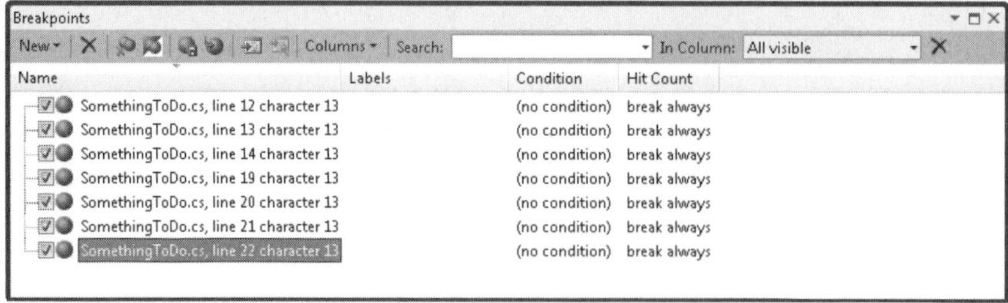

For this example, set some labels for your breakpoints (see vstipDebug0001, "Adding Labels to Breakpoints", on page 293) that have values you would like to search on:

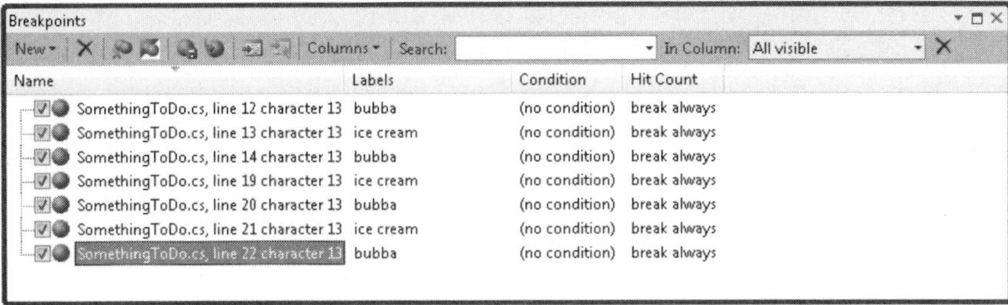

Select the column you want to search on (in this example, the Labels column):

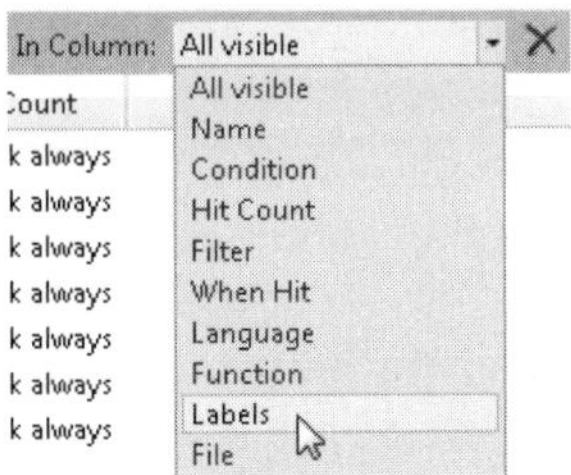

Type the string you are looking for in the search box inside the Breakpoints window, and press Enter. In this example, I'll search for any label with the letter *b* anywhere in it. This yields the following result:

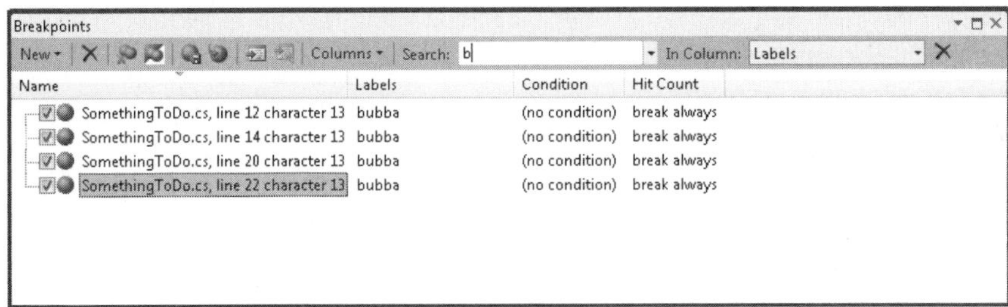

Now you can take actions on the breakpoints you can currently see. Most actions in the Breakpoints window now act on the results of the current search criteria:

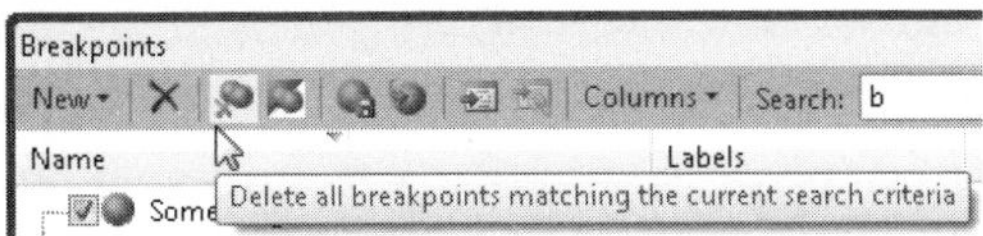

To clear the search so that you can see all the breakpoints, just click the Reset All Search Criteria So That All Breakpoints Are Shown button:

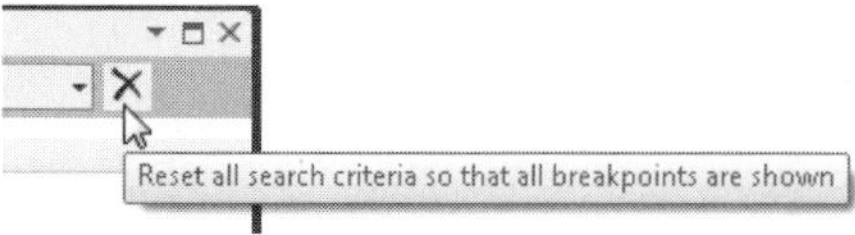

07.20 Breakpoint Hit Count

MENU	[Context Menu] | Hit Count
COMMAND	EditorContextMenus.CodeWindow.Breakpoint.BreakpointHitCount
VERSIONS	2005, 2008, 2010
CODE	vstipDebug0019

Sometimes you might not want a breakpoint to stop the first time it is encountered. This is particularly true when you are working with loops and want to stop after a number of iterations. You can set a breakpoint so that it does not break every time but only when it is hit a certain number of times. Just right-click any breakpoint, and click Hit Count:

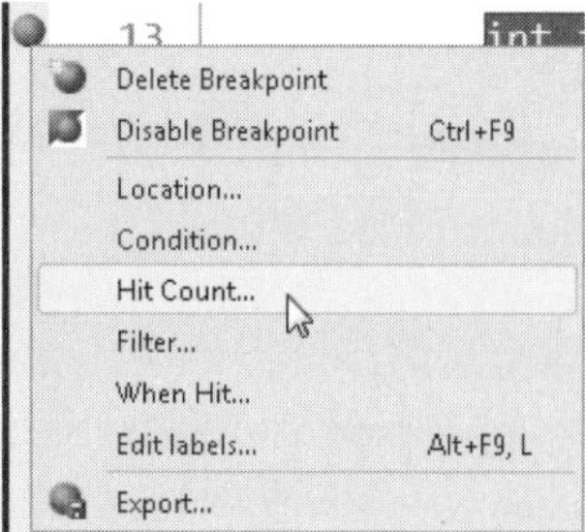

The Breakpoint Hit Count dialog box appears:

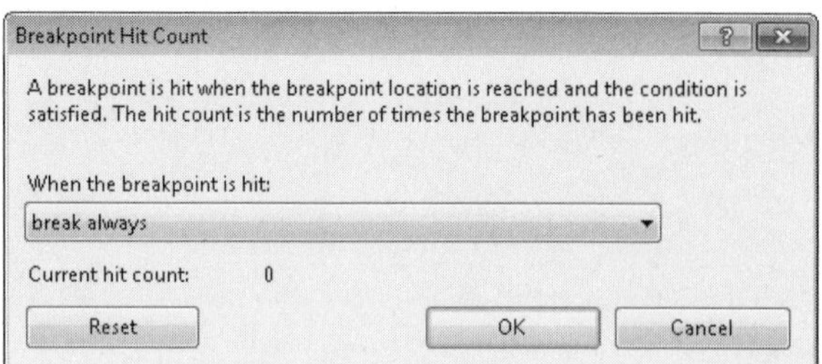

The default is to "break always," but you can change that to one of the following options:

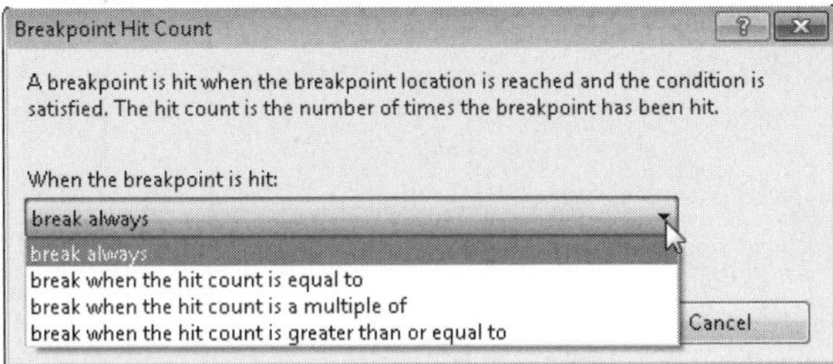

Break When The Hit Count Is Equal To

Choose this option if you want to break when the hit count reaches an exact value. So, in this example, if you put in a 5, the break does not occur until the breakpoint has been hit 5 times. This is useful when you know the number of hits you want before stopping.

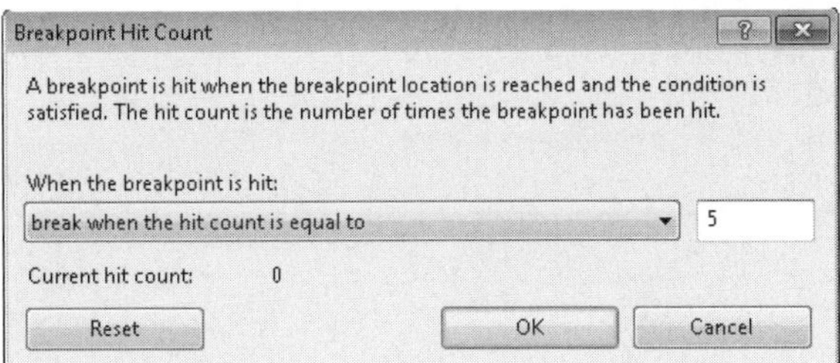

Break When The Hit Count Is A Multiple Of

This breaks every x number of times it is hit. So if you put in a 5, it breaks every 5th time (5, 10, 15, and so on). This helps when you aren't sure exactly where the problem is, so you want to skip in predefined increments as you look:

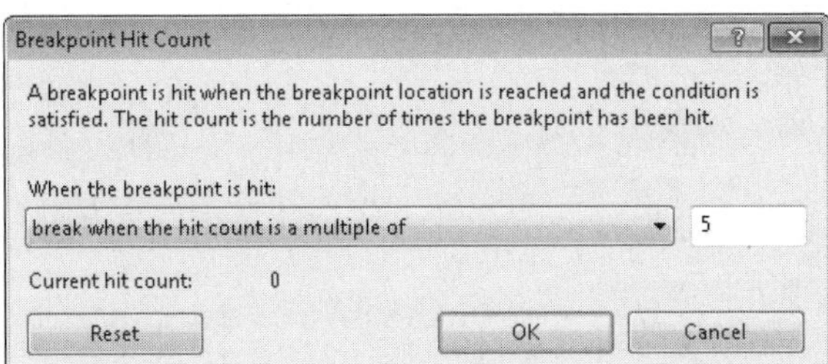

At any time, you can use the Breakpoints window to tell you the current hit count while you are debugging. In this example, the hit count is currently 15:

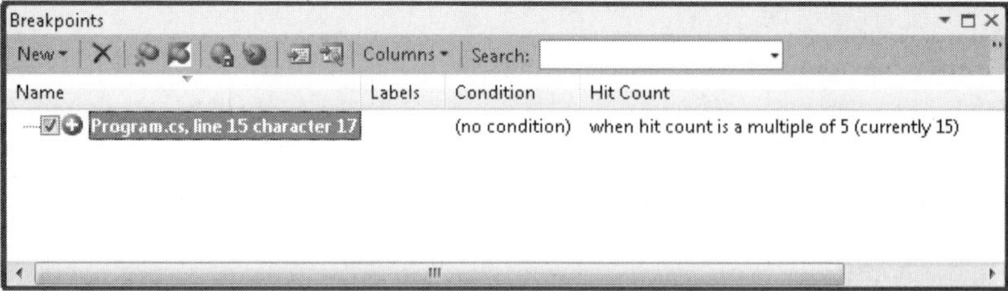

Break When The Hit Count Is Greater Than Or Equal To

This option takes any number and stops when the hit count has reached that number or higher. Use this option when you aren't exactly sure what the value should be but want to stop when it reaches an upper bound:

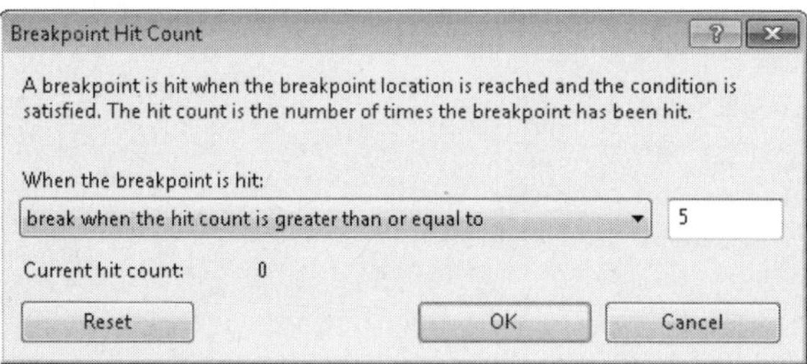

07.21 Set a Breakpoint on a Function

DEFAULT	Ctrl+B
VISUAL BASIC 6	Ctrl+B
VISUAL C# 2005	Ctrl+B; Ctrl+D, Ctrl+N; Ctrl+D, N
VISUAL C++ 2	[no shortcut]
VISUAL C++ 6	Ctrl+B
VISUAL STUDIO 6	[no shortcut]
WINDOWS	Alt,D, B, F
MENU	Debug | New Breakpoint | Break at Function
COMMAND	Debug.BreakatFunction
VERSIONS	2005, 2008, 2010
CODE	vstipDebug0020

By default, breakpoints are based on line and character position:

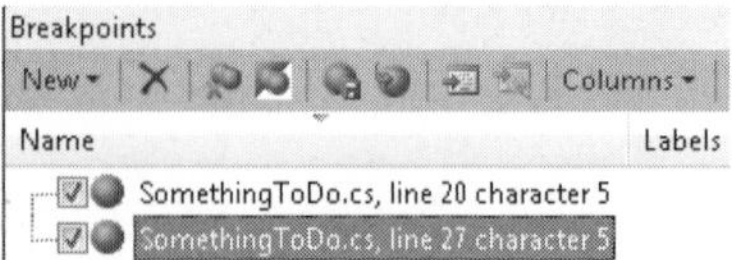

```
public void Re ( double d )
{
    d = 0.667;
    double eLocal = 0.002;
    eLocal = eLocal * d;
    Mi ( "A me so la ti do" );
}

public void Mi ( String s )
{
    s = "Hello from Mi";
    Fa ( );
}
```

But what if you don't want to break on a specific line but instead want to break when you hit a particular function? There are two ways to do this.

Breakpoints Window

In the Breakpoints window, click New and choose Break At Function (or press Ctrl+B) to bring up the New Breakpoint dialog box.

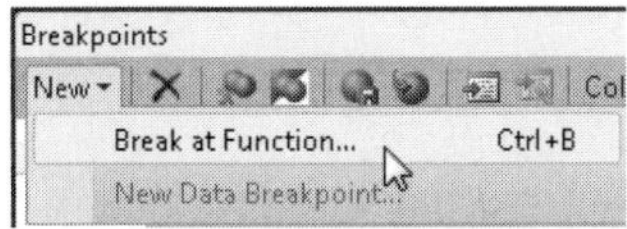

In the New Breakpoint dialog box, type in the name of the function you want to break at, and then click OK.

Warning To ensure that the correct function name is being used, always select Use IntelliSense To Verify The Function Name when you perform this action. Otherwise, the breakpoint might not work.

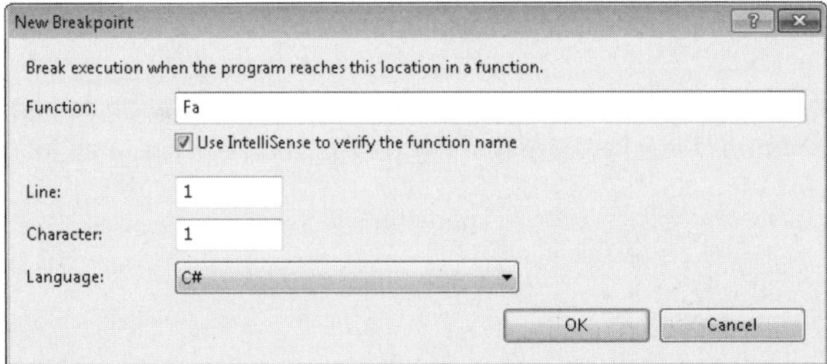

After you click OK in the New Breakpoint dialog box, you should see something similar to the following:

```
public void Fa ( )
{
    So ( );
}
```

The next illustration shows what a function breakpoint looks like in the Breakpoints window:

07.22 Set a Simple Breakpoint Condition

MENU	[Context Menu] | Condition
COMMAND	EditorContextMenus.CodeWindow.Breakpoint.BreakpointCondition
VERSIONS	2005, 2008, 2010
CODE	vstipDebug0021

Conditional breakpoints are arguably the most powerful types of breakpoints you can set. Many steps are involved in using them correctly, and knowing what steps you need to take is half the battle. Start by right-clicking on any breakpoint and choosing Condition.

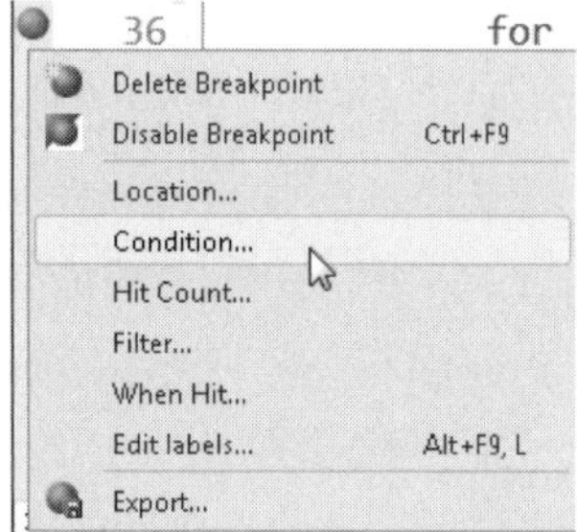

This gives us the Breakpoint Condition dialog box. Notice that the condition can be turned off by clearing the Condition check box. Additionally, two options are available for the condition that you set:

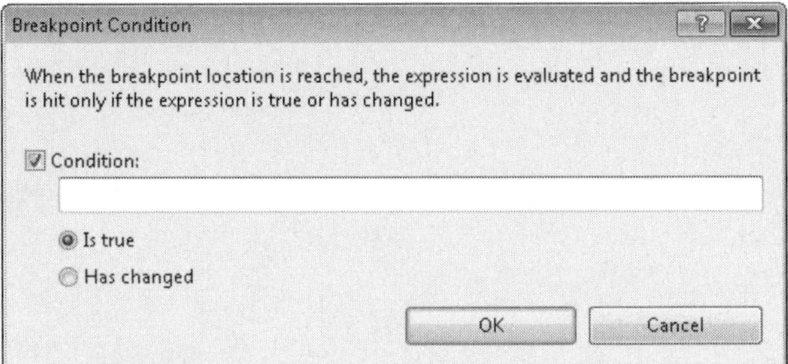

- **Is true**

  Used for Boolean expressions that evaluate to true or false.

- **Has changed**

  Used for detecting whether the value of an expression has changed at the breakpoint location.

Let's take a look at a couple of examples. Suppose we have the following For loop:

```
for ( i = 0 , m = 0 ; i < 10 ; i++ , m-- )
{
    sb.Length = 0;
    sb.AppendFormat ( "i = {0} m = {1}" , i , m );
    Trace.WriteLine ( sb.ToString ( ) );
}
```

Is True

We can set a simple "Is true" condition that says when the variable "i" is greater than 5, the code should stop:

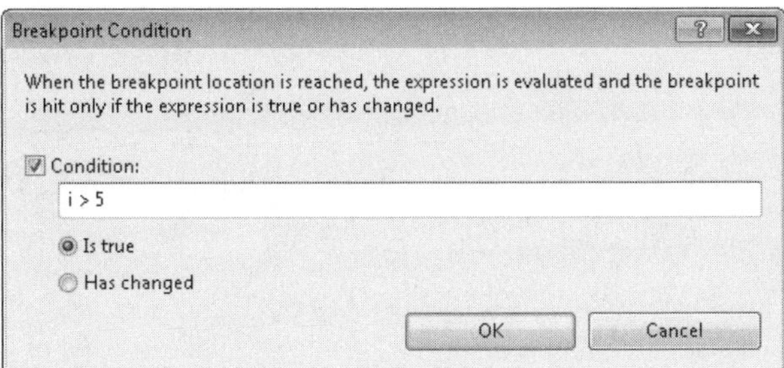

When we run the code and the breakpoint is hit, sure enough, it stops when the value of "i" is greater than 5:

```
i < 10 ;
  i 6
```

Has Changed

This one is more interesting. Basically we set up something to watch. In this case, let's just have it watch the "i" variable:

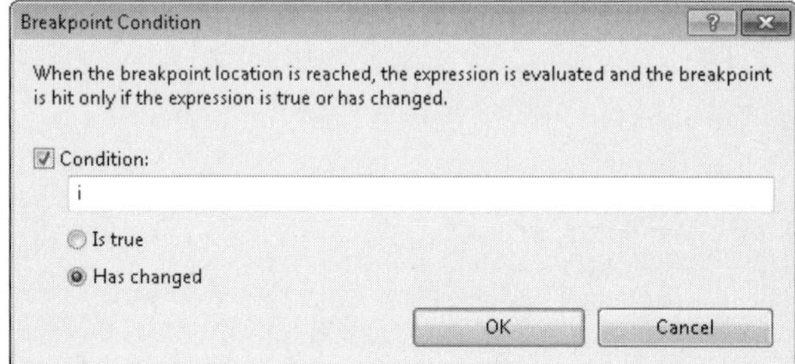

When the breakpoint is hit and the value of "i" has changed in any way, the code stops:

```
i < 10 ;
  i 0
```

Special Notes

Anytime you set an advanced breakpoint, you get a new glyph (red sphere with a plus sign in it):

You can always tell what kind of breakpoint you have by pausing your mouse over the glyph and looking at the tooltip or by looking in the Breakpoints window:

07.23 Set a Complex Breakpoint Condition

MENU	[Context Menu] | Condition
COMMAND	EditorContextMenus.CodeWindow.Breakpoint.BreakpointCondition
VERSIONS	2005, 2008, 2010
CODE	vstipDebug0022

We previously discussed how to set simple conditions. (See vstipDebug0021, "Set a Simple Breakpoint Condition," on page 318.) The real power of the Breakpoint Condition dialog box is the ability to execute any line of code from it:

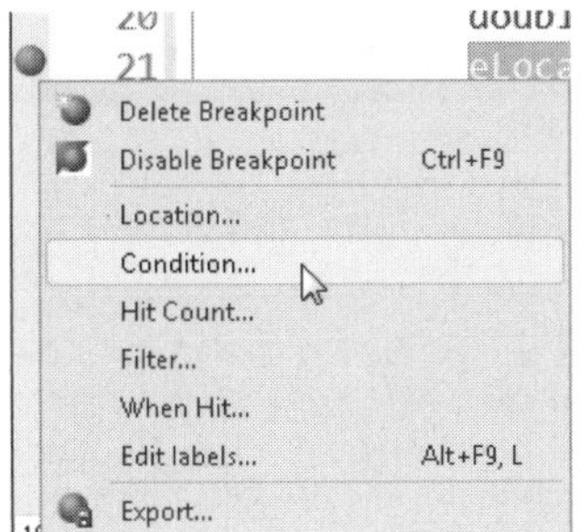

For example, you can use it to call external methods. The following example illustrates this, but bear in mind that it's a contrived example, designed to show how this works. The following illustration shows the code we want to execute:

```
public void Re(double d)
{
    d = 0.667;

    int x = 20;

    double eLocal = x + d;
    eLocal = eLocal * d;
    Mi("A me so la ti do");
}
```

Notice that a variable, x, is given a value. In this case, I hard-coded a value, but the value would presumably come as the result of some method execution. I want the breakpoint to stop only if the value of x is 20. I have a method that returns a Boolean value to test for the condition I want:

```
public bool CheckValue(int someValue)
{
    if (someValue == 20)
    {
        return true;
    }
    else
    {
        return false;
    }
}
```

I won't get into the obvious debate about whether this is a good idea or not, how the method should be constructed, or if the average rainfall in the Amazon Basin is a factor here. I'll just call the method from the Breakpoint Condition dialog box.

Notice that after typing a few characters, I use Ctrl+Space to get IntelliSense here if needed (see vstipEdit0017, "Using the New IntelliSense," on page 216):

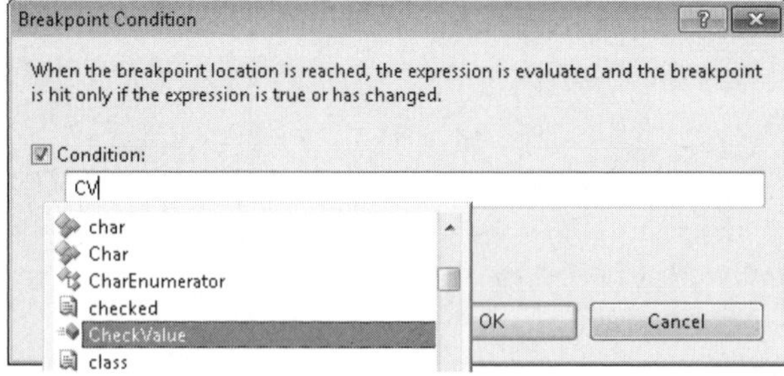

Make sure the Is True option is selected:

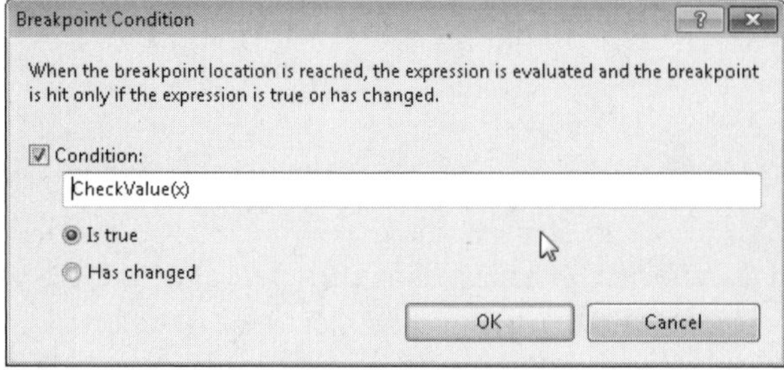

Now I have a conditional breakpoint that uses an external method to determine whether or not the code should stop. Naturally, you can add more Boolean logic here as well and include And / Or / Not / Xor:

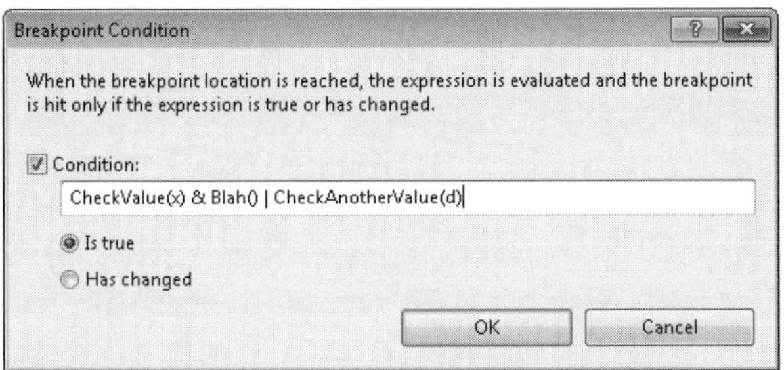

Now the really interesting part is that you can have your checking code be available only for Debug builds:

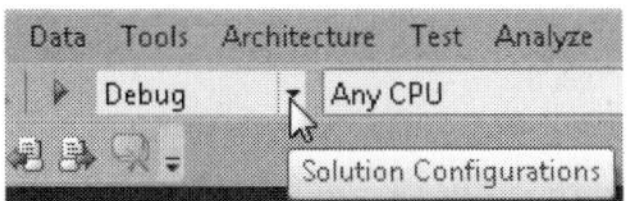

By surrounding your code with conditional compilation directives, you can easily have checking code that is around only while debugging. Following is what the checking method would look like in C#:

```
#if DEBUG
    public bool CheckValue(int someValue)
    {
        if (someValue == 20)
        {
            return true;
        }
        else
        {
            return false;
        }
    }
#endif
```

Play with this feature some, and you can see why most people (including me) think that this is one of the most powerful breakpoint features around.

07.24 Setting a Breakpoint Filter

WINDOWS	Alt,T, O (options)
MENU	Tools | Options; [Context Menu] | Filter
COMMAND	Tools.Options; EditorContextMenus.CodeWindow.Breakpoint.BreakpointFilter
VERSIONS	2005, 2008, 2010
CODE	vstipDebug0024

Breakpoint filters are used when you want to break based on thread, process, or machine information. This is particularly useful for debugging multithreaded applications. To make sure you can set them, go to Tools | Options | Debugging | General and select Enable Breakpoint Filters:

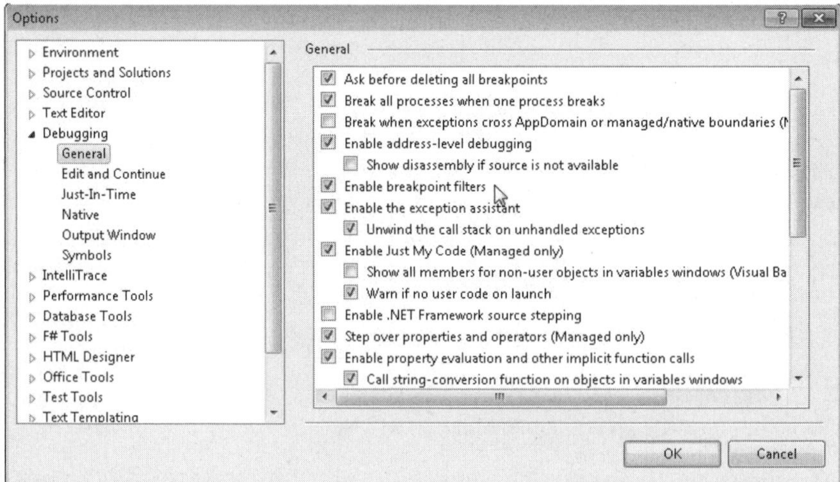

To make a breakpoint filter, just right-click any regular breakpoint and choose Filter:

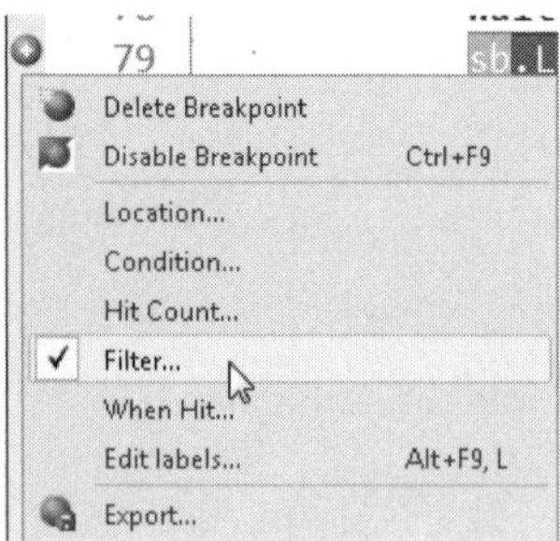

You get the Breakpoint Filter dialog box:

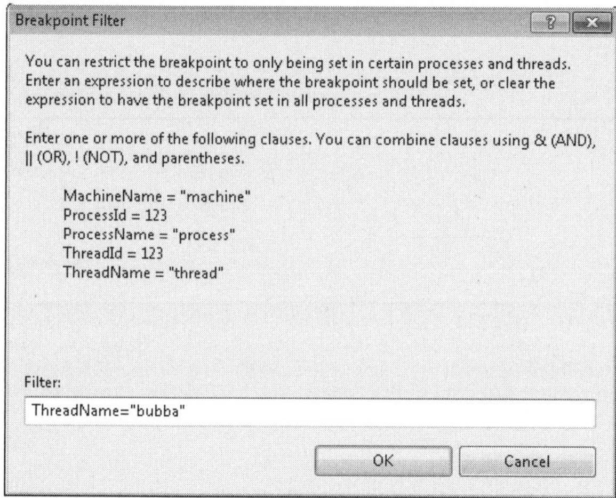

As shown in the preceding graphic, I've decided to break whenever the breakpoint is hit and the thread name is "bubba." The following illustration shows what it looks like in the Threads window when I actually run my code and the breakpoint is hit:

		1928	11	Worker Thread	Thread 2
	⇨	7912	12	Worker Thread	bubba
		7712	13	Worker Thread	Thread 4
		8648	14	Worker Thread	Thread 5

07.25 Setting a Tracepoint in Source Code

MENU	[Context Menu] | When Hit
COMMAND	EditorContextMenus.CodeWindow.Breakpoint.BreakpointWhenHit
VERSIONS	2005, 2008, 2010
CODE	vstipDebug0010

Tracepoints give you the opportunity to unobtrusively print out information during application execution. This tip shows you how to use the IDE to create tracepoints, but for detailed information about how to do this in code, see "Tracing and Instrumenting Applications" at *http://msdn.microsoft.com/en-us/library/zs6s4h68(VS.100).aspx.*

The best way to illustrate simple tracepoints is with a basic loop. I would suggest creating a new project and making a simple for loop to play with. Here is my sample code:

```
static void Main(string[] args)
{

    for (int i = 0; i < 10; i++)
    {
        Console.WriteLine("I'm doing something!");
    }


}
```

Setting Tracepoints

You have a couple of ways to set a tracepoint on a line of code.

One way is to right-click on the line and choose Breakpoint | Insert Tracepoint.

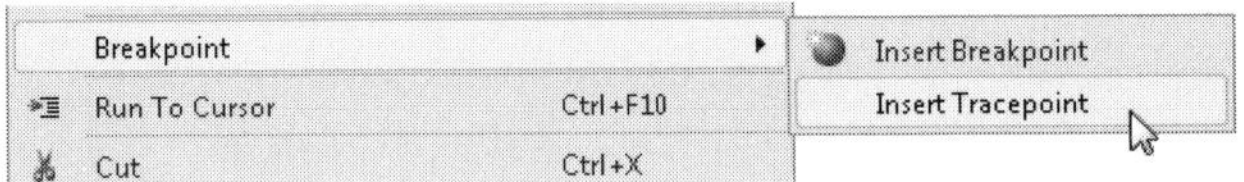

Alternatively, you can set a breakpoint (F9) and then right-click on the breakpoint in the indicator margin and choose When Hit:

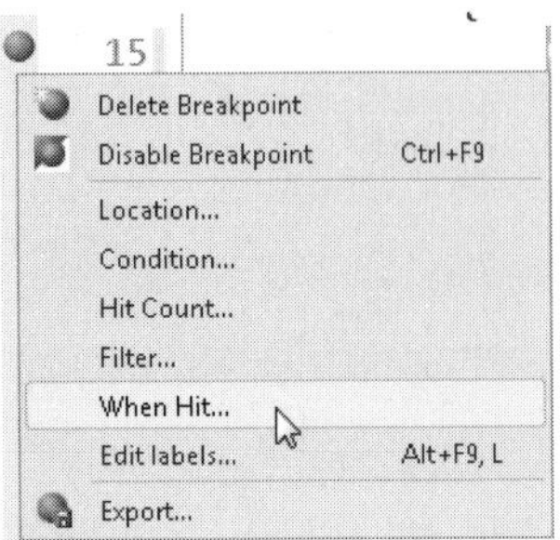

Whichever technique you use, the When Breakpoint Is Hit dialog box appears:

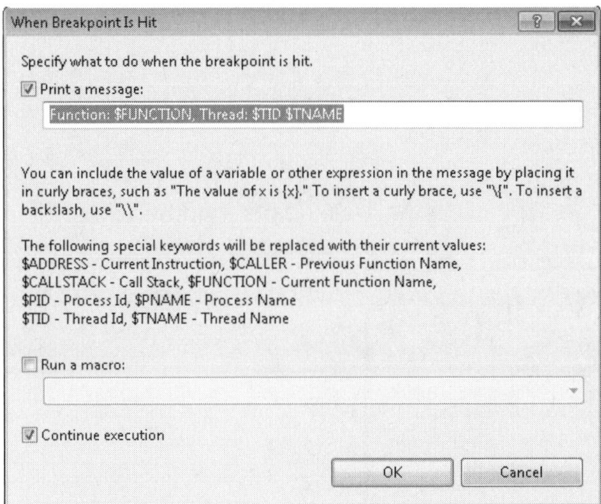

The When Breakpoint Is Hit dialog box provides three options.

Print a message

Used to print out any special variables (that begin with a $), evaluated expressions (inside curly braces), or literal text.

Run a macro

Used to actually run a macro when this tracepoint is hit and can do extended processing or kick off some other task.

Continue execution

Makes the tracepoint unobtrusive and lets the application run. If you clear the Continue Execution check box, the tracepoint becomes a breakpoint.

Click OK and notice something interesting. The normal round breakpoint indicator is now a diamond:

This is how we distinguish breakpoints (stop execution) from tracepoints (don't stop execution). For example, if I were to clear the Continue Execution check box in the When Breakpoint Is Hit dialog box, the breakpoint symbol would become round again:

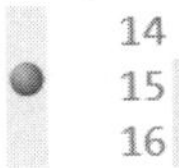

Tracepoints show up along with breakpoints in the Breakpoints window:

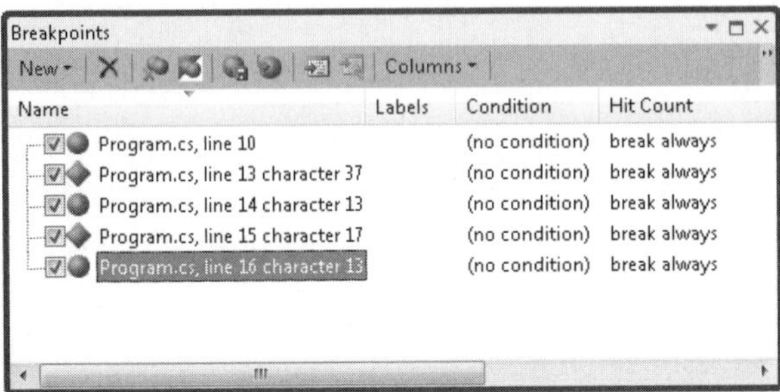

At this point, you have done enough to see tracepoints in action, so run your application. It should execute and then end. Open the Output window (Debug | Windows | Output), and notice the entries from our tracepoint:

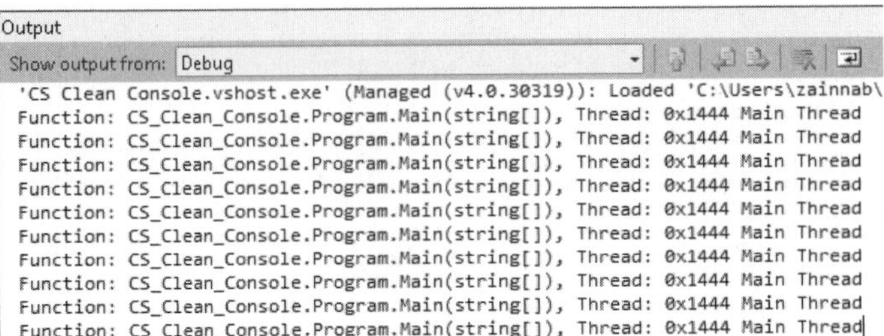

The default message isn't very helpful in this case, so let's change it to something else. In this example, let's put **The value of i is {i}**. Notice that I put the expression to be evaluated (the variable i in this case) inside curly braces:

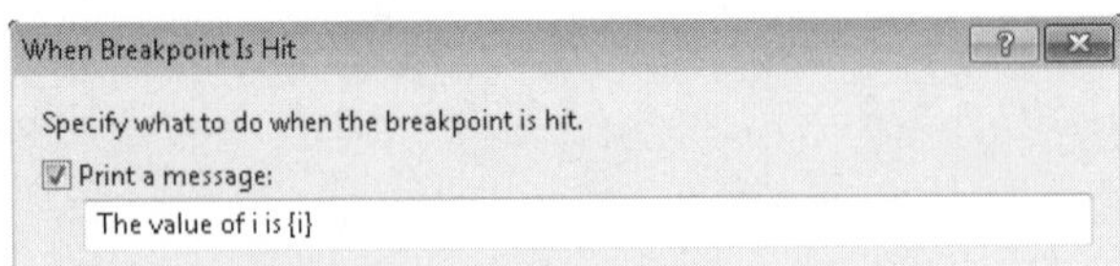

Now you should see the following in the Output window:

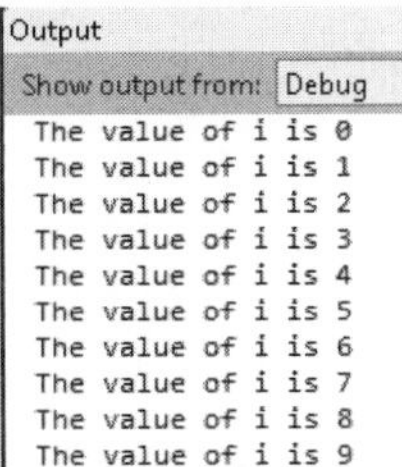

Change Default Message

There is a lot more to learn here, but you have a good start. One thing you might want to do is permanently change the default output message (currently "Function: $FUNCTION, Thread: $TID $TNAME") that you get when you set a new tracepoint. This is useful if you find that you use a certain message often across projects. You can do this by going into the registry:

```
HKEY_CURRENT_USER\Software\Microsoft\VisualStudio\<version>\Debugger
```

> **Warning** Editing the registry can cause issues with Visual Studio, so perform these steps at your own risk.

Then modify the string value called DefaultTracepointMessage to the new default you would like to have.

07.26 Import and Export Breakpoints

COMMAND	EditorContextMenus.CodeWindow.Breakpoint.BreakpointExport; DebuggerContextMenus.BreakpointsWindow.Exportselected
VERSIONS	2010
CODE	vstipDebug0003

These next features are specifically designed so that you can share breakpoints with other team members. When you do this, make sure to version your exported breakpoints with your source code for sharing.

Set one or more breakpoints in your code, and open the Breakpoints window (Ctrl+Alt+B). Notice the new Export button. It's important to understand that it exports breakpoints *matching the current search criteria*. In other words, if you don't see the breakpoint in the Breakpoints window, it will not be exported:

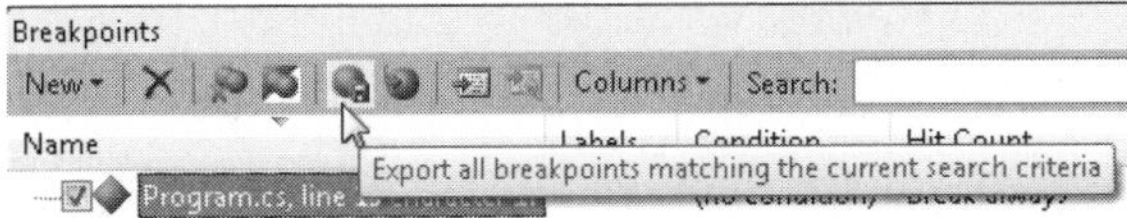

When you click the Export button, you get the classic Save As dialog box; notice that your breakpoints are saved as an XML file:

Put in some name for the file, and click Save. Give the file you created to your teammate or, if you are just practicing, you can delete your breakpoints.

Click on the new Import button:

Choose the XML file that was exported, and click Open to import your breakpoints.

07.27 Run to Cursor

DEFAULT	Ctrl+F10
VISUAL BASIC 6	Ctrl+F10; Ctrl+F8
VISUAL C# 2005	Ctrl+F10
VISUAL C++ 2	Ctrl+F10; F7
VISUAL C++ 6	Ctrl+F10
VISUAL STUDIO 6	Ctrl+F10
WINDOWS	[no shortcut]
MENU	[Context Menu] | Run To Cursor
COMMAND	Debug.RunToCursor
VERSIONS	2005, 2008, 2010
CODE	vstipDebug0023

This is one that has been around a while but seems to get lost among all the other features that are out there. Basically, if you have some code and want to quickly run it and set a temporary breakpoint at the same time, this tip is for you.

Just put the cursor on the line you want to break on:

```
static void Main(string[] args)
{

    Console.WriteLine("Go!");

}
```

Press Ctrl+F10, or right-click and choose Run To Cursor:

The application starts and a temporary Breakpoint is set on the line where you were, *but you do not see any breakpoint indicator*. The next time the code hits that line, it enters break mode:

```
static void Main(string[] args)
{

    Console.WriteLine("Go!");

}
```

Keep in mind that the application does not break until the line the temporary breakpoint is on is hit. If the line is never executed, the application will not break for debugging.

07.28 Using the Exception Assistant

VERSIONS	2005, 2008, 2010
CODE	vstipDebug0030

The Exception Assistant appears whenever a runtime exception occurs. It shows the type of exception, troubleshooting tips, and corrective actions as applicable:

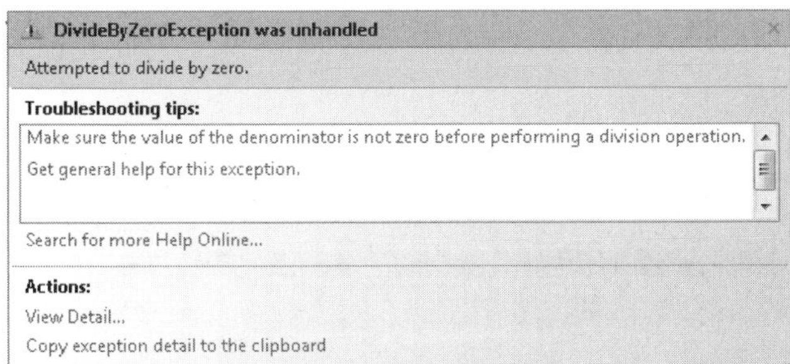

Exception Object and Description

The layout is pretty straightforward. First you have the exception object type and description:

DivideByZeroException was unhandled

Attempted to divide by zero.

Troubleshooting Tips

Then you have the Troubleshooting Tips area that provides advice about how to resolve the problem in a user-friendly format. The items are typically links to more information that can be found in the online or offline Help:

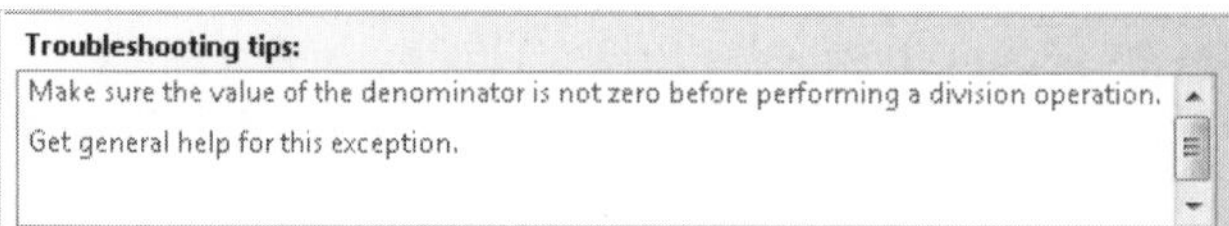

Help Online

Search For More Help Online is pretty interesting when you click the link:

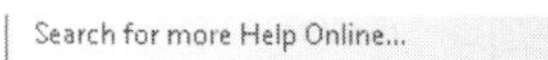

You get a dialog box asking permission to send information online:

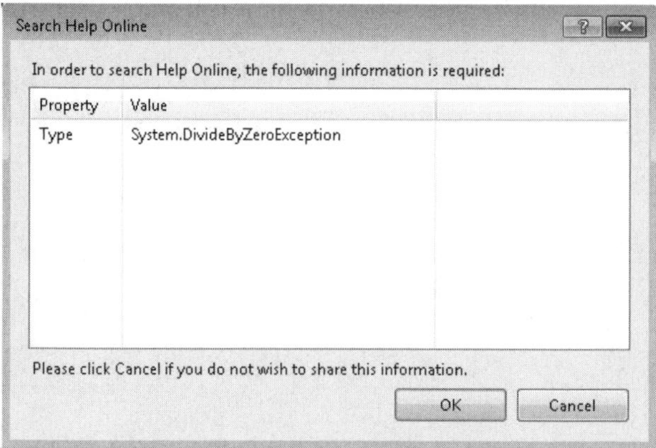

Clicking OK results in sending the information to MSDN online and performing a search:

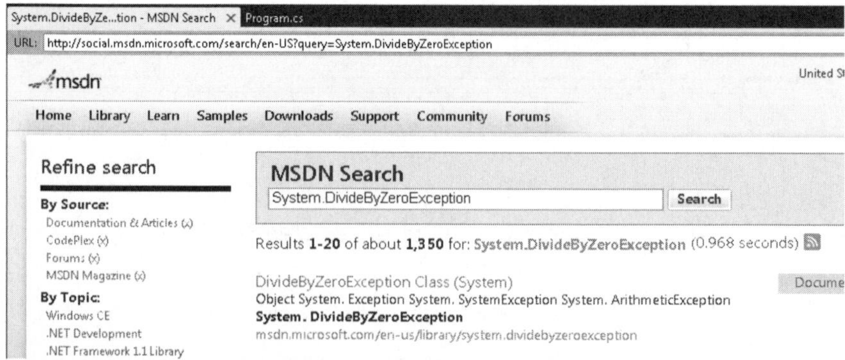

Actions

The Actions area lets you get information about the Exception Object:

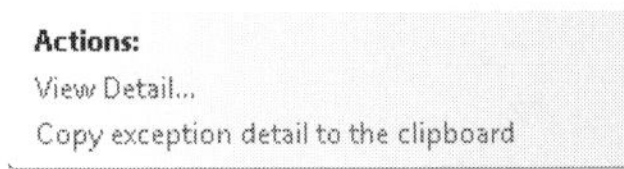

The View Detail link opens a dialog box that exposes the details of the object for you to review:

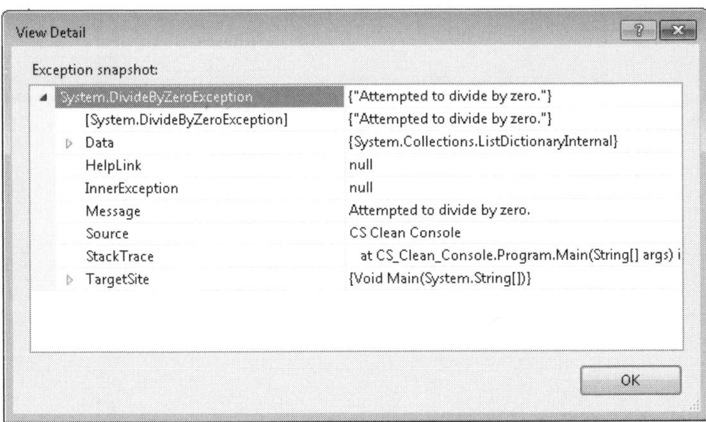

The Copy Exception Detail To The Clipboard link captures textual information you can put into any editor for analysis. It's not overly detailed but does provide a starting point for resolving the issue:

Exception Detail.txt - Notepad

File Edit Format View Help

```
System.DivideByZeroException was unhandled
  Message=Attempted to divide by zero.
  Source=CS Clean Console
  StackTrace:
       at CS_Clean_Console.Program.Main(String[] args) in C:\Users\zainnab
\Documents\Visual Studio 2010\Projects\CS Clean Console\CS Clean Console
\Program.cs:line 17
       at System.AppDomain._nExecuteAssembly(RuntimeAssembly assembly, String[]
args)
       at System.AppDomain.ExecuteAssembly(String assemblyFile, Evidence
assemblySecurity, String[] args)
       at Microsoft.VisualStudio.HostingProcess.HostProc.RunUsersAssembly()
       at System.Threading.ThreadHelper.ThreadStart_Context(Object state)
       at System.Threading.ExecutionContext.Run(ExecutionContext executionContext,
ContextCallback callback, Object state, Boolean ignoreSyncCtx)
       at System.Threading.ExecutionContext.Run(ExecutionContext executionContext,
ContextCallback callback, Object state)
       at System.Threading.ThreadHelper.ThreadStart()
  InnerException:
```

Turning Off the Exception Assistant

Although not suggested, you can actually turn this feature off. Just go to Tools | Options | Debugging | General, and clear the Enable The Exception Assistant check box:

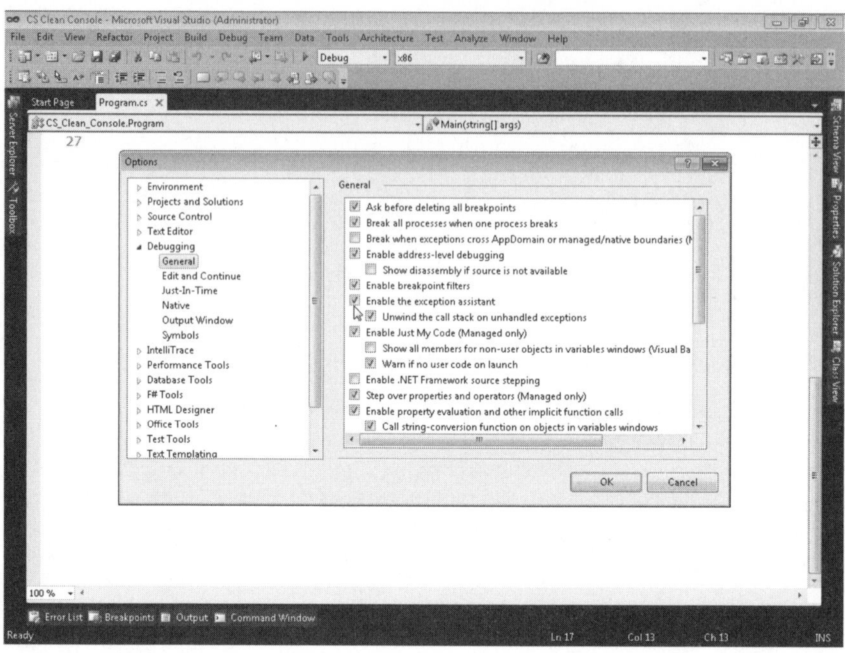

The following illustration shows what the same error looks like with the Exception Assistant off:

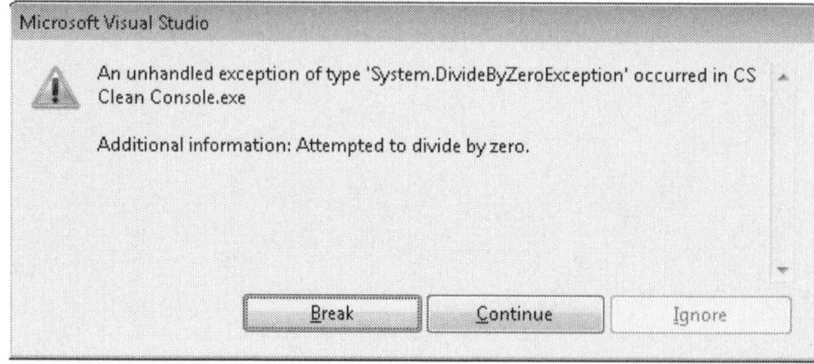

Unwind The Call Stack On Unhandled Exceptions

If you want more information about the details of this option, check out the great article by Bill Horst, at *http://blogs.msdn.com/b/vbteam/archive/2008/12/08/did-you-know-you-can-unwind-the-call-stack-from-exceptions-bill-horst.aspx.*

07.29 Use a Specific Port for the Development Server (Web Applications)

VERSIONS	2005, 2008, 2010
CODE	vstipProj0029

If you are using a firewall and want to use the same port while you do web development to accommodate a firewall rule, you can configure Visual Studio to use a fixed port. To do this, go to the project properties for any web application and click Web:

On the Web tab, go to the Servers area:

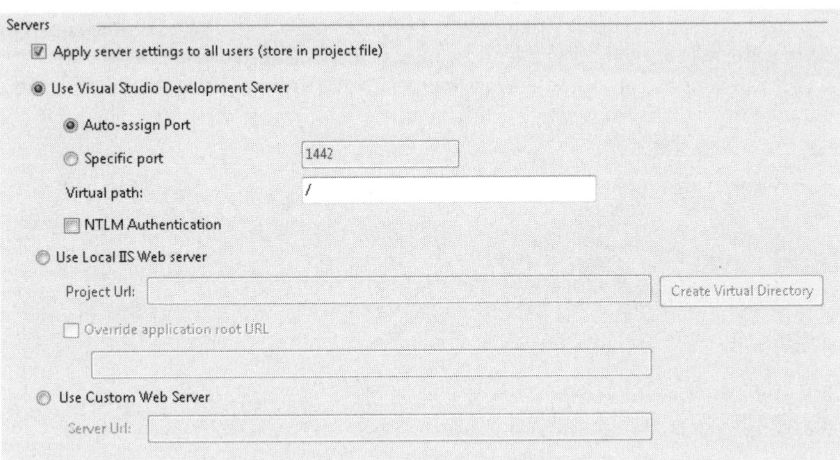

In the Servers area, choose Specific Port, and then assign a port number to use:

Use Visual Studio Development Server
Auto-assign Port
Specific port 1337
Virtual path: /

The project now continues to use the port number assigned instead of automatically assigning one.

07.30 Application and Page Level Tracing

VERSIONS	2005, 2008, 2010
CODE	vstipProj0030

When debugging any project, it's good to have as much information as possible to help deal with any issues. Working with web projects is always a challenge no matter what IDE you use. Fortunately, the folks on the web team have provided a useful tool just for web developers: tracing. Tracing can be enabled at two levels: application and page.

Warning Generally, you should not enable tracing in an production website, because this can display sensitive configuration information to anyone who views pages in the website. Tracing is intended for debugging purposes only. If the localOnly attribute is true, trace information is displayed only for localhost requests. Additionally, if <deployment retail=true> is set in the Web.config file, tracing is disabled.

Application Level Tracing

You can enable application tracing by going to Web.config and adding the <trace> element inside <system.web>:

```
<configuration>
  <system.web>

    <trace enabled="true" requestLimit="50" localOnly="true" />

  <system.web>

<configuration>
```

To access the application trace information, simply append "trace.axd" to the root of your website:

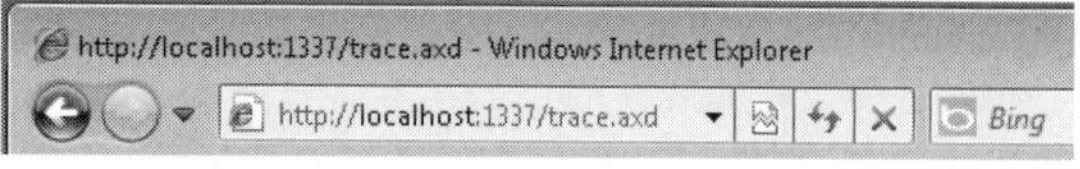

The following is a part of what you should see:

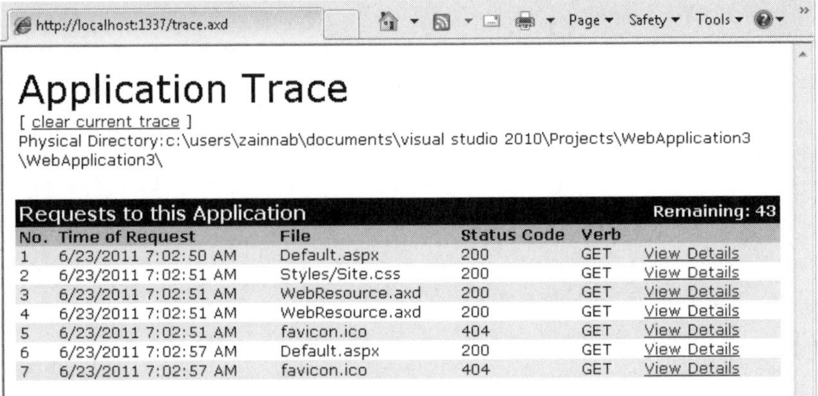

Attributes

Several attributes can be applied when using trace, all of which are optional:

- **enabled** (Boolean) Specifies whether tracing is enabled for an application. The default is false.
- **localOnly** (Boolean) Indicates whether the trace information is available only on the host web server. If false, the trace is visible from any computer, which can be a security issue. The default is true.
- **mostRecent** (Boolean) Shows whether the most recent application-level tracing output is displayed. If beyond the limits that are indicated by the requestLimit attribute, older trace data is discarded. If false, trace data is displayed for requests until the requestLimit attribute is reached. The default is false.
- **pageOutput** (Boolean) Specifies whether trace output is rendered at the end of each page. If false, trace output is accessible through the trace utility only. The default is false.
- **requestLimit** (Int32) Indicates the number of trace requests to store on the server. If the limit is reached and the mostRecent attribute is false, trace is automatically disabled. The maximum request limit is 10,000. If a value that is greater than 10,000 is specified, it is silently rounded down to 10,000 by ASP.NET. The default is 10.
- **traceMode** The order in which to display trace information. The traceMode attribute can be one of two possible values:
  - **SortByCategory** Trace information is displayed alphabetically by user-defined category.
  - **SortByTime** Trace information is displayed in the order that the trace information is processed. The default is SortByTime.

- **writeToDiagnosticsTrace** (Boolean) Indicates whether ASP.NET trace messages are forwarded to the System.Diagnostics tracing infrastructure, for any listeners that are registered to display trace messages. The default is false.

You can find more information about trace element settings at *http://msdn.microsoft.com/en-us/library/6915t83k.aspx.*

Trace Details

Additionally, you can click on the View Details link of each item and see a great deal of information:

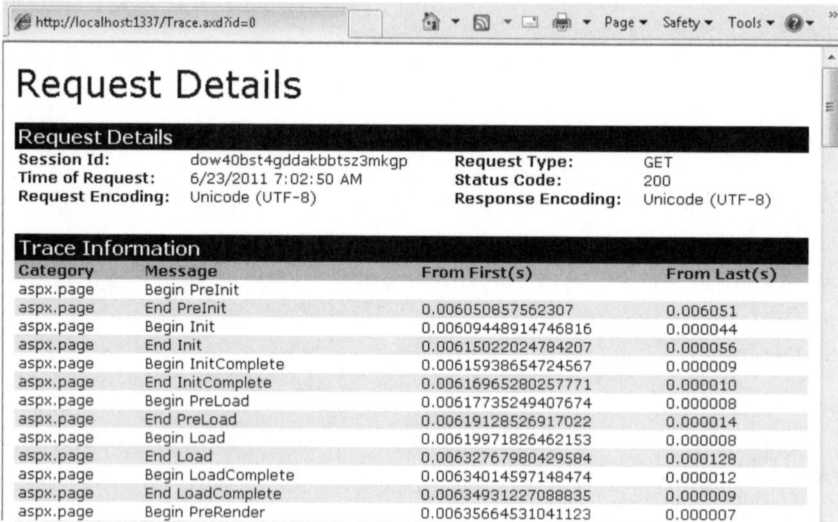

Page Level Tracing

You might not want to have tracing enabled for the entire application for a variety of reasons, such as performance, wanting to focus in on just one page, and so on. Turning on tracing for a page is very simple. Just turn on tracing in your @Page directive, as in the following example:

```
<%@ Page Title="Home Page" Language="C#" MasterPageFile="~/Site.master"
AutoEventWireup="true"
  CodeBehind="Default.aspx.cs" Inherits="WebApplication61._Default" Trace="true" %>
```

Now when you view that page, it shows the trace information on the page:

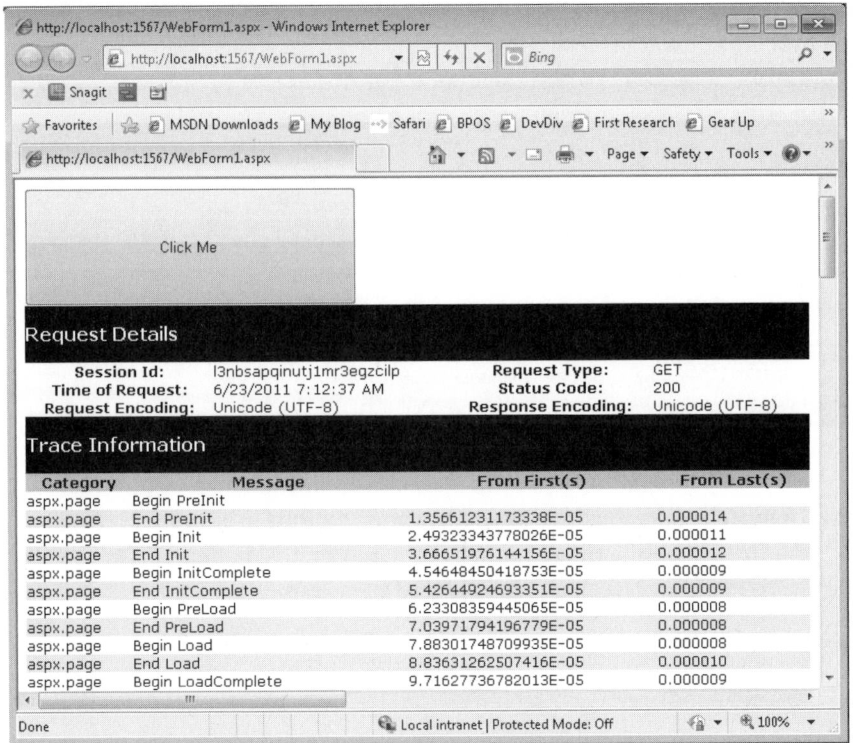

This is equivalent to setting pageOutput to true at the application level, but it affects only those pages where you have turned tracing on.

Combined Tracing

Tracing can get confusing, but the one thing to remember is that the page always wins when tracing is explicitly set. You can use the following table to help keep the tracing results in mind if you set both application and page level tracing.

Application	Page	Result for a Page
true	false	false
false	true	true

Finally

To say there is a lot going on here would be an understatement. I leave it to you to explore more of the details, which can be found at *http://msdn.microsoft.com/en-us/library/bb386420.aspx*.

07.31 The Watch Window: Watching and Changing Values

DEFAULT	Shift+F9 (QuickWatch); Ctrl+Alt+Q (QuickWatch)
VISUAL BASIC 6	Shift+F9 (QuickWatch); Ctrl+Alt+Q (QuickWatch)
VISUAL C# 2005	Shift+F9 (QuickWatch); Ctrl+Alt+Q (QuickWatch); Ctrl+D, Ctrl+Q (QuickWatch); Ctrl+D, Q (QuickWatch)
VISUAL C++ 2	Shift+F9 (QuickWatch); Ctrl+Alt+Q (QuickWatch)
VISUAL C++ 6	Shift+F9 (QuickWatch); Ctrl+Alt+Q (QuickWatch)
VISUAL STUDIO 6	Shift+F9 (QuickWatch); Ctrl+Alt+Q (QuickWatch)
WINDOWS	Alt,D, Q (QuickWatch)
MENU	Debug | QuickWatch; [Context Menu] | Add Watch
COMMAND	Debug.QuickWatch; Debug.AddWatch
VERSIONS	2005, 2008, 2010
CODE	vstipTool0104

By definition, a watch expression does exactly what it sounds like it should do: It watches something and shows you the result so that you can monitor data as you are debugging. You can use any of the following techniques to create a watch expression:

- Type it in
- QuickWatch
- Add Watch

Let's take a closer look.

Watch Expressions

First we need to define what you can watch. Essentially, you can watch any valid expression. Some examples of valid watch expressions are shown in the following illustration:

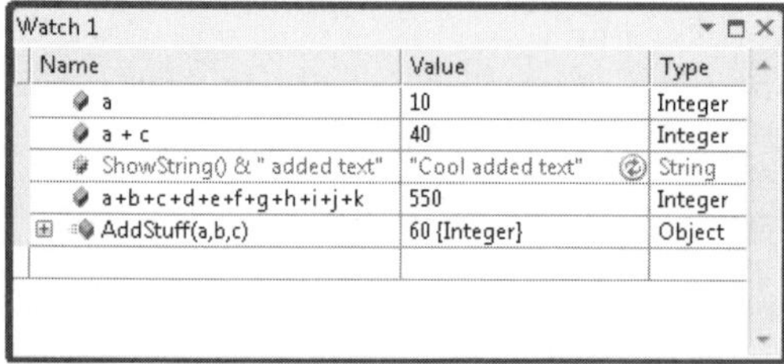

Watch Window

The easiest way to open the main Watch window is to press Ctrl+Alt+W,1 or go to Debug | Windows | Watch | Watch 1. You can have up to four Watch windows, so you can organize your watch expressions into groups if you want:

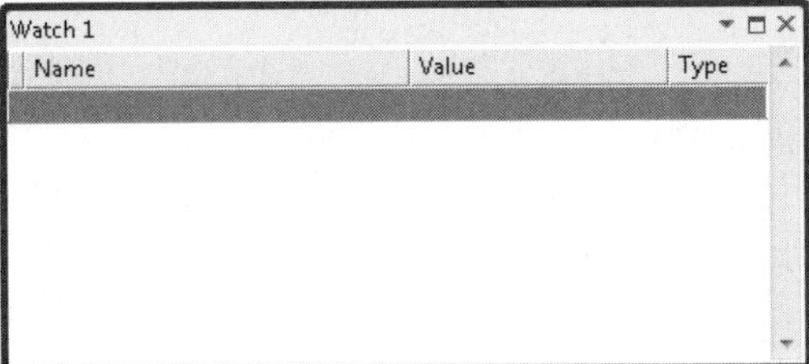

Creating a Watch Expression

Type it in

One of the quickest ways to put in most watch expressions is just to type in the variable or expression you want to watch in the Watch window:

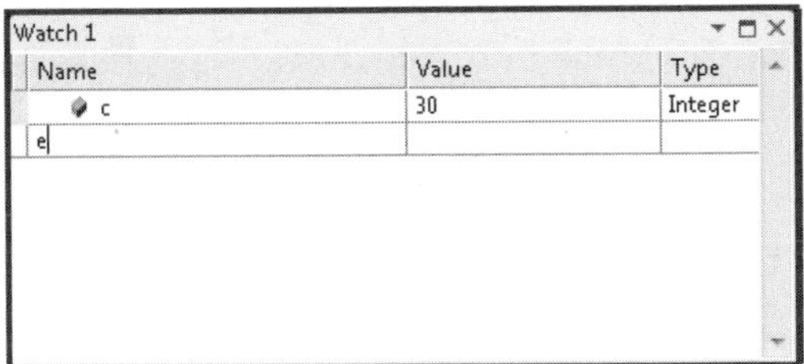

QuickWatch (Shift+F9)

Despite the name, this is actually the longest way to set a watch expression. When you press Shift+F9 or go to Debug | QuickWatch, you get the following dialog box:

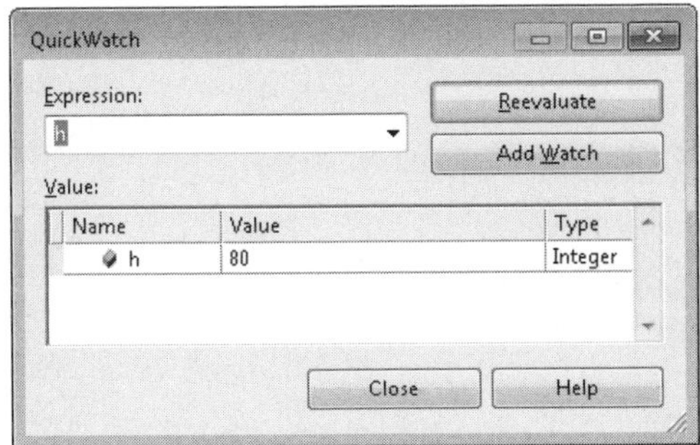

Type any expression in the Expression area, and then click Reevaluate to see the value appear in the Value area. If you are happy with what you see and want to add a watch expression to the QuickWatch window, just click Add Watch.

Add Watch

This is another pretty quick watch expression to set. Just right-click a variable or selected expression and instantly have it added to Watch 1:

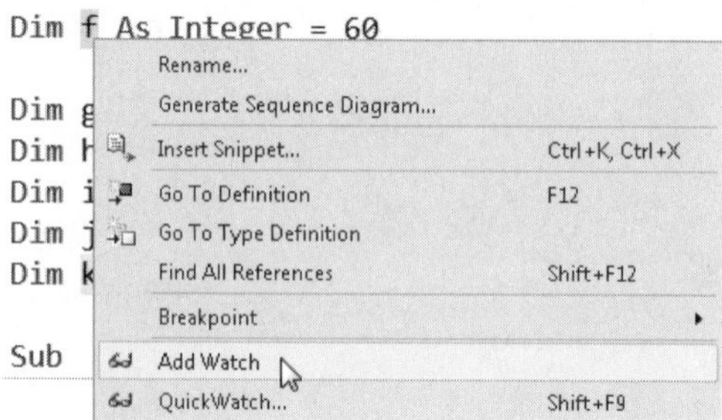

Changing Values

With any watch expression, you can change the value to suit your needs by just selecting the value you want to change:

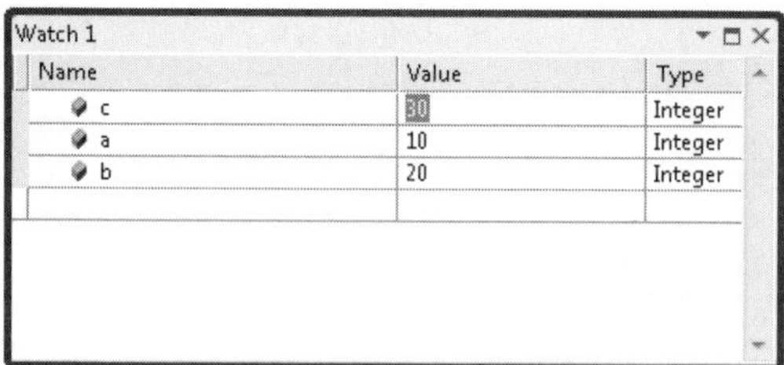

Then type in a new value, and press Enter:

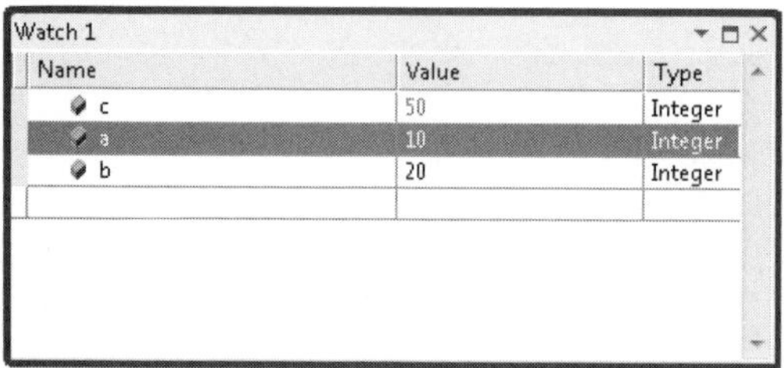

The value turns red to indicate it has changed. This makes it easy to track your changes.

07.32 Understanding QuickWatch

DEFAULT	Shift+F9; Ctrl+Alt+Q
VISUAL BASIC 6	Shift+F9; Ctrl+Alt+Q
VISUAL C# 2005	Shift+F9; Ctrl+Alt+Q; Ctrl+D, Ctrl+Q; Ctrl+D, Q
VISUAL C++ 2	Shift+F9; Ctrl+Alt+Q
VISUAL C++ 6	Shift+F9; Ctrl+Alt+Q
VISUAL STUDIO 6	Shift+F9; Ctrl+Alt+Q
WINDOWS	Alt, D, Q
MENU	Debug | QuickWatch
COMMAND	Debug.QuickWatch
VERSIONS	2005, 2008, 2010
CODE	vstipTool0108

In vstipTool0104 ("The Watch Window: Watching and Changing Values," page 340), I showed you how to use QuickWatch to get data into a Watch window. From that perspective, using QuickWatch is rather slow and cumbersome. However, QuickWatch doesn't exist for only that reason, so it is worth another look.

So, why does QuickWatch exist? It was actually created to be a dialog box that is a one-stop shop for quickly working with expressions. Think of it as a dialog box dedicated to a single watch expression. It's a modal dialog box, so you need to close it before moving on with any other debugging. Bring it up by pressing Shift+F9 or going to Debug | QuickWatch on the Menu Bar.

What Does It Do?

Like a normal watch expression, you can edit the value in it:

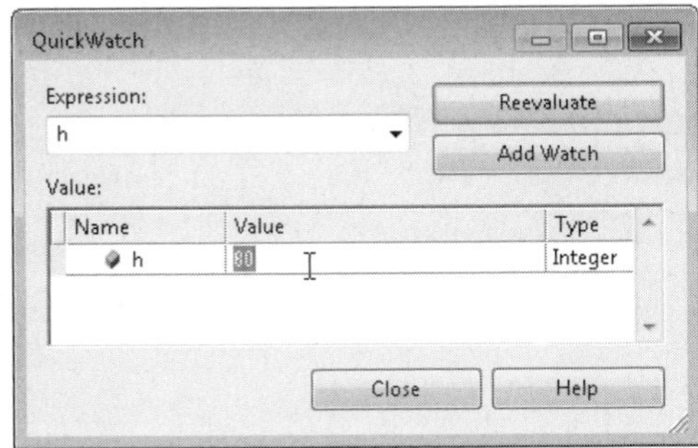

Also, you can change the expression and click Reevaluate to see a new value:

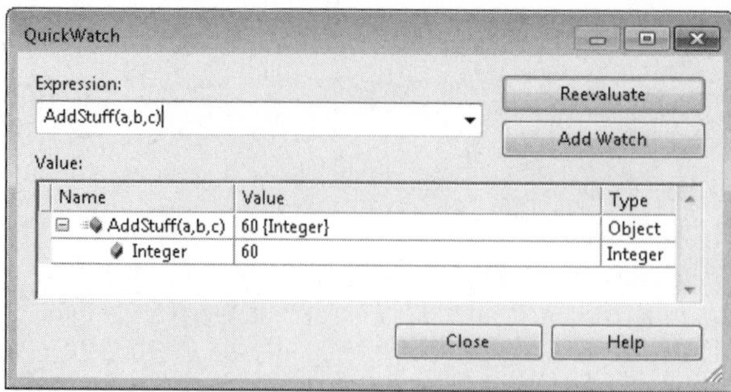

One big advantage to the QuickWatch window is the fact that it can be resized. It can be very useful when digging deep:

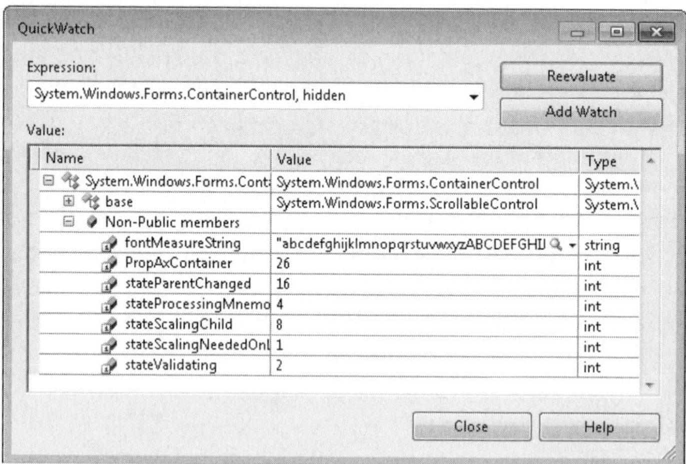

Other Options

While it is useful for specific scenarios, with the advent of DataTips (see vstipDebug0005, "Pin a DataTip to Source Code," on page 305), the usefulness of the QuickWatch dialog box has diminished somewhat, so you might choose to use DataTips instead. It all comes down to personal preference.

07.33 The Watch Window: Visualizers

DEFAULT	Ctrl+Alt+W,1; Ctrl+Alt+W,[2-4]
VISUAL BASIC 6	Ctrl+Alt+W,1; Ctrl+Alt+W,[2-4]
VISUAL C# 2005	Ctrl+Alt+W,1; Ctrl+D, Ctrl+W; Ctrl+D, W; Ctrl+Alt+W,[2-4]
VISUAL C++ 2	[no shortcut]
VISUAL C++ 6	Ctrl+Alt+W,1; Ctrl+Alt+W,[2-4]
VISUAL STUDIO 6	Ctrl+Alt+W,1; Ctrl+Alt+W,[2-4]
WINDOWS	Alt+D, W, W, [1-4]
MENU	Debug | Windows | Watch | Watch [1,2,3,4]
COMMAND	Debug.Watch[1,2,3,4]
VERSIONS	2005, 2008, 2010
CODE	vstipTool0106

When using the Watch windows, you might come across visualizers. A visualizer is a debugger component that enables the debugger to display (visualize) the contents of a data object in a meaningful, understandable form. Visualizers are pretty easy to spot because they have a magnifying glass icon:

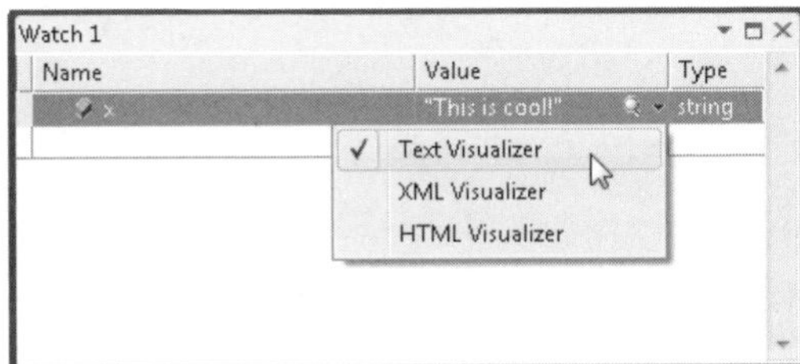

Notice that when you click on the magnifying glass, it gives you options (based on the data you are looking at) for a visualizer. If you select Text Visualizer, you get the following dialog box:

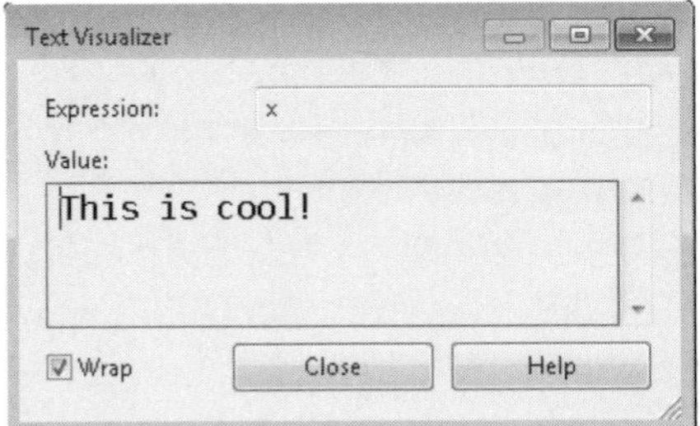

You might find it useful to leverage the power of visualizers when looking at different types of data. If this output were HTML, you would use the HTML Visualizer:

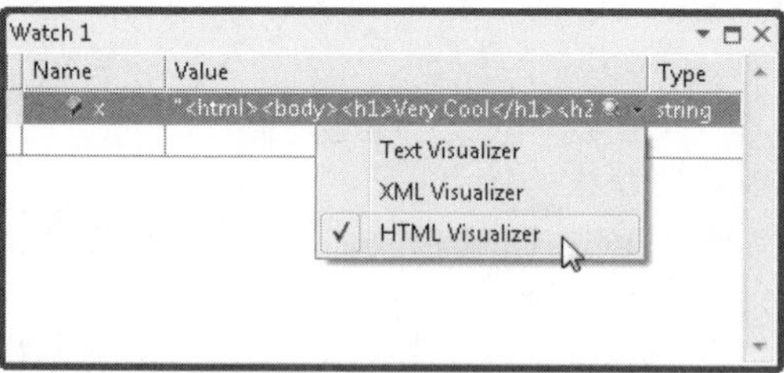

And you would see the following dialog box:

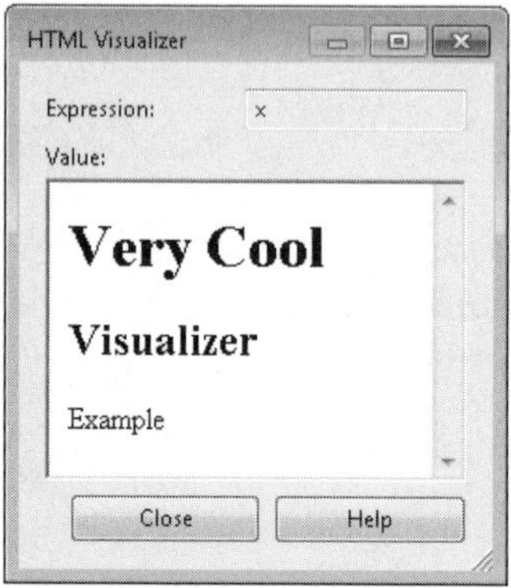

07.34 The Watch Window: Refreshing Data

WINDOWS	Alt,T, O
MENU	Tools | Options | Debugging | General
COMMAND	Tools.Options
VERSIONS	2005, 2008, 2010
CODE	vstipTool0107

When you evaluate an expression in one of the Watch windows, one of two refresh icons might appear in the Value column. One refresh icon is a circle that contains two wavy lines that resemble threads. The other icon is two circling arrows, as shown in the following example:

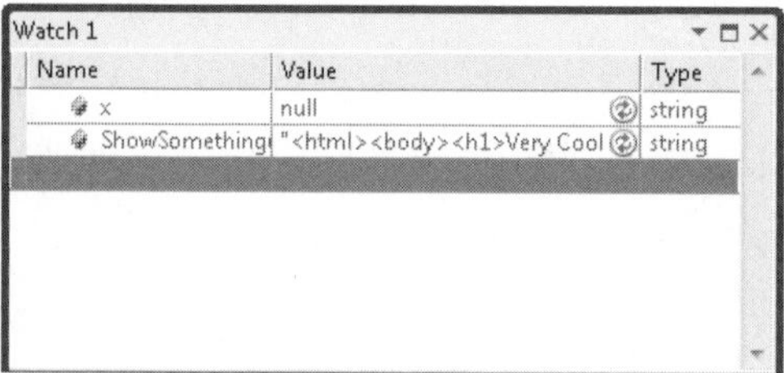

Refresh Icons

Following is what the documentation (*http://msdn.microsoft.com/en-us/library/z4ecfxd9.aspx*) has to say about these icons.

Circling arrows

If the circling arrows appear, the expression was not evaluated for one of the following reasons:

- An error occurred as the expression was being evaluated. For example, a time-out might have occurred, or a variable might have been out of scope.
- Evaluating the expression would have required evaluating a property or making an implicit function code. Evaluation of properties and implicit function calls can have side effects that affect the state of your program. Because these effects can make debugging more difficult, automatic evaluation of properties and implicit function calls by the debugger is often turned off. Occasionally, a programmer might unintentionally turn off automatic evaluation.

If you want to learn more about side effects, see the topic "Side Effects and Expressions" at *http://msdn.microsoft.com/en-us/library/a7a250bs.aspx*.

Two threads

If the two threads appear, the expression was not evaluated because of a potential cross-thread dependency. A cross-thread dependency means that evaluating the code requires other threads in your application to run temporarily. When you are in break mode, all threads in your application are typically stopped. Allowing other threads to run temporarily can have unexpected effects on the state of your program and causes the debugger to ignore events such as breakpoints.

Refreshing the data

To refresh the data, just click the icon or press the Spacebar:

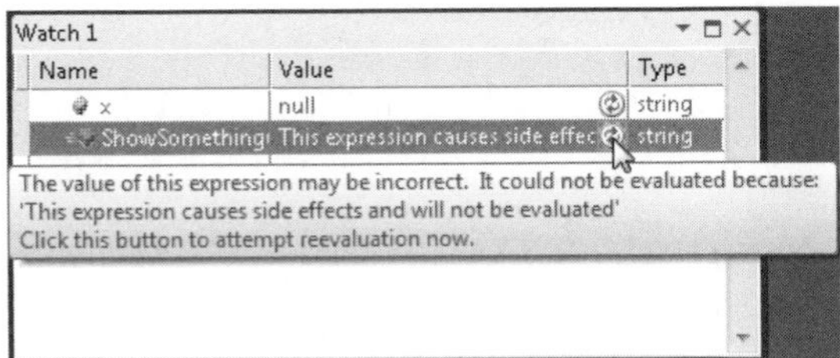

Turning It Off

Although not suggested, you can turn this feature off by going to Tools | Options | Debugging | General and clearing the Enable Property Evaluation And Other Implicit Function Calls check box:

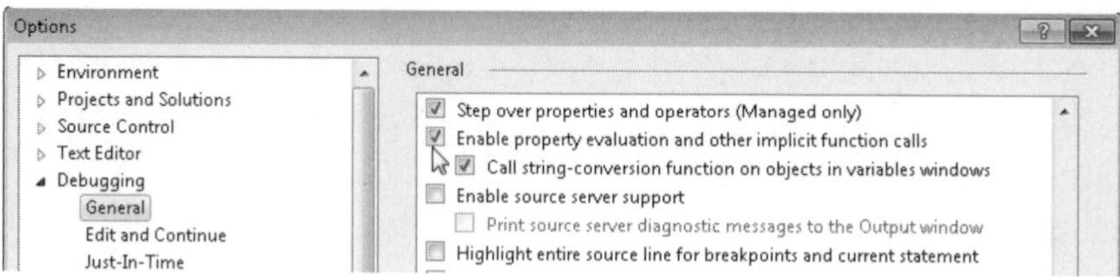

07.35 The Watch Window: Adding Watches from Variable Windows

MENU	[Context Menu] | Add Watch
COMMAND	Debug.AddWatch
VERSIONS	2005, 2008, 2010
CODE	vstipTool0109

The Locals, Autos, Watch, and QuckWatch windows are all known, collectively, as the Variable windows. Did you know that every Variable window supports the Debug.AddWatch command? This tip provides some examples.

Locals Window

Autos Window

QuickWatch

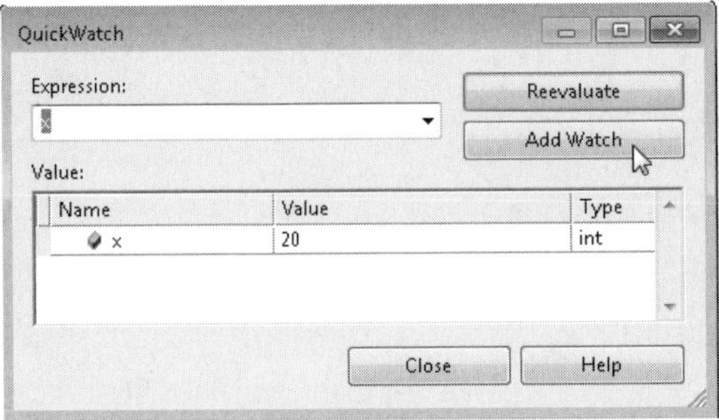

Watch [1, 2, 3, 4] Window

This is one you might not expect. The Watch windows actually have the ability to add watch expressions. Very useful if you have a complex expression and want to copy it to do a modification:

Keyboard Mapping

If you find yourself adding watch expressions frequently in break mode, you should consider mapping a keyboard shortcut. Go to Tools | Options | Environment | Keyboard, and assign a shortcut to the Debug.AddWatch command:

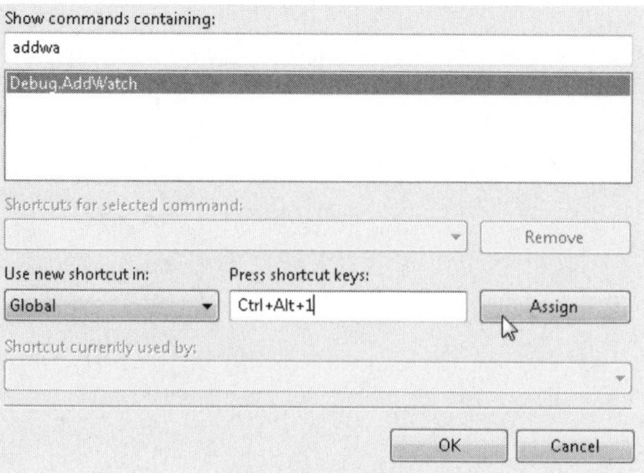

07.36 Create Folders in Class View

MENU	[Context Menu] | New Folder
COMMAND	View.ClassViewNewFolder
VERSIONS	2005, 2008, 2010
CODE	vstipTool0072

Did you know that you can create folders to easily organize items in Class View? It's pretty easy to do. Just open the Class View dialog box (Ctrl+Shift+C):

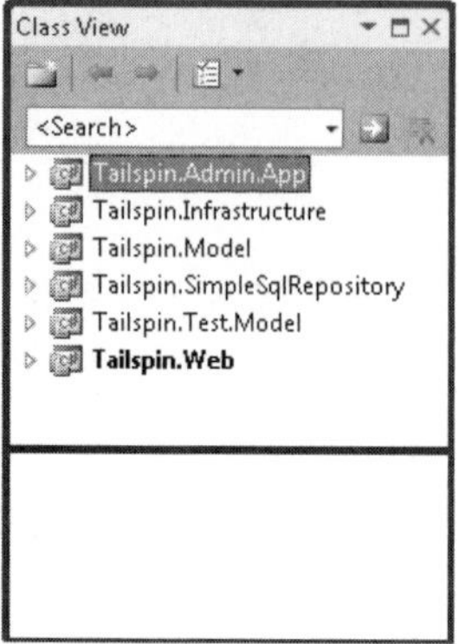

Create a New Folder

Click the Class View New Folder button:

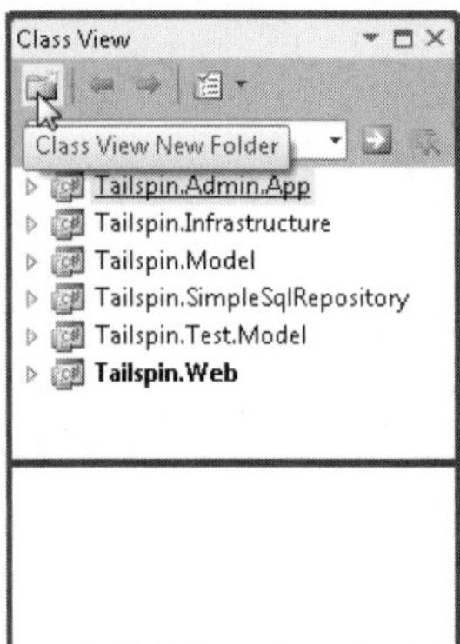

Give your new folder some logical name:

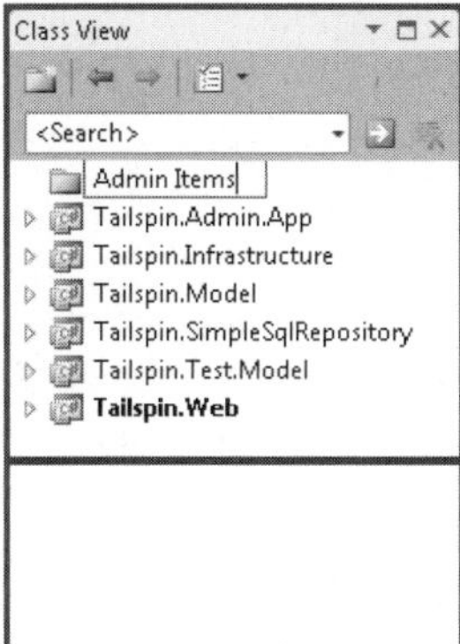

Note These folders are not created on the file system but are stored in your .suo file.

Putting Items into Your Folder

You can simply click and drag items into your new folder to organize them:

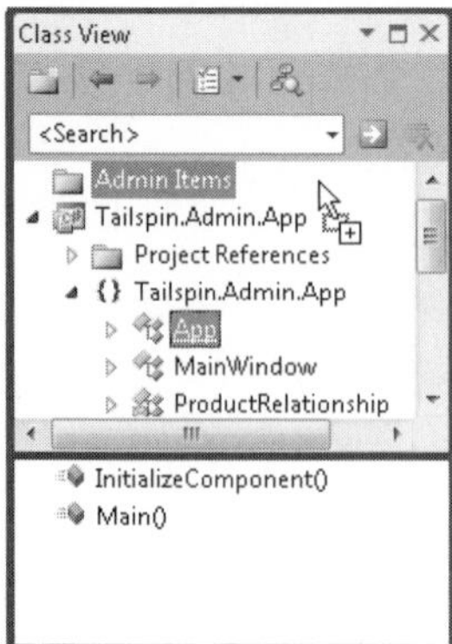

You can also copy and paste items into the folders as well. These operations are strictly organizational and don't actually make an extra copy of the item in your code.

Removing Items from Folders

You can remove items from your folder at any time by deleting them (right-click or press the Delete key).

Note This deletes only the item from the Class View and doesn't actually delete your code.

Creating Subfolders

You can even nest the folder structure by creating a new folder inside an existing one:

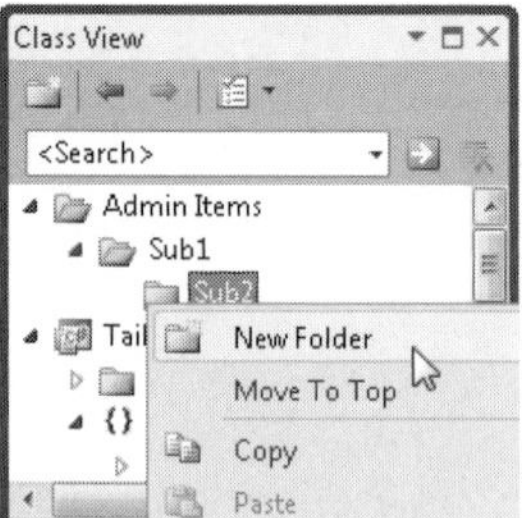

Deleting Folders

Naturally you can delete any folder by right-clicking it and choosing Delete.

07.37 Search in Class View

DEFAULT	Ctrl+K, Ctrl+V
VISUAL C++ 2	[no shortcut]
COMMAND	View.ClassViewGoToSearchCombo; View.ClassViewSearch
VERSIONS	2005, 2008, 2010
CODE	vstipTool0073

The Class View window has a search capability that finds items quickly. Just go to the Class View Search Combo box (Ctrl+K, Ctrl+V):

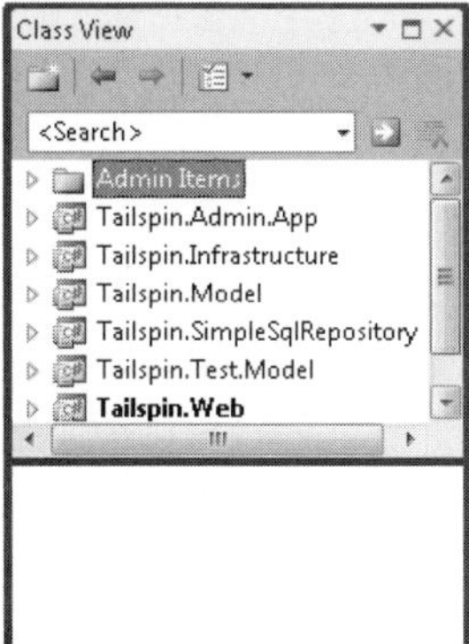

Warning I've actually had the search combo box disappear on me before. Restarting Visual Studio should bring it back if this happens to you, too.

Type in the keyword to search for, and press Enter:

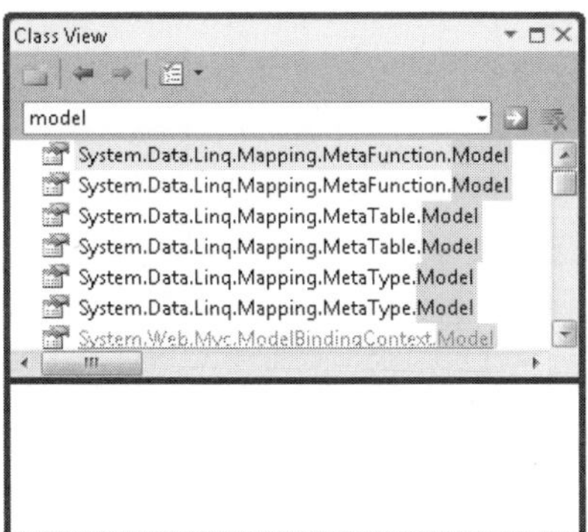

It searches for the keyword in items and shows the results while highlighting the last instance where the keyword was found in an item. The search is a contains operation, so it looks for anything that has the keyword anywhere in the result.

View.ClassViewSearch Command

If you want a quick way to do this by running a command, you can use View.ClassViewSearch with any keyword(s). First, go someplace you can run a command. I prefer to use the Find Combo box with the command character (Ctrl+/) to run my commands (see vstipTool0070, "Understanding Commands: Running Commands," on page 121, for more options):

Type in **View.ClassViewSearch [keyword(s)]**. In this case, let's look for the word "task":

Just press Enter, and we get our results in the Class View:

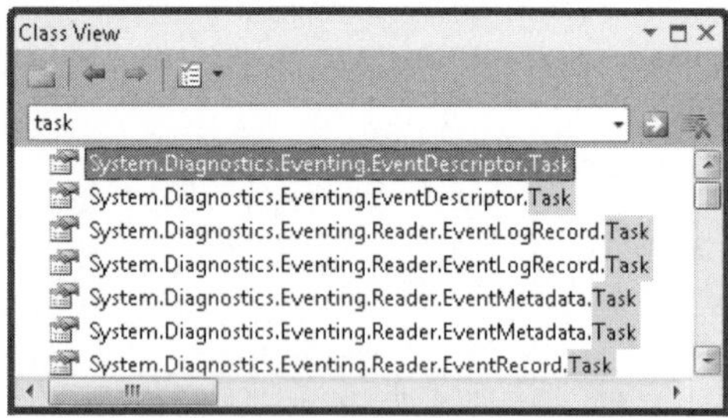

Use a Previous Search

You can repeat any previous search in Class View by using the drop-down list from the Search Combo box:

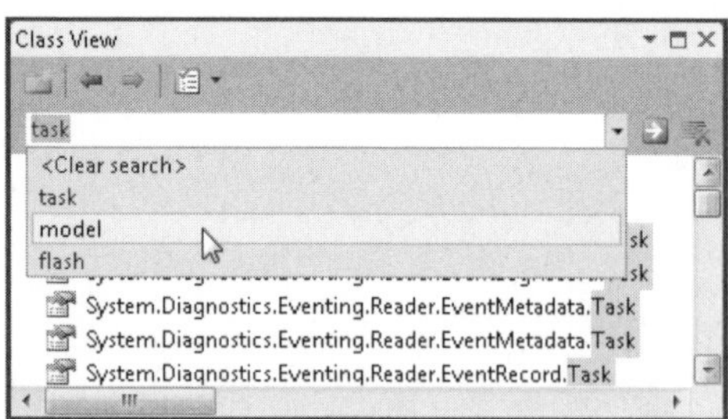

Clear Your Search

Whichever method you use, you can always clear your search by clicking the Clear Search button:

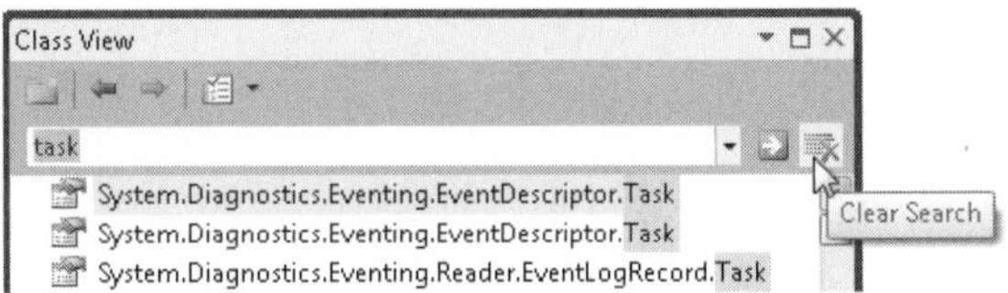

07.38 Synchronize Your Class View

COMMAND	View.SynchronizeClassView
VERSIONS	2005, 2008, 2010
CODE	vstipTool0074

When you are in your code, sometimes you would like to have Class View synchronize with your code. By default, it doesn't do this.

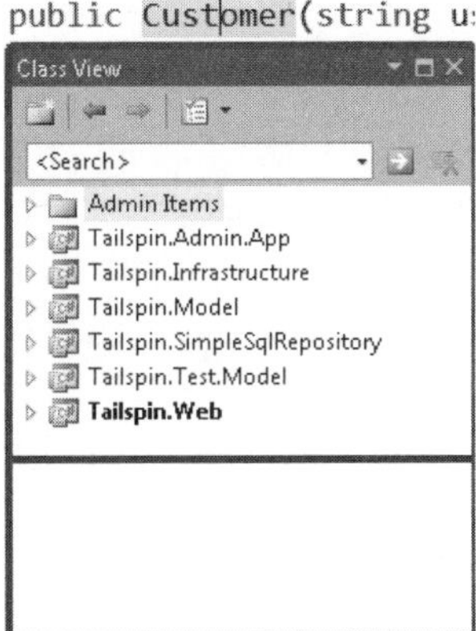

You can run the View.SynchronizeClassView command from the Find combo (Ctrl+/) to see how this works:

Note This command works only if the editor has the focus, so you need to run it from the Find drop-down box as shown in this example or assign a shortcut key to it. It does not work if you try to run it from the Command window.

It finds your current location in Class View:

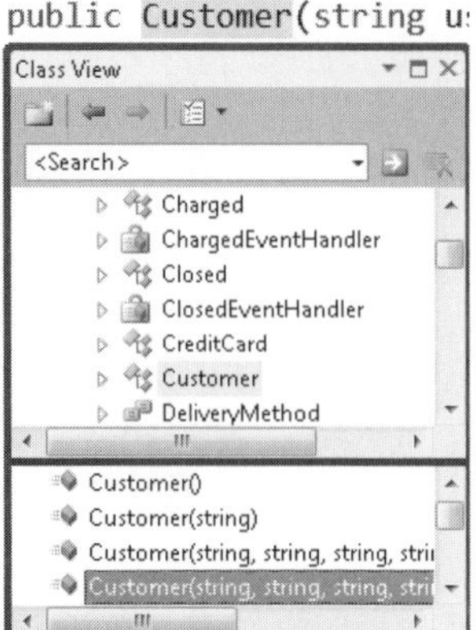

07.39 The Misnamed and Misunderstood Object Browser

DEFAULT	Ctrl+Alt+J
VISUAL BASIC 6	Ctrl+Alt+J; F2
VISUAL C# 2005	Ctrl+Alt+J; Ctrl+W, Ctrl+J; Ctrl+W, J
VISUAL C++ 2	Ctrl+Alt+J; Shift+Alt+F1
VISUAL C++ 6	Ctrl+Alt+J
VISUAL STUDIO 6	Ctrl+Alt+B; F2
WINDOWS	Alt,V, J
MENU	View | Object Browser
COMMAND	View.ObjectBrowser
VERSIONS	2005, 2008, 2010
CODE	vstipTool0077

Many people often ask why they should use the Object Browser. First and foremost, it is a way to browse to find the correct class, object, property, method, interface, and so on that is useful for your needs as you code. But the Object Browser does much, much more than its name implies.

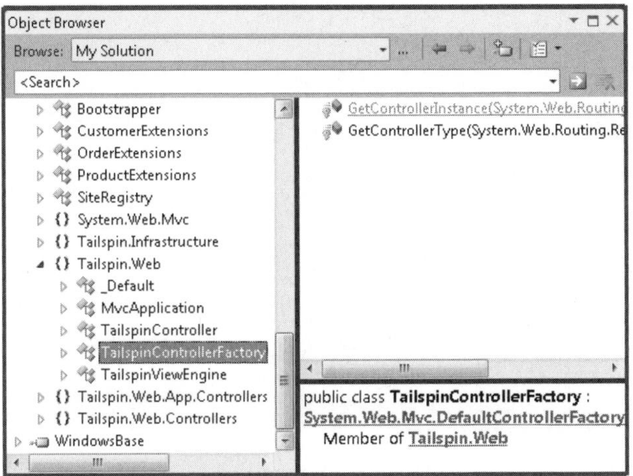

As you can see from the high-level view shown in the preceding illustration, the Object Browser is composed of several parts:

- **Toolbar** (very top) Contains various controls for manipulating the various functions available.
- **Objects pane** (left, top and bottom) Displays an expandable list of symbols whose top-level nodes represent components or namespaces available in the current browsing scope.
- **Members pane** (right, top) Displays the available members, if available, of any symbol selected in the Objects pane.
- **Description pane** (right, bottom) Displays detailed information about the currently selected object or member.

First, the name would have you think that it shows only objects. This is simply untrue. In fact, it shows many different types of symbols, which is better than just showing objects:

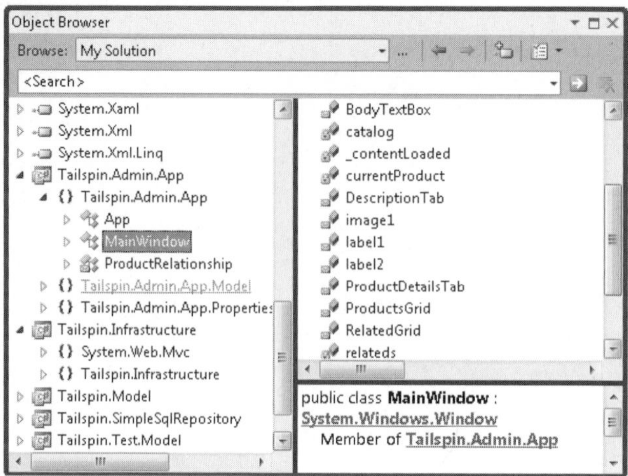

In this example, as shown in the preceding illustration, we see a couple of projects with several namespaces in them, in addition to some interfaces and classes. The classes with envelopes represent internal classes. The icons are explained in vstipTool0076, "Class View and Object Browser Icons," in Appendix B (*http://go.microsoft.com/FWLink/?Linkid=223758*).

Second, you might think that all you can do is browse items. Again, not true. For example, you can add references to your project from the Object Browser when you find something that you want to include:

The next series of tips explore, in detail, the use of the Object Browser in your work.

07.40 The Object Browser: Setting the Browsing Scope

DEFAULT	Ctrl+Alt+J
VISUAL BASIC 6	Ctrl+Alt+J; F2
VISUAL C# 2005	Ctrl+Alt+J; Ctrl+W, Ctrl+J; Ctrl+W, J
VISUAL C++ 2	Ctrl+Alt+J; Shift+Alt+F1
VISUAL C++ 6	Ctrl+Alt+J
VISUAL STUDIO 6	Ctrl+Alt+B; F2
WINDOWS	Alt, V, J
MENU	View | Object Browser
COMMAND	View.ObjectBrowser
VERSIONS	2005, 2008, 2010
CODE	vstipTool0078

When you use the Object Browser, it's a good idea to know what components you are browsing. So let's start our examination at the top, with the Browse area:

Browse

The Browse drop-down box lets you specify the browsing scope (the list of items you see in the Objects pane):

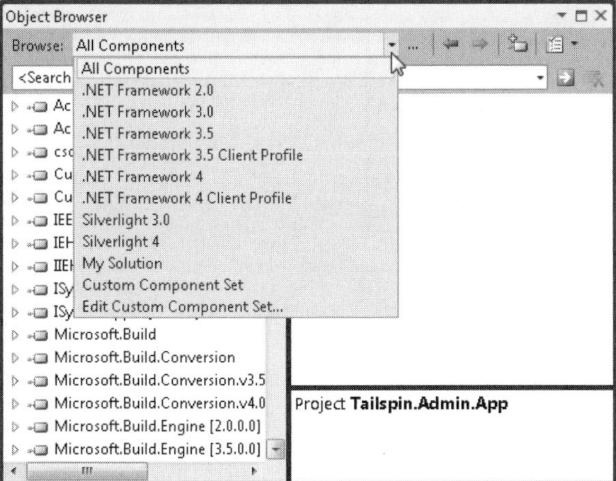

All Components

The All Components drop-down quite literally lets you browse all components, including all of the .NET Framework, the current solution and its referenced components, and any other components that you have added by selecting Edit Custom Component Set. It's a massive dose of information overload, so be prepared.

.NET Framework X / Silverlight X

Sets the browsing scope to a specific version of the Framework.

My Solution

Shows items in the current solution and referenced components.

Custom Component Set

Sets browsing scope to the list of components identified by editing the Custom Component Set. For example, if I choose NET Framework 4, I see the following:

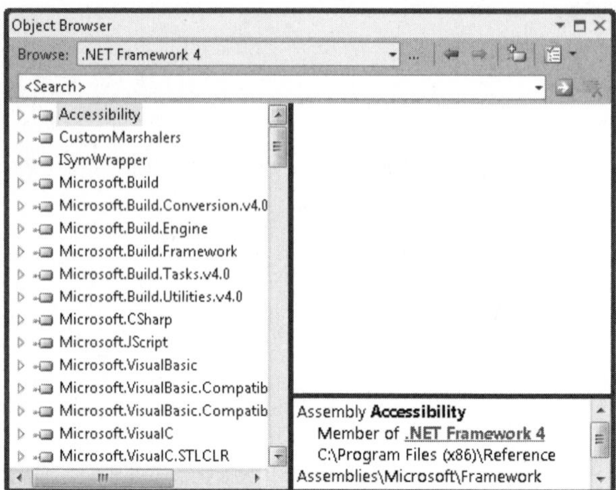

Edit Custom Component Set

You can edit the Custom Component Set to identify the components that create the browsing scope in two ways:

- Choose Edit Custom Component Set in the browse drop-down box.
- Click the "Edit Custom Component Set" button on the toolbar:

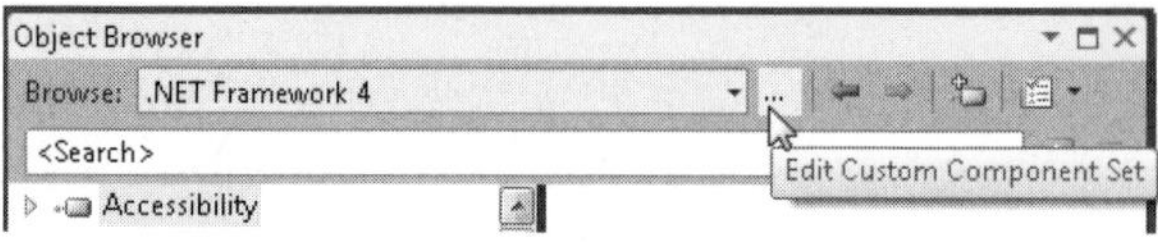

Regardless of the method used, you get the Edit Custom Component Set dialog box:

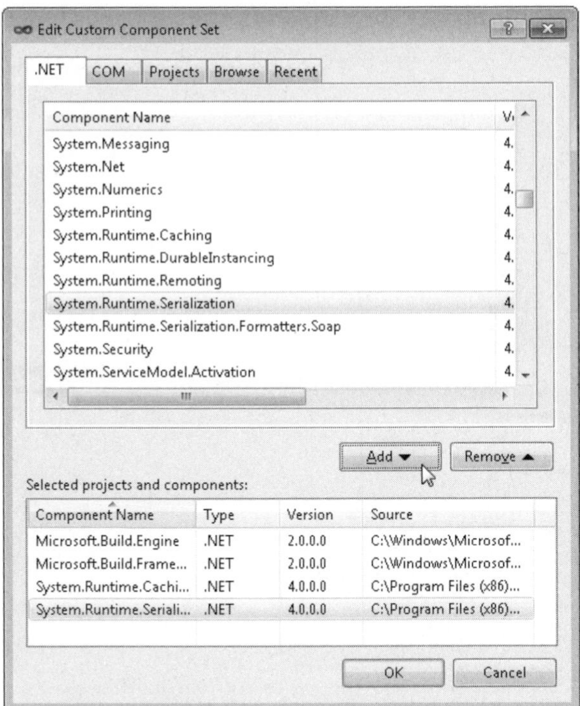

In the Edit Custom Component Set dialog box, you can add or remove components from a variety of sources. The browsing scope of the Custom Component Set is determined by the items listed in the Selected Projects And Components section of this dialog box. As you can see, information about the type, version, and source (location) is available here.

If you pick something that can't be browsed, you get the following message:

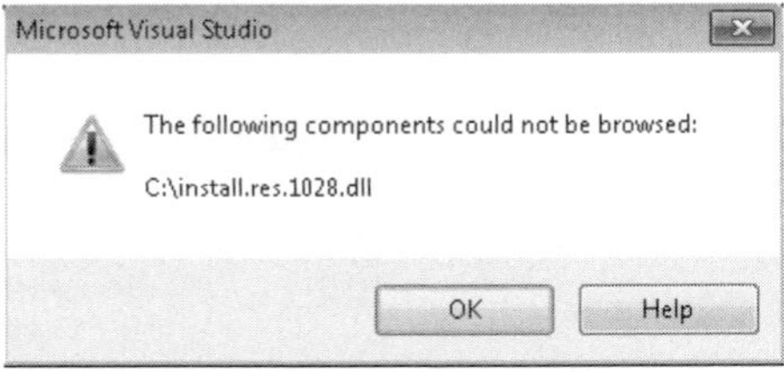

After you have successfully edited the Custom Component Set, it is automatically selected in the Browse drop-down box and becomes the current browsing scope:

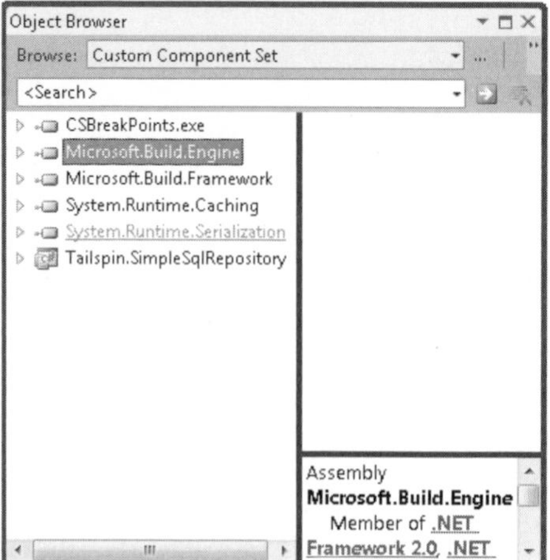

07.41 The Object Browser: Navigation and References

DEFAULT	Ctrl+Alt+J (view object browser); Alt+Right Arrow (forward); Alt+Left Arrow (back)
VISUAL BASIC 6	Ctrl+Alt+J (view object browser); F2 (view object browser); Alt+Right Arrow (forward); Alt+Left Arrow (back)
VISUAL C# 2005	Ctrl+Alt+J (view object browser); Ctrl+W, Ctrl+J (view object browser); Ctrl+W, J (view object browser); Alt+Right Arrow (forward); Alt+Left Arrow (back)
VISUAL C++ 2	Ctrl+Alt+J (view object browser); Shift+Alt+F1 (view object browser); Alt+Right Arrow (forward); Alt+Left Arrow (back)
VISUAL C++ 6	Ctrl+Alt+J (view object browser); Alt+Right Arrow (forward); Alt+Left Arrow (back)
VISUAL STUDIO 6	Ctrl+Alt+B (view object browser); F2 (view object browser); Alt+Right Arrow (forward); Alt+Left Arrow (back)
WINDOWS	Alt,V, J (view object browser)
MENU	View | Object Browser
COMMAND	View.ObjectBrowser; View.Forward; View.Backward; View.ObjectBrowserAddReference
VERSIONS	2005, 2008, 2010
CODE	vstipTool0079

Continuing our look at the Object Browser, we now turn our attention to the toolbar buttons to the right of the Browse area:

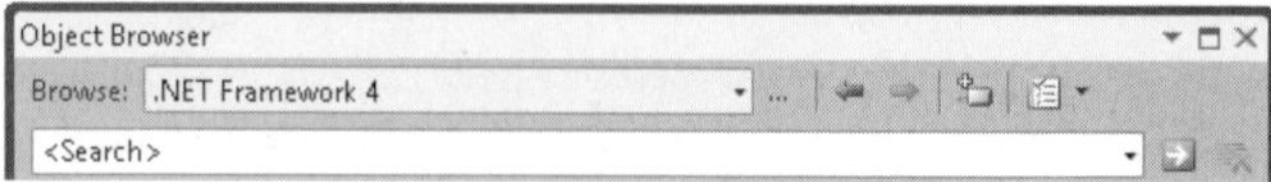

Navigation

The Forward (Alt+Right Arrow) and Back (Alt+Left Arrow) buttons can be used to easily navigate among items in the Objects pane as you browse:

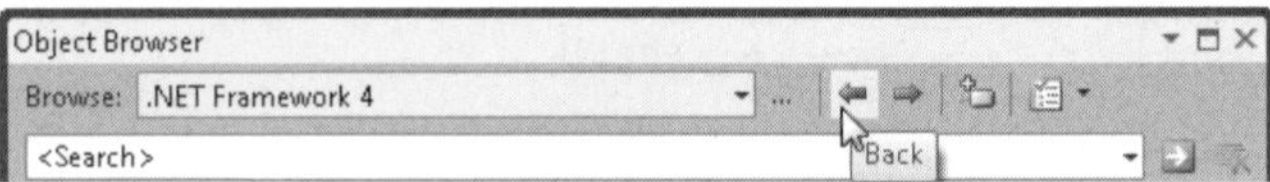

I haven't discovered any obvious upper limit to how many times you can go back. I have personally tested it to go back over 75 items, with no end in sight. The places are remembered (and more added) as long as Visual Studio remains open, regardless of which project or solution you are using.

References

You can add a reference to the currently selected item in the Objects pane to your project:

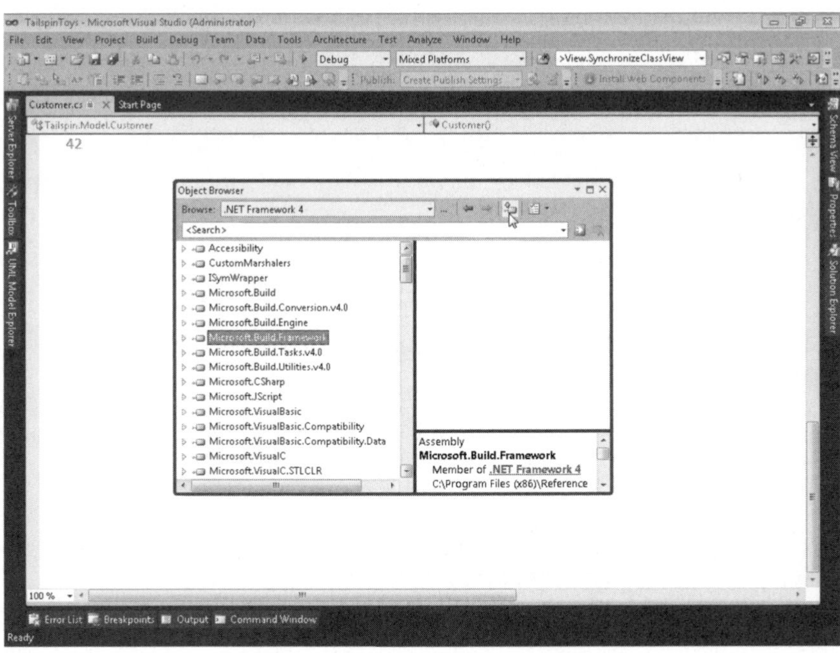

Read the tooltip carefully. Notice that it says Add To References In *Selected Project In Solution Explorer*. This might confuse you when you try to use it for the first time because you can select a reference that you want to add and then find the button disabled (top right in the following illustration):

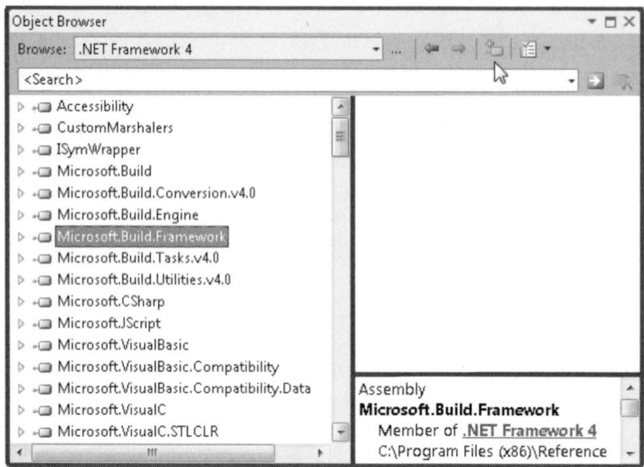

This is because you most likely don't have a project selected in Solution Explorer, as we do in the following example:

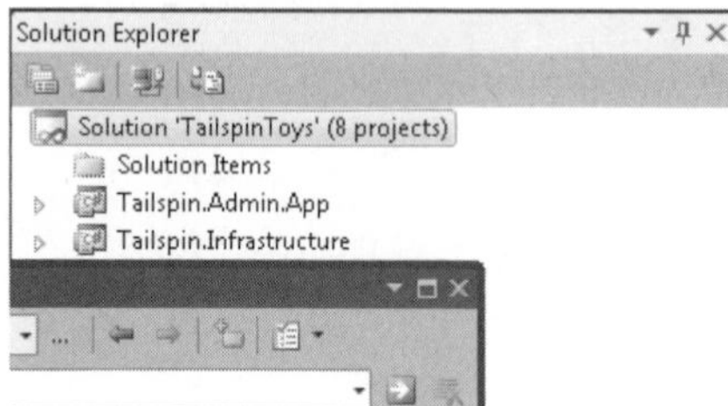

Simply click on (or in) any project, and the button becomes enabled so that you can add the reference to your project.

07.42 The Exceptions Dialog Box

DEFAULT	Ctrl+Alt+E
VISUAL BASIC 6	Ctrl+Alt+E
VISUAL C# 2005	Ctrl+Alt+E; Ctrl+D, Ctrl+E; Ctrl+D, E
VISUAL C++ 2	Ctrl+Alt+E
VISUAL C++ 6	Ctrl+Alt+E
VISUAL STUDIO 6	Ctrl+Alt+E
WINDOWS	Alt,D, X
MENU	Debug | Exceptions
COMMAND	Debug.Exceptions
VERSIONS	2005, 2008, 2010
CODE	vstipDebug0039

By default, Visual Studio breaks only when an exception is not handled by user code. This can sometimes be problematic because the exception can bubble up through several calls far away from where the actual exception originally occurred, making it harder to find the problem.

You can use the Exceptions dialog box (Ctrl+Alt+E) to configure exceptions to break when they happen rather than checking to see whether they are unhandled:

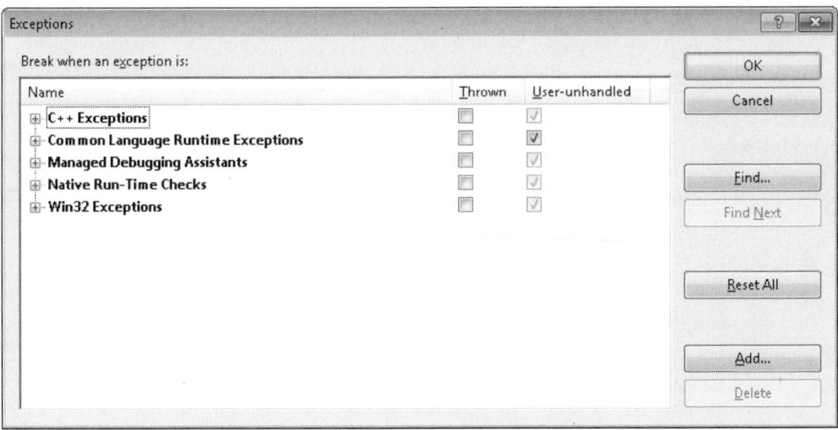

The exceptions are divided up into five broad categories. Also, as shown in the preceding illustration, two options are provided: Thrown and User-Unhandled. When you check Thrown for any category or individual exception, it breaks when the exception occurs instead of waiting to see whether the user handles the exception.

Additionally, you can use the following buttons.

Find

Helps you search for a specific exception.

Reset All

Puts exceptions back to their default settings.

Add

Allows you to add exceptions not currently in the list.

Delete

Lets you delete any added exceptions.

Special Case

You might find the User-Unhandled option missing from the Exceptions dialog box:

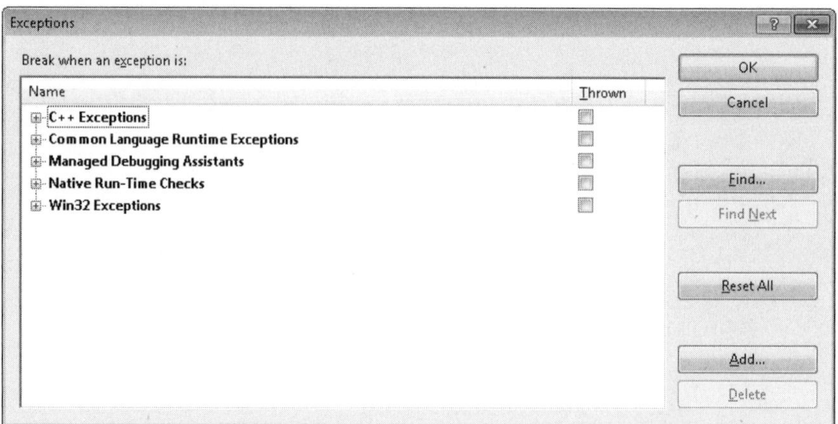

To get it back, go to Tools | Options | Debugging | General and select Enable Just My Code (Managed Only):

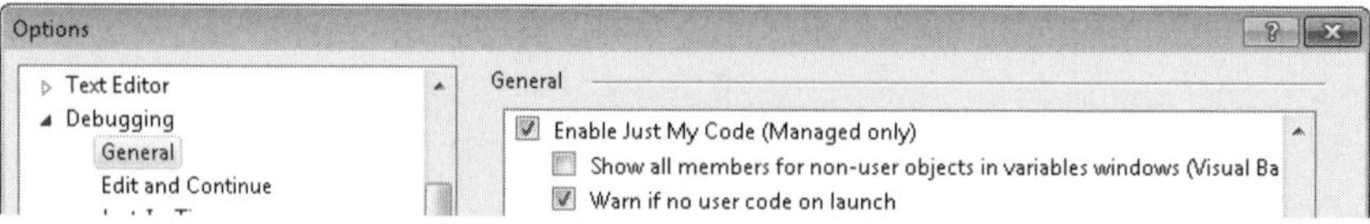

07.43 Setting a Breakpoint in the Call Stack Window

DEFAULT	Ctrl+Alt+C
VISUAL BASIC 6	Ctrl+Alt+C; Ctrl+L
VISUAL C# 2005	Ctrl+Alt+C; Ctrl+D, Ctrl+C; Ctrl+D, C
VISUAL C++ 2	Ctrl+Alt+C; Ctrl+K; Alt+6
VISUAL C++ 6	Ctrl+Alt+C; Alt+7
VISUAL STUDIO 6	Ctrl+Alt+C
WINDOWS	Alt,D, W, C
MENU	Debug | Toggle Breakpoint
COMMAND	Debug.CallStack
VERSIONS	2005, 2008, 2010
CODE	vstipDebug0008

Did you know that breakpoints can be set inside the Call Stack window? This tip shows how to do it.

First, set a breakpoint deep in series of calls to get a nice call stack.

Note If you don't have a call stack handy, just make several methods called One, Two, Three, and so forth and have them call each other, as I have done in these examples.

Run your code, and let it stop at the breakpoint. Bring up your Call Stack window (Ctrl+Alt+C or Debug | Windows | Call Stack):

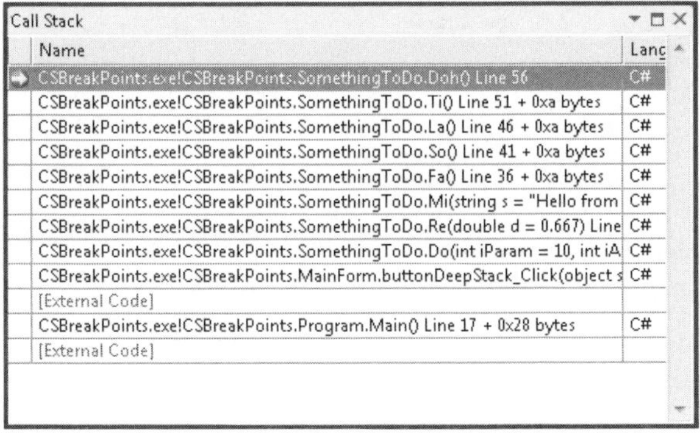

Click somewhere in the call stack you would like to stop at as it unwinds, and press F9:

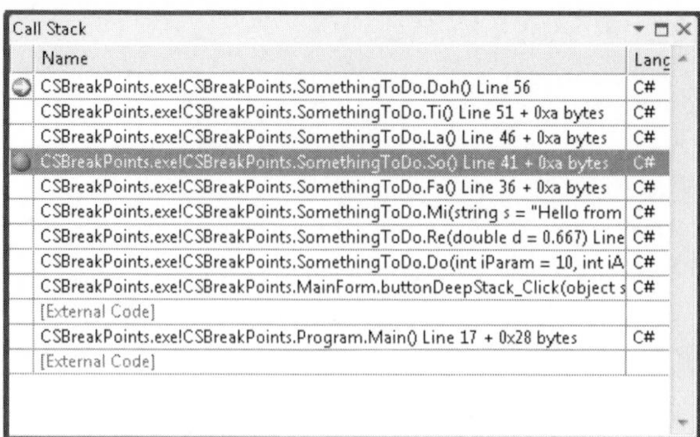

It sets a breakpoint. You can verify this by looking in your Breakpoints window:

Now just press F5 to continue, and watch as the debugger stops at the place you told it to:

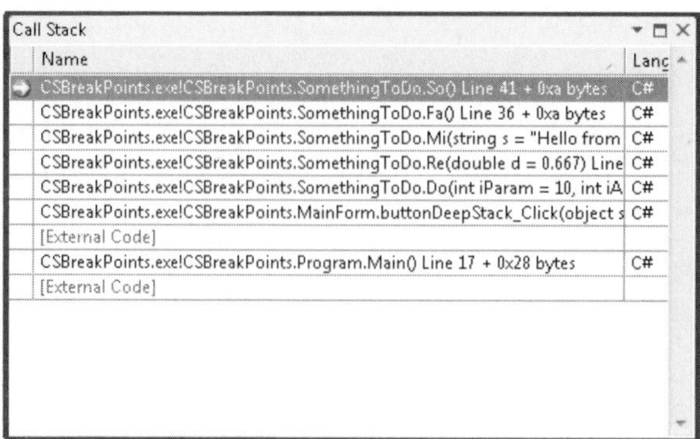

07.44 Setting a Tracepoint in the Call Stack Window

DEFAULT	Ctrl+Alt+C
VISUAL BASIC 6	Ctrl+Alt+C; Ctrl+L
VISUAL C# 2005	Ctrl+Alt+C; Ctrl+D, Ctrl+C; Ctrl+D, C
VISUAL C++ 2	Ctrl+Alt+C; Ctrl+K; Alt+6
VISUAL C++ 6	Ctrl+Alt+C; Alt+7
VISUAL STUDIO 6	Ctrl+Alt+C
WINDOWS	Alt,D, W, C
COMMAND	Debug.CallStack
VERSIONS	2005, 2008, 2010
CODE	vstipDebug0009

In vstipDebug0008 ("Setting a Breakpoint in the Call Stack Window," page 367), I showed you a classic technique of setting a breakpoint in the Call Stack window. The only problem is that breakpoints tend to be somewhat intrusive if all you want is information. So I thought it would be a good idea to also show how to set tracepoints. For more information about tracepoints, see vstipDebug0010 ("Setting a Tracepoint in Source Code," page 325).

1. Set a breakpoint deep in series of calls to get a nice call stack.

Note If you don't have a call series handy, just make several methods called One, Two, Three, and so forth, and have them call each other, as I have done in these examples.

2. Run your code, and let it stop at the breakpoint.
3. Bring up your Call Stack window (Ctrl+Alt+C or Debug | Windows | Call Stack):

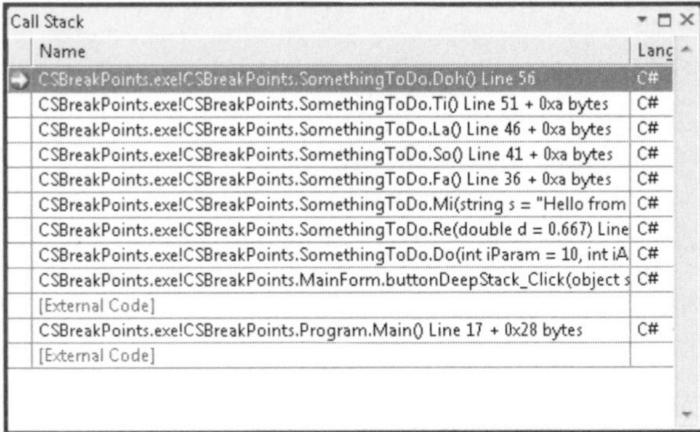

4. Right-click some place in the stack where you would like to set a tracepoint, and go to Breakpoint | Insert Tracepoint:

5. You get the When Breakpoint Is Hit dialog box:

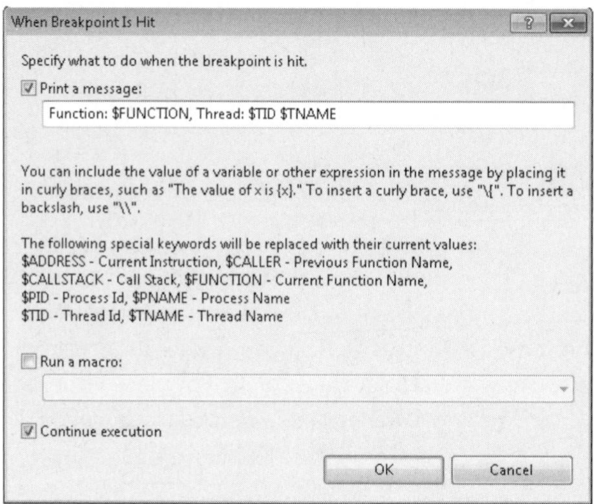

6. You definitely want to get up to speed on the details of tracepoints if you aren't familiar with them (see vstipDebug0010, "Setting a Tracepoint in Source Code," on page 325), but for now, just click OK.

7. Now we get our tracepoint. (Notice the diamond glyph.)

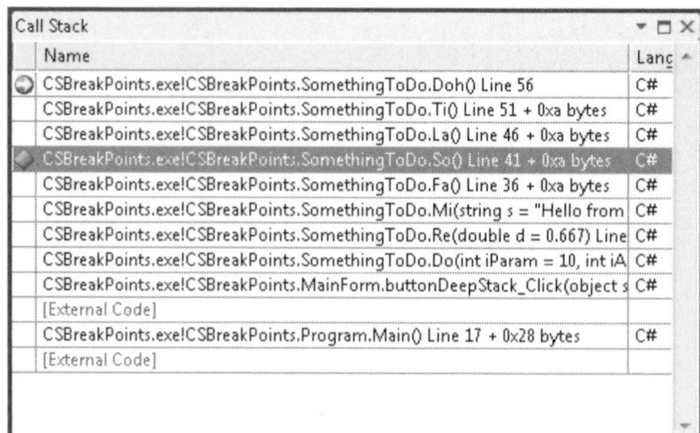

8. Press F5 to continue the program and let the call stack unwind.

9. Now bring up your Output window (Debug | Windows | Output), and notice that the trace information is in there:

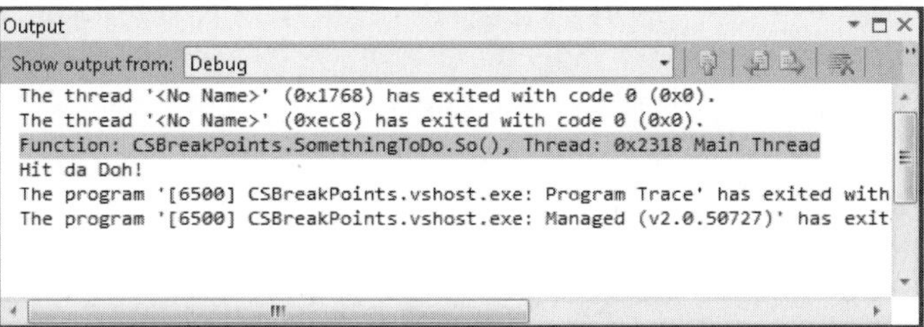

07.45 Using the WPF Tree Visualizer

VERSIONS	2010
CODE	vstipDebug0004

The WPF Tree Visualizer started out as a CodePlex project and ended up in the product itself as a visualizer. This tip shows how you can use it.

Note For those unfamiliar with WPF trees, you might want to review the article "Trees in WPF," at *http://msdn.microsoft.com/en-us/library/ms753391(VS.100).aspx.*

Enter Debug mode in any WPF project you have. Then take a look at a DataTip, the Watch window, the Autos window, or the Locals window. For this example, let's use the Autos window:

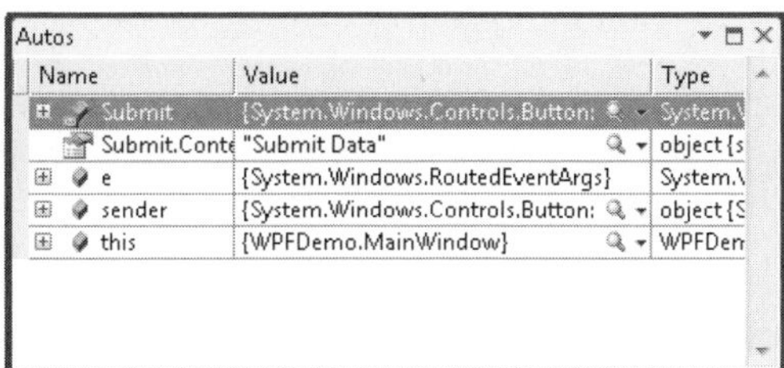

Choose any control in the Autos window, and then click the magnifying glass way over to the right of the control name:

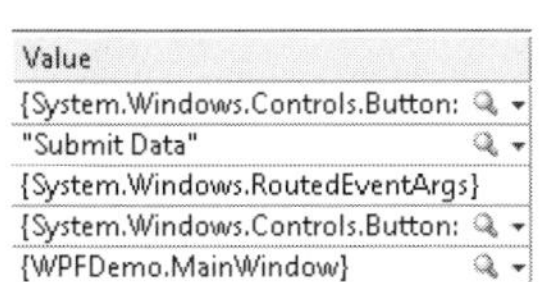

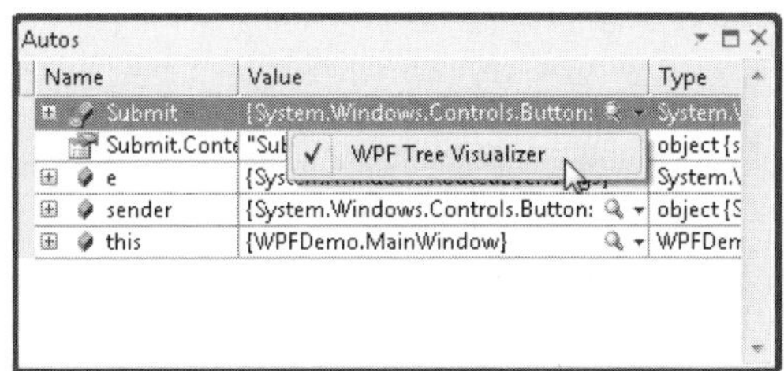

On the drop-down list, choose WPF Tree Visualizer to get the following dialog box:

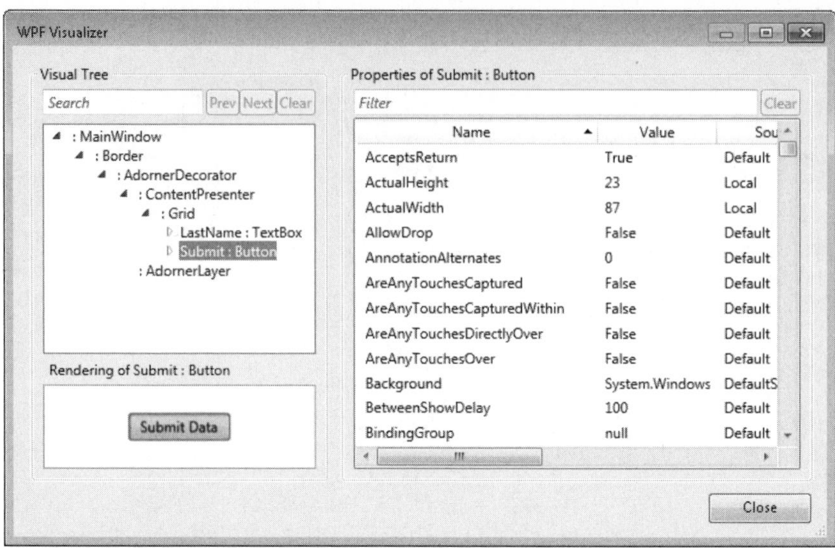

This dialog box has a lot of moving parts, so let's take a look at each one. First, the Visual Tree section shows you the hierarchy of the controls:

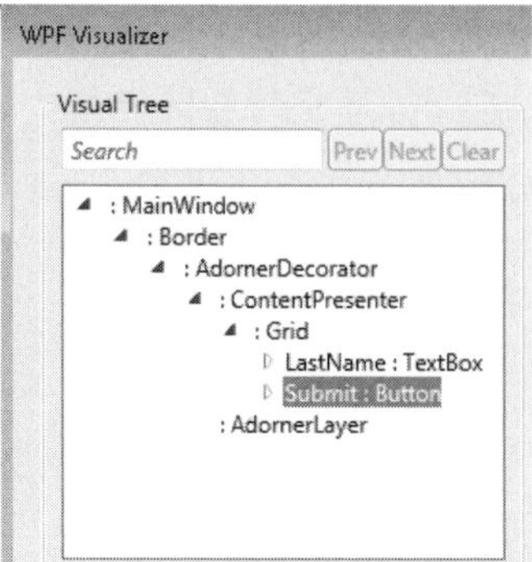

Clicking on any particular node of the tree shows you the rendering at the bottom:

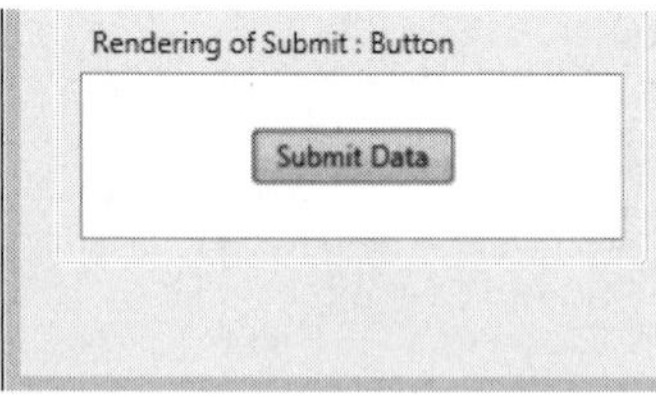

Also, the selected control has its properties displayed in the large area to the right:

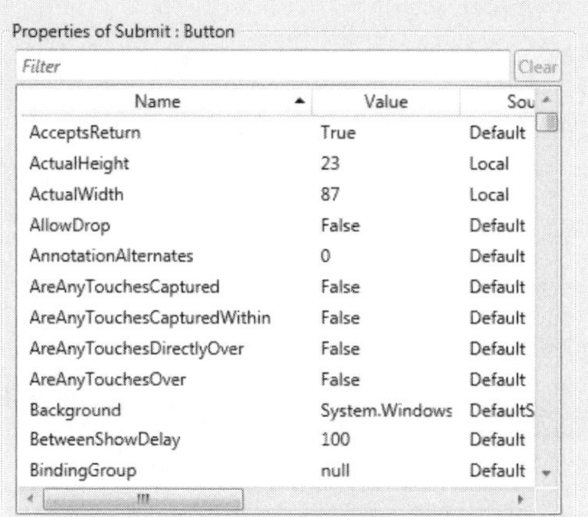

In both the Visual Tree and the Properties area, you can search or filter the results by typing into the Search or Filter text boxes respectively:

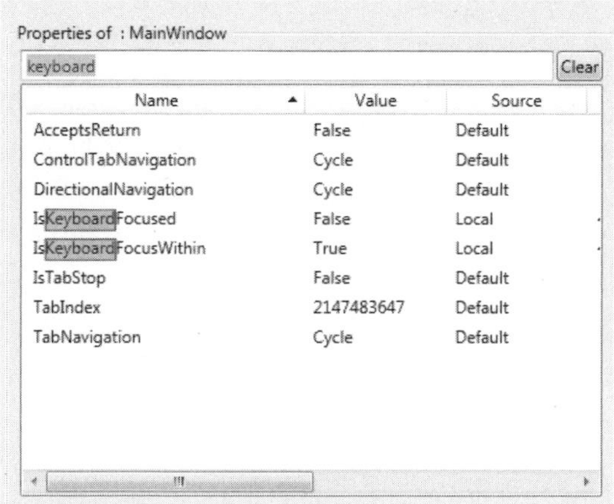

Warning Watch out for the results because they might not be what you expect. See the extra items in the list that don't have the word "keyboard" in them? How did they get there? Well, if I scroll to the right and look at other properties, you can see how it happened. Currently, there is no way that I am aware of to change this behavior.

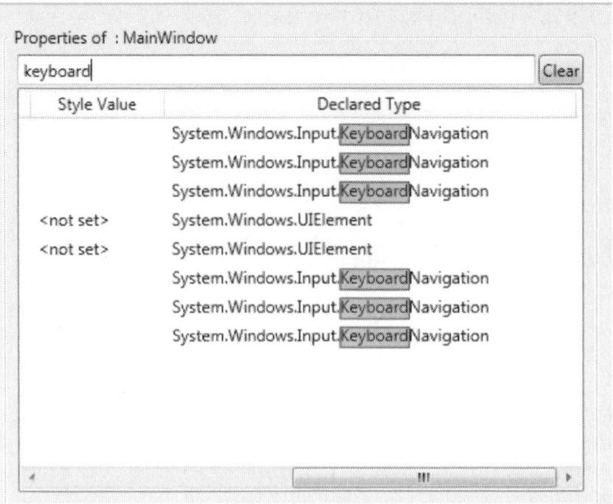

07.46 Understanding Break All Processes When One Process Breaks

MENU	Tools | Options | Debugging | General
COMMAND	Tools.Options
VERSIONS	2005, 2008, 2010
CODE	vstipDebug0029

In vstipEnv0015 ("Multiple Startup Projects," page 48), we examined how to run multiple projects at the same time. Now let's explore what happens when you go into break mode on the applications. By default, when you break one application, all the other applications break too. Let's take a look at an example.

You set a breakpoint in your first application that has a hit counter on it (see vstipDebug0019, "Breakpoint Hit Count," on page 314):

```
static void Main(string[] args)
{
    for (int counter = 0; counter <= 20; counter++)
    {
        Console.WriteLine("Server: " + counter);
        System.Threading.Thread.Sleep(1000);
    }
}
```

But you don't have any breakpoints in your second application:

```
static void Main(string[] args)
{
    for (int counter2 = 0; counter2 <= 20; counter2++)
    {
        Console.WriteLine("Client: " + counter2);
        System.Threading.Thread.Sleep(1000);
    }
}
```

When you run the applications, you get the following:

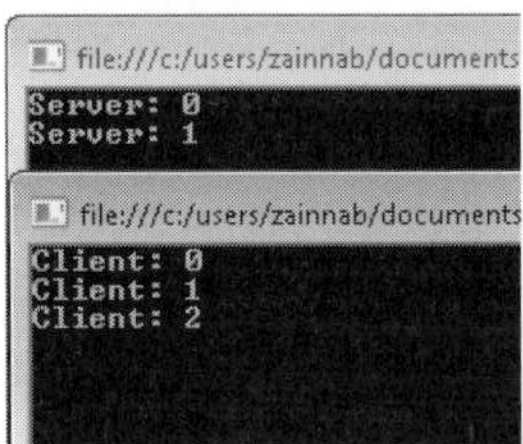

Both applications stop when one of them stops. This behavior is set in Tools | Options | Debugging | General by selecting the Break All Processes When One Process Breaks check box:

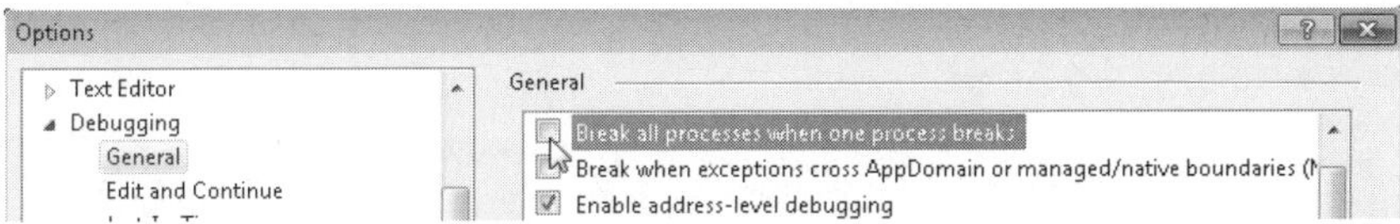

If you turn this feature off and run your applications again, you see the following (predictable) result:

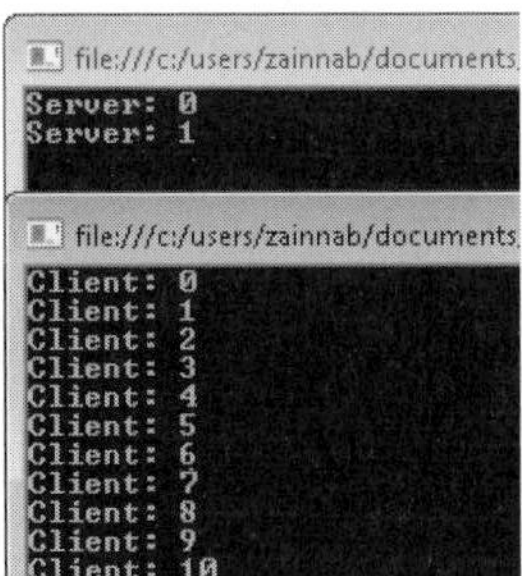

07.47 Changing Context in the Locals Window

DEFAULT	Ctrl+Alt+V, L (locals); Ctrl+5 then Alt+Down Arrow (process combo); Ctrl+6 then Alt+Down Arrow (thread combo); Ctrl+7 then Alt+Down Arrow (stack frame combo)
VISUAL BASIC 6	Ctrl+Alt+V, L (locals); Ctrl+5 then Alt+Down Arrow (process combo); Ctrl+6 then Alt+Down Arrow (thread combo); Ctrl+7 then Alt+Down Arrow (stack frame combo)
VISUAL C# 2005	Ctrl+Alt+V, L (locals); Ctrl+D, Ctrl+L (locals); Ctrl+D, L (locals); Ctrl+5 then Alt+Down Arrow (process combo); Ctrl+6 then Alt+Down Arrow (thread combo); Ctrl+7 then Alt+Down Arrow (stack frame combo)
VISUAL C++ 2	Ctrl+Alt+V, L (locals); Alt+3 (locals); Ctrl+5 then Alt+Down Arrow (process combo); Ctrl+6 then Alt+Down Arrow (thread combo); Ctrl+7 then Alt+Down Arrow (stack frame combo)
VISUAL C++ 6	Ctrl+Alt+V, L (locals); Alt+4 (locals); Ctrl+5 then Alt+Down Arrow (process combo); Ctrl+6 then Alt+Down Arrow (thread combo); Ctrl+7 then Alt+Down Arrow (stack frame combo)
VISUAL STUDIO 6	Ctrl+Alt+V, L (locals); Ctrl+Alt+L (locals); Ctrl+5 then Alt+Down Arrow (process combo); Ctrl+6 then Alt+Down Arrow (thread combo); Ctrl+7 then Alt+Down Arrow (stack frame combo)
WINDOWS	Alt,D, W, L (locals)
MENU	Debug | Windows | Locals
COMMAND	Debug.Locals; Debug.LocationToolbar.ProcessCombo; Debug.LocationToolbar.ThreadCombo; Debug.LocationToolbar.StackFrameCombo
VERSIONS	2005, 2008, 2010
CODE	vstipTool0101

Most people are familiar with the Locals window. For those who aren't, it displays variables local to the current context or scope. Information often appears in the Locals window, but the information will not be current until the next time the program breaks.

Even those who are familiar with the Locals window might not know that you can change the context. When you are in break mode, bring up the Locals window (Ctrl+Alt+V, L):

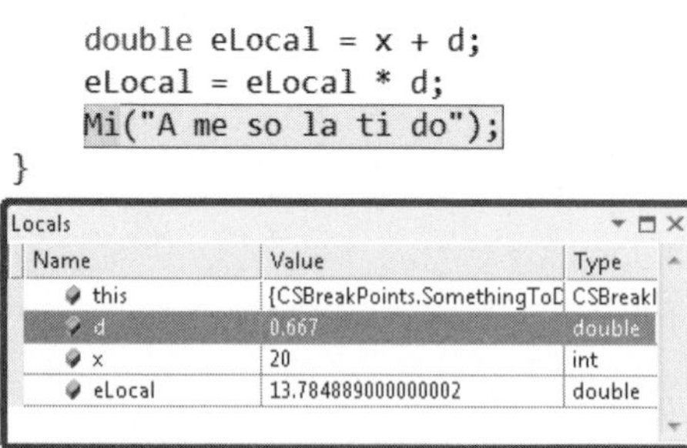

Debug Location Toolbar

You can use the Debug Location toolbar to change the context of the Locals window. If you don't have it up, you can right-click any toolbar and select Debug Location to make it appear:

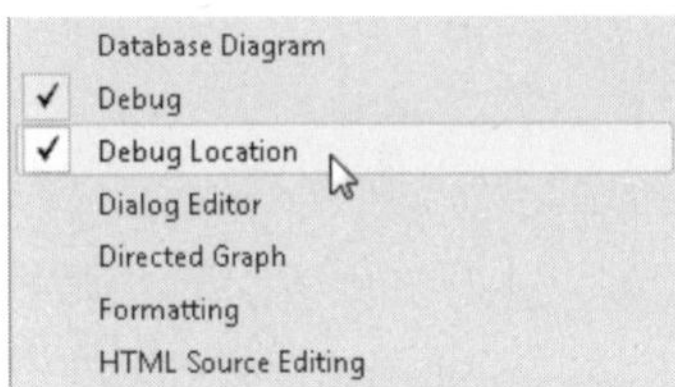

Process

If you have multiple processes running, you can use the Process combo box (Ctrl+5) to change between them. In this example, we only have one process running:

Thread

The Thread combo (Ctrl+6) lets you change the thread context to different threads. While not of much use in this example, it is very useful in debugging multithreaded applications:

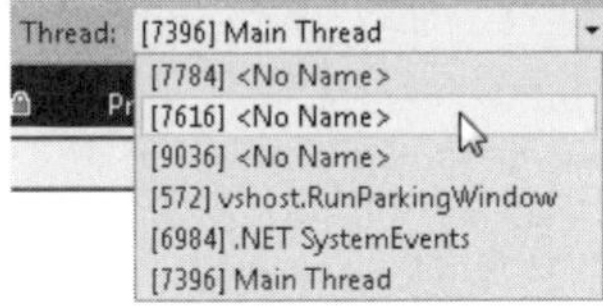

Stack Frame

The stack frame is probably the more common item you use when dealing with the Locals window. The Stack Frame combo box (Ctrl+7) allows you to switch between items in the call stack:

Currently, we're in the one method and the Locals window shows the following:

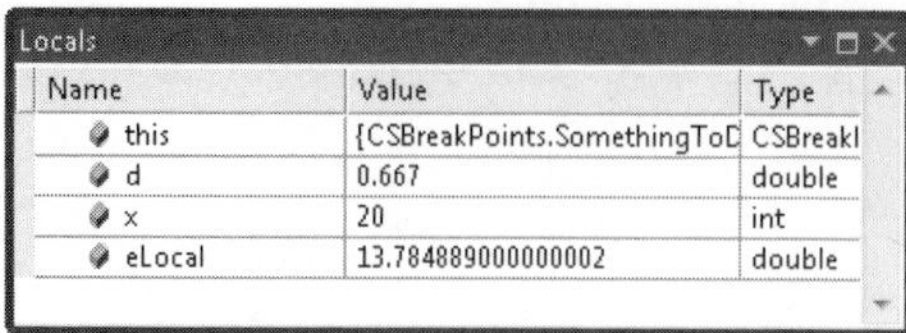

Let's change to another method in our code:

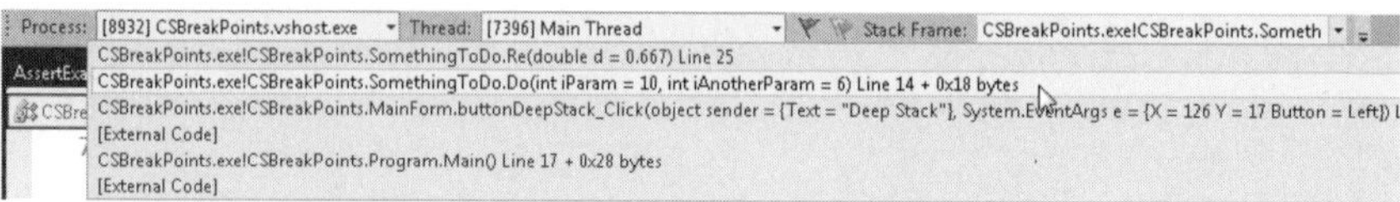

Now our Locals window shows the following:

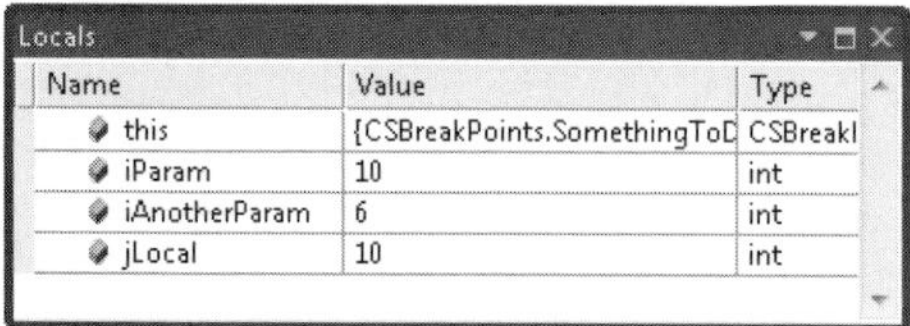

Now you too can take advantage of the Debug Location toolbar to change your context and get new information in the Locals window.

07.48 Understanding the Autos Window

DEFAULT	Ctrl+Alt+V, A
VISUAL BASIC 6	Ctrl+Alt+V, A
VISUAL C# 2005	Ctrl+Alt+V, A; Ctrl+D, Ctrl+A; Ctrl+D, A
VISUAL C++ 2:	Ctrl+Alt+V, A
VISUAL C++ 6	Ctrl+Alt+V, A
VISUAL STUDIO 6	Ctrl+Alt+V, A
WINDOWS	Alt,D, W, A
MENU	Debug | Windows | Autos
COMMAND	Debug.Autos
VERSIONS	2005, 2008, 2010
CODE	vstipTool0103

The Autos window looks a lot like the Locals window, but let's take a closer look. According to the MSDN website (*http://msdn.microsoft.com/en-us/library/aa290702(VS.71).aspx*), here is what it does:

"The Autos window displays variables used in the current statement and the previous statement. (For Visual Basic, it displays variables in the current statement and three statements on either side of the current statement.)"

The current statement is the statement at the current execution location (the statement that will be executed next if execution continues). The debugger identifies these variables for you automatically, hence the window name."

Changing Values

Just like the Locals window, you can change values in the Autos window:

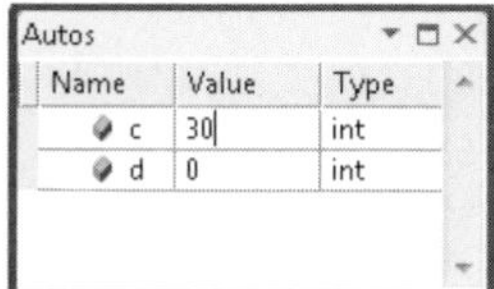

Current and Previous Statement

Simple Example

OK let's break this down. The Autos window does, in fact, show variables used in the current statement and previous statement. Following is a simple example in C# with some variables:

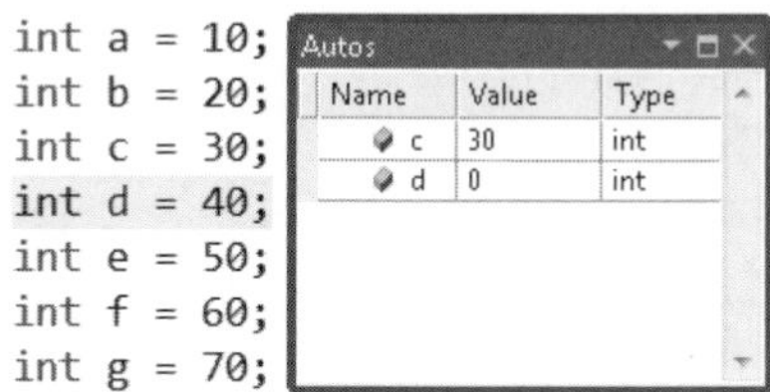

As you can see, it just shows the variable on the current line and the one before it—nothing else. Even though several lines have variables around them, the Autos window is not concerned with those variables. Now compare this to the Locals window that shows every variable in scope:

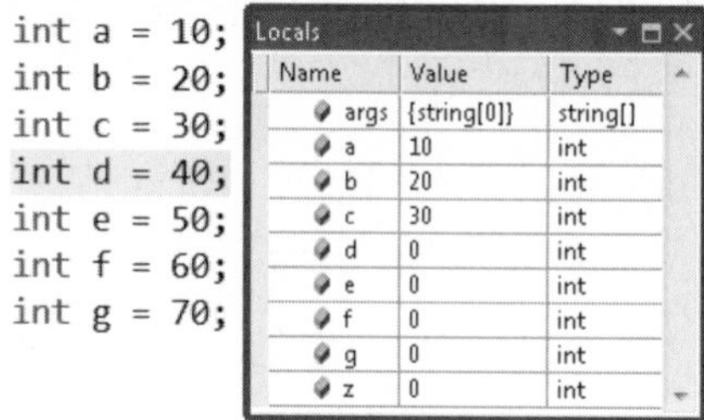

Another Example

I thought it would be instructive to see, step-by-step, how this works. Here I have stopped in some code:

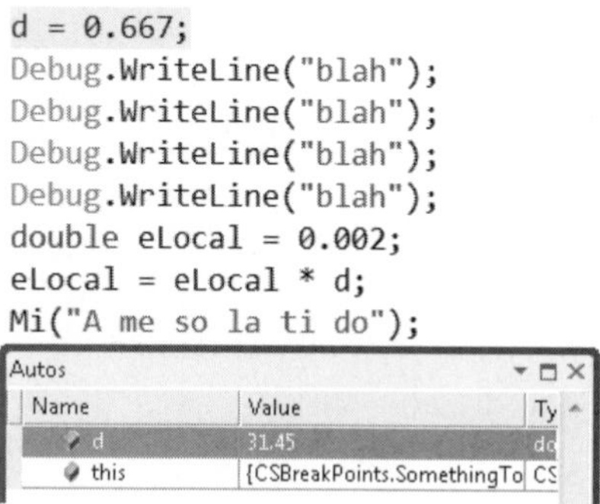

Notice that it shows the current variable and the object variable that exists all the time. Now I go down two lines:

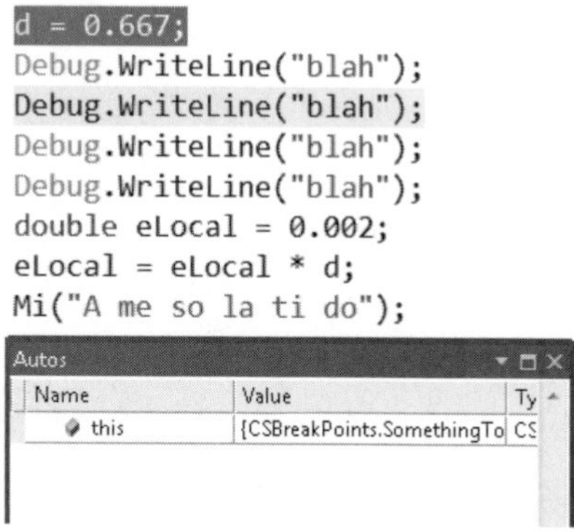

All I'm left with is the object variable. I go down another three lines:

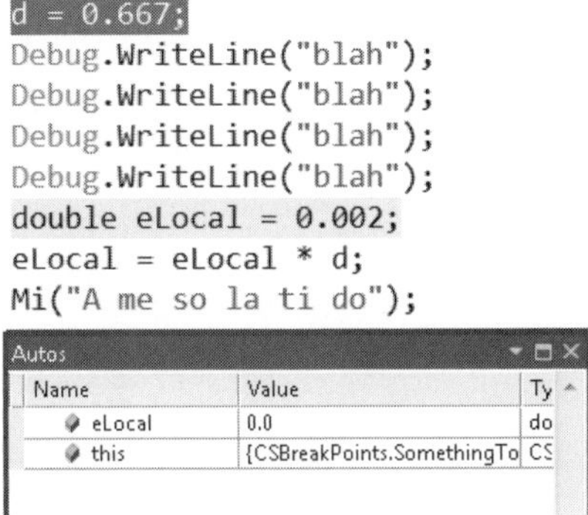

Now I can see that "eLocal" is about to be used, and I go down one more line:

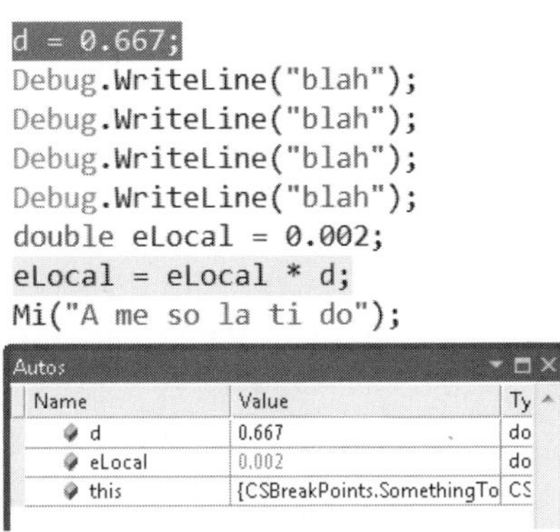

I can finally see that "eLocal" has changed, and "d" has shown up again because it is being used on the current line.

VB Shows Three Statements on Either Side

In versions prior to 2010, VB would, in fact, show three statements on either side of the current line. This is no longer true in Visual Studio 2010. The Autos window in Visual Basic acts just like the C++ and C# Autos windows and shows only the current line and the one prior.

Part II

Extensions for Visual Studio

In this part:

Chapter 8

Visual Studio Extensions

The new code editor is one of the most impressive improvements of the Visual Studio 2010 Integrated Development Environment (IDE). Built on top of Windows Presentation Foundation (WPF) and the Managed Extensibility Framework, the combination of user interface–rich flexibility plus plug-in extensibility takes innovation within Visual Studio to the next level.

Introducing Visual Studio Extensions

In addition to the editor, the Visual Studio 2010 IDE introduces a new WPF-based shell. Many core user interface features are now WPF-based, including menus, window layouts, toolbars, start page, and so forth.

Even if you've never developed any applications for use within Visual Studio, it is important to know that the SDK tooling has significantly improved, paving the way for a much richer Visual Studio ecosystem.

Gone are the days of requesting a package load key or a shell load key to develop Visual Studio applications. No more having to make modifications to the registry to install a Visual Studio plug-in.

The goals of this chapter are twofold: to provide a basic overview on how to find and install extensions and to catalogue the "must-have" extensions available for free for the Visual Studio 2010 IDE.

Welcome to the new world of Visual Studio extensions.

Installing an Extension

The development experience has greatly improved for Visual Studio 2010, providing additional ways for installing extensions. The preferred and most straightforward way to install an extension is through a new Visual Studio 2010 feature called the Extension Manager. Located within the IDE, the Extension Manager searches an online gallery, called the Visual Studio Gallery, for extensions. The Extension Manager also manages the installed and currently in-use extensions.

Installing from the Extension Manager

To open the Extension Manager from within Visual Studio, go to Tools | Extension Manager. To search for an extension online, select Online Gallery in the left navigation pane. Type in the name of the extension to search for within the Search Online Gallery text box. For example, you can search for "Color Theme Editor" to find the Visual Studio Color Theme Editor extension.

When the desired extension is found, click the Download button to install. When the install has completed, a message appears at the bottom of the Extension Manager dialog box, as shown in the following illustration.

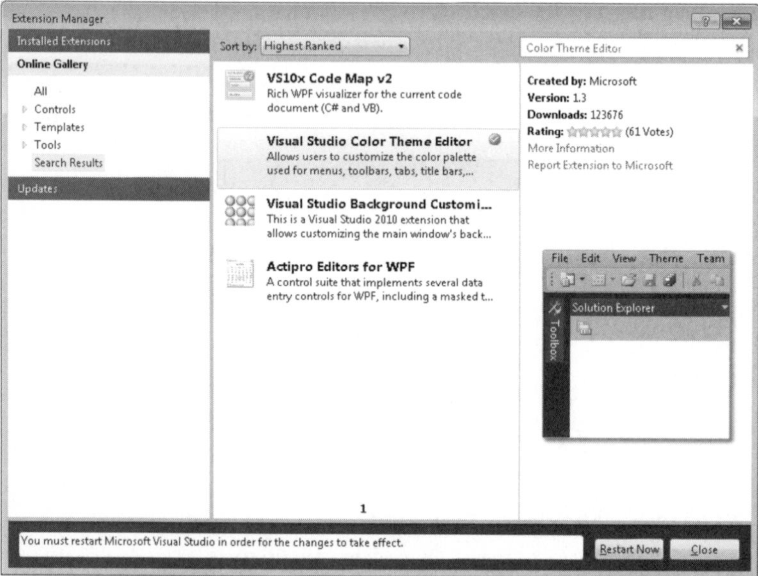

A Visual Studio restart is required for all extensions, except for templates. Click Restart Now to restart Visual Studio and enable the extension.

Installing from the Visual Studio Gallery

Another addition to Visual Studio 2010 is the Visual Studio Gallery, a website that provides a catalog of free and commercial extensions for Visual Studio. Naturally, developers writing extensions have the option of hosting the extension on their own websites, but hosting in the Visual Studio Gallery greatly increases discoverability of the extension. Additionally, you can find a significant number of tools for all past Visual Studio IDE versions from 2002 onward in the Visual Studio Gallery.

The Visual Studio Gallery is located at *www.visualstudiogallery.com*. To browse for extensions built for Visual Studio 2010, click Browse and then select Visual Studio 2010 under Visual Studio Versions in the left navigation bar.

When the desired extension is found, click the Download image link to begin the download and installation.

You can either open the .vsix file to begin the installation or save the file to install at a later time. If you chose to save the file, you can double-click the .vsix file at any time to start the installation. Otherwise, simply click Open to begin installing the extension. The Visual Studio Extension Manager prompts you to accept a license if one was provided with the extension.

A restart is required to finish installing the extension. The Extension Manager shows a "restart required" message at the bottom of the dialog box. A Visual Studio restart is required for all extensions, except for templates. Click Restart Now to restart Visual Studio and enable the extension.

Installing Through Xcopy

Because the SDK tooling has been greatly simplified, such that registry modifications are no longer necessary, it is possible to install an extension simply by copying the extension file into a specific Visual Studio folder. This method of installation through copying files is known as Xcopy deployment.

All installed extensions can be found in an unzipped format at the following location:

```
%LocalAppData%\Microsoft\VisualStudio\10.0\Extensions\<Company>\<Product>\<Version>
```

Extensions installed through the Xcopy method are disabled by default within Visual Studio. You must manually enable the extension, as described next.

To install an extension through this method, you must do the following:

1. Unzip the .vsix file.
2. Copy the .vsix raw folder into the Extensions folder.
3. Start Visual Studio, and enable the extension in the Extension Manager.

Conversely, you can uninstall any extension simply by deleting its corresponding folder from the %LocalAppData%\Microsoft\VisualStudio\10.0\Extensions directory.

Inside a .vsix File

Although creating extensions is beyond the scope of this book, it's important to be aware how content written by members of the community is installed and run on your computer, especially in the case where you need to troubleshoot a faulty extension.

All Visual Studio extensions use the .vsix file extension. A .vsix file is a .zip file (with its file extension renamed to .vsix) that uses the Open Packaging Convention to package the code and manifest for the extension. You can read more about the contents of a .vsix file on Quan To's blog at *http://blogs.msdn.com/b/quanto/archive/2009/05/26/what-is-a-vsix.aspx*.

As described on Quan To's article, the .vsix file is derived from the Visual Studio Installer found in the Visual Studio 2005 and 2008 versions. The original .vsi file launches the Content Installer from these past Visual Studio versions. The .vsi file represented many various types of content for the Visual Studio IDE (macros, add-ins, toolbox controls, code snippets, and so forth). To make the distinction clearer from this previous method of installing content, an 'x' was placed at the end of the extension, hence a .vsix file.

For more information about the Open Packaging Convention, please see the article titled "A New Standard For Packaging Your Data," at *http://msdn.microsoft.com/en-us/magazine/cc163372.aspx*.

Disabling an Extension

If you need to disable an extension for any reason—for example, the Visual Studio performance is slower than expected, the IDE crashes repeatedly, or the extension is simply not working—you can disable an extension via Extension Manager.

Select Installed Extensions in the left navigation pane of the Extension Manager, and then click Disable on any extension in the list. Again, a restart is required to disable the extension.

Note You can disable or re-enable multiple extensions at the same time within the Extension Manager, requiring only one restart of the Visual Studio IDE.

Uninstalling an Extension

The most straightforward way to uninstall an extension is through the Extension Manager. Select Installed Extension in the left navigation pane of the Extension Manager, and then click Uninstall on any extension in the list. Again, a restart is required to remove the extension.

> **Note** You can uninstall or reinstall multiple extensions at the same time within the Extension Manager, requiring only one restart of the Visual Studio IDE.

The other way to uninstall an extension is to delete the contents of the extension from the Visual Studio extension folder on your hard drive. Simply delete the extension .vsix file from the %LocalAppData%\Microsoft\VisualStudio\10.0\Extensions directory, and restart Visual Studio.

Resources for Developing Extensions

As noted, creating and developing extensions are beyond the scope of this book. However, many great resources are available, such as the following:

- **Visual Studio Extensibility Developer Center**—*http://msdn.com/vsx*
- **Extensibility samples**—*http://code.msdn.microsoft.com/vsx*

08.01 Create Themes Using All Visual Studio Elements

NAME	Visual Studio Color Theme Editor
CREATED BY	Matthew Johnson (Microsoft)
LOCATION	*http://visualstudiogallery.msdn.microsoft.com/en-us/20cd93a2-c435-4d00-a797-499f16402378?SRC=Home*

You can use the Visual Studio Color Theme Editor to create themes consisting of colors that go beyond those listed in the Tools | Options | Fonts And Colors page.

Visual Studio Color Theme Editor

The most useful feature of the Visual Studio Color Theme Editor extension is that it provides a central location for controlling almost all possible colors in the IDE. No more having to edit individual fonts and colors options under Tools | Options. Refer to the "To Customize" section later in this section for more information about how to use this feature.

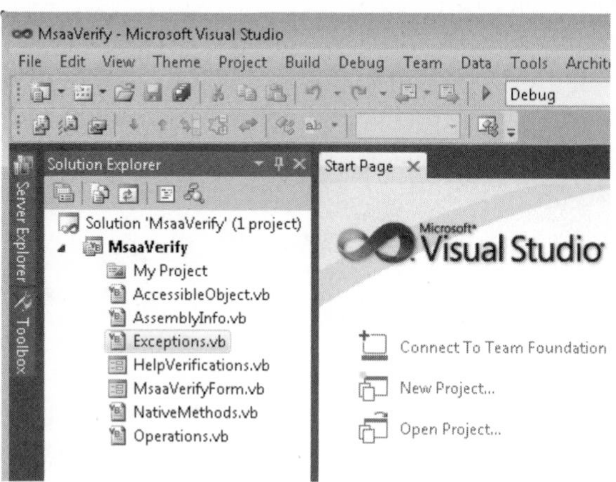

To Use

A Theme menu option is located on the Visual Studio file menu. The Theme menu lists multiple themes for you to choose from, including the Windows Classic look.

To Customize

You can create your own themes by clicking Theme | Customize Colors and choosing from hundreds of customized colors. This list of colors is significantly longer than the list found on the Tools | Options | Fonts And Colors page, because this extension lists every user interface element that implements the Visual Studio color service.

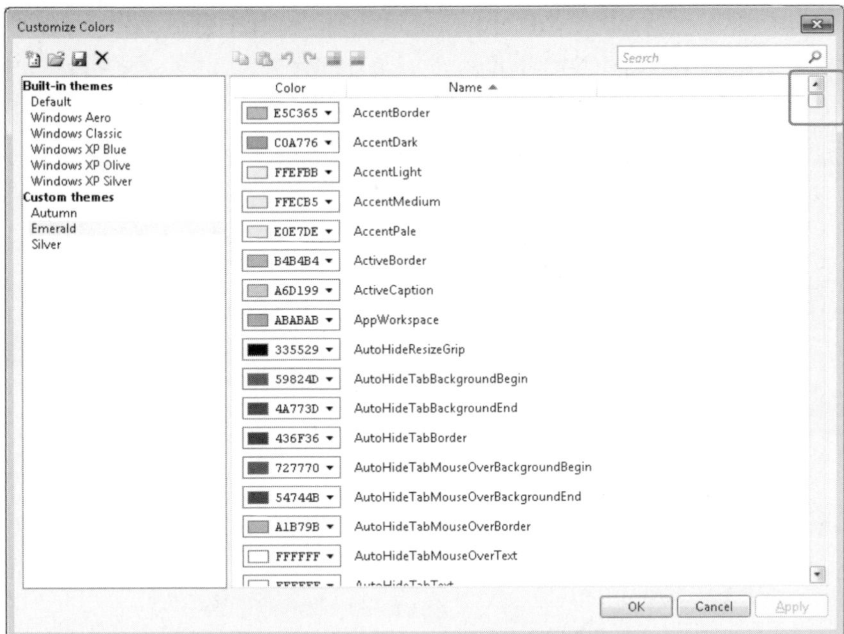

You can create new themes by clicking the Save button located in the toolbar in the upper-left corner. All themes are saved as .xml files, using the .vstheme file extension name. You can share a .vstheme file with others.

More Information

Make sure you check out the extension developer's blog post at *http://blogs.msdn.com/visualstudio/archive/2010/01/04/changing-visual-studio-s-color-palette.aspx* for an in-depth overview of the extension.

08.02 Insert Images into Your Code

NAME	Image Insertion
CREATED BY	Microsoft
LOCATION	*http://visualstudiogallery.msdn.microsoft.com/en-us/793d16d0-235a-439a-91df-4ce7c721df12*

The Image Insertion tool allows you insert images, such as a UML diagram, directly into your code. Another example is including user interface designs within your code for documentation purposes.

Image Insertion

Regardless of usage, the Image Insertion extension demonstrates that the Visual Studio 2010 editor is new and that creative extensions are possible.

Recall that the Visual Studio code editor is written using the Windows Presentation Foundation (WPF). The following illustration shows a Silverlight illustration of a hand-drawn stick figure at 100 percent zoom.

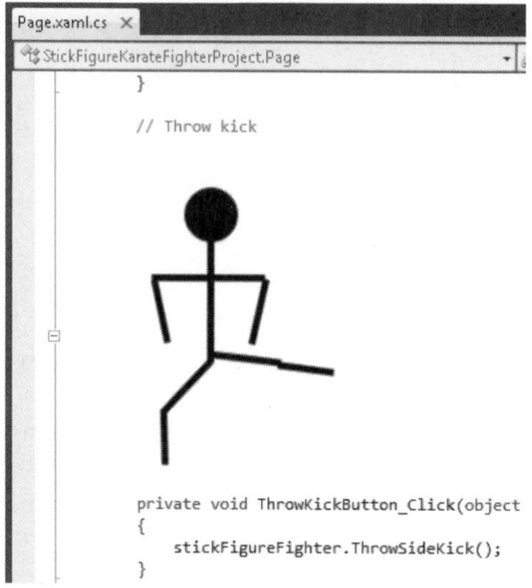

When the editor zoom is increased to 200 percent, notice how both the text *and the stick figure image* increase at the same ratio.

It is worth mentioning that this is not a separate designer built solely for this purpose. This is the actual Visual Studio code editor displaying the image.

To Use

Select an image from either a Windows Explorer window or Solution Explorer, and drag the image onto the editor surface. To successfully insert the image, you must see the blue placeholder line, as shown in the following illustration. Also note that Visual Studio inserts the image directly *above* the blue line.

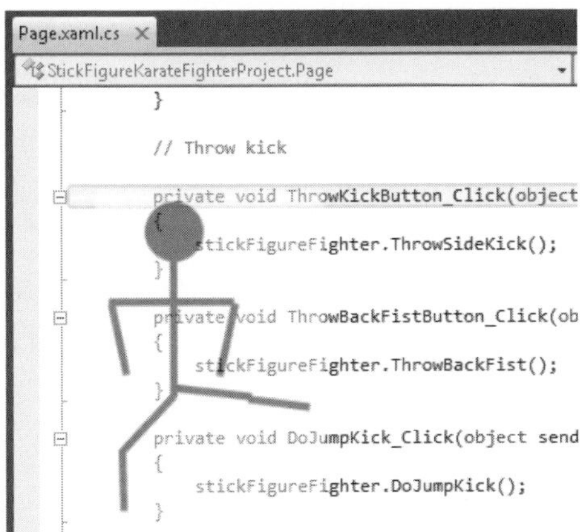

To remove the inserted image, place the mouse directly over the image until a Close button appears. Click the X button in the upper-right corner to remove the inserted image. The user interface is sensitive, so it is best to move the mouse slowly towards the X button to avoid having the controls disappear.

To resize the inserted image, use the mouse to grip the arrow controls, just as you would resize any standard window.

To Save

The images are not saved as part of the code file. The images are saved in a separate .resx file. In this example, because the image is inserted in a Page.xaml.cs file, the image is saved in a Page.xaml.Images.resx file, which is viewable in Solution Explorer. Most source control management systems allow users to customize whether .resx files should be included in a source code check-in.

To Customize

Although this extension doesn't come with any options to configure, the source code is available for tweaking at *http://editorsamples.codeplex.com*.

08.03 Add Visual Guidelines to Your Code

NAME	Editor Guidelines, Editor Guidelines UI
CREATED BY	Paul Harrington (Microsoft)
LOCATIONS	*http://visualstudiogallery.msdn.microsoft.com/0fbf2878-e678-4577-9fdb-9030389b338c* *http://visualstudiogallery.msdn.microsoft.com/en-us/7f2a6727-2993-4c1d-8f58-ae24df14ea91*

The Editor Guidelines displays vertical lines within your code to help you visualize regions, end of printable margins, and so forth.

Editor Guidelines

Although this feature has been in many previous versions of Visual Studio, it was necessary to modify the registry to use the feature. This extension brings the guidelines feature back to Visual Studio 2010 and includes options within the Visual Studio IDE to modify the guidelines.

```
#Region "Public Methods"

    ' get the control's hwnd
    Public ReadOnly Property Hwnd() As IntPtr
        Get
            If Me.m_hwnd.ToInt32 = 0 Then
                Dim handle As IntPtr

                ' get a handle from the accessible object we have
                NativeMethods.WindowFromAccessibleObject(m_msaa, handle)

                ' create an accessible object
                Dim msaa As New AccessibleObject(Me.IAccessible)

                ' cache the hwnd for future use
                m_hwnd = handle

                Return handle
            Else
                Return Me.m_hwnd
            End If
        End Get
```

To Install

The Editor Guidelines extension consists of two extensions:

- **Editor Guidelines** (*http://visualstudiogallery.msdn.microsoft.com/en-us/0fbf2878-e678-4577-9fdb-9030389b338c*)—This extension brings back the guidelines feature; however, it requires modifications to the registry to use the guidelines.
- **Editor Guidelines UI** (*http://visualstudiogallery.msdn.microsoft.com/en-us/7f2a6727-2993-4c1d-8f58-ae24df14ea91*)—This extension provides options within Visual Studio to use the guidelines, instead of manually editing the registry

Note The Editor Guidelines UI extension is an extension of the Editor Guidelines extension. The ability to extend an extension from another extension is a feature of the Managed Extensibility Framework. To install the Editor Guidelines UI extension, the Editor Guidelines extension must be installed first; otherwise, the Extension Manager displays an error message.

To Use

If you plan to use only the first extension, you need to manually edit the registry, so use at your own risk! The registry key for the guidelines feature is the same as in previous versions of Visual Studio: [HKEY_CURRENT_USER]\Software\Microsoft\VisualStudio\10.0\Text Editor.

You need to create a new REG_SZ string called "Guides" to store the information for the guideline. For example, the string "RGB(0,255,0) 100" sets a green guideline on column 100. To add additional guidelines, add the other column numbers to the Guides value separated by commas, such as RGB(0, 255, 0) 5, 60, 100.

If you have the Editor Guidelines UI extension installed, things are a lot simpler.

Right-click wherever you wish to place the guideline, and from the context menu, select **Add Guideline.**

To remove the guideline, place your cursor on the column where you wish to remove the guideline, right-click, and select **Remove Guideline.**

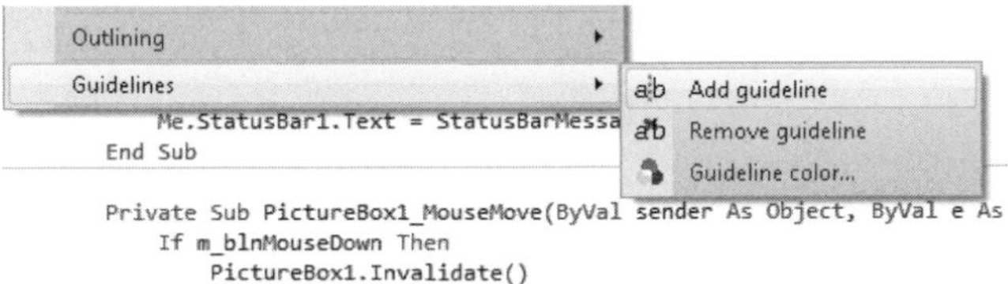

To Customize

To customize the colors for the guideline, select **Guideline Color** from the context menu, and select colors from the color palette window.

08.04 Get More IntelliSense in Your XAML Editor

NAME	XAML IntelliSense Presenter
CREATED BY	Karl Shifflett
LOCATION	*http://visualstudiogallery.msdn.microsoft.com/1a67eee3-fdd1-4745-b290-09d649d07ee0*

The XAML IntelliSense Presenter extension allows you to use the new Pascal casing and list filtering IntelliSense features in your XAML code.

XAML IntelliSense Presenter

If you've grown accustomed to the new Pascal casing and list filtering features in IntelliSense, you'll be happy to know that the Visual Studio 2010 XAML Editor IntelliSense extension gives you these features and more in the XAML editor.

To Use

Start typing in any XAML editor to bring up IntelliSense. As you start typing, you can see the Pascal case narrowing the available selection. The Pascal case narrowing filter option is enabled by default, as circled in the following illustration.

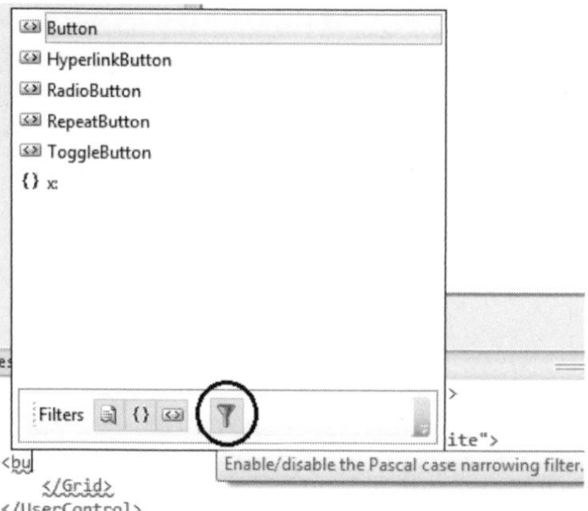

You can also toggle whether code snippets, namespaces, or element tags appear in IntelliSense.

For More Information

Check out the developer's blog post for this extension: *http://karlshifflett.wordpress.com/2010/03/21/visual-studio-2010-xaml-editor-intellisense-presenter-extension.*

08.05 Sync the Solution Explorer to the Current File

NAME	Solution Explorer Tools
CREATED BY	Chris McGraph
LOCATION	*http://visualstudiogallery.msdn.microsoft.com/ef4ac3e9-d056-4383-8ca2-11721bd879b4*

The Solution Explorer Tools extension provides you with greater control over how and when the Solution Explorer syncs to the currently opened document.

Solution Explorer Tools

The Solution Explorer Tools extension provides additional features on the Solution Explorer toolbar for controlling the opened solution.

To Use

For this extension to work properly, you must *uncheck* the Track Active Item in Solution Explorer option found on the Tools | Options | Projects and Solutions | General page.

When the Tools extension is installed, several new buttons appear on the Solution Explorer toolbar, as shown in the following illustration.

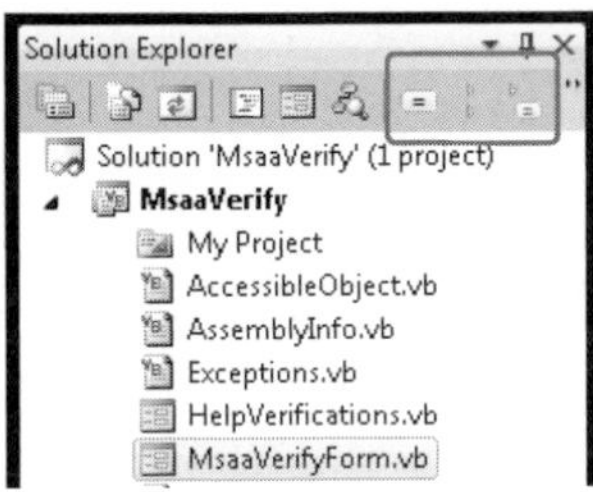

The following list describes the buttons from left to right:

- **Sync Item**—This command places the active selection in the Solution Explorer to the currently opened document.
- **Collapse All**—This command recursively collapses everything in the Solution Explorer.
- **Collapse to Item**—This command combines the two previous commands by placing the active selection in the Solution Explorer to the currently opened item and collapsing everything else in the Solution Explorer.

You can also assign keyboard shortcuts to each of the following commands on the Tools | Options | Environment | Keyboard page:

- Project.SyncItem
- Project.Collapseall
- Project.CollapseToItem

08.06 Add PowerCommands Options to the IDE

NAME	PowerCommands
CREATED BY	Microsoft
LOCATION	*http://visualstudiogallery.msdn.microsoft.com/en-us/e5f41ad9-4edc-4912-bca3-91147db95b99*

The PowerCommands extension provides additional tweaks for customizing the IDE.

PowerCommands for Visual Studio 2010

The PowerCommands have been a popular add-in for the past several previous versions of Visual Studio.

To Use

The PowerCommands extension provides additional options for customizing the IDE. These options are found on the Tools | Options | PowerCommands | General and Commands pages.

The following is a list of each of the PowerCommands options to help you discover all the ways you can further customize the IDE:

- **Format Document On Save**—Saving the file automatically formats the document.
- **Remove And Sort Usings On Save**—Saving the file automatically removes any unused using statements. This option automatically sorts all using statements in alphabetical order.
- **Remove and Sort Usings**—This command can be found on the Solution Explorer context menu at both the Solution level and at the individual project levels. It preforms the same functionality as the previous command.
- **Clear All Panes**—This command clears all Output Window subwindows at once. The Clear All Panes button is located just to the right of the Show Output From drop-down list on the Output Window toolbar.
- **Copy Path**—This command copies the full file path of the currently selected item in the Solution Explorer to the clipboard. It works with the solution node, a project node, any project item node, and any folder.
- **Email Code Snippet**—Select code in the editor, right-click to open the context menu, and select Email Code Snippet to email the code snippet. The subject of the generated email is based on the file name—for example, "Subject: CodeSnippet from Program.cs".
- **Insert Guid Attribute**—To add a GUID attribute to a class, right-click anywhere within the class and select Insert Guid Attribute from the context menu.

- **Show All Files** This option places an additional Show All Files button on the Solution Explorer toolbar. The leftmost Show All Files button is for the current project, and the rightmost Show All Files button is for the entire solution.
- **Undo Close** To reopen the most-recently closed document, go to Edit | Undo Close. The keyboard shortcut is Ctrl+Shift+Z. The cursor is placed at its last known position. To see a list of all the most-recently closed documents, go to View | Other Windows | Undo Close Window.
- **Collapse Projects** To collapse everything under a project node, including any subnodes (this being the key difference from the standard Windows behavior), right-click and select Collapse Project from the Solution Explorer context menu. This command works for solutions, projects, and solution folders.
- **Copy Class / Paste Class** To copy and paste a class, select a project item (usually a class file) on the Solution Explorer that you want to copy. Right-click and select Copy Class from the context menu. Navigate to the project node, and right-click to see the Paste Class command.
- **Copy As Project Reference** Found on the Solution Explorer context menu, this command copies a project (from its project node) and pastes it into another project node as a project reference.
- **Edit Project File** The Edit Project File option unloads a project and automatically opens the file in the editor for editing.
- **Open Containing Folder** Similar to the command found on the file tabs and in the Solution Explorer for a node, this command opens the containing folder for an item in the Solution Explorer.
- **Open Command Prompt** This option opens a Visual Studio command prompt directly from the Solution Explorer.
- **Unload Projects / Reload Projects** Similar to the built-in command for unloading a project, the Unload Projects command (found on the Solution Explorer context menu for a project node) unloads all the projects in a solution.
- **Extract Constant** Found under the Refactor menu, the Extract Constant creates a constant based on the selected text.
- **Clear Recent File List** This command removes specified recent files. In past versions of Visual Studio, this clearing required manual modifications to the registry. The command is found on the File | Recent Files menu as Clear Recent File List. This command opens a window for you to specify which files to clear.
- **Clear Recent Project List** Similar to the Clear Recent File List, this command removes projects specified by the user.

- **Close All** Found on the file tab context menu, this command closes all open documents.

For More Information

For more information about the PowerCommands extension, you can read the following blog post: *http://saraford.net/2010/09/07/power-commands-for-visual-studio-2010-extension-8*.

08.07 Use Emacs Commands in the Editor

NAME	Emacs Emulation
CREATED BY	Microsoft
LOCATION	*http://visualstudiogallery.msdn.microsoft.com/en-us/09dc58c4-6f47-413a-9176-742be7463f92*

The Emacs Commands extension provides basic support for Emacs keybindings and text editing commands.

Emacs Emulation

This extension brings back the Emacs commands for the Visual Studio 2010 editor.

To Use

To finish installing the extension, you must open a project or create a new project. Opening a project prompts you for elevated permissions to finish installing the Emacs.vsk file (the Emacs keyboard shortcut file) to the Visual Studio IDE folder located under Program Files directory. Elevated permissions are required because only user accounts with administrator privileges can reach this folder by default in Windows.

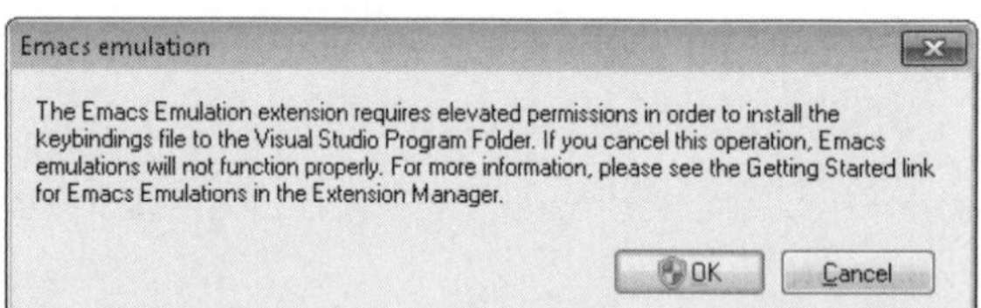

Select **Emacs** in the Tools | Options | Environment | Keyboard page's scheme drop-down list to enable the Emacs emulation experience.

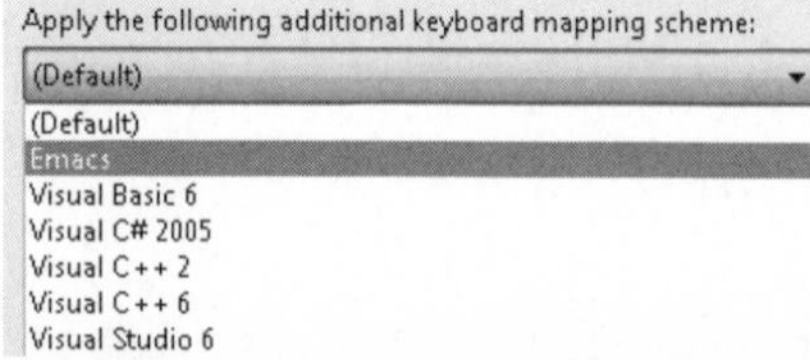

To Uninstall

When you disable or uninstall the extension, the Emacs option remains selected in the Tools | Options | Keyboard list. You must go back to the Tools | Options | Environment | Keyboard page and select the "(Default)" key bindings or your preferred keyboard mapping scheme.

If you forget to change the keyboard mapping scheme, you'll notice a great many commands and keyboard shortcuts not working in the editor, such as Ctrl+F for the Find window.

Because administrator rights were required to add this file, you also need administrator rights to remove it. Unlike the install scenario for opening or creating a project, there isn't an opportunity for the extension to prompt you to remove the .vsk file. For example, the extension cannot prompt you the next time you open a project (as in the install scenario) because the extension itself is already gone.

You can manually delete the Emacs.vsk file at your own risk, but there is no impact to Visual Studio if you decide to keep the file.

More Information

You can find more information about all the Emacs keyboard shortcuts supported by the extension at the following location: *http://visualstudiogallery.msdn.microsoft.com/en-us/09dc58c4-6f47-413a-9176-742be7463f92*.

08.08 Submit to "The Daily WTF"

NAME	The Daily WTF
CREATED BY	Inedo.com
LOCATION	*http://inedo.com/Downloads/SubmitToWTF.aspx*
SOURCE CODE LOCATION	*http://code.google.com/p/submittotdwtf*
VERSIONS	2005, 2008, 2010

Have you ever inherited source code so poorly written that you've asked a colleague to come into your office to take a look? If so, this extension is for you.

Share Bad Code with the World

Started in May 2004, "The Daily WTF" (also known as "The Daily Worse Than Failure") is a blog dedicated to poorly written code, poor project management decisions, and bizarre interview stories.

This extension allows you to submit a code snippet directly from your code editor to "The Daily WTF." It is the equivalent of using the website's contact form to submit a code suggestion.

It is a little-known fact that Sara Ford's writing style for the "Visual Studio 2008 Tip of the Day" series was inspired by Alex Papadimoulis' writing style for "The Daily WTF." The idea of providing personal commentary alongside factual information was very appealing for a daily tip series. (Thank you, Alex!)

To Install

At the time of this writing, this extension is not located on the Visual Studio Gallery.

You can download the extension from *http://inedo.com/Downloads/SubmitToWTF.aspx*. Links for both Visual Studio 2010 and Visual Studio 2005/2008 appear on the page. After you have downloaded the extension, unzip the folder and double-click the SubmitToWTF2010.vsix file.

To Use

Select code within a code editor, and open the context menu to see the Submit To TDWTF command appear. Click the Submit To TDWTF command to open a dialog box that requests additional information about the code snippet. Additionally, there is an option to request that the code snippet is not published.

More Information

You can find more information about The Daily WTF at *http://thedailywtf.com*.

08.09 Diff Files Using the Editor

NAME	CodeCompare
CREATED BY	Devart Software
LOCATION	*http://visualstudiogallery.msdn.microsoft.com/dace3633-0b51-4629-85d4-c59cdce5bb3b*
VERSIONS	2008, 2010

You can compare code side-by-side within the Visual Studio Editor by using the CodeCompare extension.

CodeCompare

The CodeCompare tool uses the Visual Studio code editor to compare two files side-by-side, allowing you to continue using all the Visual Studio code editor functionality, like syntax coloring, IntelliSense, Ctrl+Mouse Wheel zooming, and so on.

To Install

The CodeCompare tool does not use the new Visual Studio Extensibility model, so it is not found in the Extension Manager. To install, run the executable file hosted on the Visual Studio Gallery and follow the instructions in the setup wizard.

To Use

To start the CodeCompare tool, go to Tools | CodeCompare | New Comparison. This action opens a new code comparison view alongside your code files using the Visual Studio code editor. Simply select two different files to compare to start seeing a visual representation of the differences between the files.

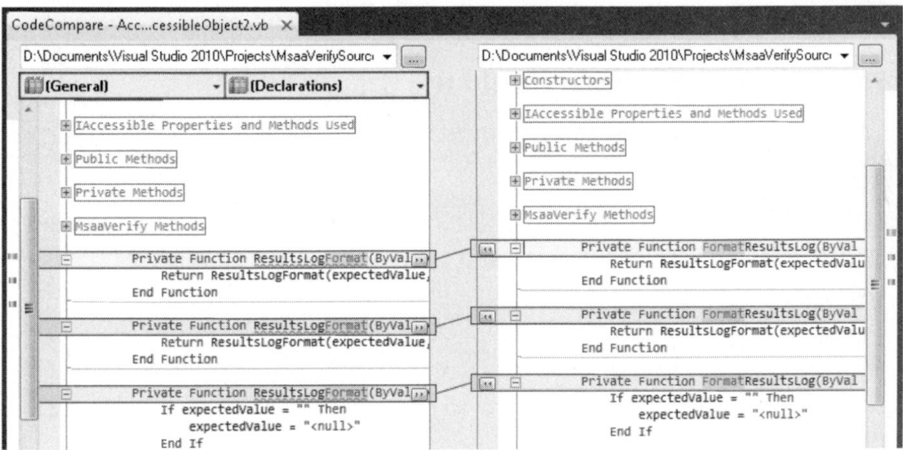

Features

CodeCompare is a fully functional code comparing tool, but a few features are worth mentioning, including the following:

- **Merge Code** Move code from one comparison view to the other. Each indicated line that is different per view has a << or a >> symbol that illustrates it is possible to merge that line or block of code to the other file.
- **Structure Comparison** Compare code by its structure, namely its classes, fields, and methods. This comparison is shown in the Difference Explorer. Oddly enough, in the free version of CodeCompare, attempting to click within the Difference Explorer clears its contents. The cursor focus must remain within the code editor for the Difference Explorer to show the structural differences between the code files.

- **New Folder Comparison** Compare code at the file level. Select two folders, and the compare tool shows you which files are different or not included. Double-click a file to do a code comparison at the file level in a new window.

To Uninstall

Go to Windows Control Panel | Uninstall A Program window, and select the Devart CodeCompare application. Click the Uninstall command on the menu to uninstall CodeCompare.

More Information

You can find more information about CodeCompare at *http://www.devart.com/codecompare.*

08.10 Run Windows PowerShell Within the IDE

NAME	PowerConsole
CREATED BY	Jianchun Xu (Microsoft)
LOCATION	*http://visualstudiogallery.msdn.microsoft.com/67620d8c-93dd-4e57-aa86-c9404acbd7b3*
VERSIONS	2010

You can use the PowerConsole extension to run both Windows PowerShell commands and Visual Studio object model (DTE) commands within the IDE.

To Use

To open the Power Console tool window, go to View | Other Windows | Power Console.

The Power Console allows you to run more than just Windows PowerShell commands. Additionally, you can call the Visual Studio object model (DTE), access Visual Studio services, interact with Visual Studio MEF components, and host your own scripting language within the Power Console.

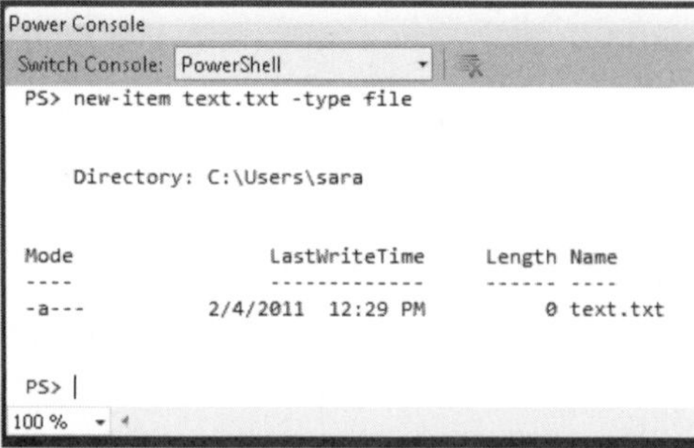

More Information

You can find more information about the Power Console at *http://visualstudiogallery.msdn.microsoft.com/67620d8c-93dd-4e57-aa86-c9404acbd7b3*.

08.11 Visualize OData in a Graphical View

NAME	Open Data Protocol Visualizer
CREATED BY	Microsoft
LOCATION	*http://visualstudiogallery.msdn.microsoft.com/f4ac856a-796e-4d78-9a3d-0120d8137722*

You can use the Open Data Protocol Visualizer extension to get a graphical view of an OData service.

Open Data Protocol Visualizer

The Open Data Protocol Visualizer provides a read-only graphical view of the types and relationships provided by a WCF Data Service.

To Use

Create a service reference through the Add Service Reference dialog box. Open the context menu for the service reference in the Solution Explorer, and select the new View In Diagram command to open the visualizer.

At the bottom of the visualizer, select the elements you want to view, or select "all" to visualize everything. You can also browse elements by using the Open Data Protocol Model Browser found under the View menu.

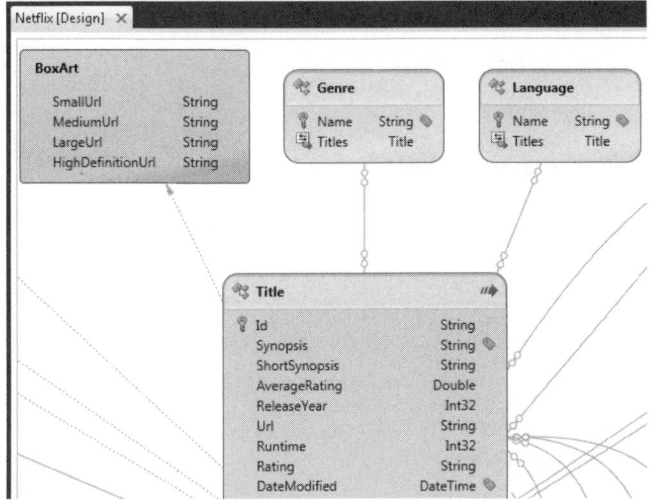

More Information

You can find a video explaining how to use the Open Data Protocol Visualizer extension located at *http://odataprimer.com/ODataVisualizerExtensionForVS2010Screencast.ashx*.

You can also find a list of OData services at *http://www.odata.org/producers*.

08.12 Run VIM Commands in the Editor

NAME	VsVim
CREATED BY	Jared Parsons (Microsoft)
LOCATION	*http://visualstudiogallery.msdn.microsoft.com/59ca71b3-a4a3-46ca-8fe1-0e90e3f79329*
SOURCE CODE	*http://github.com/jaredpar/VsVim*

The VsVim extension provides a Vim editing experience within the Visual Studio editor.

To Use

When enabled, the VIM extension immediately prompts you at the top of the editor to customize how many Visual Studio keyboard shortcut defaults you want to use. You can make additional modifications by clicking the Options button at the bottom of the editor next to the VIM extension status bar, as shown in the following illustration.

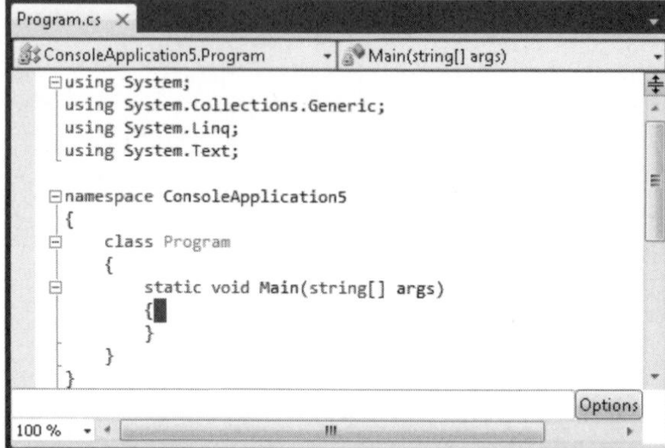

More Information

You can find a frequently asked question list for the VIM extension located at *https://github.com/jaredpar/VsVim/wiki/faq*.

08.13 Check Spelling in Your Code

NAME	Spell Checker
CREATED BY	Noah Richards with Roman Golovin and Michael Lehenbauer
LOCATION	*http://visualstudiogallery.msdn.microsoft.com/7c8341f1-ebac-40c8-92c2-476db8d523ce*

You can check for spelling errors in your code by using the Spell Checker extension.

Spell Checker

The Spell Checker extension provides a spell checker within the Visual Studio editor.

To Use

The Spell Checker extension provides spelling corrections for plain text files, comments and strings in source code, and text that isn't included within HTML tags in .html and .aspx files.

The Spell Checker uses Smart Tags, meaning that you can simply press Ctrl+. to invoke the Smart Tag window.

If you want the change the color of the red squiggles so that spelling errors are not confused with syntax errors, you can go to the Tools | Options | Environment | Fonts And Colors page, and under Display Items, select Spelling Error and change the Item Foreground color to the appropriate color.

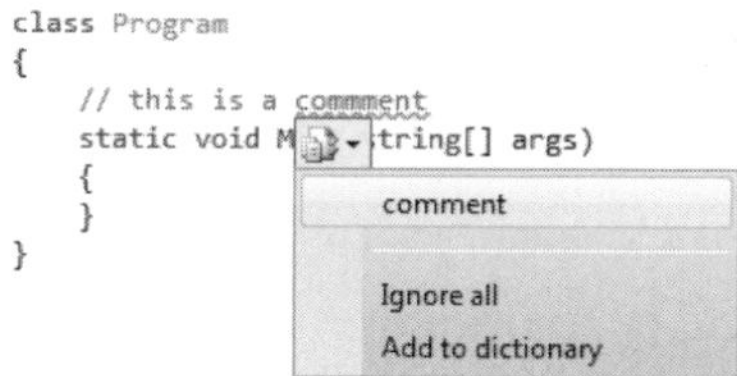

08.14 Zoom Across All Files

NAME	Presentation Zoom
CREATED BY	Chris Granger (Microsoft)
LOCATION	*http://visualstudiogallery.msdn.microsoft.com/6a7a0b57-7059-470d-bcfa-60ceb78dc752*

You can maintain a consistent zoom percentage across all open files using the Presentation Zoom extension.

Presentation Zoom

By default, the new Presentation Zoom extension in Visual Studio 2010 works only for the current file. Additional files are not affected by the zoom. This is especially noticeable when giving presentations, where the presenter has to zoom each file separately.

This extension provides a global zoom level, so all open files can share the same zoom level.

To Use

Simply use the zoom feature, either by Ctrl+Mouse wheel or updating the zoom percentage at the bottom-left corner of the editor. The next file opened or navigated to persists the same zoom percentage.

Control Zooming with a Slider Using the ZoomEditorMargin Extension

NAME	ZoomEditorMargin
CREATED BY	Benjamin Gopp
LOCATION	*http://visualstudiogallery.msdn.microsoft.com/c271d574-a481-4974-b7dd-f319404de898*

Similar to the Presentation Zoom extension discussed in the preceding section, the ZoomEditorMargin extension provides a slider control in the bottom-right corner of the editor for specifying the zoom percentage for the file in view. The ZoomEditorMargin extension works in conjunction with the Presentation Zoom extension.

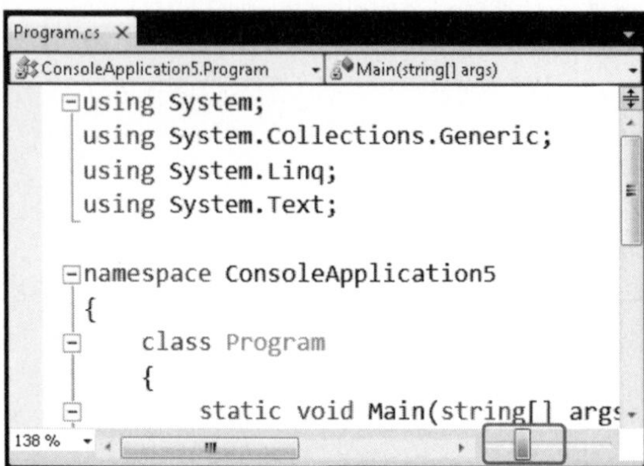

08.15 View Code Blocks Using Vertical Lines

NAME	StructureAdornment
CREATED BY	David Pugh (Microsoft)
LOCATION	*http://visualstudiogallery.msdn.microsoft.com/203f22f4-3e9f-4dbb-befc-f2606835834e*

The StructureAdornment extension displays vertical lines in the editor to show the block structure of the code file.

StructureAdornment

The StructureAdornment extension uses different colors to indicate different blocks.

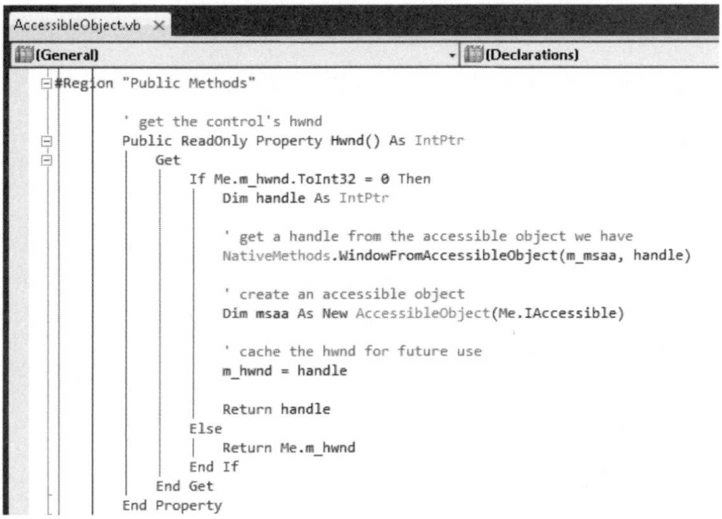

```
AccessibleObject.vb ×
(General)                                    (Declarations)
#Region "Public Methods"

    ' get the control's hwnd
    Public ReadOnly Property Hwnd() As IntPtr
        Get
            If Me.m_hwnd.ToInt32 = 0 Then
                Dim handle As IntPtr

                ' get a handle from the accessible object we have
                NativeMethods.WindowFromAccessibleObject(m_msaa, handle)

                ' create an accessible object
                Dim msaa As New AccessibleObject(Me.IAccessible)

                ' cache the hwnd for future use
                m_hwnd = handle

                Return handle
            Else
                Return Me.m_hwnd
            End If
        End Get
    End Property
```

To Use

By default, vertical lines appear in the editor. To see the beginning of a particular code block that is outside the view, mouse-over the vertical line to display the beginning of that particular code block.

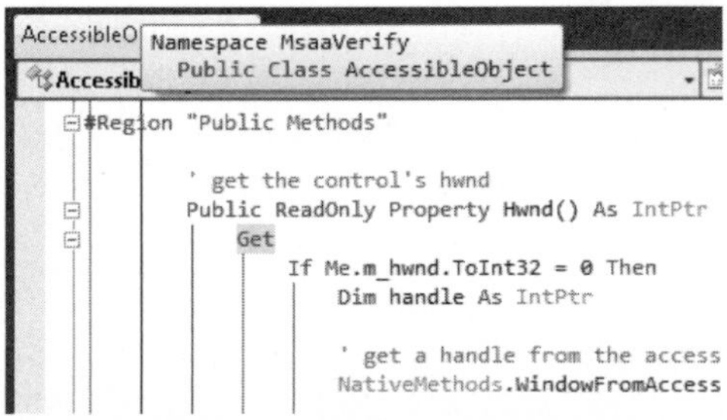

```
AccessibleO  Namespace MsaaVerify
Accessib       Public Class AccessibleObject
#Region "Public Methods"

    ' get the control's hwnd
    Public ReadOnly Property Hwnd() As IntPtr
        Get
            If Me.m_hwnd.ToInt32 = 0 Then
                Dim handle As IntPtr

                ' get a handle from the access
                NativeMethods.WindowFromAccess
```

To Customize

This extension does not have a page in Tools | Options; however, you can manually edit the registry settings for the extension. The following editor options are stored in the registry under HKEY_CURRENT_USER\Software\Microsoft\VisualStudio\10.0\Text Editor:

- **StructureAdornment/LineWidth** Width of the lines used to show the various scopes.
- **StructureAdornment/ClassColor** Color used to show the scope of class definitions as ARGB.
- **StructureAdornment/ConditionalColor** Color used to show the scope of conditionally executed code as ARGB.
- **StructureAdornment/LoopColor** Color used to show the scope of loop bodies as ARGB.
- **StructureAdornment/MethodColor** Color used to show the scope of method bodies as ARGB.
- **StructureAdornment/UnknownColor** Color used to show the scope of unknown blocks as ARGB.
- **StructureAdornment/MethodSeparatorColor** Color used draw a horizontal separator line at the end of a method as ARGB (off by default).
- **StructureAdornment/Enabled** Show structure adornments.

Modifications made to the extension appear the next time a code editor is opened.

To Uninstall

This extension installs five separate extensions. To completely remove this extension, you need to remove the following extensions:

- BlockTagger
- BlockTaggerImpl
- SettingsStore
- SettingsStoreImpl
- StructureAdornment

You can uninstall all five extensions at the same time within the Extension Manager. If prompted about a Dependence Alert, click Uninstall Anyways to continue uninstalling all extensions.

08.16 Get a Bird's-Eye View of Your Code in an Editor Margin

NAME	AllMargins
CREATED BY	David Pugh (Microsoft)
LOCATION	*http://visualstudiogallery.msdn.microsoft.com/465a0d53-5133-4edd-a0cd-94484fe3d853*

The AllMargins extension provides a complete overview of your code to improve navigation.

AllMargins

The AllMargins extension installs multiple extensions. The two most notable are the OverviewMargin extension, a bird's-eye view of the logical layout of your code all within an editor margin, and the StructureAdornment extension, which displays vertical lines in the editor, representing structural code blocks.

See the extension "View Code Blocks Using Vertical Lines" for more information about the StructureAdornment extension.

To Use

By default, both the StructureAdornment extension and the OverviewMargin extension are visible in the editor. The OverviewMargin appears on the right side of the editor.

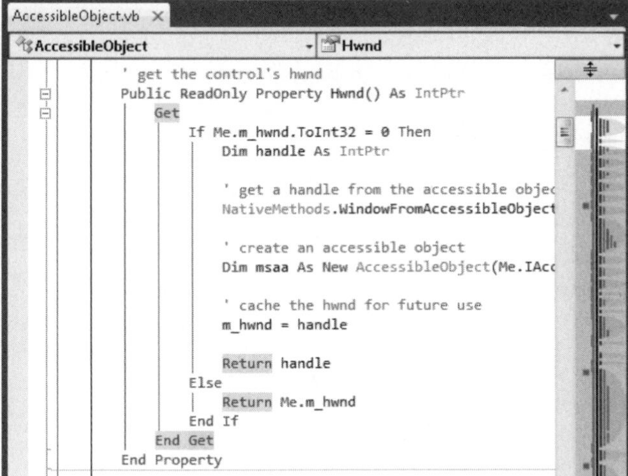

Mouse-over the left side of the OverviewMargin to see a code snippet for that particular section of code.

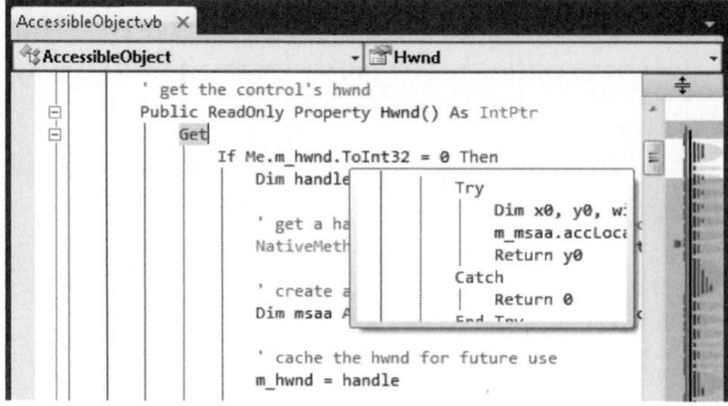

Mouse-over the right side of the OverviewMargin to see the structural code block in a condensed form.

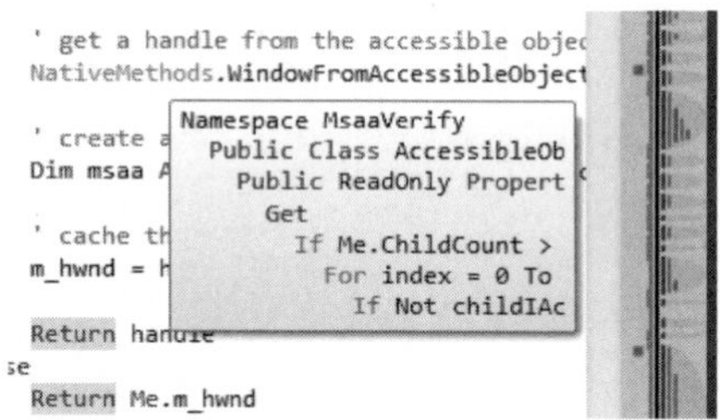

To Uninstall

This extension installs 12 separate extensions. To completely remove this extension, you need to remove the following:

- AllMargins
- BlockTagger
- BlockTaggerImpl
- CaretMargin
- ErrorsToMarks
- MarkersToMarks
- OverviewMargin
- OverviewMarginImpl
- SettingsStore
- SettingsStoreImpl
- StructureAdornment

- StructureMargin

You can uninstall all 12 extensions at the same time within the Extension Manager. If prompted about a Dependence Alert, click Uninstall Anyways to continue uninstalling all extensions.

08.17 Build Projects from the Windows 7 Taskbar

NAME	Win7 Taskbar Extension
CREATED BY	Dmitry Sitnikov
LOCATION	*http://visualstudiogallery.msdn.microsoft.com/0c92dd87-50ac-489e-882b-b99de7624502*

You can use the Win7 Taskbar Extension to start a build or debug session directly from the Windows 7 taskbar.

Win7 Taskbar Extension

The Win7 Taskbar Extension allows you to start a build or debug session for the specified Visual Studio application directly from the Windows 7 taskbar. This extension can save you time when you need to build different projects located in multiple instances of Visual Studio.

To Install

The Win7 Taskbar Extension tool is an extension of the Windows 7 taskbar, so it is not found in the Extension Manager. To install, run the executable file hosted on the Visual Studio Gallery location and follow the instructions in the setup wizard.

To Use

Mouse-over any Visual Studio window in the Windows 7 taskbar to see the extension appear. Simply click the corresponding button for Build, Start Debugging, or Start Without Debugging.

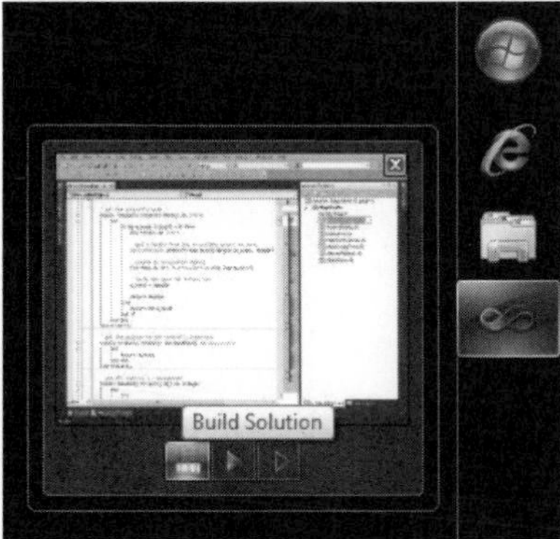

To Uninstall

Open the Windows Control Panel | Uninstall a Program window, and select the Visual Studio Win7 Taskbar Add-in application. Click the Uninstall command listed on the menu to remove the extension.

08.18 Triple-Click to Select an Entire Line

NAME	Triple Click
CREATED BY	Noah Richards
LOCATION	*http://visualstudiogallery.msdn.microsoft.com/2bbdc70c-32f7-4b69-8cff-d8190cae0cc7*
SOURCE CODE	*https://github.com/NoahRic/TripleClick*

You can use the Triple Click extension to quickly select a line of code.

Triple Click

The Triple Click extension selects an entire line of code when the left mouse button is triple-clicked.

```
' get the control's hwnd
Public ReadOnly Property Hwnd() As IntPtr
    Get
        If Me.m_hwnd.ToInt32 = 0 Then
            Dim handle As IntPtr

            ' get a handle from the accessible object we have
            NativeMethods.WindowFromAccessibleObject(m_msaa, handle)

            ' create an accessible object
            Dim msaa As New AccessibleObject(Me.IAccessible)

            ' cache the hwnd for future use
            m_hwnd = handle

            Return handle
        Else
            Return Me.m_hwnd
        End If
```

More Information

For more information, please see the extension author's blog post at *http://blogs.msdn.com/b/noahric/archive/2009/10/19/beta-2.aspx.*

08.19 Create Regular Expressions Within Your Code

NAME	Regex Editor
CREATED BY	Microsoft
LOCATION	*http://visualstudiogallery.msdn.microsoft.com/55c24bf1-2636-4f94-831d-28db8505ce00*
SOURCE CODE	*http://editorsamples.codeplex.com*

The Regex Editor helps you write regular expressions faster and easier.

Regex Editor

The Regex Editor extension is an aid for creating, testing, and saving regular expressions.

To Use

To invoke the Regex Editor window, you need to create a new Regex class within your code. For example, type in the following:

```
Regex r = new Regex(
```

This opens the Regex Editor window, shown in the following illustration.

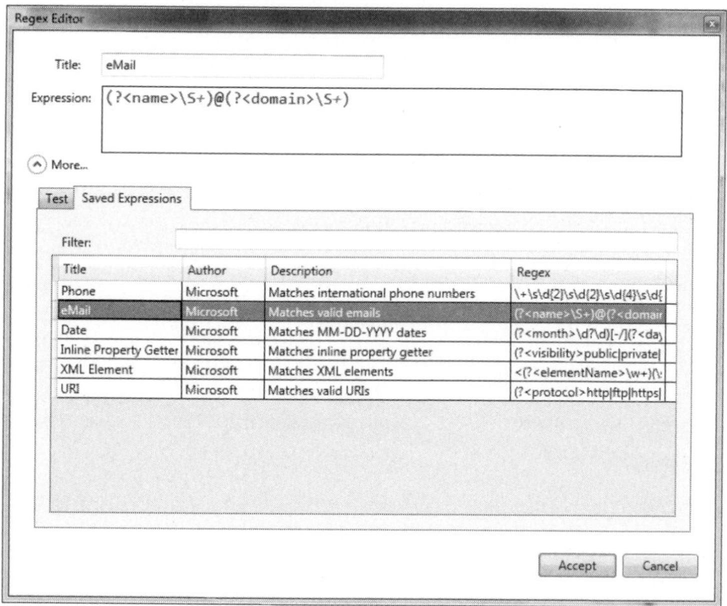

More Information

For more information, please visit the project's homepage at *http://editorsamples.codeplex.com*.

08.20 Get More Productivity Tools in the IDE

NAME	Visual Studio Productivity Power Tools
CREATED BY	Microsoft
LOCATION	*http://visualstudiogallery.msdn.microsoft.com/d0d33361-18e2-46c0-8ff2-4adea1e34fef*

The Visual Studio Productivity Power Tools are a collection of extensions intended to maximize a developer's productivity.

To Use

The tools include a variety of IDE productivity tweaks, such as the following:

- **Tools Options Support** Allows for all of the included tools to be turned on or off by selecting Tools | Options | Productivity Power Tools.
- **Document Tab Well User Interface** Customize the look and functionality of open Visual Studio tabs.
- **Searchable Add Reference Dialog** Replace the default Add Reference Dialog with a dialog box that includes a substring search of the current pane.
- **Quick Access** Search and execute common Visual Studio tasks.
- **Auto Brace Completion** Improve code productivity by automatically inserting the matching closing code construct for the following characters: (), {}, [], "", and ''.
- **Highlight Current Line** Highlight the line in the code editor where the caret is located.
- **HTML Copy** Copy code to the Windows Clipboard using the HTML Clipboard format, which makes it easy to retain code formatting.
- **Triple Click** Triple-click anywhere on a line to select the entire line.
- **Fix Mixed Tabs** Fix files that have a mix between tabs and spaces.
- **Ctrl+Click Go to Definition** Jump quickly to a symbol definition via Ctrl+Click.
- **Align Assignments** Increase code readability by aligning variable assignments. To use, press Ctrl+Alt+J.
- **Move Line Up/Down Commands** Hold down the Alt key while tapping the Up/Down arrow to move the current line of code up or down.
- **Column Guides** Everyone's favorite Visual Studio registry modification, adding a vertical line guide to the code editor, can be set via the code editor context menu.
- **Colorized Parameter Help** Add syntax color coding to Parameter Help.

To Customize the Document Tab Well User Interface

By default, the extension changes the Document Tab Well by coloring and grouping tabs based on their project, which is helpful when working with large solutions. You can customize these default settings by selecting Tools | Options | Productivity Power Tools | Document Tab Well.

Several preset configurations are available, including the following: Visual Studio 2008, Visual Studio 2010, Web Browser, Scrollable Tab Well, Vertical Tab Well, and Dynamic Tab Well.

- The Visual Studio 2008 and 2010 configurations act exactly as their names imply, causing the default tab well to behave like those versions of the IDE.
- Both the Web Browser and Dynamic Tab Wells add file type icons to what would otherwise be a typical Visual Studio 2010 tab. The difference between the two is that the Dynamic Tab Well closes the least-recently used tab when there is no more space available in the file tab channel.

- The Scrollable Tab Well is the default for the extension.

- The Vertical Tab Well has the same characteristics as the Scrollable Tab Well but places the tabs vertically, allowing for more viewable tabs.

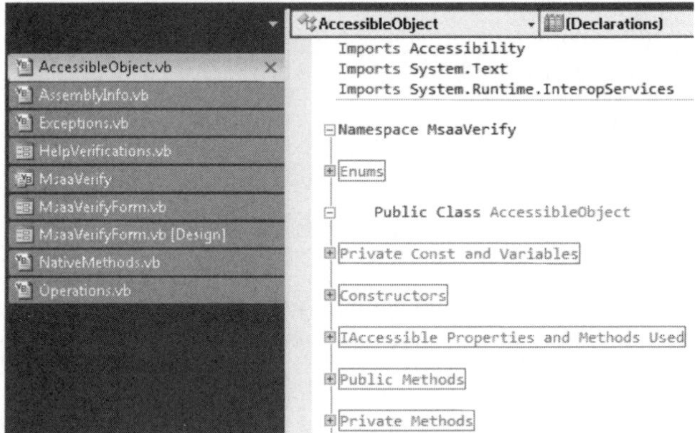

It is possible to tweak all of the configurations. The ability to *pin tabs* is probably the most useful customization. For example, you probably often want to view the contents of many files while actually working on only one or two. The ability to pin specific tabs that you are focusing on, to keep them from falling out of focus, is a huge time-saver. When you pin many tabs, you can use the Show Pinned Tabs In A Separate Row/Column option. This keeps the pinned tabs from taking up too much space.

The biggest tab productivity boost comes in the form of added keyboard navigation. In Windows, Ctrl+Tab switches to the next child window for a given program. It's known that many users do not prefer the Ctrl+Tab window that appears in Visual Studio. The Productivity Power Tools extension offers the option of moving backward and forward in visual order via Ctrl+Alt+Page Down/Up. Even more exciting, you can jump to a pinned tab via Ctrl+Num Pad 1 through 0. Talk about keyboard efficiency!

08.21 Create and Find Code Snippets

NAME	Snippet Designer
CREATED BY	Matt Manela
LOCATION	*http://visualstudiogallery.msdn.microsoft.com/B08B0375-139E-41D7-AF9B-FAEE50F68392*

The Snippet Designer is an open source extension for Visual Studio that makes it easier to create and manage code snippets.

Snippet Designer

The Snippet Designer extension adds both an editor for .snippet files as well as a tool window to search for existing code snippets.

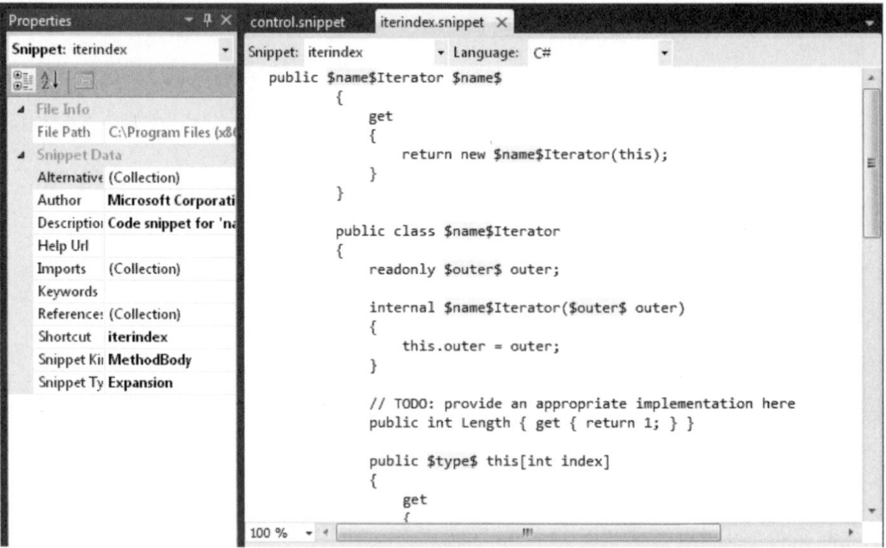

To Use

You can interact with the Snippet Designer within Visual Studio in several different ways, including the following:

- You can create a new code snippet from scratch by launching the new file dialog box (File | New File) and then choosing Snippet Designer | Code Snippet. This launches the Snippet Editor, which lets you enter the code snippet, create variable replacements, and set metadata about the snippet.
- You can create a snippet from existing code in your editor (for C#, Visual Basic, JavaScript, SQL, XML, or HTML) by highlighting the text and choosing Export As Snippet from the context menu. This launches the Snippet Editor prepopulated with the highlighted code.
- You can search for existing code snippets by launching the Snippet Explorer tool window at View | Other Windows | Snippet Explorer. This tool window enables you to perform text search on all the code snippets on your computer. From this window, you can easily preview, edit, and delete any code snippet.

More Information

For more information about the Snippet Designer extension, including documentation, source code, issue tracker, and forum discussions on its CodePlex page, visit *http://snippetdesigner.codeplex.com*.

08.22 Document Your Code with Three Keystrokes

NAME	GhostDoc
CREATED BY	SubMain
LOCATION	*http://submain.com/download/ghostdoc*

GhostDoc generates XML comments for your code by using a simple rules engine.

GhostDoc

Pairing this tool with a documentation generator such as NDoc (*http://ndoc.sourceforge.net*) or SandCastle (*http://www.sandcastledocs.com*) can automate much of the work of documenting your API.

To Use

GhostDoc adds a Document This command both to the Tools | GhostDoc menu and to the code editor context menu. By default, this command is available using the keyboard shortcut Ctrl+Shift+D.

When you invoke the command on a code element, the element's name, parameters, and context information are passed through the GhostDoc rules engine. The rules engine performs a few linguistic tricks to produce a documentation comment that makes sense in the context of your code.

GhostDoc can produce documentation comments for classes, interfaces, structs, enums, constructors, finalizers, methods, properties, fields, events, indexers, and delegates.

The generated documentation comments are not complete, but they do provide a great starting point. The documentation comments in the code below were generated by GhostDoc and have not been edited from the original output:

```
/// <summary>
///
/// </summary>
public class Request : IDisposable
{
    /// <summary>
    /// Initializes a new instance of the <see cref="Request"/> class.
    /// </summary>
    public Request() {}

    /// <summary>
    /// Performs application-defined tasks associated with
    /// freeing, releasing, or resetting unmanaged resources.
    /// </summary>
    public void Dispose() {}

    /// Gets the status for user.
    /// </summary>
    /// <param name="userId">The user id.</param>
    /// <returns>
    ///   <see cref="API.RequestStatus"/> The request status
    /// </returns>
    public RequestStatus GetStatusForUser( string userId ) {/* … */ }

    /// <summary>
    /// Gets a value indicating whether this instance is passive.
    /// </summary>
    /// <value>
    ///         <c>true</c> if this instance is passive; otherwise, <c>false</c>.
    /// </value>
    public bool IsPassive { get; private set; }

    /// <summary>
    /// Gets or sets the timeout.
    /// </summary>
    /// <value>
    /// The timeout.
    /// </value>
    public TimeSpan Timeout { get; set; }
}
```

Some conventions and niceties that drive GhostDoc:

- Code symbols, such as parameter and member names, are split into words by case changes. For example, "userId" becomes "user id."
- Certain common members, such as the Dispose method and equality members, are recognized and documented with specific verbiage.
- Method names are assumed to be describing an activity. For example, GetStatusForUser is interpreted as "Gets the status for user." When the method name contains only a verb, such as Check, GhostDoc assumes the action applies to the class and documents the method as "Checks this instance."
- Property names that start with certain words, such as "Is," "Has", "Can", and so on, are documented as state verifications. Property names containing a single word are documented as states. The documentation comment respects modifiers on property accessors, so read-only properties are documented as such.
- GhostDoc is smart enough to add references to types used in member signatures.
- Documentation comments applied to base types and members are inherited in deriving types.

To Customize

You can customize the way GhostDoc treats individual code element from the Tools | GhostDoc | Options page. The options for code-matching rules are extensive enough to adapt to any coding culture that relies on consistent naming conventions.

From the GhostDoc options dialog box, you can also configure linguistic operations and export or import your GhostDoc settings.

More Information

For more information about the GhostDoc extension, see *http://submain.com/products/ghostdoc.aspx*.

08.23 Customize Visual Studio Using Windows PowerShell

NAME	StudioShell
CREATED BY	Code Owls LLC
LOCATION	*http://studioshell.codeplex.com*

StudioShell is a deeply integrated Windows PowerShell module that simplifies access to many of the extensibility features of Visual Studio.

StudioShell

Using StudioShell, with only a few lines of PowerShell script you can perform activities that typically require an add-in.

To Use

StudioShell ships with a hosted PowerShell console available from the main menu at View | StudioShell. By default, this console is available using the keyboard shortcut Ctrl+Shift+Enter.

You can use StudioShell features in other hosted PowerShell consoles, such as NuGet (*http://nuget.codeplex.com*) or PowerGUI VSX (*http://powerguivsx.codeplex.com*). From these consoles, enter the following command in your console to activate StudioShell:

```
Import-Module StudioShell
```

StudioShell exposes many of the extensibility features of Visual Studio as a drive named "DTE." This drive lets you explore and access the extensibility features as if they were a file system on your local computer, using the same PowerShell commands you would use to manipulate files, the registry, and so on.

For example, you can see a list of existing Visual Studio window configurations by typing:

```
get-childitem dte:/windowConfigurations
```

You can create a new named window configuration by arranging your user interface and then entering:

```
new-item dte:/windowConfigurations -name MyConfig
```

You can apply the new window configuration at any time using:

```
invoke-item dte:/windowConfigurations/MyConfig
```

The standard PowerShell item commands apply to every area of the DTE drive. For example, you can use the same new-item command to create new project items:

```
new-item dte:/solution/projects/myProject -name MyClass.cs -type class
```

The Visual Studio features exposed on the DTE drive include the following:

- **User interface elements**—Manipulate windows, modify menus, add custom commands implemented in PowerShell, manage items to the task and error lists, and drop data into the output pane.
- **Visual Studio settings**—Script custom font and color settings for different environments.

- **Solutions and Projects**—Create new projects and project items, explore and manipulate your code model, or add and remove project references.
- **Breakpoints and the Debugger**—Create and remove breakpoints, set tracepoint conditions, write minidumps, or explore the current stack trace from the console.

StudioShell adds new features to Visual Studio as well, including the following:

- **Simple grid, chart, and graphing output windows usable from the console**—For example, use the console to get a list of code metrics and drop them in a graph.
- **Profile scripts for environment customization**—For example, import any other PowerShell modules you use regularly.
- **Solution script modules for per-solution environment customization**—Modify your menus and windows on a solution-by-solution basis.

To Get Help

StudioShell documentation is available within the console. To get started, type:

```
get-help about_studioshell
```

For information about using standard PowerShell commands on the DTE drive, navigate to the area of the drive where you want to work and use the **get-help** command to retrieve help for the command you want to use:

```
cd dte:/debugger/breakpoints
get-help new-item
```

To Customize

StudioShell settings are available from the Tools | Options dialog in the StudioShell pane. You can indicate a specific console to use when StudioShell is invoked, including the default StudioShell hosted console, the process console, or no console (for example, if you want to use StudioShell from NuGet). In addition, you can change the profile script behavior of StudioShell and enable startup activity logging.

You can customize your console session with any PowerShell module or script. To find scripts relevant to your needs, visit the PowerShell Code Repository at *http://www.poshcode.org*.

More Information

For more information about the StudioShell module, see *http://studioshell.codeplex.com* and *http://www.beefycode.com/post/Announcing-StudioShell.aspx*.

Appendix A

Visual Studio Keyboard Shortcut Posters

Microsoft produces keyboard shortcut posters tailored for both general use and for each major language. Knowing these shortcuts can dramatically help you in your day-to-day work. Get these now. Seriously...*now!* This appendix lists the locations where you can find the posters:

Visual Studio 2010 Shortcuts

- **All Languages 2010** *http://go.microsoft.com/FWLink/?Linkid=220091*

Visual Studio 2008 Shortcuts

- **C# 2008** *http://go.microsoft.com/FWLink/?Linkid=220094*
- **VB 2008** *http://go.microsoft.com/FWLink/?Linkid=220111*
- **C++ 2008** *http://go.microsoft.com/FWLink/?Linkid=220112*

Visual Studio 2005 Shortcuts

- **C# 2005** *http://go.microsoft.com/FWLink/?Linkid=220113*
- **VB 2005** *http://go.microsoft.com/FWLink/?Linkid=220114*
- **C++ 2005** *http://go.microsoft.com/FWLink/?Linkid=220115*

Note Wow! You've read all the tips in the book, and that's super cool! As a thank you, we would like to offer you even more tips online in the form of traditional New Orleans-style lagniappe—a little something extra on the side. Make sure to download the appendix full of lagniappe tips, free of charge, at *http://go.microsoft.com/FWLink/?Linkid=223758*.

Index

D

E

F

G

H

I

J

K

L

M

N

O

P

Q

R

U

V

Zain Naboulsi

For over 15 years, Zain, a Senior Developer Evangelist at Microsoft, has been working with the latest Microsoft technologies. He's been a consultant and trainer since 1995, and he currently creates the Visual Studio Tips and Tricks series. He pioneered aspects of online community evangelism—an effort to build communities in virtual places like LinkedIn, Facebook, and elsewhere. He is not only a proponent of the community aspect of online environments but is also a supporter of the myriad business applications that these new mediums offer.

Zain's efforts have been featured in *eWeek*, *Redmond Developer News*, and many other publications. He has been interviewed by Forrester Research, Gartner, and the Science Channel for his work. He is a frequent speaker at events on LinkedIn, Facebook, and other online venues. Zain also lectures world-wide on a variety of developer topics. You can follow his blog at *http://blogs.msdn.com/zainnab*.

Sara Ford

Sara Ford is the Senior Product Manager at Black Duck Software for Ohloh.net, the largest public destination for finding and evaluating open source software. Prior to Black Duck, she worked for nine years at Microsoft Corp., where she was responsible for CodePlex, the open source project hosting forge for Microsoft. She started her career as a software tester on Visual Studio, a software development tool, where she drove the effort to make it possible for developers who are blind or have low vision to be able to write software applications. She is the author of *Visual Studio Tips*, published by Microsoft Press (2008), from which she donated her author royalties to start a scholarship fund designed for residents of her hometown of Waveland, Miss. to attend the Mississippi Gulf Coast Community College.

What do you think of this book?

We want to hear from you!

To participate in a brief online survey, please visit:

microsoft.com/learning/booksurvey

Tell us how well this book meets your needs—what works effectively, and what we can do better. Your feedback will help us continually improve our books and learning resources for you.

Thank you in advance for your input!